Bakunin on Anarchy

Bakunin on Anarchy

Selected Works by
the Activist-Founder
of World Anarchism

Edited, Translated and with an Introduction, by
SAM DOLGOFF

Preface by Paul Avrich

Vintage Books
A Division of Random House, New York

ISBN: 0-394-71783-x

Library of Congress Catalog Card Number: 76-136351

"The Reaction in Germany" is reprinted by permission of Quadrangle Books from *Russian Philosophy*, edited by James M. Edie, James P. Scanlan, Mary-Barbara Zeldin, and George L. Kline, Copyright © 1965 by Quadrangle Books, Inc. Bakunin's Confession to the Tsar is taken from *The Doctrine of Anarchism of Michael A. Bakunin* by Eugene Pyziur, 1955, pp. 96–8, by permission of Marquette University Press, Milwaukee.

Liberty without socialism is privilege, injustice; socialism without liberty is slavery and brutality.

—MICHAEL BAKUNIN

Contents

Prefatory Note

Arranging a representative anthology of Bakunin's writings presents a number of difficult problems. *Statism and Anarchy* was the only major work he ever completed, and even many short pieces remain unfinished. For Bakunin was above all an activist: he would begin to write something, then leave off to attend to some pressing contingency; or he might complete a first draft but never find time to revise and correct it. His work abounds in repetitions and is interspersed with long digressions. His essay *God and the State*, for example, began as a critique of Marx's theory of economic determinism, was sidetracked by resentment against the defenders of established religion into an exposition of idealist philosophy, from which it digressed into a profound discussion of the interrelationship of science, authority, the state, society, and the individual—only to remain unfinished in the end. In short, Bakunin's literary output is a bewildering mass of fragments, articles, letters, speeches, essays, pamphlets, highly repetitive and full of detours and dead ends, yet flashing with insights throughout. To compile a coherent presentation of his thought is a forbidding task.

My late friend and mentor, Gregory Petrovich Maximoff, attempted a systematization of Bakunin's writings under the title *The Political Philosophy of Bakunin*, with the hopeful subtitle *Scientific Anarchism*. Unfortunately, however, there is no such thing as "scientific" anarchism. Bakunin abhorred "scientific socialism" and did not himself arrange his ideas within the constricting framework of a system. To cut up and rearrange Bakunin's writings without regard for the context or the period in which they were written risks the loss of a balanced presentation in favor of a purely personal interpretation. Moreover, Bakunin's vibrant personality, which illumines all his writings, does not come through in such a presentation. In any case, Maximoff's untimely death prevented him from writing an introduction, providing explanatory notes, and putting into final shape the results of his painstaking research. The book was completed by other hands, and eventually published in 1953.

In the preface to his excellent little book *L'Anarchisme*, the French libertarian historian-sociologist Daniel Guérin argues that since Bakunin "embraced his libertarian ideas early in 1864, after the crushing of the Polish insurrection in which he participated, his writings [before this date] have no place in an anarchist anthology. . . . The first part of his stormy career as a revolutionary conspirator has nothing to do with anarchism."

However, while the present compilation is of course primarily derived from Bakunin's anarchist period, we have also included a few short extracts from such of his early, pre-anarchist writings as foreshadow his mature ideology.

Most of the selections in the present volume have either never appeared in English at all or appeared only in disconnected excerpts. All of them have been freshly translated to convey not only the sense but also the spirit in which they were written (all translations by the editor, except as indicated below). Each selection is accompanied by a brief editorial note; editorial amplifications *within* Bakunin's texts are bracketed. The collection has been rounded out by two contributions from James Guillaume, Bakunin's comrade-in-arms and editor: a biographical sketch that helps to fill in the historical background for most of the selections; and a concluding essay, "On Building the New Social Order," that provides (what Bakunin himself never found time to do) a kind of summing up of the constructive ideas generally discussed by Bakunin and his associates in the International.

Finally, it is with the warmest appreciation that I acknowledge the contributions to the present work of the following persons:

Ida Pilat Isca, who translated from the French the following six selections: "Federalism, Socialism, Anti-Theologism," "The Paris Commune and the Idea of the State," "Program of the International Brotherhood," Extract I of Bakunin's 1872 letter to *La Liberté* of Brussels, "Appeal to the Slavs," and the speech "On the 17th Anniversary of the Polish Insurrection of 1830."

Douglas Roycroft, who translated from the French Extract

II of Bakunin's letter to *La Liberté*; Wanda Sweida and Nina Samusin, who translated from the Russian several extracts from *Statism and Anarchy*; the membership of the Libertarian Book Club, for defraying expenses incurred in the preparation of the manuscript; and Robert and Phyllis Calese and Bill and Sarah Taback, for their constant encouragement.

Murray Bookchin, my good friend, for his stimulating suggestions; my wife, Esther, without whose arduous labor in preparing the manuscript, not to mention her unceasing encouragement, this work could not have been completed; and, by no means least, my editors at Alfred A. Knopf, Angus Cameron and Sophie Wilkins, and copy editors Marguerite Raben and Mel Rosenthal, for their generous and unfailing assistance.

Preface*

A century ago anarchism was emerging as a major force within the revolutionary movement, and the name of Bakunin, its foremost champion and prophet, was as well known among the workers and radical intellectuals of Europe as that of Karl Marx, with whom he was competing for leadership of the First International. In contrast to Marx, however, Bakunin had won his reputation chiefly as an activist rather than a theorist of rebellion. He was not one to sit in libraries, studying and writing about predetermined revolutions. Impatient for action, he threw himself into the uprisings of 1848 with irrepressible exuberance, a Promethean figure moving with the tide of revolt from Paris to the barricades of Austria and Germany. Men like Bakunin, a contemporary remarked, "grow in a hurricane and ripen better in stormy weather than in sunshine."[1]

Bakunin's arrest during the Dresden insurrection of 1849 cut short his feverish revolutionary activity. He spent the next eight years in prison, six of them in the darkest dungeons of tsarist Russia, and when he finally emerged, his sentence commuted to a life term in Siberian exile, he was toothless from scurvy and his health seriously impaired. In 1861, however, he escaped his warders and embarked upon a sensational odyssey that encircled the globe and made his name a legend and an object of worship in radical groups all over Europe.

As a romantic rebel and an active force in history, Bakunin exerted a personal attraction that Marx could never rival. "Everything about him was colossal," recalled the composer Richard Wagner, a fellow participant in the Dresden uprising, "and he was full of a primitive exuberance and strength."[2] Bakunin himself speaks of his own "love for the fantastic, for

*Paper originally presented at the annual meeting of the American Historical Association, Washington, D.C., December 30, 1969, and first published in *The Russian Review*, Vol. 29 (1970), No. 2, pp. 129–42, under the title: "The Legacy of Bakunin." It appears here with certain minor revisions.

unusual, unheard-of adventures which open up vast horizons, the end of which cannot be foreseen."[3] This in turn inspired extravagant dreams in others, and by the time of his death in 1876 he had won a unique place among the adventurers and martyrs of the revolutionary tradition. "This man," said Alexander Herzen of Bakunin, "was born not under an ordinary star but under a comet."[4] His broad magnanimity and childlike enthusiasm, his burning passion for liberty and equality, his volcanic onslaughts against privilege and injustice—all this gave him enormous human appeal in the libertarian circles of his day.

But Bakunin, as his critics never tired of pointing out, was not a systematic thinker. Nor did he ever claim to be. For he considered himself a revolutionist of the deed, "not a philosopher and not an inventor of systems like Marx."[5] He refused to recognize the existence of any preconceived or preordained laws of history. He rejected the view that social change depends on the gradual unfolding of "objective" historical conditions. He believed, on the contrary, that men shape their own destinies, that their lives cannot be squeezed into a Procrustean bed of abstract sociological formulas. "No theory, no ready-made system, no book that has ever been written will save the world," Bakunin declared. "I cleave to no system. I am a true seeker."[6] By teaching the workers theories, he said, Marx would only succeed in stifling the revolutionary fervor every man already possesses—"the impulse to liberty, the passion for equality, the holy instinct of revolt." Unlike Marx's "scientific socialism," his own socialism, Bakunin asserted, was "purely instinctive."[7]

Bakunin's influence, then, as Peter Kropotkin remarked, was primarily that of a "moral personality" rather than of an intellectual authority.[8] Although he wrote prodigiously, he did not leave a single finished book to posterity. He was forever starting new works which, owing to his turbulent existence, were broken off in mid-course and never completed. His literary output, in Thomas Masaryk's description, was a "patchwork of fragments."[9]

And yet his writings, however erratic and unmethodical, abound in flashes of insight that illuminate some of the most important questions of his own time and of ours. What this preface seeks to demonstrate is that Bakunin's ideas, no less than his personality, have exerted a lasting influence, an influence that has been particularly noticeable during the past few years. If ever the spirit of Bakunin spoke, it was in the student quarter of Paris in May 1968, where the black flag of anarchism was prominently displayed and where, among the graffiti inscribed on the walls of the Sorbonne, Bakunin's famous declaration that "The urge to destroy is a creative urge" occupied a conspicuous place. In our own country Eldridge Cleaver, in *Soul on Ice*, has expressed his indebtedness to Bakunin and Nechaev's *Catechism of a Revolutionary*, which, interestingly enough, has recently been published in pamphlet form by the Black Panther organization in Berkeley. The sociologist Lewis Coser has detected a neo-Bakuninist streak in Régis Debray, whom he has cleverly dubbed "Nechaev in the Andes," after Bakunin's fanatical young disciple.[10] And Frantz Fanon's influential book, *The Wretched of the Earth*, with its Manichaean visions of the despised and rejected rising from the lower depths to exterminate their colonial oppressors, occasionally reads as though lifted straight out of Bakunin's collected works. In short, at a time when a new generation has rediscovered spontaneous, undoctrinaire insurrectionism, Bakunin's teachings have come into their own.

What are these ideas that have proved so relevant in the twentieth century—more so, perhaps, than in Bakunin's own time? Above all, Bakunin foresaw the true nature of modern revolution more clearly than any of his contemporaries, Marx not excepted. For Marx the socialist revolution required the emergence of a well-organized and class-conscious proletariat, something to be expected in highly industrialized countries like Germany or England. Marx regarded the peasantry as the social class least capable of constructive revolutionary action: together with the *Lumpenproletariat* of the urban slums, the peasants were benighted and primitive barbarians, the bulwark of counter-revolution. For Bakunin, by contrast, the peasantry and *Lumpenproletariat*, having been least exposed to the corrupting influences of bourgeois civilization, retained their primitive vigor and turbulent instinct for revolt. The real proletariat, he said, did not consist in the skilled artisans and organized factory workers, who were tainted by the pretensions and aspirations of the middle classes, but in the great mass of "uncivilized, disinherited, and illiterate" millions who truly had nothing to lose but their chains. Thus, while Marx believed in an organized revolution led by a trained and disciplined working class, Bakunin set his hopes on a peasant jacquerie combined with a spontaneous rising of the infuriated urban mobs, a revolt of the uncivilized masses driven by an instinctive passion for justice and by an unquenchable thirst for revenge. Bakunin's model had been set by the great rebellions of Razin and Pugachev in the seventeenth and eighteenth centuries. His vision was of an all-embracing upheaval, a true revolt of the masses, including, besides the working class, the darkest elements of society—the *Lumpenproletariat*, the primitive peasantry, the unemployed, the outlaws—all pitted against those who throve on their misery and enslavement.

Subsequent events have, to a remarkable extent, confirmed the accuracy of Bakunin's vision. It is small wonder, then, that contemporary historians have shown a new appreciation of the role of spontaneous and primitive movements in shaping history. From the work of Barrington Moore, who has recently investigated the relationship between modernization and agrarian revolt, as well as that of Eric Hobsbawm, George Rudé, E. P. Thompson, and others, we are coming to understand that most modern revolutions, like those of the past, have been largely unplanned and spontaneous, driven by mass movements of urban and rural laborers, and in spirit predominantly anarchistic. No longer can these naïve, primitive, and irrational groups be written off as fringe elements to be ignored by the historian. They lie, rather, at the very basis of social change.

Bakunin foresaw that the great revolutions of our time would emerge from the "lower depths" of comparatively undeveloped countries. He saw decadence in advanced civilization and vitality in backward, primitive nations. He insisted that the revolutionary impulse was strongest where men had no property, no regular employment, and no stake in things as they were; and this meant that the universal upheaval of his dreams would start in the south and east of Europe rather than in such prosperous and disciplined countries as England or Germany.

These revolutionary visions were closely related to Bakunin's early pan-Slavism. In 1848 he spoke of the decadence of Western Europe and saw hope in the more primitive, less industrialized Slavs for its regeneration. Convinced that the breakup of the Austrian Empire was an essential condition for a European revolution, he called for its destruction and replacement by independent Slavic republics, a dream realized seventy years later. He correctly anticipated the future importance of Slavic nationalism, and he saw, moreover, that a revolution of Slavs would precipitate the social transformation of Europe. He prophesied, in particular, a messianic role for his native Russia akin to the Third Rome of the past and the Third International of the future. "The star of revolution," he wrote in 1848, "will rise high above Moscow from a sea of blood and fire, and will turn into the lodestar to lead a liberated humanity."[11]

We can see then why it is Bakunin, rather than Marx, who can claim to be the true prophet of modern revolution. The three greatest revolutions of the twentieth century—in Russia, Spain, and China—have all occurred in relatively backward countries and have largely been "peasant wars" linked with spontaneous outbursts of the urban poor, as Bakunin predicted. The peasantry and unskilled workers, those primitive groups for whom Marx expressed withering contempt, have become the mass base of twentieth-century social upheavals—upheavals which, though often labeled "Marxist," are far more accurately described as "Bakuninist." Bakunin's visions, moreover, have anticipated the social ferment within the "Third World" as a whole, the modern counterpart on a global scale of Bakunin's backward, peripheral Europe.

It is hardly surprising, therefore, that the spirit of Bakunin should pervade the writings of such contemporary theorists of mass revolt as Frantz Fanon and Régis Debray and, to a lesser degree, of Eldridge Cleaver and Herbert Marcuse. Fanon, no less than Bakunin, was convinced that the working class had been corrupted by the values of the establishment and had thus lost its revolutionary fervor. "The great mistake," he wrote, "the inherent defect in the majority of political parties of the under-developed regions has been, following traditional lines, to approach in the first place those elements which are the most politically conscious: the working classes in the towns, the skilled workers and the civil servants—that is to say, a tiny portion of the population, which hardly represents more than one percent."[12] Fanon, like Bakunin, pinned his hopes on the great mass of unprivileged and un-Europeanized village laborers and *Lumpenproletariat* from the shanty towns, uprooted, impoverished, starving, and with nothing to lose. For Fanon, as for Bakunin, the more primitive the man, the purer his revolutionary spirit. When Fanon refers to "the hopeless dregs of humanity" as natural rebels, he is speaking the language of Bakunin. With Bakunin, moreover, he shares not only a common faith in the revolutionary potential of the underworld, but also a vision of rebirth through fire and a thoroughgoing rejection of European civilization as decadent and repressive—in place of which, he says, the Third World must begin "a new history of man." The Black Panthers, in turn, have appropriated many of Fanon's ideas, and Eldridge Cleaver and Huey Newton freely acknowledge their debt to him—and indirectly to Bakunin—when describing the blacks in America as an oppressed colony kept in check by an occupation army of white policemen and exploited by white businessmen and politicians.

In a similar vein, Herbert Marcuse writes in *One Dimensional Man* that the greatest hope of revolutionary change lies in "the substratum of the outcasts and outsiders, the exploited and persecuted of other races and other colors, the unemployed and the unemployables." If these groups, he adds, should ally themselves with the radical intellectuals, there might occur an uprising of "the most advanced consciousness of humanity and its most exploited force."[13] Here again, it is Bakunin rather than Marx whose influence is apparent. For Bakunin set great store by the disaffected students and intellectuals and assigned them a key role in the impending world revolution. Bakunin's prophetic vision of an all-encompassing class war, in contrast to Marx's more narrowly conceived struggle between proletariat and bourgeoisie, made ample room for this additional fragmented element of society for which Marx had only disdain. In Marx's view, rootless intellectuals did not comprise a class of their own, nor were they an integral component of the bourgeoisie. They were merely "the dregs" of the middle class, "a bunch of *déclassés*" —lawyers without clients, doctors without patients, petty journalists, impecunious students, and their ilk—with no vital role to play in the historical process of class conflict.[14] For Bakunin, on the other hand, the intellectuals were a valuable revolutionary force, "fervent, energetic youths, totally *déclassé*, with no career or way out."[15] The *déclassés*, Bakunin pointed out, like the jobless *Lumpenproletariat* and the landless peasantry, had no stake whatever in things as they were and no prospect for improvement except through an immediate revolution that would demolish the existing order.

In general, then, Bakunin found the greatest revolutionary potential in uprooted, alienated, *déclassé* elements, elements either left behind by, or refusing to fit into, modern society. And here again he was a truer prophet than his contemporaries. For the alliance of estranged intellectuals with the dispossessed masses in guerrilla-style warfare has been a central feature of modern revolutions. Régis Debray, in *Revolution in the Revolution?*, another influential manual of modern rebellion, carries this idea to its ultimate conclusion. People who have jobs, says Debray, who lead more or less normal working lives in town or village, however poor and oppressed, are essentially bourgeois because they have something to lose—their work, their homes, their sustenance. For Debray only the rootless guerrilla, with nothing to lose but his life, is the true proletarian, and the revolutionary struggle, if it is to be successful, must be conducted by bands of professional guerrillas—i.e., *déclassé* intellectuals— who, in Debray's words, would "initiate the highest forms of class struggle."[16]

Bakunin differed with Marx on still another point that is of considerable relevance for the present. Bakunin was a firm believer in immediate revolution. He rejected the view that revolutionary forces will emerge gradually, in the fullness of time. What he demanded, in effect, was "freedom now." He would countenance no temporizing with the existing system. The old order was rotten, he argued, and salvation could be achieved only by destroying it root and branch. Gradualism and reformism in any shape were futile, palliatives and compromises of no use. Bakunin's was a dream of immediate and universal destruction, the leveling of all existing values and institutions, and the creation of a new libertarian society on their ashes. In his view, parliamentary democracy was a shameless fiction so long as men were being subjected to economic exploitation. Even in the freest of states, he declared, such as Switzerland and the United States, the civilization of the few is founded on the travail and degradation of the many. "I do not believe in constitutions and laws," he said. "The best constitution in the world would not be able to satisfy me. We need something different: inspiration, life, a new lawless and therefore free world."[17]

In rejecting the claim of parliamentary democracy to represent the people, Bakunin, as his biographer E. H. Carr has noted, "spoke a language which has become more familiar in the twentieth century than it was in the nineteenth."[18] Sounding still another modern note, Bakunin saw the ideal moment for popular revolution in time of war—and ultimately during a world war. In 1870 he regarded the Franco-Prussian War as the harbinger of an anarchist revolution in which the state would be smashed and a free federation of communes arise on its ruins. The one thing that could save France, he wrote in his *Letters to a Frenchman,* was "an elemental, mighty, passionately energetic, anarchistic, destructive, unrestrained uprising of the popular masses,"[19] a view with which Daniel Cohn-Bendit and his fellow rebels of May 1968 would enthusiastically agree. Bakunin believed, like Lenin after him, that national war must be converted into social rebellion. He dreamt of a general European war, which he felt was imminent and would destroy the bourgeois world. His timing, of course, was faulty. As Herzen once remarked, Bakunin habitually "mistook the third month of pregnancy for the ninth." But his vision was at length fulfilled when the First World War brought about the collapse of the old order and released revolutionary forces that have yet to play themselves out.

Let us focus for a moment on the Russian Revolution, the prototype of twentieth-century social upheavals. Here, in essence, was the spontaneous "revolt of the masses" that Bakunin had foreseen some fifty years before. In 1917 Russia experienced a virtual breakdown of political authority, and councils of workers and peasants sprang up which might form the basis of libertarian communes. Lenin, like Bakunin before him, encouraged the raw and untutored elements of Russian society to sweep away what remained of the old regime. Bakunin and Lenin, for all their differences of temperament and doctrine, were alike in their refusal to collaborate with the liberals or moderate socialists, whom they regarded as incurably counterrevolutionary. Both men were anti-bourgeois and anti-liberal to the roots. Like Bakunin, Lenin called for instant socialism, without any prolonged capitalist phase of development. He too believed that the global revolution might be centered on backward peasant Russia. In his *April Theses*, moreover, he put forward a number of specifically Bakuninist propositions: the transformation of the world war into a revolutionary struggle against the capitalist system; the renunciation of parliamentary government in favor of a regime of soviets patterned after the Paris Commune; the abolition of the police, the army, and the bureaucracy; and the leveling of incomes. Lenin's appeal for "a breakup and a revolution a thousand times more powerful than that of February" had a distinctly Bakuninist ring—so much so, that one anarchist leader in Petrograd was convinced that Lenin intended to "wither away the state" the moment he got hold of it.[20]

And, indeed, Lenin's greatest achievement was to return to the anarcho-populist roots of the Russian revolutionary tradition, to adapt his Marxist theories to suit the conditions of a relatively backward country in which a proletarian revolution made little sense. While the Marxist in Lenin told him to be patient, to let Russia evolve in accordance with the laws of historical materialism, the Bakuninist in him insisted that the revolution must be made at once, by fusing the proletarian revolution with the revolutions of a land-hungry peasantry and a militant elite of *déclassé* intellectuals, social elements for which Marx, as we have seen, had expressed contempt. Small wonder that Lenin's orthodox Marxist colleagues accused him of becoming an anarchist and "the heir to the throne of Bakunin."[21] Small wonder, too, that several years later a leading Bolshevik historian could write that Bakunin "was the founder not only of European anarchism but also of Russian populist insurrectionism and therefore of Russian Social Democracy from which the Communist party emerged," and that Bakunin's methods "in many respects anticipated the emergence of Soviet power and forecast, in general outline, the course of the great October Revolution of 1917."[22]

But if Bakunin foresaw the anarchistic nature of the Russian Revolution, he also foresaw its authoritarian consequences. If 1917 began, as Bakunin had hoped, with a spontaneous mass revolt, it ended, as Bakunin had feared, with the dictatorship of a new ruling elite. Long before Machajski or Djilas or James Burnham, Bakunin had warned that a "new class" of intellectuals and semi-intellectuals might seek to replace the landlords and capitalists and deny the people their freedom. In 1873 he prophesied with startling accuracy that under a so-called dictatorship of the proletariat "the leaders of the Communist party, namely Mr. Marx and his followers, will proceed to liberate humanity in their own way. They will concentrate the reins of government in a strong hand. . . . They will establish a single state bank, concentrating in its hands all commercial, industrial, agricultural, and even scientific production, and then divide the masses into two armies—industrial and agricultural—under the direct command of state engineers, who will constitute a new privileged scientific and political class."[23]

And yet, for all his assaults on revolutionary dictatorship, Bakunin was determined to create his own secret society of conspirators, whose members would be "subjected to a strict hierarchy and to unconditional obedience." This clandestine organization, moreover, would remain intact even after the revolution had been accomplished in order to forestall the establishment of any "official dictatorship."[24] Thus Bakunin committed the very sin he so bitterly denounced. He himself was one of the principal originators of the idea of a secret and closely knit revolutionary party bound together by implicit obedience to a revolutionary dictator, a party that he likened at one point to the Jesuit Order. While he recognized the intimate connection between means and ends, while he saw that the methods used to make the revolution must affect the nature of society *after* the revolution, he nonetheless resorted to methods which were the precise contradiction of his own libertarian principles. His ends pointed towards freedom, but his means—the clandestine revolutionary party—pointed towards totalitarian dictatorship. Bakunin, in short, was trapped in a classic dilemma: he understood that the lack of an efficient revolutionary organization would spell inevitable failure, but the means he chose inevitably corrupted the ends towards which he aspired.

More than that, on the question of revolutionary morality Bakunin, under the influence of his disciple Sergei Nechaev, preached in effect that the ends justify the means. In his *Catechism of a Revolutionary*, written with Nechaev exactly a hundred years ago, the revolutionist is depicted as a complete immoralist, bound to commit any crime, any treachery, any baseness to bring about the destruction of the existing order. The revolutionist, wrote Bakunin and Nechaev, "despises and hates present-day social morality in all its forms. He regards everything as moral that favors the triumph of the revolution. . . . All soft and enervating feelings of friendship, love, gratitude, even honor must be stifled in him by a cold passion for the revolutionary cause. . . . Day and night he must have one thought, one aim—merciless destruction."[25] Eldridge Cleaver tells us in *Soul on Ice* that he "fell in love" with Bakunin and Nechaev's *Catechism* and took it as a revolutionary bible, incorporating its principles into his everyday life by employing "tactics of ruthlessness in my dealings with everyone with whom I came into contact."[26] (The *Catechism*, as mentioned above, has recently been published as a pamphlet by Cleaver's Black Panther organization in Berkeley.)

Here again, as in his belief in a clandestine organization of revolutionaries as well as a "temporary" revolutionary dictatorship, Bakunin was a direct forebear of Lenin. This makes it easier to understand how it was possible for many anarchists in 1917 to collaborate with their Bolshevik rivals to overthrow the Kerensky government. After the October Revolution, in fact,

One anarchist leader even tried to work out an "anarchist theory of the dictatorship of the proletariat."[27] There is tragic irony in the fact that, as in Spain twenty years later, the anarchists should have helped to destroy the fragile embryo of democracy, thus preparing the way for a new tyranny which was to be the author of their downfall. For once in power the Bolsheviks proceeded to suppress their libertarian allies, and the revolution turned into the opposite of all Bakunin's hopes. Among the few anarchist groups allowed to remain in existence was one which solemnly declared its intention to launch the stateless society "in interplanetary space but not upon Soviet territory"[28]—which raises some interesting prospects in this era of Armstrong and Aldrin! For most anarchists, however, there remained only the melancholy consolation that their mentor Bakunin had predicted it all fifty years before.

Bakunin's legacy, then, has been an ambivalent one. This was because Bakunin himself was a man of paradox, possessed of an ambivalent nature. A nobleman who yearned for a peasant revolt, a libertarian with an irresistible urge to dominate others, an intellectual with a powerful anti-intellectual streak, he could preach unrestrained liberty while spinning from his brain a whole network of secret organizations and demanding from his followers unconditional obedience to his will. In his *Confession* to the tsar, moreover, he was capable of appealing to Nicholas I to carry the banner of Slavdom into Western Europe and do away with the effete parliamentary system. His pan-Slavism and anti-intellectualism, his pathological hatred of Germans and Jews (Marx, of course, being both), his cult of violence and revolutionary immoralism, his hatred of liberalism and reformism, his faith in the peasantry and *Lumpenproletariat*—all this brought him uncomfortably close to later authoritarian movements of both the Left and the Right, movements from which Bakunin himself would doubtless have recoiled in horror had he lived to see their mercurial rise.

Yet, for all his ambivalence, Bakunin remains an influential figure. Herzen once called him "a Columbus without an America, and even without a ship."[29] But the present revolutionary movement owes him a good deal of its energy, its audacity, and its tempestuousness. His youthful exuberance, his contempt for middle-class conventions, and his emphasis on deeds rather than theories exert considerable appeal among today's rebellious youth, for whom Bakunin provides an example of anarchism in action, of revolution as a way of life. His ideas, too, continue to be relevant—perhaps more relevant than ever. Whatever his defects as a scholar, especially when compared with Marx, they are more than outweighed by his revolutionary vision and intuition. Bakunin was the prophet of primitive rebellion, of the conspiratorial revolutionary party, of terrorist amoralism, of guerrilla insurrectionism, of revolutionary dictatorship, and of the emergence of a new ruling class that would impose its will on the people and rob them of their freedom. He was the first Russian rebel to preach social revolution in cosmic terms and on an international scale. His formulas of self-determination and direct action exercise an increasing appeal, while his chief *bête noire*, the centralized bureaucratic state, continues to fulfill his most despairing predictions. Of particular note, after the lessons of Russia, Spain, and China, is Bakunin's message that social emancipation must be attained by libertarian rather than dictatorial means. Moreover, at a time when workers' control is again being widely discussed, it is well to remember that Bakunin, perhaps even more than Proudhon, was a prophet of revolutionary syndicalism, insisting that a free federation of trade unions would be "the living germ of the new social order which is to replace the bourgeois world."[30]

But above all Bakunin is attractive to present-day students and intellectuals because his libertarian brand of socialism provides an alternative vision to the bankrupt authoritarian socialism of the twentieth century. His dream of a decentralized society of autonomous communes and labor federations appeals to those who are seeking to escape from a centralized, conformist, and artificial world. "I am a human being: do not fold, spindle, or mutilate" has a distinctive Bakuninist flavor. Indeed, student rebels, even when professed Marxists, are often closer in spirit to Bakunin, whose black flag has occasionally been unfurled in campus demonstrations from Berkeley to Paris. Their stress on the natural, the spontaneous, the unsystematic, their urge towards a simpler way of life, their distrust of bureaucracy and of centralized authority, their belief that all men should take part in decisions affecting their lives, their slogans of "participatory democracy," "freedom now," "power to the people," their goals of community control, workers' management, rural cooperation, equal education and income, dispersal of state power —all this is in harmony with Bakunin's vision. Even the ambivalence among so many youthful rebels, who combine the antithetical methods of libertarian anarchism and authoritarian socialism, reflects the ambivalence within Bakunin's own revolutionary philosophy and personal makeup.

Finally, Bakunin has found an echo wherever young dissidents question our uncritical faith in self-glorifying scientific progress. A hundred years ago Bakunin warned that scientists and technical experts might use their knowledge to dominate others, and that one day ordinary citizens would be rudely awakened to find that they had become "the slaves, the playthings, and the victims of a new group of ambitious men."[31] Bakunin therefore preached a "revolt of life against science, or rather, against the rule of science." Not that he rejected the validity of scientific knowledge. But he recognized its dangers. He saw that life cannot be reduced to laboratory formulas and that efforts in this direction would lead to the worst form of tyranny. In a letter written barely a year before his death, he spoke of the "evolution and development of the principle of evil" throughout the world and forewarned of what we now call the "military-industrial complex." "Sooner or later," he wrote, "these enormous military states will have to destroy and devour each other. But what a prospect!"[32]

How justified were his fears can be appreciated now in an age of nuclear and biological weapons of mass destruction. At a time when the idealization of primitive social elements is again in fashion, when mass rebellion is again being widely preached, and when modern technology threatens Western civilization with extinction, Bakunin clearly merits a reappraisal. We are fortunate, then, to have at our disposal this fine new collection of his writings. It is the fullest Bakunin anthology available in English. With its rich selection of his essays, speeches, and letters, as well as substantial extracts from his major works, it amply reveals the wide range and continued vitality of Bakunin's thought. As Max Nettlau, the foremost historian of anarchism, noted thirty years ago, Bakunin's "ideas remain fresh and will live forever."[33]

PAUL AVRICH

Bakunin on Anarchy

Introduction

Every command slaps liberty in the face.—Bakunin[1]

As the current reevaluation of traditional socialist theory proceeds, the ideas of Michael Bakunin, founder of the international anarchist movement, are arousing increasing interest.[2] The present anthology is designed to acquaint the English-speaking reader with the range of his thought, a mode of thought most relevant to those growing numbers of people who are alarmed by the unprecedented proliferation, and misuse, of the political, economic, and military powers of the state, and the concomitant regimentation of the individual. Clearly, the old nineteenth-century theories of socialism as tested in twentieth-century practice seem no longer applicable to the realities of our cybernetic age and must be revised in a libertarian direction.

By now it is all too evident that the nationalization of property and the means of production does not fundamentally alter the basic inequality between those wielding power and those subject to it. Lenin's notion that "freedom is a bourgeois middle-class virtue" is giving way to the conviction that freedom is a greater necessity than even the most efficient concentration of political and economic power, and no one any longer believes that the state will "wither away." The dogma that science, philosophy, ethics, and democratic institutions are mere reflections (an "ideological superstructure" in Marxist jargon) of the economic mode of production is equally losing ground to the conviction that these phenomena have an independent share in shaping human history. It is this shift in social thinking that generated the Hungarian Revolution of 1956 and other resistance movements in Eastern Europe, in Czechoslovakia, in the Soviet Union itself. It is echoed in student unrest throughout the world, and everywhere the most radical elements are questioning the concept of state sovereignty as well as that of all centralized authority.

This is precisely the point of view first espoused by Bakunin in his polemics with the Marxists a hundred years ago. Bakunin's critique of the State and authoritarian socialism in general revolves around what has since become the crucial issue of our time, Socialism and Freedom, which he formulates as follows:

> . . . Equality without freedom is the despotism of the State.
> . . . the most fatal combination that could possibly be formed, would be to unite socialism to absolutism; to unite the aspiration of the people for material well-being . . . with the dictatorship or the concentration of all political and social power in the State. . . . We must seek full economic and social justice only by way of freedom. There can be nothing living or human outside of liberty, and a socialism that does not accept freedom as its only creative principle . . . will inevitably . . . lead to slavery and brutality.[3]

As for the consequences of authoritarian socialism, Bakunin predicted that "all work will be performed in the employ of the State . . . following a certain period of transition . . . the State will become the only banker, capitalist, and organizer. It will be the director of all national labor and the distributor of its products." The State would organize its subject population into two armies, one agricultural, the other industrial, under the direct command of the State engineers who would constitute the new, scientific-political ruling class. Thus, as early as 1873, Bakunin foresaw the rise of Technocracy.

In criticizing Marx's theory of the State, Bakunin maintained that the State is not merely an agent of the dominant economic class, but also constitutes a class in itself, and the most powerful of all by virtue of its monopoly of armed force and its sovereignty over all other social institutions. "The trouble," he declared, "lies not in any particular form of government, but in . . . the very existence of government itself." In a socialist state, the political structures and the bureaucracy exercise the functions of the deposed classes and enjoy their privileges. Bakunin argued that the State was not only the product but, contrary to Marx's view, also the creator and perpetuator of economic, political, and social inequality. And his critique in this respect has been sustained by modern social thinkers. Thus, Rudolf Hilferding, a noted Marxist economist, has written: "It is the essence of a totalitarian state that it subjects the economy to its aims . . . the Marxist sectarian cannot grasp the idea that present-day state power, having achieved independence, is unfolding its enormous strength according to its own laws, subjecting other social forces and compelling them to serve its ends. . . ."[4]

Freedom is the keystone of Bakunin's thought. The goal of history is the realization of freedom, and its driving force is the "instinct of revolt." Freedom is implicit in the social nature of Man and can be developed only in society, through the practice of mutual aid, which Bakunin calls "solidarity." Freedom is indissolubly linked to equality and justice in a society based on reciprocal respect for individual rights.

> History consists in the progressive negation of the primitive animality of Man by the development of his humanity.[5]
> I am truly free only when all human beings . . . are equally free. The freedom of other men, far from negating or limiting my freedom, is, on the contrary, its necessary condition and confirmation.[6]

Like Marx, Bakunin emphasized the importance of the economic factor in social evolution. But he accepted Marx's materialist "laws of history" only insofar as they harmonized with man's deepest aspirations; that is, for freedom. It is true that some of Marx's own earlier writings concerning freedom, alienation, and the State—resurrected long after his death (his economic-philosophical manuscripts were first published in 1927) —could well have been produced by an anarchist; and many "Marxist humanists" have tried to use these writings to show that Marx was really a libertarian. Typical in this regard is

Herbert Marcuse's assertion that "Once the humanistic idea is seen . . . as the very substance of Marx's theory, the deep-rooted libertarian and anarchistic elements of Marxian theory come to life."[7]

As Marx elaborated his system, however, the element of freedom dwindled in importance as against the inexorable laws of historical evolution underlying the progressive development of society. Hence Marx, like Engels, thought that the Swiss fighting for their emancipation from the Habsburgs were reactionary, because the "laws of history" demanded centralization, and to take the side of freedom and federalism was therefore mere bourgeois idealism or sentimentality.

While Marx was concentrating on the formulation of these "laws," Bakunin was championing the primacy of Man's life, the aspirations of the individual human being to ultimate fulfillment and development. For Bakunin, all systems are necessarily abstractions, and all generalization violates the living reality of the individual. Bakunin was more interested in the nature of Man than in speculation about the "laws of history":

> The lord of the Bible had more insight into the nature of man than Auguste Comte and his disciples, who counseled him to be "reasonable and not attempt the impossible." To entice man to eat of the forbidden fruit of the tree of knowledge, God had but to command him: "Thou Shalt Not!" This immoderation, this disobedience, this rebellion of the human spirit against all imposed limits, be it in the name of science, be it in the name of God, constitutes his glory, the source of his power and of his liberty. By reaching for the impossible, man discovers the possible, and those who limit themselves to what seems possible will never advance a single step.[8]

Bakunin's concept of "natural society," which he contrasts to the "artificial society of the State," could be defined as a social organization governed by customs, mores, traditions, and moral norms acquired and expanded through the ages in the course and in the practice of daily life. This idea was derived from Proudhon and, according to G. D. H. Cole, was later expanded and clarified by Kropotkin in his *Mutual Aid*. It must be stressed, however, that Bakunin did not think a society necessarily good because it was "natural"—it could be either good or bad, depending on the material, intellectual, and ethical level of its members. If a society is bad, the enlightened individual is morally bound to revolt against it. When public opinion is poisoned by ignorance and prejudice, it can be even more tyrannical than the most despotic State.

It is true that Marx, like Bakunin, looked upon the State as a "parasitic excrescence which battens on society and inhibits its free movement."[9] But Marx and most authoritarian socialists did not give much thought to the forms of organization that might concretize or translate into reality the ideal of a free, stateless society. They naïvely assumed that the "Workers' State" would in some natural, spontaneous fashion eventually evolve into the ideal. But the revolutions of the twentieth century and the rise of totalitarian and "welfare" states have demonstrated— as Bakunin foresaw—how central planning and centralized state structures create new bureaucracies and a new "scientific-political class," the modern commissarocracy.

Proudhon, Bakunin, Kropotkin, and their successors—the collectivist, communist, and syndicalist anarchists—understood that freedom (paradoxical as this may seem) must be organized, must systematically permeate every cell of the social body. Freedom is inseparable from local autonomy, workers' control, community control; but such self-governing local units and groups can function, survive, and prosper only by coordinating their activities. A vast network of free associations, federated at every level and preserving the maximum degree of local autonomy, was therefore envisaged as the only feasible alternative to the suffocating centralized State. Bakunin, like his predecessor Proudhon—and unlike some modern anarchists who tend to reject *all* forms of organization—saw in federalism the structure, coordination, and implementation without which freedom would remain only a subject for political oratory. He insisted that federalism would foster unity on a higher plane than would compulsion and regimentation. This approach, so long regarded as utopian, is now daily becoming more realistic.

For Bakunin, federalism without the right to secede would be meaningless, this being inseparable from the basic right of groups and individuals to create their own forms of association. Anticipating the objection that the right to secede would paralyze the functions of society, Bakunin reasoned that by a natural process people with strong common interests will cooperate, and those who stand to lose more than they gain by seceding will resolve their differences; while those who secede because they have little or nothing in common will not hurt the collectivity, but will, on the contrary, eliminate a source of friction.

Bakunin maintained that the remedy for excessive centralization lies not in rejecting organization, but in the humanistic and libertarian perfection of the means of organization, in constant improvement both of its methods, and of the capacity of men to apply them. This problem, like the problem of power in general, will probably never be fully resolved. But it is the merit of Bakunin, and of the libertarian movement as a whole, that they endeavored to reduce it to a minimum.

Bakunin understood that the organic structures vital to social life could easily take on an authoritarian character through the concentration of power in a minority of specialists, scientists, officials, and administrators. In the age of Darwin, a time when science was becoming a new religion, Bakunin was already warning against the potential dictatorship of the scientists. And in the scientists who today actively oppose such perversions of science as State-subsidized research to perfect weapons of destruction, we see men imbued with Bakunin's spirit.

But it was with regard to the theory of revolution itself that Bakunin made some of his greatest contributions.

Among the most vexing problems affecting all revolutionary organizations is the relationship between a mass movement and the doctrinaire minorities that each strive to lead the revolution in its particular direction. Authoritarians simplify matters for themselves by concentrating on the conquest of power—which, however, leads inevitably to the abortion of the revolution. For anarchists, intent upon guiding the revolution in a libertarian direction by libertarian means, the question of how to stop authoritarians from seizing power without instituting a dictatorship of their own becomes increasingly complicated.

Bakunin understood that the people tend to be gullible and

oblivious to the early harbingers of dictatorship until the revolutionary storm subsides and they awake to find themselves in shackles. He therefore set about forming a network of secret cadres whose members would prepare the masses for revolution by helping them to identify their enemies and by fostering their confidence in their own creative capacities, and who would fight with them on the barricades. These militants would seek no power for themselves but insist unceasingly that all power must derive and flow back to the grass-roots organizations spontaneously created by the revolution itself. Such secret cadres could not be formed in the heat of revolution, when it would be too late to act effectively. They must be organized long in advance and the members must have a clear understanding of their aims and be organizationally prepared to exert maximum influence over the masses. The creation of such vanguard associations, animated by libertarian principles, is indispensable to the success of the Social Revolution.

However, this concept of an anarchist vanguard to forestall the seizure of power by a minority raises, as already hinted, a number of perplexing problems, problems debated to this day in the anarchist movement. Any vanguard movement constitutes an elite; and every elite—particularly when organized as a secret society—tends to separate itself from the masses and willy-nilly develop a kind of leadership complex. Would not this state of mind lead the vanguard to mistake its own will for the will of the people? Would it not thereby paralyze the spontaneity and initiative of the popular movement? How could demagogues and would-be dictators be kept from infiltrating and corrupting the vanguard? How could authoritarian groups (e.g., the Bolsheviks) be prevented from coming to power by cleverly using the same language as the anarchists, echoing the same essentially libertarian demands of the workers and peasants only as a means of achieving control over them? (Lenin, for example, was so adroit at speaking like an anarchist that he even deceived some anarchists, while men of his own party accused him of "Bakuninism"; but he subsequently "redeemed" himself by engineering the establishment of a counterrevolutionary, totalitarian "workers' and peasants' state.")

Like most radicals of his period, Bakunin believed that the revolution was imminent, that it was urgently necessary to define clearly the problems facing it, and that there were no perfect solutions. In his extensive writings, he seeks to outline a program of revolutionary transition, as a basis for building a realistic movement capable of coping with the immediate problems of the social revolution. To have laid the rough foundations for such a movement, to have asked the right questions and suggested a good many answers, is no mean achievement.

Bakunin's views on the revolutionary role of anarchists, as repeatedly stressed in almost all his writings, are typically put forth in such passages as the following:

> Our aim is the creation of a powerful but always invisible revolutionary association which will prepare and direct the revolution. But never, even during open revolution, will the association as a whole, or any of its members, take any kind of public office, for it has no aim other than to destroy all government and to make government impossible everywhere. . . . It will keep watch so that authorities, governments, and states can never be built again.[10]
>
> I wonder how Marx fails to see that the establishment of a . . . dictatorship to perform, in one way or another, as chief engineer of the world revolution, regulating and directing a revolutionary movement of the masses in all countries in a machinelike fashion— that the establishment of such a dictatorship would be enough of itself to kill the revolution and distort all popular movements.[11]
>
> . . . in the Social Revolution, individual action was to be almost nil, while the spontaneous action of the masses had to be everything. All that the individual can do is to formulate and propagate ideas expressing the instinctive desires of the people, and contribute their constant efforts to the revolutionary organization of the natural power of the masses. This, and nothing more: all the rest can only be accomplished by the people. Otherwise we would end up with a political dictatorship—the reconstitution of the State. . . .[12]

Disregarding these unequivocal denunciations of dictatorship, however, historians like Steklov, Nomad, Pyziur, and Cunow still insist that Bakunin was at heart an authoritarian, a precursor of Lenin. They base this assertion not upon an overall assessment of his writings or the basic tenets of his doctrine, but primarily upon the internal rules that Bakunin wrote for the International Brotherhood in 1865, and upon his references to "invisible collective dictatorship," "well-conducted revolution," and a few similar scattered remarks taken out of context and refuted by the very writings from which they are extracted. It is true that the internal Brotherhood rules constituted a violation of Bakunin's own anarchist principles, but to stress this contradiction as the essence of Bakunin's doctrine is a gross distortion. Even more irresponsible are charges of dictatorship whose authors fail to specify that they are based on Bakunin's early, nonanarchist writings (for example, the *Confession* of 1851). As Franco Venturi points out, this was the period of "Bakunin's temporary adherence . . . to the dictatorship of the Blanqui type, and when it came to an end . . . Bakunin found himself an anarchist."[13] Not Bakunin, but Robespierre, Blanqui, Tkachev, and Nechaev are Lenin's forebears. Professor Isaiah Berlin, for example, declares that "When Lenin organized the Bolshevik Revolution in 1917, the technique he adopted, 'prima facie' at least, resembled those commended by the Russian Jacobins, Tkachev and his followers, who had learnt from Blanqui and Buonarroti. . . ."[14]*

Even with regard to the Brotherhood rules, what Bakunin's critics fail to realize is that in his time all revolutionary organizations were forced to operate in secret—that the survival of such a group and the safety of its members depended on strict adherence to certain rules of conduct which the members voluntarily accepted. The elaborate style of the statutes that Bakunin worked out for the Brotherhood, in the manner of the Freemasons and the Carbonari, is largely attributable to his romantic temperament and to the generally conspiratorial atmosphere then prevailing in Italy. Nor is due consideration given to the fact that Bakunin was only beginning to formulate his ideas and that these statutes represent only a passing phase in the maturing of his thought. Such secret societies were actually informal, loosely organized groups of individuals connected by personal

---

*For further discussion on this point, see selection and postscript to "Letter to Albert Richard," p. 177.

contact and correspondence. No account is taken, moreover, of the frequently loose sense in which the term "dictatorship" was used by nineteenth-century socialists—to mean simply the preponderant influence of a social class, as in Marx's "dictatorship of the proletariat." Similarly, Bakunin refers, in his letter to Albert Richard (see selection), to an "invisible collective dictatorship" of socialists which would act to *forestall* the reestablishment of the State. (The term is still used in this way by certain modern writers—G. D. H. Cole, for example.)

Such historians as Joll, Eltzbacher, Cole, Woodcock, and Nettlau have provided a more balanced view, and placed the whole question in its proper perspective. Thus, Cole writes:

> Bakunin agreed with Marx in advocating a dictatorship of the proletariat over the exploiting classes; but he held that this dictatorship must be a spontaneous dictatorship of the entire uprisen working class and not by any body of leaders set in authority over them. . . .

> Bakunin hated formal organization. What he loved was the sense of being bound together with friends and fellow workers in an association too intimate to need . . . any rules written down—or indeed, any clearly defined membership at all.[15]

Joll argues similarly: "While Bakunin admitted that discipline would be necessary in a revolution—though it was not a quality for which he had any natural respect—the discipline he wanted in the revolutionary movement would not be the dictatorial, dogmatic discipline of the communists," and here he quotes Bakunin's own reflections on

> . . . the voluntary and considered agreement of individual effort toward the common aim. . . . Hierarchical order and promotion do not exist, so that the commander of yesterday can become a subordinate tomorrow. No one rises above the other, or if one does rise, it is only to fall back again a moment later, like the waves of the sea returning to the salutary level of equality.[16]

Another major argument of the critics rests on Bakunin's brief association with the unscrupulous Sergei Nechaev and their alleged coauthorship of the infamous *Rules That Must Inspire* *the Revolutionist* (better known as *The Catechism of the Revolutionary*). It is on this basis that Bakunin has been accused of advocating a despotic Machiavellian approach, with the "Jesuits" of the revolution required to be unprincipled, devoid of all moral feeling, and contemptuous of all ethical obligations. Actually, however, recent research by Michael Confino has conclusively shown that Nechaev was the sole author of *The Catechism*. The essential point, in any case, is that Bakunin shortly repudiated both Nechaev and his ruthless amoralism in the strongest possible terms, warning all his friends to sever relations with him as well. Moreover, all reliable historians agree that the measures advocated in *The Catechism* are in flagrant contradiction to everything else Bakunin ever wrote or did.*

Some historians give the impression that Bakunin advocated indiscriminate violence against persons. To the contrary, he opposed regicide and repeatedly stressed that destruction must be directed not against persons but against institutions: ". . . It will then become unnecessary to destroy men and reap the inevitable reaction which massacres of human beings have never failed and never will fail to produce in every society."[17]†

Bakunin had no blanket formula covering all revolutions. Revolutions in underdeveloped countries with large peasant populations would take on a character different from those in relatively advanced industrial nations with well-organized labor movements, a substantial middle class, and great numbers of affluent farmers. In contrast to Marx, Bakunin believed that the revolution would be sparked by people with "the 'devil' in them"; by the "unchaining of the 'evil' passions" of those Marx called the *Lumpenproletariat*. Bakunin's *Lumpenproletariat*, however, was broader than Marx's, since it included all the submerged classes: unskilled, unemployed, and poor workers, poor peasant proprietors, landless agricultural laborers, oppressed racial

---

*For more information about the relationship between Bakunin and Nechaev, see Notes 13 and 14 to Guillaume's "Biographical Sketch," pp. 386–9.

†The reader will have noted a certain divergence, in the discussion of the preceding paragraphs, from the views expressed by Paul Avrich in his Preface. This divergence in no way reflects on the high esteem in which the editor holds Professor Avrich, both professionally and personally. After discussing our differences at some length, we decided, in the true anarchist spirit, simply to exercise mutual tolerance.

minorities, alienated and idealistic youth, déclassé intellectuals, and "bandits" (by whom Bakunin meant insurrectionary "Robin Hoods" like Pugachev, Stenka Razin, and the Italian Carbonari):

> Marx speaks disdainfully of this *Lumpenproletariat* . . . but in them, and only in them—and not in the bourgeois-minded strata of the working class—is crystallized the whole power and intelligence of the Social Revolution. In moments of crisis, the masses will not hesitate to burn down their own homes and neighborhoods . . . they develop a passion for destruction . . . of itself this negative passion is not nearly enough to attain the revolutionary heights. . . . But without it, revolution would be impossible. Revolution requires extensive and widespread destruction, a fecund and renovating destruction, since in this way, and only in this way, are new worlds born.[18]

Bakunin had faith in the latent revolutionary "instincts" of the masses which could be brought to the surface by their misery, by spontaneous outbursts, and by the propaganda and activist initiative of conscious, dedicated revolutionists. (For Bakunin, "instinct" could denote spontaneity, impulse, or aspiration, depending on the context.) Instinct and spontaneity, however are not enough:

> . . . For if instinct alone sufficed to liberate peoples, they would long since have freed themselves. These instincts did not prevent them from accepting . . . all the religious, political, and economic absurdities of which they have been the eternal victims. They are ineffectual because they lack two things . . . organization and knowledge.[19]

> . . . poverty and degradation are not sufficient to generate the Social Revolution. They may call forth sporadic local rebellions, but not great and widespread mass uprisings. . . . It is indispensable that the people be inspired by a universal ideal, . . . that they have a general idea of their rights, and a deep, passionate . . . belief in the validity of these rights. When this idea and this popular faith are joined to the kind of misery that leads to desperation then the Social Revolution is near and inevitable and no force on earth can stop it.[20]

Although Bakunin believed that only the great masses of the people could make a revolution, he envisaged an important role for those he described as "intelligent and noble youths who, though belonging by birth to the privileged classes, by their generous convictions and ardent sympathies embrace the cause of the people."[21] Here, Bakunin had in mind his own aristocratic background and that of other revolutionaries who, in his time as in our own, left comfortable and even luxurious homes behind to fight for an all-embracing humanitarian ideal. Such educated youth, by learning from the common people, could in turn render invaluable service to the people's cause.

Despite some impressions to the contrary, Bakunin was not a "putschist," a promoter of phony revolutions. With his views about the revolutionary potential of the *Lumpenproletariat*, he saw revolutions as most likely to occur in "backward" countries, rather than in the relatively affluent industrial nations, with their large elements of bourgeois-minded workers. In this respect, history has proved Bakunin right and Marx wrong; for the most notable revolutions of this century have been those that broke out in preindustrial Russia and China. And more recently, revolutionary ferment has proved to be greatest in African, Asian, and Central and South American lands.

Bakunin also attached great importance to psychological factors in revolution, insisting that revolution was impossible for people who had "lost the habit of freedom," and thereby adding another dimension to revolutionary theory. As against Marx's economic determinism, he left more room for Man's will, his aspiration to freedom and equality, and his "instinct of revolt," which constitutes the "revolutionary consciousness" of oppressed peoples. On the other hand, he did overstress the importance of "temperament" in revolution, asserting, for example, that Latin and Slavic peoples were libertarian by nature—incapable of forming a strong state of their own, the Slavs' statism was, so to speak, imported from Germany. Yet we see that Russia and Spain are today notably totalitarian states. And in Italy, where fascism first took hold, Mussolini was deposed only when he and his ally Hitler faced certain defeat.

Bakunin applied all that he had learned from his study of past upheavals such as the French Revolution and, above all, from his direct participation in the Revolution of 1848, to the

problems generated by the Franco-Prussian War of 1870. It was
during this period that Bakunin developed the idea of turning
such a war between national states into a civil war for the Social
Revolution. He believed that only a widespread guerrilla war
waged by the whole population could simultaneously repulse a
tyrannical foreign army and defend the Social Revolution against
domestic enemies: "When a nation of thirty-eight million people rises to defend itself, determined to destroy everything, and
ready to sacrifice their lives and possessions rather than submit
to slavery, no army in the world, however powerful, however
well organized and equipped with the most extraordinary weapons, will be able to conquer it."[22] The recent history of Algeria
and Vietnam certainly bears him out in this regard.

Bakunin's warnings to the Bolsheviks of his day, the Jacobins
and the Blanquists, as to where their policies could lead, read
almost like a preview of the general course of the Russian Revolution from its inception to the final seizure of power and the
establishment of a totalitarian state:

> . . . the construction of a powerfully centralized revolutionary
> State . . . would inevitably lead to the establishment of a military
> dictatorship . . . it would again condemn the masses, governed by
> edict, to immobility . . . to slavery and exploitation by a new, quasi-
> revolutionary aristocracy . . . hence the triumph of the Jacobins or
> the Blanquists would be the death of the revolution.[23]

To save the Revolution, Bakunin worked out a libertarian
strategy based on the principle that the forms of the new society
are generated by the Revolution itself. Thus, a revolution directed from a single center, or even a number of urban centers,
by means of commissars and with military expeditions to enforce
decrees, must inevitably produce a new authoritarian regime:
today's commissars will become tomorrow's rulers. Bakunin
believed, therefore, in a general revolution embracing both the
cities and the countryside, and directed by the workers and
peasants in each locality. Properly coordinated at every level,
such a revolution would from the outset naturally assume a
libertarian and federalist character.

Among Bakunin's most significant contributions to modern revolutionary theory was his confidence in the revolutionary capacities of the peasantry. To be sure, he did not idealize them: he knew that they were ignorant, superstitious, and conservative. But he believed that if the radicals and progressive city workers would abandon their snobbish attitudes and try to understand the peasants' problems, the latter could be won over to the side of the Revolution. And, indeed, since poor peasants and landless laborers constituted the overwhelming mass of the rural population, the very fate of the Revolution—as Bakunin well realized—hinged upon actively involving them in the struggle, not as second-class citizens, but in brotherly solidarity with the urban workers. If the revolutionaries called instead for the immediate confiscation of their little parcels of land, and refused to redistribute the estates of rich landowners and Church and State properties among the millions of landless peasants, the latter would reinforce the armies of reaction, and the Revolution would be nipped in the bud. And over and above purely practical considerations, Bakunin feared the corrupting effect of ruthless measures against the peasants on the revolutionaries themselves. The erosion of moral and ethical principles would alone be sufficient to undermine the Social Revolution.

Bakunin repeatedly warned against the usurpation of the Revolution by even a socialist government, which would institute collectivization (or any other measures) by decree. Its commissars and military expeditions would fan out over the countryside to expropriate the poorer peasants and institute a reign of terror like that which precipitated the collapse of the French Revolution.

Within our own lifetimes, we have witnessed Stalin's reign of terror instituted as a means of forced collectivization. The Russian landworkers, unable to revolt by force of arms, resorted to an unrelenting, silent, but no less effective war of nonviolent resistance. By acts of sabotage, slowdowns, and other means, the peasants greatly cut agricultural production. This is one of the main reasons why a regime capable of launching sputniks is still unable to solve its agricultural problems, even half a century after the Revolution. More generally, we may say that the Russian Revolution was doomed to fail when it lost its local and spontaneous character. The emerging creative forms of social life, the soviets and other associations of the people, were aborted by the concentration of power in the State.

Bakunin's views on this subject are still relevant to the revolutionary struggles in the underdeveloped countries that comprise two-thirds of the world's population.[24] He himself summed up these views in the following words: "The constructive tasks of the Social Revolution, the new forms of social life, can emerge only from the living experience of the grass-roots organizations which will themselves build the new society according to their manifold needs and desires."[25]

Bakunin's intense concern with the peasant problem has given rise to yet another false impression—namely, that he expounded a sort of primitive peasant anarchism and did not pay enough attention to the problems of the industrial proletariat in the comparatively advanced industrial nations of Western Europe. To the contrary, he counted on the urban workers to play a leading role in radicalizing the peasants. Indeed, the First International (the International Workingmen's Association, founded in September 1864) arose precisely out of the need for effective organization of the proletariat in increasingly industrialized countries. Perhaps the most fruitful years of Bakunin's life were those dedicated to promoting libertarian principles in the International. No revolutionary was more concerned than he with the problems of the labor movement, and his analysis, among other things, of the root causes of the evils afflicting the modern labor movement remains as timely as ever.[26]

It is impossible, in fact, to write a history of the international labor movement without taking into account the enormous influence of Bakunin's ideas in Spain, Italy, France, Belgium, Central and South America, and even the United States. It was Bakunin and the other libertarian members of the International who worked out the fundamental principles of the revolutionary syndicalist movements which flourished in these countries from the 1890's till the defeat of the Spanish Revolution in 1939. As Professor Paul Brissenden long ago pointed out:

There is no doubt that all the main ideas of modern revolutionary unionism as exhibited in the I.W.W. may be found in the old International Workingmen's Association. The I.W.W. organ *Industrial Worker* asserts that we: ". . . must trace the ideas of modern revolutionary unionism to the International. . . . Many items in the program originally drafted by the famous anarchist, Michael Bakunin, for the International in 1868 were similar to the twentieth century slogans of the I.W.W."[27]

The clash of personalities between Marx and Bakunin has been overemphasized, at least as an essential element in their running controversy during the congresses of the International. They should be seen, rather, as embodying two diametrically opposed tendencies in the theory and tactics of socialism—the authoritarian and the libertarian schools, respectively, the two main lines of thought that have helped shape the character of the modern labor movement.

Many socialists of both camps, Bakunin included, then believed the collapse of capitalism and the social revolution to be imminent. Although this was an illusion, the debate they conducted on fundamental principles has remained pertinent, and in various forms, still goes on. To many others at the time —as a French political scientist, Michel Collinet, has pointed out—the issues discussed by the authoritarian Marxists and the libertarian Bakuninists seemed to be merely abstract speculation about what might happen in the distant future; but the problems which then seemed so far-fetched, he says, ". . . are today crucial; they are being decisively posed not only in totalitarian regimes, which relate themselves to Marx, but also in the so-called capitalist nations which are being dominated by the growing power of the state."[28]

Collinet lists the basic points in question: How can liberty and free development be assured in an increasingly industrialized society? How can capitalist exploitation and oppression by the State be eliminated? Must power be centralized, or should it be diffused among multiple federated units? Must the capitalist State be supplanted by a workers' State, or should the workers destroy *all* forms of State power? Should the International be the model of a new society or simply an instrument of the State or of political parties? At the Congress of Lausanne in 1867, the Belgian delegate, Caesar de Paepe, raised just such a question regarding "the efforts now being made by the International for the emancipation of the workers. Could this not," he inquired, "result in the creation of a new class of ex-workers who wield State power, and would not the situation of the workers be much more miserable than it is now?"[29]

Collinet remarks that "In this respect, the criticisms of Bakunin and the Belgian collectivists were singularly cogent. Is it not in the name of 'socialism' that the people in the totalitarian countries are so heavily oppressed?"[30]

Bakunin was deeply concerned over the internal organization of the International, which he insisted must correspond to the new society that it was struggling to bring about (a concern amply justified, if we consider the many autocratically organized unions of today, which constitute in themselves miniature States). He maintained that the workers, by constructing their unions in accordance with libertarian principles, would "create within the old society the living seeds of the new social order . . . they are creating not only the ideas, but the facts of the future itself. . . ."[31]

Although a strong advocate of revolutionary syndicalist principles, Bakunin did not see it as either practicable or desirable that society be controlled solely by unions or by any other single agency: the abuse of power is a perpetual temptation. He maintained that a free society must be a pluralistic society in which the infinite needs of Man will be reflected in an adequate variety of organizations. Geoffrey Osterrgard, in a significant article, "The Relevance of Syndicalism," quotes the historian of socialism G. D. H. Cole as saying toward the end of his life: "I am neither a Communist nor a Social-Democrat because I regard both as creeds of totalitarianism, and . . . society must rest on the widest possible diffusion of power and responsibility. . . ."[32] Osterrgard, who shares Cole's view, concludes that:

   . . . the socialists of this generation will have to take a long step backwards if they are to move forward again in the right direction. They will have to reassess the whole libertarian tradition . . .

and from this reassessment draw sustenance for a new third camp movement.[33]

In such a reexamination, much can still be learned from the failures as well as the achievements of Bakunin and the other pioneers who fought for freedom a century ago.

Michael Bakunin

———◆————

A Biographical Sketch
by James Guillaume
1844–1916

James Guillaume, Bakunin's friend and comrade-in-arms, edited the last five volumes of the six-volume French edition of his collected works. Guillaume's biographical sketch of Bakunin, here Englished in its entirety for the first time, originally appeared in his introduction to Volume II of that edition.

This sketch is a primary source not only on the life of Bakunin, but also on the most significant events in the socialist movement of that period. It incidentally contributes valuable background information for many of the other selections in the present volume. Guillaume, who did not limit himself to recording events but also took part in shaping them, had been inclined toward anarchism even before he met Bakunin in 1869. Earlier, he had been one of the founders of the First International in Switzerland, where it held its first congress, in Geneva, in 1866. He attended all its congresses, and eventually published a four-volume history of the International which has become an indispensable source on the socialist movement of the period as well as on the origins of the revolutionary syndicalist movement of the early 1900's in France and elsewhere. Guillaume also wrote widely on libertarian theory and practice (see selection, p. 356) and edited a number of periodicals. His extensive writings on cultural subjects included substantial contributions to the theory of libertarian progressive education as represented particularly by the early-nineteenth-century Swiss educator Johann Pestalozzi.

MICHAEL ALEXANDROVICH BAKUNIN was born on May 18, 1814[1] on his family's estate in the little village of Premukhino, in the province of Tver. His father was a career diplomat who, as a young attaché, had lived for years in Florence and Naples. Upon his return to Russia, he settled down on his paternal estate where, at the age of forty, he married an eighteen-year-old girl from the prominent Muraviev family. Given to liberal ideas, he was for a while platonically involved with one of the Decembrist[2] clubs. After Nicholas I became Tsar, however, Bakunin gave up politics and devoted himself to the care of his estate and the education of his children, five girls and five boys, the oldest of whom was Michael.

At fifteen, Michael entered the Artillery School in St. Petersburg where, three years later, he was commissioned a junior officer and sent to garrison in the provinces of Minsk and of Grodno, in Poland. He arrived in the latter post shortly after the Polish insurrection of 1832 had been crushed. The spectacle of Poland terrorized shocked the gently bred young officer and deepened his hatred of despotism. Two years later, he resigned from the army and went to Moscow, where he lived for the next six years, spending some summer vacations on the family estate.

In Moscow, Bakunin studied philosophy and began to read the French Encyclopedists. His enthusiasm for the philosophy of Fichte, shared with his friends Stankevich and Belinsky,[3] led Bakunin to translate, in 1836, Fichte's *Vorlesungen über die Bestimmung des Gelehrten (Lectures on the Vocation of the Scholar)*. From Fichte, Bakunin went on to immerse himself in the philosophy of Hegel, then the most influential thinker among German intellectuals. The young man wholeheartedly embraced Hegelianism, bedazzled by the famous maxim that "Everything that exists is rational"—even though it also served to justify the Prussian state. In 1839 he met Alexander Herzen and the latter's friend Nicholas Ogarev, who had returned from exile to Moscow; but their ideas and his were too divergent at the time for a meeting of minds.

In 1840, aged twenty-six, Bakunin went to St. Petersburg and thence to Germany, to study and prepare himself for a professorship in philosophy or history at the University of Moscow. When, in the same year, Nicholas Stankevich died in Italy, Bakunin still believed in the immortality of the soul (letter to Herzen, October 23, 1840). In the course of his intellectual evolution, however, he came to interpret the philosophy of Hegel as a revolutionary theory. As Ludwig Feuerbach, in his *The Essence of Christianity*, arrived at atheism by means of Hegelian doctrine, so Michael Bakunin applied Hegel to his own political and social ideas and arrived at social revolution.

From Berlin, Bakunin moved in 1842 to Dresden. There he collaborated with Arnold Ruge[4] in publishing the *Deutsche Jahrbücher* ("German Yearbooks"), in which he first began to formulate his revolutionary ideas. His article "Reaction in Germany: A Fragment by a Frenchman" concluded with the famous declaration:

> Let us put our trust in the eternal spirit which destroys and annihilates only because it is the unfathomable and eternally creative source of all life. The desire for destruction is also a creative desire.

Herzen believed at first that the article had actually been written by a Frenchman, and wrote in his personal diary that "this is a powerful and firm appeal, a victory for the democratic party. The article is from beginning to end bound to arouse wide interest."

The illustrious German poet Georg Herwegh visited Bakunin in Dresden, and the two men formed a lasting friendship. A resident of Dresden who also became Bakunin's devoted friend was the musician Adolf Reichel.

Within a short time the Saxon government became overtly hostile toward Ruge and his collaborators, and Bakunin and Herwegh left Saxony for Switzerland. There Bakunin came into contact with the German communists grouped around Wilhelm Weitling.[5] In Bern during the winter of 1843–44, a lifelong friendship developed with Adolf Vogt, who later became professor of medicine at the University of Bern. When the Russian government demanded that the Swiss authorities deport Bakunin to Russia, he left Bern in February 1844, stopping first in Brussels and then in Paris, where he remained until 1847.

II

In Paris Bakunin again met Herwegh, the latter's wife, Emma Siegmund, and Karl Marx, who had arrived there in 1843. Marx at first collaborated with Arnold Ruge, but he and Engels soon went their own way and began to formulate their own ideology. Bakunin saw much of Proudhon, with whom he held night-long discussions, and was also on friendly terms with George Sand. The years in Paris were the most fruitful for Bakunin's intellectual development—it was then that the basic outlines of the ideas underlying his revolutionary program began to take shape, though it was not until much later that he freed himself entirely of metaphysical idealism. Bakunin himself informs us, in a manuscript written in 1871, of his intellectual relations with Marx and Proudhon during this period. He recalls that:

> As far as learning was concerned, Marx was, and still is, incomparably more advanced than I. I knew nothing at that time of political economy, I had not yet rid myself of my metaphysical aberrations, and my socialism was only instinctive. Although younger than I, he was already an atheist, a conscious materialist, and an informed socialist. It was precisely at this time that he was elaborating the foundations of his system as it stands today. We saw each other often. I greatly respected him for his learning and for his passionate devotion—though it was always mingled with vanity—to the cause of the proletariat. I eagerly sought his conversation, which was always instructive and witty when it was not inspired by petty hate, which alas! was only too often the case. There was never any frank intimacy between us—our temperaments did not permit it. He called me a sentimental idealist, and he was right; I called him vain, perfidious, and cunning, and I also was right.

Bakunin offers the following characterization of Engels in his book *Statism and Anarchy*:

In 1845 Marx was the leader of the German communists. While his devoted friend Engels was just as intelligent as he, he was not as erudite. Nevertheless, Engels was more practical, and no less adept at political calumny, lying, and intrigue. Together they founded a secret society of German communists or authoritarian socialists.

In a French manuscript of 1870, Bakunin evaluates Proudhon, comparing him to Marx:

As I told him a few months before his death, Proudhon, in spite of all his efforts to shake off the tradition of classical idealism, remained all his life an incorrigible idealist, immersed in the Bible, in Roman law and metaphysics. His great misfortune was that he had never studied the natural sciences or appropriated their method. He had the instincts of a genius and he glimpsed the right road, but hindered by his idealistic thinking patterns, he fell always into the old errors. Proudhon was a perpetual contradiction: a vigorous genius, a revolutionary thinker arguing against idealistic phantoms, and yet never able to surmount them himself. . . . Marx as a thinker is on the right path. He has established the principle that juridical evolution in history is not the cause but the effect of economic development, and this is a great and fruitful concept. Though he did not originate it—it was to a greater or lesser extent formulated before him by many others—to Marx belongs the credit for solidly establishing it as the basis for an economic system. On the other hand, Proudhon understood and felt liberty much better than he. Proudhon, when not obsessed with metaphysical doctrine, was a revolutionary by instinct; he adored Satan and proclaimed Anarchy. Quite possibly Marx could construct a still more rational system of liberty, but he lacks the instinct of liberty—he remains from head to foot an authoritarian.

On November 29, 1847, at a banquet in Paris commemorating the Polish insurrection of 1830, Bakunin delivered a speech in which he severely denounced the Russian government. At the request of the Russian Ambassador, Kiselev, he was expelled from France. To counteract the widespread protests of those who sympathized with Bakunin, Kiselev circulated the rumor that he had been employed by the Russian government to pose as a revolutionary, but that he had gone too far. (This is related by Bakunin in a letter to Fanelli, May 29, 1867.) Bakunin then went to Brussels, where he again met Marx. Of Marx and his circle, Bakunin wrote to his friend Herwegh:

> The German workers, Bornstadt, Marx, Engels—especially Marx—poison the atmosphere. Vanity, malevolence, gossip, pretentiousness and boasting in theory and cowardice in practice. Dissertations about life, action, and feeling—and complete absence of life, action, and feeling—and complete absence of life. Disgusting flattery of the more advanced workers—and empty talk. According to them, Feuerbach is a "bourgeois," and the epithet BOURGEOIS! is shouted *ad nauseam* by people who are from head to foot more bourgeois than anyone in a provincial city—in short, foolishness and lies, lies and foolishness. In such an atmosphere no one can breathe freely. I stay away from them and I have openly declared that I will not go to their *Kommunistischer Handwerkerverein* [Communist Trade Union Society] and will have nothing to do with this organization.

III

The revolution of February 24, 1848, opened the doors of France once again to Bakunin. Just as he was about to return to Paris, however, events in Vienna and Berlin caused him to change his plans, and he left for Germany in April. He was also then hoping to participate in the Polish insurrectionary movement. In Cologne, he again met Marx and Engels, who had begun publication of their *Neue Rheinische Zeitung*. It was at this time that the "Democratic Legion of Paris" organized an expedition to Germany to stage an insurrection in the Grand Duchy of Baden. The attempt was a disastrous failure. Marx and Engels violently attacked Bakunin's friend Herwegh, who together with other German exiles was one of the leaders of this ill-fated expedition. Bakunin came to his defense. Much later—in 1871—Bakunin wrote that "I must openly admit that in this controversy Marx and Engels were in the right. With characteristic insolence, they attacked Herwegh personally when he was not there to defend himself. In a face-to-face confrontation with them, I heatedly defended Herwegh, and our mutual dislike began then."

Later, in June 1848, Bakunin went to Berlin and Breslau and then to Prague, where he tried to influence the Slav Congress in a revolutionary democratic direction. After participating in the week-long insurrection, which was brutally suppressed, he returned to Breslau. He was still there when the *Neue Rheinische Zeitung*—controlled by Marx—published in its July 6 issue a letter from a Paris correspondent which read, in part:

> In regard to pro-Slav propaganda, we were told yesterday that George Sand possesses documents which greatly compromise the Russian exile Michael Bakunin and reveal him as an instrument or newly enrolled AGENT OF RUSSIA, who played a key part in the arrest of the unfortunate Poles. George Sand has shown these documents to some of her friends.

Bakunin immediately protested this infamous slander in a letter published in the *Allgemeine Oder Zeitung* of Breslau, and reprinted in the *Neue Rheinische Zeitung* on July 16. He also wrote to George Sand asking for an explanation. She replied in an open letter to the editor of the *Neue Rheinische Zeitung*:

> The allegations of your correspondent are entirely false. There are no documents. I do not have the slightest proof of the insinuations that you make against M. Bakunin. I have never had, nor have I ever authorized any one else to cast, the slightest doubt on his personal integrity and devotion to his principles. I appeal to your sense of honor and to your conscience to print this letter immediately in your paper.

Marx printed her letter together with the comment: "We have fulfilled the obligation of the press to exercise strict vigilance over prominent public individuals and at the same time given M. Bakunin the opportunity to dispel suspicions which have been current in certain Paris circles."

It is useless to elaborate on the singular theory that it is the duty of the press to publish false and libelous accusations without attempting to verify the facts!

The next month Bakunin and Marx met again in Berlin, and a reluctant reconciliation was effected. Bakunin recalled the incident in 1871: "Mutual friends induced us to embrace, and during our conversation Marx remarked, half-smilingly, 'Do you know that I am now the chief of a secret communist society, so well disciplined that had I said to any member, "Kill Bakunin," you would be dead?' "

Expelled from Prussia and Saxony, Bakunin spent the rest of the year 1848 in the principality of Anhalt. There he published, in German, the pamphlet *Appeal to the Slavs: By a Russian Patriot, Michael Bakunin, Member of the Slav Congress*. In this work he proposed that revolutionary Slavs unite with the revolutionaries of other nations—Hungarians, Germans, Italians—to overthrow the three major autocracies of the time: the Russian Empire, the Austro-Hungarian Empire, and the Kingdom of Prussia; this would be followed by the free federation of the emancipated Slavic peoples. Marx criticized these ideas in the *Neue Rheinische Zeitung* of February 14, 1849:

> Bakunin is our friend, but this does not prevent us from criticizing his pamphlet. Apart from the Russians, the Poles, and perhaps the Turkish Slavs, no Slavic people has a future, for the simple reason that they lack the indispensable historical, geographical, political, and industrial conditions for independence and vitality.

Regarding the difference between Marx's and his own views on the Slavic question, Bakunin wrote, in 1871:

> In 1848 we disagreed, and I must admit that his reasoning was more correct than mine. Carried away, enraptured by the atmosphere of the revolutionary movement, I was much more interested in the negative than in the positive aspect of the revolution. Nevertheless, there is one point on which Marx was wrong, and I was right. As a Slav, I wanted the emancipation of the Slavic race from the German yoke, and as a German patriot he did not admit then, nor will he admit now, the right of the Slavs to free themselves from German domination. He thought then, as he does now, that the mission of the Germans is to civilize—that is to say, Germanize—the Slavs, for better or for worse.[6]

In January 1849 Bakunin secretly arrived in Leipzig. There, together with a group of young Czechs from Prague, he occupied himself with preparations for an uprising in Bohemia. In spite of the growing reaction in Germany and France, hope still lived, for there was more than one place in Europe where the revolution had not yet been crushed. Pope Pius IX, expelled from Rome, had been replaced by the Roman Republic, headed by the triumvirate of Mazzini, Saffi, and Armellini, with Garibaldi in command of the army. Venice, its freedom regained, heroically repulsed the siege of the Austrians; the Hungarians, rebelling against Austria under the leadership of Kossuth, proclaimed the defeat of the Habsburgs. And on May 3, 1849, a popular rebellion broke out in Dresden, provoked by the refusal of the King of Saxony to accept the constitution of the German Empire approved by the Frankfurt Parliament. The King fled, and a provisional government was proclaimed. For five days the rebels controlled the city. Bakunin, who had left Leipzig for Dresden in the middle of April, became one of the leaders of the rebellion and inspired the highest measure of heroism in the men defending the barricades against the Prussian troops. A gigantic figure of a man, already renowned as a revolutionary, Bakunin became the focus of all eyes. An aura of legend soon enveloped him. To him alone were attributed the fires set by the rebels; about him it was written that he was "the very soul of the Revolution," that he initiated widespread terrorism, that to stop the Prussians from shooting into the barricades he advised the defenders to take the art treasures from the museums and galleries and display them from the barricades—the stories were endless.

On May 9 the rebels—greatly outnumbered and outgunned—retreated to Freiberg. There Bakunin pleaded in vain with Stephen Born (organizer of the Arbeiter Verbrüderung, the first organization of German workers) to take his remaining troops to Bohemia and spark a new uprising. Born refused, and disbanded his forces. Seeing that there was nothing more to be done, Bakunin, the composer Richard Wagner, and Heubner—a democrat, very loyal to Bakunin—went to Chemnitz. There, during the night, armed bourgeois arrested Heubner and Bakunin and turned them over to the Prussians. Wagner hid in his sister's house and escaped.

The role of Bakunin in this rebellion had been that of a determined fighter as well as a leading strategist. Even the hostile Marx felt obliged to acknowledge his outstanding contribution in one of his letters, some years later, to the New York *Daily Tribune* (October 2, 1852), entitled "Revolution and Counter-revolution in Germany":

> In Dresden, the battle in the streets went on for four days. The shopkeepers of Dresden, organized into "community guards," not only refused to fight, but many of them supported the troops against the insurrectionists. Almost all of the rebels were workers from the surrounding factories. In the Russian refugee Michael Bakunin they found a capable and cool-headed leader.

IV

Conducted to the Königstein fortress, Bakunin spent many months in detention, and eventually was condemned to death, on January 14, 1850. In June his sentence was commuted to life imprisonment, and the prisoner was then extradited to Austria, at the request of the Austrian authorities. Bakunin was first jailed in Prague and then, in March 1851, transferred to Olmütz, where he was sentenced to hang. Once again his sentence was commuted to life imprisonment. He was brutally treated in the Austrian prisons: his hands and feet were chained, and in Olmütz he was chained to the prison wall.

Shortly thereafter, the Austrians handed Bakunin over to Russia, where he was imprisoned in the dreadful dungeons of the Fortress of Peter and Paul. At the beginning of his captivity, Count Orlov, an emissary of the Tsar, visited Bakunin and told him that the Tsar requested a written confession, hoping that the confession would place Bakunin spiritually as well as physically in the power of the Russian Bear. Since all his acts were known, he had no secrets to reveal, and so he decided to write to the Tsar:

> You want my confession; but you must know that a penitent sinner is not obliged to implicate or reveal the misdeeds of others. I have only the honor and the conscience that I have never betrayed anyone who has confided in me, and this is why I will not give you any names.

When the Tsar, Nicholas I, read Bakunin's letter, he remarked, "He is a good lad, full of spirit, but he is a dangerous man and we must never cease watching him."[7]

With the outbreak of the Crimean War in 1854, the Fortress of Peter and Paul was exposed to bombardment by the English, and Bakunin was transferred to Schlüsselberg prison. There he was attacked by scurvy, and all his teeth fell out. Let me now interject what I myself wrote the day after Bakunin died, stating only what he personally told me about the last period of his imprisonment:

> The atrocious prison diet had completely ruined his stomach (scurvy) so that anything he ate caused nausea and vomiting, and he could digest only finely chopped sour cabbage. But if his body was debilitated, his spirit was indomitable. It was this above all he feared, that prison life would break his spirit; that he would no longer hate injustice and feel in his heart the passion for rebellion that sustained him; that the day would come when he would pardon his tormentors and accept his fate. But he need not have feared: not for a single moment did his spirit waver, and he emerged from the purgatory of his confinement as he entered, undaunted and defiant. . . .

> He recounted to us, also, that to distract his mind from his long, loathsome solitude, he found pleasure in mentally reenacting the legend of Prometheus the Titan, benefactor of mankind, who while chained to the Caucasian Rock by order of Olympus, heard the sweet plaintive melody of the ocean nymphs bringing consolation and joy to the victim of Jupiter's vengeance.[8]

It was hoped that with the death of Nicholas I Bakunin's situation would be to some extent alleviated. However, the new Tsar, Alexander II, personally crossed Bakunin's name off the amnesty list. Much later, Bakunin's mother went before the Tsar and begged him to have mercy on her son; but the autocrat answered, "Madame, while your son remains alive, he will not be freed." One day Alexander, while reading the letter that Bakunin had written his predecessor in 1851, remarked to his aide, Prince Goncharov, "But I don't see the least sign of repentance."

In 1857 Alexander was at last induced to relent, and Bakunin was released from prison and sentenced to perpetual exile in

Siberia. He was given permission to reside in the Tomsk region. In the latter part of 1858 he married a young Polish girl, Antonia Kwiatkowski. Somewhat later—through the intervention of a relative on his mother's side, Nicholas Muraviev, Governor General of Eastern Siberia—Bakunin was permitted to move to Irkutsk. There he was at first employed by a government agency, the Amur Development Authority, and later in a mining enterprise.

Bakunin had expected to be freed quickly and allowed to return to Russia. But Muraviev, who was trying to help him, lost his post because he opposed the bureaucracy, and Bakunin realized that he could regain his liberty in only one way: escape. Leaving Irkutsk in mid-June 1861 on the pretext of business— alleged commercial negotiations and a government-authorized study—Bakunin arrived in Nikolaevsk in July. From there he sailed on the government vessel *Strelok* to Kastri, a southern port, where he managed to board the American merchant ship *Vickery*, which took him to Hakodate, Japan. He went next to Yokohama, then in October to San Francisco, and in November to New York. On December 27, 1861, Bakunin arrived in London, where he was welcomed like a long-lost brother by Herzen and Ogarev.

V

I will briefly summarize Bakunin's activity during the six years after his return to Western Europe. He soon realized that despite his personal friendship with Herzen and Ogarev, he could not associate himself with the political line of their journal, *Kolokol* ("The Bell"). During the year 1862, Bakunin expounded his current ideas in two pamphlets: *To My Russian, Polish, and Other Slav Friends* and *Romanov, Pugachev, or Pestel?*[9]

The outbreak of the Polish insurrection of 1863 found Bakunin trying to unite all men of action to render effective aid and deepen the revolution. But attempts to organize a Russian legion failed, and the expedition of Colonel Lapinski came to naught. Bakunin then went to Stockholm—where he was reunited with his wife—hoping to get help from Sweden. His plans all failed, however, and he returned to London. He next went to Italy, and in the middle of 1864 returned to Sweden. Thence he went back once more to London, where he again saw Marx, and then to Paris, where he was reunited with Proudhon. Finally he went back to Italy.

As a consequence of the war of 1859 and Garibaldi's heroic expedition of 1860, Italy then stood on the threshold of a new era. Bakunin remained there until 1867, living first in Florence and then in and around Naples. It was during this period that he conceived the plan of forming a secret organization of revolutionaries to carry on propaganda work and prepare for direct action at a suitable time. From 1864 onward he steadily recruited Italians, Frenchmen, Scandinavians, and Slavs into a secret society known as the International Brotherhood, also called the Alliance of Revolutionary Socialists. He and his friends also combated the devoutly religious followers of the republican Mazzini, whose watchword was "God and Country." In Naples, Bakunin established the journal *Libertà e Giustizia* ("Liberty and Justice"), in which he developed his revolutionary program.[10]

In July 1866 he informed his friends Herzen and Ogarev about the secret society and its program, on which he had been concentrating all his efforts for two years. According to Bakunin, the society then had members in Sweden, Norway, Denmark, Belgium, England, France, Spain, and Italy, as well as Polish and Russian members.

In 1867 bourgeois democratic pacifists of many lands (though preponderantly French and German) founded The League for Peace and Freedom and convened a congress in Geneva which aroused wide interest. Although Bakunin had few illusions about the new organization, he hoped to propagandize its members in favor of revolutionary socialism. He attended the congress, addressed the delegates, and became a member of the Central Committee of the League. For a whole year he tried to induce the Committee to adopt a social revolutionary program. At the second congress of the League, in Bern in 1868, Bakunin and his colleagues in the Alliance of Revolutionary Socialists tried to persuade the congress to adopt unambiguously revolutionary resolutions. After several days of heated debate, however, the resolutions were voted down. The minority faction of revolutionary socialists then resigned from the League, on September 25, 1868, and that same day founded a new, open—not secret —organization, called the International Alliance of Socialist Democracy. The Alliance's Declaration of Principles was written by Bakunin; a summary of his ideas, it was the product and culmination of the long period of ideological development he had begun in Germany in 1842. Among other things, it stated that:

> The alliance declares itself atheist; it seeks the complete and definitive abolition of classes and the political, economic, and social equality of both sexes. It wants the land and the instruments of labor (production), like all other property, to be converted into the collective property of the whole society for utilization by the workers; that is, by agricultural and industrial associations. It affirms that all the existing political and authoritarian States, which are to be reduced to simple administrative functions dealing with public utilities in their respective countries, must eventually be replaced by a worldwide union of free associations, agricultural and industrial.

The New Alliance affirmed its desire to become a branch of the International, whose statutes it accepted.

Just a few weeks earlier (September 1) the first issue of a Russian-language journal, *Narodnoye Dyelo* ("Public Affairs"), had appeared, under the editorship of Bakunin and Nicholas Zhukovsky, and had published a "Program of Russian Socialist Democracy"—a program that coincided, in the main, with that of the Alliance. With the second issue, however, the editorship changed hands: the paper fell under the control of Nicholas Utin, who gave it an entirely different orientation.[11]

VI

The International Workingmen's Association was founded in London on September 23, 1864, but its structure and its constitution were not formally adopted until the first congress convened in Geneva, September 3–8, 1866. In October 1864

Bakunin again met Marx, whom he had not seen since 1848. Marx requested this meeting to reestablish friendly relations with Bakunin who had been estranged when, in 1853, Marx's *Neue Rheinische Zeitung* repeated the old libel that Bakunin was a Russian agent. Mazzini and Herzen defended Bakunin, who was at that time in a Russian prison. Later in 1853 Marx had declared in the English paper *Morning Advertiser* that he was Bakunin's friend and had personally assured Bakunin that this was still the case. At their reunion in 1864, Marx invited Bakunin to join the International, but Bakunin preferred to return to Italy to devote himself to his secret organization. Bakunin's decision was understandable. At that time the International, outside of the General Council in London and a few Mutualist workers from Paris, could hardly be considered an international organization, and no one could foresee the importance it later assumed. It was only after the second congress at Lausanne in September 1867, the two strikes in Paris, and the great strike at Geneva (1868) that it drew serious attention and its revolutionary capabilities could no longer be ignored. In its third congress, in Brussels in 1868, the theories of cooperativism and Proudhonist Mutualism were seriously challenged by those of revolution and collective ownership.

In July 1868 Bakunin became a member of the Geneva section of the International, and after resigning from the "League for Peace and Freedom" at its Bern Congress, he settled in Geneva in order to participate actively in the labor movement of the city. Intensive propaganda sparked the growth of the International. A trip to Spain by Fanelli (an Italian revolutionary socialist and coworker of Bakunin) resulted in the establishment of the International in Madrid and Barcelona. The French sections of French-speaking Switzerland united into a federation under the name "Romance Federation of the International" and in January 1869 launched their official organ, the magazine *L'Égalité*. *L'Égalité* attacked the false socialists of the Swiss Jura (mountains) and won the enthusiastic support of a majority of the region's workers for revolutionary socialism. On various occasions, Bakunin came to the Jura to denounce what he called "collaboration between workers and employers, alliances—masked as cooperation—with bourgeois political parties and reactionary groups," gradually forming a lasting friendship with the militant workers. In Geneva itself, a conflict took place between construction workers, who were instinctively revolutionary, and the better-paid and highly skilled watch and jewelry workers, who called themselves "Fabrica" and who wanted to participate in election campaigns with the bourgeois radicals. Those of a revolutionary tendency had the powerful encouragement of Bakunin, who, in addition to his public addresses, formulated his program and exposed the opportunists in a series of notable articles such as "The Policy of the International" [see selection in present volume], printed in L'Égalité. As a result, the Bakuninists won out—although this victory proved, regrettably, temporary. Nonetheless, since the Belgian, Spanish, French, and French-Swiss sections of the International all favored collectivism, its adoption by a large majority at the next congress was assured.

The General Council of London refused to admit the Alliance as a branch of the International because the Alliance would constitute what amounted to a second international body in the International, thereby causing confusion and disorganization. Unquestionably one of the motives for this decision was Marx's ill will toward Bakunin, whom the German regarded as a schemer aiming to "break up the International and convert it into his own tool." But in any case, irrespective of Marx's personal sentiments, Bakunin's idea of forming a dual organization was unfortunate. When this was explained to him by his Belgian and Swiss comrades, he recognized the justice of the General Council's decision. The Central Bureau of the Alliance, after consulting the members, dissolved the Alliance, and the local group in Geneva became a simple section of the International which was then admitted to membership by the General Council in July 1869.

The fourth general congress of the International (Basel, September 6–12, 1869) almost unanimously endorsed the principle of collective property, but it soon became evident that the delegates were divided into two distinct ideological groups. The Germans, Swiss-Germans, and English were state communists.

The opposing group—Belgians, Swiss-French, French, and Spaniards—were antiauthoritarian communists, federalists, or anarchists who took the name "Collectivists." Bakunin, naturally, belonged to this faction, which included the Belgian De Paepe and the Parisian Varlin.[12]

The secret organization founded by Bakunin in 1864 was dissolved in January 1869 because of an internal crisis, but many of its members kept in touch with each other. The intimate circle attracted new friends, Swiss, Spaniards, and Frenchmen, Varlin among them. This free contact of men united for collective action in an informal revolutionary fraternity was continued in order to strengthen and give more cohesion to the great revolutionary movement which the International represented.

In the summer of 1869, Borkheim, a friend of Marx, repeated in the Berlin journal *Zukunft* ("The Future") the old libel that Bakunin was a Russian agent, and Wilhelm Liebknecht, a founder of the German Social Democratic party, at various times continued to spread this falsehood. When Bakunin met Liebknecht at the Basel Congress, he challenged him to prove his charges before an impartial "court of honor." Liebknecht explained that he had never personally slandered Bakunin, but had only repeated what he read in the papers, primarily the *Zukunft*. The court of honor unanimously found Liebknecht guilty and signed a statement to that effect. Liebknecht admitted that he was wrong and shook hands with Bakunin, who then set fire to the statement, using it to light his cigarette.

After the Basel Congress, Bakunin moved to Locarno, where he could live cheaply and where he would not be distracted while making a number of Russian translations for a St. Petersburg publisher (the first was of volume one of Marx's *Das Kapital*).[13] Unfortunately, Bakunin's departure from Geneva left the field open for the political machinations of a group headed by the Russian immigrant Nicholas Utin. In a few months they disrupted the Russian section of the International, occupied the key posts, and seized control of its organ, *L'Égalité*. Marx entered into an alliance with Utin and his camarilla of pseudosocialists of the "Temple Unico," the old Masonic hall used as a meeting place for the Geneva International. Meanwhile, on March 28,

Marx addressed his notorious "Confidential Communication" to his German friends in order to stir up hatred among the German Democratic Socialists against Bakunin. He represented him as an agent of the pan-Slavist party, from which, Marx declared, Bakunin received twenty-five thousand francs per year.

In April 1870, Utin and his Geneva conspirators engineered a split of the Romance Federation into two factions. The first faction, which took the name "Jura Federation," was in agreement with the Internationalists of France, Belgium, and Spain. They adopted a revolutionary antiauthoritarian position, declaring that "all participation of the working class in the politics of bourgeois governments can result only in the consolidation and perpetuation of the existing order." The other, the Temple Unico faction, backed by the London General Council as well as by the Germans and Swiss-Germans, believed in "electoral action and workers' candidates for political posts."

Bakunin was at that time preoccupied with Russian events. In the spring of 1869 he became friendly with the fiery young revolutionist Sergei Nechaev. Bakunin still believed at that time in the possibility of a vast peasant uprising in Russia, much like that of Stenka Razin. The second centennial of this great revolt of 1669 seemed almost like a prophetic coincidence. It was then that Bakunin wrote in Russian the manifesto *Some Words to My Young Brothers in Russia* and the pamphlet *Science and the Present Revolutionary Cause*. Nechaev soon returned to Russia, but was forced to flee again after the arrest of almost all his friends and the destruction of his organization. He reached Switzerland in January 1870. Nechaev then prevailed upon Bakunin to abandon the translation of Marx's *Das Kapital* which he had already begun, and to concentrate entirely upon Russian revolutionary propaganda. Nechaev also succeeded in obtaining money for his alleged "Russian Committee" from the remainder of the Bakhmetiev Fund for Russian revolutionary propaganda, which was administered by Ogarev.

Bakunin also wrote, in Russian, the pamphlet *To the Officers of the Russian Army*, and, in French, *The Bears of Bern and the Bear of St. Petersburg*. He edited a few issues of the new series of *Kolokol* and engaged in feverish activity for many months. In July 1870, when Bakunin realized that Nechaev was using him to attain a personal dictatorship by Jesuitical methods, he broke off all relations with the young revolutionist. He had been the victim of excessive trustfulness and of his admiration for Nechaev's savage energy. Bakunin wrote to Ogarev on August 21, 1870:

> We have been pretty fine fools. How Herzen would have laughed at us if he were still alive, and how right he would have been!! Well, all we can do is to swallow this bitter pill, which will make us more cautious in the future.[14]

VII

When the Franco-Prussian War of 1870–71 broke out, Bakunin passionately followed the course of battle. To his friend Ogarev he wrote in a letter dated August 11, 1870, "You are only a Russian, but I am an Internationalist." To Bakunin, the crushing of France by feudal, militarist Germany would mean the triumph of the counterrevolution; and this defeat could only be avoided by calling upon the French people to rise en masse and throw out both the foreign invader and their own domestic tyrants who were holding them in economic and political bondage. To his socialist friends in Lyons, Bakunin wrote:

> The patriotic movement is nothing in comparison with what you must now do if you want to save France. Therefore, arise my comrades to the strains of the *Marseillaise* which today is once again the true anthem of France palpitating with life, the song of liberty, the song of the people, the song of humanity. In acting patriotically we are (also) saving universal liberty. Ah! if I were young again, I would not be writing letters. I would be among you!

A correspondent of the *Volksstaat* (Wilhelm Liebknecht's paper) had reported that the Parisian workers were "indifferent toward the war." Bakunin felt that it was perverse to accuse the workers of an apathy which, if actually present, would be criminal on their part. He wrote to the workers that they could not remain indifferent to the German invasion, that they must absolutely defend their liberty against the armed gangs of Prussian militarism.

If France were invaded by an army of German, English, Belgian, Spanish, or Italian proletarians, holding high the banner of revolutionary socialism and proclaiming to the world the final emancipation of labor, I would have been the first to cry to the workers of France: "Open your arms, embrace them, they are your brothers, and unite with them to sweep away the rotten remains of the bourgeois world!" . . . But the invasion that today dishonors France is an aristocratic, monarchic, military invasion. . . . If they remain passive before this invasion, the French workers will betray not only their own liberty, they will also betray the cause of the workers of the world, the sacred cause of revolutionary socialism.

Bakunin's ideas about the situation facing French workers and the means that should be employed to save France and the cause of liberty were expressed by him in a small pamphlet which appeared anonymously, in September 1870, under the title *Letters to a Frenchman on the Present Crisis*. [See selection in this volume.]

Bakunin left Locarno on September 9, 1870, and arrived in Lyons on the fifteenth. On his arrival, a Committee for the Salvation of France, whose most active and determined member was Bakunin, was immediately organized to mount a revolutionary insurrection. The program of the movement was printed on a huge red poster and was signed by the delegates of Lyons, St.-Étienne, Tarare, and Marseilles. Although Bakunin was a foreigner and his position therefore more precarious, he did not hesitate to add his signature to those of his friends, thus sharing their perils and their responsibilities. The poster proclamation first declares that "The administrative and governmental machinery of the State having become impotent is abolished," and that "The people of France [have] regained full control over their own affairs. . . ." It then immediately proposes the formation in all the federated communes of Committees for the Salvation of France, and the immediate dispatch to Lyons of two delegates from each committee in the capital of each department of France, to form the Revolutionary Convention for the Salvation of France.

On September 28, a popular uprising put the revolutionists in possession of the Lyons City Hall; but the treason of General Cluseret, in helping to suppress an uprising he had endorsed, and the cowardice of some of those who had betrayed the trust of the people caused the defeat of the revolutionists. Bakunin, against whom the prosecutor of the Republic, Andrieux, had issued an order of arrest, fled to Marseilles where he remained in hiding for some time, trying to prepare a new uprising. In the meantime, the French authorities spread the rumor that Bakunin was a paid agent of Prussia and that the Government of National Defense could prove it. On its part, Liebknecht's *Volksstaat*, commenting on the twenty-eighth of September and the red poster proclamation, declared that "Not even the Berlin [government's] press could have better served Bismarck's plans."

On October 24, Bakunin, in despair over events in France, sailed from Marseilles on a ship returning to Locarno by way of Genoa and Milan. The day before his departure he had written the following to the Spanish Socialist Sentinon, who had come to France hoping to participate in the revolutionary movement:

> The French people are no longer revolutionary at all. . . . Militarism and Bureaucracy, the arrogance of the nobility and the Protestant Jesuitry of the Prussians, in affectionate alliance with the knout of my dear sovereign and master, the Emperor of all the Russias, are going to command all Europe, God knows for how many years. Goodbye to all our dreams of impending Revolution!!

The uprising that broke out in Marseilles on October 31, only seven days after Bakunin's departure, confirmed his pessimistic prediction: the Revolutionary Commune which had been established when news of the capitulation of Bazaine reached Marseilles held out for only five days before surrendering to Alfonso Gent, who had been sent by Gambetta.

In Locarno, where he spent the winter in seclusion, battling against poverty and despair, Bakunin wrote the continuation of his *Letters to a Frenchman*, an analysis of the new situation in Europe. It was published in the spring of 1871 with the characteristic title, *The Knouto-Germanic Empire and the Social Revolution*. News of the Parisian insurrection of March 18, 1871 (the Paris Commune) lightened his pessimism. The Paris proletariat, at least, had lost neither their energy nor their spirit of revolt. But France, exhausted and defeated, could not be galvanized by the heroism of the people of Paris. The attempts in various provinces to spread the communalist movement (self-governing communes) failed, and the Parisian insurrectionists were finally crushed by their innumerable enemies. Bakunin, who had gone to stay with friends in the Jura to be nearer the French frontier, was unable to help and was compelled to return to Locarno.

But this time Bakunin did not give way to discouragement. The Commune of Paris, upon which all the reactionary forces concentrated their furious, venomous hatred, kindled a spark of hope in the hearts of all the exploited. The proletariat of the world saluted the heroic people whose blood ran in torrents for the emancipation of humanity. "The modern Satan, the great rebellion, suppressed, but not pacified!" exclaimed Bakunin. The Italian patriot Mazzini added his voice to those who cursed the Commune and the International. Bakunin wrote the *Response of an Internationalist to Mazzini* which appeared in August 1871 in both Italian and French. This work made a deep impression in Italy, and produced among the youth and the workers of Italy a climate of opinion which gave birth, toward the end of 1871, to many new sections of the International. A second pamphlet, *The Political Theology of Mazzini and the International*, even further consolidated and extended the International. Bakunin, who by sending Fanelli to Spain had created the International there, was by his polemic with Mazzini also the creator of the International in Italy. Now he threw himself passionately into the struggle not only against the domination of the bourgeoisie over the proletariat, but against the men who were trying to install the principle of authority in the International Working-men's Association.

VIII

The split in the Romance Federation (French-speaking Switzerland), which could have been healed if the London General Council had so desired and if the agents of that Council had been less perfidious, was aggravated to the point of irreversibility. In August 1870 Bakunin and three of his friends were expelled from the Geneva section because they had declared their sympathy for the Jura Federationists. Soon after the end of the Franco-Prussian War Marx's agents came to Geneva to revive the discords. The members of the now-dissolved Geneva section of the Alliance believed that they had given sufficient proof of their friendly intentions by dissolving their section. But the party of Marx and Utin did not cease its harassments: a new section, called "Propaganda and Revolutionary Socialist Action," formed by refugees from the Paris Commune and including old members of the Alliance section, was promptly refused admission to the International by the General Council. Instead of a general congress of the International, the General Council, controlled by Marx and his friend Engels, in September 1871 convened a secret conference in London, attended almost entirely by partisans of Marx. The conference adopted resolutions destroying the autonomy of the sections and federations of the International and giving the General Council powers that violated the fundamental statutes of the International and the conference. At the same time it tried to promote and organize, under the direction of the General Council, what it called "the political [parliamentary] action of the working class."

Immediate action was necessary. The International, a vast federation of groups organized to fight the economic exploitation of the capitalist system, was in imminent danger of being derailed by a little band of Marxist and Blanquist sectarians.[15] The sections of the Jura, together with the "Propaganda and Revolutionary" section of Geneva, met in Sonvilier (November 12, 1871) and established the Jurassian Federation of the International. This association sent a circular to all the federations of the International urging them to jointly resist the usurpations of the General Council and to energetically reconquer their autonomy. The circular, among other things, declared:[16]

> If there is an undeniable fact, attested to a thousand times by experience, it is the corrupting effect produced by authority on those who manipulate it. It is absolutely impossible for a man who wields power to remain a moral man. . . .

The General Council could not escape this inevitable law. These men, accustomed to march at our head and to speak in our name, have been led by the very demands of their situation to desire that their particular program, their particular doctrine, should prevail in the International. Having become in their own eyes a sort of government, it was natural that their own particular ideas should appear to them as official theory, as they had the sole "freedom of the city" [unlimited power] in the Association whilst divergent views expressed by other groups appeared no longer the legitimate expression of opinions with rights equal to their own, but as veritable heresies. . . .

We do not impugn the intentions of the General Council. The persons who compose it found themselves the victims of an inevitable necessity. They wanted in good faith, and for the triumph of their particular doctrine, to introduce into the International the principle of authority. Circumstances appeared to favor their doctrine, and it appears to us quite natural that this school, whose ideal is THE CONQUEST OF POLITICAL POWER BY THE WORKING CLASS, should have believed that the International was going to alter its original structure and transform itself into a hierarchical organization directed and governed by the General Council. . . .

But while we understand these tendencies we feel obliged to fight them in the name of that Social Revolution whose program is "Emancipation of the workers by the workers themselves." . . .

The future society must be nothing else than the universalization of the organization that the International has formed for itself. We must therefore strive to make this organization as close as possible to our ideal. How could one expect an egalitarian society to emerge out of an authoritarian organization? It is impossible. The International, embryo of the future society, must from now on faithfully reflect our principles of federation and liberty, and must reject any principle tending toward authority and dictatorship.

Bakunin enthusiastically welcomed the Sonvilier circular and devoted all his energies to actively propagating its principles in the Italian sections of the International. Spain, Belgium, most of the French sections (secretly reorganized in spite of the Versailles reaction following the defeat of the Paris Commune), and most of the United States sections declared themselves in agreement with the Swiss-Jura Federation. It was soon certain that the attempts of Marx and his allies to capture the International would be repulsed. The first half of 1872 was marked by a "confidential circular" issued by the General Council, written by Karl Marx and printed as a pamphlet entitled *Les prétendues scissions dans l'Internationale* ("The Alleged Splits in the International"). Prominent Federalist militants and others seeking independence from the General Council were personally slandered, and the widespread protests against certain acts of the General Council were depicted as sordid intrigues by members of the old International Alliance of the Social Democracy (the Alliance) who, directed by "the Pope of Locarno" (Bakunin), were working for the destruction of the International. Bakunin gave his reaction to this circular in a letter: "The sword of Damocles that hung over us so long has at last fallen over our heads. It is not really a sword, but the habitual weapon of Marx, a heap of filth."

Bakunin passed the summer and autumn of 1872 in Zurich, where on his initiative a Slavic section was founded, composed almost entirely of Serbian and Russian students, which joined the Jura Federation of the International. Since April Bakunin had been in contact with Russian émigré youths in Locarno who organized themselves into a secret action and propaganda group. The most militant member of this group was Armand Ross (Michael Sazhin). In intimate contact with Bakunin from the summer of 1870 to the spring of 1876, Ross was the principal intermediary between the great revolutionary agitator and Russian youth.

Bakunin's propaganda during this period was an inspiration to the young Russians in the following years. Bakunin's dictum that the youth must "GO TO THE PEOPLE" had become an axiom within the populist movement. In Zurich, Ross established a Russian-language printing plant which in 1873 published *Istoricheskoye Razvitiye Internatsionala* ("The Historical Development of the International"), a collection of articles translated from Swiss and Belgian socialist papers, with explanatory notes by different writers, and a chapter on the Alliance written by Bakunin. In 1874 Ross's press printed *Gosudarstvennost i Anarkhiya* ("Statism and Anarchy"). [See selection in this volume.] A conflict with Peter Lavrov and personal dissensions among some of its members led to the dissolution of the Zurich Slav section of the International in 1873.[17]

In the meantime the General Council decided to convene a general congress for September 2, 1872. It chose to meet at The Hague for two main reasons: it was a location close to London, and thus allowed many delegates who agreed with Marx's policies or held fictitious credentials to get to the congress easily; at the same time, the location made it more difficult for delegates representing remote or legally banned federations to attend; there was no possibility, for example, of Bakunin's attending. The newly constituted Italian Federation refused to send delegates. The Spanish Federation sent four, the Jura Federation two, the Belgian Federation seven, the Dutch Federation four, the English Federation five. These twenty-two delegates, the only ones truly representing constituents of the International, made up the core of the minority. The majority of forty who, in reality, represented only themselves had already pledged themselves in advance to faithfully carry out the orders of the clique headed by Marx and Engels. The only decision of the congress with which we deal here is the expulsion of Bakunin [Guillaume was also expelled] from the International. This action was taken on the last day of the congress, September 7, after one-third of the delegates had already gone home, by a vote of twenty-seven for and seven against, with eight abstentions. A mock inquiry by a five-member commission, held behind closed doors, found Bakunin guilty of the charges made by the Marxist clique, and he was expelled on two grounds:

1. That a draft of principles and letters signed "Bakunin" proves that said citizen has tried to establish, and perhaps has succeeded in establishing, a society in Europe named "The Alliance" with rules on social and political matters entirely different from those of the International.
2. That Citizen Bakunin has made use of deceptive tricks in order to appropriate some portion of another person's fortune, which constitutes fraud; that further he or his agents resorted to threats lest he be compelled to meet his obligations.[18]

The second Marxist accusation refers to the three hundred rubles advanced to Bakunin for the translation of Marx's *Das Kapital* and the letter written by Nechaev to the publisher Poliakov.

A protest against this infamy, immediately published by a group of Russian immigrants, made these points:

> Geneva and Zurich, October 4, 1872. They have dared to accuse our friend Michael Bakunin of fraud and blackmail. We do not deem it necessary or opportune to discuss the alleged facts on which these strange accusations against our friend and compatriot are based. The facts are well known in all details and we will make it our duty to establish the truth as soon as possible. Now we are prevented from so doing by the unfortunate situation of another compatriot who is not our friend, but whose persecution at this very moment by the Russian government renders him sacred to us. [This refers to Nechaev, who was arrested in Zurich on August 14, 1872, and extradited to Russia via Switzerland on October 27, 1872.] Mr. Marx, whose cleverness we do not, like others, question, has this time at least shown very bad judgment. Honest hearts in all lands will doubtless beat with indignation and disgust at so shameful a conspiracy and so flagrant a violation of the most elementary principles of justice. As to Russia, we can assure Mr. Marx that all his maneuvers will inevitably end in failure. Bakunin is too well esteemed and known there for calumny to touch him. Signed: Nicholas Ogarev, Bartholomy Zaitsev, Vladimir Ozerov, Armand Ross, Vladimir Holstein, Zemphiri Ralli, Alexander Oelsnitz, Valerian Smirnov.

The day after the Hague Congress of September 5, 1872, another congress of the International—comprising delegations from the Italian, Spanish, Swiss-Jura federations, as well as representatives from American and French sections—convened in St.-Imier, Switzerland. The congress stated that it unanimously:

> Rejects absolutely all resolutions of the Hague Congress and does not recognize to any extent the powers of the new General Council named by it. [The General Council had been transferred to New York.][19]

The Italian Federation had already affirmed, on August 4,

1872, the resolutions of the St.-Imier Congress, which the Jura Federation also adopted at a special meeting held the same day as that of the congress. Most of the French sections hastened to express their complete approval. The Spanish and Belgian federations endorsed the resolutions at their congresses held respectively in Cordoba and Brussels during Christmas week of 1872. The American Federation did likewise at its meeting in New York City on January 12, 1873. The English Federation, which included Marx's old friends Eccarius and Jung, refused to recognize the decisions of the Hague Congress and the new General Council.[20]

On June 5, 1873, the General Council in New York, exercising the powers vested in it by the Hague Congress, suspended the Jura Federation, declaring it subversive. As a result, the Dutch Federation, which had been neutral, joined the other seven federations of the International, declaring on February 14, 1873, that it refused to recognize the "suspension" of the Jura Federation.

The publication by Marx and the little group that still remained faithful to him of a pamphlet filled with gross lies, entitled *The Alliance of the Social Democracy and the International* [written in French in the second half of 1873], only provoked the disgust of all those who read this product of blind hatred.[21]

On September 1, 1873, the sixth congress of the International opened in Geneva. The Belgian, Dutch, Italian, French, English, and Swiss-Jura federations were represented and the Lasallian socialists of Berlin sent a telegram of greetings. The congress concerned itself with the revision of the statutes of the International, pronounced the dissolution of the General Council, and made the International a free federation without any directing authority over it:

The federations and sections comprising the International each reclaims its complete autonomy, the right to organize itself as it sees fit, to administer its own affairs without any outside interference, and to determine the best and most efficient means for the emancipation of labor. [Article 3 of the new statutes]

His lifelong battles had left Bakunin exhausted. Prison had aged him before his time, his health had seriously deteriorated, and he now craved repose and retirement. When he saw the International reorganized in a way that fulfilled the principle of free federation, he felt that the time had come to take leave of his comrades. On October 12, 1873, he addressed a letter to the members of the Jura Federation:

> I beg you to accept my resignation as a member of the Jura Federation and the International. I no longer feel that I have the strength needed for the struggle: I would be a hindrance in the camp of the Proletariat, not a help . . . I retire then, dear comrades, full of gratitude to you and sympathy for your great cause —the cause of humanity. I will continue to follow, with brotherly anxiety, all your steps and I will greet with joy each of your new victories. Till death I will be yours. [For full text, see p. 351.]

He had but three years to live.

His friend, the Italian revolutionist Carlo Cafiero,[22] invited him to stay in his villa near Locarno. There Bakunin lived until the middle of 1874, apparently absorbed by his new life, one in which he had at last found tranquillity, security, and relative well-being. But he still regarded himself as a soldier of the revolution. When his Italian friends launched an insurrectionary movement, Bakunin went to Bologna in July 1874 to participate. But the insurrection, poorly planned, collapsed and Bakunin returned in disguise to Switzerland.

At this time Bakunin and Cafiero became estranged. Cafiero, having sacrificed his entire fortune for the cause of the revolution, found himself ruined and was forced to sell the villa. Bakunin, unable to stay in Locarno, settled in Lugano where, thanks to his paternal inheritance sent to him by his brothers, he was able to support himself and his family. The temporary coolness between Bakunin and Cafiero did not last long, and friendly relations were soon reestablished. But Bukanin's illness progressed, ravaging both spirit and body, so that by 1875 he was only a shadow of his former self. Hoping to find relief, Bakunin left Locarno for Bern to consult his old friend, Vogt, to whom he said, "I have come to be restored to health or to die." He was taken to a hospital, where he was affectionately attended by Dr. Vogt and another close friend, the musician Reichel.

In one of his last conversations, recalled by Reichel, Bakunin in speaking of Schopenhauer remarked:

> All our philosophy starts from a false base; it begins always by considering man as an individual, and not as he should be considered—that is, as a being belonging to a collectivity; most of the philosophical (and mistaken) views stemming from this false premise either are led to the conception of a happiness in the clouds, or to a pessimism like that of Schopenhauer and Hartmann.

In another conversation, Reichel expressed his regret that Bakunin could never find time to write his memoirs. Bakunin replied:

> And why should you want me to write them? It is not worth the effort. Today the people in all lands have lost the instinct of revolution. No, if I get a bit of strength back again, I would rather write an ethic based on the principles of collectivism, making no use of philosophical or religious phrases.

He died at noon on July 1, 1876.

On July 3, socialists from all parts of Switzerland arrived in Bern to pay their last respects to Michael Bakunin. At his graveside, eulogies were offered by some of his friends from the Jura Federation: Adhemar Schwitzguebel, James Guillaume, Élisée Reclus; by Nicholas Zhukovsky, representing the Russians; by Paul Brouse for the French Revolutionary Youth; by Betsien for the German proletariat. At a meeting after the funeral all were moved by one sentiment: to forget, upon the grave of Bakunin, all personal bickering, and to unite on the basis of liberty and mutual tolerance all the socialist factions in both camps. The following resolution received unanimous approval:

> The workers gathered in Bern on the occasion of the death of Michael Bakunin belong to five different nations. Some are partisans of a Worker's State, while others advocate the free federation of groups of producers. But all feel that a reconciliation is not only very essential and very desirable, but also easy to estab-

lish on the basis of the principles of the International, as formulated in Article 3 of the revised statutes adopted at the Geneva Congress of 1873.

Therefore this assembly, meeting in Bern, calls upon all workers to forget the vain and unfortunate dissensions of the past and to unite on the basis of strict adherence to the principles enunciated in Article 3 of the above-mentioned statutes [autonomy of the sections].

Do you want to know how this moving appeal to forget past hatreds and to unite in liberty was answered? The Marxist *Tagwacht* of Zurich on July 8 printed the following:

Bakunin was regarded by many fair-minded men and good socialists as a Russian agent. This suspicion, doubtless erroneous, was aroused by the fact that Bakunin greatly harmed the revolutionary movement; it was the reaction which benefited most from his activity.

Similar malevolent accusations vented by the *Volksstaat* of Leipzig and the Russian-language *Vpered* of London compelled the friends of Bakunin to conclude that his enemies did not intend to desist from their campaign of hatred. Hence the Bulletin of the Jura Federation on September 10, 1876, faced with hostile manifestations, declared:

We desire, as our conduct has always established, the most complete reconciliation possible of all socialist groups: we are ready to extend our hand in friendship to all those who sincerely wish to struggle for the emancipation of labor. But we are at the same time determined not to allow anyone to insult our dead.

Will the time come when posterity will assess the personality and achievements of Bakunin with the impartiality that we have a right to expect? Further, can one hope that the wishes expressed by his friends on his freshly covered grave will someday be realized?

I

The
Pre-Anarchist
Period

Revolutionary
Pan-Slavism

1842

The Reaction in Germany

The first of the following four selections is an extract from Bakunin's pivotal essay The Reaction in Germany: From the Notebooks of a Frenchman written in October 1842 under the pseudonym Jules Elysard.[1] It marks his emergence from purely philosophical studies to active participation in revolutionary sociopolitical movements. Criticized by his friends as being too abstract, the essay employs Hegelian philosophic language to justify a concept of permanent social and political revolution tailored to Bakunin's temperament. Its polemics are aimed at the "compromisers," those who, like the stereotype of today's liberal, would take an intermediate position between the conservatives—whom Bakunin called "positivists" as opposed to the radical "negativists" with regard, of course, to the status quo or establishment—and the radicals. The religious tone of some passages mark the essay as belonging to the period before his study of socialist ideas, a study which led to his public advocacy of atheism in 1860. Despite its vagueness and philosophic phrasing, the essay is a call for social revolution, for the realization of human freedom as the supreme end of history, and an assertion of faith in the revolutionary capabilities of the lowest classes in society, the poor. Too many people are fond of repeating Bakunin's celebrated phrase "The passion for destruction is a creative passion, too!" without regard for the social and political meaning he attached to it.

Freedom, the realization of freedom: who can deny that this is what today heads the agenda of history? . . . Revolutionary propaganda is in its deepest sense the NEGATION of the existing conditions of the State; for, with respect to its innermost nature, it has no other program than the destruction of whatever order prevails at the time. . . . We must not only act politically, but in our politics act religiously, religiously in the sense of freedom, of which the one true expression is justice and love. Indeed, for us alone, who are called the enemies of the Christian religion, for us alone it is reserved, and even made the highest duty . . . really to exercise love, this highest commandment of Christ and this only way to true Christianity.

To the compromisers we can apply what was said in a French journal: "The Left says, two times two are four; the Right, two times two are six; and the middle-of-the-road compromisers say two times two are five." They never answer yes or no; they say: "To a certain extent you are right, but on the other hand. . . ." And if they have nothing left to say, they say: "Yes, it is a curious thing." . . . And as it is said of the Polish Jews that in the last Polish war they wanted to serve both warring parties simultaneously, the Poles as well as the Russians, and consequently were hanged by both sides impartially, so these poor souls vex themselves with the impossible business of the outward reconciliation of opposites, and are despised by both parties for their pains. No, the spirit of revolution is not subdued, it has only sunk into itself in order soon to reveal itself again as an affirmative, creative principle, and right now it is burrowing—if I may avail myself of this expression of Hegel's—like a mole under the earth.

Nevertheless, visible manifestations are stirring around us, hinting that the spirit, that old mole, has brought its underground work to completion and that it will soon come again to pass judgment. Everywhere, especially in France and England, social and religious societies are being formed which are wholly alien to the world of present-day politics, societies that derive their life from new sources quite unknown to us and that grow and diffuse themselves without fanfare. The people, the poor class, which without doubt constitutes the greatest part of humanity; the class whose rights have already been recognized in theory but which is nevertheless still despised for its birth, for its ties with poverty and ignorance, as well as indeed with actual slavery—this class, which constitutes the true people, is everywhere assuming a threatening attitude and is beginning to count the ranks of its enemy, far weaker in numbers than itself, and to demand the actualization of the right already conceded to it by everyone. All people and all men are filled with a kind of premonition, and everyone whose vital organs are not paralyzed faces with shuddering expectation the approaching future which will utter the redeeming word. Even in Russia, the boundless snow-covered kingdom so little known, and which perhaps also has a great future in store, even in Russia dark clouds are gathering, heralding storm. Oh, the air is sultry and pregnant with lightning.

And therefore we call to our deluded brothers: Repent, repent, the Kingdom of the Lord is at hand!

To the Positivists we say: "Open the eyes of your mind; let the dead bury the dead, and convince yourselves at last that the Spirit, ever young, ever newborn, is not to be sought in fallen ruins!" And we exhort the compromisers to open their hearts to truth, to free themselves of their wretched and blind circumspection, of their intellectual arrogance, and of the servile fear which dries up their souls and paralyzes their movements.

Let us therefore trust the eternal Spirit which destroys and annihilates only because it is the unfathomable and eternal source of all life. The passion for destruction is a creative passion, too!

1847

———◆◆———

On the 17th Anniversary
of the Polish Insurrection
# of 1830

It is a long step forward from "The Reaction in Germany" to Bakunin's speech on the seventeenth anniversary of the Polish insurrection of 1830,[2] given on November 29, 1847, at a great banquet in Paris to commemorate that first Polish uprising—the step from philosophy to political action. Indeed, for giving that speech Bakunin was expelled from France at the request of the Russian ambassador—definite proof that he had begun to be taken seriously. Its importance for his ideological career is suggested by what he wrote, much later, to Herzen and Ogarev: "Since 1846 the Slavo-Polish cause has become my idée fixe." Here he himself locates the beginning of his revolutionary pan-Slavism, his particular blend of nationalism for the sake of revolution, of which the third extract in this section, the "Appeal to the Slavs,"[3] is a full-blown expression. And of course Bakunin's pan-Slavism was meant to trigger a general European revolution, the final objective and leitmotif behind all his activities on the Slavic front.

The speech appeared in full on December 14, 1847, in the journal La Réforme, and was also summarized in the following introduction.

At a meeting held in Paris on November 29 last, for the purpose of celebrating the seventeenth anniversary of the Polish revolution, a Russian refugee, M. Bakunin, delivered an address couched in the most generous terms, which contained the latest and boldest views on the Russian situation.

We quote the most striking passages of this sensational statement:

Gentlemen: This is indeed a solemn moment for me. I am a Russian, and I come to this great assembly, gathered here to celebrate the anniversary of the Polish revolution. Your very presence here is a sort of defiance, a threat and a curse thrown into the face of all the oppressors of Poland. I have come here, gentlemen, inspired by a profound love and unshakable respect for my country.

I am not unaware of how unpopular Russia is in Europe. The Poles consider her, not without reason, as perhaps one of the principal causes of all their misfortunes. Men of independent opinion from other countries view the very rapid development of her power as an ever-growing danger to the liberty of peoples. . . .

Russia figures as the synonym for brutal oppression; thanks to the execrable policies of our sovereigns, the name "Russian," in the official sense of the word, stands for "slave and executioner." (It is on this theme that Bakunin enlarges in the first part of his address, not without referring, in this tragic period for the Poles,[4] to the martyrdom of Postel, of Ryleev, of Muraviev-Apostol, of Bestuzhev-Ryumin, of Dohovsky, who had been hanged in St. Petersburg twenty-two years before for having been "the first citizens of Russia.")

Almost a year ago (continued Bakunin)—I believe it was after the massacre of Galicia, a Polish nobleman made you an extraordinary proposition, in a highly eloquent letter addressed to Prince Metternich, which has since become famous. No doubt carried away by his hatred for the Austrians which, by the way, was quite justified, he suggested nothing less than that you should submit to the Tsar, surrender yourselves, body and soul, to him, without drawback and without reservation. He advised you to do voluntarily what you had so far done under duress, and he promised you, in compensation, that as soon as you ceased to pose as slaves, your master would, in spite of himself, become your brother. Your

brother, gentlemen, do you hear this? Emperor Nicholas your
brother! (No! No! Great commotion in the hall)

The oppressor, your bitterest enemy, the personal enemy of
Poland, the executioner of so many victims (Bravo! Bravo!), the
man who ravished your liberty, the man who is pursuing you with
relentless perseverance, as much through hate and by instinct as
through political strategy—would you accept him as your brother?
(Cries from all directions, No! No! No!) Each one of you would
rather see Poland perish than consent to such a monstrous alliance.
(Prolonged bravos)

And the speaker went on to draw the following argument
from his earlier remarks:

Yes, it is just because you are the enemies of Emperor Nicholas,
the enemies of official Russia, that you are, in the nature of things,
even without wishing it, the friends of the Russian people. (Applause) There is a general belief in Europe, I know, that we Russians form an indivisible unit with our government, that we are
quite happy under the regime of Nicholas; that he and his system,
oppressor within the country and invader beyond its frontiers, are
the perfect expression of our national genius. Nothing of the kind.
No, gentlemen, the Russian people are not happy! I say this joyfully and proudly. For if happiness were possible for the Russians
in their present abject state, ours would be the basest, vilest people
in the world.

As he developed the idea of a revolutionary alliance between
Poland and Russia, Mr. Bakunin came to the following conclusion:

To the extent that we have remained disunited, we have
mutually paralyzed ourselves. Together we shall be all-powerful
for the good. Nothing could resist our common and united action.
The reconciliation of Russia and Poland is a tremendous task, well
worth our total devotion. This will be the emancipation of sixty
million men, the deliverance of all the Slav peoples who are groaning under a foreign yoke. It will be, in the end, the fall, the definitive collapse of despotism in Russia. (Applause)

"The Appeal to the Slavs," together with its preparatory drafts, forms a comprehensive statement of Bakunin's opinions as they emerged from the shock and disappointment of the 1848 revolution. His ideas may be briefly summarized in three sentences. First, he believed the bourgeoisie had revealed itself as a specifically counterrevolutionary force, and that the future hopes of revolution lay with the working class. Secondly, he believed that an essential condition of the revolution was the breakup of the Austrian Empire, and the establishment in Central and Eastern Europe of a federation of free Slav republics. Thirdly, he believed that the peasantry, and in particular the Russian peasantry, would prove a decisive force in bringing about the final and successful revolution.[5] Referring to Bakunin's call for the dissolution of the Habsburg and Russian Empires, E. H. Carr adds: "For this, if for no other reason, the Appeal to the Slavs is a landmark in European history. It was the first occasion on which, exactly seventy years before November 1918, the destruction of the Austrian Empire and the building of new Slav states on its ruins was publicly advocated."[6]

The bourgeois democrats did not like Bakunin's call for the social revolution that would enfranchise the lower classes, and all such "subversive" sections were eliminated from the official version of the "Appeal to the Slavs." The most "objectionable" section has been included at the end of the selection. Today the "Appeal to the Slavs" might seem curiously contemporary to the oppressed Slavic peoples of Eastern Europe once again under Kremlin domination.

Arrested and jailed in Austria for his participation in the unsuccessful revolution of March 1848, Bakunin was eventually handed over to the Russian authorities. In the Peter and Paul fortress that had once held Dostoyevsky, among others, Bakunin was invited, as a Russian nobleman, to write a confession for the Tsar, Nicholas I, not as a criminal to his judge but as a son to his spiritual father. The paragraphs here included already pre-figure Bakunin's later recommendations for anarchist strategy.[7]

Taken together, the extracts from these four works dating from, respectively, 1842, 1847, 1848, and 1851, of which the first two were written before Bakunin entered upon a total of twelve years of imprisonment both in Austria and Russia, and the last in prison, mark Bakunin's development during the stormy mid-century years of revolutions and their setbacks. They foreshadow many of his later anarchist ideas on the necessity for revolution, on the peasants as a revolutionary force, on the destruction of the bourgeois social order, on antiparliamentarianism and federalism. However, what he wrote when "confessing" under pressure to the enemy in person, the most autocratic of all the Tsars, especially the plans for dictatorship, may be attributed partly to his being still under the influence of Blanquist ideas, partly to his seeking formulations that might be comprehensible and even possibly impressive to the Tsar. As Venturi has pointed out, such passages need not be taken too literally. Bakunin's letters from prison to his family prove that he remained faithful to his anarchist principles throughout: "When Bakunin's temporary adherence . . . to the dictatorship of the Blanqui type, came to an end . . . [he] found himself an anarchist."[8]

1848

Appeal to the Slavs

BROTHERS! This is the hour of decision. It is for you to take a stand, openly either for the old world, in ruins, which you would prop up for yet another little while, or for the new world whose radiance has reached you and which belongs to the generations and centuries to come. It is up to you, too, to determine whether the future is to be in your hands or, if you want, once more to sink into impotence, into the night of hopes abandoned, into the inferno of slavery. On the choice you will make hangs the fate of other peoples who long for emancipation. Your decision will inspire them to advance toward their goal with quickened steps, and without drawbacks, or this goal—which will never disappear—will again retreat into a shadowy distance.

The eyes of all are fixed upon you with breathless anxiety. What you decide will determine the realization of the hopes and destinies of the world—to arrive soon or to drift away to a remote and uncertain future. It is to be your welfare or your loss, the blessings of the peoples upon you or their condemnation of you; make your choice!

The world is split into two camps; on one side the revolution, on the other the counterrevolution. And the clear alternatives are before you. Each of us must choose his camp, you as well as ourselves. There is no middle road. Those who point to a middle road and recommend it to you are either self-deceived or deceivers.

They are self-deceived if they place their credence in this lie that we can glide smoothly and surely along toward our goal if we grant some little accommodations to each of the great antagonists in the struggle, so as to appease both of them and thereby avert the explosion of the conflict which is both inevitable and necessary.

They are deceivers if they seek to persuade you that, in accordance with the tactics of diplomacy, you should remain neutral for a time, and then choose the stronger side, making sure of your personal advantage with the help of those you have assisted.

Brothers, do not put your trust in the art of diplomacy. It is this which has brought about the ruin of Poland. The same fate will be reserved for you. What does diplomatic chicanery tell you? That you can make use of it in order to overcome your enemies. But do you not see that, rather than being able to make use of this means, you are yourselves but a tool in the hands of the diplomats, a tool they use to crush their own enemies? Once they have got rid of them they will turn upon you, now that you stand weak and alone, and will thrust your own heads under the yoke. Do you not see that there it is, the shameful tactic, the ruse employed by the counterrevolution? Do you not know the old maxim of all oppressors: *Divide and rule?*

What could you expect from diplomacy, anyway? Can it deny its origin, which is none other than despotism? Can it have other interests to fight for than those to which it owes its origin? Can it work for the creation of a new world, which will be its condemnation and its death? Never. Look it plainly in the face; before this visage, the prototype of evil, of duplicity, of treason, you will be seized with the most profound disgust.

You will reject it, for truth is never born of a lie. Nothing truly great has ever been accomplished by eunuchs, and freedom can only be won by freedom.

You have good reason for cursing the old German politics, which deserved your rightful hatred, for it never desired anything but your ruin. It held you shackled for centuries and, even before Frankfurt, responded with irony to your well-justified hopes and your appeals . . . and rejoiced, in Vienna, at the dissolution of the Prague Congress. But do not be deceived and listen carefully. *This old politics which we condemn, which we curse as you do, against which we vow terrible vengeance, this politics will never be part of the future German people. It is not the German revolution, not a part of German democracy.* It is merely the politics of the old state chancellorships, of the rights of monarchs, of aristocrats and privileged persons of all kinds. It is the politics of the camarillas and the generals directed by them as though they were war machines. It is the politics whose fall we are preparing—all of us who are animated by the spirit of youth and of the future, all those who will joyfully grasp the hands of the democrats of all countries, so that we may together, closely united, fight for the common good, for the future of all peoples.

All the reactionaries work united for an evil cause; should we not do likewise for our good cause? When reaction conspires throughout Europe, when it works without stint, with the help of an organization slowly and carefully prepared, stretching all over the land, the revolution should create for itself a power capable of fighting it.

It is a sacred duty for all of us, soldiers of the revolution, democrats of all countries, to unite our forces, to come to an understanding and to organize.

At the first sign of life of the revolution, as you know, there was a long outburst of hatred against the old politics of the oppressors, a long cry of sympathy and of love for all oppressed nationalities.

The peoples that had so long been driven by the chains of diplomacy finally became aware of their shameful condition. They realized that the welfare of nations could not be assured so long as there still existed, anywhere in Europe, a single people bowed under the yoke; that the liberty of peoples, in order to be won anywhere, had to be won everywhere. And, for the first time, the peoples demanded in one united voice a liberty that was true and complete, liberty without reservations, without exceptions, without limitations.

Away with the oppressors! was the universal cry. Liberty for the oppressed, for the Poles, the Italians, for all! No more wars of conquest, nothing but the last supreme war, the war of the revolution for the emancipation of all the peoples! Away with the narrow frontiers forcibly imposed by the congress of despots, in accordance with the so-called historic, geographic, commer-

*cial, strategic necessities! There should be no other frontiers but
those which respond simultaneously to nature and to justice, in
accordance with the spirit of democracy—frontiers which the peoples themselves in their sovereign will shall trace, founded upon
their national sympathies. Such was the unanimous cry of the
peoples.*

*Brothers! did you hear it then, that sublime cry? Right there
in Vienna, do you remember? You heard it and understood it on
that day when, still fighting with the others for the welfare of all,
you erected, in the midst of the German barricades, that great
Slav barricade over which floated your national banner, with the
device:* TO OUR FUTURE LIBERTY!

How great, how beautiful was that movement, which swept
over all of Europe and made it tremble! Animated by the revolutionary spirit, Italians, Poles, Slavs, Germans, Magyars, Walachians from Austria and Walachians from Turkey—all those
who suffered under the yoke of foreign powers—arose, thrilled
with joy and hope. The most audacious dreams were to be fulfilled. The peoples saw the boulder which for centuries had covered their independence finally rolling away into the distance,
as though pushed by an invisible hand. The enchanted seal was
broken, and the dragon that had been standing guard over the
melancholy torpor of so many living dead peoples lay mortally
wounded, writhing in its death throes. The old politics of the
kings had vanished; a new one, the politics of the peoples, was
coming into life.

*The Revolution, in its omnipotence, declared the dissolution
of the States of the despots; the dissolution of the Prussian
Empire, which abandoned one of the fragments of Poland; the
dissolution of the Empire of Austria, that monster composed of
various nations which had been all chained together by ruse, by
crime: the dissolution of the Turkish Empire, within which
seven million Osmanlis[9] had packed and trampled upon a population of twelve million Slavs, Walachians and Greeks; and
finally, the dissolution of the last stronghold of despotism, the
last private domain of Machiavellism and of diplomacy, struck
at its very heart, the Russian Empire, so that the three great
nations so long enslaved within its borders, Great Russia, Little*

*Russia, and Poland, liberated at last and rendered to themselves,
might stretch their free hands to all their brothers of the Slav
race.*

*Thus, dissolution, overturn, and régeneration in the entire
North and East of Europe, a free Italy, and as the last result, the
Universal Federation of European Republics.*

We then met in Prague, like brothers who, after a long separation, came together to say to each other that their paths
would never again lead them apart. Strongly animated by the
common bonds of history and of blood, we vowed never to let
our destinies divide us. We forswore the politics of the despots
whose victims we had been for so long and ourselves established
our right to absolute independence. We promised ourselves that
this independence would be shared by all the Slav peoples. We
recognized Bohemia and Moravia as nations. We rejected the
absurd claims of the Frankfurt [parliament], which has now
become the laughingstock of Europe, which had wanted to make
Germans of us all, while we stretched our fraternal hands out to
the German people, to democratic Germany. In the name of the
Slavs who lived in Hungary, we offered a fraternal alliance to the
Magyars, those fiery enemies of our race, who with a total population of some four million wanted to enslave eight million Slavs.
Nor did we forget, in our pact for liberation, those of our brothers who are groaning under Turkish domination. We solemnly
condemned that criminal politics which thrice tore Poland
asunder and now wants once more to rend its sad remainder. We
expressed an ardent wish soon to see the resurrection of that
noble and saintly martyred people as a sign of deliverance of all
of us. Finally, we made a strong appeal to that great Russian
people which, alone of all the Slavs, has been able to preserve
its national existence. We entreated the Russians to give serious
thought to what they know only too well—that their nationality
and their greatness mean nothing so long as they themselves are
not free, so long as they permit their power to be used as a
scourge against unhappy Poland and as a perpetual threat to
European civilization.

This is what we have done and what, jointly with the democrats of all countries, we have demanded: LIBERTY, EQUALITY,

FRATERNITY OF NATIONS, within which the Slav peoples, free like these and in fraternal contact with all, but united in a closer alliance among themselves, may soon be transformed into a vast democratic State.

Two great questions have moved to the forefront, as though arising spontaneously, from the very first days of the spring! The social question, on the one hand, and the question of independence of all the nations, the emancipation of the peoples, on the other hand, signifying emancipation within and outside. These were not just some few individuals, nor was it a party. It was the admirable instinct of the masses, which had raised these two questions above all the others and demanded their prompt solution. Everybody had come to the realization that liberty was merely a lie where the great majority of the population is reduced to a miserable existence, where, deprived of education, of leisure, and of bread, it is fated to serve as an underprop for the powerful and the rich. The social revolution, therefore, appears as a natural, necessary corollary of the political revolution. It has likewise been felt that, so long as there may be a single persecuted nation in Europe, the decisive and complete triumph of democracy will not be possible anywhere. The oppression of one is the oppression of all, and we cannot violate the liberty of one being without violating the freedom of all of us. The social question, a very difficult question, bristling with dangers and heavy with portents of storms, cannot be resolved either by a preconceived theory or by any isolated system. Its solution calls for goodwill and unanimous cooperation. It calls for the faith of all the people in the right of all to equal liberty. We need to transform the material and moral conditions of our present-day existence, to overturn, from top to bottom, this decrepit social world which has grown impotent and sterile and incapable of containing or supporting so great a mass of liberty. We must, first, purify our atmosphere and make a complete transformation of our environment, for it corrupts our instincts and our will by constricting our hearts and our minds. The social question thus appears to be first and foremost the question of the complete overturn of society.

1851

From the *Confession*
to *Tsar Nicholas I*

In Bohemia I wanted a decisive radical revolution which would overthrow everything and turn everything upside down, so that after our victory the Austrian government would not find anything in its old place. . . . I wanted to expel the whole nobility, the whole of the hostile clergy, after confiscating without exception all landed estates. I wanted to distribute part of these among the landless peasants in order to incite them to revolution, and to use the rest as a source of additional financing for the revolution. I wanted to destroy all castles, to burn all files of documents in all of Bohemia without exception, including all administrative, legal, and governmental papers, and to proclaim all mortgages paid, as well as all other debts not exceeding a certain sum, e.g., one or two thousand gulden. In short, the revolution I planned was terrible and unprecedented, although directed more against things than against people.

But my plans did not stop there. I wanted to transform all Bohemia into a revolutionary camp, to create a force there capable not only of defending the revolution within the country, but also of taking the offensive outside Bohemia. . . .

All clubs, newspapers, and all manifestations of an anarchy of mere talk were to be abolished, all submitted to one dictatorial power; the young people and all able-bodied men divided into categories according to their character, ability, and inclination were to be sent throughout the country to provide a provisional revolutionary and military organization. The secret society directing the revolution was to consist of three groups, independent of and unknown to each other: one for the townspeople, another for the youth, and a third for the peasants.

Each of these societies was to adapt its action to the social character of the locality to which it was assigned. Each was to be organized on strict hierarchical lines, and under absolute discipline. These three societies were to be directed by a secret central committee composed of three or, at the most, five persons. In case the revolution was successful, the secret societies were not to be liquidated; on the contrary, they were to be strengthened and expanded, to take their place in the ranks of the revolutionary hierarchy.

Such a revolution, not limited to one nationality, would by its example and its fiery propaganda, attract not only Moravia, but . . . in general all adjacent German territory.

In Russia I wanted a republic, but what kind of republic? Not a parliamentary one!! I believe that in Russia, more than anywhere else, a strong dictatorial power will be indispensable, but one which would concern itself solely with raising the standard of living and education of the peasant masses; a power free in direction and spirit but without parliamentary privileges; free to print books expressing the ideas of the people, hallowed by their Soviets, strengthened by their free activity, and unconstricted by anything or anyone.

II

The
Anarchism of
Michael Bakunin

While there are many indications of the libertarian direction of Bakunin's thought before and after his escape from Siberia in 1861, it was not until the period between 1864 and 1867, when he lived in Italy, that his anarchist ideas took final shape. This period marks the last step in Bakunin's transition from revolutionary nationalism to the mature revolutionary anarchism expounded by him toward the end of his eventful life.

In 1864 Bakunin founded the secret International Revolutionary Association (better known as the International Fraternity) which published its program and statutes in 1865–66 in three related documents: The International Family, the Revolutionary Catechism,[1] and the National Catechism,[2] in which Bakunin outlined the basic tenets of his doctrine. They are, as H. E. Kaminski writes, "the spiritual foundation of the entire anarchist movement. . . ."[3] As Bakunin's ideas evolved, he modified some and elaborated others, but never departed from the fundamental principles defined in these documents. They were reproduced in the original French in Dr. Max Nettlau's definitive biography of Bakunin. Nettlau made fifty copies of them which he deposited in the principal libraries of the world. They were then included in the excellent anthology of the anarchist movement, Ni Dieu, Ni Maître, edited by the noted libertarian-socialist historian and sociologist Daniel Guérin.[4] In his introduction Guérin remarks that these texts are ". . . the least known and the most important of Bakunin's writings . . . they should not be confused with the Rules That Should Inspire a Revolutionist, written much later in 1869, during Bakunin's brief association with the young Russian nihilist Sergei Nechaev whose credo was 'the end justifies the means.' . . . The men who, in Italy, founded the Fraternity with Bakunin were former disciples of the republican nationalist Giuseppe Mazzini, from whom they acquired their fondness for secret societies. They left their mentor because they rejected his Deism and his purely 'political' conception of the revolution as bourgeois and devoid of social content. . . ."

It is necessary to point out that when dissent is outlawed, revolutionaries are forced to organize secret societies. Bakunin was not alone; everybody conspired—the Poles, the. Italians, the Russians, the Blanquists, and the nascent unions camouflaged as "social clubs."

Like all radicals at that time, Bakunin believed that the fall or death of Napoleon III would precipitate a new revolution, a new 1848. He directed all his energy toward safeguarding the expected revolution from the mistakes which had led to the collapse of the revolution of 1848. Despite the encouraging revival of the socialist and labor movements, Bakunin saw that the workers were still very far from attaining the necessary revolutionary consciousness. To imbue the masses with this consciousness and to prevent the deformation of the revolution, Bakunin felt that the only alternative was to organize the secret International Fraternity. Bakunin was convinced that this kind of vanguard movement was indispensable to the success of the Social Revolution; that the Revolution must simultaneously destroy the old order and take on a federalist and anarchistic direction.

The Revolutionary Catechism is primarily concerned with the immediate practical problems of the revolution. It was meant to sketch out for new and prospective members of the International Fraternity both the fundamental libertarian principles and a program of action. The Revolutionary Catechism does not attempt to picture the perfect anarchist society—the anarchist heaven. Bakunin had in mind a society in transition toward anarchism. The building of a full-fledged anarchist society is the work of future generations.

The Revolutionary Catechism indicates that Bakunin did not at first favor the direct expropriation of those sectors of private industry which did not employ hired labor. He expected that with the abolition of the right of inheritance, private ownership would disappear within a generation, to be gradually superseded by workers' productive associations. He feared that an immediate massive expropriation might find the workers unprepared to take control. This would leave the way open for a bureaucratic administrative apparatus. It would lead to a worse evil, namely, the restoration of authoritarian institutions. The fact that Bakunin called for the destruction of all oppressive institutions does not mean that he favored premature changes in certain areas. However, some years later he included expropriation in his program when the workers demanded it.

In touching on the constructive potentialities of cooperative workers' associations, Bakunin speculated that in the future mankind would not be politically organized into nations. National frontiers would be abolished. Human society would be organized industrially according to the needs of production. In view of the existing situation, it was not a matter of immediate concern and he merely mentioned it in passing. Later on, this idea occupied a key place in Bakunin's anarcho-syndicalist program for the International.

To avoid misunderstanding, the reader should know that before anarchism became an organized movement, Bakunin and the anarchists in general used the term "State" and allied expressions in a twofold sense: with reference to the social collectivity or social order, and as designating the complex of repressive institutions exercising intrusive political authority over society and the individual. To avoid this confusion, anarchists today use the word "State" only in the second, negative sense.

1866

Revolutionary Catechism

. . .

II. Replacing the cult of God by *respect and love of humanity*, we proclaim *human reason* as the only criterion of truth; *human conscience* as the basis of justice; *individual and collective freedom* as the only source of order in society.

III. Freedom is the absolute right of every adult man and woman to seek no other sanction for their acts than their own conscience and their own reason, being responsible first to themselves and then to the society which they have *voluntarily* accepted.

IV. It is not true that the freedom of one man is limited by that of other men. Man is really free to the extent that his freedom, fully acknowledged and mirrored by the free consent of his fellowmen, finds confirmation and expansion in their liberty. Man is truly free only among equally free men; the slavery of even one human being violates humanity and negates the freedom of all.

V. The *freedom* of each is therefore realizable only in the equality of all. The realization of freedom through equality, in principle and in fact, is *justice*.

VI. If there is one fundamental principle of human morality, *it is freedom*. To respect the freedom of your fellowman *is duty*; to love, help, and serve him *is virtue*.

VII. *Absolute rejection of every authority including that which sacrifices freedom for the convenience of the state.* Primitive society had no conception of freedom; and as society evolved, *before* the full awakening of human rationality and freedom, it passed through a stage controlled by human and divine authority. The political and economic structure of society must now be reorganized on the basis of freedom. Henceforth, *order in society must result from the greatest possible realization of individual liberty, as well as of liberty on all levels of social organization.*

VIII. The political and economic organization of social life must not, as at present, be directed from the summit to the base —the center to the circumference—imposing unity through forced centralization. On the contrary, it must be reorganized to issue *from the base to the summit—from the circumference to the center—according to the principles* of free association and federation.

IX. *Political organization.* It is impossible to determine a concrete, universal, and obligatory norm for the internal development and political organization of every nation. The life of each nation is subordinated to a plethora of different historical, geographical, and economic conditions, making it impossible to establish a model of organization equally valid for all. Any such attempt would be absolutely impractical. It would smother the richness and spontaneity of life which flourishes only in infinite diversity and, what is more, contradict the most fundamental principles of freedom. However, without certain *absolutely essential conditions* the practical realization of freedom will be forever impossible.

These conditions are:

A. *The abolition of all state religions and all privileged churches, including those partially maintained or supported by state subsidies.* Absolute liberty of every religion to build temples to their gods, and to pay and support their priests.

B. The churches considered as religious corporations must never enjoy the *same* political rights accorded to the productive associations; nor can they be entrusted with the education of children; for they exist merely to negate morality and liberty and to profit from the lucrative practice of witchcraft.

C. *Abolition of monarchy; establishment of a commonwealth.*

D. *Abolition of classes, ranks, and privileges; absolute equality of political rights for all men and women; universal suffrage.* [Not in the state, but in the units of the new society. Note by Max Nettlau]

E. *Abolition,* dissolution, and moral, political, and economic dismantling of the *all-pervasive, regimented, centralized State,* the alter ego of the Church, and as such, the permanent cause of the impoverishment, brutalization, and enslavement of the multitude. This naturally entails the following: *Abolition of all state universities:* public education must be administered only by the communes and free associations. *Abolition of the state judiciary:* all judges must be elected by the people. *Abolition of all criminal, civil, and legal codes now administered in Europe:* because the code of liberty can be created only by *liberty itself. Abolition of banks and all other institutions of state credit. Abolition of all centralized administration, of the bureaucracy, of all permanent armies and state police.*

F. Immediate direct election of all judicial and civil functionaries as well as representatives (national, provincial, and communal delegates) by the universal suffrage of both sexes.

G. *The internal reorganization* of each country on the basis of the *absolute freedom of individuals, of the productive associations, and of the communes.* Necessity of recognizing the *right of secession: every individual, every association, every commune, every region, every nation has the absolute right to self-determination, to associate or not to associate, to ally themselves with whomever they wish and repudiate their alliances without regard to so-called historic rights* [rights consecrated by legal precedent] *or the convenience of their neighbors.* Once the right to secede is established, secession will no longer be necessary. With the dissolution of a "unity" imposed by violence, the units of society will be drawn to unite by their powerful mutual attraction and by inherent necessities. Consecrated by liberty, these new federations of communes, provinces, regions, and nations will then be truly strong, productive, and indissoluble.[5]

H. *Individual rights.*

1. The right of every man and woman, from birth to adulthood, to complete upkeep, clothes, food, shelter, care, guidance, education (public schools, primary, secondary, higher education, artistic, industrial, and scientific), all at the expense of society.

2. The equal right of adolescents, while freely choosing their careers, to be helped and to the greatest possible extent supported by society. After this, society will exercise no authority or supervision over them except to respect, and if necessary defend, their freedom and their rights.

3. The freedom of adults of both sexes must be absolute and complete, freedom to come and go, to voice all opinions, to be lazy or active, moral or immoral, in short, to dispose of one's person or possessions as one pleases, being accountable to no one. Freedom to live, be it honestly, by one's own labor, even at the expense of individuals who *voluntarily* tolerate one's exploitation.

4. Unlimited freedom of propaganda, speech, press, public or private assembly, with no other restraint than the natural salutary power of public opinion. Absolute freedom to organize associations even for allegedly immoral purposes including even those associations which advocate the undermining (or destruction) of individual and public freedom.

5. Freedom can and must be defended only by freedom: to advocate the restriction of freedom

on the pretext that it is being defended is a dangerous delusion. As morality has no other source, no other object, no other stimulant than freedom, all restrictions of liberty in order to protect morality have always been to the detriment of the latter. Psychology, statistics, and all history prove that individual and social immorality are the inevitable consequences of a false private and public education, of the degeneration of public morality and the corruption of public opinion, and above all, of the vicious organization of society. An eminent Belgian statistician [Quételet] points out that society opens the way for the crimes later committed by malefactors. It follows that all attempts to combat social immorality by rigorous legislation which violates individual freedom must fail. Experience, on the contrary, demonstrates that a repressive and authoritarian system, far from preventing, only increases crime; that public and private morality falls or rises to the extent that individual liberty is restricted or enlarged. It follows that in order to regenerate society, we must first completely uproot this political and social system founded on inequality, privilege, and contempt for humanity. After having reconstructed society on the basis of the most complete liberty, equality, and justice—not to mention work for all and an enlightened education inspired by respect for man—public opinion will then reflect the new humanity and become a natural guardian of the most absolute liberty [and public order. Ed.].

6. Society cannot, however, leave itself completely defenseless against vicious and parasitic individuals. Work must be the basis of all political rights. The units of society, each within its own jurisdiction, can deprive all such antisocial adults of political rights (except the old, the sick, and those

dependent on private or public subsidy) and will
be obliged to restore their political rights as soon
as they begin to live by their own labor.

7. The liberty of every human being is inalienable
and society will never require any individual to
surrender his liberty or to sign contracts with
other individuals except on the basis of the most
complete equality and reciprocity. Society cannot
forcibly prevent any man or woman so devoid
of personal dignity as to place him- or herself in
voluntary servitude to another individual; but it
can justly treat such persons as parasites, not
entitled to the enjoyment of political liberty,
though only *for the duration of their servitude.*

8. Persons losing their political rights will also lose
custody of their children. Persons who violate
voluntary agreements, steal, inflict bodily harm, or
above all, violate the freedom of any individual,
native or foreigner, will be penalized according to
the laws of society.

. . .

10. Individuals condemned by the laws of any and
every association (commune, province, region, or
nation) reserve the right to escape punishment
by declaring that they wish to resign from that
association. But in this case, the association will
have the equal right to expel him and declare him
outside its guarantee and protection.

I. *Rights of association* [*federalism*]. The cooperative
workers' associations are a new fact in history. At this
time we can only speculate about, but not determine,
the immense development that they will doubtlessly
exhibit in the new political and social conditions of
the future. It is possible and even very likely that they
will someday transcend the limits of towns, provinces,
and even states. They may entirely reconstitute society, dividing it not into nations but into different

industrial groups, organized not according to the needs of politics but to those of production. But this is for the future. Be that as it may, we can already proclaim this fundamental principle: *irrespective of their functions or aims, all associations, like all individuals, must enjoy absolute freedom.* Neither society, nor any part of society—commune, province, or nation —has the right to prevent free individuals from associating freely for any purpose whatsoever: political, religious, scientific, artistic, or even for the exploitation or corruption of the naïve or alcoholics, provided that *they are not minors.* To combat charlatans and pernicious associations is the special affair of public opinion. But society is obliged to refuse to guarantee civic rights of any association or collective body whose aims or rules violate the fundamental principles of human justice. Individuals shall not be penalized or deprived of their full political and social rights solely for belonging to such unrecognized societies. The difference between the recognized and unrecognized associations will be the following: the juridically recognized associations will have the right to the protection of the community against individuals or recognized groups who refuse to fulfill their voluntary obligations.[6] The juridically unrecognized associations will not be entitled to such protection by the community and none of their agreements will be regarded as binding.

J. The division of a country into regions, provinces, districts, and communes, as in France, will naturally depend on the traditions, the specific circumstances, and the particular nature of each country. We can only point out here the two fundamental and indispensable principles which *must* be put into effect by any country seriously trying to organize a free society. *First: all organizations must proceed by way of federation from the base to the summit, from the commune to the coordinating association of the country*

or nation. Second: there must be at least one auton-
omous intermediate body between the commune
and the country, the department, the region, or the
province. Without such an autonomous intermediate
body, the commune (in the strict sense of the term)
would be too isolated and too weak to be able to resist
the despotic centralistic pressure of the State, which
will inevitably (as happened twice in France) restore
to power a despotic monarchical regime. Despotism
has its source much more in the centralized organization of the State, than in the despotic nature of kings.

K. *The basic unit of all political organization in each*
country must be the completely autonomous com-
mune, constituted by the majority vote of all adults of
both sexes. No one shall have either the power or the
right to interfere in the internal life of the commune.
The commune elects all functionaries, lawmakers, and
judges. It administers the communal property and
finances. Every commune should have the incontestable right to create, without superior sanction, its own
constitution and legislation. But in order to join and
become an integral part of the provincial federation,
the commune must conform its own particular charter to the fundamental principles of the provincial
constitution and be accepted by the parliament of the
province. The commune must also accept the judgments of the provincial tribunal and any measures
ordered by the government of the province. (All
measures of the provincial government must be rati-
fied by the provincial parliament.) Communes refusing to accept the provincial laws will not be entitled
to its benefits.

L. *The province must be nothing but a free federation*
of autonomous communes. The *provincial* parliament
could be composed either of a single chamber with
representatives of each of the communes or of two
chambers, the other representing the population of
the province, independent of the communes. The pro-

vincial parliament, without interfering in any manner whatsoever in the internal decisions of the communes will formulate the provincial constitution (based on the principles of this catechism). This constitution must be accepted by all communes wishing to participate in the provincial parliament. The provincial parliament will enact legislation defining the rights and obligations of individuals, communes, and associations in relation to the provincial federation, and the penalties for violations of its laws. It will reserve, however, the right of the communes to diverge on secondary points, though not on fundamentals.

The provincial parliament, in strict accordance with the *Charter of the Federation of Communes*, will define the rights and obligations existing between the communes, the parliament, the judicial tribunal, and the provincial administration. It will enact all laws affecting the whole province, pass on resolutions or measures of the national parliament, without, however, violating the autonomy of the communes and the province. Without interfering in the internal administration of the communes, it will allot to each commune its share of the provincial or national income, which will be used by the commune as its members decide. The provincial parliament will ratify or reject all policies and measures of the *provincial* administration which will, of course, be elected by universal suffrage. The *provincial tribunal* (also elected by universal suffrage) will adjudicate, without appeal, all disputes between communes and individuals, communes and communes, and communes and the provincial administration or parliament. [These arrangements will thus] lead not to dull, lifeless uniformity, but to a real living unity, to the enrichment of communal life. A unity will be created which reflects the needs and aspirations of the communes; in short, we will have individual and collective freedom. This unity cannot be achieved by the *com-*

pulsion or violence of provincial power, for even truth and justice when coercively imposed must lead to falsehood and iniquity.

M. *The nation must be nothing but a federation of autonomous provinces.* [The organizational relations between the provinces and the nation will, in general, be the same as those between the communes and the province—Nettlau]

N. *Principles of the International Federation.* The union of nations comprising the International Federation will be based on the principles outlined above. It is probable, and strongly desired as well, that when the hour of the People's Revolution strikes again, every nation will unite in brotherly solidarity and forge an unbreakable alliance against the coalition of reactionary nations. This alliance will be the germ of the future Universal Federation of Peoples which will eventually embrace the entire world. The International Federation of revolutionary peoples, with a parliament, a tribunal, and an international executive committee, will naturally be based on the principles of the revolution. Applied to international polity these principles are:

1. Every land, every nation, every people, large or small, weak or strong, every region, province, and commune has the absolute right to self-determination, to make alliances, unite or secede as it pleases, regardless of so-called historic rights and the political, commercial, or strategic ambitions of States. The unity of the elements of society, in order to be genuine, fruitful, and durable, must be absolutely free: it can emerge only from the internal needs and mutual attractions of the respective units of society. . . .

2. Abolition of alleged historic right and the horrible right of conquest.

3. Absolute rejection of the politics of aggrandizement, of the power and the glory of the State. For

this is a form of politics which locks each country into a self-made fortress, shutting out the rest of humanity, organizing itself into a closed world, independent of all human solidarity, finding its glory and prosperity in the evil it can do to other countries. A country bent on conquest is necessarily a country internally enslaved.

4. The glory and grandeur of a nation lie only in the development of its humanity. Its strength and inner vitality are measured by the degree of its liberty.

5. The well-being and the freedom of nations as well as individuals are inextricably interwoven. Therefore, there must be free commerce, exchange, and communication among all federated countries, and abolition of frontiers, passports, and customs duties [tariffs]. Every citizen of a federated country must enjoy the same civic rights and it must be easy for him to acquire citizenship and enjoy political rights in all other countries adhering to the same federation. If liberty is the starting point, it will necessarily lead to unity. But to go from unity to liberty is difficult, if not impossible; even if it were possible, it could be done only by destroying a spurious "unity" imposed by force. . . .

• • •

7. No federated country shall maintain a permanent standing army or any institution separating the soldier from the civilian. Not only do permanent armies and professional soldiers breed internal disruption, brutalization, and financial ruin, they also menace the independence and well-being of other nations. All able-bodied citizens should, if necessary, take up arms to defend their homes and their freedom. Each country's military defense and equipment should be organized locally by the

commune, or provincially, somewhat like the militias in Switzerland or the United States of America [circa 1860–7].

8. The International Tribunal shall have no other function than to settle, without appeal, all disputes between nations and their respective provinces. Differences between two federated countries shall be adjudicated, without appeal, only by the International Parliament, which, in the name of the entire revolutionary federation, will also formulate common policy and make war, if unavoidable, against the reactionary coalition.

9. No federated nation shall make war against another federated country. If there is war and the International Tribunal has pronounced its decision, the aggressor must submit. If this doesn't occur, the other federated nations will sever relations with it and, in case of attack by the aggressor, unite to repel invasion.

10. All members of the revolutionary federation must actively take part in approved wars against a non-federated state. If a federated nation declares unjust war on an outside State against the advice of the International Tribunal, it will be notified in advance that it will have to do so alone.

11. It is hoped that the federated states will eventually give up the expensive luxury of separate diplomatic representatives to foreign states and arrange for representatives to speak in the name of all the federated States.

12. Only nations or peoples accepting the principles outlined in this catechism will be admitted to the federation.

X. *Social Organization.* Without political equality there can be no real political liberty, but political equality will be possible only when there is *social and economic equality*.

A. Equality does not imply the leveling of individual differences, nor that individuals should be made physically, morally, or mentally identical. Diversity in capacities and powers—those differences between races, nations, sexes, ages, and persons—far from being a social evil, constitutes, on the contrary, the abundance of humanity. Economic and social equality means the equalization of personal wealth, but not by restricting what a man may acquire by his own skill, productive energy, and thrift.

B. Equality and justice demand only *a society so organized that every single human being will—from birth through adolescence and maturity—find therein equal means, first for maintenance and education, and later, for the exercise of all his natural capacities and aptitudes.* This equality from birth that justice demands for everyone will be impossible as long as the right of inheritance continues to exist.

· · ·

D. *Abolition of the right of inheritance.* Social inequality —inequality of classes, privileges, and wealth—not by right but in *fact*, will continue to exist until such time as the right of inheritance is abolished. It is an inherent social law that *de facto* inequality inexorably produces inequality of rights; social inequality leads to political inequality. And without political equality—in the true, universal, and libertarian sense in which we understand it—society will always remain divided into two unequal parts. The first, which comprises the great majority of mankind, the masses of the people, will be oppressed by the privileged, exploiting minority. *The right of inheritance violates the principle of freedom and must be abolished.*

· · ·

G. When inequality resulting from the right of inheritance is abolished, there will still remain inequalities [of wealth] due to the diverse amounts of energy and skill possessed by individuals. These inequalities will never entirely disappear, but will become more and more minimized under the influence of education and of an egalitarian social organization, and, above all, when the right of inheritance no longer burdens the coming generations.

H. Labor being the sole source of wealth, everyone is free to die of hunger, or to live in the deserts or the forests among savage beasts, but whoever wants to live in society must earn his living by his own labor, or be treated as a parasite who is living on the labor of others.

I. Labor is the foundation of human dignity and morality. For it was only by free and intelligent labor that man, overcoming his own bestiality, attained his humanity and sense of justice, changed his environment, and created the civilized world. The stigma which, in the ancient as well as the feudal world, was attached to labor, and which to a great extent still exists today, despite all the hypocritical phrases about the "dignity of labor"—this stupid prejudice against labor has two sources: the first is the conviction, so characteristic of the ancient world, that in order to give one part of society the opportunity and the means to humanize itself through science, the arts, philosophy, and the enjoyment of human rights, another part of society, naturally the most numerous, must be condemned to work as slaves. This fundamental institution of ancient civilization was the cause of its downfall.

The city, corrupted and disorganized on the one hand by the idleness of the privileged citizens, and undermined on the other by the imperceptible but relentless activity of the disinherited world of slaves who, despite their slavery, through common labor developed a sense of mutual aid and solidarity against oppression, collapsed under the blows of the barbarian peoples.

Christianity, the religion of the slaves, much later

destroyed ancient forms of slavery only to create a new slavery. Privilege, based on inequality and the right of conquest and sanctified by divine grace, again separated society into two opposing camps: the "rabble" and the nobility, the serfs and the masters. To the latter was assigned the noble profession of arms and government; to the serfs, the curse of forced labor. The same causes are bound to produce the same effects; the nobility, weakened and demoralized by depraved idleness, fell in 1789 under the blows of the revolutionary serfs and workers. The [French] Revolution proclaimed the dignity of labor and enacted the rights of labor into law. But only in law, for in fact labor remained enslaved. The first source of the degradation of labor, namely, the dogma of the political inequality of men, was destroyed by the Great Revolution. The degradation must therefore be attributed to a second source, which is nothing but the *separation* which still exists *between manual and intellectual labor*, which reproduces in a new form the ancient inequality and divides the world into two camps: *the privileged minority*, privileged not by law but by *capital*, and *the majority of workers*, no longer captives of the law but of hunger.

The dignity of labor is today theoretically recognized, and public opinion considers it disgraceful to live without working. But this does not go to the heart of the question. Human labor, in general, is still divided into two exclusive categories: the first —solely intellectual and managerial—includes the scientists, artists, engineers, inventors, accountants, educators, governmental officials, and their subordinate elites who enforce labor discipline. The second group consists of the great mass of workers, people prevented from applying creative ideas or intelligence, who blindly and mechanically carry out the orders of the intellectual-managerial elite. This economic and social division of labor has disastrous consequences for

members of the privileged classes, the masses of the
people, and for the prosperity, as well as the moral
and intellectual development, of society as a whole.

For the privileged classes a life of luxurious idleness gradually leads to moral and intellectual degeneration. It is perfectly true that a certain amount of
leisure is absolutely necessary for the artistic, scientific, and mental development of man; creative leisure
followed by the healthy exercise of daily labor, one
that is well earned and is socially provided for all
according to individual capacities and preferences.
Human nature is so constituted that the propensity
for evil is always intensified by external circumstances,
and the morality of the individual depends much
more on the conditions of his existence and the
environment in which he lives than on his own will.
In this respect, as in all others, the law of social solidarity is essential: there can be no other moralizer for
society or the individual than freedom in absolute
equality. Take the most sincere democrat and put him
on the throne; if he does not step down promptly, he
will surely become a scoundrel. A born aristocrat (if
he should, by some happy chance, be ashamed of his
aristocratic lineage and renounce privileges of birth)
will yearn for past glories, be useless in the present,
and passionately oppose future progress. The same
goes for the bourgeois: this dear child of capital and
idleness will waste his leisure in dishonesty, corruption, and debauchery, or serve as a brutal force to
enslave the working class, who will eventually unleash
against him a retribution even more horrible than that
of 1793.

The evils that the worker is subjected to by the
division of labor are much easier to determine: forced
to work for others because he is born to poverty and
misery, deprived of all rational upbringing and education, morally enslaved by religious influence. He is
catapulted into life, defenseless, without initiative and

without his own will. Driven to despair by misery, he sometimes revolts, but lacking that unity with his fellow workers and that enlightened thought upon which power depends, he is often betrayed and sold out by his leaders, and almost never realizes who or what is responsible for his sufferings. Exhausted by futile struggles, he falls back again into the old slavery.

This slavery will last until capitalism is overthrown by the collective action of the workers. They will be exploited as long as education (which in a free society will be equally available to all) is the exclusive birthright of the privileged class; as long as this minority monopolizes scientific and managerial work and the people—reduced to the status of machines or beasts of burden—are forced to perform the menial tasks assigned to them by their exploiters. This degradation of human labor is an immense evil, polluting the moral, intellectual, and political institutions of society. History shows that an uneducated multitude whose natural intelligence is suppressed and who are brutalized by the mechanical monotony of daily toil, who grope in vain for any enlightenment, constitutes a mindless mob whose blind *turbulence* threatens the very existence of society itself.

The artificial separation between manual and intellectual labor must give way to a new social synthesis. When the man of science performs manual labor and the man of work performs intellectual labor, free intelligent work will become the glory of mankind, the source of its dignity and its rights.

K. *Intelligent and free labor will necessarily be collective labor.* Each person will, of course, be free to work alone or collectively. But there is no doubt that (outside of work best performed individually) in industrial and even scientific or artistic enterprises, collective labor will be preferred by everyone. For association marvelously multiplies the productive capacity of each worker; hence, a cooperating member of a productive association will earn much more in much less time. When the free productive associations (which will include members of cooperatives and labor organizations) voluntarily organize according to their needs and special skills, they will then transcend all national boundaries and form an immense worldwide economic federation. This will include an industrial parliament, supplied by the associations with precise and detailed global-scale statistics; by harmonizing supply and demand the parliament will distribute and allocate world industrial production to the various nations. Commercial and industrial crises, stagnation (unemployment), waste of capital, etc., will no longer plague mankind; the emancipation of human labor will regenerate the world.

L. *The land, and all natural resources, are the common property of everyone, but will be used only by those who cultivate it by their own labor.* Without expropriation, only through the powerful pressure of the worker's associations, capital and the tools of production will fall to those who produce wealth by their own labor. [Bakunin means that private ownership of production will be permitted only if the owners do the actual work and do not employ anyone. He believed that collective ownership would gradually supersede private ownership.]

M. *Equal political, social, and economic rights, as well as equal obligations for women.*

N. Abolition not of the natural family but of the *legal* family founded on law and property. Religious and civil marriage to be replaced by *free* marriage. Adult men and women have the right to unite and separate as they please, nor has society the right to hinder their union or to force them to maintain it. With the abolition of the right of inheritance and the education of children assured by society, all the legal reasons for the irrevocability of marriage will disappear. The union of a man and a woman must be free, for a free choice is the indispensable condition for moral sincerity. In marriage, man and woman must enjoy absolute liberty. Neither violence nor passion nor rights surrendered in the past can justify an invasion by one of the liberty of another, and every such invasion shall be considered a crime.

O. From the moment of pregnancy to birth, a woman and her children shall be subsidized by the communal organization. Women who wish to nurse and wean their children shall also be subsidized.

P. Parents shall have the right to care for and guide the education of their children, under the ultimate control of the commune which retains the right and the obligation to take children away from parents who, by example or by cruel and inhuman treatment, demoralize or otherwise hinder the physical and mental development of their children.

Q. Children belong neither to their parents nor to society. They belong to themselves and to their own future liberty. Until old enough to take care of themselves, children must be brought up under the guidance of their elders. It is true that parents are their natural tutors, but since the very future of the commune itself depends upon the intellectual and moral training it gives to children, the *commune must be the tutor*. The freedom of adults is possible only when the free society looks after the education of minors.

R. *The secular school must replace the Church,* with the difference that while religious indoctrination perpetuates superstition and divine authority, the sole purpose of secular public education is the gradual, progressive initiation of children into liberty by the triple development of their physical strength, their minds, and their will. Reason, truth, justice, respect for fellowmen, the sense of personal dignity which is inseparable from the dignity of others, love of personal freedom and the freedom of all others, the conviction that work is the base and condition for rights

—these must be the fundamental principles of all public education. Above all, education must make men and inculcate human values first, and then train specialized workers. As the child grows older, authority will give way to more and more liberty, so that by adolescence he will be completely free and will forget how in childhood he had to submit unavoidably to authority. Respect for human worth, the germ of freedom, must be present even while children are being severely disciplined. The essence of all moral education is this: inculcate children with respect for humanity and you will make good men. . . .

S. Having reached the age of adulthood, the adolescent will be proclaimed autonomous and free to act as he deems best. In exchange, society will expect him to fulfill only these three obligations: that he remain *free*, that he *live by his own labor*, and that he *respect the freedom of others*. And, as the crimes and vices infecting present society are due to the evil organization of society, it is certain that in a society based on reason, justice, and freedom, on respect for humanity and on complete equality, the good will prevail and the evil will be a morbid exception, which will diminish more and more under the pervasive influence of an enlightened and humanized public opinion.

T. The old, sick, and infirm will enjoy all political and social rights and be bountifully supported at the expense of society.

XI. *Revolutionary policy*. It is our deep-seated conviction that since the freedom of all nations is indivisible, national revolutions must become international in scope. Just as the *European and world reaction is unified*, there should no longer be *isolated revolutions*, but *a universal, world-wide revolution*. Therefore, all the particular interests, the vanities, pretensions, jealousies, and hostilities between and among nations must now be transformed into *the unified, common, and universal interest of the revolution*, *which alone can assure the freedom and independence of each nation by the solidarity of all.* We believe also that the holy alliance of the world counterrevolution and the conspiracy of kings, clergy, nobility, and the bourgeoisie, based on enormous budgets, on permanent armies, on formidable bureaucracies, and equipped with all the monstrous apparatus of modern centralized states, constitutes an overwhelming force; indeed, that this formidable reactionary coalition can be destroyed only by the greater power of the *simultaneous revolutionary alliance and action of all the people of the civilized world*, that against this reaction *the isolated revolution of a single people will never succeed*. Such a revolution would be folly, a catastrophe for the isolated country and would, in effect, constitute a crime against all the other nations. It follows that the uprising of a single people must have in view not only itself, but the whole world. This demands a worldwide program, as large, as profound, as true, as human, in short, as all-embracing as the interests of the whole world. And in order to energize the passions of all the popular masses of Europe, regardless of nationality, this *program can only be the program of the social and democratic revolution*.

Briefly stated, the objectives of *the social and democratic revolution* are: Politically: the abolition of the historic rights of states, the rights of conquest, and diplomatic rights [statist international law. Tr.]. It aims at the full emancipation of individuals and associations from divine and human bondage; it seeks the absolute destruction of all compulsory unions, and all agglomerations of communes into provinces and conquered countries into the State. Finally, it requires the radical dissolution of the centralized, aggressive, authoritarian State, including its military, bureaucratic, governmental, administrative, judicial, and legislative institutions. The revolution, in short, has this aim: *freedom for all, for individuals as well as collective bodies, associations, communes, provinces, regions, and nations,* and *the mutual guarantee of this freedom by federation.*

Socially: *it seeks the confirmation of political equality by economic equality.* This is not the removal of natural individual differences, but *equality in the social rights of every individual from birth;* in particular, equal means of subsistence, support, education, and opportunity for every child, boy or girl, until maturity, and equal resources and facilities in adulthood to create his own well-being by his own labor.

1866

—•—

National Catechism

THE national catechisms of different countries may differ on secondary points, but there are certain fundamental points which must be accepted by the national organizations of all countries as the basis of their respective catechisms. These points are:

1. That it is absolutely necessary for any country wishing to join the free federations of peoples to replace its centralized, bureaucratic, and military organizations by a federalist organization based only on the absolute liberty and autonomy of regions, provinces, communes, associations, and individuals. This federation will operate with elected functionaries directly responsible to the people; it will not be a nation organized from the top down, or from the center to the circumference. Rejecting the principle of imposed and regimented unity, it will be directed from the bottom up, from the circumference to the center, according to the principles of free federation. Its free individuals will form voluntary associations, its associations will form autonomous communes, its communes will form autonomous provinces, its provinces will form the regions, and the regions will freely federate into countries which, in turn, will sooner or later create the universal world federation.

2. Recognition of the absolute right of every individual, commune, association, province, and nation to secede from any body with which it is affiliated. [Bakunin believed that voluntary association, impelled by common needs, will be more durable than compulsory unity imposed from above. Volun-

tary unity, says Bakunin, "will then be truly strong, fecund, and indissoluble."—Tr.]

3. The impossibility of political liberty without political equality. Political freedom and equality are impossible without social and economic equality.

The Necessity of the Social Revolution

The spread and depth of this revolution will more or less differ in each country, according to the political and social situation and the level of revolutionary development. Nevertheless, there are CERTAIN PRINCIPLES which can today attract and inspire the masses to action, regardless of their nationality or the condition of their civilization. These principles are:

1. The land is the common property of society. But its fruits and use shall be open only to those who cultivate it by their labor; accordingly, ground rents must be abolished.
2. Since all social wealth is produced by labor, he who consumes without working, if able to work, is a thief.
3. Only honest people should be entitled to political rights. Such rights shall belong only to the workers. . . .
4. Today no revolution can succeed in any country if it is not at the same time both a political and a social revolution. Every exclusively political revolution—be it in defense of national independence or for internal change, or even for the establishment of a republic—that does not aim at the immediate and real political and economic emancipation of people will be a false revolution. Its objectives will be unattainable and its consequences reactionary.
5. The Revolution must be made not *for* but *by* the people and can never succeed if it does not enthusiastically involve all the masses of the people, that is, in the rural countryside as well as in the cities.
6. Organized by the idea and the identity of a common program for all countries; coordinated by a secret organization which will rally not a few, but all, countries into a single plan of action; unified, furthermore, by simultaneous revolutionary uprisings in most of the rural areas and in the cities,

the Revolution will from the beginning assume and retain a LOCAL character. And this in the sense that it will not originate with a preponderance of the revolutionary forces of a country spreading out, or focused from, a single point or center, or ever take on the character of a bourgeois quasi-revolutionary expedition in Roman imperial style [i.e., sending dictatorial commissars to impose the "party line"]. On the contrary, the Revolution will burst out from all parts of a country. It will thus be a true people's revolution involving everybody—men, women, and children—and it is this that will make the Revolution invincible.

7. At the outset (when the people, for just reasons, spontaneously turn against their tormentors) the Revolution will very likely be bloody and vindictive. But this phase will not last long and will never [degenerate into] cold, systematic terrorism. . . . It will be a war, not against particular men, but primarily against the antisocial institutions upon which their power and privileges depend.

8. The Revolution will therefore begin by destroying, above all, all the institutions and all the organizations, churches, parliaments, tribunals, administrations, banks, universities, etc., which constitute the lifeblood of the State. The State must be entirely demolished and declared bankrupt, not only financially, but even more politically, bureaucratically, militarily (including its police force). At the same time, the people in the rural communes as well as in the cities will confiscate for the benefit of the Revolution all state property. They will also confiscate all property belonging to the reactionaries and will burn all deeds of property and debts, declaring null and void every civil, criminal, judicial, and official document and record, leaving each in the status quo possession (of property). This is the manner in which the Social Revolution will be made, and once the enemies of the Revolution are deprived of all their resources it will no longer be necessary to invoke bloody measures against them. Further, the unnecessary employment of such unfortunate measures must inevitably lead to the most horrible and formidable reaction.

9. The Revolution being localized, it will necessarily assume a FEDERALIST CHARACTER. Thus, upon overthrowing the established government, the communes must reorganize themselves in a revolutionary manner, electing the administrators and revolutionary tribunals on the basis of universal suffrage and on the principle that all officials must be made directly and effectively responsible to the people.

10. In order to prepare for this revolution it will be necessary to conspire and to organize a strong secret association coordinated by an international nucleus. [See the "Program of the International Brotherhood."]

1867

———•◆•———

Federalism, Socialism, Anti-Theologism

"Federalism, Socialism, Anti-Theologism"[7] was presented as a "Reasoned Proposal to the Central Committee of the League for Peace and Freedom, by M. Bakunin, Geneva." The League was an international bourgeois-pacifist organization founded in September 1867 to head off a war between Prussia and France over Luxembourg which threatened to engulf all Europe. Among the sponsors of the League were Victor Hugo, Garibaldi, John Stuart Mill, and other prominent individuals. At the first congress held in Geneva, Bakunin delivered a long address. The text was either lost or destroyed and Bakunin wrote this work in the form of a speech, never finished, like most of his works. It was divided into three parts. The first and second parts, which follow, deal with federalism and socialism, respectively; the third part, on "anti-theologism," is omitted here, except for the diatribe against Rousseau's theory of the state. Bakunin analyzes Rousseau's doctrine of the social contract, makes distinctions between state and society, and discusses the relationship between the individual and the community, and the nature of man in general.

As noted in the "Biographical Sketch," Bakunin had no illusions about the revolutionary potentialities of the League, but he hoped to influence as many members as possible and propagandize his principles. In order not to alienate the members

Bakunin purposely moderated his language, but not his ideas. While the Central Committee of the League accepted Bakunin's thesis, the congress rejected it and Bakunin and his supporters resigned in 1868.

"Federalism, Socialism, Anti-Theologism" differs from the Catechism in some important ways. While the Catechism is primarily a program of action based on Bakunin's main ideas, "Federalism" is a major theoretical work in which these and other concepts barely mentioned in the Catechism are analyzed. Bakunin introduces the idea of a transitional stage in which the full realization of socialism "will no doubt be the work of centuries" which history has placed on the agenda and which "we cannot afford to ignore." He also registers his "protest against anything that may in any way resemble communism or state socialism." Bakunin's conception of a United States of Europe (the objective of the League and the name of its official publication), far from constituting an endorsement of the State, renders the existence of any state, in the accepted sense of the word, impossible. He rejects the idea of state sovereignty as an "attempt at a social organization devoid of the most complete liberty for individuals as well as associations." Bakunin also formulated ideas about the nature of man and the relationship of the individual to society which are only hinted at in the Catechism but are further developed in his subsequent writings. Bakunin's occasionally extravagant praise of American democracy in the Northern States can be ascribed partly to ignorance, but mostly to his passionate sympathy for the North in the Civil War.

Federalism

We are happy to be able to report that the principle of federalism has been unanimously acclaimed by the Congress of Geneva. . . . Unfortunately, this principle has been poorly formulated in the resolutions of the congress. It has not even been mentioned except indirectly . . . while in our opinion, it should have taken first place in our declaration of principles.

This is a most regrettable gap which we should hasten to

fill. In accordance with the unanimous sense of the Congress of Geneva, we should proclaim:

1. That there is but one way to bring about the triumph of liberty, of justice, and of peace in Europe's international relations, to make civil war impossible between the different peoples who make up the European family; and that is the formation of the *United States of Europe*.

2. That the United States of Europe can never be formed from the states as they are now constituted, considering the monstrous inequality which exists between their respective forces.

3. That the example of the now defunct Germanic Confederation has proved once and for all that a confederation of monarchies is a mockery, powerless to guarantee either the peace or the liberty of populations.

4. That no centralized state, being of necessity bureaucratic and militarist, even if it were to call itself republican, will be able to enter an international confederation with a firm resolve and in good faith. Its very constitution, which must always be an overt or covert negation of enduring liberty, would necessarily remain a declaration of permanent warfare, a threat to the existence of its neighbors. Since the State is essentially founded upon an act of violence, of conquest, what in private life goes under the name of housebreaking—an act blessed by all institutionalized religions whatsoever, eventually consecrated by time until it is even regarded as an historic right—and supported by such divine consecration of triumphant violence as an exclusive and supreme right, every centralized State therefore stands as an absolute negation of the rights of all other States, though recognizing them in the treaties it may conclude with them for its own political interest. . . .

5. That all members of the League should therefore bend all their efforts toward reconstituting their respective countries, in order to replace their old constitution—founded from top to bottom on violence and the principle of authority—with a new organization based solely upon the interests, the needs, and the natural preferences of their populations—having no other principle but the free federation of individuals into

communes, of communes into provinces,[8] of the provinces into nations, and, finally, of the nations into the United States of Europe first, and of the entire world eventually.

6. Consequently, the absolute abandonment of everything which is called the historic right of the State; all questions relating to natural, political, strategic, and commercial frontiers shall henceforth be considered as belonging to ancient history and energetically rejected by all the members of the League.

7. Recognition of the absolute right of each nation, great or small, of each people, weak or strong, of each province, of each commune, to complete autonomy, provided its internal constitution is not a threat or a danger to the autonomy and liberty of neighboring countries.

8. The fact that a country has been part of a State, even if it has joined that State freely and of its own will, does not create an obligation for that country to remain forever so attached. No perpetual obligation could be accepted by human justice, the only kind of justice that may have authority amongst us, and we shall never recognize other rights or duties than those founded upon liberty. The right of free union and of equally free secession is the first, the most important, of all political rights, the one right without which the federation would never be more than a centralization in disguise.

9. From all that has been said, it follows that the League must openly prohibit any alliance of any national faction whatsoever of the European democracy with the monarchical State, even if the aim of such an alliance were to regain the independence or liberty of an oppressed country. Such an alliance could only lead to disappointment and would at the same time be a betrayal of the revolution.

10. On the other hand, the League, precisely because it *is* the League for Peace and Freedom, and because it is convinced that peace can only be won by and founded upon the closest and fullest solidarity of peoples in justice and in liberty, should openly proclaim its sympathy with any national insurrection, either foreign or native, provided this insurrection

is made in the name of our principles and in the political as well as the economic interests of the masses, but not with the ambitious intent of founding a powerful State.

11. The League will wage a relentless war against all that is called the glory, the grandeur, and the power of States. It will be opposed to all these false and malevolent idols to which millions of human victims have been sacrificed; the glories of human intelligence, manifested in science, and universal prosperity founded upon labor, justice, and liberty.

12. The League will recognize *nationality* as a natural fact which has an incontestable right to a free existence and development, but not as a principle, since every principle should have the power of universality, while nationality, a fact of exclusionist tendency, separates. The so-called *principle of nationality*, such as has been declared in our time by the governments of France, Russia, Prussia, and even by many German, Polish, Italian, and Hungarian patriots, is a mere derivative notion born of the reaction against the spirit of revolution. It is aristocratic to the point of despising the folk dialects spoken by illiterate peoples. It implicitly denies the liberty of provinces and the true autonomy of communes. Its support, in all countries, does not come from the masses, whose real interests it sacrifices to the so-called public good, which is always the good of the privileged classes. It expresses nothing but the alleged historic rights and ambitions of States. The right of nationality can therefore never be considered by the League except as a natural consequence of the supreme principle of liberty; it ceases to be a right as soon as it takes a stand either against liberty or even outside liberty.

13. Unity is the great goal toward which humanity moves irresistibly. But it becomes fatal, destructive of the intelligence, the dignity, the well-being of individuals and peoples whenever it is formed without regard to liberty, either by violent means or under the authority of any theological, metaphysical, political, or even economic idea. That patriotism which tends toward unity without regard to liberty is an evil patriotism, always disastrous to the popular and real interests of the country it claims to exalt and serve. Often,

without wishing to be so, it is a friend of reaction—an enemy of the revolution, i.e., the emancipation of nations and men. The League can recognize only one unity, that which is freely constituted by the federation of autonomous parts within the whole, so that the whole, ceasing to be the negation of private rights and interests, ceasing to be the graveyard where all local prosperities are buried, becomes the confirmation and the source of all these autonomies and all these prosperities. The League will therefore vigorously attack any religious, political, or economic organization which is not thoroughly penetrated by this great principle of freedom; lacking that, there is no intelligence, no justice, no prosperity, no humanity.

Such, gentlemen of the League for Peace and Freedom, as we see it and as you no doubt see it, are the developments and the natural consequences of that great principle of federalism which the Congress of Geneva has proclaimed. Such are the absolute conditions for peace and for freedom.

Absolute, yes—but are they the only conditions? We do not think so.

The Southern states in the great republican confederation of North America have been, since the Declaration of Independence of the republican states, democratic par excellence[9] and federalist to the point of wanting secession. Nevertheless, they have drawn upon themselves the condemnation of all friends of freedom and humanity in the world, and with the iniquitous and dishonorable war they fomented against the republican states of the North [the Civil War], they nearly overthrew and destroyed the finest political organization that ever existed in history. What could have been the cause of so strange an event? Was it a political cause? No, it was entirely social. The internal political organization of the Southern states was, in certain respects, even freer than that of the Northern states. It was only that in this magnificent organization of the Southern states there was a black spot, just as there was a black spot in the republics of antiquity; the freedom of their citizens was founded upon the forced labor of slaves. This sufficed to overthrow the entire existence of these states.

Citizens and slaves—such was the antagonism in the ancient world, as in the slave states of the new world. Citizens and slaves, that is, forced laborers, slaves not *de jure* but *de facto* [not in law but in fact], such is the antagonism in the modern world. And just as the ancient states perished through slavery, the modern states will likewise perish through the proletariat.

It is in vain that we try to console ourselves with the idea that this is a fictitious rather than a real antagonism, or that it is impossible to establish a line of demarcation between the owning and the disowned classes, since these two classes merge through many intermediate imperceptible degrees. In the world of nature such lines of demarcation do not exist either; in the ascending scale of life, for instance, it is impossible to indicate the point at which the vegetable kingdom ends and the animal kingdom starts, where bestiality ceases and Man begins. Nevertheless, there is a very real difference between plant and animal, between animal and Man. In human society likewise, in spite of the intermediate stages which form imperceptible transitions between one type of political and social life and another, the difference between classes is nonetheless strongly marked. Anyone can distinguish the aristocracy of noble birth from the aristocracy of finance, the upper bourgeoisie from the petty bourgeoisie, the latter from the proletariat of factories and cities, just as one can distinguish the great landowner, the man who lives on his income, from the peasant landowner who himself tills the soil, or the farmer from the landless agricultural laborer.

All these varying types of political and social life may nowadays be reduced to two main categories, diametrically opposed, and natural enemies to each other: the *political classes*, i.e. *privileged classes* constituting all those whose privilege stems from land and capital or only from bourgeois education,[10] and the disinherited *working classes*, deprived of capital and land and even elementary schooling.

One would have to be a sophist to deny the existence of the abyss which separates these two classes today. As in the ancient world, our modern civilization, which contains a comparatively limited minority of privileged citizens, is based upon the forced labor (forced by hunger) of the immense majority of the population who are fatally doomed to ignorance and to brutality.

It is in vain, too, that we would try to persuade ourselves that the abyss could be bridged by the simple diffusion of light among the masses. It is well enough to set up schools among the masses. It is well enough to set up schools for the people. But we should also question whether the man of the people, feeding his family by the day-to-day labor of his hands, himself deprived of the most elementary schooling and of leisure, dulled and brutalized by his toil—we should question whether this man has the idea, the desire, or even the possibility of sending his children to school and supporting them during the period of their education. Would he not need the help of their feeble hands, their child labor, to provide for all the needs of his family? It would be sacrifice enough for him to send to school one or two of them, and give them hardly enough time to learn a little reading and writing and arithmetic, and allow their hearts and minds to be tainted with the Christian catechism which is being deliberately and profusely distributed in the official public schools of all countries—would this piddling bit of schooling ever succeed in lifting the working masses to the level of bourgeois intelligence? Would it bridge the gap?

Obviously this vital question of primary schooling and higher education for the people depends upon the solution of the problem, difficult in other ways, of radical reform in the present economic condition of the working classes. Improve working conditions, render to labor what is justly due to labor, and thereby give the people security, comfort, and leisure. Then, believe me, they will educate themselves; they will create a larger, saner, higher civilization than this.

It is also in vain that we might say, with the economists, that an improvement in the economic situation of the working classes depends upon the general progress of industry and commerce in each country, and their complete emancipation from the supervision and protection of the State. The freedom of industry and of commerce is certainly a great thing, and one of the essential foundations of the future international alliance of all the peoples of the world. As we love freedom, all types of freedom, we should equally love this. On the other hand, however, we must recognize that so long as the present states exist, and so long as labor continues to be the slave of property and of capital, this particular freedom, while it enriches a minimum portion of the bourgeoisie to the detriment of the immense majority, would produce one benefit alone; it would further enfeeble and demoralize the small number of the privileged while increasing the misery, the grievances, and the just indignation of the working masses, and thereby hasten the hour of destruction for states.

England, Belgium, France, and Germany are those European countries where commerce and industry enjoy comparatively the greatest liberty and have attained the highest degree of development. And it is precisely in these countries where poverty is felt most cruelly, where the abyss between the capitalist and the proprietor on the one hand and working classes on the other seems to have deepened to a degree unknown elsewhere. In Russia, in the Scandinavian countries, in Italy, in Spain, where commerce and industry have had but slight development, people seldom die of hunger, except in cases of extraordinary catastrophe. In England, death from starvation is a daily occurrence. Nor are those isolated cases; there are thousands, and tens and hundreds of thousands, who perish. Is it not evident that in the economic conditions now prevailing in the entire civilized world —the free development of commerce and industry, the marvelous applications of science to production, even the machines intended to emancipate the worker by facilitating his toil—all these inventions, this progress of which civilized man is justly proud, far from ameliorating the situation of the working classes, only worsen it and make it still less endurable?

North America alone is still largely an exception to this rule. Yet far from disproving the rule, this exception actually serves to confirm it. If the workers in that country are paid more than those in Europe, and if no one there dies of hunger, and if, at the same time, the antagonism between classes hardly exists there; if all its workers are citizens and if the mass of its citizens truly constitutes one single body politic, and if a good primary and even secondary education is widespread among the masses, it should no doubt be largely attributed to that traditional spirit of freedom which the early colonists brought with them from England. Heightened, tested, strengthened in the great religious struggles, the principle of individual independence and of communal and provincial *self-government* was still further favored by the rare circumstance that once it was transplanted into a wilderness, delivered, so to speak, from the obsessions of the past, it could create a new world—the world of liberty. And liberty is so great a magician, endowed with so marvelous a power of productivity, that under the inspiration of this spirit alone, North America was able within less than a century to equal, and even surpass, the civilization of Europe. But let us not deceive ourselves: this marvelous progress and this so enviable prosperity are due in large measure to an important advantage which America possesses in common with Russia: its immense reaches of fertile land which even now remain uncultivated for lack of manpower. This great territorial wealth has been thus far as good as lost for Russia since we have never had liberty there. It has been otherwise in North America; offering a freedom which does not exist anywhere else, it attracts every year hundreds of thousands of energetic, industrious, and intelligent settlers whom it is in a position to admit because of this wealth. It thereby keeps poverty away and at the same time staves off the moment when the social question will arise. A worker who finds no work or is dissatisfied with the wages which capital offers him can in the last resort always make his way to the Far West and set about clearing a patch of land in the wilderness.

Since this possibility is always open as a way out for all the workers of America, it naturally keeps wages high and affords to each an independence unknown in Europe. This is an advantage; but there is also a disadvantage. As the good prices for industrial goods are largely due to the good wages received by labor, American manufacturers are not in a position in most cases to compete with the European manufacturers. The result is that the industry of the Northern states finds it necessary to impose a protectionist tariff. This, however, first brings about the creation of a number of artificial industries, and particularly the oppression and ruination of the nonmanufacturing Southern states, which drives them to call for secession. Finally, the result is the crowding together in cities such as New York, Philadelphia, Boston, and others of masses of workers who gradually begin to find themselves in a situation analogous to that of workers in the great manufacturing states of Europe. And, as a matter of fact, we now see the social question confronting the Northern states just as it has confronted us a great deal earlier.

We are thus forced to admit that in our modern world the civilization of the few is still founded, though not as completely as in the days of antiquity, upon the forced labor and the comparative barbarism of the many. It would be unjust to say that this privileged class is a stranger to labor. On the contrary, in our time they work hard and the number of idle people is diminishing appreciably. They are beginning to hold work in honor; those who are most fortunate realize today that one must work hard in order to remain at the summit of the present civilization and even in order to know how to profit by one's privileges and retain them. But there is this difference between the work done by the comfortable classes and that done by the laboring classes: the former is rewarded in an incomparably greater proportion and affords the privileged the opportunity for *leisure*, that supreme condition for all human development, both intellectual and moral—a condition never attained by the working classes. Also, the work done in the world of the privileged is almost exclusively *mental* work—the work involving imagination, memory, the thinking process. The work done by millions of proletarians, on the other hand, is *manual* work; often, as in all factories, for instance, it is work that does not even exercise man's entire muscular system at one time, but tends to develop one part of the body to the detriment of all the others, and this labor is generally performed under conditions harmful to his health and to his harmonious development. The laborer on the land is in this respect much more fortunate: his nature is not vitiated by the stifling, often tainted atmosphere of a factory; it is not deformed by the abnormal development of one of his powers at the expense of the others; it remains more vigorous, more complete. On the other hand, his mind is almost always slower, more sluggish, and much less developed than that of the worker in the factories and in the cities.

In sum, workers in the crafts, in the factories, and workers on the land all represent *manual labor*, as opposed to the privileged representatives of *mental labor*. What is the consequence of this division, not a fictitious but a real one, which lies at the very foundation of the present political and social situation?

To the privileged representatives of mental work—who, incidentally, are not called upon in the present organization of society to represent their class because they may be the most intelligent, but solely because they were born into the privileged class—to them go all the benefits as well as all the corruptions of present-day civilization: the wealth, the luxury, the comfort, the well-being, the sweetness of family life, the exclusive political liberty with the power to exploit the labor of millions of workers and to govern them as they please and as profits them—all the inventions, all the refinements of imagination and intellect . . . and, along with the opportunity for becoming complete men, all the depravities of a humanity perverted by privilege. As to the representatives of *manual labor*, those countless millions of proletarians or even the small landholders, what is left for them? To them go misery without end, not even the joys of family life—since the family soon becomes a burden for the poor man—ignorance, barbarity, and we might say even an inescapable brutality, with the dubious consolation that they serve as a pedestal to civilization, to the liberty and corruption of the few. Despite this, they have preserved a freshness of the spirit and of the heart. Morally strengthened by labor, forced though it may be, they have retained a sense of justice of quite another kind than the justice of lawgivers and codes. Being miserable themselves, they keenly sympathize with the misery of others; their common sense has not been corrupted by the sophisms of a doctrinaire science or by the mendacity of politics—and since they have not yet abused life, or even used it, they have faith in life.

But what of the objection that this contrast, this gulf

between the small number of the privileged and the vast numbers of the disinherited has always existed and still exists; just what has changed? It is only that this gulf used to be filled with the great fog banks of religion, so that the masses were deceived into thinking there was a common ground for all. Nowadays, the Great Revolution has begun to sweep the mists away; the masses, too, are beginning to see the abyss and to ask the reason why. This is a stupendous realization.

Since the Revolution has confronted the masses with its own gospel, a revelation not mystical but rational, not of heaven but of earth, not divine but human—the gospel of the Rights of Man; since it has proclaimed that all men are equal and equally entitled to liberty and to a humane life—ever since then, the masses of people in all Europe, in the entire civilized world, slowly awakening from the slumber in which Christianity's incantations had held them enthralled, are beginning to wonder whether they, too, are not entitled to equality, to liberty, and to their humanity.

From the moment this question was asked, the people everywhere, led by their admirable good sense as well as by their instinct, have realized that the first condition for their real emancipation or, if I may be permitted to use the term, their *humanization*, was, above all, a radical reform of their economic condition. The question of daily bread is for them the principal question, and rightly so, for, as Aristotle has said: "Man, in order to think, to feel freely, to become a man, must be free from worry about his material sustenance." Furthermore, the bourgeois who so loudly protest against the materialism of the common people, and who continually preach to them of abstinence and idealism, know this very well; they preach by word and not by example.

The second question for the people is that of leisure after labor, a condition *sine qua non* for humanity. But bread and leisure can never be made secure for the masses except through a radical transformation of society as presently constituted. That is why the Revolution, impelled by its own logical insistency, has given birth to *socialism*.

Socialism[11]

The French Revolution, having proclaimed the right and the duty of each human individual to become a man, culminated in Babouvism. Babeuf—one of the last of the high-principled and energetic citizens that the Revolution created and then assassinated in such great numbers, and who had the good fortune to have counted men like Buonarotti among his friends—had brought together, in a singular concept, the political traditions of France and the very modern ideas of a social revolution. Disappointed with the failure of the Revolution to bring about a radical change in society, he sought to save the spirit of this Revolution by conceiving a political and social system according to which the republic, the expression of the collective will of the citizens, would confiscate all individual property and administer it in the interest of all. Equal portions of such confiscated property would be allotted to higher education, elementary education, means of subsistence, entertainment, and each individual, without exception, would be compelled to perform both muscular and mental labor, each according to his strength and capacity. Babeuf's conspiracy failed; he was guillotined, together with some of his old friends. But his ideal of a socialist republic did not die with him. It was picked up by his friend Buonarotti, the arch-conspirator of the century, who transmitted it as a sacred trust to future generations. And thanks to the secret societies Buonarotti founded in Belgium and France, communist ideas germinated in popular imagination. From 1830 to 1848 they found able interpreters in Cabet and M. Louis Blanc, who established the definitive theory of *revolutionary socialism*. Another socialist movement, stemming from the same revolutionary source, converging upon the same goal though by means of entirely different methods, a movement which we should like to call *doctrinaire socialism*, was created by two eminent men, Saint-Simon and Fourier. Saint-Simonianism was interpreted, developed, transformed, and established as a quasi-practical system, as a church, by Le Père Enfantin, with many of his friends who have now become financiers and statesmen, singularly devoted to the

Empire. Fourierism found its commentator in *Démocratie Pacifique,* edited until December by M. Victor Considérant.

The merit of these two socialist systems, though different in many respects, lies principally in their profound, scientific, and severe critique of the present organization of society, whose monstrous contradictions they have boldly revealed, and also in the very important fact that they have strongly attacked and subverted Christianity for the sake of rehabilitating our material existence and human passions, which were maligned and yet so thoroughly indulged by Christianity's priesthood. The Saint-Simonists wanted to replace Christianity with a new religion based upon the mystical cult of the flesh, with a new hierarchy of priests, new exploiters of the mob by the privilege inherent in genius, ability, and talent. The Fourierists, who were much more democratic, and, we may say, more sincerely so, envisioned their phalansteries as governed and administered by leaders elected by universal suffrage, where everyone, they thought, would personally find his own work and his own place in accordance with the nature of his own feelings.

The defects of Saint-Simonianism are too obvious to need discussion. The twofold error of the Saint-Simonists consisted, first, in their sincere belief that though their powers of persuasion and their pacific propaganda they would succeed in so touching the hearts of the rich that these would willingly give their surplus wealth to the phalansteries; and, secondly, in their belief that it was possible, theoretically, a priori, to construct a social paradise where all future humanity would come to rest. They had not understood that while we might enunciate the great principles of humanity's future development, we should leave it to the experience of the future to work out the practical realization of such principles.

In general, regulation was the common passion of all the socialists of the pre-1848 era, with one exception only. Cabet, Louis Blanc, the Fourierists, the Saint-Simonists, all were inspired by a passion for indoctrinating and organizing the future; they all were more or less authoritarians. The exception is Proudhon.

The son of a peasant, and thus instinctively a hundred times more revolutionary than all the doctrinaire and bourgeois socialists, Proudhon armed himself with a critique as profound and penetrating as it was merciless, in order to destroy their systems. Resisting authority with liberty, against those state socialists, he boldly proclaimed himself an anarchist; defying their deism or their pantheism, he had the courage to call himself simply an atheist or rather, with Auguste Comte, a *positivist*.

His own socialism was based upon liberty, both individual and collective, and on the spontaneous action of free associations obeying no laws other than the general laws of social economy, already known and yet to be discovered by social science, free from all governmental regulation and state protection. This socialism subordinated politics to the economic, intellectual, and moral interests of society. It subsequently, by its own logic, culminated in federalism.

Such was the state of social science prior to 1848. The polemics of the left carried on in the newspapers, circulars, and socialist brochures brought a mass of new ideas to the working classes. They were saturated with this material and, when the 1848 revolution broke out, the power of socialism became manifest.

Socialism, we have said, was the latest offspring of the Great Revolution; but before producing it, the revolution had already brought forth a more direct heir, its oldest, the beloved child of Robespierre and the followers of Saint-Just—*pure republicanism*, without any admixture of socialist ideas, resuscitated from antiquity and inspired by the heroic traditions of the great citizens of Greece and Rome. As it was far less humanitarian than socialism, it hardly knew man, and recognized the citizen only. And while socialism seeks to found a *republic of men*, all that republicanism wants is a *republic of citizens*, even though the citizens—as in the constitutions which necessarily succeeded the constitution of 1793 in consequence of that first constitution's deliberately ignoring the social question—even though the citizens, I say, by virtue of being *active citizens*, to borrow an expression from the Constituent Assembly, were to base their civic privilege upon the exploitation of the labor of *passive citizens*. Besides, the political republican is not at all egotistic in his own behalf, or at least is not supposed to be so; he must be an egotist in behalf of his fatherland which he must value above himself, above all other individuals, all nations, all humanity. Consequently, he will always ignore international justice; in all debates, whether his country be right or wrong, he will always give it first place. He will want it always to dominate and to crush all the foreign nations by its power and glory. Through natural inclination he will become fond of conquest, in spite of the fact that the experience of centuries may have proved to him that military triumphs must inevitably lead to Caesarism.

The socialist republican detests the grandeur, the power, and the military glory of the State. He sets liberty and the general welfare above them. A federalist in the internal affairs of the country, he desires an international confederation, first of all in the spirit of justice, and second because he is convinced that the economic and social revolution, transcending all the artificial and pernicious barriers between states, can only be brought about, in part at least, by the solidarity in action, if not of all, then at least of the majority of the nations constituting the civilized world today, so that sooner or later all the nations must join together.

The strictly political republican is a stoic; he recognizes no rights for himself but only duties; or, as in Mazzini's republic, he claims one right only for himself, that of eternal devotion to his country, of living only to serve it, and of joyfully sacrificing himself and even dying for it, as in the song Dumas dedicated to the Girondins: "To die for one's country is the finest, the most enviable fate."

The socialist, on the contrary, insists upon his positive rights to life and to all of its intellectual, moral, and physical joys. He loves life, and he wants to enjoy it in all its abundance. Since his convictions are part of himself, and his duties to society are indissolubly linked with his rights, he will, in order to remain faithful to both, manage to live in accordance with justice like Proudhon and, if necessary, die like Babeuf. But he will never say that the life of humanity should be a sacrifice or that death is the sweetest fate.

Liberty, to the political republican, is an empty word; it is the liberty of a willing slave, a devoted victim of the State. Being always ready to sacrifice his own liberty, he will willingly sacrifice the liberty of others. Political republicanism, therefore, neces-sarily leads to despotism. For the socialist republican, liberty linked with the general welfare, producing a humanity of all through the humanity of each, is everything, while the State, in his eyes, is a mere instrument, a servant of his well-being and of everyone's liberty. The socialist is distinguished from the bourgeois by *justice*, since he demands for himself nothing but the real fruit of his own labor. He is distinguished from the strict republican by his *frank and human egotism*; he lives for himself, openly and without fine-sounding phrases. He knows that in so living his life, *in accordance with justice*, he serves the entire society, and, in so serving it, he also finds his own welfare. The republican is rigid; often, in consequence of his patriotism, he is cruel, as the priest is often made cruel by his religion. The socialist is natural; he is moderately patriotic, but nevertheless always very human. In a word, between the political republican and the socialist republican there is an abyss; the one, as a *quasi-religious phenomenon*, belongs to the past; the other, whether *positivist* or *atheist*, belongs to the future.

The natural antagonism of these two kinds of republican came plainly into view in 1848. From the very first hours of the Revolution, they no longer understood each other; their ideals, all their instincts, drew them in diametrically opposite directions. The entire period from February to June was spent in skirmishes which, carrying the civil war into the camp of the revolutionaries and paralyzing their forces, naturally strengthened the already formidable coalition of all kinds of reactionaries; fear soon welded them into one single party. In June the republicans, in their turn, formed a coalition with the reaction in order to crush the socialists. They thought they had won a victory, yet they pushed their beloved republic down into the abyss. General Cavaignac, the flagbearer of the reaction, was the precursor of Napoleon III. Everybody realized this at the time, if not in France then certainly everywhere else, for this disastrous victory of the republicans against the workers of Paris was celebrated as a great triumph in all the courts of Europe, and the officers of the Prussian Guards, led by their generals, hastened to convey their fraternal congratulations to General Cavaignac.

Terrified of the red phantom, the bourgeoisie of Europe permitted itself to fall into absolute serfdom. By nature critical and liberal, the middle class is not fond of the military, but, facing the threatening dangers of a popular emancipation, it chose militarism. Having sacrificed its dignity and all its glorious conquests of the eighteenth and early nineteenth centuries, it fancied that it had at least the peace and tranquillity necessary for the success of its commercial and industrial transactions. "We are sacrificing our liberty to you," it seemed to be saying to the military powers who again rose upon the ruins of this third revolution. "Let us, in return, peacefully exploit the labor of the masses, and protect us against their demands, which may appear theoretically legitimate but which are detestable so far as our interests are concerned." The military, in turn, promised the bourgeoisie everything; they even kept their word. Why, then, is the bourgeoisie, the entire bourgeoisie of Europe, generally discontented today?

The bourgeoisie had not reckoned with the fact that a military regime is very costly, that through its internal organization alone it paralyzes, it upsets, it ruins nations, and moreover, obeying its own intrinsic and inescapable logic, it has never failed to bring on *war*; dynastic wars, wars of honor, wars of conquest or wars of national frontiers, wars of equilibrium—destruction and unending absorption of states by other states, rivers of human blood, a fire-ravaged countryside, ruined cities, the devastation of entire provinces—all this for the sake of satisfying the ambitions of princes and their favorites, to enrich them to occupy territories, to discipline populations, and to fill the pages of history.

Now the bourgeoisie understands these things, and that is why it is dissatisfied with the military regime it has helped so much to create. It is indeed weary of these drawbacks, but what is it going to put in the place of things as they are?

Constitutional monarchy has seen its day, and, anyway, it has never prospered too well on the European continent. Even in England, that historic cradle of modern institutionalism, battered by the rising democracy it is shaken, it totters, and will soon be unable to contain the gathering surge of popular passions and demands.

A republic? What kind of republic? Is it to be political only, or democratic and social? Are the people still socialist? Yes, more than ever.

What succumbed in June 1848 was not socialism in general. It was only *state socialism*, authoritarian and regimented socialism, the kind that had believed and hoped that the State would fully satisfy the needs and the legitimate aspirations of the working classes, and that the State, armed with its omnipotence, would and could inaugurate a new social order. Hence it was not socialism that died in June; it was rather the State which declared its bankruptcy toward socialism and, proclaiming itself incapable of paying its debt to socialism, sought the quickest way out by killing its creditor. It did not succeed in killing socialism but it did kill the faith that socialism had placed in it. It also, at the same time, annihilated all the theories of authoritarian or doctrinaire socialism, some of which, like *L'Icarie* by Cabet, and like *L'Organisation du Travail* by Louis Blanc, had advised the people to rely in all things upon the State—while others demonstrated their worthlessness through a series of ridiculous experiments. Even Proudhon's bank, which could have prospered in happier circumstances, was crushed by the strictures and the general hostility of the bourgeoisie.

Socialism lost this first battle for a very simple reason. Although it was rich in instincts and in negative theoretical ideas, which gave it full justification in its fight against privilege, it lacked the necessary positive and practical ideas for erecting a new system upon the ruins of the bourgeois order, the system of popular justice. The workers who fought in June 1848 for the emancipation of the people were united by instinct, not by ideas—and such confused ideas as they did possess formed a tower of Babel, a chaos, which could produce nothing. Such was the main cause of their defeat. Must we, for this reason, hold in doubt the future itself, and the present strength of socialism? Christianity, which had set as its goal the creation of the kingdom of justice in heaven, needed several centuries to triumph in

Europe. Is there any cause for surprise if socialism, which has set itself a more difficult problem, that of creating the kingdom of justice on earth, has not triumphed within a few years?

Is it necessary to prove that socialism is not dead? We need only see what is going on all over Europe today. Behind all the diplomatic gossip, behind the noises of war which have filled Europe since 1852, what serious question is facing all the countries if it is not the social question? It alone is the great unknown; everyone senses its coming, everyone trembles at the thought, no one dares speak of it—but it speaks for itself, and in an ever louder voice. The cooperative associations of the workers, these mutual aid banks and labor credit banks, these trade unions, and this international league of workers in all the countries—all this rising movement of workers in England, in France, in Belgium, in Germany, in Italy, and in Switzerland—does it not prove that they have not in any way given up their goal, nor lost faith in their coming emancipation? Does it not prove that they have also understood that in order to hasten the hour of their deliverance they should not rely on the States, nor on the more or less hypocritical assistance of the privileged classes, but rather upon themselves and their independent, completely spontaneous associations?

In most of the countries of Europe, this movement, which, in appearance at least, is alien to politics, still preserves an exclusively economic and, so to say, private character. But in England it has already placed itself squarely in the stormy domain of politics. Having organized itself in a formidable association, The Reform League, it has already won a great victory against the politically organized privilege of the aristocracy and the upper bourgeoisie. The Reform League, with a characteristically British patience and practical tenacity, has outlined a plan for its campaign; it is not too straitlaced about anything, it is not easily frightened, it will not be stopped by any obstacle. "Within ten years at most," they say, "and even against the greatest odds, we shall have universal suffrage, and then . . . then we will make the social revolution!"

In France, as in Germany, as socialism quietly proceeded along the road of private economic associations, it has already achieved so high a degree of power among the working classes that Napoleon III on the one side and Count Bismarck on the other are beginning to seek an alliance with it. In Italy and in Spain, after the deplorable fiasco of all their political parties, and in the face of the terrible misery into which both countries are plunged, all other problems will soon be absorbed in the economic and social question. As for Russia and Poland, is there really any other question facing these countries? It is this question which has just extinguished the last hopes of the old, noble, historic Poland; it is this question which is threatening and which will destroy the pestiferous Empire of All the Russias, now tottering to its fall. Even in America, has not socialism been made manifest in the proposition by a man of eminence, Mr. Charles Sumner, Senator from Massachusetts, to distribute lands to the emancipated Negroes of the Southern states?

You can very well see, then, that socialism is everywhere, and that in spite of its June defeat it has by force of underground work slowly infiltrated the political life of all countries, and succeeded to the point of being felt everywhere as the latent force of the century. Another few years and it will reveal itself as an active, formidable power.

With very few exceptions, almost all the peoples of Europe, some even unfamiliar with the term "socialism," are socialist today. They know no other banner but that which proclaims their economic emancipation ahead of all else; they would a thousand times rather renounce any question but that. Hence it is only through socialism that they can be drawn into politics, a good politics.

Is it not enough to say, gentlemen, that we may not exclude socialism from our program, and that we could not leave it out without dooming all our work to impotence? By our program, by declaring ourselves federalist republicans, we have shown ourselves to be revolutionary enough to alienate a good part of the bourgeoisie, all those who speculate upon the misery and the misfortunes of the masses and who even find something to gain in the great catastrophes which beset the nations more than ever today. If we set aside this busy, bustling, intriguing, speculating section of the bourgeoisie, we shall still keep the majority of decent, industrious bourgeois, who occasionally do some harm by necessity rather than willfully or by preference, and who would want nothing better than to be delivered from this fatal necessity, which places them in a state of permanent hostility toward the working masses and, at the same time, ruins them. We might truthfully say that the petty bourgeoisie, small business, and small industry are now beginning to suffer almost as much as the working classes, and if things go on at the same rate, this respectable bourgeois majority could well, through its economic position, soon merge with the proletariat. It is being destroyed and pushed downward into the abyss by big commerce, big industry, and especially by large-scale, unscrupulous speculators. The position of the petty bourgeoisie, therefore, is growing more and more revolutionary; its ideas, which for so long a time had been reactionary, have been clarified through these disastrous experiences and must necessarily take the opposite course. The more intelligent among them are beginning to realize that for the decent bourgeoisie the only salvation lies in an alliance with the people—and that the social question is as important to them, and *in the same way*, as to the people.

This progressive change in the thinking of the petty bourgeoisie in Europe is a fact as cheering as it is incontestable. But we should be under no illusion; the initiative for the new development will not belong to the bourgeoisie but to the people—in the West, to the workers in the factories and the cities; in our country, in Russia, in Poland, and in most of the Slav countries, to the peasants. The petty bourgeoisie has grown too fearful, too timid, too skeptical to take any initiative alone. It will let itself be drawn in, but it will not draw in anyone, for while it is poor in ideas, it also lacks the faith and the passion. This passion, which annihilates obstacles and creates new worlds, is to be found in the people only. Therefore, the initiative for the new movement will unquestionably belong to the people. And are we going to repudiate the people? Are we going to stop talking about socialism, which is the new religion of the people?

But socialism, they tell us, shows an inclination to ally itself with Caesarism. In the first place, this is a calumny; it is

Caesarism, on the contrary, which, on seeing the menacing power of socialism rising on the horizon, solicits its favors in order to exploit it in its own way. But is not this still another reason for us to work for socialism, in order to prevent this monstrous alliance, which would without doubt be the greatest misfortune that could threaten the liberty of the world?

We should work for it even apart from all practical considerations, because socialism is *justice*. When we speak of justice we do not thereby mean the justice which is imparted to us in legal codes and by Roman law, founded for the most part on acts of force and violence consecrated by time and by the blessings of some church, Christian or pagan and, as such, accepted as an absolute, the rest being nothing but the logical consequence of the same.[12] I speak of that justice which is based solely upon human conscience, the justice which you will rediscover deep in the conscience of every man, even in the conscience of the child, and which translates itself into simple *equality*.

This justice, which is so universal but which nevertheless, owing to the encroachments of force and to the influence of religion, has never as yet prevailed in the world of politics, of law, or of economics, should serve as a basis for the new world. Without it there is no liberty, no republic, no prosperity, no peace! It should therefore preside at all our resolutions in order that we may effectively cooperate in establishing peace.

This justice bids us take into our hands the people's cause, so miserably maltreated until now, and to demand in its behalf economic and social emancipation, together with political liberty.

We do not propose to you, gentlemen, one or another socialist system. What we ask of you is to proclaim once more that great principle of the French Revolution: that every man is entitled to the material and moral means for the development of his complete humanity—a principle which, we believe, translates itself into the following mandate:

To organize society in such a manner that every individual endowed with life, man or woman, may find almost equal means for the development of his various faculties and for their utilization in his labor; to organize a society which, while it makes it impossible for any individual whatsoever to exploit the labor of others, will not allow anyone to share in the enjoyment of social wealth, always produced by labor only, unless he has himself contributed to its creation with his own labor.

The complete solution of this problem will no doubt be the work of centuries. But history has set the problem before us, and we can now no longer evade it if we are not to resign ourselves to total impotence.

We hasten to add that we energetically reject any attempt at a social organization devoid of the most complete liberty for individuals as well as associations, and one that would call for the establishment of a ruling authority of any nature whatsoever, and that, in the name of this liberty—which we recognize as the only basis for, and the only legitimate creator of, any organization, economic or political—we shall always protest against anything that may in any way resemble communism or state socialism.

The only thing we believe the State can and should do is to change the law of inheritance, gradually at first, until it is entirely abolished as soon as possible. Since the right of inheritance is a purely arbitrary creation of the State, and one of the essential conditions for the very existence of the authoritarian and divinely sanctioned State, it can and must be abolished by liberty—which again means that the State itself must accomplish its own dissolution in a society freely organized in accordance with justice. This right must necessarily be abolished, we believe, for as long as *inheritance* is in effect, there will be *hereditary* economic inequality, not the natural inequality of individuals but the artificial inequality of classes—and this will necessarily always lead to the hereditary inequality of the development and cultivation of mental faculties, and continue to be the source and the consecration of all political and social inequalities. Equality from the moment life begins—insofar as this equality depends on the economic and political organization of society, and in order that everyone, in accordance with his own natural capacities, may become the heir and the product of his own labor—this is the problem which justice sets before us. We believe that the public funds for the education and elementary schooling of all children of both sexes, as well as their maintenance from birth until they come of age, should be the sole inheritors of all the deceased. As Slavs and Russians, we may add that for us the social idea, based upon the general and traditional instinct of our populations, is that the earth, the property of all the people, should be owned only by those who cultivate it with the labor of their own hands.

We are convinced that this principle is a just one, that it is an essential and indispensable condition for any serious social reform, and hence that Western Europe, too, cannot fail to accept and recognize it, in spite of all the difficulties its realization may encounter in certain countries. In France, for instance, the majority of the peasants already own their land; most of these same peasants, however, will soon come to own nothing, because of the parceling out which is the inevitable result of the politico-economic system now prevailing in that country. We are making no proposal on this point, and indeed we refrain, in general, from making any proposals, dealing with any particular problem of social science or politics. We are convinced that all these questions should be seriously and thoroughly discussed in our journal. We shall today confine ourselves to proposing that you make the following declaration:

As we are convinced that the real attainment of liberty, of justice, and of peace in the world will be impossible so long as the immense majority of the populations are dispossessed of property, deprived of education and condemned to political and social nonbeing and a de facto if not a de jure slavery, through their state of misery as well as their need to labor without rest or leisure, in producing all the wealth in which the world is glorying today, and receiving in return but a small portion hardly sufficient for their daily bread;

As we are convinced that for all these populations, hitherto so terribly maltreated through the centuries, the question of bread is the question of intellectual emancipation, of liberty, and of humanity;

As we are convinced that liberty without socialism is privilege, injustice; and that socialism without liberty is slavery and brutality;

Now therefore, the League highly proclaims the need for a radical social and economic reform, whose aim shall be the deliverance of the people's labor from the yoke of capital and property, upon a foundation of the strictest justice—not juridical, not theological, not metaphysical, but simply human justice, of positive science and the most absolute liberty.

The League at the same time decides that its journal will freely open its columns to all serious discussions of economic and social questions, provided they are sincerely inspired by a desire for the greatest popular emancipation, both on the material and the political and intellectual levels.

Rousseau's Theory of the State

. . . We have said that man is not only the most individualistic being on earth—he is also *the most social*. It was a great mistake on the part of Jean Jacques Rousseau to have thought that primitive society was established through a free agreement among savages. But Jean Jacques is not the only one to have said this. The majority of jurists and modern publicists, either of the school of Kant or any other individualist and liberal school, those who do not accept the idea of a society founded upon the divine right of the theologians nor of a society determined by the Hegelian school as a more or less mystical realization of objective morality, nor of the naturalists' concept of a primitive animal society, all accept, *nolens volens,* and for lack of any other basis, *the tacit agreement or contract* as their starting point.

According to the theory of the social contract primitive men enjoying absolute liberty only in isolation are antisocial by nature. When forced to associate they destroy each other's freedom. If this struggle is unchecked it can lead to mutual extermination. In order not to destroy each other completely, they conclude a *contract,* formal or tacit, whereby they surrender some of their freedom to assure the rest. This contract becomes the foundation of society, or rather of the State, for we must point out that in this theory there is no place for society; only the State exists, or rather society is completely absorbed by the State.

Society is the natural mode of existence of the human collectivity, independent of any contract. It governs itself through the customs or the traditional habits, but never by laws. It progresses slowly, under the impulsion it receives from individual initiatives and not through the thinking or the will of the lawgiver. There are a good many laws which govern it without its being aware of them, but these are natural laws, inherent in the body social, just as physical laws are inherent in material bodies. Most of these laws remain unknown to this day; nevertheless, they have governed human society ever since its birth, independent of the thinking and the will of the men composing the society. Hence they should not be confused with the political and juridical laws proclaimed by some legislative power, laws that are supposed to be the logical sequelae of the first contract consciously formed by men.

The state is in no wise an immediate product of nature. Unlike society, it does not precede the awakening of reason in men. The liberals say that the first state was created by the free and rational will of men; the men of the right consider it the work of God. In either case it dominates society and tends to absorb it completely.

One might rejoin that the State, representing as it does the public welfare or the common interest of all, curtails a part of the liberty of each only for the sake of assuring to him all the remainder. But this remainder may be a form of security; it is never liberty. Liberty is indivisible; one cannot curtail a part of it without killing all of it. This little part you are curtailing is the very essence of my liberty; it is all of it. Through a natural, necessary, and irresistible movement, all of my liberty is concentrated precisely in the part, small as it may be, which you curtail. It is the story of Bluebeard's wife, who had an entire palace at her disposal, with full and complete liberty to enter everywhere, to see and to touch everything, except for one dreadful little chamber which her terrible husband's sovereign will had forbidden her to open on pain of death. Well, she turned away from all the splendors of the palace, and her entire being concentrated on the dreadful little chamber. She opened that forbidden door, for good reason, since her liberty depended on her doing so, while the prohibition to enter was a flagrant violation of precisely that liberty. It is also the story of Adam and Eve's fall. The prohibition to taste the fruit from the tree of the knowledge of good and evil, for no other reason than that such was the will of the Lord, was an act of atrocious despotism on the part of the good Lord. Had our first parents obeyed it, the entire human race would have remained plunged in the most humiliating slavery. Their disobedience has emancipated and saved us. Theirs, in the language of mythology, was the first act of human liberty.

But, one might say, could the State, the democratic State, based upon the free suffrage of all its citizens, be the negation of their liberty? And why not? That would depend entirely on the mission and the power that the citizens surrendered to the State. A republican State, based upon universal suffrage, could be very despotic, more despotic even than the monarchical State, if, under the pretext of representing everybody's will, it were to bring down the weight of its collective power upon the will and the free movement of each of its members.

However, suppose one were to say that the State does not restrain the liberty of its members except when it tends toward injustice or evil. It prevents its members from killing each other, plundering each other, insulting each other, and in general from hurting each other, while it leaves them full liberty to do good. This brings us back to the story of Bluebeard's wife, or the story of the forbidden fruit: what is good? what is evil?

From the standpoint of the system we have under examination, the distinction between good and evil did not exist before the conclusion of the contract, when each individual stayed deep in the isolation of his liberty or of his absolute rights, having no consideration for his fellowmen except those dictated by his relative weakness or strength; that is, his own prudence and self-interest.[13] At that time, still following the same theory, egotism was the supreme law, the only right. The good was determined by success, failure was the only evil, and justice was merely the consecration of the *fait accompli*, no matter how horrible, how cruel or infamous, exactly as things are now in the political morality which prevails in Europe today.

The distinction between good and evil, according to this system, commences only with the conclusion of the social contract. Thereafter, what was recognized as constituting the common interest was proclaimed as good, and all that was contrary to it as evil. The contracting members, on becoming citizens, and bound by a more or less solemn undertaking, thereby assumed an obligation: to subordinate their private interests to the common good, to an interest inseparable from all others. Their own rights were separated from the public right, the sole representative of which, the State, was thereby invested with the power to repress all illegal revolts of the individual, but also with the obligation to protect each of its members in the exercise of his rights insofar as these were not contrary to the common right.

We shall now examine what the State, thus constituted, should be in relation to other states, its peers, as well as in relation to its own subject populations. This examination appears to us all the more interesting and useful because the State, as it is here defined, is precisely the modern State insofar as it has separated itself from the religious idea—*the secular* or *atheist State* proclaimed by modern publicists. Let us see, then: of what does its morality consist? It is the modern State, we have said, at the moment when it has freed itself from the yoke of the Church, and when it has, consequently, shaken off the yoke of the universal or cosmopolitan morality of the Christian religion; at the moment when it has not yet been penetrated by the humanitarian morality or idea, which, by the way, it could never do without destroying itself; for, in its separate existence and isolated concentration, it would be too narrow to embrace, to contain the interests and therefore the morality of all mankind.

Modern states have reached precisely this point. Christianity serves them only as a pretext or a phrase or as a means of deceiving the idle mob, for they pursue goals which have nothing to do with religious sentiments. The great statesmen of our days, the Palmerstons, the Muravievs, the Cavours, the Bismarcks, the Napoleons, had a good laugh when people took their religious pronouncements seriously. They laughed harder when people attributed humanitarian sentiments, considerations, and intentions to them, but they never made the mistake of treating these ideas in public as so much nonsense. Just what remains to constitute their morality? The interest of the State, and nothing else. From this point of view, which, incidentally, with very few exceptions, has been that of the statesmen, the *strong men* of all times and of all countries—from this point of view, I say, whatever conduces to the preservation, the grandeur and the power of the State, no matter how sacrilegious or morally revolting it may seem, *that is the good.* And conversely, whatever opposes the State's interests, no matter how holy or just otherwise, *that is evil.* Such is the secular morality and practice of every State.

It is the same with the State founded upon the theory of the social contract. According to this principle, the good and the just commence only with the contract; they are, in fact, nothing but the very contents and the purpose of the contract; that is, *the common interest* and *the public right* of all the individuals who have formed the contract among themselves, *with the exclusion of all those who remain outside the contract.* It is, consequently, *nothing but the greatest satisfaction given to the collective egotism of a special and restricted association,* which, being founded upon the partial sacrifice of the individual egotism of each of its members, rejects from its midst, as strangers and natural enemies, the immense majority of the human species, whether or not it may be organized into analogous associations.

The existence of one sovereign, exclusionary State necessarily supposes the existence and, if need be, provokes the formation of other such States, since it is quite natural that individuals who find themselves outside it and are threatened by it in their existence and in their liberty, should, in their turn, associate themselves against it. We thus have humanity divided into an indefinite number of foreign states, all hostile and threatened by each other. There is no common right, no social contract of any kind between them; otherwise they would cease to be independent states and become the federated members of one great state. But unless this great state were to embrace all of humanity, it would be confronted with other great states, each federated within, each maintaining the same posture of inevitable hostility.

War would still remain the supreme law, an unavoidable condition of human survival.

Every state, federated or not, would therefore seek to become the most powerful. It must devour lest it be devoured, conquer lest it be conquered, enslave lest it be enslaved, since two powers, similar and yet alien to each other, could not coexist without mutual destruction.

The State, therefore, is the most flagrant, the most cynical, and the most complete negation of humanity. It shatters the universal solidarity of all men on the earth, and brings some of them into association only for the purpose of destroying, conquering, and enslaving all the rest. It protects its own citizens only; it recognizes human rights, humanity, civilization within its own confines alone. Since it recognizes no rights outside itself, it logically arrogates to itself the right to exercise the most ferocious inhumanity toward all foreign populations, which it can plunder, exterminate, or enslave at will. If it does show itself generous and humane toward them, it is never through a sense of duty, for it has no duties except to itself in the first place, and then to those of its members who have freely formed it, who freely continue to constitute it or even, as always happens in the long run, those who have become its subjects. As there is no international law in existence, *and as it could never exist in a meaningful and realistic way without undermining to its foundations the very principle of the absolute sovereignty of the State,* the State can have no duties toward foreign populations. Hence, if it treats a conquered people in a humane fashion, if it plunders or exterminates it halfway only, if it does not reduce it to the lowest degree of slavery, this may be a political act inspired by prudence, or even by pure magnanimity, but it is never done from a sense of duty, for the State has an absolute right to dispose of a conquered people at will.

This flagrant negation of humanity which constitutes the very essence of the State is, from the standpoint of the State, its supreme duty and its greatest virtue. It bears the name *patriotism*, and it constitutes the entire *transcendent morality* of the State. We call it transcendent morality because it usually goes beyond the level of human morality and justice, either of the community or of the private individual, and by that same token often finds itself in contradiction with these. Thus, to offend, to oppress, to despoil, to plunder, to assassinate or enslave one's fellowman is ordinarily regarded as a crime. In public life, on the other hand, from the standpoint of patriotism, when these things are done for the greater glory of the State, for the preservation or the extension of its power, it is all transformed into duty and virtue. And this virtue, this duty, are obligatory for each patriotic citizen; everyone is supposed to exercise them not against foreigners only but against one's own fellow citizens, members or subjects of the State like himself, whenever the welfare of the State demands it.

This explains why, since the birth of the State, the world of politics has always been and continues to be the stage for unlimited rascality and brigandage, brigandage and rascality which, by the way, are held in high esteem, since they are sanctified by patriotism, by the transcendent morality and the supreme interest of the State. This explains why the entire history of ancient and modern states is merely a series of revolting crimes; why kings and ministers, past and present, of all times and all countries—statesmen, diplomats, bureaucrats, and warriors—if judged from the standpoint of simple morality and human justice, have a hundred, a thousand times over earned their sentence to hard labor or to the gallows. There is no horror, no cruelty, sacrilege, or perjury, no imposture, no infamous transaction, no cynical robbery, no bold plunder or shabby betrayal that has not been or is not daily being perpetrated by the representatives of the states, under no other pretext than those elastic words, so convenient and yet so terrible: *"for reasons of state."*

These are truly terrible words, for they have corrupted and dishonored, within official ranks and in society's ruling classes, more men than has even Christianity itself. No sooner are these words uttered than all grows silent, and everything ceases; honesty, honor, justice, right, compassion itself ceases, and with it logic and good sense. Black turns white, and white turns black. The lowest human acts, the basest felonies, the most atrocious crimes become meritorious acts.

The great Italian political philosopher Machiavelli was the first to use these words, or at least the first to give them their true meaning and the immense popularity they still enjoy among our rulers today. A realistic and positive thinker if there ever was one, he was the first to understand that the great and powerful states could be founded and maintained by crime alone—by many great crimes, and by a radical contempt for all that goes under the name of honesty. He has written, explained, and proven these facts with terrifying frankness. And, since the idea of humanity was entirely unknown in his time; since the idea of fraternity—not human but religious—as preached by the Catholic Church, was at that time, as it always has been, nothing but a shocking irony, belied at every step by the Church's own actions; since in his time no one even suspected that there was such a thing as popular right, since the people had always been considered an inert and inept mass, the flesh of the State to be molded and exploited at will, pledged to eternal obedience; since there was absolutely nothing in his time, in Italy or elsewhere, except for the State—Machiavelli concluded from these facts, with a good deal of logic, that the State was the supreme goal of all human existence, that it must be served at any cost and that, since the interest of the State prevailed over everything else, a good patriot should not recoil from any crime in order to serve it. He advocates crime, he exhorts to crime, and makes it the *sine qua non* of political intelligence as well as of true patriotism. Whether the State bear the name of a monarchy or of a republic, crime will always be necessary for its preservation and its triumph. The State will doubtless change its direction and its object, but its nature will remain the same: always the energetic, permanent violation of justice, compassion, and honesty, for the welfare of the State.

Yes, Machiavelli is right. We can no longer doubt it after an experience of three and a half centuries added to his own experience. Yes, so all history tells us: while the small states are virtuous only because of their weakness, the powerful states sustain themselves by crime alone. But our conclusion will be entirely different from his, for a very simple reason. We are the children of the Revolution, and from it we have inherited the religion of humanity, which we must found upon the ruins of the religion of divinity. We believe in the rights of man, in the dignity and the necessary emancipation of the human species. We believe in human liberty and human fraternity founded upon justice. In a word, we believe in the triumph of humanity upon the earth. But this triumph, which we summon with all our longing, which we want to hasten with all our united efforts— since it is by its very nature the negation of the crime which is intrinsically the negation of humanity—this triumph cannot be achieved until crime ceases to be what it now is more or less everywhere today, *the real basis of the political existence of the nations absorbed and dominated by the ideas of the State*. And since it is now proven that no state could exist without committing crimes, or at least without contemplating and planning them, even when its impotence should prevent it from perpetrating crimes, we today conclude in favor of the *absolute need of destroying the states*. Or, if it is so decided, their radical and complete transformation so that, ceasing to be powers centralized and organized from the top down, by violence or by authority of some principle, they may recognize—with absolute liberty for all the parties to unite or not to unite, and with liberty for each of these always to leave a union even when freely entered into—from the bottom up, according to the real needs and the natural tendencies of the parties, through the free federation of individuals, associations, communes, districts, provinces, and nations within humanity.

Such are the conclusions to which we are inevitably led by an examination of the external relations which the so-called free states maintain with other states. Let us now examine the relations maintained by the State founded upon the free contract arrived at among its own citizens or subjects.

We have already observed that by excluding the immense majority of the human species from its midst, by keeping this majority outside the reciprocal engagements and duties of morality, of justice, and of right, the State denies humanity and, using that sonorous word patriotism, imposes injustice and cruelty as a supreme duty upon all its subjects. It restricts, it mutilates, it kills humanity in them, so that by ceasing to be men, they may be solely citizens—or rather, and more specifically, that through the historic connection and succession of facts, they may never rise above the citizen to the height of being man.

We have also seen that every state, under pain of destruction and fearing to be devoured by its neighbor states, must reach out toward omnipotence, and, having become powerful, must conquer. Who speaks of conquest speaks of peoples conquered, subjugated, reduced to slavery in whatever form or denomination. Slavery, therefore, is the necessary consequence of the very existence of the State.

Slavery may change its form or its name—its essence remains the same. Its essence may be expressed in these words: *to be a slave is to be forced to work for someone else, just as to be a master is to live on someone else's work*. In antiquity, just as in Asia and in Africa today, as well as even in a part of America, slaves were, in all honesty, called slaves. In the Middle Ages, they took the name of serfs: nowadays they are called *wage earners*. The position of this latter group has a great deal more dignity attached to it, and it is less hard than that of slaves, but they are nonetheless forced, by hunger as well as by political and social institutions, to maintain other people in complete or relative idleness, through their own exceedingly hard labor. Consequently they are slaves. And in general, no state, ancient or modern, has ever managed or will ever manage to get along without the forced labor of the masses, either wage earners or slaves, as a principal and absolutely necessary foundation for the leisure, the liberty, and the civilization of the political class: *the citizens*. On this point, not even the United States of North America can as yet be an exception.

Such are the internal conditions that necessarily result for the State from its objective stance, that is, its natural, permanent, and inevitable hostility toward all the other states. Let us now see the conditions resulting directly for the State's citizens from that free contract by which they supposedly constituted themselves into a State.

The State not only has the mission of guaranteeing the safety of its members against any attack coming from without; it must also defend them within its own borders, some of them against

the others, *and each of them against himself*. For the State—
and this is most deeply characteristic of it, of every state, as of
every theology—presupposes man to be essentially evil and
wicked. In the State we are now examining, *the good*, as we have
seen, commences only with the conclusion of the social contract and, consequently, is merely the product and very content
of this contract. The *good* is not the product of liberty. On the
contrary, so long as men remain isolated in their absolute individuality, enjoying their full natural liberty to which they recognize no limits but those of fact, not of law, they follow one law
only, that of their natural egotism. They offend, maltreat, and
rob each other; they obstruct and devour each other, each to the
extent of his intelligence, his cunning, and his material resources,
doing just as the states do to one another. By this reasoning,
human liberty produces not *good* but *evil;* man is by nature evil.
How did he become evil? That is for theology to explain. The
fact is that the Church, at its birth, finds man already evil, and
undertakes to make him good, that is, to transform the natural
man into the citizen.

To this one may rejoin that, since the State is the product of
a contract freely concluded by men, and since the good is the
product of the State, it follows that the good is the product of
liberty! Such a conclusion would not be right at all. The State
itself, by this reasoning, is not the product of liberty; it is, on
the contrary, the product of the voluntary sacrifice and negation of liberty. Natural men, completely free from the sense of
right but exposed, *in fact*, to all the dangers which threaten
their security at every moment, in order to assure and safeguard
this security, sacrifice, or renounce more or less of their own liberty, and, to the extent that they have sacrificed liberty for security and have thus become citizens, they become the *slaves of
the State*. We are therefore right in affirming that, *from the viewpoint of the State, the good is born not of liberty but rather of
the negation of liberty*.

Is it not remarkable to find so close a correspondence between
theology, that science of the Church, and politics, that science of
the State; to find this concurrence of two orders of ideas and of
realities, outwardly so opposed, nevertheless holding the same

conviction: *that human liberty must be destroyed if men are to be moral, if they are to be transformed into saints (for the Church) or into virtuous citizens (for the State)?* Yet we are not at all surprised by this peculiar harmony, since we are convinced, and shall try to prove, that politics and theology are two sisters issuing from the same source and pursuing the same ends under different names; and that every state is a terrestrial church, just as every church, with its own heaven, the dwelling place of the blessed and of the immortal God, is but a celestial state.

Thus the State, like the Church, starts out with this fundamental supposition, that men are basically evil, and that, if delivered up to their natural liberty, they would tear each other apart and offer the spectacle of the most terrifying anarchy, where the stronger would exploit and slaughter the weaker—quite the contrary of what goes on in our model states today, needless to say! The State sets up the principle that in order to establish public order, there is need of a superior authority; in order to guide men and repress their evil passions, there is need of a guide and a curb.

. . . In order to assure the observance of the principles and the administration of laws in any human society whatsoever, there has to be a vigilant, regulating, and, if need be, repressive power at the head of the State. It remains for us to find out who should and who could exercise such power.

For the State founded upon divine right and through the intervention of any God whatever, the answer is simple enough; the men to exercise such power would be the priests primarily, and secondarily the temporal authorities consecrated by the priests. For the State founded on the free social contract, the answer would be far more difficult. In a pure democracy of equals—all of whom are, however, considered incapable of self-restraint on behalf of the common welfare, their liberty tending naturally toward evil—who would be the true guardian and administrator of the laws, the defender of justice and of public order against everyone's evil passions? In a word, who would fulfill the functions of the State?

The best citizens, would be the answer, the most intelligent and the most virtuous, those who understand better than the others the common interests of society and the need, the duty, of everyone to subordinate his own interests to the common good. It is, in fact, necessary for these men to be as intelligent as they are virtuous; if they were intelligent but lacked virtue, they might very well use the public welfare to serve their private interests, and if they were virtuous but lacked intelligence, their good faith would not be enough to save the public interest from their errors. It is therefore necessary, in order that a republic may not perish, that it have available throughout its duration a continuous succession of many citizens possessing both virtue and intelligence.

But this condition cannot be easily or always fulfilled. In the history of every country, the epochs that boast a sizable group of eminent men are exceptional, and renowned through the centuries. Ordinarily, within the precincts of power, it is the insignificant, the mediocre, who predominate, and often, as we have observed in history, it is vice and bloody violence that triumph. We may therefore conclude that if it were true, as the theory of the so-called rational or liberal State clearly postulates, that the preservation and durability of every political society depend upon a succession of men as remarkable for their intelligence as for their virtue, there is not one among the societies now existing that would not have ceased to exist long ago. If we were to add to this difficulty, not to say impossibility, those which arise from the peculiar demoralization attendant upon power, the extraordinary temptations to which all men who hold power in their hands are exposed, the ambitions, rivalries, jealousies, the gigantic cupidities by which particularly those in the highest positions are assailed by day and night, and against which neither intelligence nor even virtue can prevail, especially the highly vulnerable virtue of the isolated man, it is a wonder that so many societies exist at all. But let us pass on.

Let us assume that, in an ideal society, in each period, there were a sufficient number of men both intelligent and virtuous to discharge the principal functions of the State worthily. Who would seek them out, select them, and place the reins of power in their hands? Would they themselves, aware of their intelligence and their virtue, take possession of the power? This was done by two sages of ancient Greece, Cleobulus and Periander;

notwithstanding their supposed great wisdom, the Greeks applied to them the odious name of tyrants. But in what manner would such men seize power? By persuasion, or perhaps by force? If they used persuasion, we might remark that he can best persuade who is himself persuaded, and the best men are precisely those who are least persuaded of their own worth. Even when they are aware of it, they usually find it repugnant to press their claim upon others, while wicked and mediocre men, always satisfied with themselves, feel no repugnance in glorifying themselves. But let us even suppose that the desire to serve their country had overcome the natural modesty of truly worthy men and induced them to offer themselves as candidates for the suffrage of their fellow citizens. Would the people necessarily accept these in preference to ambitious, smooth-tongued, clever schemers? If, on the other hand, they wanted to use force, they would, in the first place, have to have available a force capable of overcoming the resistance of an entire party. They would attain their power through civil war which would end up with a disgruntled opposition party, beaten but still hostile. To prevail, the victors would have to persist in using force. Accordingly the free society would have become a despotic state, founded upon and maintained by violence, in which you might possibly find many things worthy of approval—but never liberty.

If we are to maintain the fiction of the free state issuing from a social contract, we must assume that the majority of its citizens must have had the prudence, the discernment, and the sense of justice necessary to elect the worthiest and the most capable men and to place them at the head of their government. But if a people had exhibited these qualities, not just once and by mere chance but at all times throughout its existence, in all the elections it had to make, would it not mean that the people itself, as a mass, had reached so high a degree of morality and of culture that it no longer had need of either government or state? Such a people would not drag out a meaningless existence, giving free rein for all its instincts; out of its life, justice and public order would rise spontaneously and naturally. The State, in it, would cease to be the providence, the guardian, the educator, the regulator of society. As it renounced all its repressive power and sank to the subordinate position assigned to it by Proudhon, it would turn into a mere business office, a sort of central accounting bureau at the service of society.

There is no doubt that such a political organization, or rather such a reduction of political action in favor of the liberty of social life, would be a great benefit to society, but it would in no way satisfy the persistent champions of the State. To them, the State, as providence, as director of the social life, dispenser of justice, and regulator of public order, is a necessity. In other words, whether they admit it or not, whether they call themselves republicans, democrats, or even socialists, they always must have available a more or less ignorant, immature, incompetent people, or, bluntly speaking, a kind of *canaille* to govern. This would make them, without doing violence to their lofty altruism and modesty, keep the highest places for themselves, so as always to devote themselves to the common good, of course. As the privileged guardians of the human flock, strong in their virtuous devotion and their superior intelligence, while prodding the people along and urging it on for its own good and well-being, they would be in a position to do a little discreet fleecing of that flock for their own benefit.

Any logical and straightforward theory of the State is essentially founded upon the principle of *authority*, that is, the eminently theological, metaphysical, and political idea that the masses, *always* incapable of governing themselves, must at all times submit to the beneficent yoke of a wisdom and a justice imposed upon them, in some way or other, from above. Imposed in the name of what, and by whom? Authority which is recognized and respected as such by the masses can come from three sources only: force, religion, or the action of a superior intelligence. As we are discussing the theory of the State founded upon the free contract, we must postpone discussion of those states founded on the dual authority of religion and force and, for the moment, confine our attention to authority based upon a superior intelligence, which is, as we know, always represented by minorities.

What do we really see in all states past and present, even those endowed with the most democratic institutions, such as the United States of North America and Switzerland? Actual self-government of the masses, despite the pretense that the people hold all the power, remains a fiction most of the time. It is always, in fact, minorities that do the governing. In the United States, up to the recent Civil War and partly even now, and even within the party of the present incumbent, President Andrew Johnson, those ruling minorities were the so-called Democrats, who continued to favor slavery and the ferocious oligarchy of the Southern planters, demagogues without faith or conscience, capable of sacrificing everything to their greed, to their malignant ambition. They were those who, through their detestable actions and influence, exercised practically without opposition for almost fifty successive years, have greatly contributed to the corruption of political morality in North America.

Right now, a really intelligent, generous minority—but always a minority—the Republican party, is successfully challenging their pernicious policy. Let us hope its triumph may be complete; let us hope so for all humanity's sake. But no matter how sincere this party of liberty may be, no matter how great and generous its principles, we cannot hope that upon attaining power it will renounce its exclusive position of ruling minority and mingle with the masses, so that popular self-government may at last become a fact. This would require a revolution, one that would be profound in far other ways than all the revolutions that have thus far overwhelmed the ancient world and the modern.

In Switzerland, despite all the democratic revolutions that have taken place there, government is still in the hands of the well-off, the middle class, those privileged few who are rich, leisured, educated. The sovereignty of the people—a term, incidentally, which we detest, since all sovereignty is to us detestable —the government of the masses by themselves, is here likewise a fiction. The people are sovereign in law, but not in fact; since they are necessarily occupied with their daily labor which leaves them no leisure, and since they are, if not totally ignorant, at least quite inferior in education to the propertied middle class, they are constrained to leave their alleged sovereignty in the hands of the middle class. The only advantage they derive from this situation, in Switzerland as well as in the United States of North America, is that the ambitious minorities, the seekers of political power, cannot attain power except by wooing the people, by pandering to their fleeting passions, which at times can be quite evil, and, in most cases, by deceiving them.

Let no one think that in criticizing the democratic government we thereby show our preference for the monarchy. We are firmly convinced that the most imperfect republic is a thousand times better than the most enlightened monarchy. In a republic, there are at least brief periods when the people, while continually exploited, is not oppressed; in the monarchies, oppression is constant. The democratic regime also lifts the masses up gradually to participation in public life—something the monarchy never does. Nevertheless, while we prefer the republic, we must recognize and proclaim that whatever the form of government may be, so long as human society continues to be divided into different classes as a result of the *hereditary* inequality of occupations, of wealth, of education, and of rights, there will always be a class-restricted government and the inevitable exploitation of the majorities by the minorities.

The State is nothing but this domination and this exploitation, well regulated and systematized. We shall try to prove this by examining the consequences of the government of the masses by a minority, intelligent and dedicated as you please, in an ideal state founded upon the free contract.

Once the conditions of the contract have been accepted, it remains only to put them into effect. Suppose that a people recognized their incapacity to govern, but still had sufficient judgment to confide the administration of public affairs to their best citizens. At first these individuals are esteemed not for their official position but for their good qualities. They have been elected by the people because they are the most intelligent, capable, wise, courageous, and dedicated among them. Coming from the mass of the people, where all are supposedly equal, they do not yet constitute a separate class, but a group of men privileged only by nature and for that very reason singled out for election by the people. Their number is necessarily very limited, for in all times and in all nations the number of men endowed with qualities so remarkable that they automatically command the unanimous respect of a nation is, as experience teaches us, very small. Therefore, on pain of making a bad choice the people will be forced to choose its rulers from among them.

Here then is a society already divided into two categories, if not yet two classes. One is composed of the immense majority of its citizens who freely submit themselves to a government by those they have elected; the other is composed of a small number of men endowed with exceptional attributes, recognized and accepted as exceptional by the people and entrusted by them with the task of governing. As these men depend on popular election, they cannot at first be distinguished from the mass of citizens except by the very qualities which have recommended them for election, and they are naturally the most useful and the most dedicated citizens of all. They do not as yet claim any privilege or any special right except that of carrying out, at the people's will, the special functions with which they have been entrusted. Besides, they are not in any way different from other people in their way of living or earning their means of living, so that a perfect equality still subsists among all.

Can this equality be maintained for any length of time? We claim it cannot, a claim that is easy enough to prove.

Nothing is as dangerous for man's personal morality as the habit of commanding. The best of men, the most intelligent, unselfish, generous, and pure, will always and inevitably be corrupted in this pursuit. Two feelings inherent in the exercise of power never fail to produce this demoralization: *contempt for the masses, and, for the man in power, an exaggerated sense of his own worth.*

"The masses, on admitting their own incapacity to govern themselves, have elected me as their head. By doing so, they have clearly proclaimed their own *inferiority* and my *superiority*. In this great crowd of men, among whom I hardly find any who are my equals, I alone am capable of administering public affairs. The people need me; they cannot get along without my services, while I am sufficient unto myself. They must therefore obey me for their own good, and I, by deigning to command them, create their happiness and well-being." There is enough here to turn anyone's head and corrupt the heart and make one swell with pride, isn't there? That is how power and the habit of commanding become a source of aberration, both intellectual and moral, even for the most intelligent and most virtuous of men.

All human morality—and we shall try, further on, to prove the absolute truth of this principle, the development, explanation, and widest application of which constitute the real subject of this essay—all collective and individual morality rests essentially upon *respect for humanity*. What do we mean by respect for humanity? We mean the recognition of human right and human dignity in every man, of whatever race, color, degree of intellectual development, or even morality. But if this man is stupid, wicked, or contemptible, can I respect him? Of course, if he is all that, it is impossible for me to respect his villainy, his stupidity, and his brutality; they are repugnant to me and arouse my indignation. I shall, if necessary, take the strongest measures against them, even going so far as to kill him if I have no other way of defending against him my life, my right, and whatever I hold precious and worthy. But even in the midst of the most violent and bitter, even mortal, combat between us, I must respect his human character. My own dignity as a man depends on it. Nevertheless, if he himself fails to recognize this dignity in others, must we recognize it in him? If he is a sort of ferocious beast or, as sometimes happens, worse than a beast, would we not, in recognizing his humanity, be supporting a mere fiction? No, for whatever his present intellectual and moral degradation may be, if, organically, he is neither an idiot nor a madman—in which case he should be treated as a sick man rather than as a criminal—if he is in full possession of his senses and of such intelligence as nature has granted him, his humanity, no matter how monstrous his deviations might be, nonetheless really exists. *It exists as a lifelong potential capacity to rise to the awareness of his humanity, even if there should be little possibility for a radical change in the social conditions which have made him what he is.*

Take the most intelligent ape, with the finest disposition; though you place him in the best, most humane environment, you will never make a man of him. Take the most hardened criminal or the man with the poorest mind, provided that neither has any organic lesion causing idiocy or insanity; the criminality of the one, and the failure of the other to develop an awareness of his humanity and his human duties, *is not their fault, nor is it due to their nature; it is solely the result of the social environment in which they were born and brought up.*

1869

The Program
of the International
Brotherhood

All the evidence indicates that the secret "International Brotherhood," also called "Secret Alliance," was formally dissolved early in 1869. In reply to accusations made by Marx and the General Council of the International, both Bakunin and Guillaume denied its existence. There was undoubtedly an informal group of "advanced men" adhering to Bakunin's ideas, but as a formal organization, says Guillaume, "[the International Brothers] existed only theoretically in Bakunin's brain as a kind of dream indulged in with delight. . . ."[14] But this does not lessen the importance of the ideas formulated in the program which Bakunin wrote for it.

While the Program[15] does not cover all the subjects discussed in the Revolutionary Catechism, it contains a more precise and advanced formulation of Bakunin's ideas about revolutionary strategy; about the expropriation of private, Church, and State property, and its transfer into the collective property of federated workers' industrial and agricultural associations; faith in the creative capacity of the masses; revolutionary violence and terrorism; revolution by a centralized "socialist" state; and above all, the tasks of the anarchist vanguard movement (International Brotherhood) in the Social Revolution. In addition to its theo-

retical value, the Program is inspired by a profound humanitarian spirit totally at variance with the stereotype pictured by Bakunin's enemies.

THE association of the International Brothers desires a revolution that shall be at the same time universal, social, philosophical, and economic, so that no stone may remain unturned, in all of Europe first, and then in the rest of the world, to change the present order of things founded on property, on exploitation, domination, and the principle of authority, be it religious, metaphysical, and doctrinaire in the bourgeois manner or even revolutionary in the Jacobin manner. Calling for peace for the workers and liberty for all, we want to destroy all the states and all the churches, with all their institutions and their religious, political, financial, juridical, police, educational, economic, and social laws, so that all these millions of wretched human beings, deceived, enslaved, tormented, exploited, may be released from all their official and officious directors and benefactors—both associations and individuals—and at last breathe in complete freedom.

Convinced as we are that individual and social evil resides much less in individuals than in the organization of material things and in social conditions, we will be humane in our actions, as much for the sake of justice as for practical considerations, and we will ruthlessly destroy what is in our way without endangering the revolution. We deny society's free will and its alleged right to punish. Justice itself, taken in its widest, most humane sense, is but an idea, so to say, which is not an absolute dogma; it poses the social problem but it does not think it out. It merely indicates the only possible road to human emancipation, that is the humanization of society by liberty in equality. The positive solution can be achieved only by an increasingly rational organization of society. This solution, which is so greatly desired, our ideal for all, is liberty, morality, intelligence, and the welfare of each through the solidarity of all: human fraternity, in short.

Every human individual is the involuntary product of a

natural and social environment within which he is born, and to the influence of which he continues to submit as he develops. The three great causes of all human immorality are: political, economic, and social inequality; the ignorance resulting naturally from all this; and the necessary consequence of these, *slavery*.

Since the social organization is always and everywhere the only cause of crimes committed by men, the punishing by society of criminals who can never be guilty is an act of hypocrisy or a patent absurdity. The theory of guilt and punishment is the offspring of theology, that is, of the union of absurdity and religious hypocrisy. The only right one can grant to society in its present transitional state is the natural right to kill in self-defense the criminals it has itself produced, but not the right to judge and condemn them. This cannot, strictly speaking, be a right, it can only be a natural, painful, but inevitable act, itself the indication and outcome of the impotence and stupidity of present-day society. The less society makes use of it, the closer it will come to its real emancipation. All the revolutionaries, the oppressed, the sufferers, victims of the existing social organization, whose hearts are naturally filled with hatred and a desire for vengeance, should bear in mind that the kings, the oppressors, exploiters of all kinds, are as guilty as the criminals who have emerged from the masses; like them, they are evildoers who are not guilty, since they, too, are involuntary products of the present social order. It will not be surprising if the rebellious people kill a great many of them at first. This will be a misfortune, as unavoidable as the ravages caused by a sudden tempest, and as quickly over; but this natural act will be neither moral nor even useful.

History has much to teach us on this subject. The dreadful guillotine of 1793, which cannot be reproached with having been idle or slow, nevertheless did not succeed in destroying the French aristocracy. The nobility was indeed shaken to its roots, though not completely destroyed, but this was not the work of the guillotine; it was achieved by the confiscation of its properties. In general, we can say that carnage was never an effective means to exterminate political parties; it was proved particularly ineffective against the privileged classes, since power resides less in men themselves than in the circumstances created for men of privilege by the organization of material goods, that is, the institution of the State and its natural basis, *individual property*.

Therefore, to make a successful revolution, it is necessary to attack conditions and material goods; to destroy property and the State. It will then become unnecessary to destroy men and be condemned to suffer the sure and inevitable reaction which no massacre has ever failed and ever will fail to produce in every society.

It is not surprising that the Jacobins and the Blanquists—who became socialists by necessity rather than by conviction, who view socialism as a means and not as the goal of the revolution, since they desire dictatorship and the centralization of the State, hoping that the State will lead them necessarily to the reinstatement of property—dream of a bloody revolution against men, inasmuch as they do not desire the revolution against property. But such a bloody revolution, based on the construction of a powerfully centralized revolutionary State, would inevitably result in military dictatorship and a new master. Hence the triumph of the Jacobins or the Blanquists would be the death of the revolution.

We are the natural enemies of such revolutionaries—the would-be dictators, regulators, and trustees of the revolution—who even before the existing monarchical, aristocratic, and bourgeois states have been destroyed, already dream of creating new revolutionary states, as fully centralized and even more despotic than the states we now have. These men are so accustomed to the order created by an authority, and feel so great a horror of what seems to them to be disorder but is simply the frank and natural expression of the life of the people, that even before a good, salutary disorder has been produced by the revolution they dream of muzzling it by the act of some authority that will be revolutionary in name only, and will only be a new reaction in that it will again condemn the masses to being governed by decrees, to obedience, to immobility, to death; in other words, to slavery and exploitation by a new pseudorevolutionary aristocracy.

What we mean by revolution is an outburst of what today

is called "evil passions" and the destruction of the so-called public order.

We do not fear anarchy, we invoke it. For we are convinced that anarchy, meaning the unrestricted manifestation of the liberated life of the people, must spring from liberty, equality, the new social order, and the force of the revolution itself against the reaction. There is no doubt that this new life—the popular revolution—will in good time organize itself, but it will create its revolutionary organization from the bottom up, from the circumference to the center, in accordance with the principle of liberty, and not from the top down or from the center to the circumference in the manner of all authority. It matters little to us if that authority is called Church, Monarchy, constitutional State, bourgeois Republic, or even revolutionary Dictatorship. We detest and reject all of them equally as the unfailing sources of exploitation and despotism.

The revolution as we understand it will have to destroy the State and all the institutions of the State, radically and completely, from its very first day. The natural and necessary consequences of such destruction will be:

a. the bankruptcy of the State
b. the discontinuance of payments of private debts through the intervention of the State, leaving to each debtor the right to pay his own debts if he so desires
c. the discontinuance of payments of all taxes and of the levy of any contributions, direct or indirect
d. the dissolution of the arms, the judicial system, the bureacracy, the police, and the clergy
e. the abolition of official justice, the suspension of everything called juridically the law, and the carrying out of these laws; consequently, the abolition and burning of all titles to property, deeds of inheritance, deeds of sale, grants, of all lawsuits —in a word, all the judicial and civil red tape; everywhere and in all things, the revolutionary fact replacing the right created and guaranteed by the State
f. the confiscation of all productive capital and of the tools of

production for the benefit of workers' associations, who will
have to have them produced collectively

g. the confiscation of all the property owned by the Church
and the State as well as the precious metals owned by individuals, for the benefit of the federative Alliance of all the
workers' associations, which will constitute the commune.
(In return for the goods which have been confiscated, the
commune will give the strict necessities of life to all the individuals so dispossessed, and they will later gain more by their
own labor if they can and if they wish.)

h. for the purpose of effecting the organization of the revolutionary commune by permanent barricades, and the office of a
council of the revolutionary commune by the delegation of
one or two deputies for each barricade, one per street or per
district, there will be provided deputies invested with imperative, always responsible, and always revocable mandates. The
communal council thus organized will be able to choose, from
its own members, executive committees, one for each branch
of the revolutionary administration of the commune

i. declaration by the capital city, rebellious and organized as a
commune, to the effect that, having destroyed the authoritarian, controlled State, which it had the right to do, having
been enslaved just like all the other localities, it therefore
renounces the right, or rather any claim, to govern the provinces

j. an appeal to all the provinces, communes, and associations to
let everything go and follow the example set by the capital:
first, to reorganize themselves on a revolutionary basis, then
to delegate their deputies, likewise invested with imperative,
responsible, and revocable mandates, to a set meeting place,
for the purpose of constituting the federation of associations,
communes, and provinces which have rebelled in the name
of the same principles, and in order to organize a revolutionary force capable of overcoming the reaction. There will be
no dispatching of official revolutionary commissars with rib-
bons decorating their chests but revolutionary propagandists
will be sent to all the provinces and communes, particularly

to the peasants, who cannot be excited to rebellion by principles or decrees of a dictatorship but solely by the revolutionary fact itself; that is, by the inevitable consequences in all the communes of the complete cessation of the juridical official life of the State. Also, the abolition of the national state in the sense that any foreign country, province, commune, association, or even an isolated individual, that may have rebelled in the name of the same principles will be received into the revolutionary federation regardless of the present frontiers of the states, although they may belong to different political or national systems; and their own provinces, communes, associations, or individuals who defend the reaction will be excluded. It is through the expansion and organization of the revolution for mutual defense of the rebel countries that the universality of the revolution, founded upon the abolition of frontiers and on the ruins of the states, will triumph.

No political or national revolution can ever triumph unless it is transformed into a social revolution, and unless the national revolution, precisely because of its radically socialist character, which is destructive of the State, becomes a universal revolution.

Since the Revolution must everywhere be achieved by the people, and since its supreme direction must always rest in the people, organized in a free federation of agricultural and industrial associations, the new revolutionary State, organized from the bottom up by revolutionary delegations embracing all the rebel countries in the name of the same principles, irrespective of old frontiers and national differences, will have as its chief objective the administration of public services, not the governing of peoples. It will constitute the *new party*, the alliance of the universal revolution, as opposed to the alliance of the reaction.

This revolutionary alliance excludes any idea of dictatorship and of a controlling and directive power. It is, however, necessary for the establishment of this revolutionary alliance and for the triumph of the Revolution over reaction that the unity of ideas and of revolutionary action find an *organ* in the midst of the popular anarchy which will be the life and the energy of the

Revolution. This organ should be *the secret and universal association of the International Brothers.*

This association has its origin in the conviction that revolutions are never made by individuals or even by secret societies. They make themselves; they are produced by the force of circumstances, the movement of facts and events. They receive a long preparation in the deep, instinctive consciousness of the masses, then they burst forth, often seemingly triggered by trivial causes. All that a well-organized society can do is, first, to assist at the birth of a revolution by spreading among the masses ideas which give expression to their instincts, and to organize, not the army of the Revolution—the people alone should always be that army—but a sort of revolutionary general staff, composed of dedicated, energetic, intelligent individuals, sincere friends of the people above all, men neither vain nor ambitious, but capable of serving as intermediaries between the revolutionary idea and the instincts of the people.

There need not be a great number of these men. One hundred revolutionaries, strongly and earnestly allied, would suffice for the international organization of all of Europe. Two or three hundred revolutionaries will be enough for the organization of the largest country.

Bakunin on the Revolutionary Labor Movement

Bakunin's Revolutionary Catechism of 1866 and other works written before he joined the International in 1868 did not deal with the specific problems of the industrial proletariat. In 1864, when the International was founded, the labor movement was in its infancy, and in Italy, where Bakunin lived until 1867, it hardly existed. The International developed very slowly, and only after 1868 did it become a potential revolutionary force. Twenty-six of the sixty-four delegates to the Lausanne Congress of the International also attended the first Geneva Congress of the League for Peace and Freedom which was in session shortly after the Congress of the International adjourned. It was then that Bakunin became acquainted with the most active members of the International and became aware of its revolutionary potential. Bakunin's entry into the International marked a turning point in his revolutionary career and in the history of the modern anarchist movement. He applied the ideas formulated in the Revolutionary Catechism and in "Federalism, Socialism, Anti-Theologism" to the concrete practical problems facing the European proletariat.

The revolutionary syndicalist labor movements which flourished in a number of European countries, in Central and South America, to some extent in the United States, and in Spain during the Spanish Civil War (1936–9) derived their orientation from the libertarian sections of the International. Professor Paul Brissenden illustrates this point by a quotation from the IWW organ Industrial Worker of June 18, 1910:

> We must trace the origins of the ideas of modern revolutionary unionism to the International. . . . Many ideas originally drafted for the International by the famous anarchist Michael Bakunin in 1868 were similar to the twentieth-century slogans of the IWW.[16]

The principles of revolutionary syndicalism, also called

"Anarcho-Syndicalism," *worked out by Bakunin and his com-rades in the International are discussed in the selections* The Policy of the International, The Program of the Alliance, *and* The International and Karl Marx.

Scattered statements by Bakunin that the workers are "social-ist by instinct," "socialists without knowing it," implying that the workers automatically become revolutionists as they unite in their struggle against their employers for immediate economic improvements, do not accurately reflect his views on these points. Such exaggerated assertions were made to propagandize unso-phisticated workers or made in the heat of argument against bourgeois class-collaborationists or Marxists who advocated par-liamentary political action. All the evidence indicates that what Bakunin really meant was that the economic situation of the workers only renders them receptive to socialist revolutionary ideas. "The theoretical propagandizing of socialist ideas," he says, "is also necessary to prepare the masses for the Social Revolution." These ideas must be planted by a specific organization of con-scious, dedicated revolutionists unified by a common ideological program, in this case by Bakunin's "Alliance." Bakunin defines the relationship between the International and the Alliance as follows:

The Alliance is the necessary complement to the International. But the International and the Alliance, while having the same ultimate aims, perform different functions. The International endeavors to unify the working masses, the millions of workers, regardless of nationality and national boundaries or religious and political beliefs, into one compact body; the Alliance, on the other hand, tries to give these masses a really revolutionary direction. The programs of one and the other, without being in any way opposed, differ only in the degree of their revolutionary develop-ment. The International contains in germ, but only in germ, the whole program of the Alliance. The program of the Alliance rep-resents the fullest unfolding of the International.[17]

There is a good deal of confusion about whether Bakunin and the anti-authoritarian members of the International were "collectivists" or what has been variously called "anti-authori-tarian communists," "federalist communists," or "communist-

anarchists." This question is clarified by James Guillaume in a
hitherto unpublished letter dated August 24, 1909. A copy of
this letter was lately sent to the editor of the present volume
from Montevideo, Uruguay, by the anarchist historian Vladimir
Muñoz. We translate the following excerpts:

At first [1868 Congress of the International] the term "collectivists" designated the partisans of collective property: all those
who, in opposition to the partisans of individual property, declared
that mines, land, communications and transportation, machines,
etc., should be collectively owned. . . . at the Basel Congress
(1869) the partisans of collective ownership split into two opposing factions. Those who advocated ownership of collective property
by the State were called "state" or "authoritarian communists."
Those who advocated ownership of collective property directly by
the workers' associations were called "anti-authoritarian communists" or "communist federalists" or "communist anarchists." To
distinguish themselves from the authoritarians and avoid confusion,
the anti-authoritarians called themselves "collectivists." . . . Varlin,
the editor of the projected anarchist paper *La Marseillaise*, wrote
me in December 1869 that: "The principles espoused in this
journal will be the same as those adopted almost unanimously by
the delegates to the Basel congress of the International held a few
months ago: *collectivism or non-authoritarian communism.*" The
year before, at the 1868 Congress of the League for Peace and
Freedom, Bakunin called himself a "collectivist" and stated: "I
want society and collective or social property to be organized from
the bottom up by way of free association, and not from the top
down by means of any authority whatsoever. In this sense I am a
collectivist."

As to the distribution of the products of collective labor, I
wrote: ". . . Once the worker owns the instruments of labor, all
the rest is of secondary importance. How the products of collective
labor will be equitably shared must be left to the judgment of each
group." . . . The collectivists knew very well that when the instruments of production are common property, labor becomes a
social act and therefore the products are social products. In 1871
Bakunin wrote: "Only collective labor creates wealth. *Collective*
wealth must be collectively owned." . . . In my essay "On Building the New Social Order" [see selection, p. 356] I stated clearly
that in the collectivist society, when machines will triple produc-

tion, goods will not be sold to consumers but distributed according to their needs. . . . These, and many other quotations that I could easily supply, show clearly that the collectivist Internationalists never accepted the theory of "to each according to the product of his labor."

Guillaume saw no difference in principle between collectivism and anti-State communism. The collectivists understood that full communism would not be immediately realizable. They were convinced that the workers themselves would gradually introduce communism as they overcame the obstacles, both psychological and economic.

1869

———•—•———

The Policy of
the International

The Policy of the International[18] consists of four articles
written by Bakunin for L'Égalité, the organ of the French-
speaking libertarian Romance Federation of the International,
August 7–28, 1869. It is written in the popular style suitable for
the intelligent workers of the period.

Bakunin begins by outlining in simple language the main
principles of the International and then goes on to discuss the
nature of the bourgeoisie and its relationship to the International,
to parliamentarianism, and to immediate problems. His astute
remarks about working-class politicians, bourgeoisified workers,
and the bourgeoisie in general are still cogent. Bakunin's practical
proposals show how well he understood the mind of the average
worker.

Bakunin's references to "the June days" and "the December
days" require some elucidation. The revolution of 1848 began
with the uprising of the Parisian workers on February 24.
When the government fell, King Louis Philippe abdicated and
fled to England. The Second Republic was then declared. When
the National Workshops program for the unemployed (similar
to the WPA program of Franklin Roosevelt) collapsed, a new
uprising of hundreds of thousands of starving Parisian workers
was crushed by General Cavaignac, who had been invested with
dictatorial powers by the republican National Assembly. This
slaughter, which took place between the 22nd and the 24th of

June, became known as "the June days." "The December days"
signify the accession to power of Louis Napoleon (later to
become Emperor Napoleon III). In the national plebiscite of
December 10, he was elected president of France with the
support of the peasants and other reactionary classes. He ban-
ished or imprisoned the radicals as well as the liberal democrats
and the republican opposition, and established "the reign of
Caesarism and militarism" referred to by Bakunin.

I

THE International, in accepting a new member, does not
ask him whether he is an atheist or a believer, whether or not
he belongs to any political party. It asks only this: are you a
worker, or if not, do you sincerely desire and will you fully
embrace the cause of the workers to the exclusion of all causes
contrary to its principles?

Do you feel that the workers, the sole producers of all the
world's wealth, who have created civilization and won all the
liberties the bourgeoisie enjoy, should be themselves condemned
to poverty, ignorance and servitude? Do you understand that the
principal source of all the evils the workers must now endure is
poverty, and that this poverty, the lot of all the workers in the
world, is the necessary consequence of the existing economic
order of society, and primarily of the submission of labor to the
yoke of capital, i.e., to the bourgeoisie?

Do you understand that there is an irreconcilable antagonism between the proletariat and the bourgeoisie which is the
necessary consequence of their respective economic positions?
That the wealth of the bourgeois class is incompatible with the
well-being and freedom of the workers, because this excessive
wealth can be founded only upon the exploitation and subjugation of labor, and that for this reason, the prosperity and dignity
of the working masses demands the abolition of the bourgeoisie
as a class. . . . Do you understand that no worker, however intelligent or energetic, can fight all by himself against the well-
organized power of the bourgeoisie, a power sustained by all
states?

Do you understand that faced with the formidable coalition of all the privileged classes, all the capitalists, and all the states, an isolated workers' association, local or national, even in one of the greatest European nations, can never triumph, and that faced with this coalition, victory can only be achieved by a union of all the national and international associations into a single universal association which is none other than the great International Workingmen's Association?

If you thoroughly understand and truly want all this, then irrespective of your national loyalties and religious beliefs, come to us and you will be welcomed. But you must first pledge:

a. to subordinate your personal and family interests as well as your political and religious beliefs to the supreme interests of our association: to the struggle of labor against capital, i.e., the economic struggle of the workers against the bourgeoisie.
b. never to compromise with the bourgeoisie for your personal gain.
c. never to satisfy your vanity by displaying your disdain for the rank and file. If you do so, you will be treated as a bourgeois, an enemy of the proletariat, for the bourgeois shuns the collectivity, and the proletarian seeks only the solidarity of all who work and are exploited by capitalism.
d. to remain always faithful to the solidarity of labor. The least betrayal of this solidarity will be considered by the International as the greatest crime that any worker could commit; in short, you must fully and without reservation accept our general statutes and pledge yourself to conform to them in all the acts of your life.

We think that the founders of the International showed great wisdom in eliminating all religious and national questions from its program. They purposely refrained from injecting their very definite antireligious and national convictions into the program because their main concern was to unite the oppressed and the exploited workers of the civilized world in one common effort. They had necessarily to find a common basis, and formulate a set of elementary principles acceptable to all workers regardless of the political and economic aberrations still infecting the minds of so many toilers.

The inclusion of the antireligious and political program of any group or party in the program of the International, far from uniting the European workers, would have divided them even more than they are at present. . . . Taking advantage of the ignorance of the workers, the priests, the governments, and all the bourgeois parties, including the most leftwing of them, have succeeded in indoctrinating the workers with all sorts of false ideas whose sole purpose was to brainwash them into voluntarily serving the privileged classes against their own best interests.

Besides, the difference in the degree of industrial, political, and moral development of the working masses in the different countries is still too great for them to unite on the basis of one political and antireligious program. To make such a program an absolute condition for membership would be to establish a sect and not to organize a universal association. It could only destroy the International at the outset.

There is yet another important reason for eliminating all political tendencies, at least formally *and only formally*. Until now there has never been a true politics of the people, and by the "people" we mean the lowly classes, the "rabble," the poorest workers whose toil sustains the world. There has been only the politics of the privileged classes, those who have used the physical prowess of the people to overthrow and replace each other in the never-ending struggle for supremacy. The people have shifted support from one side to the other in the vain hope that in at least one of these political changes . . . their century-old poverty and slavery would be lightened. Even the great French Revolution did not basically alter their status. It did away with the nobility only to replace it with the bourgeoisie. The people are no longer *called* serfs. They are proclaimed free men, legally entitled to all the rights of free-born citizens; but they remain poverty-stricken serfs in fact.

And they will remain enslaved as long as the working masses continue to serve as tools of bourgeois politics, whether conservative or liberal, even if those politics pretend to be revolutionary. For all bourgeois politics whatever the label or color have only one purpose: to perpetuate domination by the bourgeoisie, and *bourgeois domination is the slavery of the proletariat*.

What was the International to do? It had to separate the working masses from all bourgeois politics and expunge from its program the political programs of the bourgeoisie. When the International was first organized, the only institutions exerting major pressure were the church, the monarchy, the aristocracy, and the bourgeoisie. The latter, particularly the liberal bourgeoisie, were undoubtedly more humane than the others, but they too depended upon the exploitation of the masses, and their sole purpose was also to fight their rivals for the privilege of monopolizing the exploitation. The International had first to clear the ground. Since all politics, as far as the emancipation is concerned, is infected with reactionary elements, the International had first to purge itself of all political systems, and then build upon the ruins of the bourgeois social order the new politics of the International. [*L'Égalité*, August 7, 1869]

II

It was for these reasons that the founders of the International based the organization only on the economic struggle of the workers against capitalist exploitation. They reasoned that once the workers, drawing confidence from the justice of their cause as well as from their numerical superiority, become involved with their fellow workers in their common struggle against the employing class, the force of events and the intensification of the struggle will soon impel them to recognize all the political, socialist, and philosophical principles of the International, principles which are in fact only the true reflection of their own experiences and aspirations.

From the political and social angle, the necessary consequences of these principles are the abolition of all territorial states and the erection upon their ruins of the great international confederation of all national and productive groups. Philosophically it means nothing less than the realization of human felicity, equality, liberty, and justice. And these ideals will tend to render superfluous all religious phantasies and vain dreams of a better life in heaven. . . .

But to proclaim these two ultimate aims prematurely to ignorant workers whose minds are poisoned by the demoralizing doctrines and propaganda of the State and the priesthood would surely shock and repel them. . . . They would not even suspect that these aims are actually the truest expression of their own interests, that the pursuit of these objectives will lead to the realization of their most cherished yearnings, and that precisely those religious and political prejudices in whose name they spurn these ideas are perhaps the direct cause of their prolonged poverty and slavery.

It is necessary to clearly distinguish the prejudices of the privileged classes. The prejudices of the masses . . . militate against their own interests, while those of the bourgeoisie are based precisely on their class interests. . . . The people want, but do not know. The bourgeoisie know, but do not want. Of the two, which is incurable? The bourgeoisie, of course.

General rule: you can convince only those who already feel the need for change by virtue of their instincts and their miserable circumstances, but never those who feel no need for change. Nor can you convince those who may desire to escape from an intolerable situation, but are attracted to ideas totally at variance with yours, owing to the nature of their social, intellectual, and moral habits.

You cannot win over to socialism a money-mad noble or a bourgeois whose sole ambition is to climb into the nobility, or a worker who is heart and soul bent on becoming a bourgeois. Nor can you win over an intellectual snob, or a self-styled "savant" vaunting his scientific knowledge after half-digesting a few books. Such people seethe with contempt and arrogance toward the unlettered masses, and imagine themselves ordained to form a new dominant caste.

No amount of reasoning or agitation will succeed in converting these moral unfortunates. The only effective way to overcome their resistance is through *action:* to close off the avenues for privileged positions, exploitation, and domination. Only the Social Revolution, sweeping away all inequality, can moralize them and bring them to seek their happiness in equality and in solidarity.

Things are different with serious workers. And by serious workers, I mean those who are crushed under the burden of toil; all those whose position is so precarious that they can never (barring extraordinary circumstances) even hope to attain a better station in life. . . . Also in this category are those rare and generous workers who, though they have the opportunity to raise themselves out of the working class, prefer nevertheless to suffer and struggle with their brother workers against the bourgeoisie. Such workers do not have to be converted; they are already true socialists.

The great mass of workers, exhausted by daily drudgery, are miserable and ignorant. Yet this mass, despite its political and social prejudices, is socialistic *without knowing it*. Because of its social position, it is more truly socialist than all the scientific and bourgeois socialists combined. It is socialistic by virtue of the material conditions and the needs of its being, while the latter are only intellectually socialist. In real life, the material needs exert a much greater power than the needs of the intellect, which are always and everywhere the expression of the being, the reflection of the successive developments of life, but never its vital principle. . . .

What the workers lack is not a sense of reality or socialist aspirations, but only socialist thought. Deep in his heart, every worker aspires to a full life, to material well-being and intellectual development, based on justice or equality for every human being longing to live and work in an atmosphere of freedom. Obviously this ideal cannot be realized under the present social system, based as it is on the cynical exploitation of the toiling masses. Since his emancipation can be attained only by the overthrow of the existing social order, every earnest worker is potentially a revolutionary socialist.

The seeds of socialist thought are subconsciously planted in the mind of every serious worker. The socialist aim is to make the worker fully conscious of what he wants, to awaken in him an intelligence which will correspond to his inner yearnings. Once the intelligence of the workers is raised to the level of what they instinctively feel, their will is bound to be concentrated and their power irresistible. It is axiomatic that ignorance and religious and political prejudices . . . slow up the development of this intelligence among the working masses. How to dissipate this ignorance? How to root out these prejudices? By education? By propaganda?

Propaganda and education are excellent but insufficient means. The isolated worker weighed down by toil and daily cares cannot attend to his education. And who will make this propaganda? Will it be a handful of socialists but lately emerged from their bourgeois environment? They are undoubtedly dedicated and motivated by generous impulses, but far too few in number to adequately propagandize the masses.

Besides, the workers will receive guardedly at best the propaganda of intellectuals who come from a totally different and hostile social background. The preamble of the statutes of the International states: "The emancipation of the workers is the task of the workers themselves." It is absolutely right. This is the fundamental principle of our great association. But the workers know little about theory and are unable to grasp the implications of this principle. The only way for the workers to learn theory is through practice: *emancipation through practical action.* It requires the full solidarity of the workers in their struggle against their bosses, through the *trade unions and the building up of resistance* [strike funds]. [*L'Égalité,* August 14, 1869]

III

If the International from its inception tolerated the reactionary political and religious ideas of the workers who joined it, it was not because it was by any means indifferent toward these ideas. As I have already demonstrated, it could not be indifferent, because all reactionary ideas entertained by the membership undermine the basic principle and with it the very existence of the International itself.

The founders of the International, I repeat, acted wisely in adopting this tolerant policy. They reasoned . . . that a worker involving himself in the struggle will necessarily be led to realize that there is an unbridled antagonism between the . . . reaction and his most cherished aspirations . . . and having realized this, will openly declare himself a revolutionary socialist.

This is not the case with the bourgeoisie. All their interests are contrary to the economic transformation of society. And if their ideas are also contrary to it they are reactionaries, or to use a term much more in vogue today, "moderates"; they will always remain reactionaries and it is necessary to keep them out of the International. A worker can recognize the bourgeois who sincerely seeks membership in the International by the relations he keeps up with the bourgeois world. The great majority of the bourgeois capitalists and landed proprietors, those who have the courage to come out openly and manifest their abhorrence of the labor movement are, at least, resolute and sincere enemies and less dangerous for the International than the hypocrites.

But there is another category of bourgeois socialist who is not so frank or courageous. Enemies of social liquidation (the abolition of authoritarian exploitative institutions), they, like all reactionary bourgeois, defend the institutions responsible for the slavery of the proletariat and still pose as the apostles for the emancipation of the working class.

The radical and liberal bourgeois socialists who founded the League for Peace and Freedom [see selection] belong to this category. In its first year, 1867, the League rejected socialism with horror. Last year, 1868, at the Bern Congress, they again overwhelmingly rejected economic equality. Now, in 1869, seeing that the League is about to expire and wishing to stave off death a little longer, they finally realize that they must deal with the social problem. They now call themselves "socialists," but they are bourgeois socialists because they would resolve all social questions on the basis of *social equality*. They want to preserve interest on capital and land rents and still call for the emancipation of the workers.

What impels them to undertake so hopeless and ridiculous a task? Most of the bourgeoisie are tired of the reign of Caesarism and militarism, which they themselves, out of fear of the proletariat, helped to initiate in the 1848 revolution.

You need only recall the June days, precursors of the December days, when this *National Assembly*, with one voice, cursed the illustrious and heroic socialist Proudhon, the only one who had the courage to defy and expose this rabid herd of bourgeois conservatives, liberals, and radicals; nor should you now forget that among his traducers were a number of citizens still living, and today more militant than ever, who received their revolutionary baptism during the persecutions of the December days, and many who have since become martyrs to liberty. But notwithstanding these honorable exceptions, the whole bourgeoisie, including the radical bourgeois, have themselves created the very Caesarism and militarism whose effects they now deplore. After having used these elements against the proletariat, they now want to get rid of them. Why? Because the regime has humiliated them and encroached upon their interests. But how can they free themselves? *Then*, they were brave and powerful enough to challenge them. *Now*, they are cowardly, senile, and impotent.

Help can come only from the proletariat. But how can they be won over? By promises of liberty and equality? These promises will no longer move the workers. They have learned by bitter experience that these fine-sounding words mean only the perpetuation of an economic slavery no less hard than before. To touch the heart of these millions of wage slaves, you must speak to them about economic emancipation. There is no worker who today does not understand that economic freedom is the basis for all his other freedoms. This being the case, the bourgeois must now speak to the workers about the economic reform of society.

The bourgeois members of the League for Peace and Freedom say to themselves:

Very well, we must also call ourselves socialists. We must promise the workers social and economic reforms, always on the condition that they respect the civilization and the omnipotence of the bourgeoisie, private and hereditary property, interest on capital and on landed property, and all the rest of it. We must find some way to convince them that only under these conditions will our domination be assured and (strange as it may seem) the workers be emancipated. We will even convince them that to realize all these social and economic reforms, it is above all necessary to make a good political revolution, exclusively political, as red as they could possibly wish, if necessary even with a great chopping-off of heads, but always with scrupulous respect for the sanctity of property; an entirely Jacobin revolution; in short . . . we will make ourselves the masters of the situation and then grant the workers what we think they are entitled to.

There is an infallible sign by which workers can recognize a phony socialist, a bourgeois socialist; if he says that the political must *precede* the social and economic transformation; if he denies that both must be made at the same time, or shrugs his shoulders when told that the political revolution will be meaningful only when it begins with a full, immediate and direct *social liquidation.* . . . [*L'Égalité*, August 21, 1869]

IV

If the International is to remain true to its principles, it cannot deviate from the only road that can lead it to victory; it must above all counteract the influence of two kinds of bourgeois socialists: the advocates of bourgeois politics, including the revolutionary bourgeois, and the "practical men" with their bourgeois cooperation. The politics of the International is summed up in these words from our preamble:

. . . that the submission of labor to capital is the source of all *political, moral, and material servitude,* and that for this reason the economic emancipation of the workers is the great objective to which every political movement must be subordinated. . . .

It is clear that every political movement whose objective is not the immediate, direct, *definitive, and complete* economic emancipation of the workers, and which does not clearly and unmistakably proclaim the principle of *economic equality,* i.e., *restitution of capital to labor* or *social liquidation*—that every such political movement is a bourgeois movement and must therefore be excluded from the International. The politics of the bourgeois democrats and the bourgeois socialists is based on the idea that political liberty is the *preliminary condition* for economic emancipation. These words can have only one meaning. ... The workers must ally themselves with the radical bourgeois to first make the political revolution; and then, later, fight against their former allies to make the economic revolution.

We emphatically repudiate this disastrous theory which will once again make the workers the instrument of their own enslavement and submit themselves anew to the exploitation of the bourgeoisie. To conquer political liberty *first* can mean only that the social and economic relations will at least "temporarily" remain untouched. In short, the capitalists keep their wealth and the workers their poverty.

We will be told that once political liberty is won, it will much later serve the workers as the instrument to win *equality* and *economic justice*. Freedom is, of course, a magnificent and powerful force, provided the workers will have the opportunity to make use of it and provided that it is effectively in their possession. But if not, this political freedom will as always remain a transparent fraud, a fiction. One must live in a dream world to imagine that a worker, under the prevailing economic and social conditions, can really and effectively exercise political liberty. He lacks both the time and the material means to do so.

What did we see in France the day after the 1848 revolution, from the political point of view the most radical revolution that can be desired? The French workers were certainly neither indifferent nor unintelligent, yet though they had universal suffrage they left everything to the bourgeois politicians. Why? Because they lacked the material means necessary to make political liberty a reality; ... while the bourgeois radicals and liberals, including the conservatives, the newly minted republicans of the day before yesterday, and other such converts, connived and schemed—the one thanks to income from property or their lucrative positions, the other thanks to their state positions in which they naturally remained and in which they entrenched themselves more solidly than ever. ...

Let us suppose that the workers, made wiser by experience, instead of electing the bourgeois to constituent or legislative assemblies will send simple workers from their own ranks. Do you know what will happen? The new worker deputies, trans-planted into a bourgeois environment, living and soaking up all the bourgeois ideas and acquiring their habits, will cease being workers and statesmen and become converted into bourgeois, even more bourgeois-like than the bourgeois themselves. Because men do not make positions; positions, contrariwise, make men. And we know from experience that worker bourgeois are no less egotistic than exploiter bourgeois, no less disastrous for the International than the bourgeois socialists, no less vain and ridiculous than bourgeois who become nobles. . . .

To urge workers to win political liberty without first dealing with the burning question of socialism, without pronouncing the phrase that makes the bourgeoisie tremble—*social liquidation* —is simply to say: "Conquer political liberty for us, so that we can use it against you later on."

Just as the bourgeois socialists strive to organize a formidable campaign among the workers to win political liberty, *using socialism as the bait* to hook them; so must the working masses, fully aware of their position, clarified and guided by the princi-ples of the International, begin to organize themselves effectively and constitute a true power, not national, but international, to replace the policy of the bourgeoisie with their own policy; and just as the bourgeoisie need a revolution to institute their own ideal of full political liberty under republican institutions, and no revolution can succeed without the people . . . it is necessary that the workers' movement cease pulling chestnuts out of the fire for the benefit of the bourgeois gentlemen and make that revolution serve only for the triumph of the people, for the cause of all who toil against the exploiters of labor.

True to its principles, the International Workingmen's Associ-ation will never endorse or support any political agitation which does not aim at the immediate, direct, and complete *economic emancipation* of the workers, the abolition of the bourgeoisie as a class economically separate from the great mass of the people. The International will not support any revolution which from the very first day does not inscribe upon its banner . . . *social liquidation*.

But revolutions are not improvised or made arbitrarily,

neither by individuals nor by the most powerful associations. Independent of all will and of all conspiracies, they are always brought about by the natural force of events. They can be foreseen, their imminence can sometimes be sensed, but their explosion can never be artificially accelerated. Convinced of this truth, we ask, "What policy should the International pursue during this more or less extended interval separating us from the overwhelming Social Revolution which everyone awaits?"

Ignoring all local and national politics, the International endeavors to imbue the labor agitation of all lands with an *exclusively economic character*. To achieve its immediate aim—reduction of working hours and higher wages—it prepares for strikes, sets up strike funds, and tries to unite the workers into one organization.

[Let us enlarge our association. But at the same time, let us not forget to consolidate and reinforce it so that our solidarity, which is our whole power, grows stronger from day to day. Let us have more of this solidarity in study, in our work, in civic action, in life itself. Let us cooperate in our common enterprise to make our lives a little more supportable and less difficult. Let us, whenever possible, establish producer-consumer cooperatives and mutual credit societies which, though under the present economic conditions they cannot in any real or adequate way free us, are nevertheless important inasmuch as they train the workers in the practice of managing the economy and plant the precious seeds for the organization of the future.][19]

The International will continue to propagandize its principles, because these principles, being the purest expression of the collective interests of the workers of the whole world, are the soul and living, dynamic power of our association. It will spread its propaganda without regard for the susceptibilities of the bourgeoisie, so that every worker, emerging from the intellectual and moral torpor in which he has been kept, will understand his situation and know what he wants and what to do, and under what conditions he can obtain his rights as a man. The International will have to conduct its propaganda even more energetically, because within the International itself we encounter influences which express disdain for these principles, deprecating them as empty, useless theory and trying to mislead the workers into returning to the economic and religious catechism of the bourgeoisie.

The International will expand and organize itself strongly; so that when the Revolution, ripened by the force of events, breaks out, there will be a real force ready which knows what to do and is therefore capable of guiding the revolution in the direction marked out by the aspirations of the people: a serious international organization of workers' associations of all lands, capable of replacing this departing world of *states*.

We conclude this faithful exposition of the policy of the International, by quoting the concluding paragraph from the preamble to our general statutes:

> The movement brought into being among the industrialized countries of Europe, in giving rise to new hopes, gives a solemn warning not to fall again into old errors. [*L'Égalité*, August 28, 1869]

———— •◆• ————

III

———— •◆• ————

The Franco-
Prussian War
and the
Paris Commune

1870

—•◦•—

Letter to Albert Richard

Written shortly before the outbreak of the Franco-Prussian War (July 19, 1870–January 28, 1871) and the ill-fated uprising in Lyons of September 5, 1870, led by Bakunin, Richard, and other members of the secret vanguard organization the Alliance, this selection,[1] both in subject matter and in timing, belongs to Bakunin's Letters to a Frenchman on the Present Crisis (September, 1870). The "Letter to Albert Richard" is important primarily because it deals with the crucial question of the relationship between the revolutionary minority and the masses. It is also relevant because in so doing it anticipates the general course of the Russian Revolution and because it sums up Bakunin's alternative to authoritarian revolutions. Since this letter provides the necessary background information, explanatory comments will in this instance follow the text.

Albert Richard (1846–1925) was a French anarchist from Lyons, where he was an active member of the Alliance and a pioneer organizer of the International. Bakunin accused him of betraying the Lyons uprising by collaborating with the provisional government. After the fall of the Paris Commune of May 1871 in which he fought, Richard wrote a pamphlet urging the restoration of Napoleon III. (On the Lyons uprising see Biographical Sketch, by James Guillaume.)

Many historians blame Bakunin and his "irresponsible adventurism" for the collapse of the Lyons revolt. But the official *biographer of Karl Marx, Franz Mehring, defends Bakunin's conduct:*

The ridiculing of this unsuccessful attempt [Marx was one of the worst offenders in this regard] might reasonably have been left to the reaction, and an opponent of Bakunin whose opposition to anarchism did not rob him of all capacity to form an objective judgment wrote:

"Unfortunately mocking voices have been raised even in the social democratic press, although Bakunin's attempt certainly does not deserve this. Naturally, those who do not share the anarchist opinions of Bakunin and his followers must adopt a critical attitude towards his baseless hopes, but apart from that, his action in Lyons was a courageous attempt to awaken the sleeping energies of the French proletariat and to direct them simultaneously against the foreign enemy and the capitalist system. Later the Paris Commune attempted something of the sort also and was warmly praised by Marx." . . .[2]

You keep on telling me that we both agree on fundamental points. Alas! my friend, I am very much afraid that we find ourselves in absolute disagreement. . . . I must, more than ever, consider you as a believer in centralization, and in the revolutionary State, while I am more than ever opposed to it, and have faith only in revolutionary anarchy, which will everywhere be accompanied by an invisible collective power, the only dictatorship I will accept, because it alone is compatible with the aspirations of the people and the full dynamic thrust of the revolutionary movement!

Your revolutionary strategy could be summed up as follows: as soon as the revolution breaks out in Paris, Paris organizes the Provisional Revolutionary Commune. Lyons, Marseilles, Rouen, and other large cities revolt at the same time, immediately send their revolutionary delegations to Paris, and set up a sort of national assembly, or People's Committee of Public Safety for all of France. This committee decrees the revolution for all of France. This committee decrees the revolution, the abolition of the old state and social liquidation of all exploitative institutions, be they governmental, religious, or economic. The committee also decrees, at the same time, the collectivization of property and the organization of a new revolutionary state with dictatorial power in order to suppress internal and external reaction: Is this not your idea?

Our idea, our plan is exactly the opposite—there is no reason to assume that the revolutionary uprising must necessarily begin in Paris. It may well begin in the provinces. But let us assume that the revolution, as usual, begins in Paris. It is our conviction that Paris should then play only a negative role, i.e., initiate the destruction of the old order, but not organize the new order (in the rest of France). If Paris itself stages a successful uprising, it would then have the obligation and the right to call for solidarity in the complete political, juridical, financial, and administrative liquidation of the State, and of political and privately owned or controlled (but not strictly) personal property; the demolition of all the functions, services, and powers of the State; the public burning of all public and private legal documents and records. Paris will immediately and to the greatest possible extent organize itself in a revolutionary manner. The newly formed workers' associations would then take possession of all the tools of production as well as all buildings and capital, arming and organizing themselves into regional sections made up of groups based on streets and neighborhood boundaries. The federally organized sections would then associate themselves to form a federated commune. And it will be the duty of the commune to declare that it has neither the right nor the desire to organize or govern all of France. This commune, on the contrary, will appeal to all the people, to all the communes, and to what up till now was considered foreign territory, to follow its example, to make its own revolution in as radical a manner as possible and to destroy the state, juridical institutions, privileged ownership, and so forth.

Paris will then invite these French or foreign communes to meet either in Paris or in some other place, where their delegations will collectively work out the necessary arrangements to lay the groundwork for equality, the indispensable precondition for all freedom. They will formulate an absolutely negative program

which will stress what must be abolished, organize the common
defense and propaganda against the enemies of the Revolution,
and develop practical revolutionary solidarity with its friends in
all lands.

The constructive tasks of the Social Revolution, the creation
of new forms of social life, can emerge only from the living
practical experience of the grass-roots organizations which will
build the new society according to their manifold needs and
aspirations.

The provinces, at least such main centers as Lyons, Marseilles, Saint-Étienne, Rouen, and others do not have to wait for
decrees from Paris before organizing the Revolution. They must
revolt and, like Paris, make the negative, i.e., the destructive
phase of the Revolution. They must organize themselves spontaneously, without outside interference, so that the Revolutionary Federal Assembly or Provincial and Communal Delegations
do not attempt to govern and regulate all of France; the Revolutionary Assembly is, on the contrary, the creation of local and
spontaneous organizations in each of the revolutionary centers
of France. In short, the Revolution emanating from all points
should not, and must not, depend on a single directing center.
The center must not be the source, but the product; not the
cause, but the effect of the revolution.

There must be anarchy, there must be—if the revolution is
to become and remain alive, real, and powerful—the greatest
possible awakening of all the local passions and aspirations; a
tremendous awakening of spontaneous life everywhere. After
the initial revolutionary victory the political revolutionaries,
those advocates of brazen dictatorship, will try to squelch the
popular passions. They appeal for *order*, for trust in, for submission to those who, in the course and in the name of the Revolution, seized and legalized their own dictatorial powers; this is
how such political revolutionaries reconstitute the State. We, on
the contrary, must awaken and foment all the dynamic passions
of the people. We must bring forth anarchy, and in the midst
of the popular tempest, we must be the invisible pilots guiding
the Revolution, not by any kind of overt power but by the collective dictatorship of all our allies [members of the anarchist

vanguard organization International Alliance of Social Democracy], a dictatorship without tricks, without official titles, without official rights, and therefore all the more powerful, as it does not carry the trappings of power. This is the only dictatorship I will accept, but in order to act, it must first be created, it must be prepared and organized in advance, for it will not come into being by itself, neither by discussions, nor by theoretical disputations, nor by mass propaganda meetings. . . .

If you will build this collective and invisible power you will triumph; the well-directed revolution will succeed. Otherwise, it will not! ! If you will play around with welfare committees, with official dictatorship, then the reaction which you yourself have built will engulf you . . . who are already talking yourselves into becoming the Dantons, the Robespierres, and the Saint-Justs of revolutionary socialism, and you are already preparing your beautiful speeches, your brilliant "coups d'états," which you will suddenly foist on an astonished world. . . .

Postscript to the
Letter to Albert Richard

Whether Bakunin's concept of "invisible collective dictatorship" contradicts his libertarian principles is a matter of controversy. To back up the contention that Bakunin was basically an authoritarian, some critics quote only this passage and ignore the rest of the letter. The Bolshevik historian Steklov, basing his opinion only on Bakunin's early nonanarchist writings, when he temporarily favored a Blanquist-type dictatorship, naturally counts Bakunin as one of the forerunners of Lenin's theory of party dictatorship. G. D. H. Cole stresses, to the contrary, that

> Bakunin agreed with Marx in advocating a dictatorship of the proletariat over the exploiting classes; but he held that this dictatorship must be a spontaneous dictatorship of the entire uprisen working class, and not by any body of leaders set in authority over them.[3]

Lenin would agree that an organization exercising no overt authority, without a state, without official status, without the machinery of institutionalized power to enforce its policies, cannot be defined as a dictatorship. It would certainly not measure up to Lenin's specifications as formulated in his *State and Revolution.* Moreover, if it is borne in mind that this passage is part of a letter repudiating in the strongest terms the State and the authoritarian statism of the "Robespierres, the Dantons, and the Saint-Justs (whom Lenin admired) of the revolution," it is then reasonable to conclude that Bakunin used the word "dictatorship" to denote preponderant influence or guidance exercised largely by example, not in order to usurp but to safeguard the people's revolution. In line with this conclusion, Bakunin used the words "invisible" and "collective" to denote the underground movement exerting this influence in an organized manner. Bakunin explained that according to the statutes of the Alliance

no member . . . is permitted, even in the midst of full revolution, to take public office of any kind, nor is the organization permitted to do so . . . it will at all times be on the alert, making it impossible for authorities, governments, and states to be reestablished.[4]

Bakunin's well-known predilection for the establishment of tightly organized secret hierarchical organizations, for which he worked out elaborate statutes in the style of the Freemasons and the Carbonari, can be attributed partly to his romantic temperament and partly to the fact that all revolutionary and progressive groups were forced to operate secretly. Bakunin's secret organizations were actually quite informal fraternities of loosely organized individuals and groups connected by personal contact and correspondence, as preferred by his closest associates who considered his schemes for elaborate, centralized secret societies incompatible with libertarian principles.

1870

——— •••• ———

Letters to a Frenchman on the Present Crisis

These "Letters to a Frenchman" were not actually addressed to anyone in particular, but were merely the form the author used to indicate the informality and personal quality of what he had to say.

This long extract[5] naturally divides itself into three distinct sections: a) General Problems of the Social Revolution, with special emphasis on the organization of the peasants in relation to the urban working class in predominantly agrarian countries, capitalist war between states, and civil war; b) The Revolutionary Temper and Its Matrix;[6] c) A Critique of the German Social-Democratic Program.

His Letters to a Frenchman are among the most important of Bakunin's writings. For it is in this major work that Bakunin made his unique contributions to the theory and practice of revolution. It was written during the stormy period of the Franco-Prussian War when France faced certain defeat. The government of Napoleon III had collapsed and the succeeding provisional republican government was hopelessly demoralized. The French armies were in full retreat and the Prussian troops were at the gates of Paris. It was in the midst of this crisis that Bakunin developed ideas which have since become the watchwords of libertarian revolutionary movements and to which even the authoritarians still pay lip service—ideas such as turning the wars between states into civil wars for the Social Revolution; the people-in-arms fighting a guerrilla war to repulse a foreign army and simultaneously defending the revolution against its domestic enemies; all power to the grass-roots organizations spontaneously created by the revolution; a federalist alternative to centralized statist revolution-by-decree, among others.

One of Bakunin's most significant contributions to modern revolutionary theory was his confidence in the revolutionary capabilities of the peasants. He worked out ways of winning them over to the side of the revolution, with particular emphasis on establishing harmonious relations between the peasants and the more sophisticated urban workers. As in all his other writings on revolution, he reiterates his views on the proper relation between the anarchist vanguard organization and the masses. While fully appreciating the importance of the economic situation in revolution, Bakunin nevertheless attached equal weight to the will, the revolutionary consciousness of the people. The section on The Revolutionary Temper and Its Matrix differs substantially from the Marxist interpretation and occupies a key place in Bakunin's revolutionary ideology.

General Problems of the
Social Revolution

I have already shown that France cannot be saved . . . by the State. But outside the parasitic, artificial institution of the State, a nation consists only of its people; consequently, *France can be saved only by the immediate, nonpartisan action of the people,* by a mass uprising of all the French people, spontaneously organized from the bottom upward, a war of destruction, a merciless war to the death.

When a nation of thirty-eight million people rises to defend itself, determined to destroy everything and ready even to sacrifice lives and possessions rather than submit to slavery, no army in the world, however powerful, however well organized and equipped with the most extraordinary weapons, will be able to conquer it.

Everything depends on the ability of the French people to make such an effort. To what extent have blandishments of bourgeois civilization affected their revolutionary capacities?

Have such factors rendered them incapable of summoning up the requisite heroism and primitive tenacity, do they prefer peace at the price of freedom, or freedom at the cost of immense privations? Do they still retain at least some of the natural strength and primitive energy which makes a nation powerful?

If France had been composed solely of the bourgeoisie, I would have unhesitatingly replied in the negative. The French bourgeoisie, as in most of the countries of Western Europe, comprise an immense body, far more numerous than is generally assumed, even penetrating the proletariat and to some extent corrupting its upper strata.

In France, the workers are much less attached to the bourgeois class than in Germany, and are daily increasing their separation from it. Nevertheless, the deleterious influence of bourgeois civilization continues to corrupt some sections of the French proletariat. This accounts for the indifference and the egoism observed within certain better paying occupations. These workers are semibourgeois, because of self-interest and self-delusion, and they oppose the Revolution because they fear that the Revolution will ruin them.

The bourgeoisie, accordingly, constitute a very influential and a very considerable section of French society. But if at this moment all Frenchmen were bourgeois, the Prussian invasion would envelop Paris and France would be lost. The bourgeoisie has long since outlived its heroic age; it lacks the dynamism, the supreme heroism that carried it to victory in 1793, and, since then, having become complacent and satiated, it has steadily degenerated. In case of extreme necessity it will sacrifice even its sons, but it will never sacrifice its social position and its property for the realization of a great ideal. It would rather submit to the German yoke than renounce its social privileges and accept economic equality with the proletariat. I do not say that the bourgeoisie is unpatriotic; on the contrary, patriotism, in the narrowest sense, is its essential virtue. But the bourgeoisie love their country only because, for them, the country, represented by the State, safeguards their economic, political, and social privileges. Any nation withdrawing this protection would be disowned by them. Therefore, for the bourgeoisie, the country *is* the State. Patriots of the State, they become furious enemies of the masses if the people, tired of sacrificing themselves, of being used as a passive footstool by the government, revolt against it. If the bourgeoisie had to choose between the masses who rebel against the State and the Prussian invaders of France, they would surely choose the latter. This would be a disagreeable option but they are, nevertheless, defenders of the principle of the State against the worthless rabble, the masses of the world. Did not the bourgeoisie of Paris and all France champion Louis Bonaparte in 1848 for the same reason? And did they not support Napoleon III, until it became plain to everyone that his government had brought France to the brink of ruin? The bourgeoisie of France ceased supporting him only when they became afraid that his downfall would be the signal for the people's revolution, i.e., that he could not prevent the Social Revolution. And their fear of this is so great as to lead them to betray their country. They are intelligent enough to fully understand that the present regime [the government which succeeded Napoleon III] cannot save France, that the new rulers have neither the will, nor the intelligence, nor the power to do so. Yet, despite all this, they continue to support this government; they are more afraid of the invasion of their bourgeois civilization by the people of France than they are of the Prussian invasion of France.

This being said, the French bourgeoisie in general is, at present, sincerely patriotic. They cordially hate the Prussians. To drive the insolent invaders from the soil of France they are ready to make great sacrifices of soldiers, most of them from the lower classes, and of money, which will sooner or later be recovered from the people. But they absolutely insist that all contributed wealth and manpower should be concentrated in the hands of the State and that, as far as possible, all the armed volunteers should become soldiers in the regular army. They insist that all private voluntary organizations involved in war operations, whether financial, military, administrative, or medical, be permitted to function only under the direct supervision of the State. They also demand that nongovernmental citizens' militias and all irregular military bodies shall be organized by and under the personal supervision of *authorized leaders*, *licensed by the State,* property owners, well-known bourgeois "gentlemen," and other solid citizens. In this way those workers and peasants in the unofficial forces who might rebel or participate in insurrection will no longer be dangerous. What is more, the leaders will, if necessary, dispatch these troops to suppress uprisings against the authorities, as happened in June 1790 when the mobile guards opposed the people.

On this one point, the bourgeois of all denominations—from the most reactionary vigilantes to the most rabid Jacobins—together with the authoritarian State Communists, are unanimous: *that the salvation of France can and must be achieved only by and through the State.* But France can be saved only by drastic measures which require the dissolution of the State. . . .

[Bakunin here points out that for fear of a mass insurrection, the government did not institute even the most elementary measures to halt the advance of the Prussian armies, and therewith begins his discussion of his practical revolutionary program.]

In spite of the inferiority of the two French armies, they were still able to halt the enemy in other parts of France and to repulse the Prussian armies before they approached the walls of Paris. If the government and military authorities had done what all the French press, from the very beginning of the military crisis, had urged them to do; if, as soon as the news of the disastrous defeat of the French armies reached Paris, instead of proclaiming a state of siege in the capital and in the eastern departments, they had called for mass uprisings in all those departments; if, instead of restricting the fighting to the two armies, these armies had become the base of support for a formidable insurrection by guerrillas or, if necessary, by brigands; if the peasants and the workers had been armed with guns instead of scythes; if the two armies, casting aside all military pomp and snobbery, had entered into fraternal relations with the innumerable irregular fighting units . . . by fighting together in solidarity even without the help of unoccupied France, they would have been able to save Paris. At the very least, the enemy would have been halted long enough to permit the provisional government to mobilize strong forces. . . .

To sum up the main points: the administrative and governmental machinery must be permanently smashed and not replaced by another. Give complete freedom of initiative, movement, and organization to all the provinces, and to all the communes of France, which is equivalent to dissolving the State, and initiating the Social Revolution. . . .

It is clear that Paris at this time cannot occupy itself with the formulation and practical application of revolutionary ideas, that it must concentrate all its efforts and resources exclusively on defense. The entire population of besieged Paris must organize itself into a great army, disciplined by the common sense of danger and the necessities of defense—an immense city at war, determined to fight the enemy at every point. . . . But an army does not discuss and theorize. It does not make revolution, it fights.

Paris, preoccupied with defense, will be absolutely unable to lead or organize the national revolutionary movement. If Paris were to make so ridiculous and absurd an attempt, it would kill all revolutionary activity. Moreover, the rest of France, the provinces and the communes, would be obliged, in the supreme interests of national salvation, to disobey all orders issued by Paris and to resist all attempts to enforce them. The best and only thing that Paris can do, in order to save itself, is to proclaim and encourage the absolute autonomy and spontaneity of all the provincial movements, and should Paris forget or neglect to do so for any reason whatsoever, the provinces, in order to save France and Paris itself, *will have to rebel and spontaneously organize themselves independent of Paris*.

It is evident from all this that if France is to be saved, it will require spontaneous uprisings in all the provinces. Are such uprisings possible? Yes, if the workers in the great provincial cities—Lyons, Marseilles, Saint-Étienne, Rouen, and many others—have blood in their veins, brains in their heads, energy in their hearts, and if they are not doctrinaires but revolutionary socialists. *Only the workers in the cities can now [spearhead the movement to] save France*. Faced with mortal danger from within and without, *France can be saved only by a spontaneous, uncompromising, passionate, anarchic, and destructive uprising of the masses of the people all over France*.

I believe that the only two classes now capable of so mighty an insurrection are *the workers and the peasants*. Do not be surprised that I include the peasants. The peasants, like other Frenchmen, do wrong, not because they are by nature evil but because they are ignorant. Unspoiled by overindulgence and indolence, and only slightly affected by the pernicious influence of bourgeois society, the peasants still retain their native energy and simple unsophisticated folkways. It is true that the peasants, being petty landlords, are to a considerable extent egoistic and reactionary, but this has not affected their instinctive hatred of the "fine gentlemen" [country squires], and they hate the bourgeois landlords, who enjoy the bounty of the earth without cultivating it with their own hands. On the other hand, the peasant is intensely patriotic, i.e., he is passionately attached to his land, and I think that nothing would be easier than to turn him against the foreign invader.

It is clear that in order to win over the peasants to the side of the Revolution, it is necessary to use great prudence; for ideas and propaganda which are enthusiastically accepted by the city workers will have the opposite effect on the peasants. It is essential to talk to the peasants in simple language suitable to their sentiments, their level of understanding, and mindful of the nature of their prejudices, inculcated by the big landlords, the priests, and the state functionaries. Where the Emperor [Napoleon III] is loved, almost worshipped, by the peasants, one should not arouse antagonism by attacking him. It is necessary to *undermine in fact* and not in words the authority of the State and the Emperor, by undermining the establishment through which they wield their influence. To the greatest possible extent, the functionaries of the Emperor—the mayors, justices of the peace, priests, rural police, and similar officials, should be discredited.

It is necessary to tell the peasants that the Prussians must be ousted from France (which they probably know without being told) and that they must arm themselves and organize volunteer guerrilla units and attack the Prussians. But they must first follow the example set by the cities, which is to get rid of all the parasites and counterrevolutionary civil guards; turn the defense of the towns over to the armed people's militias; con-fiscate State and Church lands and the holdings of the big landowners for redistribution by the peasants; suspend all public and private debts. . . . Moreover, before marching against the Prussians, the peasants, like the industrial city workers, should unite by federating the fighting battalions, district by district, thus assuring a common coordinated defense against internal and external enemies.

This, in my opinion, is the most effective way of dealing with the peasant problem; for while they are defending the land they are, at the same time, unconsciously but effectively destroy-ing the state institutions rooted in the rural communes, and therefore making the Social Revolution. . . .

I am not at all disturbed by the seeming Bonapartist sympa-thies of the French peasants. Such sympathies are merely a superficial manifestation of deep socialist sentiments, distorted by ignorance and the malevolent propaganda of the exploiters; a rash of measles, which will yield to the determined treatment of revolutionary socialism. The peasants will donate neither their land nor their money nor their lives just to keep Napoleon III on his throne; but they are willing to kill the rich and to take and give their property to the Emperor because they hate the rich in general. They harbor the thoroughgoing and intense socialistic hatred of laboring men against the men of leisure, the "upper crust." I recall a tragic incident, where the peasants in the commune of Dordogne burned a young aristocratic land-owner. The quarrel began when a peasant said: "Ah! noble sir, you stay comfortably and peacefully at home because you are rich; you have money and we are going to send your wealth to the poor and use it for the war. Very well, let us go to your house, and see what we can find there!" In these few words we can see the living expression of the traditional rancor of the peasant against the rich landlord, but not by any means the fanatical desire to sacrifice themselves and kill for the Emperor; on the contrary, they naturally try to escape military service.

This is not the first time that a government has exploited for its own purposes the legitimate hatred of the peasants for the rich landholders and urban bourgeoisie. For example, at the

end of the eighteenth century, Cardinal Ruffo, of bloody memory, incited an insurrection of the peasants of Calabria against
the newly installed liberal republican government of Naples. . . .
The Calabrian peasants began by looting the castles [estates]
and the city mansions of the wealthy bourgeois, but took nothing
from the people. In 1846, the agents of Prince Metternich
engineered an insurrection of the peasants of Galicia against
the powerful Polish aristocrats and landlords, who themselves
were plotting a nationalistic insurrection; and before that, the
Empress Catherine [the Great] of Russia encouraged the Ukrain-
ian peasants to kill thousands of Polish nobles. Finally, in 1786,
the Russian government organized a "jacquerie" [peasant revolt]
in the Ukraine against the Polish patriots, most of them nobles.

You see, then, that the rulers, these official guardians of
public order, property, and personal security, had no scruples
about using these deceptive methods when it suited their purposes. The peasants are made revolutionary by necessity, by the
intolerable realities of their lives; their violent hatreds, their
socialist passions have been exploited, illegitimately diverted to
support the reactionaries. And we, the revolutionary socialists,
could we not direct these same passions toward their true end,
to an objective in perfect harmony with the deep-seated needs
that aroused these passions? I repeat, these instincts are profoundly socialist because they express the irrepressible conflict
between the workers and the exploiters of labor, and the very
essence of socialism, the real, natural inner core of all socialism,
lies there. The rest, the different systems of economic and social
organization, are only experimental, tentative, more or less
scientific—and, unfortunately, often too doctrinaire—manifestations of this primitive and fundamental instinct of the people.

If we really want to be practical; if, tired of daydreaming, we
want to promote the Revolution; we must rid ourselves of a
number of dogmatic bourgeois prejudices which all too many
city workers unfortunately echo. Because the city worker is more
informed than the peasant, he often regards peasants as inferiors
and talks to them like a bourgeois snob. But nothing enrages
people more than mockery and contempt, and the peasant reacts
to the city worker's sneers with bitter hatred. This is most unfor-

tunate, for this contempt and hatred divide the people into two antagonistic camps, each paralyzing and undermining the other. In fact, there is no real conflict of interests between these two camps; there is only an immense and tragic gulf which must be bridged at all costs.

The more sophisticated—and by that very circumstance, slightly bourgeois-tinged—socialism of the city workers, misunderstands, scorns, and mistrusts the vigorous, primitive peasant socialism, and tries to overshadow it. This lack of communication is responsible for the dense ignorance of urban socialism so prevalent among the peasants, who are unable to distinguish between this socialism and the bourgeois character of the cities. The peasants regard the city workers as contemptible lackeys of the bourgeoisie; this hatred renders the peasants blind tools of reaction.

Such is the fatal antagonism that has up till now paralyzed the revolutionary forces of France and of Europe. Everyone seriously concerned with the triumph of the Social Revolution must first strive to eliminate this antagonism. Since the estrangement between the two camps is due only to misunderstanding, one of them must take the initiative to effect a reconciliation. The city workers must first ask themselves what they have against the peasants. What are their grievances?

There are three grievances. The *first* is that the peasants are ignorant, superstitious, and fanatically religious, and that they allow the priests to lead them by the nose. The *second* is that they are zealously devoted to their emperor. The *third* is that the peasants are obstinate supporters of individual property.

It is true that the peasants are extremely ignorant. But is this their fault? Has anyone tried to provide schools for them? Is this a reason for despising and mistreating them? If this were so, the bourgeois, who are far better educated than the industrial workers, would have the right to mistreat the workers; and we know many bourgeois who say just this, on the pretext that their superior education entitles them to dominate the city workers and that these workers are obliged to recognize their right to do so. The superiority of the workers over the bourgeoisie lies not in their education, which is slight, but in their human feelings and their realistic, highly developed conception of what is just. But do the peasants lack this feeling for justice? Look carefully: though they express it in many different ways, you will find that they are endowed with the same feeling for what is right. You will see that alongside their ignorance there is an innate common sense, an admirable skillfulness, and it is this capacity for honest labor which constitutes the dignity and the salvation of the proletariat.

The peasants, you say, are superstitious, fanatically religious, and controlled by their priests. Their superstition is due to their ignorance, artificially and systematically implanted by all the bourgeois governments. Besides, the peasants are not as superstitious and religious as you assume; only their wives are so. But are the wives of city workers actually more liberated from the superstitions and the doctrines of the Roman Catholic religion? As to the priests, their influence is by no means as great as is generally supposed. The peasants give lip service to the Church to avoid domestic bickering and only if their formal adherence in no way conflicts with their material interests. In spite of the frantic maledictions of the Church, the religious superstition of the peasants did not stop them in 1789 from buying church property that had been confiscated by the State. Whence we conclude that, to root out the influence of the priests in the rural areas, the revolution has only to do this one thing: place the material interests of the peasants in direct and intense opposition to the vital interests of the Church.

It always angers me to hear not only the revolutionary Jacobins but also the enlightened socialists of the school of Blanqui, and even some of our intimate friends, indirectly influenced by the Blanquists, advancing the completely *antirevolutionary* idea that it will be necessary in the future to decree the abolition of all religious cults and the violent expulsion of all priests. I feel this way because *I am above all an absolute enemy of revolution by decrees*, which derives from the idea of the *revolutionary State*, i.e., *reaction disguised as revolution*. To the system of revolution by decree *I counterpose revolutionary action*, the only consistent, true, and effective program. The authoritarian system of decrees in trying *to impose* freedom and equality obliterates both. *The anarchistic system of revolutionary deeds and action naturally and unfailingly evokes the emergence and flowering of freedom and equality, without any necessity whatever for institutionalized violence or authoritarianism.* The authoritarian system necessarily leads to the triumph of naked reaction. The second will erect the Revolution on natural and unshakeable foundations.

By way of illustration, we maintain that if the abolition of religious cults and the expulsion of the priests is decreed by law, even the least religious peasants will come to their defense, primarily because there is in men an inborn irresistible urge—the source of all freedom—to rebel against any arbitrary measure, even if imposed in the name of liberty. You can therefore be entirely certain that if the cities commit the colossal folly of decreeing the extermination of religious cults and the banishment of priests, the peasants will revolt en masse against the cities and become a terrible weapon in the hands of the reaction. But does this mean that the priests should be left in full possession of their power? By no means! They must be fought not because they are ministers of the Roman Catholic religion but because they are *agents of Prussia* [or the rich]. In the rural areas, as in the cities, no revolutionary authorities, not even the Revolutionary Committees of Public Safety, should attack the priests. *This must be done only by the people themselves: the workers in the cities and the peasants in the countryside must themselves take the offensive against the priests.* The revolutionary authorities can help them indirectly, by upholding their right to do so, ostensibly out of respect for freedom of conscience. Let us, at least to some extent, adopt the prudent tactics of our adversaries. See, for example, how every government supports freedom in words but is at the same time reactionary in deeds. Let the revolutionary authorities dispense with violent phrases; but while using as moderate a language as possible, let them at the same time *act and make* the revolution.

In all lands, authoritarian revolutionists have always behaved in a totally different manner. While they have most often been ultrarevolutionary in words, they have at the same time been very moderate, if not entirely reactionary, in deeds. It can even be said that *their bombastic language has, in most instances, been used as a mask to deceive the people, to hide the paucity of their ideas and the inconsistency of their acts.* There are men, many of them among the so-called revolutionary bourgeoisie, who by mouthing revolutionary slogans think that they are making the Revolution. Feeling that they have thus adequately fulfilled their revolutionary obligations, they now proceed to be careless in action and, in flagrant contradiction to principles, commit what are in effect wholly reactionary acts. We who are truly revolutionary must behave in an altogether different manner. Let us *talk less* about revolution and *do* a great deal *more.* Let others concern themselves with the theoretical development of the principles of the Social Revolution, while we content ourselves with spreading these principles everywhere, *incarnating them into facts.*

My intimate friends and allies [members of the Alliance] will probably be surprised that I speak this way—I, who have been so concerned with the theory, who have at all times been a jealous and vigilant guardian of revolutionary principles. Ah! How times have changed! *Then,* not quite a year ago, we were only preparing for a revolution, which some expected sooner and others later; but now even the blind can tell that we are in the midst of a revolution. *Then,* it was absolutely necessary to stress theoretical principles, to expound these principles clearly and in all their purity, and thus to build a party which, though small in number, would be composed of sincere men, fully and passionately dedicated to these principles, so that in time of crisis each could count on the solidarity of all the others.

But it is now too late to concentrate on the enrollment of new men into such an organization. We have for better or worse built a small party: small, in the number of men who joined it with full knowledge of what we stand for; immense, if we take into account those who instinctively relate to us, if we take into account the popular masses, whose needs and aspirations we reflect more truly than does any other group. All of us must now embark on stormy revolutionary seas, and from this very moment we must spread our principles, not with words *but with deeds,* *for this is the most popular, the most potent, and the most irresistible form of propaganda.* Let us say less about principles, whenever circumstances and revolutionary policy demand it— i.e., during our momentary weakness in relation to the enemy— but let us at all times and under all circumstances be adamantly consistent in our action. For in this lies the salvation of the revolution.

Throughout the world the authoritarian revolutionists have done very little to promote revolutionary activity, primarily because *they always wanted to make the Revolution by themselves, by their own authority and their own power.* This could not fail to severely constrict the scope of revolutionary action because it is impossible, even for the most energetic and enterprising authoritarian revolutionary, to understand and deal effectively with all the manifold problems generated by the Revolution. For every dictatorship, be it exercised by an individual or collectively by relatively few individuals, is necessarily very circumscribed, very shortsighted, and its limited perception cannot, therefore, penetrate the depth and encompass the whole complex range of popular life; just as it is impossible for even the most gigantic vessel to contain the depths and vastness of the ocean. . . .

What should the revolutionary authorities—and there should be as few of them as possible—do to organize and spread the Revolution? They must promote the Revolution not by issuing decrees but by stirring the masses to action. They must under no circumstances foist any artificial organization whatsoever upon the masses. On the contrary, they should foster the self-organization of the masses into autonomous bodies, federated from the bottom upward. This could be done by winning the cooperation of the most influential, the most intelligent, and the most dedicated individuals in each locality, to ensure that these organizations, as far as possible, conform to our principles. Therein lies the secret of our triumph.

Who can doubt that the Revolution will be faced with many difficult problems? Do you think that a revolution is child's play, that it will not have to overcome innumerable obstacles? The revolutionary socialists of our day should not follow the pattern set by the revolutionary Jacobins of 1793. Very few, if any, of their tactics are worth imitating. Revolutionary routine would ruin them. They must create everything anew and base their policies and activities on living experiences.

As I have already said, I am not at all alarmed by the platonic attachment of the peasants to the Emperor [Napoleon III]. This attachment is merely a negative expression of their hatred for the landed gentry and the bourgeois of the cities; it need not seriously hinder the development of the Social Revolution.

The last principal grievance of the city proletariat against the peasants concerns their avarice, their unbridled egoism, and their fanatical commitment to the individual ownership of land. Workers who reprimand the peasants for all these faults should first reflect and ask themselves: who is not an egoist? Who in present society is not avaricious, in the sense that he holds on passionately to the little property that he has been able to scrape together, so that he and his loved ones shall not die of hunger and privation in the economic jungle of this merciless society? It is true that the peasants are not communists. They hate and fear those who would abolish private property, because they have something to lose—at least, in their imagination, and imagination is a very potent factor, though generally underestimated today. The vast majority of the city workers, owning no property, are immeasurably more inclined towards communism than are the peasants. Nothing is more natural; the communism of the one is just as natural as the individualism of the other, but this is no reason to praise the workers for their communist inclinations, nor to reproach the peasants for their individualism. The ideas and the passions of both are conditioned by their different environments. Besides, are all the city workers communists?

There is no point in extolling or denigrating the peasants. *It is a question of establishing a program of action which will overcome the individualism and conservatism of the peasants, and not only prevent their individualism from propelling them into the camp of the reaction but enable that individualism to serve and ensure the triumph of the Revolution.*

Remember, my dear friends, and repeat to yourselves a hundred, a thousand times a day that the triumph or defeat of the Revolution depends on the establishment of this program of action.

You will agree with me that it is already too late to convert the peasants by theoretical propaganda. There remains then, apart from what I have already suggested, this one tactic: *terrorism of the cities against the countryside.* This is the method par excellence advocated by our dear friends, the workers of the great cities of France, who do not realize that this revolutionary—I was about to say reactionary—tactic was taken from the arsenal of revolutionary Jacobinism, and that if they ever have the misfortune of using it, they will destroy not only themselves but, what is far worse, the Revolution itself. For what would be the inevitable and fatal consequence of such a policy? The whole rural population, ten million strong, would go over to the other side of the barricades, and these innumerable and invincible masses would reinforce the armies of the reaction.

Viewed from this as well as other angles, I regard the Prussian invasion as a piece of good fortune for France and for world revolution. If this invasion had not taken place, and if the revolution in France had been made without it, the French socialists themselves would have attempted once again—and this time on their own account—to stage a state revolution [*putsch, coup d'état*]. This would be absolutely illogical, it would be fatal for socialism; but they certainly would have tried to do it, so deeply have they been influenced by the principles of Jacobinism. Consequently, among other measures of public safety decreed by a convention of delegates from the cities, they would no doubt try to *impose* communism or collectivism on the peasants. This would spark an armed rebellion, which would be obliged to depend upon an immense, well-disciplined, and well-organized army. As a result, the socialist rulers would not only give another army of rebellious peasants to the reaction, they would also beget the formation of a reactionary militarist caste of power-hungry generals within their own ranks. Thus replenished, the machinery of the State would soon have to have a leader, a dictator, an emperor, to direct this machine. All this would be inevitable, for it springs not from the caprice of an individual but from the logic of the situation, a logic that never errs.

Fortunately, events themselves will now force the urban workers to open their eyes and reject this fatal procedure copied from the Jacobins. Under the prevailing circumstances, only madmen would even dream of unleashing a reign of terror against the countryside. If the countryside should rise up against the cities, the cities, and France with them, would be lost. This is understood by the working masses of Lyons, Marseilles, and other great cities of France; indeed, it partly accounts for their incredible and shameful apathy in this terrible crisis, when only the combined efforts of all the inhabitants of France can save the country and, with it, French socialism. [Another possible reason for the apathy is that Marseilles, Lyons, and the other cities referred to were not invaded by the Prussians, who stopped short at Paris, where the peace was concluded.] The French workers have lost their Latin impetuousness. As of now, they have patiently tolerated their sufferings. Furthermore, their ideals, their hopes, their principles, their political and social imaginations, their practical plans and projects—which they dreamed of putting into effect in the near future—all this came more from books, from current theories ceaselessly discussed, than from their own spontaneous thoughts derived from their concrete living experience. They have viewed the facts of their daily life in abstract terms, and have lost the faculty of drawing inspiration and ideas from the real situations they confront. Their ideas are based upon a particular theory, traditionally and uncritically accepted, with full confidence in its validity. And this theory aims at nothing other than the political system of the Jacobins, somewhat modified to suit the revolutionary socialists. This theory of revolution is now completely bankrupt, since its base, the power of the State, has collapsed. Under these circumstances the use of terroristic methods against the peasants, as advocated by the Jacobins, is absolutely out of question. And the workers of France, knowing of no other alternative, are disoriented and confused. They say, not without reason, that it is impossible to unleash a legal, official reign of terror and institute draconic measures against the peasants; that it is impossible to establish a revolutionary state, a central committee of public salvation for all France, at a moment when the foreign invader is not at the frontier, as in 1792, but in the very heart of France, a few steps from Paris. Seeing the collapse of the whole official apparatus, they rightly feel that it would be hopeless to create another one. And these revolutionists, unable to understand how the salvation of France is possible without the State, these champions of the people, having not even the slightest conception of the tremendous dynamic power of what statists of all colors from white to red scornfully call "anarchy," fold their arms and exclaim: "We are lost, France is doomed."

But my dear friends, we are not lost. *France can be saved by anarchy.*

Let loose this mass anarchy in the countryside as well as in the cities, aggravate it until it swells like a furious avalanche destroying and devouring everything in its path, both internal enemies and Prussians. This is a bold and desperate measure, I know. But it is the only feasible alternative. Without it, there is no salvation for France. All the ordinary means having failed, there is left only the primitive ferocious energy of the French people who must now choose between the slavery of bourgeois civilization and the political and primitive ferocity of the proletariat.

I have never believed that the workers in the cities, even under the most favorable conditions, will ever be able to impose communism or collectivism on the peasants; and I have never believed in this method of bringing about socialism, because I abhor every imposed system and because I am a sincere and passionate lover of freedom. This false idea and this ill-conceived hope are destructive of liberty and constitute the fundamental fallacy of authoritarian communism. For the imposition of violence, systematically organized, leads to the restitution of the principle of authority and makes necessary the State and its privileged ranks. Collectivism could be imposed only on slaves, and this kind of collectivism would then be the negation of humanity. In a free community, collectivism can come about only through the pressure of circumstances, not by imposition from above but by a free spontaneous movement from below, and only when the conditions of privileged [state-supported or subsidized] individualism, the politics of the State, criminal and civil codes, the juridical family, and the law of inheritance will have been swept away by the revolution. . . .

What are the principal grievances of the peasants, the main causes of their sullen and deep hatred of the city? They are:

1. The peasants feel that they are despised by the city workers.
2. The peasants imagine, not without many and good reasons, and many historical examples to support their view, *that the cities want to exploit them and force them to accept a political system that they abhor.*
3. In addition, the peasants think that the city workers favor the collectivization of property and fear that the socialists will confiscate their lands, which they love above all else.

What should the city workers do to overcome the distrust and animosity of the peasants? They must first of all abandon their contemptuous attitude. This is absolutely necessary for the salvation of the Revolution and for the workers themselves, for the peasants' hatred constitutes an immense danger. If it were not for this distrust and hatred, the Revolution would have succeeded long ago, for it is the animosity between the city and the land which in all countries sustains the reaction and is its main base of support. City workers must overcome their antipeasant prejudices not only in the interests of the Revolution, or for strategic reasons, but as an act of elementary justice. There is no justification for these prejudices. The peasants are not parasites; they too are hard workers, except that they toil under different conditions. The city workers who are exploited by bourgeois masters should realize that the peasants, who are also exploited, are their brothers. . . .

Bear this in mind. The peasant hates all governments and obeys the laws only because it is prudent to do so. He pays his taxes regularly and tolerates the conscription of his sons into the army only because he sees no alternative. And he is averse to change, because he thinks that new governments, regardless of their forms and programs, will be no better than their predecessors, and because he wants to avoid the risks and expenses involved in what may very well be a useless or even more harmful change.

The peasant will make common cause with the city workers

only when he is sure that the city workers are not going to foist their political and social system upon him, allegedly for his benefit. He will become an ally as soon as he is convinced that the industrial workers will not force his land to be surrendered [to the State]. . . .

And when the workers, abandoning the pretentious scholastic vocabulary of doctrinaire socialism, themselves inspired with revolutionary fervor, come to the peasants and explain in simple language, without evasions and fancy phrases, what they want; when they come to the country villages, not as conceited preceptors and instructors but as brothers and equals, trying to spread the Revolution but not imposing it on the land workers; when they burn all the official documents, judgments, court orders, and titles to property, and abolish rents, private debts, mortgages, criminal and civil law books, etc. . . . When this mountain of useless old papers symbolizing the poverty and enslavement of the proletariat goes up in flames—then, you can be sure, the peasants will understand and join their fellow revolutionists, the city workers.

What gives the urban workers the right to impose their preferred form of government or economic system on the peasants? They claim that the Revolution gives them that right. But revolution is no longer revolution when it becomes despotic, and when, instead of promoting freedom, it begets reaction.

The immediate, if not the ultimate, goal of the Revolution is the extirpation of the principle of authority in all its possible manifestations; this aim requires the abolition and, if necessary, the violent destruction of the State, because the State, as Proudhon demonstrated so well, is the younger brother of the Church, it is the historical consecration of all despotism and all privilege, the political reason for all economic and social servitude, the very essence and center of all reaction. Whoever in the name of the Revolution wants to establish a State—even a provisional State—establishes reaction and works for despotism, not freedom; for privilege, not for equality. . . .

Where did the French socialists get the preposterous, arrogant, and unjust idea that they have the right to flout the will of ten million peasants and impose their political and social system upon them? What is the theoretical justification for this fictitious right? This alleged right, in fact, is another bourgeois gift, a political inheritance from bourgeois revolutionism. And it is based on the alleged or real superiority of intelligence and education, i.e., the supposed superiority of urban over rural civilization. But you should realize that this principle can easily be invoked to justify every conquest, and consecrate all oppression. The bourgeoisie have always used this principle to prove that it is their exclusive mission and their exclusive right to *govern* (or what adds up to the same thing), to exploit all the workers. In conflicts between nations as well as between classes, this fatal principle sanctions all invasive authority. Did not the Germans repeatedly invoke this principle to excuse their onslaughts against the liberty and independence of the Slavic and other peoples and to legitimize their violent and imposed Germanization? Was it not their claim that such subjugation is the triumph of civilization over barbarism?

Beware! The Germans are already saying that German Protestant civilization is far superior to the Catholic civilization of the Latin peoples in general and to French civilization in particular. Take heed! The Germans may soon feel morally obliged to civilize you, just as you are now telling us that you are duty-bound to civilize and forcefully emancipate your countrymen, your brothers, the French peasants. To me, both claims are equally odious, and I openly declare that in relations between nations as in relations between classes, I will always be on the side of those whom you intend to civilize by these tyrannical methods. I will join them in rebellion against all such arrogant civilizers, be they workers or Germans; and in so doing, I will be serving the Revolution against the reaction.

This being the case, I will then be asked, Must we then abandon the ignorant and superstitious peasants to the reaction? By no means! ! Reaction must be uprooted in the country as well as in the rural areas. I will then be told: In order to do this, it is not enough to say we want to destroy the reaction; it must be eliminated, and this can be accomplished only by decrees. Again

I say, *by no means*! ! On the contrary, and all history proves it, decrees, like all authority in general, abolish nothing; they only perpetuate that which they were supposed to destroy.

What, then, should be done? Since the revolution cannot be *imposed* upon the rural areas, it must *be germinated within the agricultural communities, by stirring up a revolutionary movement of the peasants themselves, inciting them to destroy, by direct action, every political, judicial, civil, and military institution, and to establish and organize anarchy through the whole countryside.*

This can be done in only one way, by speaking to the peasants in a manner which will *impel them in the direction of their own interests.* They love the land? Let them take the land and throw out those landlords who live by the labor of others! ! They do not like paying mortgages, taxes, rents, and private debts? Let them stop paying! ! And lastly, they hate conscription? Don't force them to join the army! !

And who will fight the Prussians? You need not worry about that. Once the peasants are aroused and actually see the advantages of the Revolution, they will voluntarily give more money and more men to defend the Revolution than it would be possible to extract from them by compulsory official measures. The peasants will, as they did in 1792, again repel the Prussian invaders. It is necessary only that they have the opportunity to raise hell, and only the anarchist revolution can inspire them to do it.

But will not the institution of private property be even more firmly entrenched when the peasants divide up the land expropriated from the bourgeoisie? No, for with the abolition of the State and all its juridical institutions, together with the legal family and the law of inheritance—all of which will be swept away in the maelstrom of the anarchist revolution—property will no longer be protected and sanctioned by the State. There will be neither political nor juridical rights; there will be only established revolutionary facts.

You will ask, Since private landed property will no longer be protected by the State or any other external power and will be defended only by each owner himself, will not every man grab what he can from the other and the strong rob the weak? Furthermore, what will stop the weak from uniting to plunder the other landholder? "There is no way out of this," you will exclaim. "This means civil war!"

Yes, there will be civil war. But why be so afraid of civil war? Bearing in mind historical evidence, I ask, have great ideas, great personalities, and great nations emerged from civil war or from a social order imposed by some tutelary government? Having been spared civil war for over twenty years, haven't you, a great nation, now fallen so low that the Prussians could devour you in one gulp?

Civil war, so destructive to the power of states, is, on the contrary, and because of this very fact, always favorable to the awakening of popular initiative and to the intellectual, moral, and even the material interests of the populace. And for this very simple reason: civil war upsets and shakes the masses out of their sheepish state, a condition very dear to all governments, a condition which turns peoples into herds to be utilized and shorn at the whims of their shepherds. Civil war breaks through the brutalizing monotony of men's daily existence, and arrests that mechanistic routine which robs them of creative thought. . . .

Do you wish to see ten million peasants united against you in a single, solid, and unanimous mass, incensed by the hatred which your decrees and revolutionary violence has aroused? Or would you prefer a cleavage, a division in their ranks, to be opened by the anarchist revolution; one which will enable you to exert influence and build a powerful base of support among the peasants? Do you not realize that the peasants are backward, precisely because they have not been shaken out of their torpor by a civil war which would have aroused strife in the stagnant rural villages? Compact masses are human herds, little susceptible to the developing influence of ideas and propaganda. Civil war, on the contrary, creates diversity of ideas, interests, and aspirations. The peasants lack neither humanitarian feeling nor innate hatred of injustice; what they lack is revolutionary spirit and determination. The civil war will give them this spirit.

The civil war will make the whole countryside receptive to your revolutionary socialist propaganda. You will have created,

I repeat, what you have never yet had—a party which, on a grand scale, can organize true socialism, a collective society, animated by the most complete freedom. You will organize it from below upward by *encouraging the spontaneous action of the peasants* themselves in accord with these precepts.

Do not fear that the civil war, i.e., anarchy, will devastate the countryside. There is in every human society a strong instinct of self-preservation, a powerful collective inertia which safeguards it from self-annihilation, and it is precisely this inertia which accounts for the slow and difficult progress of the Revolution. Under the deadening weight of the State, European society, in the countryside as well as in the cities (though more so in the countryside), has today lost all its vigor, all spontaneity of thought and action, and if this situation continues for a few more decades, European society may wither away. . . .

Do not fear that the peasants will slaughter each other unless restrained by public authority and respect for criminal and civil law. They might start off in this direction, but they will quickly realize that it is economically and physically impossible to persist in doing so. They will then stop fighting each other, come to an understanding, and form some kind of organization to avoid future strife and to further their mutual interests. The overriding need to feed themselves and their families (and therefore to resume cultivation of their land), the necessity to defend their homes, their families, and their own lives against unforeseen attack—all these considerations will undoubtedly soon compel them to contract new and mutually suitable arrangements.

And do not think, because these arrangements will be made by the pressure of circumstances and not by official decrees, that the richest peasants will therefore exercise an excessive influence. For, no longer protected by the law, the influence of the great landowners will be undermined. They are powerful only because they are protected by the State, and once the State is abolished their power will also disappear. As to more astute and relatively affluent peasants, their power will be successfully annulled by the great mass of small and poorer peasants and, as well, by the landless agricultural laborers. This group, an enslaved mass forced to suffer in silence, will be regenerated and made potent by revolutionary anarchy.

In short, I do not say that the peasants, freely reorganized from the bottom up, will miraculously create an ideal organization, conforming in all respects to our dreams. But I am convinced that what they construct will be living and vibrant, a thousand times better and more just than any existing organization. Moreover, this peasant organization, being on the one hand open to the revolutionary propaganda of the cities, and on the other, not petrified by the intervention of the State—for there will be no State—will develop and perfect itself through free experimentation as fully as one can reasonably expect in our times.

With the abolition of the State, the spontaneous self-organization of popular life, for centuries paralyzed and absorbed by the omnipotent power of the State, will revert to the communes. The development of each commune will take as its point of departure the actual condition of its civilization. And since the diversity between levels of civilization [culture, technology] in different communes of France, as in the rest of Europe, is very great, there will first be civil war between the communes themselves, inevitably followed by mutual agreement and equilibrium between them. But in the meantime, will not the internal struggle within the communes and between the communes themselves paralyze French resistance, thus surrendering France to the Prussians?

By no means. History shows that nations never feel so self-confident and powerful in their foreign relations as when they are racked and deeply divided internally; and that, on the contrary, nations are never so weak as when they are apparently united under a seemingly invincible authority.

To convince yourself of this, you have but to compare two historical periods: the first, a France tempered and invigorated from the internal wars of the Fronde, under the young King Louis XIV; the second, a France in the King's old age, with the monarchy entrenched, pacified and unified by this great French leader. Contrast the first France, flushed with victories, with the second France marching from defeat to defeat, marching to her ruin. Compare also the France of 1792 with the France of today [1870]. The France of 1792–1793 was torn apart by civil war, the whole Republic locked in mortal combat, fighting furiously to survive. And in spite of this civil strife France victoriously repelled an invasion by almost every European power. But in 1870, France, unified and pacified under the Empire, finds itself battered by the Prussian armies and so demoralized that its very existence is imperiled. . . . The inhuman, lustful compulsion to become the greatest and mightiest nation in the world is comparable to the frantic, superhuman exertions of a delirious patient, who rallies all his temporary energy, only to fall back again, utterly exhausted. . . .

The Revolutionary Temper
and Its Matrix

France can no longer be resuscitated, galvanized into action by vain dreams of national greatness and glory. All this is already a thing of the past. The government of Napoleon III, undermined by internal degeneration, corruption, and intrigue, has disintegrated under the blows of the Prussians. . . .

Except in England and Scotland where there are, strictly speaking, no peasants, or in Ireland, Italy, and Spain, where the peasants because of their utter poverty are spontaneously inclined to be socialistic and revolutionary, the petty peasant proprietors of Western Europe—particularly in France and Germany—are semisatisfied. They cherish their property and feel that they must defend their imaginary advantages against the attacks of the Social Revolution; and although they have no real benefits, they still cling to the illusion of ownership, to their vain dreams of wealth. In addition to these drawbacks, the peasants are systematically kept in a condition of brutish ignorance by their churches and governments. The peasants now constitute the principal, almost the only, base for the security and power of states. Because of this, their governments carefully and consistently nurture their prejudices, implant Christian faith and loyalty to authority, and incite hatred against the progressive nonconformist elements in the cities. In spite of all these obstacles, the peasants, as I have already explained, can eventually be won over to the side of the Social Revolution. To accomplish this, the initiative must be taken by the revolutionary city proletarians, for they are the only ones who today embody the aroused idea and spirit, the understanding and the conscious will to make the Social Revolution. Hence the greatest threat to the existence of states is now concentrated solely in the city proletariat. . . .

It is of course obvious that if this war ends in a disastrous and shameful defeat for France, the workers will be immeasurably more dissatisfied than they are at present. But does this mean that they would be disposed to become more revolutionary? And even if this were so, would the revolutionary struggle be any less difficult than it is today?

My answer is an unhesitating no, for the following reason: the revolutionary temper of the working masses does not depend solely on the extent of their misery and discontent, but also on their faith in the justice and the triumph of their cause. The working masses, from the dawn of history through our own times, have been poverty-stricken and discontented. For all political societies, all states, republics as well as monarchies, have been based on the open or thinly disguised misery and forced labor of the proletariat. . . . But this discontent rarely produces revolutions. Even peoples reduced to the utmost poverty, despite their tribulations, fail to show signs of stirring. Why don't they revolt? Is it because they are satisfied with their lot? Of course not. They do not revolt because they have no adequate perception of their rights nor any confidence in their own powers; and lacking both, they became helpless and endured slavery for centuries. How can these revolutionary qualities be acquired by the masses? The educated individual becomes aware of his rights both by theoretical reasoning and the practical experience of life. The first condition, i.e., the ability to think abstractly, has not yet been attained by the masses. . . . How can the working masses acquire any knowledge of their rights? Only through their great historical experiences, through this great tradition, unfolded over the centuries and transmitted from generation to generation, continually augmented and enriched by new sufferings and new injustices, finally permeating and enlightening the great proletarian masses. As long as a people have not yet sunk into a state of hopeless decadence, its progress is always due to this great beneficent tradition, to this unequaled teacher of the masses. . . . But peoples in different historical epochs do not progress at a steady or equal pace. On the contrary, the rate of progress fluctuates, being sometimes rapid, deep, and far-reaching; at other times it is barely perceptible, or else it grinds to a halt and seems even to take a backward course. How can this phenomenon be explained?

It can be ascribed to the kind of events which shape each historical period. There are events that energize people and propel them in a forward direction. Other events have a discouraging, depressing effect on the morale and general attitude of the masses, distorting their sense of judgment, perverting their minds, and leading them in self-destructive directions. In studying general historical patterns in the development of peoples, one can detect two contrasting movements comparable to the ebb and flow of the oceanic tides.

In certain epochs, events occur which herald the coming of great historical changes, of great expectations and triumphs for humanity. At these points everything seems to move at a quickened pace. An air of vigor and power seems to pervade the social atmosphere; minds, hearts, and wills coalesce into one mighty upsurge as humanity marches toward the conquest of new horizons. It is as though an electric current were galvanizing the whole society, uniting the feelings of temperamentally different individuals into one common sentiment, forging totally different minds and wills into one. At such times the individual is brimful of confidence and courage because his feelings are reciprocated and heightened by the emotions of his fellowmen. Citing but a few examples from modern history, such was the period at the end of the eighteenth century, the eve of the French Revolution. So also, but to a considerably lesser extent, were the years preceding the revolution of 1848. And such, I believe, is the character of our present era, which may be the

prelude to events which will perhaps outshine the glorious days
of 1789 and 1793. . . .

But there are also somber, disheartening, disastrous epochs,
when everything reeks of decadence, exhaustion, and death, pre-
saging the exhaustion of public and private conscience. These
are the ebb tides following historic catastrophes. Such was the
time of the First Empire and the restoration of Napoleon I.
Such were the twenty or thirty years following the catastrophe of
June 1848. Such would be the twenty or thirty years following
the conquest of France by the armies of Prussian despotism. . . .

Under such conditions, a handful of workers may remain
revolutionary, but they will lack enthusiasm and confidence; for
confidence is possible only when the sentiments of an individual
find an echo, a support in the wholehearted revolutionary spirit
and will of the populace. . . . But the populace will be completely
disorganized, demoralized, and crushed by the reaction. . . . All
the workers' associations, in and out of the factories and workshops, will be suppressed. There will be no discussion groups, no
cooperative educational circles, no way to revive the collective
will of the workers. . . . Each worker will be intellectually and
morally isolated, condemned to impotence.

To make sure that the workers will not reorganize themselves, the government will arrest and deport several hundred,
or perhaps several thousand, of the most intelligent, militant,
and dedicated workers to Devil's Island [the former French
penal colony]. With the working masses facing so deplorable a
situation, it will be a long time before they are capable of making the Revolution!

Even if, despite this most unfavorable situation, and impelled
by that French heroism which refuses to accept defeat, and
driven even more by desperation, the French workers revolt,
they are likely to be taught a lesson by the most deadly of modern
weapons. Against this dreadful "persuasion," neither intelligence
nor the collective will can avail the workers, driven to resistance
by suicidal desperation alone, a resistance likely to leave them
infinitely worse off than ever.

And then? French socialism will no longer be able to take

its place in the vanguard of the European revolutionary move-ment, fighting for the emancipation of the proletariat. The new government may, for reasons of its own, grudgingly tolerate a few remaining socialist periodicals and writers in France. But neither the writers, nor the philosophers, nor their books are enough to build a living, powerful, socialist movement. Such a movement can be made a reality only by the awakened revolu-tionary consciousness, the collective will, and the organization of the working masses themselves. Without this, the best books in the world are nothing but theories spun in empty space, impo-tent dreams.

A Critique of the German Social Democratic Program

It would be difficult, if not impossible, to write a history of modern times without taking into account the absorption of the social-democratic movement into the structure of modern "wel-fare" democratic capitalism. Aside from revisionist socialists like Eduard Bernstein, who foresaw this development, nineteenth-and early twentieth-century radicals expected the imminent col-lapse of capitalism. But capitalism has not only been able to survive, it has actually grown stronger by adopting in various degrees social-democratic measures, and integrating them into the capitalist economic system. It could never have done this without the collaboration of the social-democratic parties. In so doing, capitalism changed its form and the old-line socialist movement lost its identity.

How and why this tendency developed in Germany, once the stronghold of social democracy, is discussed by Bakunin in the selection A Critique of the German Social-Democratic Pro-gram. Because it is so important and so fundamental to the social-democratic program, the idea of Representative Govern-ment and Universal Suffrage is analyzed by Bakunin separately.

Let us examine the situation in countries outside France where the socialist movement has become a real power. . . . The German Social-Democratic Workers party (S.D.W.P.) and the General Association of German Workers (G.A.G.W.), founded by Ferdinand Lassalle, are both socialist in the sense that they want to alter the relations between capital and labor in a socialist manner [abolish capitalism]. The Lassalleans as well as the Eisenach party [named after the congress held in Eisenach, August 7–9, 1869] agree fully that in order to effect this change, it will be absolutely necessary *first to reform the State*, and if this cannot be done by widespread propaganda and a legal peaceful labor movement, then the State will have to be reformed by force, i.e., by a political revolution.

All the German socialists believe that the political revolution must precede the Social Revolution. This is a fatal error. For any revolution made *before* a social revolution will necessarily be a bourgeois revolution, which can lead only to bourgeois socialism —a new, more efficient, more cleverly concealed form of the exploitation of the proletariat by the bourgeoisie. [By "bourgeois socialism," Bakunin as well as Marx meant a partnership between capital and labor, the "public" and the State. It was introduced in Germany by Bismarck and advocated in our times by right-wing democratic socialists, "enlightened capitalists," and liberals in general.]

This false principle—the idea that a political revolution must precede a social revolution—is, in effect, an open invitation to all the German bourgeois liberal politicians to infiltrate the S.D.W.P. And this party was on many occasions pressured by its leaders—not by the radical-minded rank and file members—to fraternize with the bourgeois democrats of the *Volkspartei* (People's Party), an opportunist party concerned only with politics and virulently opposed to the principles of socialism. This hostility was amply demonstrated by the vicious attacks of its patriotic orators and official journals against the revolutionary socialists of Vienna.

These onslaughts against revolutionary socialism aroused the indignation and opposition of almost all the Germans and seri-

ously embarrassed Liebknecht and the other leaders of the
S.D.W.P. They wanted to calm the workers and thus stay in
control of the German labor movement and, at the same time,
remain on friendly terms with the leaders of the bourgeois democrats of the *Volkspartei*, who soon realized that they had made a
serious tactical error by antagonizing the German labor movement without whose support they could not hope to attain
political power.

In this respect the *Volkspartei* followed the tradition of the
bourgeoisie never to make a revolution by themselves. Their
tactics, however ingeniously applied, are always based on this
principle: to enlist the powerful help of the people in making a
political revolution but to reap the benefit for themselves. It
was this sort of consideration which induced the *Volkspartei* to
reverse its antisocialist stand and proclaim that it too, is now a
socialist party. . . . After a year of negotiations, the top leaders of
the workers' and the bourgeois parties adopted the famous
Eisenach Program and formed a single party retaining the name
S.D.W.P. This program is really a strange hybrid of the revolutionary program of the International Workingmen's Association
(the International) and the well-known opportunistic program
of the bourgeois democracy. . . .

Article I of the program is in fact contradictory to the fundamental policy and spirit of the International. The S.D.W.P.
wants to institute *a free People's State*. But the words *free* and
People's are annulled and rendered meaningless by the word
State; the name International implies the negation of the State.
Are the framers of the program talking about an international or
universal state, or do they intend to set up only a state embracing
all the countries of Western Europe—England, France, Germany, the Scandinavian countries, Holland, Switzerland, Spain,
Portugal, and the Slavic nations subjected to Austria?[7] No. Their
political stomachs cannot digest so many countries at one time.
With a passion they do not even attempt to conceal, the social
democrats proclaim that they want to erect the great pan-
Germanic fatherland. And this is why the only aim of the
S.D.W.P., the construction of an all-German state, is the very
first article of their program. They are above all *German patriots*.

Instead of dedicating themselves to the creation of the all-German State, the German workers should join their exploited brothers of the entire world in defense of their mutual economic and social interests; the labor movement of each country must be based solely on the principle of international solidarity. . . . If, in case of conflict between two states, the workers would act in accordance wtih Article I of the social-democratic program, they would, against their better inclinations, be *joining their own bourgeoisie* against their fellow workers in a foreign country. They would thereby sacrifice the international solidarity of the workers to the national patriotism of the State. This is exactly what the German workers are now doing in the Franco-Prussian War. As long as the German workers seek to set up a national state—even the freest People's State—they will inevitably and utterly sacrifice the freedom of the people to the glory of the State, socialism to politics, justice and international brotherhood to patriotism. It is impossible to go in two different directions at the same time. Socialism and social revolution involve the destruction of the State; consequently, those who want a state must sacrifice the economic emancipation of the masses to the political monopoly of a privileged party.

The S.D.W.P. would sacrifice the economic, and with it, the political emancipation of the proletariat—or more correctly said, its *emancipation from politics and the State*—to the triumph of bourgeois democracy. This follows plainly from the second and third articles of the social-democratic program. The first three clauses of Article 2 conform in every respect to the socialist principles of the International: the abolition of capitalism; full political and social equality; every worker to receive the full product of his labor. But the fourth clause, by declaring that political emancipation is the *preliminary* condition for the economic emancipation of the working class, that the solution of the social question is possible only in a democratic state, nullifies these principles and makes it impossible to put them into practice. The fourth clause amounts to saying:

"Workers, you are slaves, victims of capitalist society. Do you want to free yourself from this economic straitjacket? Of course you do, and you are absolutely right. But to attain your just demands, *you must first help us make the political revolution. Afterwards, we will help you make the Social Revolution.* Let us first, with your strength, erect the democratic State, a good democratic State, as in Switzerland: and then we promise to give you the same benefits that the Swiss workers now enjoy. . . . (Witness the strikes in Basel and Geneva, ruthlessly suppressed by the bourgeoisie.)"

To convince yourself that this incredible delusion accurately reflects the tendencies and spirit of German social democracy, you have but to examine Article 3, which lists all the immediate and proximate goals to be advanced in the party's legal and peaceful propaganda and election campaigns. These demands merely duplicate the familiar program of the bourgeois democrats: universal suffrage with direct legislation by the people;[8] abolition of all political privileges; replacement of the permanent standing army by the volunteers' and citizens' militias; separation of Church from State, and the schools from the Church; free and compulsory elementary education; freedom of the press, assembly, and association; and replacement of all indirect taxation by a single, direct, and progressively higher income tax based on earnings.

Does not this program prove that the social democrats are interested in the exclusively political reform of the institutions and laws of the State, and that for them socialism is but an empty dream, which may at best be realized in the distant future?

Were it not for the fact that the true aspirations and radical sentiments of its members, the German workers, go much further than this program, would we not be justified in saying that the S.D.W.P. was created for the sole purpose of using the working masses as the unconscious tool to promote the political ambitions of the German bourgeois democrats?

There are only two planks in this program which free-enterprise capitalists will dislike. The first appears in the latter half of clause 8, Article 3; it demands *establishment of a normal working day* (limitation of hours), *abolition of child labor, and limitation of women's work*; measures which make the free enterprisers shudder. As passionate lovers of all freedom which they can use to their advantage, they demand the unlimited right to exploit the proletariat and bitterly resent state interference. However, the poor capitalists have fallen upon evil days. They have been forced to accept state intervention even in England, which is by no stretch of the imagination a socialist society.

The other plank—clause 10, Article 3—is even more important and socialistic. It demands state help, protection, and credit for workers' cooperatives, particularly producers' cooperatives, with all necessary guarantees, i.e., freedom to expand. Free enterprise is not afraid of successful competition from workers' cooperatives because the capitalists know that workers, with their meager incomes, will never by themselves be able to accumulate enough capital to match the immense resources of the employing class . . . but the tables will be turned when the workers' cooperatives, backed by the power and well-nigh unlimited credit of the State, begin to fight and gradually absorb both private and corporate capital (industrial and commercial). For the capitalist will in fact be competing with the State, and the State is, of course, the most powerful of all capitalists. [It will be seen from the context of the next paragraph that Bakunin regards state subsidy of workers' cooperatives as part of the transition from capitalism to state socialism.]

Labor employed by the State—such is the fundamental principle of authoritarian communism, of state socialism. The State, having become the sole proprietor—at the end of a period of transition necessary for allowing society to pass, without too great dislocation, from the present organization of bourgeois privilege to the future organization of official equality for all—the State will then become the only banker, capitalist, organizer, and director of all national labor, and the distributor of all its products. Such is the ideal, the fundamental principle of modern communism.

Representative Government
and Universal Suffrage

Bakunin opposed workers' participation in bourgeois politics because he feared that participation would corrode the proletariat and perpetuate the establishment (as it did in Germany till Hitler's victory). His opposition to parliamentary government was sharpened during his polemics with the Marxist parties, who favored parliamentary action by the workers while in effect ignoring the supreme importance of direct revolutionary action.° Bakunin did not oppose universal suffrage in principle but only insofar as it reinforced the bourgeois democratic state. But he never raised abstention from the electoral process to an inflexible article of faith. Under certain exceptional circumstances, he advocated temporary alliance with progressive political parties for specific, limited objectives. In a letter to his friend the Italian anarchist Carlo Gambuzzi, a former lawyer, Bakunin advised him to become a candidate for Deputy from Naples:

> You will perhaps be surprised that I, a determined and passionate abstentionist from politics, should now advise my friends [members of the Alliance] to become deputies—this is because circumstances have changed. First, all my friends, and most assuredly yourself, are so inspired by our ideas, our principles, that there is no danger that you will forget, deform, or abandon them, or that you will fall back into the old political habits. Second, times have become so grave,

the danger menacing the liberty of all countries so formidable, that all men of goodwill must step into the breach, and especially our friends, who must be in a position to exercise the greatest possible influence on events. . . .[10]

In a letter to another Italian anarchist, Celso Cerretti, written during the reaction that occurred in all of Europe after the fall of the Paris Commune in 1871, Bakunin noted that Spain was the only country where a revolutionary situation existed and in view of the special circumstances prevailing in that country advised temporary collaboration with the progressive political parties:

> . . . Letters that I receive from different parts of Spain indicate that the socialist workers are very effectively organized. And not only the workers but the peasants of Andalusia, among whom socialist ideas [have fortunately] been successfully spread—these peasants too are prepared to take a very active part in the coming revolution. While maintaining our identity, we must, at this time, help the political parties and endeavor later to give this revolution a clearly socialist character. . . . If the Revolution triumphs in Spain, it will naturally tremendously accelerate and spread the Revolution in all of Europe. . . .[11]

M ODERN society is so convinced of this truth: *every state, whatever its origin or form, must necessarily lead to despotism*, that countries which have in our time wrested a measure of freedom from the State have hastened to subject their rulers, even when these rulers emerged from revolution and were elected by all the people, to the strictest possible control. To safeguard their freedom, they depend on the real and effective control exercised by the popular will over those invested with public and repressive authority. In all nations living under representative government freedom can be real only when this control is real and effective. It follows, therefore, that if such control is fictitious, then the freedom of the people becomes likewise a complete fiction.

It would be easy to prove that nowhere in Europe is there real popular control of government, but we shall confine ourselves to Switzerland and see how popular control over the Swiss government is exercised. For what is true in this respect for Switzerland must hold even more for any other country. Around 1830, the most progressive cantons in Switzerland tried to safeguard their liberties by instituting universal suffrage. There were solid grounds for this movement. As long as our legislative councils were chosen by privileged citizens, and unequal voting rights between cities and rural areas, between patricians and plebeians, continued to exist, the officials appointed by these councils as well as the laws enacted by them could not have failed to perpetuate the domination of the ruling aristocracy over the nation. It therefore became necessary to abolish this regime and replace it by one honoring the sovereignty of the people, i.e., universal suffrage.

It was generally expected that once universal suffrage was established, the political liberty of the people would be assured. This turned out to be a great illusion. In practice, universal suffrage led to the collapse, or at least the flagrant demoralization, of the Radical party, which is so glaringly obvious today. The radicals [liberals] did not intend to cheat the people, but they did cheat themselves. They were quite sincere when they promised to provide popular freedom by means of universal suffrage. Fired by this conviction, they were able to stir up the masses to overthrow the entrenched aristocratic government. Today, demoralized by the exercise of power, they have lost their faith in themselves and in their ideals; this explains the depth of their depression and the profundity of their corruption.

And, indeed, at first glance the idea of universal suffrage seemed so reasonable and so simple; once the legislative and executive powers emanate directly from popular elections, would not these powers faithfully reflect the will of the people? And how could this popular will fail to produce anything other than freedom and general well-being?

The whole system of representative government is an immense fraud resting on this fiction: that the executive and legislative bodies elected by universal suffrage of the people must or even can possibly represent the will of the people. The people instinctively reach out for two things: the greatest possible prosperity coupled with the greatest possible freedom to live their own lives, to choose, to act. They want the best organization of their economic interests coupled with the complete absence of all political power and all political organization, since every political organization must inescapably nullify the freedom of the people. Such is the dynamic aspiration of all popular movements.

But the ambitions of those who govern, those who formulate and enforce the laws, are diametrically opposed to the popular aspirations. Irrespective of their democratic sentiments or intentions, the rulers by virtue of their elevated position look down upon society as a sovereign regarding his subjects. But there can be no equality between the sovereign and the subject. On one side there is the feeling of superiority necessarily induced by a high position; on the other, that of inferiority resulting from the sovereign's superior position as the wielder of executive and legislative power. Political power means domination. And where there is domination, there must be a substantial part of the population who remain subjected to the domination of their rulers; and subjects will naturally hate their rulers, who will then naturally be forced to subdue the people by even more oppressive measures, further curtailing their freedom. Such is the nature of political power ever since its origin in human society. This also explains why and how men who were the reddest democrats, the most vociferous radicals, once in power become the most moderate conservatives. Such turnabouts are usually and mistakenly regarded as a kind of treason. Their principal cause is the inevitable change of position and perspective. We should never forget that the institutional positions and their attendant privileges are far more powerful motivating forces than mere individual hatred or ill will. If a government composed exclusively of workers were elected tomorrow by universal suffrage, these same workers, who are today the most dedicated democrats and socialists, would tomorrow become the most determined aristocrats, open or secret worshippers of the principle of authority, exploiters and oppressors.

In Switzerland, as in all other nations, however egalitarian its political institutions may be, it is the bourgeoisie who rule and it is the working masses, including the peasants, who must obey the laws made by the bourgeoisie. The people have neither the time nor the requisite knowledge to participate in governmental functions. The bourgeoisie possess both; hence, not by right, but in fact, they hold the exclusive privilege of governing. Political equality in Switzerland, as in all other countries, is therefore a puerile fiction, an absolute fraud.

Now, since the bourgeoisie by virtue of their economic and political privileges are so far removed from the people, how can their governing and their laws truly express the feelings, ideas, and will of the people? It is impossible, and daily experience demonstrates that in the legislative and all other branches of government, the bourgeoisie is primarily concerned with promoting its own interests and not the legitimate interests of the people. True, all district officials and legislators are directly or indirectly elected by the people. True, on election day even the proudest bourgeois office seekers are forced to court their majesty, The Sovereign People. They come to the sovereign populace, hat in hand, professing no other wish than to serve them. For the office seeker this is an unpleasant chore, soon over and therefore to be patiently endured. The day after election everybody goes about his business, the people go back to toil anew, the bourgeoisie to reaping profits and to political conniving. They seldom meet and never greet each other till the next election when the farce is repeated. . . . Since popular control in the representative system is the sole guarantee of popular freedom, it is obvious that this freedom too is wholly spurious.

To correct the obvious defects of this system, the radical democrats of the Zurich Canton introduced the *referendum*, direct legislation by the people. The referendum is also an ineffective remedy; another fraud. In order to vote intelligently on proposals made by legislators or measures advanced by interested groups, the people must have the time and the necessary knowledge to study these measures thoroughly. . . . The referendum is meaningful only on those rare occasions when the proposed legislation vitally affects and arouses all the people, and the issues involved are clearly understood by everyone. But almost all the proposed laws are so specialized, so intricate, that only political experts can grasp how they would ultimately affect the people. The people, of course, do not even begin to understand or pay attention to the proposed laws and vote for them blindly when urged to do so by their favorite orators.

Even when the representative system is improved by referendum, there is still no popular control, and real liberty—under representative government masquerading as self-government—is an illusion. Due to their economic hardships the people are ignorant and indifferent and are aware only of things closely affecting them. They understand and know how to conduct their daily affairs. Away from their familiar concerns they become confused, uncertain, and politically baffled. They have a healthy, practical common sense when it comes to communal affairs. They are fairly well informed and know how to select from their midst the most capable officials. Under such circumstances, effective control is quite possible, because the public business is conducted under the watchful eyes of the citizens and vitally and directly concerns their daily lives. This is why municipal elections always best reflect the real attitude and will of the people. [It can be gathered from the context that Bakunin, without explicitly saying so, refers not to great cities with hundreds of thousands or millions of inhabitants but to small or medium-sized communities where face-to-face democracy is practical.] Provincial and county governments, even when the latter are directly elected, are already less representative of the people. Most of the time, the people are not acquainted with the relevant political, juridical, and administrative measures; those are beyond their immediate concern and almost always escape their control. The men in charge of local and regional governments live in a different environment, far removed from the people, who know very little about them. They do not know these leaders' characters personally, and judge them only by their public speeches, which are packed with lies to trick the people into supporting them. . . . If popular control over regional and local affairs is exceedingly difficult, then popular control over the federal or national government is altogether impossible.

Most of the public affairs and laws, especially those dealing with the well-being and material interests of the local communities and associations are settled in ways beyond the grasp of the people, without their knowledge or concern, and without their intervention. The people are committed to ruinous policies, all without noticing. They have neither the experience nor the time to study all these laws and so they leave everything to their elected representatives. These naturally promote the interests of their class rather than the prosperity of the people, and their greatest talent is to sugarcoat their bitter measures, to render them more palatable to the populace. Representative government is a system of hypocrisy and perpetual falsehood. Its success rests on the stupidity of the people and the corruption of the public mind.

Does this mean that we, the revolutionary socialists, do not want universal suffrage—that we prefer limited suffrage, or a single despot? Not at all. What we maintain is that universal suffrage, considered in itself and applied in a society based on economic and social inequality, will be nothing but a swindle and snare for the people; nothing but an odious lie of the bourgeois democrats, the surest way to consolidate under the mantle of liberalism and justice the permanent domination of the people by the owning classes, to the detriment of popular liberty. We deny that universal suffrage could be used by the people for the conquest of economic and social equality. It must always and necessarily be an instrument hostile to the people, one which supports the *de facto* dictatorship of the bourgeoisie.

1871

———◆●◆———

God and the State

The following extract from The Knouto-Germanic Empire and the Social Revolution, entitled "God and the State"[12] by Bakunin's intimate associates, Carlo Cafiero and Élisée Reclus, but better called "Authority and Science," goes to the core of Bakunin's ideology. Bakunin's views on the nature of authority and its relation to science, the function of science in society, its role in the state and vis-à-vis the individual, are still cogent and place him far ahead of his Darwinian contemporaries who had begun to regard science as something of a new religion. Bakunin concerned himself not with "humanity in general" but with the uniqueness and the feelings of actual living persons, all the anonymous "little fellows" threatened with becoming mere ciphers lost in the mazes of the technotronic superstate.

"Man, Society, and Freedom"[13] is taken from a long unfinished note to the same work, and illustrates Bakunin's profound differences with those individualists who believe that there exists a fundamental antagonism between the individual and society, and that man is a free agent anterior to and apart from society. It is here that he defines his key concept, freedom. Realist that he was, Bakunin had no illusions either about individual man or about society. Neither is naturally "good" or naturally "bad"— they are both. Because men have, on the one hand, an innate urge toward conformity with their fellows, "Social tyranny [i.e., public opinion] can be even more tyrannical than the official, legalized despotism of the State." Fortunately, however, there exists in every human being, latently or actively, a counter-balancing will "to revolt against all divine, collective, and individual authority."

Authority and Science[14]

What is authority? Is it the inevitable power of the natural laws which manifest themselves in the necessary concatenation and succession of phenomena in the physical and social worlds? Indeed, against these laws revolt is not only forbidden, it is impossible. We may misunderstand them or not know them at all, but we cannot disobey them; for they constitute the basic conditions of our existence; they envelop us, penetrate us, regulate all our movements, thoughts, and acts; even when we believe we disobey them, we are only showing their omnipotence.

Yes, we are the absolute slaves of these laws. But in such slavery there is no humiliation, or rather, it is not slavery at all. For slavery presupposes an external master, an authority apart from the subject whom he commands. But these laws are not something apart; they are inherent in us; they constitute our whole being, physically, intellectually, and morally; we breathe, we act, we think, we wish, only in accordance with these laws. Without them we are nothing, *we are not*. Whence, then, could we derive the power and the wish to rebel against them?

Man has but one liberty with respect to natural laws, that of recognizing and applying them on an ever-extending scale in conformity with the object of collective and individual emancipation or humanization which he pursues. These laws, once recognized, exercise an authority which is never disputed by the mass of men. One must, for instance, be at bottom either a fool or a theologian or at least a metaphysician, jurist, or bourgeois economist to rebel against the law by which twice two makes four. One must have faith to imagine that fire will not burn nor water drown, except, indeed, recourse be had to some subterfuge founded in its turn on some other natural law. But these revolts, or, rather, these attempts at, or foolish fancies of, an impossible revolt, are decidedly the exception; for, in general it may be said that the mass of men in their daily lives acknowledge the government of common sense—that is, of the sum of natural laws generally recognized—in an almost absolute fashion.

The great misfortune is that a large number of natural laws, already established as such by science, remain unknown to the masses, thanks to the watchfulness of the tutelary governments that exist, as we know, only for the "good of the people." There is another difficulty, namely, that the major portion of the natural laws connected with the development of human society, which are quite as necessary, invariable, fatal, as the laws that govern the physical world, have not been duly established or recognized by science itself.

Once they are recognized by science, and have then passed into the consciousness of all men, the question of liberty will be entirely solved. The most stubborn authorities must admit that then there will be no need either of political organization or direction or legislation, three things which are always equally fatal and inimical to the liberty of the people inasmuch as they impose upon them a system of external and therefore despotic laws. This is so whether they are imposed by a sovereign or a democratically elective parliament.

The liberty of man consists solely in this: that he obeys natural laws because he has *himself* recognized them as such, and not because they have been externally imposed upon him by any extrinsic will whatever, divine or human, collective or individual.

Suppose a learned academy, composed of the most illustrious scientists, were charged with the lawful organization of society, and that, inspired only by the purest love for truth, it framed only laws in absolute harmony with the latest discoveries of science. Such legislation, I say, and such organization would be a monstrosity, first, because human science is always and necessarily imperfect, since, comparing what it has discovered, it is still in its cradle. So that were we to try to force the practical life of men, collective as well as individual, into strict conformity with the latest data of science, we should condemn society as well as individuals to suffer martyrdom on a Procrustean bed.

Secondly, a society which obeyed legislation emanating from a scientific academy, not because it understood its rational character but because this legislation was imposed by the academy in the name of a science which the people venerated without comprehending it, would be a society not of men but of brutes. It would be another version of those missions in Paraguay which submitted so long to the government of the Jesuits. It would surely and rapidly descend to the lowest stage of idiocy.

And there is still a third reason which would render such a government impossible—namely, that a scientific academy invested with absolute sovereignty, even if it were composed of the most illustrious men, would infallibly and soon end in its own moral and intellectual corruption. For such is the history of all academies even today, with the few privileges allowed them. From the moment he becomes an academician, an officially licensed "servant," the greatest scientific genius inevitably lapses into sluggishness. He loses his spontaneity, his revolutionary hardihood, and that troublesome and savage energy characteristic of the genius, ever called to destroy tottering old worlds and lay the foundations of the new. He undoubtedly gains in politeness, in utilitarian and practical wisdom, what he loses in power of originality. In a word, he becomes corrupted.

It is the characteristic of privilege and of every privileged position to kill the hearts and minds of men. The privileged man, whether politically or economically, is a man depraved in mind and heart. That is a social law which admits of no exception, and it is applicable to entire nations as to classes, corporations, and individuals. It is the law of equality, the supreme condition of liberty and humanity. The principle object of this treatise is precisely to demonstrate this truth in all the manifestations of human life.

A scientific body to which has been confided the government of society would soon end by devoting itself no longer to science at all, but to quite another matter; and, as in the case of all established powers, that would be its own eternal perpetuation by rendering the society confided to its care ever more stupid and consequently more dependent upon the scientists' authority.

But that which is true of scientific academies is also true of constituent assemblies, even those chosen by universal suffrage. They may change in composition, of course, but this does not prevent the formation in a few years' time of a body of privileged politicians exclusively intent upon the direction of public affairs as a sort of political aristocracy or oligarchy. Witness what has happened in the United States of America and in Switzerland.

Therefore let us have no external legislation and no authority. The one is inseparable from the other, and both tend to create a slavish society.

Does it follow that I reject all authority? Perish the thought. In the matter of boots, I defer to the authority of the bootmaker; concerning houses, canals, or railroads, I consult the architect or the engineer. For such special knowledge I apply to such a "savant." But I allow neither the bootmaker nor the architect nor the "savant" to impose his authority on me. I listen to them freely and with all the respect merited by their intelligence, their character, their knowledge, reserving always my incontestable right of criticism and censure. I do not content myself with consulting a single authority in any special branch; I consult several; I compare their opinions and choose that which seems to me soundest. But I recognize no *infallible* authority, even in special questions; consequently, whatever respect I may have for the honesty and the sincerity of an individual, I have no absolute faith in any person. Such a faith would be fatal to my reason, to my liberty, and even to the success of my undertakings; it would immediately transform me into a stupid slave, the tool of other people's will and interests.

If I bow before the authority of the specialists, willing to accept their suggestions and their guidance for a time and to a degree, I do so only because I am not compelled to by anyone. Otherwise I would repel them with horror and bid the devil take their counsels, their directions, and their services, certain that they would make me pay, by the loss of my liberty and self-respect, for such scraps of truth, wrapped in a multitude of lies, as they might give me.

I bow before the authority of specialists because it is imposed upon me by my own reason. I am conscious of my inability to grasp any large portion of human knowledge in all its details and developments. The greatest intelligence would not be equal to a comprehension of the whole, whence the necessity of the division and association of labor. I receive and I give; such is human life.

Each directs and is directed in his turn. Therefore there is no fixed and constant authority, but a continual fluctuation of mutual, temporary, and above all voluntary authority and sub-ordination.

To accept a fixed, constant, and universal authority is ruled out precisely because there is no "universal" man capable of grasping, in that wealth of detail without which the application of a science to life is impossible, all the sciences and all the aspects of social life. And indeed if a single man could ever attain such an all-encompassing understanding, and if he wished to use it to impose his authority upon us, it would be necessary to drive this man out of society, because his authority would inevitably reduce all the others to slavery and imbecility. I do not think that society ought to maltreat men of genius as it has done hitherto; but neither do I think it should indulge them too far, still less accord them any special privileges or exclusive rights whatsoever, for three reasons: first, because it would often mistake a charlatan for a man of genius; second, because, through such a system of privileges, it might transform into a charlatan even a real man of genius, and thus demoralize and degrade him; and, finally, because it would establish a master over itself.

To sum up: we do recognize the absolute authority of science, for the sole object of science is the thorough and systematic formulation of all the natural laws inherent in the material, intellectual, and moral life of both the physical and social worlds, which are one and the same world. Apart from this, the sole legitimate authority—legitimate because it is rational and in harmony with human liberty—we declare all other authorities false, arbitrary, and deadly. . . .

But while rejecting the absolute, universal, and infallible authority of men of science, we willingly accept the respectable, although relative, temporary, and restricted authority of scientific specialists, asking nothing better than to consult them by turns, and grateful for their precious information as long as they are willing to learn from us in their turn. In general, we ask nothing better than to see men endowed with great knowledge, with great experience, great minds, and above all great hearts, exercise over us a natural and legitimate influence, freely accepted, and never imposed in the name of any official authority or established right; for every authority or established right, officially imposed as such, becomes at once an oppression and a falsehood, and would inevitably impose upon us . . . slavery and absurdity.

In a word, we reject all legislation, all authority, and all privileged, licensed, official, and legal powers over us, even though arising from universal suffrage, convinced that this can serve only to the advantage of a dominant minority of exploiters against the interests of the immense majority in subjection to them.

This is the sense in which we are all anarchists. . . .

The immense advance of positive science over theology, metaphysics, politics, and judicial right consists in this: that, in place of the false abstractions set up by these doctrines, it posits true generalizations that express the nature and logic of things, their relations, and the laws of their development. This profoundly distinguishes science from all earlier modes of thought and will forever assure its importance to society: science will constitute in a certain sense society's collective consciousness. But in one respect it resembles all the other disciplines: since it, too, deals in abstractions, it is forced by its very nature to ignore real men, apart from whom the abstractions have no existence. To remedy this radical defect, positive science will have to proceed by a new method. The doctrines of the past have always taken advantage of the people's ignorance and gladly sacrificed them to their abstractions, which are incidentally very lucrative to their actual flesh-and-bone proponents. Positive science, admitting its absolute inability to conceive and take an interest in real individuals, must renounce all claims to the government of societies. By meddling in this, it would only sacrifice continually the living men it ignores to the abstractions which constitute the sole object of its legitimate preoccupations.

A pure science of history, for instance, does not yet exist; we have barely begun today to glimpse its extremely complicated possibilities. But suppose it were fully developed, what could it give us? It could give us a faithful and rational picture of the natural development of the general conditions—material and ideal, economic, political and social, religious, philosophical, aesthetic, and scientific—of historical societies. But this universal picture of human civilization, however detailed it might be, would never show anything beyond general and consequently *abstract* estimates. The millions of individuals who furnished the *living and suffering materials* of this history at once triumphant and dismal—triumphant by its general results, dismal by the immense hecatomb of human victims "crushed under its jugger-naut"—those billions of obscure individuals without whom none of the great general advances in history would have happened— and who, remember, have never benefited by any of these advances—will find not the slightest place in our annals. They lived and they were sacrificed, crushed for the good of humanity in general, that is all.

Shall we blame the science of history? That would be unjust and ridiculous. Individuals cannot be grasped by thought, by reflections, or even by human speech, which is capable of express-ing abstractions only; they cannot be so grasped in the present any more than in the past. Therefore social science itself, the science of the future, will necessarily continue to ignore them. All that we have a right to demand of it is that it shall point us with a faithful and sure hand to the *general causes of suffering.* Among these causes it will not forget the immolation and subordination (still too frequent, alas!) of living individuals to abstract gen-eralities, at the same time showing us the *general conditions necessary to the real individuals living in society.* That is its mis-sion; those are its limits, beyond which the action of social science can be only impotent and deadly. Beyond these limits are the doctrinaire tensions to governing authority of its licensed repre-sentatives, its priests. It is time to have done with all the popes and priests; we want no more of them, even if they call them-selves "Social Democrats." . . .

On the one hand, science is indispensable to the rational organization of society; on the other, being incapable of concern for the real and living, it must not interfere with the real or prac-tical organization of society. How to solve this antinomy?

This contradiction can be resolved in only one way: by the liquidation of science as a moral authority apart from the life of the people, and represented by a body of accredited "savants." It

must spread among the masses. Science, being called upon henceforth to represent society's collective consciousness, must really
become the property of everybody. Thereby, without losing anything of its universal character, of which it can never divest itself
without ceasing to be science, and while continuing to concern
itself exclusively with general causes, the conditions, and the fixed
interrelations of individuals and things, it will fuse in fact with
the immediate and real life of all individuals. . . .

Again, it is life, not science, that created life; only the spontaneous action of the people themselves can create liberty. It
would be splendid, to be sure, if science could begin at once to
illuminate the spontaneous march of the people towards their
emancipation. But better no light at all than a false and feeble
light, kindled only to mislead those who follow it. After all, the
people will not lack light. Not in vain have they traveled a long
historic road and paid for their errors with centuries of misery.
The practical summary of their painful experiences constitutes a
sort of traditional knowledge, which in some respects is worth as
much as theoretical knowledge. Last of all, a portion of the youth
—those of the bourgeois students who feel hatred enough for the
falsehood, hypocrisy, injustice, and cowardice of the bourgeoisie
to find courage to turn their backs upon it, and passion enough
to unreservedly embrace the just and humane cause of the
proletariat—will assume the role of fraternal instructors of the
people: *thanks to them, there will be no occasion for the
government of the "savants."* Science, in becoming the patrimony of everybody, will wed itself in a certain sense to the
immediate and real life of each individual. It will gain in utility
and grace what it loses in pride, ambition, and doctrinaire ped-
antry. This, however, will not prevent men of genius, better
organized for scientific speculation than the majority of their
fellows, from devoting themselves exclusively to the cultivation
of the sciences and rendering great services to humanity. Only,
they will be ambitious for no other social influence than the
natural influence exercised on its surroundings by every superior
intelligence, and for no other reward than the high delight which
a noble mind always finds in the satisfaction of a noble passion.

Man, Society, and Freedom

. . . The doctrinaire liberals, reasoning from the premises of individual freedom, pose as the adversaries of the State. Those among them who maintain that the government, i.e., the body of functionaries organized and designated to perform the functions of the State is a *necessary evil,* and that the progress of civilization consists in always and continuously diminishing the attributes and the rights of the States, are inconsistent. Such is the theory, but in practice these same doctrinaire liberals, when the existence or the stability of the State is seriously threatened, are just as fanatical defenders of the State as are the monarchists and the Jacobins.

Their adherence to the State, which flatly contradicts their liberal maxims, can be explained in two ways: in practice, their class interests make the immense majority of doctrinaire liberals members of the bourgeoisie. This very numerous and respectable class demand, only for themselves, the exclusive rights and privileges of complete license. The socioeconomic base of its political existence rests upon no other principle than the unrestricted license expressed in the famous phrases *laissez faire* and *laissez aller* [the economic doctrine of absolute "free enterprise" without interference, or "Devil take the hindmost"]. But they want this anarchy only for themselves, not for the masses who must remain under the severe discipline of the State because they are "too ignorant to enjoy this anarchy without abusing it." For if the masses, tired of working for others, should rebel, the whole bourgeois edifice would collapse. Always and everywhere, when the masses are restless, even the most enthusiastic liberals immediately reverse themselves and become the most fanatical champions of the omnipotence of the State.

In addition to this practical reason, there is still another of a theoretical nature which also leads even the most sincere liberals back to the cult of the State. They consider themselves liberals because their theory on the origin of society is based on the principle of individual freedom, and it is precisely because of this that they must inevitably recognize the absolute right [sovereignty] of the State.

According to them individual freedom is not a creation, a historic product of society. They maintain, on the contrary, that individual freedom is anterior to all society and that all men are endowed by God with an immortal soul. Man is accordingly a complete being, absolutely independent, apart from and outside society. As a free agent, anterior to and apart from society, he necessarily forms his society by a voluntary act, a sort of contract, be it instinctive or conscious, tacit or formal. In short, according to this theory, individuals are not the product of society but, on the contrary, are led to create society by some necessity such as work or war.

It follows from this theory that society, strictly speaking, does not exist. The natural human society, the beginning of all civilization, the only milieu in which the personality and the liberty of man is formed and developed does not exist for them. On the one hand, this theory recognizes only self-sufficient individuals living in isolation, and on the other hand, only a society arbitrarily created by them and based only on a formal or tacit contract, i.e., on the State. (They know very well that no state in history has ever been created by contract, and that all states were established by conquest and violence.)

The mass of individuals of whom the State consists are seen as in line with this theory, which is singularly full of contradictions. Each of them is, considered on the one hand, an immortal soul endowed with free will. All are untrammeled beings altogether sufficient unto themselves and in need of no other person, not even God, for, being immortal, they are themselves gods. On the other hand, they are brutal, weak, imperfect, limited, and altogether subject to the forces of nature which encompass them and sooner or later carry them off to their graves. . . .

Under the aspect of their earthly existence, the mass of men present so sorry and degrading a spectacle, so poor in spirit, in will and initiative, that one must be endowed with a truly great capacity for self-delusion, to detect in them an immortal soul, or even the faintest trace of free will. They appear to be absolutely determined: determined by exterior nature, by the stars, and by all the material conditions of their lives; determined by laws and by the whole world of ideas or prejudices elaborated in past centuries, all of which they find ready to take over their lives at birth.

The immense majority of individuals, not only among the ignorant masses but also among the civilized and privileged classes, think and want only what everybody else around them thinks and wants. They doubtlessly believe that they think for themselves, but they are only slavishly repeating by rote, with slight modifications, the thoughts and aims of the other conformists which they imperceptibly absorb. This servility, this routine, this perennial absence of the will to revolt and this lack of initiative and independence of thought are the principle causes for the slow, desolate historical development of humanity. For us, materialists and realists who believe in neither the immortality of the soul nor in free will, this slowness, as disastrous as it may be, is a natural fact. Emerging from the state of the gorilla, man has only with great difficulty attained the consciousness of his humanity and his liberty. . . . He was born a ferocious beast and a slave, and has gradually humanized and emancipated himself only in society, which is necessarily anterior to the birth of his thought, his speech, and his will. He can achieve this emancipation only through the collective effort of all the members, past and present, of society, which is the source, the natural beginning of his human existence.

Man completely realizes his individual freedom as well as his personality only through the individuals who surround him, and thanks only to the labor and the collective power of society. Without society he would surely remain the most stupid and the most miserable among all the other ferocious beasts. . . . Society, far from decreasing his freedom, on the contrary creates the individual freedom of all human beings. Society is the root, the tree, and liberty is its fruit. Hence, in every epoch, man must seek his freedom not at the beginning but at the end of history. It can be said that the real and complete emancipation of every individual is the true, the great, the supreme aim of history. . . .

The materialistic, realistic, and collectivist conception of freedom, as opposed to the idealistic, is this: Man becomes conscious of himself and his humanity only in society and only by the collective action of the whole society. He frees himself from the yoke of external nature only by collective and social labor, which alone can transform the earth into an abode favorable to the development of humanity. Without such material emancipation the intellectual and moral emancipation of the individual is impossible. He can emancipate himself from the yoke of his own nature, i.e., subordinate his instincts and the movements of his body to the conscious direction of his mind, the development of which is fostered only by education and training. But education and training are preeminently and exclusively social . . . hence the isolated individual cannot possibly become conscious of his freedom.

To be free . . . means to be acknowledged and treated as such by all his fellowmen. The liberty of every individual is only the reflection of his own humanity, or his human right through the conscience of all free men, his brothers and his equals.

I can feel free only in the presence of and in relationship with other men. In the presence of an inferior species of animal I am neither free nor a man, because this animal is incapable of conceiving and consequently recognizing my humanity. I am not myself free or human until or unless I recognize the freedom and humanity of all my fellowmen.

Only in respecting their human character do I respect my own. A cannibal who devours his prisoner . . . is not a man but a beast. A slave owner is not a man but a master. By denying the humanity of his slaves he also abrogates his own humanity, as the history of all ancient societies proves. The Greeks and the Romans did not feel like free men. They did not consider themselves as such by human right. They believed in privileges for Greeks and Romans and only for their own countries, while they remained unconquered and conquered other countries. Because they believed themselves under the special protection of their national gods, they did not feel that they had the right to revolt . . . and themselves fell into slavery. . . .

I am truly free only when all human beings, men and women, are equally free. The freedom of other men, far from negating or limiting my freedom, is, on the contrary, its necessary premise and confirmation. It is the slavery of other men that sets up a barrier to my freedom, or what amounts to the same thing, it is their bestiality which is the negation of my humanity. For my dignity as a man, my human right which consists of refusing to obey any other man, and to determine my own acts in conformity with my convictions is reflected by the equally free conscience of all and confirmed by the consent of all humanity. My personal freedom, confirmed by the liberty of all, extends to infinity.

The materialistic conception of freedom is therefore a very positive, very complex thing, and above all, eminently social, because it can be realized only in society and by the strictest equality and solidarity among all men. One can distinguish the main elements in the attainment of freedom. The first is eminently social. It is the fullest development of all the faculties and powers of every human being, by education, by scientific training, and by material prosperity; things which can only be provided for every individual by the collective, material, intellectual, manual, and sedentary labor of society in general.

The second element of freedom is negative. It is the revolt of the individual against all divine, collective, and individual authority.

The first revolt is against the supreme tyranny of theology, of the phantom of God. As long as we have a master in heaven, we will be slaves on earth. Our reason and our will will be equally annulled. As long as we believe that we must unconditionally obey—and vis-à-vis God, no other obedience is possible— we must of necessity passively submit, without the least reservation, to the holy authority of his consecrated and unconsecrated agents, messiahs, prophets, divinely inspired lawmakers, emperors, kings, and all their functionaries and ministers, representatives and consecrated servitors of the two greatest institutions which impose themselves upon us, and which are established by God himself to rule over men; namely, the Church and the State. All temporal or human authority stems directly from spiritual and/or divine authority. But authority is the negation of freedom. God, or rather the fiction of God, is the consecration and the intellectual and moral source of all slavery on earth, and the freedom of mankind will never be complete until the disastrous and insidious fiction of a heavenly master is annihilated.

This is naturally followed by the revolt against the tyranny of men, individual as well as social, represented and legalized by the State. At this point, we must make a very precise distinction between the official and consequently dictatorial prerogatives of society organized as a state, and of the natural influence and action of the members of a nonofficial, nonartificial society.

The revolt against this natural society is far more difficult for the individual than it is against the officially organized society of the State. Social tyranny, often overwhelming and baneful, does not assume the violent imperative character of the legalized and formalized despotism which marks the authority of the State. It is not imposed in the form of laws to which every individual, on pain of judicial punishment, is forced to submit. The action of social tyranny is gentler, more insidious, more imperceptible, but no less powerful and pervasive than is the authority of the State. It dominates men by customs, by mores, by the mass of prejudices, by the habits of daily life, all of which combine to form what is called public opinion.

It overwhelms the individual from birth. It permeates every facet of life, so that each individual is, often unknowingly, in a sort of conspiracy against himself. It follows from this that to revolt against this influence that society naturally exercises over him, he must at least to some extent revolt against himself. For, together with all his natural tendencies and material, intellectual, and moral aspirations, he is himself nothing but the product of society, and it is in this that the immense power exercised by society over the individual lies.

From the angle of absolute morality, i.e., of human respect, this power of society can be beneficent and it can also be injurious. It is beneficial when it tends to the development of science, of material prosperity, of freedom, equality, and solidarity. It is baneful when it tends in the opposite direction. A man born into a society of brutes tends to remain a brute; born into a society ruled by priests, he becomes an idiot, a sanctimonious hypocrite; born into a band of thieves, he will probably become a thief; and if he is unfortunately born into a society of demigods who rule this earth, nobles, princes, he will become a contemptible enslaver of society, a tyrant. In all these cases, revolt against the society in which he was born is indispensable for the humanization of the individual.

But, I repeat, the revolt of the individual against society is much more difficult than revolt against the State. The State is a transitory, historic institution, like its brother institution, the Church, the regulator of the privileges of a minority and the real enslavers of the immense majority.

Revolt against the State is much less difficult because there is something in the very nature of the State that provokes revolt. The State is *authority, force*. It is the ostentation and infatuation with force. It does not insinuate itself. It does not seek to convert; and if at times it meliorates its tyranny, it does so with bad grace. For its nature is not to persuade, but to impose itself by force. Whatever pains it takes to mask itself, it is by nature the legal violator of the will of men, the permanent negator of their freedom. Even when the State commands the good it brings forth evil; for every command slaps liberty in the face; because when the good is decreed, it becomes evil from the standpoint of human morality and liberty. Freedom, morality, and the human dignity of the individual consists precisely in this; that he does good not because he is forced to do so, but because he freely conceives it, wants it, and loves it.

The authority of society is imposed not arbitrarily or officially, but naturally. And it is because of this fact that its effect on the individual is incomparably much more powerful than that of the State. It creates and molds all individuals in its midst. It passes on to them, slowly, from the day of birth to death, all its material, intellectual, and moral characteristics. Society, so to speak, individualizes itself in every individual.

The real individual is from the moment of his gestation in his mother's womb already predetermined and particularized by a confluence of geographic, climatic, ethnographic, hygienic, and economic influences, which constitute the nature of his family, his class, his nation, his race. He is shaped in accordance with his aptitudes by the combination of all these exterior and physical influences. What is more, thanks to the relatively superior organization of the human brain, every individual inherits at birth, in different degrees, not ideas and innate sentiments, as the idealists claim, but only the capacity to feel, to will, to think, and to speak. There are rudimentary faculties without any content. Whence comes their content? From society . . . impressions, facts, and events coalesced into patterns of thought, right or wrong, are transmitted from one individual to another. These are modified, expanded, mutually complimented and integrated by all the individual members and groups of society into a unique system, which finally constitutes the common consciousness, the collective thought of a society. All this, transmitted by tradition from one generation to another, developed and enlarged by the intellectual labors of centuries, constitutes the intellectual and moral patrimony of a nation, a class, and a society. . . .

Every new generation upon reaching the age of mature thought finds in itself and in society the established ideas and conceptions which serve it as the point of departure, giving it, as it were, the raw material for its own intellectual and moral labor. . . . These are the conceptions of nature, of man, of justice, of the duties and rights of individuals and classes, of social conventions, of the family, of property, and of the State, and many other factors affecting the relations between men. All these ideas are imprinted upon the mind of the individual, and conditioned by the education and training he receives even before he becomes fully aware of himself as an entity. Much later, he rediscovers them, consecrated and explained, elaborated by theory, which expresses the universal conscience or the collective prejudices of the religious, political, and economic institutions of the society to which he belongs. He is himself so imbued with these prejudices that he is, involuntarily, by virtue of all his intellectual and moral habits, the upholder of these iniquities, even if he were not personally interested in defending them.

It is certainly not surprising that the ideas passed on by the collective mind of society should have so great a hold upon the masses of people. What is surprising, on the contrary, is that there are among these masses individuals who have the ideas, the will, and the courage to go against the stream of conformity. For the pressure of society on the individual is so great that there is no character so strong, nor an intelligence so powerful as to be entirely immune to this despotic and irresistible influence. . . .

Nothing demonstrates the social nature of man better than this influence. It can be said that the collective conscience of any society whatever, embodied in the great public institutions, in all the details of private life, serves as the base of all its theories. It constitutes a sort of intellectual and moral atmosphere: harmful though it may be, yet absolutely necessary to the existence of all its members, whom it dominates while sustaining them, and reinforcing the banality, the routine, which binds together the great majority of the masses.

The greatest number of men, and not only the masses of people but the privileged and enlightened classes even more, feel ill at ease unless they faithfully conform and follow tradition and routine in all the acts of their lives. They reason that "Our father thought and acted in this way, so we must think and do the same. Everybody else thinks and acts this way. Why should we think and act otherwise?"

1871

———◆———

The Program of the Alliance

The overall theme of The Program of the Alliance[15] is the relationship between the conscious revolutionary vanguard, Bakunin's Alliance, and the working masses in and out of the International whom it is trying to influence in a revolutionary direction. How to organize the unorganized and how to radicalize them when they are organized is the main theme, though Bakunin digresses to other matters not strictly related to it. Since the text deals with different subjects, it has for the sake of clarity been divided into three sections (our subtitles).

The Program of the Alliance opens with a discussion of union bureaucracy, a description of how the executive committees elected by the sections of rank-and-file local unions tend to become transformed from being the intended agents to the masters of the membership. He stresses that no organization, however free, can long withstand the lethargy and indifference of the membership without degenerating into some form of dictatorship—a warning all too relevant in our own time.

Bakunin's "Fabrica sections" were composed of native citizens, the highly skilled, better-paid watchmakers and jewelry workers, most of whom favored parliamentary action and class collaboration. The construction and other heavy manual workers, mostly unskilled, low-paid foreigners, favored direct economic action. Not being allowed to vote, they were naturally not interested in parliamentary action. Their disenfranchisement, and the indignities they suffered, often on the part of the snobbish

Fabrica workers, engaged the support of Bakunin and the Swiss libertarian sections of the International.

The second section deals with the internal organization of the International. The so-called central sections referred to are the ideological-activist vanguard groups animating the organization of the masses. In discussing the connection between this revolutionary minority and the general membership of the International, Bakunin deals with the structure and the internal problems of the International and its ultimate objectives. The vast mass of the workers were quite unorganized and only a tiny fraction of the organized minority were affiliated with the International. The organization was to a considerable extent infiltrated by bourgeois-minded elements who advocated class-collaboration, and by Marxist and other authoritarian socialists. How to surmount these difficulties and forge the International into a massive revolutionary labor movement capable of spearheading and carrying through the Social Revolution was the question.

In the third section here, Bakunin anticipates the objection that his recommendations would make the International a miniature replica of the State. As so often elsewhere, Bakunin stresses the need for an organized revolutionary minority to guard against the usurpation of power. He insists that such a minority is not the same as the governing oligarchy of the State, and defines the essential differences between libertarian organization and state organization. Transcending the labor question as such, he goes on into a fruitful digression on the relationship of the individual to society and the nature of society and the State.

Centralization and decentralization, the monopoly of power and the diffusion of power among the many units of society and the individuals who compose it, is more than a recurrent theme in all anarchist literature: it underlies the deepest problems of our times.

Union Bureaucracy

Having convinced themselves that what they would like their sections to do is what the membership actually wants, the committees make decisions for them without even bothering to consult them. This illusion is bound to have unfortunate effects, particularly on the social morality of the leaders themselves. The leaders regard themselves as the absolute masters of their constituents, as permanent chiefs, whose power is sanctioned by their services as well as the length of their tenure in office.

Even the best of men are rendered corruptible by the temptations of power and the absence of a serious, consistent opposition. In the International there can be no mercenary corruption, for the association is too poor to pay high, or even adequate, salaries to its officials. . . . But the International is unfortunately subject to corruption by another kind of temptation: *vanity and ambition.*

. . . If there is a devil in human history, that devil is the principle of command. It alone, sustained by the ignorance and stupidity of the masses, without which it could not exist, is the source of all the catastrophes, all the crimes, and all the infamies of history.

Everyone, even the best of men, carries within himself the germs of this accursed affliction and every germ must necessarily quicken and grow if it finds even the slightest favorable conditions. In human society these conditions are the stupidity, the ignorance, and the servile habits of the masses. It can well be said that the masses themselves create their own exploiters, their own despots, their own executioners of humanity. When they are quiescent and patiently endure their humiliation and slavery, the best men emerging from their ranks—the most intelligent, the most energetic, the very men who in better circumstances could render great services to humanity—become despots even while deluding themselves that they are actually working for the benefit of their victims. By contrast, in an intelligent and alert society, jealous of its liberties and ready to defend its rights, even the most malevolent, the most egotistic individuals, necessarily become good. Such is the power of society, a thousand times stronger than the strongest individual.

It is thus clear that the absence of opposition and control and of continuous vigilance inevitably becomes a source of depravity for all individuals vested with social power. And those among them who cherish and would safeguard their personal morality should, in the first place, not stay too long in power, and in the second place, while still in power encourage this vigilant and salutary opposition.

This is what the committees of Geneva (doubtless unaware of this threat to their personal morality) generally failed to do. Through self-sacrifice, initiative, and ability, they attained leadership, and by a species of self-hallucination, almost inevitable in all those holding office too long, they ended by imagining themselves indispensable. This is how a sort of governmental aristocracy was imperceptibly nurtured in the very heart of sections so democratic as the construction workers. . . . With the growing authority of the committees, the workers become increasingly indifferent to all matters except strikes and the payment of dues, which are collected with great difficulty. . . .

The construction workers' section simply left all decision-making to their committees. "We have elected a committee. The committee will decide." This is what they told anyone who tried to get their opinion on any subject. Soon they never had any opinion at all—like blank sheets of paper on which the committees could write whatever they wanted. As long as the committees did not ask for too much money and did not press the workers too hard to pay back dues, the committee could do almost anything with impunity. This is very good for the committees, but not at all favorable for the social, intellectual, and moral progress of the collective power of the International. In this manner power gravitated to the committees, and by a species of fiction characteristic of all governments the committees substituted their own will and their own ideas for that of the membership. They represented only themselves. Such power, based on the ignorance and indifference of the workers, is its inevitable and detestable consequence. Once introduced into the internal organization of the International, it prepares the ground for the spawning of all sorts of intrigues, vanities, ambitions, and personal interests. It is a fine way to inspire a puerile self-satisfaction and a sense of security as ridiculous as it is baneful for the proletariat; and sure, also, to frighten the timid souls among the bourgeoisie. But it is not a potent force. It will in no way promote the life-and-death struggle that the European proletariat must now wage against the all-too-real world of the bourgeoisie.

This indifference to general problems manifesting itself more and more every day, this lassitude which leaves all problems to the decision of committees, and the habit of automatic sub-ordination which is its natural consequence, infects not only the sections but also the committees themselves. Most of the committee members become the unthinking instruments of three or two, or even just one of their colleagues. Some are more intelligent and aggressive than the others. Thus a majority of the sections as well as their committees are in fact ruled by oligarchs or individuals who mask their absolute power even in organizations which have constitutions and procedures as safeguards. . . . In solidly organized sections like the Fabrica sections (whatever their other shortcomings) where there is real autonomy, they have been able to drastically curtail the arbitrary power of the Geneva Central Committee (representing all the local unions in the Geneva branch of the International) . . . even though they nevertheless exert a predominant influence—and this, for many reasons: first, that the Geneva workers are much better informed, have much more political understanding, and are far more articulate than the construction workers; second, that the Fabrica sections always delegated to the Central Committee their most intelligent and capable workers in whom they had full confidence; delegates who conscientiously fulfilled all their obligations to their respective sections as stipulated in the statutes; reporting regularly to the membership the proposals made and how they voted; asking for further instructions (plus instant recall of unsatisfactory delegates). . . .

Among the construction workers these conditions did not obtain, and where revolt against the tyranny was squelched before it could be effectively organized, the sections could defend their rights and their autonomy in only one way: the workers called general membership meetings. Nothing arouses the antipathy of the committees more than these popular assemblies, which the committees always try to counteract by staging *assemblies of all the committees of the sections*. . . .

In these great meetings of the sections, the items on the agenda were amply discussed and the most progressive opinion prevailed. Most of the time, when the spirit of the masses was not corrupted by the skillful and slanderous propaganda of the committees, these assemblies were inspired by a sort of collective instinct propelling the people irresistibly toward truth and justice. Even the most recalcitrant were swept into the current of generous sentiment. The mighty ones, the connivers who maneuvered the workers in secret meetings, lost their cocksure smugness when challenged by these assemblies, where popular good sense . . . made naught of their sophisms. In these assemblies of all the sections, great numbers of previously passive workers, caught up in the general camaraderie, repudiated their leaders and voted against their resolutions. . . .

The Structure of the
International

The rise of modern industry sparked the founding of the International in 1864 in almost all European countries, particularly in highly industrialized England, France, Germany, Switzerland, and Belgium. Two factors brought about the creation of the International. The first was the simultaneous awakening of the spirit, courage, and consciousness of the workers in these countries which followed the catastrophic defeat of the 1848 and 1851 uprisings. The second factor was the phenomenal enrichment of the bourgeoisie and the concomitant poverty of the workers. But, as is often the case, this renascent faith did not at once manifest itself among the proletarian masses. The first feeble, widely scattered associations were pioneered by a few of the most intelligent, educated militants—most of them tempered in the crucible of past struggles, It was they who, upon returning from the founding conference of the International in London, organized the first central sections of the International in their respective countries.

The central sections represent no specific industry, but comprise the most advanced workers from all the industries. What do these sections represent? The idea behind the International. What is its mission? The elaboration and propagandizing of this idea. What is this idea? It is the full emancipation of all those

who eke out their miserable sustenance by any form of productive labor, who are economically exploited and politically oppressed by the capitalists and their privileged intermediaries.
Such is the negative, combative, or revolutionary force of this
idea. And what is the positive force? It is the founding of a new
social order resting on emancipated labor, one which will spontaneously erect upon the ruins of the Old World the free federation of workers' associations. These two aspects of the same
question are inseparable.

For no one can destroy without having at least a remote conception, true or false, of the new order of things which should
replace the existing one. The more fantastic the conception, the
more ruthless must be the destructive force. The more this concept approximates reality and conforms to the necessary, creative
development of existing society, the more useful and salutary
will be the effects of this destructive action. Destructive action
is always determined not only by its purpose and its intensity but
also by the means employed. It is conditioned by the constructive
ideal from which it draws its initial inspiration, which constitutes its soul.

The central sections are the active nuclei which retain,
develop, and clarify the new faith. No one joins them as a
specialized worker in this or that trade. All join as workers in
general to promote the general organization of labor in all countries. They *are* workers in "general." Workers for what? Workers
for the idea, for propaganda, and for the organization of the
economic and militant might of the International, workers for
the Social Revolution.

If the International Workingmen's Association were composed solely of central sections, it would never have attained
even one hundredth of the power of which it can now be so
proud. The central sections would have been mere debating
societies where all kinds of social questions, including of course
that of workers' organizations, would have been perpetually discussed without the least attempt being made or the slightest
possibility existing of putting these ideas into practice. And this
for the simple reason that "labor in general" is an abstract idea
which is realized only in the immense diversity of specialized

trades and industries. Each industry has its own special problems which cannot be determined by abstract formulas, and which are revealed only through actual development and practice.

The relationship of these industries to labor in general results from the vital combinations of all particular trades and functions, and is not based on an abstract, a priori principle, dogmatically or violently imposed.

If the International had been composed only of the central sections, the latter probably would have succeeded in organizing conspiracies for the overthrow of the existing order but would have been unable to achieve its goal. For it could have attracted only a mere handful of heroic workers while the remaining millions of workers would have remained outside this small circle. And the social order cannot be destroyed without winning the support of these millions. Only a relatively small number of individuals are moved by an abstract idea. The millions, the proletarian masses (and this is true also for the privileged classes) are moved only by the force of facts . . . by their immediate interests and their momentary passions.

In order to interest and involve the whole proletariat in the work of the International, it is necessary to approach them not with vague generalizations but with realistic understanding of their daily concerns. To win the confidence of uninformed workers, and the vast majority of the proletariat are unfortunately in this group, it is necessary to begin by talking to the worker, not of the general troubles of the proletariat of the world, nor the general causes responsible for them, but only of his own trade and the working conditions in his own locality, his working hours, the cost of living, and to suggest practical measures to alleviate these evils and better his conditions. It would be a mistake to speak to him first about things like the abolition of hereditary property, the abolition of the juridical rights of the State, and the replacement of the State by the free federation of producers' associations. He probably will not understand these theories. No! Propose in simple language such ideas as will appeal to his good sense and which he can verify by his daily experiences. These measures are: the establishment of complete solidarity with his workmates in order to defend his rights and resist the aggression of the employer. Next, the extension of this solidarity from·his place of work to embrace the trades in his own locality, i.e., his formal entry as an active member in the section of his trade or profession, a section affiliated with the International Workingmen's Association.

Having joined his section of the International, the newly enlisted worker learns many things. He learns that the same solidarity that exists within his section is also established among all the different sections and trades in the whole area; that this wider solidarity has become necessary because all the employers in all the industries have established a united front to cut wages and drive down the living standards of the workers. He will learn later that this solidarity is not confined to his area but extends much further, beyond all frontiers, and embraces the workers of the world, powerfully organized for their defense, for waging war against exploitation by the bourgeoisie.

A worker does not need much intellectual preparation to become a member of a trade union section which is affiliated to the International. He is already, unconsciously and in a perfectly natural manner, conditioned to become one. All he has to know is that hard work is wearing him down, that his wages are barely enough to provide for his family, that his employer is a ruthless exploiter whom he detests with all the hatred of the slave rebelling against his master. This feeling will, when the final struggle has been won, give place to a feeling of justice and goodwill toward his former employer, as is befitting one who is now among the fraternity of free men.

The worker easily understands that he cannot possibly fight alone. To defend his rights he must unite with his fellow workers in his place of work, and pledge his solidarity in the common struggle. He learns that a union in one shop is not enough, and that it is necessary for all workers in the same trade and in the same locality to join forces. Even the least informed workers will, as a result of their shared experience, soon realize that solidarity must transcend narrow local limits.

The workers in the same trade and locality declare a strike for shorter hours and more pay. The boss imports strikebreakers from other places in and even outside the country who will work for less pay and longer hours. To compete with foreign producers who can sell their goods more cheaply because of lower working costs, employers are forced to reduce wages and lengthen working hours. Better working conditions in one country can be maintained only if the conditions in all other countries are comparable. Repeated experience eventually teaches even the most simple-minded workers that it is not enough to be organized locally, and that the workers in the same trade must be unionized not only in one region or in one country, but in all countries. . . .

If only a single trade is internationally organized, while other trades remain unorganized . . . the employer making less money in the unionized enterprises will gradually transfer his capital to the more sparsely organized and even altogether nonunion shops and industries. This situation creates unemployment in organized trades and compels the workers either to starve or to accept lower wages and increased hours. Conditions in any particular trade or industry will sooner or later affect the workers in all other branches of production. These factors demonstrate to the workers in all occupations in all lands that they are unbreakably linked by ties of economic solidarity and fraternal sentiment. . . .

The International Workingmen's Association did not spring ready-made out of the minds of a few erudite theoreticians. It developed out of actual economic necessity, out of the bitter tribulations the workers were forced to endure and the natural impact of these trials upon the minds of the toilers. For the International to come into being, it was necessary that the elements which went into its making—the economic factors, the experiences and aspirations and attitude of the proletariat—should have already provided a solid base for it. It was necessary that all over the world there should be pioneering groups or associations of advanced workers who were willing to initiate this great workers' movement of self-emancipation. . . . It is not enough that the workers can free themselves by way of international solidarity. It is also necessary that they have confidence in the effectiveness of this solidarity and in their coming deliverance. In the workers' world this economic solidarity is also expressed emotionally by a deep passionate sentiment. As the political and social consequences of the economic oppression are felt by the proletariat in all trades and lands, this sentiment of emotional solidarity grows ever more intense.

The new member learns more from his own personal experience than he does from the verbal explanation of his fellow workers, explanations that are confirmed by his own experience and the experiences of all the members of his section. The workers of his trade, no longer willing to put up with the greed of their bosses, declare a strike. For a worker living only on his meager wages, every strike is a misfortune. His earnings stop and he has no savings. . . . The strike fund of his union, built up with great difficulty, cannot sustain a strike lasting many days or even weeks. The strikers must either starve or give in to the harsh conditions imposed by their insolent employers, if help does not come quickly.

But who will offer to help the strikers? Help can come only from workers in other trades and other countries. Lo and behold! Help arrives. The International sends out a call for help, and local as well as foreign sections respond. . . . This experience, renewed many times, demonstrates to the worker more powerfully than words the blessings of the international solidarity of labor.

To share in the advantages of this solidarity, the worker is not asked about his political or religious beliefs. He is asked only one question: with the benefits, will you also accept the sometimes inconvenient obligations of membership? Will you practice *economic solidarity in the widest sense of the word*?

But once this solidarity is seriously and firmly established, it produces all the rest, all the sublime and the most subversive principles of the International which becomes the most ruthless enemy of religion, of the juridical rights of the State, of authority, divine as well as human—from the socialist point of view, the natural result of this economic solidarity. And the immense practical advantage of the trade sections over the central sections consists precisely in this: that these developments, these principles, are demonstrated to the workers not by theoretical reasoning, but by the living and tragic experience of a struggle which becomes each day more profound and more terrible. The least educated worker, the least prepared, driven by the very conse-

quences of this struggle, ends by recognizing himself as a revolutionist, an anarchist, and an atheist, without in the least
knowing how he became such.

It is clear that only the trade union sections can give a practical education to their members and that this alone can lead to
the organization of the proletarian masses into the International,
without whose powerful participation the Social Revolution will
never be realized. If the International, I repeat, consisted only of
central sections, they would be souls without a body, magnificent
unrealizable dreams. . . .

Fortunately, the central sections . . . were founded, not by
bourgeois, not by professional scholars, nor by politicians, but by
socialist workers [as against the bourgeois youth]. The socialist
workers had a highly positive and practical [approach to the
organization of the workers]. . . . This fortunate circumstance
enabled them to avoid the two pitfalls which wrecked all bourgeois revolutionary attempts: empty academic wrangling and
platonic conspiracies. They could not wait for the masses. They
had to induce the various trades already organized [but not in
the International] . . . to affiliate with the general organization
[the International] while still retaining their autonomy. . . . And
they succeeded in organizing around every central section as
many trade union sections as there were different industries. [The
central sections also induced unorganized workers to join the
International as members-at-large.]

The immense task to which the International Workingmen's
Association has dedicated itself is not only economic or purely
material. It has, at the same time and in the highest degree, a
social, philosophic, and moral objective. . . . Far from dissolving,
the central sections must pursue this objective and continue to
spread the new social philosophy, theoretically inspired by real
science—experimental and rational—based on humanistic principles in harmony with the eternal instincts of equality, liberty,
and social solidarity.

Social science as a moral doctrine is the development and the
formulation of these instincts. Between these instincts and this
science there is a gap which must be bridged. For if instinct alone
had been sufficient for the liberation of peoples, they would

have long since freed themselves. These instincts did not prevent the masses from accepting, in the melancholy and tragic course of their history, all the religious, political, economic, and social absurdities of which they have been the eternal victims. The masses are a force, or at least the essential elements of a force. What do they lack? They lack two things which up till now constituted the power of all government: organization and knowledge.

The organization of the International, having for its objective not the creation of new despotisms but the uprooting of all domination, will take on an essentially different character from the organization of the State. Just as the State is authoritarian, artificial, violent, foreign, and hostile to the natural development of the popular instincts, so must the organization of the International conform in all respects to these instincts and these interests. But what is the organization of the masses? It is an organization based on the various functions of daily life and of the different kinds of labor. It is the organization by professions and trades. Once all the different industries are represented in the International, including the cultivation of the land, its organization, the organization of the mass of the people, will have been achieved.

The organization of the trade sections and their representation in the Chambers of Labor creates a great academy in which all the workers can and must study economic science; these sections also bear in themselves the living seeds of the new society which is to replace the old world. They are creating not only the ideas, but also the facts of the future itself.[16]

*The Structure of the State
Contrasted with That of the International*

When the International has organized a half, a third, or even a tenth of the European proletariat, states will have ceased to exist. . . . For if even one worker out of ten joins the International seriously and with full knowledge of the cause, the rest would come under its pervasive influence, and in the first crisis all would follow the International in working to achieve the emancipation of the proletariat.

Could such a mobilization of the International's influence over the masses lead to a new system of state domination? No, for the essential difference between the organized action of the International and the action of all states, is that the International is not vested with any official authority or political power whatever. It will always be the natural organization of action, of a greater or lesser number of individuals, inspired and united by the general aim of influencing [by example] the opinion, the will, and the action of the masses. Governments, by contrast, impose themselves upon the masses and force them to obey their decrees, without for the most part taking into consideration their feelings, their needs, and their will. There exists between the power of the State and that of the International the same difference that exists between the official power of the State and the natural activity of a club. The International is not and never will be anything but the organization of the unforced action of individuals upon the masses. The opposite is true of the State and all its institutions: church, university, law courts, bureaucracy, taxation, police, and military . . . all corrupt the minds and will of its subjects and demand their passive obedience. . . .

The State is the organized authority, domination, and power of the possessing classes over the masses . . . the International wants only their complete freedom, and calls for their revolt. But in order that this rebellion be powerful and capable enough to overthrow the domination of the State and the privileged classes, the International has to organize itself. To attain its objective, it employs only two means, which, if not always legal, are completely legitimate from the standpoint of human rights. These two means are the dissemination of the ideas of the International and the natural influence of its members over the masses.

Whoever contends that such action, being a move to create a new authoritarian power, threatens the freedom of the masses must be a sophist or a fool. All social life is nothing but the incessant mutual interdependence of individuals and of masses. All individuals, even the strongest and the most intelligent, are at every moment of their lives both the producers and the products of the will and action of the masses.

The freedom of each individual is the ever-renewing result of numerous material, intellectual, and moral influences of the surrounding individuals and of the society into which he is born, and in which he grows up and dies. To wish to escape this influence in the name of a transcendental, divine, absolutely self-sufficient freedom is to condemn oneself to nonexistence; to forgo the exercise of this freedom upon others is to renounce all social action and all expression of one's thoughts and sentiments, and to end in nothingness. Such absolute independence and such a freedom, the brainchild of idealists and metaphysicians, is a wild absurdity.

In human society, as in nature, every being lives only by the supreme principle of the most positive intervention in the existence of every other being. The character and extent of this intervention depend upon the nature of the individual. To abolish this mutual intervention would mean death. And when we demand the freedom of the masses, we do not even dream of obliterating any of the natural influences that any individual or group of individuals exercise upon each other. We want only the abolition of artificial, privileged, legal, and official impositions. If the Church and the State were private institutions, we would, no doubt, be against them, but we would not contest their right to exist. We fight them because they are organized to exploit the collective power of the masses by official and violent superimposition. If the International were to became a State we, its most zealous champions, would become its most implacable enemies.

But the point is precisely that the International cannot organize itself into a State. It cannot do so because the International, as its name implies, means the abolition of all frontiers, and there can be no State without frontiers, without sovereignty. The universal State, the dream of the greatest despots in the world, has been proven by history to be unrealizable. The universal State, or the *People's State*, of which the German Communists dream, can therefore signify only one thing: *the destruction of the State*.

The International Workingmen's Association would be totally devoid of meaning if it did not aim at the abolition of the State. It organizes the masses only to facilitate the destruction of the State. And how does it organize them? Not from the top down, not by constricting the manifold functions of society which reflect the diversity of labor, not by forcing the natural life of the masses into the straitjacket of the State, not by imposing upon them a fictitious unity. On the contrary, it organizes them from the bottom up, beginning with the social life of the masses and their real aspirations, and inducing them to group, harmonize, and balance their forces in accordance with the natural diversity of their occupations and circumstances. . . . This is the true function of the trade union section.

We have already said that in order to organize the masses and with them solidly to establish the influence of the International, it would be sufficient, strictly speaking, that one out of ten workers should join. . . . In moments of great political or economic crisis, when the rebellious instincts of the masses boil over, at a time when these herds of human slaves . . . rise up at last to throw off their yoke, they find themselves bewildered, powerless because they are completely unorganized. They are in the mood to listen to all worthwhile suggestions; ten, twenty, or thirty well-organized militants, acting together, knowing what they want and how to get it, can easily rally several hundred courageous activists. We saw an example of this during the Paris Commune [1871]. A serious organization coming to life only during the siege, nowhere near as strong as the situation demanded, was, despite these drawbacks, able to constitute a formidable power with a vast resistance potential.

What will happen when the International is better organized, when a great many more sections—above all, agricultural sections—are enrolled in its ranks, when each section triples its membership? What will happen when each and every member knows better than he does now the ultimate objectives and true principles of the International, as well as the means to insure its triumph? The International will have become an invincible power.

1871

——— • ———

The Paris Commune and
the Idea of the State

"The Paris Commune and the Idea of the State"[17] is Bakunin's preamble to the second part of his major work The Knouto-Germanic Empire and the Social Revolution. The Paris Commune of 1871 is a landmark in the history of the socialist movement, a standard by which all socialist theory is evaluated, a climactic event whose significance is still being debated. Karl Marx, in Civil War in France, and V. I. Lenin, in State and Revolution, hailed it as the model for the proletarian revolution. But while the Marxists and Blanquists cited it as proof of their theories, the anarchists maintained that the Paris Commune demonstrated the bankruptcy of authoritarian socialism and the validity of their own approach. As James Guillaume observed,

> This [Civil War in France] is a surprising declaration of principles wherein Marx seems to have abandoned his own program and gone over to the side of the federalists [now known as the anarchists]. Was this a sincere conversion on the part of the author of Capital, or a temporary maneuver dictated by events—an apparent adhesion to the Commune to benefit from the prestige attached to its name?

Arthur Müller Lehning, the editor of the massive edition of the Archives of Bakunin now being issued in the Netherlands, states that

It is an irony of history that at the very moment when the battle between the authoritarians and the antiauthoritarians in the International reached its apogee, Marx should in effect endorse the program of the antiauthoritarian tendency. . . . The Commune of Paris had nothing in common with the state socialism of Marx and was more in accord with the ideas of Proudhon and the federalist theories of Bakunin. *Civil War in France* is in full contradiction with all Marx's writings on the question of the State.[18]

Marx's admirer and official biographer, Franz Mehring, agrees:

. . . The opinions of the *Communist Manifesto* could not be reconciled with the praise lavished by [*Civil War in France*] for the vigorous fashion in which it began to exterminate the parasitic State. . . . Both Marx and Engels were well aware of the contradiction, and in a preface to a new edition of the *Communist Manifesto* issued in June 1872, they revised their opinions. . . . After the death of Marx, Engels in fighting the Anarchists once again took his stand on the original basis of the *Manifesto*. . . . if an insurrection was able to abolish the whole oppressive machinery of the State by a few simple decrees, was not that a confirmation of Bakunin's steadfastly maintained standpoint?[19]

Bakunin did not unreservedly praise everything done by the Commune, and did not hesitate to point out some of its major mistakes, but in contrast to some of his colleagues, he made allowances for its shortcomings.

From discussing the Commune, Bakunin turns to "the notion of the State" and outlines a stateless social order that would "affirm and reconcile the interests of individuals and society"—a harmony actively prevented by the State which sacrifices the many to the few. He discusses the connection between church and state, those twin evils institutionalizing the "lust for power," and his comments upon the nature of man, society, order, the State, religious belief, and the concept of freedom add up to an outline of his main themes.

THIS work, like all my published work, of which there has not been a great deal, is an outgrowth of events. It is the natural continuation of my *Letters to a Frenchman* (September 1870), wherein I had the easy but painful distinction of foreseeing and foretelling the dire calamities which now beset France and the whole civilized world, the only cure for which is the Social Revolution.

My purpose now is to prove the need for such a revolution. I shall review the historical development of society and what is now taking place in Europe, right before our eyes. Thus all those who sincerely thirst for truth can accept it and proclaim openly and unequivocally the philosophical principles and practical aims which are at the very core of what we call the Social Revolution.

I know my self-imposed task is not a simple one. I might be called presumptuous had I any personal motives in undertaking it. Let me assure my reader, I have none. I am not a scholar or a philosopher, not even a professional writer. I have not done much writing in my life and have never written except, so to speak, in self-defense, and only when a passionate conviction forced me to overcome my instinctive dislike for any public exhibition of myself.

Well, then, who am I, and what is it that prompts me to publish this work at this time? I am an impassioned seeker of the truth, and as bitter an enemy of the vicious fictions used by the established order—an order which has profited from all the religious, metaphysical, political, juridical, economic, and social infamies of all times—to brutalize and enslave the world. I am a fanatical lover of liberty. I consider it the only environment in which human intelligence, dignity, and happiness can thrive and develop. I do not mean that formal liberty which is dispensed, measured out, and regulated by the State; for this is a perennial lie and represents nothing but the privilege of a few, based upon the servitude of the remainder. Nor do I mean that individualist, egoist, base, and fraudulent liberty extolled by the school of Jean Jacques Rousseau and every other school of bourgeois liberalism, which considers the rights of all, represented by the State, as a limit for the rights of each; it always, necessarily, ends up by reducing the rights of individuals to zero. No, I mean the only liberty worthy of the name, the liberty which implies the full development of all the material, intellectual, and moral capacities latent in every one of us; the liberty which knows no other restrictions but those set by the laws of our own nature. Consequently there are, properly speaking, no restrictions, since these laws are not imposed upon us by any legislator from outside, alongside, or above ourselves. These laws are subjective, inherent in ourselves; they constitute the very basis of our being. Instead of seeking to curtail them, we should see in them the real condition and the effective cause of our liberty—that liberty of each man which does not find another man's freedom a boundary but a confirmation and vast extension of his own; liberty through solidarity, in equality. I mean liberty triumphant over brute force and, what has always been the real expression of such force, the principle of authority. I mean liberty which will shatter all the idols in heaven and on earth and will then build a new world of mankind in solidarity, upon the ruins of all the churches and all the states.

I am a convinced advocate of economic and social equality because I know that, without it, liberty, justice, human dignity, morality, and the well-being of individuals, as well as the prosperity of nations, will never amount to more than a pack of lies. But since I stand for liberty as the primary condition of mankind, I believe that equality must be established in the world by the spontaneous organization of labor and the collective ownership of property by freely organized producers' associations, and by the equally spontaneous federation of communes, to replace the domineering paternalistic State.

It is at this point that a fundamental division arises between the socialists and revolutionary collectivists on the one hand and the authoritarian communists who support the absolute power of the State on the other. Their ultimate aim is identical. Both equally desire to create a new social order based first on the organization of collective labor, inevitably imposed upon each and all by the natural force of events, under conditions equal for all, and second, upon the collective ownership of the tools of production.

The difference is only that the communists imagine they can attain their goal by the development and organization of the political power of the working classes, and chiefly of the proletariat of the cities, aided by bourgeois radicalism. The revolutionary socialists, on the other hand, believe they can succeed only through the development and organization of the non-political or antipolitical social power of the working classes in city and country, including all men of goodwill from the upper classes who break with their past and wish openly to join them and accept their revolutionary program in full.

This divergence leads to a difference in tactics. The communists believe it necessary to organize the workers' forces in order to seize the political power of the State. The revolutionary socialists organize for the purpose of destroying—or, to put it more politely—liquidating the State. The communists advocate the principle and the practices of authority; the revolutionary socialists put all their faith in liberty. Both equally favor science, which is to eliminate superstition and take the place of religious faith. The former would like to impose science by force; the latter would try to propagate it so that human groups, once convinced, would organize and federalize spontaneously, freely, from the bottom up, of their own accord and true to their own interests, never following a prearranged plan imposed upon "ignorant" masses by a few "superior" minds.

The revolutionary socialists hold that there is a great deal more practical good sense and wisdom in the instinctive aspirations and real needs of the masses than in the profound intelligence of all the doctors and guides of humanity who, after so many failures, still keep on trying to make men happy. The revolutionary socialists, furthermore, believe that mankind has for too long submitted to being governed; that the cause of its troubles does not lie in any particular form of government but in the fundamental principles and the very existence of government, whatever form it may take.

Finally, there is the well-known contradiction between communism as developed scientifically by the German school and accepted in part by the Americans and the English, and Proudhonism, greatly developed and taken to its ultimate conclusion by the proletariat of the Latin countries. Revolutionary socialism has just attempted its first striking and practical demonstration in the Paris Commune.

I am a supporter of the Paris Commune, which, for all the bloodletting it suffered at the hands of monarchical and clerical reaction, has nonetheless grown more enduring and more powerful in the hearts and minds of Europe's proletariat. I am its supporter, above all, because it was a bold, clearly formulated negation of the State.

It is immensely significant that this rebellion against the State has taken place in France, which had been hitherto the land of political centralization par excellence, and that it was precisely Paris, the leader and the fountainhead of the great French civilization, which took the initiative in the Commune. Paris, casting aside her crown and enthusiastically proclaiming her own defeat in order to give life and liberty to France, to Europe, to the entire world; Paris reaffirming her historic power of leadership, showing to all the enslaved peoples (and are there any masses that are not slaves?) the only road to emancipation and health; Paris inflicting a mortal blow upon the political traditions of bourgeois radicalism and giving a real basis to revolutionary socialism against the reactionaries of France and Europe! Paris shrouded in her own ruins, to give the solemn lie to triumphant reaction; saving, by her own disaster, the honor and the future of France, and proving to mankind that if life, intelligence, and moral strength have departed from the upper classes, they have been preserved in their power and promises in the proletariat! Paris inaugurating the new era of the definitive and complete emancipation of the masses and their real solidarity across state frontiers; Paris destroying nationalism and erecting the religion of humanity upon its ruins; Paris proclaiming herself humanitarian and atheist, and replacing divine fictions with the great realities of social life and faith in science, replacing the lies and inequities of the old morality with the principles of liberty, justice, equality, and fraternity, those eternal bases of all human morality! Paris heroic, rational and confident, confirming her strong faith in the destinies of mankind by her own glorious downfall, her death; passing down her faith, in all its power, to the generations to come! Paris, drenched in the blood of her noblest children—this is humanity itself, crucified by the united international reaction of Europe, under the direct inspiration of all the Christian churches and that high priest of iniquity, the

Pope. But the coming international revolution, expressing the solidarity of the peoples, shall be the resurrection of Paris.

This is the true meaning, and these are the immense, beneficent results of two months which encompassed the life and death of the ever memorable Paris Commune.

The Paris Commune lasted too short a time, and its internal development was too hampered by the mortal struggle it had to engage in against the Versailles reaction to allow it at least to formulate, if not apply, its socialist program theoretically. We must realize, too, that the majority of the members of the Commune were not socialists, properly speaking. If they appeared to be, it was because they were drawn in this direction by the irresistible course of events, the nature of the situation, the necessities of their position, rather than through personal conviction. The socialists were a tiny minority—there were, at most, fourteen or fifteen of them; the rest were Jacobins. But, let us make it clear, there are Jacobins and Jacobins. There are Jacobin lawyers and doctrinaires, like Mr. Gambetta; their positivist . . . presumptuous, despotic, and legalistic republicanism had repudiated the old revolutionary faith, leaving nothing of Jacobinism but its cult of unity and authority, and delivered the people of France over to the Prussians, and later still to native-born reactionaries. And there are Jacobins who are frankly revolutionaries, the heroes, the last sincere representatives of the democratic faith of 1793; able to sacrifice both their well-armed unity and authority rather than submit their conscience to the insolence of the reaction. These magnanimous Jacobins led naturally by Delescluze,[20] a great soul and a great character, desire the triumph of the Revolution above everything else; and since there is no revolution without the masses, and since the masses nowadays reveal an instinct for socialism and can only make an economic and social revolution, the Jacobins of good faith, letting themselves be impelled increasingly by the logic of the revolutionary movement, will end up becoming socialists in spite of themselves.

This precisely was the situation in which the Jacobins who participated in the Paris Commune found themselves. Delescluze, and many others with him, signed programs and proclamations whose general import and promise were of a positively socialist nature. However, in spite of their good faith and all their goodwill, they were merely socialists impelled by outward circumstances rather than by an inward conviction; they lacked the time and even the capacity to overcome and subdue many of their own bourgeois prejudices which were contrary to their newly acquired socialism. One can understand that, trapped in this internal struggle, they could never go beyond generalities or take any of those decisive measures that would end their solidarity and all their contacts with the bourgeois world forever.

This was a great misfortune for the Commune and for these men. They were paralyzed, and they paralyzed the Commune. Yet we cannot blame them. Men are not transformed overnight; they do not change their natures or their habits at will. They proved their sincerity by letting themselves be killed for the Commune. Who would dare ask more of them?

They are no more to be blamed than the people of Paris, under whose influence they thought and acted. The people were socialists more by instinct than by reflection. All their aspirations are in the highest degree socialist but their ideas, or rather their traditional expressions, are not. The proletariat of the great cities of France, and even of Paris, still cling to many Jacobin prejudices, and to many dictatorial and governmental concepts. The cult of authority—the fatal result of religious education, that historic source of all evils, deprivations, and servitude—has not yet been completely eradicated in them. This is so true that even the most intelligent children of the people, the most convinced socialists, have not freed themselves completely of these ideas. If you rummage around a bit in their minds, you will find the Jacobin, the advocate of government, cowering in a dark corner, humble but not quite dead.

And, too, the small group of convinced socialists who participated in the Commune were in a very difficult position. While they felt the lack of support from the great masses of the people of Paris, and while the organization of the International Association, itself imperfect, compromised hardly a few thousand persons, they had to keep up a daily struggle against the Jacobin majority. In the midst of the conflict, they had to feed and provide work for several thousand workers, organize and arm them, and keep a sharp lookout for the doings of the reactionaries. All this in an immense city like Paris, besieged, facing the threat of starvation, and a prey to all the shady intrigues of the reaction, which managed to establish itself in Versailles with the permission and by the grace of the Prussians. They had to set up a revolutionary government and army against the government and army of Versailles; in order to fight the monarchist and clerical reaction they were compelled to organize themselves in a Jacobin manner, forgetting or sacrificing the first conditions of revolutionary socialism.

In this confusing situation, it was natural that the Jacobins, the strongest section, constituting the majority of the Commune, who also possessed a highly developed political instinct, the tradition and practice of governmental organization, should have had the upper hand over the socialists. It is a matter of surprise that they did not press their advantage more than they did; that they did not give a fully Jacobin character to the Paris insurrection; that, on the contrary, they let themselves be carried along into a social revolution.

I know that many socialists, very logical in their theory, blame our Paris friends for not having acted sufficiently as socialists in their revolutionary practice. The yelping pack of the bourgeois press, on the other hand, accuse them of having followed their program too faithfully. Let us forget, for a moment, the ignoble denunciations of that press. I want to call the attention of the strictest theoreticians of proletarian emancipation to the fact that they are unjust to our Paris brothers, for between the most correct theories and their practical application lies an enormous distance which cannot be bridged in a few days. Whoever had the pleasure of knowing Varlin,[21] for instance (to name just one man whose death is certain), knows that he and his friends were guided by profound, passionate, and well-considered socialist convictions. These were men whose ardent zeal, devotion, and good faith had never been questioned by those who had known them. Yet, precisely because they were men of good faith, they were filled with self-distrust in the face of the immense task to which they had devoted their minds and their lives; they thought too little of themselves! And they were convinced that in the Social Revolution, diametrically opposite to a political revolution in this as in other ways, individual action was to be almost nil, while the spontaneous action of the masses had to be everything. All that individuals can do is formulate, clarify, and propagate ideas expressing the instinctive desires of the people, and contribute their constant efforts to the revolutionary organization of the natural powers of the masses. This and nothing more; all the rest can be accomplished only by the people themselves. Otherwise we would end up with a political dictatorship—the reconstitution of the State, with all its privileges, inequalities, and oppressions; by taking a devious but inevitable path we would come to reestablish the political, social, and economic slavery of the masses.

Varlin and all his friends, like all sincere socialists, and generally like all workers born and bred among the people, shared this perfectly legitimate feeling of caution toward the continuous activity of one and the same group of individuals and against the domination exerted by superior personalities. And since they were just and fair-minded men above all else, they turned this foresight, this mistrust, against themselves as much as against other persons.

Contrary to the belief of authoritarian communists—which I deem completely wrong—that a social revolution must be decreed and organized either by a dictatorship or by a constituent assembly emerging from a political revolution, our friends, the Paris socialists, believed that revolution could neither be made nor brought to its full development except by the spontaneous and continued action of the masses, the groups and the associations of the people.

Our Paris friends were right a thousand times over. In fact, where is the mind, brilliant as it may be, or—if we speak of a collective dictatorship, even if it were formed of several hundred individuals endowed with superior mentalities—where are the intellects powerful enough to embrace the infinite multiplicity and diversity of real interests, aspirations, wishes, and needs which sum up the collective will of the people? And to invent a social organization that will not be a Procrustean bed upon which the violence of the State will more or less overtly force unhappy society to stretch out? It has always been thus, and it is exactly this old system of organization by force that the Social Revolution should end by granting full liberty to the masses, the groups, the communes, the associations and to the individuals as well; by destroying once and for all the historic cause of all violence, which is the power and indeed the mere existence of the State. Its fall will bring down with it all the inequities of the law and all the lies of the various religions, since both law and religion have never been anything but the compulsory consecration, ideal and real, of all violence represented, guaranteed, and protected by the State.

It is obvious that liberty will never be *given* to humanity, and that the real interests of society, of all groups, local associations, and individuals who make up society will never be satisfied until there are no longer any states. It is obvious that all the so-called general interests of society, which the State is supposed to represent and which are in reality just a general and constant negation of the true interests of regions, communes, associations, and individuals subject to the State, are a mere abstraction, a fiction, a lie. The State is like a vast slaughterhouse or an enormous cemetery, where all the real aspirations, all the living forces of a country enter generously and happily, in the shadow of that abstraction, to let themselves be slain and buried. And just as no abstraction exists for and by itself, having no legs to stand on, no arms to create with, no stomach to digest the mass of victims delivered to it, it is likewise clear that the celestial or religious abstraction, God, actually represents the very real interests of a privileged class, the clergy, while its terrestrial complement, that political abstraction, the State, represents the no less real interests of the exploiting class which tends to absorb all the others— the bourgeoisie. As the clergy has always been divisive, and nowadays tends to separate men even further into a very powerful and wealthy minority and a subjected and rather wretched majority, so likewise the bourgeoisie, with its various social and political organizations in industry, agriculture, banking, and commerce, as well as in all administrative, financial, judiciary, education, police, and military functions of the State tend increasingly to weld all of these into a really dominant oligarchy on the one hand, and on the other hand into an enormous mass of more or less hopeless creatures, defrauded creatures who live in a perpetual illusion, steadily and inevitably pushed down into the proletariat by the irresistible force of the present economic development, and reduced to serving as blind tools of this all-powerful oligarchy.

The abolition of the Church and the State should be the first and indispensable condition for the real enfranchisement of society which can and should reorganize itself, not from the top down according to an ideal plan dressed up by wise men or scholars nor by decrees promulgated by some dictatorial power or even by a national assembly elected through universal suffrage. Such a system, as I have already said, would inevitably lead to the creation of a new state and, consequently, to the formation of a ruling aristocracy, that is, an entire class of persons who have nothing in common with the masses. And, of course, this class would exploit and subject the masses, under the pretext of serving the common welfare or saving the State.

The future social organization should be carried out from the bottom up, by the free association or federation of workers, starting with the associations, then going on to the communes, the regions, the nations, and, finally, culminating in a great international and universal federation. It is only then that the true, life-giving social order of liberty and general welfare will come into being, a social order which, far from restricting, will affirm and reconcile the interests of individuals and of society.

It is said that the harmony and universal solidarity of individuals with society can never be attained in practice because their interests, being antagonistic, can never be reconciled. To this objection I reply that if these interests have never as yet come to mutual accord, it was because the State has sacrificed the interests of the majority for the benefit of a privileged minority. That is why this famous incompatibility, this conflict of personal interests with those of society, is nothing but a fraud, a political lie, born of the theological lie which invented the doctrine of original sin in order to dishonor man and destroy his self-respect. The same false idea concerning irreconcilable interests was also fostered by the dreams of metaphysics which, as we know, is close kin to theology. Metaphysics, failing to recognize the social character of human nature, looked upon society as a mechanical and purely artificial aggregate of individuals, suddenly brought together in the name of some formal or secret compact concluded freely or under the influence of a superior power. Before uniting in society, these individuals, endowed with some sort of immortal soul, enjoyed complete liberty, according to the metaphysicians. We are convinced that all the wealth of man's intellectual, moral, and material development, as well as his apparent independence, is the product of his life in society. Outside society, not only would he not be a free man, he would not even become genuinely human, a being conscious of himself, the only being who thinks and speaks. Only the combination of intelligence and collective labor was able to force man out of that savage and brutish state which constituted his original nature, or rather the starting point for his further development. We are profoundly convinced that the entire life of men—their interests, tendencies, needs, illusions, even stupidities, as well as every bit of violence, injustice, and seemingly voluntary activity—merely represent the result of inevitable societal forces. People cannot reject the idea of mutual independence, nor can they deny the reciprocal influence and uniformity exhibiting the manifestations of external nature.

In nature herself, this marvelous correlation and interdependence of phenomena certainly is not produced without struggle. On the contrary, the harmony of the forces of nature appears only as the result of a continual struggle, which is the real condition of life and of movement. In nature, as in society, order without struggle is death.

If order is natural and possible in the universe, it is only because the universe is not governed according to some preimagined system imposed by a supreme will. The theological hypothesis of divine legislation leads to an obvious absurdity, to the negation not only of all order but of nature herself. Natural laws are real only in that they are inherent in nature; that is, they are not established by any authority. These laws are but simple manifestations, or rather continuous variations, of the uniformi-

ties constituting what we call "nature." Human intelligence and
its science have observed them, have checked them experiment-
ally, assembled them into a system and called them laws. But
nature as such knows no laws. She acts unconsciously; she represents in herself the infinite variety of phenomena which appear
and repeat themselves inevitably. This inevitability of action is
the reason the universal order can and does exist.

Such an order is also apparent in human society, which
seems to have evolved in an allegedly antinatural way but actually is determined by the natural animal's needs and his capacity
for thinking that have contributed a special element to his
development—a completely natural element, by the way, in the
sense that men, like everything that exists, represent the material
product of the union and action of natural forces. This special
element is reason, the capacity for generalization and abstraction,
thanks to which man is able to project himself in his thought,
examining and observing himself like a strange, external object.
By lifting himself in thought above himself, and above the
world around him, he reaches the representation of perfect
abstraction, the absolute void. And this absolute is nothing less
than his capacity for abstraction, which disdains all that exists
and finds its repose in attaining complete negation. This is the
ultimate limit of the highest abstraction of the mind; this absolute nothingness is God.

This is the meaning and the historical foundation of every
theological doctrine. As they did not understand the nature and
the material causes of their own thinking, and did not even
grasp the conditions or natural laws underlying such thinking,
these early men and early societies had not the slightest suspicion
that their absolute notions were simply the result of their own
capacity for formulating abstract ideas. Hence they viewed these
ideas, drawn from nature, as real objects, next to which nature
herself ceased to amount to anything. They began to worship
their fictions, their improbable notions of the absolute, and to
honor them. But since they felt the need of giving some concrete
form to the absolute idea of nothingness or of God, they created
the concept of divinity and, furthermore, endowed it with all the
qualities and powers, good and evil, which they found only in

nature and in society. Such was the origin and historical development of all religions, from fetishism on down to Christianity.

We do not intend to undertake a study of the history of religious, theological, and metaphysical absurdities or to discuss the procession of all the divine incarnations and visions created by centuries of barbarism. We all know that superstition brought disaster and caused rivers of blood and tears to flow. All these revolting aberrations of poor mankind were historical, inevitable stages in the normal growth and evolution of social organizations. Such aberrations engendered the fatal idea, which dominated men's imagination, that the universe was governed by a supernatural power and will. Centuries came and went, and societies grew accustomed to this idea to such an extent that they finally destroyed any urge toward or capacity to achieve further progress which arose in their midst.

The lust for power of a few individuals originally, and of several social classes later, established slavery and conquest as the dominant principle, and implanted this terrible idea of divinity in the heart of society. Thereafter no society was viewed as feasible without these two institutions, the Church and the State, at its base. These two social scourges are defended by all their doctrinaire apologists.

No sooner did these institutions appear in the world than two ruling classes—the priests and the aristocrats—promptly organized themselves and lost no time in indoctrinating the enslaved people with the idea of the utility, indispensability, and sacredness of the Church and of the State.

1872

———— ·•·• ————

Letter to La Liberté

This long letter to La Liberté (dated October 5, 1872), never completed and never sent, was written about a month after the expulsion of Bakunin and Guillaume from the International by the Hague Congress of September 2–7, 1872. In extract I,[22] Bakunin protests Marx's high-handed procedure and "the sentence of excommunication just pronounced against me"; he also sums up the fundamental disagreements between the two opposing tendencies in the International, as well as his position on Marx's theories of revolutionary dictatorship, the transitional period, provisional governments, constituent assemblies, and related themes.

Extract II[23] offers a condensed and acute critique of practically the whole range of Marxist theory of history, economic determinism, the nature of the State, parliamentary action, the "Dictatorship of the Proletariat," urban workers and rural masses, the possibilities of revolution in "advanced" and "backward" countries, etc. Bakunin also outlines the difference between the anarchist and Marxist conceptions of freedom and social cohesion, as well as the federalist-decentralized versus centralized statist form of organization.

I

To the Editors of *La Liberté*

Gentlemen:

Since you published the sentence of excommunication which the Marxian Congress of the Hague has just pronounced against me, you will surely, in all fairness, publish my reply. Here it is.

The triumph of Mr. Marx and his group has been complete. Being sure of a majority which they had been long preparing and organizing with a great deal of skill and care, if not with much respect for the principles of morality, truth, and justice as often found in their speeches and so seldom in their actions, the Marxists took off their masks. And, as befits men who love power, and always in the name of that sovereignty of the people which will, from now on, serve as a stepping-stone for all those who aspire to govern the masses, they have brazenly decreed their dictatorship over the members of the International.

If the International were less sturdy and deeply rooted, if it had been based, as they imagine, only upon the formally organized official leadership and not on the real solidarity of the effective interests and aspirations of the proletariat of all the countries of the civilized world, on the free and spontaneous federation of workers' sections and associations, independent of any government control, the decrees of this pernicious Hague Congress, a far too indulgent and faithful incarnation of the Marxist theories and practice, would have sufficed to kill it. They would have reduced to ridicule and odium this magnificent association, in the foundation of which, I am pleased to state, Mr. Marx had taken an intelligent and energetic part.

A state, a government, a universal dictatorship! The dreams of Gregory VII, Boniface VII, Charles V, and the Napoleons reappearing in new forms, but ever with the same claims, in the Social Democratic camp! Can one imagine anything more burlesque and at the same time more revolting? To claim that a group of individuals, even the most intelligent and best-intentioned, would be capable of becoming the mind, the soul, the directing and unifying will of the revolutionary movement and the economic organization of the proletariat of all lands—this is such heresy against common sense and historical experience that one wonders how a man as intelligent as Mr. Marx could have conceived it!

The popes at least had the excuse of possessing absolute truth, which they stated they held in their hands by the grace of the Holy Ghost and in which they were supposed to believe. Mr.

Marx has no such excuse, and I shall not insult him by suggesting that he imagines he has scientifically invented something that comes close to absolute truth. But from the moment that absolute truth is eliminated, there can be no infallible dogma for the International, and, consequently, no official political or economic theory, and our congresses should never assume the role of ecumenical councils which proclaim obligatory principles for all their members and believers to follow.

There is but one law that is really obligatory upon all the members, individuals, sections, and federations of the International, for all of which this law is the true and the only basis. In its most complete form with all its consequences and applications, this law advocates *the international solidarity of workers of all trades and all countries in their economic struggle against the exploiters of labor*. The living unity of the International resides solely in the real organization of this solidarity by the spontaneous action of the workers' groups and by the absolutely free federation of the masses of workers of all languages and all nations, all the more powerful because it is free; the International cannot be unified by decrees and under the whip of any sort of government whatsoever.

Who can entertain any doubt that out of this ever-growing organization of the militant solidarity of the proletariat against bourgeois exploitation there will issue forth the political[24] struggle of the proletariat against the bourgeoisie? Both the Marxists and ourselves are in unanimous agreement on this point. But here a question comes up which separates us completely from the Marxists.

We believe that the policy of the proletariat, necessarily revolutionary, should have the destruction of the State for its immediate and only goal. We cannot understand how one can speak of international solidarity when there is a wish to preserve the State, unless one dreams of the Universal State, that is, of universal slavery, such as the great emperors and popes dreamed of. For the State is, by its very nature, a breach of this solidarity and hence a permanent cause of war. Nor can we understand how anyone could speak of the liberty of the proletariat, or the real emancipation of the masses, within the State and by the

State. State means domination, and any domination presupposes the subjugation of the masses and, consequently, their exploitation for the benefit of some ruling minority.

We do not accept, even for the purposes of a revolutionary transition, national conventions, constituent assemblies, provisional governments, or so-called revolutionary dictatorships, because we are convinced that revolution is sincere and permanent only within the masses; that when it is concentrated in the hands of a few ruling individuals, it inevitably and immediately turns into reaction. Such is our belief; this is not the proper time for enlarging upon it. The Marxists profess quite contrary ideas. As befits good Germans, they are worshippers of the power of the State, and are necessarily also the prophets of political and social discipline, champions of the social order built from the top down, always in the name of universal suffrage and the sovereignty of the masses upon whom they bestow the honor of obeying their leaders, their elected masters. The Marxists admit of no other emancipation but that which they expect from their so-called People's State (*Volksstaat*).

Between the Marxists and ourselves there is an abyss. They are the governmentalists; we are the anarchists, in spite of it all.

Such are the two principal political tendencies which at present separate the International into two camps. On one side there is nothing, properly speaking, but Germany; on the other we find, in varying degrees, Italy, Spain, the Swiss Jura, a large part of France, Belgium, Holland, and in the very near future, the Slav peoples. These two tendencies came into direct confrontation at the Hague Congress, and, thanks to Mr. Marx's great tactical skill, thanks to the thoroughly artificial organization of his last congress, the Germanic tendency has prevailed.

Does this mean that the obnoxious question has been resolved? It was not even properly discussed; the majority, having voted like a well-drilled regiment, crushed all discussions under its vote. Thus the contradiction still remains, sharper and more alarming than ever, and Mr. Marx himself, intoxicated as he may be by his victory, can hardly imagine that he has disposed of it at so small a price. And if he did, for a moment, entertain such a foolish hope, he must have been promptly undeceived by the united stand of the delegates from the Jura, Spain, Belgium, and Holland (not to mention Italy, which did not even deign to send delegates to this so blatantly fraudulent congress), a protest quite moderate in tone, yet all the more powerful and deeply significant.

But what is to be done today? Today, since solution and reconciliation in the field of politics are impossible, we should practice mutual toleration, granting to each country the incontestable right to follow whatever political tendencies it may prefer or find most suitable for its own particular situation. Consequently, by rejecting all political questions from the obligatory program of the International, we should seek to strengthen the unity of this great association solely in the field of economic solidarity. Such solidarity unites us while political questions inevitably separate us.

That is where the real unity of the International lies; in the common economic aspirations and the spontaneous movement of the masses of all the countries—not in any government whatsoever nor in any uniform political theory imposed upon these masses by a general congress. This is so obvious that one would have to be dazzled by the passion for power to fail to understand it.

I could understand how crowned or uncrowned despots might have dreamed of holding the sceptered world in their hands. But what can one say of a friend of the proletariat, a revolutionary who claims he truly desires the emancipation of the masses, when he poses as a director and supreme arbiter of all the revolutionary movements that may arise in different countries and dares to dream of subjecting the proletariat to one single idea hatched in his own brain?

I believe that Mr. Marx is an earnest revolutionary, though not always a very consistent one, and that he really desires the revolt of the masses. And I wonder how he fails to see how the establishment of a universal dictatorship, collective or individual, a dictatorship that would in one way or another perform the task of chief engineer of the world revolution, regulating and directing an insurrectionary movement of the masses in all countries pretty much as one would run a machine—that the establishment of such a dictatorship would be enough of itself to kill the revolution, to paralyze and distort all popular movements.

Where is the man, where is the group of individuals, however great their genius, who would dare flatter themselves that they alone could encompass and understand the infinite multitude of diverse interests, tendencies, and activities in each country, in each province, in each locality, in each profession and craft, and which in their immense aggregate are united, but not regimented, by certain fundamental principles and by a great common aspiration, the same aspiration [economic equality without loss of autonomy] which, having sunk deep into the conscience of the masses, will constitute the future Social Revolution?

And what can one think of an International Congress which, in the alleged interest of this revolution, imposes on the proletariat of the whole civilized world a government invested with dictatorial power, with the inquisitorial and pontifical right to suspend the regional federations of the International and shut out whole nations in the name of an alleged official principle which is in fact only the idea of Marx, transformed by the vote of a fictitious majority into an absolute truth? What can one think of a Congress which, to render its folly even more glaring, relegates to America this dictatorial government [the General Council of the International] composed of men who, though probably honest, are ignorant, obscure, absolutely unknown even to the Congress itself? Our enemies, the bourgeoisie, would be right if they mocked the Congress and maintained that the International Workingmen's Association combats existing tyranny only to set up a new tyranny over itself; that in rightfully trying to replace old absurdities, it creates new ones!

II

Why men like Messrs. Marx and Engels should be indispensable to the partisans of a program consecrating political power and opening the door to all their ambitions is understandable. Since there will be political power, there will necessarily be subjects, who will be forced to obey, for without obedience there can be no power. One may object that they will obey not men but the laws which they have themselves made. But to that I reply that everybody knows how people make these laws and set up standards of obedience to these laws even in the most democratic and free countries. Anyone not involved in a party which takes fiction for reality will remember that even in these countries the people obey not the laws made by themselves but the laws made in their name; and that their obedience to these laws can never be anything but obedience to the arbitrary will of some tutelary and governing minority, or, in a word, a voluntary servitude.

We revolutionary anarchists who sincerely want full popular emancipation view with repugnance another expression in this program: it is the designation of the proletariat, the workers, as a *class* and not a mass. Do you know what this signifies? It is no more nor less than the aristocratic rule of the factory workers and of the cities over the millions who constitute the rural proletariat, who, in the anticipations of the German Social Democrats, will in effect become the subjects of their so-called People's State. "Class," "power," "state" are three inseparable terms, one of which presupposes the other two, and which boil down to this: *the political subjection and economic exploitation of the masses*.

The Marxists think that just as in the eighteenth century the bourgeoisie dethroned the nobility in order to take its place and gradually absorb and then share with it the domination and exploitation of the workers in the cities as well as in the country-side, so the proletariat in the cities is exhorted to dethrone and absorb the bourgeoisie, and then jointly dominate and exploit the land workers. . . .

Though differing with us in this respect, they do not entirely reject our program. They only reproach us for wanting to hasten, to outstrip the slow march of history, and for ignoring the scientific law of successive revolutions in inevitable stages. Having proclaimed in their works of philosophical analysis of the past that the bloody defeat of the insurgent peasants of Germany and the triumph of the despotic states in the sixteenth century constituted a great revolutionary move forward, they now have the nerve to call for the establishment of a new despotism, allegedly for the benefit of the urban workers and to the detriment of the toilers in the countryside.

This same logic leads the Marxists directly and fatally to what we call *bourgeois socialism* and to the conclusion of a new political pact between the bourgeois who are "radicals," or who are forced to become such, and the "intelligent," "respectable" bourgeoisified minority of city workers, to the detriment of the proletarian masses, not only in the country but also in the cities.

Such is the meaning of workers' candidacies to the parliaments of existing states, and of the conquest of political power. Is it not clear that the popular nature of such power will never be anything but a fiction? It will obviously be impossible for hundreds or even tens of thousands or indeed only a few thousand to exercise this power effectively. They will necessarily have to exercise power by proxy, to entrust this power to a group of men elected to represent them and govern them. . . . After a few brief moments of freedom or revolutionary euphoria, these new citizens of a new state will awake to find themselves again the pawns and victims of the new power clusters. . . .

I am fully confident that in a few years even the German workers will go the way that seems best to them, provided they allow us the same liberty. We even recognize the possibility that their history, their particular nature, their state of civilization, and their whole situation today impel them to follow this path. Let the German, American, and English toilers and those of other nations march with the same energy toward the destruction of all political power, liberty for all, and a natural respect for that liberty; such are the essential conditions of international solidarity.

To support his program for the conquest of political power, Marx has a very special theory, which is but the logical consequence of his whole system. He holds that the political condition of each country is always the product and the faithful expression of its economic situation; to change the former it is necessary only to transform the latter. Therein lies the whole secret of historic evolution according to Marx. He takes no account of other factors in history, such as the ever-present reaction of political, juridical, and religious institutions on the economic situation. He says: "Poverty produces political slavery, the State." But he does not allow this expression to be turned around, to say: "Political slavery, the State, reproduces in its turn, and maintains poverty as a condition for its own existence; so that to destroy poverty, it is necessary to destroy the State!" And strangely enough, Marx, who forbids his disciples to consider political slavery, the State, as a real cause of poverty, commands his disciples in the Social Democratic party to consider the conquest of political power as the absolutely necessary preliminary condition for economic emancipation!

[We insert here a paragraph from Bakunin's speech at the September 1869 Congress of the International, giving another objection to Marx's theory of economic determinism:]

The report of the General Council of the International [drawn up by Marx] says that the judicial fact being nothing but the consequence of the economic fact, it is therefore necessary to transform the latter in order to eliminate the former. It is incontestable that what has been called juridical or political right in history has always been the expression and the product of an accomplished fact. But it is also incontestable that after having been the effect of acts or facts previously accomplished, this right causes in its turn further effects, becoming itself a very real and powerful fact which must be eliminated if one desires an order of things different from the existing one. It is thus that the right of inheritance, after having been the natural consequence of the violent appropriation of natural and social wealth, becomes later the basis for the political state and the juridical family, which guarantees and sanctions private property. . . .

Likewise, Marx completely ignores a most important element in the historic development of humanity, that is, the temperament and particular character of each race and each people, a temperament and a character which are themselves the natural product of a multitude of ethnological, climatological, economic, and historic causes, but which exercise, even apart from and independent of the economic conditions of each country, a considerable influence on its destinies and even on the development of its economic forces. Among these elements, and these so-called natural traits, there is one whose action is completely decisive in the particular history of each people; it is the intensity of the spirit of revolt, and by that I mean the token of liberty with which a people is endowed or which it has conserved. This instinct is a fact which is completely primordial and animalistic; one finds it in different degrees in every living being, and the energy and vital power of each is to be measured by its intensity. In Man this instinct, in addition to the economic needs which urge him on, becomes the most powerful agent of total human emancipation. And since it is a matter of temperament rather than intellectual and moral culture, although these ordinarily complement each other, it sometimes happens that civilized peoples possess it only in a feeble degree, either because they have exhausted it during their previous development, or have been depraved by their civilization, or possibly because they were originally less fully endowed with it than other peoples. . . .

The reasoning of Marx ends in absolute contradiction. Taking into account only the economic question, he insists that only the most advanced countries, those in which capitalist production has attained greatest development, are the most capable of making social revolution. These civilized countries, to the exclusion of all others, are the only ones destined to initiate and carry through this revolution. This revolution will expropriate either by peaceful, gradual, or by violent means, the present property owners and capitalists. To appropriate all the landed property and capital, and to carry out its extensive economic and political programs, the revolutionary State will have to be very powerful and highly centralized. The State will administer and direct the cultivation of the land, by means of its salaried officials commanding armies of rural workers organized and disciplined for this purpose. At the same time, on the ruins of the existing banks, it will establish a single state bank which will finance all labor and national commerce.

It is readily apparent how such a seemingly simple plan of organization can excite the imagination of the workers, who are as eager for justice as they are for freedom; and who foolishly imagine that the one can exist without the other; as if, in order to conquer and consolidate justice and equality, one could depend on the efforts of others, particularly on governments, regardless of how they may be elected or controlled, to speak and act for the people! For the proletariat this will, in reality, be nothing but a barracks: a regime, where regimented workingmen and women will sleep, wake, work, and live to the beat of a drum; where the shrewd and educated will be granted government privileges; and where the mercenary-minded, attracted by the immensity of the international speculations of the state bank, will find a vast field for lucrative, underhanded dealings.

There will be slavery within this state, and abroad there will be war without truce, at least until the "inferior" races, Latin and Slav, tired of bourgeois civilization, no longer resign themselves to the subjection of a State, which will be even more despotic than the former State, although it calls itself a People's State.

The Social Revolution, as envisioned and hoped for by the Latin and Slav workers, is infinitely broader in scope than that advanced by the German or Marxist program. For them it is not a question of the emancipation of the working class, parsimoniously doled out and realizable only in the remote future, but rather the completed and real emancipation of all workers, not only in some but in all nations, "developed" and "undeveloped." And the first watchword of this emancipation can be none other than *freedom*. Not the bourgeois political freedom so extolled and recommended as the first step in the conquest of full freedom by Marx and his followers, but *a broad human freedom*, a freedom destroying all the dogmatic, metaphysical, political, and juridical fetters by which everyone today is loaded down, which will give everybody, collectives as well as individuals, full autonomy in their activities and their development, delivered once and for all from inspectors, directors, and guardians.

The second watchword of this emancipation is *solidarity*, not Marxian solidarity, decreed from the top down by some government, by trickery or force, upon the masses; not that unity of all which is the negation of the liberty of each, and which by that very fact becomes a falsehood, a fiction, hiding the reality of slavery; but that solidarity which is, on the contrary, the confirmation and realization of every freedom, having its origin not in any political law whatsoever but in the inherent social nature of Man, in virtue of which no man is free if all men who surround him and exercise an influence, direct or indirect, on his life, are not equally free. . . .

The solidarity which is sought, far from being the product of any artificial authoritarian organization whatsoever, can only be the spontaneous product of social life, economic as well as moral; the result of the free federation of common interests, aspirations, and tendencies. . . . It has for its essential basis *equality and collective labor*—obligatory not by law, but by the force of realities—and collective property; as a guiding light, it has experience, the practice of the collective life, knowledge, and learning; as a final goal, the establishment of a free humanity, beginning with the downfall of all states.

This is the ideal, not divine, not metaphysical, but human and practical,[25] which corresponds to the modern aspirations of the Latin and Slav peoples. They want full freedom, complete solidarity, complete equality; in short, they want a full-scale humanity, and they will not accept less, even on the pretext that limited freedom is only temporary. The Marxists will denounce these aspirations as folly, as they have been doing for a long time . . . but the Latins and Slavs will never exchange these magnificent objectives for the completely bourgeois platitudes of Marxian socialism.

1872

———◆———

The International
and Karl Marx

The following selection, The International and Karl Marx,[26] embodies—together with the selection The Paris Commune and the Idea of the State, and the two extracts apiece from the letter to La Liberté and Statism and Anarchy—Bakunin's critique of Marxism, which is becoming increasingly relevant as the current reevaluation of Marxism on all sides continues.

This selection was written when the decisive struggle between the authoritarian and antiauthoritarian sections in the International had reached its climax with the expulsion of Bakunin and Guillaume from the International by the notorious Hague Congress in 1872. The first part concerns Marx's conduct in the International and pinpoints the differences of principle and tactics between the two opposing factions. It also deals with the basic principles of revolutionary syndicalism, including a critique of Marxism, particularly in relation to the labor movement. Bakunin takes up such still-vital matters as 1) pro-labor bourgeois liberals; 2) should the General Council assume dictatorial powers over the International; 3) should the International be a model of the new society it is trying to build, or a replica of the State; 4) the relatively prosperous "semibourgeois caste of crafts and industrial workers" who could easily constitute the "fourth governing class" (the other three being the Church, the State bureaucracy, and the capitalists); and 5) Bakunin's confidence in the revolutionary *potential of the 'most oppressed, poorest, and alienated masses whom he calls "the flower of the proletariat."*

The second part deals primarily with Bakunin's critique of Marx's theory of historical materialism and economic determinism, holding that decisive events which conform to Marx's fatalistic "laws of history" are neither inevitable nor necessarily progressive.

WHEN it comes to exploitation the bourgeoisie practice solidarity. In combating them the exploited must do likewise; and the organization of this solidarity is the sole aim of the International. This aim, so simple and so clearly expressed in our original statutes, is the only legitimate obligation that all the members, sections, and federations of the International must accept. That they have done so willingly is shown by the fact that in barely eight years more than a million workers have joined and united their forces under the banner of this organization, which has in fact become a real power, a power with which the mightiest monarchs are now forced to reckon.

But all power entices the ambitious, and Mr. Marx and company, it seems, having never taken into account the nature and source of this prodigious power of the International, imagine that they can make it a stepping-stone or an instrument for the realization of their own political pretensions. Mr. Marx, who was one of the principal initiators of the International (a title to glory that no one will contest) and who for the last eight years has practically monopolized the whole General Council, should have understood better than anyone two things which are self-evident and which only those blinded by vanity and ambition could ignore: 1) that the marvelous growth of the International is due to the *elimination from its official program and rules* of all political and philosophic questions, and 2) that basing itself on the principle of the autonomy and freedom of all its sections and federations the International has happily been spared the ministrations of a *centralizer* or director who would naturally impede and paralyze its growth. Before 1870, precisely in the period of the International's greatest expansion, the General Council of

the International did not interfere with the freedom and autonomy of the sections and federations—not because it lacked the
will to dominate, but only because it did not have the power to
do so and no one would have obeyed it. The General Council
was an appendage trailing behind the spontaneous movement of
the workers of France, Switzerland, Spain, and Italy.

As far as the political question is concerned, everyone knows
that if it was eliminated from the program of the International,
it was not the fault of Mr. Marx. Nor is it due to any change of
mind on the part of the author of that famous *Manifesto* of the
German Communists published in 1848 by him and his friend
and accomplice, Mr. Engels. Nor did he fail to emphasize this
question in the Inaugural Proclamation—a circular addressed to
all the workers of all lands—published in 1864 by the London
Provisional General Council. The sole author of the Proclamation[27] was Mr. Marx.

In this proclamation the chief of the German authoritarian
communists stressed that "the conquest of political power is the
first task of the proletariat. . . ."

The First Congress of the International (Geneva, 1866)
nipped in the bud the attempt of Marx—who now poses as the
dictator of our great association—to inject this political plank. It
has been completely eliminated from the program and statutes[28]
adopted by this congress which remain the foundation of the
International. Take the trouble to reread the magnificent "Considerations" which are the Preamble to our general statutes and
you will see that the political question is dealt with in these
words:

> Considering that the emancipation of the workers must be the
> task of the workers themselves; that the efforts of the workers to
> achieve their emancipation must not be to reconstitute new privi-
> leges, but to establish, once for all, equal duties and equal rights;
> that the enslavement of the workers to capital is the source of all
> servitude—political, moral, and material; that for this reason the
> *economic emancipation of the workers is the great aim to which
> must be subordinated every political movement, etc.*[29] [All emphases
> are Bakunin's.]

This key phrase of the whole program of the International

breaks the links which chain the proletariat to the politics of the bourgeoisie. The proletariat, in recognizing this truth, will further widen the gap that separates them from the bourgeoisie with each step they take.

The Alliance,[30] the Geneva section of the International, has interpreted this paragraph of the "Considerations" in these terms:

> The Alliance rejects all political action which has not for its immediate and direct aim the triumph of the workers over capitalism. Consequently it fixes as its ultimate aim the abolition of the state, of all states, [these to be replaced] by the universal federation of all local associations through and in freedom.

Contrary to this, the German Social Democratic Workers party, founded in 1869, under the auspices of Mr. Marx, by Mr. Liebknecht and Mr. Babel, announced in its program that "the conquest of political power was the indispensable condition for the economic emancipation of the proletariat" and that consequently, the immediate objective of the party must be the organization of a big legal campaign to win universal suffrage and all other political rights. The final aim was the establishment of the Great Pan-Germanic State, the so-called People's State.

Between these two tendencies there exist the same conflicting conceptions and the same abyss that separate the proletariat and the bourgeoisie. Is it surprising, therefore, that these irreconcilable adversaries clashed in the International, that the struggle between them, in all forms and on all possible occasions, is still going on? The Alliance, true to the program of the International, disdainfully rejected all collaboration with bourgeois politics, in however radical and socialist a disguise. They advised the proletariat that the only real emancipation, the only policy truly beneficial for them, is the exclusively *negative* policy of demolishing political institutions, political power, government in general, and the State, and that to do this it is necessary to unify the scattered forces of the proletariat into an International organization, a revolutionary power directed against the entrenched power of the bourgeoisie.

The German Social Democrats advocated a completely opposite policy. They told these workers, who unfortunately heeded them, that the first and most pressing task of their organization must be to win political rights by legal agitation. They thus subordinated the movement for economic emancipation to an exclusively political movement, and by this obvious reversal of the whole program of the International they filled in at a single stroke the abyss that the International had opened between the proletariat and the bourgeoisie. They have done more. They have tied the proletariat to the bourgeois towline. For it is evident that this whole political movement so enthusiastically extolled by the German Socialists, since it must precede the economic revolution, can only be directed by the bourgeoisie, or what is still worse, by *workers transformed into bourgeois by their vanity and ambition*. And, in fact, this movement, like all its predecessors, will once more supersede the proletariat and condemn them to be the blind instruments, the victims, to be used and then sacrificed in the struggle between the rival bourgeois parties for the power and right to dominate and exploit the masses. To anyone who doubts this we have only to show what is happening now in Germany, where the organs of social democracy sing hymns of joy on seeing a congress of professors of bourgeois political economy entrusting the proletariat to the paternal protection of states, and it has occurred in parts of Switzerland where the Marxian program prevails—at Geneva, Zurich, Basel, where the International has declined to the point of being only an electoral ballot box for the profit of the radical bourgeois. These incontestable facts seem to me to be more eloquent than any words.

These facts are real and they are a natural effect of the triumph of Marxian propaganda. And it is for this reason that we fight the Marxian theories to the death, convinced that if they should triumph throughout the International, they would at the least kill its spirit, as they have already in great part done in the places I have referred to.

Certainly we have deplored and still deeply deplore the immense confusion and demoralization which these ideas have caused in arresting the promising and marvelous growth of the International and almost wrecking the organization. In spite of this none of us ever dreamed of stopping Mr. Marx and his fanatical disciples from propagating their ideas in our great association. If we did so, we would violate our fundamental principle: *absolute freedom to propagandize political and philosophic ideas.*

The International permits no *censor* and no *official truth* in whose name this censorship can be imposed. So far, the International has refused to grant this privilege either to the Church or to the State, and it is precisely because of this fact that the unbelievably rapid growth of the International has surprised the world.

This is what the Geneva Congress (1866) understood better than Mr. Marx. The effective power of our association, the International, was based on eliminating from its program all political and philosophical planks, *not as subjects for discussion and study* but as *obligatory principles* which all members must accept.

It is true that in the second congress of the International (Lausanne, 1867), misinformed friends, not adversaries, moved for the adoption of a political plank. But most fortunately the question of politics was harmlessly formulated in this platonic statement: "that the political question was inseparable from the economic question"—a declaration to which any of us could subscribe. For it is evident that politics, that is, the institutions of and relations between states, has no other object than to assure to the governing classes the legal exploitation of the proletariat. Consequently, from the moment that the proletariat becomes aware that it must emancipate itself, it must of necessity concern itself with the game of politics in order to fight and defeat it. This is not the sense in which our adversaries understand this problem. What they have sought and still want is the *constructive* politics of the State. But not finding the sentiment favorable at Lausanne, they wisely abstained from pressing the question.[31]

In 1868 they tried again at the Brussels Congress. The Belgian Internationalists, being communalists, i.e., antiauthoritarians and anticentralists by tradition and history, offered our opponents no chance of success. Once again, they did not press the political question.

Three years of defeats! This was too much for the impatient ambition of Mr. Marx. He commanded his army to make a direct attack, which order was carried out at the Basel Congress (1869). The chances seemed favorable. The Social Democratic party had enough time to organize itself in Germany under the leadership of Mr. Liebknecht and Mr. Babel. The party had links with German Switzerland, at Zurich and Basel, and even in the German section of the International in Geneva. It was the first time that German delegates were present in any great number in a congress of the International.

. . . Though well prepared for the great battle, the Marxists lost. . . . Soon after his defeat at this congress, the General Council, which was in effect Marx's puppet, awoke from its enforced lethargy (so healthful for the International) and opened an offensive. It began with a torrent of odious falsehoods, character assassinations, and plots against all those who dared to disagree with Marx's clique, disseminated by the German papers and in the other countries by secret letters and confidential circulars, and by all sorts of agents recruited in various ways into the Marxist camp.

This was followed by the London Conference (September 1871), which, prepared by the long arm of Mr. Marx, approved all that he wished—the conquest of political power as an integral part of the obligatory program of the International and the dictatorship of the General Council, that is, the personal dictatorship of Marx, and consequently the transformation of the International into an immense and monstrous state with himself as chief.

The legitimacy of this conference has been contested. Mr. Marx, a very able political conniver, doubtless anxious to prove to the world that though he lacked firearms and cannons the masses could still be governed by lies, by libels, and by intrigues, organized his Congress of the Hague in September 1872. Barely two months have passed since this congress,[32] and already in all of Europe (with the exception of Germany where the workers are brainwashed by the lies of their leaders and their press) and its free federations—Belgian, Dutch, English, American, French, Spanish, Italian—without forgetting our excellent Jura Federation [Switzerland]—there has arisen a cry of indignation and contempt against this cynical burlesque which dares to call itself a true Congress of the International. Thanks to a rigged, fictitious majority, composed almost exclusively of members of the General Council, cleverly used by Mr. Marx, all has been travestied, falsified, brutalized. Justice, good sense, honesty, and the honor of the International brazenly rejected, its very existence endangered—all this the better to establish the dictatorship of Mr. Marx. It is not only criminal—it is sheer madness. Yet Mr. Marx who thinks of himself as the father of the International (he was unquestionably one of its founders) cares not a whit, and permits all this to be done! This is what personal vanity, the lust for power, and above all, political ambition can lead to. For all these deplorable acts Marx is personally responsible. Marx, in spite of all his misdeeds, has unconsciously rendered a great service to the International by demonstrating in the most dramatic and evident manner that if anything can kill the International, it is the introduction of politics into its program.

The International Workingmen's Association, as I have said, would not have grown so phenomenally if it had not eliminated from its statutes and program all political and philosophical questions. This is clear and it is truly surprising that it must again be demonstrated.

I do not think that I need show that for the International to be a real power, it must be able to organize within its ranks the immense majority of the proletariat of Europe, of America, of all lands. But what political or philosophic program can rally to its banner all these millions? Only a program which is very general, hence vague and indefinite, for every theoretical definition necessarily involves elimination and in practice exclusion from membership.

For example: there is today no serious philosophy which does not take as its point of departure not positive but *negative* atheism. (Historically it became necessary to negate the theological and metaphysical absurdities.) But do you believe that if this simple word "atheism" had been inscribed on the banner of the International this association would have been able to attract more than a few hundred thousand members? Of course not— not because the people are truly religious, but because they believe in a Superior Being; and they will continue to believe in a

Superior Being until a social revolution provides the means to achieve all their aspirations here below. It is certain that if the International had demanded that all its members must be atheists, it would have excluded from its ranks the flower of the proletariat.

To me the flower of the proletariat is not, as it is to the Marxists, the upper layer, the aristocracy of labor, those who are the most cultured, who earn more and live more comfortably than all the other workers. Precisely this semibourgeois layer of workers would, if the Marxists had their way, constitute their *fourth governing class*. This could indeed happen if the great mass of the proletariat does not guard against it. By virtue of its relative well-being and semibourgeois position, this upper layer of workers is unfortunately only too deeply saturated with all the political and social prejudices and all the narrow aspirations and pretensions of the bourgeoisie. Of all the proletariat, this upper layer is the least social and the most individualist.

By the *flower of the proletariat*, I mean above all that great mass, those millions of the uncultivated, the disinherited, the miserable, the illiterates, whom Messrs. Engels and Marx would subject to their paternal rule by a *strong government*[33]—naturally for the people's own salvation! All governments are supposedly established only to look after the welfare of the masses! By flower of the proletariat, I mean precisely that eternal "meat" (on which governments thrive), that great *rabble of the people* (underdogs, "dregs of society") ordinarily designated by Marx and Engels in the picturesque and contemptuous phrase *Lumpenproletariat*. I have in mind the "riffraff," that "rabble" almost unpolluted by bourgeois civilization, which carries in its inner being and in its aspirations, in all the necessities and miseries of its collective life, all the seeds of the socialism of the future, and which alone is powerful enough today to inaugurate and bring to triumph the Social Revolution.

In almost all countries, this "rabble" would refuse to join the International if that association had an official commitment to atheism. It would be a heavy blow if they should reject the International, for on them rests the entire success of our great association.

It is absolutely the same in respect to all political policies. No matter how hard Messrs. Marx and Engels may try, they will not change what is now plainly and universally apparent: there does not exist any political principle capable of inspiring and stirring the masses to action. Attempts to spear the masses collapsed after a number of years, even in Germany. What the masses want above all is their immediate economic emancipation; this emancipation is for them equivalent to freedom and human dignity, a matter of life or death. If there is an ideal that the masses are today capable of embracing with passion, it is economic equality. And the masses are a thousand times right, for as long as the present condition is not replaced by economic equality, all the rest, all that constitutes the value and dignity of human existence —liberty, science, love, intelligence, and fraternal solidarity—will remain for them a horrible and cruel deception.

The instinctive passion of the masses for economic equality is so great that if they had hopes of receiving it from a despotic regime, they would indubitably and without much reflection, as they have often done before, deliver themselves to despotism. Happily, historic experience has been of service even to the masses. Today they are everywhere beginning to understand that no despotism has had or can have either the will or the power to give them economic equality. The program of the International is very happily explicit on this question: *the emancipation of the workers can be achieved only by the workers themselves.*

Is it not astonishing that Mr. Marx has believed it possible to graft onto this precise declaration, which he himself probably wrote, his scientific socialism? For this—the organization and the rule of the new society by socialist savants—is the worst of all despotic governments!

But thanks to the great, beloved common people, the "rabble," who are moved by an instinct invincible as well as just, all the governmental schemes of this little working-class minority already disciplined and marshaled to become the myrmidons of a new despotism, the scientific socialism of Mr. Marx will never be inflicted upon them and is doomed to remain only a dream. This new experience, perhaps the saddest of all experiences, will be spared society because the proletariat in all countries is today animated by a deep distrust against everything political, and against all politicians—whatever their party color. All of them, from the "reddest" republicans to the most absolutist monarchists, have equally deceived, oppressed, and exploited the people.

Taking into consideration these feelings of the masses, how can anyone hope to attract them to any political program? And supposing that the masses allow themselves to be drawn into the International even so, as they do, how can anyone hope that the proletariat of all lands, who differ so greatly in temperament, in culture, in economic development, would shoulder the yoke of a uniform political program? Only the demented could imagine such a possibility. Yet Mr. Marx not only enjoys imagining it, he wanted to accomplish this feat. By a despotic sneak attack,[34] he tore to shreds the pact of the International, hoping thereby, as he still does today, to impose a uniform political program, *his own program*, upon all the federations of the International, and hence upon the proletariat of all countries.

This has caused a great split in the International. Let us not deceive ourselves; the basic unity of the International has been fractured. This was accomplished, I repeat, by the acts of the Marxist party which throughout the Hague Congress has tried to impose the will, the thought, and the policy of its chief upon the whole International.

If the declarations of the Hague Congress are to be taken seriously our great association would have no alternative but to dissolve. For we cannot imagine that the workers of England, Holland, Belgium, France, the Swiss Jura, Spain, America, not to mention the Slavs, would submit to Marxist discipline.

Nevertheless, if one agrees with the various politicians in the International—with the revolutionary Jacobins, the Blanquists, the democratic republicans, not to mention the social democrats or Marxists—that the political question must be an integral part of the program of the International, he must admit that Marx is right. The International can be powerful only if it acts as a unit, with only one political program for all. Otherwise there would be as many different Internationals as there were programs.

But as it is clearly impossible for all the workers of all the different countries to unite voluntarily and spontaneously under the same political programs, this single program would have to be imposed upon them. To avoid the impression that it was foisted on the International by the Marxist-dominated General Council, a rigged Marxian congress "voted" it in, thus demonstrating in a new way this old truth about the representative system and universal suffrage: in the name of the free choice of all will be decreed the slavery of all. This is what really happened in the Hague Congress.

It was for the International what the battle and surrender of Sedan was for France:[35] the victorious invasion of pan-Germanism, not Bismarckian but Marxist, imposing the political program of the authoritarian communists or social democrats of Germany and the dictatorship of their chief over the world proletariat. The better to hide his scheme and sweeten the bitter pill, this notorious congress sent to America a dummy general council, chosen and rehearsed by Mr. Marx himself, always obeying his secret instructions, to assume all the trappings, the drudgery, and appearances of power, while from behind the scenes Mr. Marx will exercise the real power.

But disgusting as this scheme may appear to delicate and timorous souls, it became absolutely necessary from the moment the proposal was made to anchor the political question in the program of the International. Since unity of political action is considered necessary, and since it cannot and will not freely emerge through the spontaneous and voluntary agreement of the federations and sections of the different countries, it must be imposed on them. Only in this way can this most desired and highly touted political unity be created. But at the same time slavery is also being created.

To sum up: By introducing the political question in the official and obligatory programs and statutes of the International, the Marxists have put our association in a terrible dilemma. Here are the two alternatives: *Either political unity with slavery or liberty with division and dissolution.* What is the way out? Quite simply: we must return to our original principles and omit the specific political issue, thus leaving the sections and federations free to develop their own policies. But then would not each section and each federation follow whatever political policy it wants?

No doubt. But then, will not the International be transformed into a tower of Babel? On the contrary, only then will it attain real unity, basically economic, which will necessarily lead to real political unity. Then there will be created, though of course not all at once, the grand policy of the International—not from a single head, ambitious, erudite, but nevertheless, incapable of embracing the thousand needs of a proletariat no matter how brainy it may be[36] but by the absolutely free, spontaneous, and concurrent action of the workers of all countries.

The foundation for the unity of the International, so vainly looked for in the current political and philosophical dogmas, has already been laid by the common sufferings, interests, needs, and real aspirations of the workers of the whole world. This solidarity does not have to be artificially created. It is a fact, it is life itself, a daily experience in the world of the worker. And all that remains to be done is to make him understand this fact and help him to organize it consciously. This fact is *solidarity for economic demands*. This slogan is in my opinion the only, yet at the same time a truly great, achievement of the first founders of our association, among whom, as I always like to remember, Mr. Marx has played so useful and preponderant a part—excepting his political schemes which the Geneva Congress (1866) wisely eliminated from the program he presented.

I have always avoided calling Mr. Marx and his numerous collaborators the "founders" of the International, not because I am motivated by mean sentiments to deprecate or minimize their merits: on the contrary, I gladly give them full credit. Rather, I am convinced that the International has been not their work but the work of the proletariat itself. They (Marx and Company) were somewhat like midwives rather than parents. The great author (unaware, as authors of great things usually are) was the proletariat, represented by a few hundred anonymous workers, French, English, Belgian, Swiss, and German. It was their keen and profound instinct as workers, sharpened by the sufferings inherent in their situation, which impelled them to find the true principle and true purpose of the International. They took the common needs already in existence as the foundation and saw the *international organization of economic conflict against capi-*

talism as the true objective of this association. In giving it exclusively this base and aim, the workers at once established the entire power of the International. They opened wide the gates to all the millions of the oppressed and exploited, regardless of their beliefs, their degree of culture, or their nationality.

One cannot commit a greater mistake than to demand more than a thing, an institution, or a man can give. By demanding more than that from them one demoralizes, impedes, perverts, and renders them totally useless for any constructive action. The International in a short time produced great results. It organized and will continue to organize ever greater masses of the proletariat for economic struggles. Does it follow from this that the proletariat can also be used as an instrument for the political struggle? Because he thought so, Mr. Marx nearly killed the International at the Hague Congress. It is the old story of the goose that laid golden eggs. At the summons to unite for the economic struggle, masses of workers from different countries hastened to join forces under the banner of the International, and Mr. Marx imagined that the masses would stay under it—what do I say?— that they would rush to join in even greater numbers, when he, the new Moses, had inscribed the commandments of his new decalogue on our banner, in the official and binding program of the International.

This was his mistake. The masses, regardless of their degree of culture, religious beliefs, country, or native tongue, understood the language of the International when it spoke to them of their poverty, their sufferings, and their slavery under the yoke of capitalism. They responded when the necessity to unite in a great common struggle was explained to them. But here they were being told about a political program—most learned and above all quite authoritarian—which for the sake of their own salvation was attempting—in the very International by means of which they were to organize their own emancipation—to impose on them a dictatorial government (only temporarily, of course!) directed by an extraordinarily brainy man.

It is sheer madness to hope that the working masses of Europe and America will stay in the International in such circumstances. But, you may ask, "Has not the remarkable success [of the

International] shown that Mr. Marx was right, and didn't the
Hague Congress vote in favor of all his demands?"

No one knows better than Mr. Marx himself how little the
resolutions approved by the unfortunate congress at the Hague
expressed the true thoughts and aspirations of the federations of
all countries. The composition and the manipulation of this congress have caused so much pain and disappointment that no one
has the least illusion about its real value. Outside of the German
Social Democratic party, the federations of all countries—the
American, the English, the Dutch, the Belgian, the French,
the Jura-Swiss, the Spanish, and the Italian—protested all the
resolutions of this disastrous and disgraceful congress and vehe-
mently denounced its ignoble intrigues.

But let us set aside the moral question and deal only with the
main points. A political program has no value if it deals only with
vague generalities. It must specify precisely what institutions are
to replace those that are to be overthrown or reformed. Marx's
program is a complete network of political and economic institutions rigidly centralized and highly authoritarian, sanctioned, no
doubt, like all despotic institutions in modern society, by universal suffrage, but nevertheless subordinate to a *very strong*
government—to quote Engels, Marx's alter ego, the autocrat's
confidant.

But why should this particular program be injected into the
official and binding statutes of the International? Why not that
of the Blanquists? Why not ours? Could it be because Mr. Marx
concocted it? That is no reason. Or is it because the German
workers seem to like it? But the anarchist program is with very
few exceptions accepted by all the Latin federations; the Slavs
would never accept any other. Why, then, should the program of
the Germans dominate the International, which was conceived in
liberty and can only prosper in and by liberty? . . .

It is clear that the wish to force the federations—be it by
violence, by intrigue, or both—to accept a single arbitrary political
program must fail; the most likely result would be the dissolution
of the International and its division into many political parties,
each promoting its own political program. To save its integrity
and assure its progress, there is only one procedure: to follow and

preserve the original policy and *keep the political question out of the official and obligatory program and statutes of the International Workingmen's Association—which was organized not for the political struggle but only for economic ends—and absolutely refuse to let it be used by anyone as a political instrument.* Those who would [capture the International] and commit it to a positive political policy in the struggle between the rival political parties [for the attainment of state power] will be immediately demoralized. Those who foolishly imagine that they really have this power will see it gradually slip from their fingers and dissolve before their very eyes.

But would the International then cease to concern itself with political and philosophical questions? Would the International ignore progress in the world of thought as well as the events which accompany or arise from the political struggle in and between states, concerning itself only with the economic problem? Would the International limit itself to gathering statistics, studying the laws of production and the distribution of wealth, regulating wages, gathering strike funds, organizing local, national, and international strikes, establishing national and international trade unions, and founding mutual-credit and consumers'-production cooperatives wherever possible?

We hasten to say that it is absolutely impossible to ignore political and philosophical questions. An exclusive preoccupation with economic questions would be fatal for the proletariat. Doubtless the defense and organization of its economic interests —a matter of life and death—must be the principal task of the proletariat. But it is impossible for the workers to stop there without renouncing their humanity and depriving themselves of the intellectual and moral power which is so necessary for the conquest of their economic rights. In the miserable circumstances in which the worker now finds himself, the main problem he faces is most likely bread for himself and his family. But much more than any of the privileged classes today, he is a human being in the fullest sense of this word; he thirsts for dignity, for justice, for equality, for liberty, for humanity, and for knowledge, and he passionately strives to attain all these things together with the full enjoyment of the fruits of his own labor. Therefore, if political and philosophical questions have not yet been posed in the International, it is the proletariat itself who will pose them.

On the one hand, the political and philosophical questions must be excluded from the program of the International. On the other, they must necessarily be discussed. How can this seeming contradiction be resolved?

This problem will solve itself by liberty. No political or philosophical theory should be considered a fundamental principle, or be introduced into the official program of the International. Nor should acceptance of any political or philosophical theory be obligatory as a condition for membership, since as we have seen, to impose any such theory upon the federations composing the International would be slavery, or it would result in division and dissolution, which is no less disastrous. But it does not follow from this that free discussion of all political and philosophical theories cannot occur in the International. On the contrary, it is precisely the very existence of an official theory that will kill such discussion by rendering it absolutely useless instead of living and vital, and by inhibiting the expression and development of the worker's own feelings and ideas. As soon as an *official truth* is pronounced—having been scientifically discovered by this great brainy head laboring all alone—a truth proclaimed and imposed on the whole world from the summit of the Marxist Sinai, why discuss anything?

All that remains to be done is to learn by heart the commandments of the new decalogue. On the other hand, if people do not have and cannot claim that they have the truth, they will try to find it. Who searches for the truth? Everyone, and above all the proletariat, which thirsts for and needs it more than all others. Many do not believe that the proletariat can itself spontaneously find and develop true philosophical principles and political policies. I will now try to show how this is being done by the workers at the very core of the International.

The workers, as I have said, originally join the International for one very practical purpose: solidarity in the struggle for full economic rights against the oppressive exploitation by the bourgeoisie of all lands. Note that by this single act, though at first without realizing it, the proletariat takes a decisively negative position on politics. And this in two ways. First of all, it under-mines the concept of political frontiers and international politics of states, the existence of which depends upon the sympathies, the voluntary cooperation, and the fanatical patriotism of the enslaved masses. Secondly, it digs a chasm between the bour-geoisie and the proletariat and places the proletariat outside the activity and political conniving of all the parties within the State; but in placing itself outside all bourgeois politics, the proletariat necessarily turns against it.

The proletariat, by its adherence to the International, has unconsciously taken up a very definite political position. How-ever, this is an absolutely *negative* political position; and the great mistake, not to say the treason and the crime of the Social Democrats—who are urging the German workers to follow the Marxist program—is that they tried to transform this negative attitude into positive collaboration with bourgeois politics.

The International, in placing the proletariat outside the politics of the State and of the bourgeois world, thereby con-structed a new world, the world of the united proletarians of all lands. This is the new world of the future: the legitimate inher-itor, but at the same time the gravedigger of all former civiliza-tions, which, founded on privilege, are completely bankrupt, exhausted, and doomed to extinction. On the ruins of the old world, on the demolition of all oppressions divine and human, of all slavery, of all inequality, the International is destined to create a new civilization. This is the mission, and therefore the true program of the International—not the official, artificial pro-gram, from which may all the Christian and pagan gods protect us—but that which is inherent in the very nature of the organiza-tion itself.

The true program, I will repeat it a thousand times, is quite simple and moderate: *the organization of solidarity in the eco-nomic struggle of labor against capitalism*. On this foundation, at first exclusively material, will rise the intellectual and moral pillars of the new society. To bring such a society into being, all the thoughts, all the philosophical and political tendencies of the International, born out of the womb of the proletariat itself, must originate, and take as their principal point of departure this economic base which constitutes the very essence and the declared, obvious aim of the International. Is this possible?

Yes, and this process is now taking place. Whoever has kept in touch with developments in the International during the last few years will notice how this is slowly taking place, sometimes at a quickened, sometimes at a slower pace, and always in three different, but firmly connected, ways: *first*, by the establishment and coordination of strike funds and the international solidarity of strikes; *second*, by the organization and the international (federative) coordination of trade and professional unions; *third*, by *the spontaneous and direct development of philosophical and sociological ideas in the International*, ideas which inevitably develop side by side with and are produced by the first two movements.

Let us now consider these three ways, different but inseparable, and begin with the organization of strike funds and strikes.

Strike funds aim only at collecting resources which make it possible to organize and maintain strikes, always a costly undertaking. The strike is the beginning of the social war of the proletariat against the bourgeoisie, a tactic that remains within the limits of legality. Strikes are a valuable tactic in two ways. First they electrify the masses, reinforcing their moral energy and awakening in them the sense of profound antagonism between their interests and those of the bourgeoisie. Thus strikes reveal to them the abyss which from this time on irrevocably separates the workers from the bourgeoisie. Consequently they contribute immensely by arousing and manifesting between the workers of all trades, of all localities, and of all countries the consciousness and the fact itself of solidarity. Thus a double action, the one negative, the other positive, tending to create directly the new world of the proletariat by opposing it in an almost absolute manner to the bourgeois world.

It is significant that in this connection the radical and bourgeois socialists have always bitterly opposed the idea of strikes and made desperate efforts to discourage the proletariat from striking. Mazzini never could bear any talk of strikes; and if his disciples, many of whom have become demoralized, disoriented, and disorganized since his death [March 10, 1872], today timidly endorse the strike, it is only because the propaganda for the Social Revolution has so stirred the Italian masses, and social and economic demands have manifested themselves with such power in the strikes that have simultaneously erupted all over Italy, that they fear to oppose this movement lest they become isolated and lose all influence among the people.

Mazzini, together with all the bourgeois socialists and radicals of Europe, was *from his point of view* right in condemning strikes. For what is it the Mazzinisti want who today are so imbued with the spirit of conciliation that they are about to unite with those who call themselves "the Radicals" in the Italian parliament? They want the establishment of a single great democratic republican state. To establish this state they must first overthrow the present one, and for that the powerful support of the people is indispensable. Once the people have performed this great service to the politicians of the school of Mazzini, they will naturally be sent back to their factories and workshops or to their fields to resume their essential labors. There they will submit not to the paternal monarchy but to the fraternal protection of the new but no less authoritarian republican government. Today the workers must renounce the strike and make appeal to their new rulers. But how can the bourgeois radicals and socialists be stirred to act on behalf of the workers?

By appealing to their socialist instincts? Impossible! This would be the surest way to stir up the hatred and bitter opposition of all the capitalists and proprietors against both themselves and the republic of their dreams. Also impossible because it is precisely with these exploiters that the bourgeois and radical socialists want to collaborate and with them they wish to constitute the new government. They cannot establish an orderly new government with the "barbaric, ignorant" anarchical masses, especially when these masses have been roused and stirred in the course of their economic struggles by the passion for justice, for equality, and for their real freedom, which is incompatible with any and all governments. The radical and bourgeois socialists must, therefore, avoid the social (economic) question and concentrate on inciting the political and patriotic passions of the workers. This will cause their hearts to beat in unison with the hearts of the bourgeoisie, and the workers will then be psychologically prepared to render to the radical politicians the precious service demanded of them: that of overthrowing the monarchical government.

But we have seen that the first effect of strikes is to destroy this touching and very profitable harmony with the bourgeoisie. Strikes have the effect of reminding the workers that between them and their rulers there exists an abyss and of awakening in the hearts of the proletariat socialist passions and aspirations which are absolutely incompatible with patriotic and political fanaticism. Yes, from this perspective Mazzini was a thousand times right: Strikes must be prohibited!

Mazzini, for reasons which I have just indicated, clearly wishes to put an end to the antagonism between classes. But does Mr. Marx really want to preserve this antagonism, which renders all participation of the masses in the politics of the State absolutely impossible? For such political action cannot succeed unless the bourgeoisie enter into it, and will succeed only when this class develops and directs it. Of this, Marx cannot be ignorant. It is impossible for me to believe he is unaware of this, after the speech he recently delivered in Amsterdam in which he declared that in certain countries, perhaps in Holland itself, the social question can be peaceably resolved; that is, in an altogether friendly, legal way, without force. This can mean only that the social problem can be resolved by a series of successive, tranquil, and judicious compromises between the bourgeoisie and the proletariat. Mazzini has never differed from this.

In the end, Mazzini and Marx agree on a cardinal point: that the great social reforms which are to emancipate the proletariat can be put into effect only by a great democratic, republican, and very powerful, highly centralized state. This state, they allege, must impose upon the people a very strong government, this being in the people's interest, to secure their education and well-being.

Between Mazzini and Marx there has always been an enormous difference, and it is all to the honor of Mazzini. Mazzini was a profoundly sincere and passionate believer. He adored his God, to whom he devoted all that he felt, thought, did. In regard to his own style of life, he was the simplest of men, the most modest, the most unselfish. But he became inflexible, furious, when anyone touched his God.

Mr. Marx does not believe in God, but he believes deeply in himself. His heart is filled not with love but with rancor. He has very little benevolence toward men and becomes just as furious, and infinitely more spiteful, than Mazzini when anyone dares question the omniscience of the divinity whom he adores, that is to say, Mr. Marx himself. Mazzini would like to impose on humanity the absurdity of God; Mr. Marx tries to impose himself. I believe in neither, but if I were forced to choose, I would prefer the Mazzinian God.

I believe it is my duty to give this explanation, so that the friends and disciples of Mazzini cannot accuse me of dishonoring the memory of their master by likening him to Mr. Marx. I return to my subject.

I say then that for all the reasons I have given, it would not surprise me if we soon hear talk of a reconciliation between the Mazzinian agitation and the Marxist intrigue in Italy. I maintain that if the Marxist party, the so-called Social Democrats, continues along the road of political action, it will sooner or later be forced to oppose economic action—the tactic of strikes—so incompatible are these two methods in reality. . . .

Political Consciousness
and Statist Civilization

Is it possible even by means of the most cleverly devised and energetically expressed propaganda to imbue the great masses of a nation with tendencies, aspirations, passions, and thoughts that are absolutely foreign to them, that are not the product of their own history, of their customs and traditions? It seems to me that when the question is so posed, any reasonable and sensitive man who has even the least idea of how the popular conscience is developed, can answer only in the negative. Ultimately, no propaganda has ever artificially created a source or basis for a people's aspirations and ideas, which are always the product of their spontaneous development and the actual conditions of life.

What, then, can propaganda do? It can, in general, express the proletariat's own instincts in a new, more definite and more apt form. It can sometimes precipitate and facilitate the awakening consciousness of the masses themselves. It can make them conscious of what they are, of what they feel, and of what they already instinctively wish; but never can propaganda make them what they are not, nor awaken in their hearts passions which are foreign to their own history.

Now to discuss the question whether by means of propaganda it is possible to make a people politically conscious for the first time, we must specify what political consciousness is *for the masses of the people*. I emphasize *for the masses of the people*. For we know very well that for the privileged classes, political consciousness is nothing but the right of conquest, guaranteed and codified, of the exploiter of the labor of the masses and the right to govern them so as to assure this exploitation. But for the masses, who have been enslaved, governed, and exploited, of what does political consciousness consist? It can be assured by only one thing—the goddess of revolt. This mother of all liberty, the tradition of revolt, is the indispensable historical condition for the realization of any and all freedoms.

We see then that this phrase *political consciousness*, throughout the course of historical development, possesses two absolutely different meanings corresponding to two opposing viewpoints. From the viewpoint of the privileged classes, political consciousness means conquest, enslavement, and the indispensable mechanism for this exploitation of the masses: *the coextensive organization of the State*. From the viewpoint of the masses, it means the destruction of the State. It means, accordingly, two things that are diametrically and inevitably opposed.

Now it is absolutely certain that there has never existed a people, no matter how low-spirited or maltreated by circumstances, who did not feel at least at the beginning of their slavery some spark of revolt. To revolt is a natural tendency of life. Even a worm turns against the foot that crushes it. In general, the vitality and relative dignity of an animal can be measured by the intensity of its instinct to revolt. In the world of beasts as in the human world there is no habit more degrading, more stupid, or more cowardly than the habit of supine submission and obedience to another's oppression. I contend that there has never existed a people so depraved that they did not at some time, at least at the beginning of their history, revolt against the yoke of their slave drivers and their exploiters, and against the yoke of the State.

But it must be acknowledged that since the bloody wars of the Middle Ages, the State has crushed all popular revolts. With the exception of Holland and Switzerland, the State reigns triumphant in all the countries of Europe. In our "new" civilization there is the enforced slavery of the masses and, for reasons of profit, the more or less voluntary allegiance of the economically privileged classes to the State. All the so-called revolutions of the past—including the great French Revolution, despite the magnificent concepts that inspired it—all these revolutions have been nothing but the struggle between rival exploiting classes for the exclusive enjoyment of the privileges granted by the State. They express nothing but a fight for the domination and exploitation of the masses.

And the masses? Alas! It must be acknowledged that the masses have allowed themselves to become deeply demoralized, apathetic, not to say castrated, by the pernicious influence of our corrupt, centralized, statist civilization. Bewildered, debased, they have contracted the fatal habit of obedience, of sheepish resignation. They have been turned into an immense herd, artificially segregated and divided into cages for the greater convenience of their various exploiters.

Critique of Economic Determinism and Historical Materialism

The Marxist sociologists, men like Engels and Lassalle, in objecting to our views contend that the State is not at all the cause of the poverty, degradation, and servitude of the masses; that both the miserable condition of the masses and the despotic power of the State are, on the contrary, the effect of a more general underlying cause. In particular, we are told that they are both the products of an inevitable stage in the economic evolution of society; a stage which, historically viewed, constitutes an immense step forward to what *they* call the "Social Revolution." To illustrate how far the obsession with this doctrine has already gone: the crushing of the formidable revolts of the peasants in Germany in the sixteenth century led inevitably to the triumph of the centralized, despotic State, from which dates the centuries-old slavery of the German people. This catastrophe is hailed by Lassalle as a victory for the coming Social Revolution! Why? Because, say the Marxists, the peasants are the natural represen-tatives of reaction, while the modern, military, bureaucratic state, beginning in the second half of the sixteenth century, initiated the slow, but always progressive, transformation of the ancient feudal and land economy into the industrial era of production, in which capital exploits labor. This State, therefore, has been an essential condition for the coming Social Revolution.

It is now understandable why Mr. Engels, following this logic, wrote in a letter to our friend Carlo Cafiero that Bismarck as well as King Victor Emmanuel of Italy (inadvertently) had greatly helped the revolution because both of them created polit-ical centralization in their respective countries. I urge the French allies and sympathizers of Mr. Marx to carefully examine how this Marxist concept is being applied in the International.

We who, like Mr. Marx himself, are materialists and deter-minists, also recognize the inevitable linking of economic and political facts in history. We recognize, indeed, the necessity and inevitable character of all events that occur but we no longer bow before them indifferently, and above all we are very careful about praising them when, by their nature, they show themselves in flagrant contradiction to the supreme end of history. This is a thoroughly human ideal which is found in more or less recog-nizable form in the instincts and aspirations of the people and in all the religious symbols of all epochs, because it is inherent in the human race, the most social of all the species of animals on earth. This ideal, today better understood than ever, is *the triumph of humanity, the most complete conquest and establish-ment of personal freedom and development—material, intellec-tual, and moral—for every individual, through the absolutely unrestricted and spontaneous organization of economic and so-cial solidarity.*

Everything in history that shows itself conformable to that end, from the human point of view—and we can have no other—is good; all that is contrary to it is bad. We know very well, in any case, that what we call good and bad are always the natural results of natural causes, and that consequently one is as inevitable as the other. But in what is properly called nature we recognize many necessities that we are little disposed to bless, such as the necessity of dying when one is bitten by a mad dog. In the same way, in that immediate continuation of the life of nature called history, we encounter many necessities which we find much more worthy of opprobrium than benediction, and which we believe we should stigmatize with all the energy of which we are capable in the interest of our social and individual morality. We recognize, however, that from the moment they have been accomplished, even the most detestable facts have that character of inevitability which is found in all the phenomena of nature as well as those of history.

To clarify my thought, I shall give some examples. When I study the social and political conditions of the Romans and the Greeks in the period of the decline of antiquity, I conclude that the conquest of Greece by the military and political barbarism of the Romans and the consequent destruction of a comparatively higher standard of human liberty was a natural and inevitable fact. But this does not prevent me from taking, retrospectively and firmly, the side of Greece against Rome in that struggle. For I find that the human race has gained absolutely nothing by the triumph of Rome.

Likewise, that the Christians in their holy fury destroyed all the libraries of the pagans and all their treasures of art, ancient philosophy, and science is an absolutely natural and therefore inevitable fact. But it is impossible for me to see how this fact has in any manner whatsoever furthered our political and social development. I am even very much disposed to doubt the inevitable process of economic facts in which, if one were to believe Mr. Marx, there must be sought to the exclusion of all other considerations the only cause of all of history's moral and intellectual phenomena. Further, I am strongly disposed to think that these acts of holy barbarity, or rather that long series of barbarous acts and crimes which the first Christians, divinely inspired, committed against the human spirit, were among the principal causes of the intellectual and moral degradation, as well as the political and social slavery, which filled that long series of centuries called the Middle Ages. Be sure of this, that if the first Christians had not destroyed the libraries, the museums, and the temples of antiquity, we should not have been condemned today to fight the mass of horrible and shameful absurdities which still clog men's brains to such a degree that I sometimes doubt the possibility of a more humane future.

Continuing my protests against the kinds of historical facts whose inevitability I myself also acknowledge, I pause before the splendor of the Italian republics and before the magnificent awakening of human genius during the Renaissance. Then I see two friends, as ancient as history itself, approaching; the same two serpents which up till now have devoured everything beautiful and virtuous that mankind has created. They are called the Church and the State, the *papacy* and the *empire*. Eternal evils and inseparable allies, embracing each other and together devouring that unfortunate, most beautiful Italy, condemning her to three centuries of death. Well, though I again find it all natural and inevitable, I nevertheless curse both emperor and pope.

Let us pass on to France. After a century of struggle, Catholicism, supported by the State, finally triumphed over Protestantism. Do I not still find in France today some politicians or historians of the fatalist school who, calling themselves revolutionists, consider this victory of Catholicism—a bloody and inhuman victory if ever there was one—a veritable triumph for the cause of the Revolution? Catholicism, they insist, was then the State representing democracy, while Protestantism represented the revolt of the aristocracy against the State and consequently against democracy. This sort of sophism is completely identical to the Marxist sophism, which also considers the triumph of the State to be a victory for social democracy. It is with these disgusting and revolting absurdities that the mind and moral sense of the masses are perverted, habituating them to hail their bloodthirsty exploiters, the masters and servants of the State, as their saviors and emancipators.

It is a thousand times right to say that Protestantism, not as a Calvinist theology but as an energetic and armed protest, represented revolt, liberty, humanity, the destruction of the State; while Catholicism was public order, authority, divine law, the mutual salvation of the Church and the State, the condemnation of human society to protracted slavery.

Hence, while recognizing the inevitability of the accomplished fact I do not hesitate to say that the victory of Catholicism in France in the sixteenth and seventeenth centuries was a great misfortune for the entire human race. The massacre of Saint Bartholomew and the revocation of the Edict of Nantes were facts as disastrous for France as were, in our times, the defeat and massacre of the people of Paris in the Commune of Paris. I have actually heard very intelligent and very worthy Frenchmen ascribe the defeat of Protestantism in France to the revolutionary nature of the French people. "Protestantism," they allege, "was only a semirevolution; we need a complete revolution; it is for this reason that the French neither wanted nor could prevent the Reformation. France preferred to remain Catholic till the moment when it could proclaim atheism. This is why the French people, with true Christian resignation, tolerated both the horrors of Saint Bartholomew and the no less abominable revocation of the Edict of Nantes."

These worthy patriots either fail to or do not want to consider one thing. A people who for any reason whatsoever tolerates tyranny will finally lose the salutary habit and even the very instinct of revolt. Once a people loses the inclination for liberty, it necessarily becomes, not only in its external conditions but in the very essence of its own being, a people of slaves. It was because Protestantism was defeated in France that the French people lost, or perhaps never acquired, the habit of liberty. It is because this habit is wanting that France today lacks what we call *political consciousness*, and it is because it lacks this consciousness that all the revolutions it has made up till now have failed to achieve its political liberty. With the exception of its great revolutionary days, which are its festival days, the French people remain today as they were yesterday, a people of slaves.

Going on to other cases, I take up the partition of Poland. Here I am very glad, at least on this question, to agree with Mr. Marx; for he, like myself and everyone else, considers this partition a *great crime*. I would only like to know why, given both his fatalistic and his optimistic point of view, he contradicts himself by condemning a great event which already belong to the historical past. Proudhon, whom he loved so much,[37] was much more logical and consistent than Marx. Trying with might and main to establish an historical justification for his conclusion, he wrote an unfortunate pamphlet[38] in which he first showed quite decisively that the Poland of the nobility must perish, because it carries within itself the germs of its own dissolution. He then attempted to contrast this nobility unfavorably with the Tsarist Empire, which he deemed a harbinger of the triumphant socialist democracy. This was much more than a mistake. I do not hesitate to say, in spite of my tender respect for the memory of Proudhon, that it was a crime, the crime of a sophist who, in order to win a dispute, dared to insult a martyred nation at the very moment when it was for the hundredth time revolting against its Russian and German debauchers and for the hundredth time lying prostrate under their blows. . . .[39]

Why does Marx, in contradiction to his own ideas, favor the establishment of an independent Polish state? Mr. Marx is not only a learned socialist, he is also a very clever politician and a patriot no less ardent than Bismarck, though he would approach his goals through somewhat different means. And like many of his compatriots, both socialist and otherwise, he desires the establishment of a great Germanic state, one that will glorify the German people and benefit world civilization. Now among the obstacles to the realization of this aim is the Prussian Empire which, with menacing power, poses as the protector of the Slavic peoples against German civilization.

The policy of Bismarck is that of the present; the policy of Marx, who considers himself at least as Bismarck's successor, is that of the future.[40] And when I say that Mr. Marx considers

himself the continuation of Bismarck, I am far from defaming
Marx. If he did not consider himself as such, he could not have
permitted Engels, the confidant of all his thoughts, to write that
Bismarck serves the cause of the Social Revolution. He serves it
now, inadvertently, in his own way; Mr. Marx will serve it later,
in another way.

Now let us examine the particular character of Mr. Marx's
policy. Let us ascertain the essential points in which it differs
from the policy of Bismarck. The principal point and, one might
say, the only one, is this: Mr. Marx is a democrat, an authoritarian socialist, and a republican. Bismarck is an out-and-out
aristocratic, monarchical Junker. The difference is therefore very
great, very serious, and both sides are sincere in their differences.
On this point, there is no agreement or reconciliation possible
between Bismarck and Mr. Marx. Even apart from Marx's lifelong dedication to the cause of social democracy, which he has
demonstrated on numerous occasions, his very position and his
ambitions are a positive guarantee on this point. In a monarchy,
however liberal, or even in a conservative republic like that of
Thiers,[41] there can be no role for Mr. Marx, and much less so in
the Prussian Germanic Empire founded by Bismarck, with a
militarist and bigoted bugbear of an emperor as chief, and all the
barons and bureaucrats as guardians. Before he can come to
power, Mr. Marx will have to sweep all that away. He is therefore
forced to be a revolutionary.

The concepts of the form and the conditions of the government, these ideas separate Bismarck from Mr. Marx. One is an
out-and-out monarchist and the other is an out-and-out democrat
and republican and, into the bargain, a socialist democrat and
socialist republican.

Let us now see what unites them. *It is the out-and-out cult
of the State.* I have no need to prove it in the case of Bismarck.
The proofs are there. He is completely a state's man, and nothing
but a state's man. But neither is it difficult to prove that Mr.
Marx is also a state's man. He loves government to such a degree
that he even wanted to institute one in the International Workingmen's Association; and he worships power so much that he
wanted, and still intends today, to impose his dictatorship upon

us. His socialist political program is a very faithful expression of his personal attitude. The supreme objective of all his efforts, as is proclaimed in the fundamental statutes of his party in Germany, is the establishment of the great People's State [*Volksstaat*].

But whoever says state necessarily says a particular limited state, doubtless comprising, if it is very large, many different peoples and countries, but excluding still more. For unless he is dreaming of a universal state, as did Napoleon and the Emperor Charles the Fifth, or the papacy, which dreamed of the Universal Church, Marx will have to content himself with governing a single state. Consequently, whoever says state says *a* state, and whoever says *a* state affirms by that the existence of other states, and whoever says *other* states immediately says: competition, jealousy, truceless and endless war. The simplest logic as well as all history bears witness to this truth.

Any state, under pain of perishing and seeing itself devoured by neighboring states, must tend toward complete power, and having become powerful, it must embark on a career of conquest so that it will not itself be conquered; for two similar but competing powers cannot coexist without trying to destroy each other. Whoever says "conquest," under whatever form or name, says conquered peoples, enslaved and in bondage.

It is in the nature of the State to break the solidarity of the human race. The State cannot preserve itself as an integrated entity and in all its strength unless it sets itself up as the supreme be-all and end-all for its own subjects, though not for the subjects of other unconquered states. This inevitably results in the supremacy of state morality and state interests over universal human reason and morality, thus rupturing the universal solidarity of humanity. The principle of political or state morality is very simple. The State being the supreme objective, everything favorable to the growth of its power is good; everything contrary to it, however humane and ethical, is bad. This morality is called *patriotism*. The International is the negation of patriotism and consequently the negation of the State. If, therefore, Mr. Marx and his friends of the German Social Democratic party should succeed in introducing the State principle into our program, they would destroy the International.

The State, for its own preservation, must necessarily be powerful as regards foreign affairs, but if it is so in regard to foreign relations, it will unfailingly be so in regard to domestic matters. The morality of every state must conform to the particular conditions and circumstances of its existence, a morality which restricts and therefore rejects any human and universal morality. It must see to it that all its subjects think and, above all, act in total compliance with the patriotic morality of the State and remain immune to the influence and teachings of true humanistic morality. This makes state censorship absolutely necessary; for too much liberty of thought and opinion is incompatible with the unanimity of adherence demanded by the security of the State, and Mr. Marx, in conformity with his eminently political point of view, considers this censorship reasonable. That this is in reality Mr. Marx's opinion is sufficiently demonstrated by his attempts to introduce censorship into the International, even while masking these efforts with plausible pretexts.

But however vigilant this censorship may be, even if the State were to have an exclusive monopoly over education and instruction for all the people, as Mazzini wished, and as Mr. Marx wishes today, the State can never be sure that prohibited and dangerous thoughts may not somehow be smuggled into the consciousness of its subjects. Forbidden fruit has such an attraction for men, and the demon of revolt, that eternal enemy of the State, awakens so easily in their hearts when they are not entirely stupefied, that neither the education nor the instruction nor even the censorship of the State sufficiently guarantees its security. It must still have a police, devoted agents who watch over and direct, secretly and unobtrusively, the current of the people's opinions and passions. We have seen that Mr. Marx himself is so convinced of this necessity that he planted his secret agents in all the regions of the International, above all in Italy, France, and Spain. Finally, however perfect from the point of view of preserving the State, of organizing the education and indoctrination of its citizens, of censorship, and of the police, the State cannot be secure in its existence while it does not have an armed force to defend itself against its *enemies at home*.

The State is the government from above downwards of an

immense number of men, very different from the point of view of the degree of their culture, the nature of the countries or localities that they inhabit, the occupations they follow, the interests and aspirations directing them—the State is the government of all these by one or another minority. This minority, even if it were a thousand times elected by universal suffrage and controlled in its acts by popular institutions, unless it were endowed with omniscience, omnipresence, and the omnipotence which the theologians attribute to God, could not possibly know and foresee the needs of its people, or satisfy with an even justice those interests which are most legitimate and pressing. There will always be discontented people because there will always be some who are sacrificed.

Besides, the State, like the Church, is by its very nature a great sacrificer of living beings. It is an arbitrary being in whose heart all the positive, living, unique, and local interests of the people meet, clash, destroy each other, become absorbed into that abstraction called the *common interest* or the *common good* or the *public welfare*, and where all the real wills cancel each other in that abstraction that bears the name *will of the people*. It follows from this that the so-called will of the people is never anything but the negation and sacrifice of all the real wills of the people, just as the so-called public interest is nothing but the sacrifice of their interests. But in order for this omnivorous abstraction to impose itself on millions of men, it must be represented and supported by some real being, some living force. Well, this force has always existed. In the Church it is called the clergy, and in the State the ruling or governing class.

And, in fact, what do we find throughout history? The State has always been the patrimony of some privileged class: a priestly class, an aristocratic class, a bourgeois class. And finally, when all the other classes have exhausted themselves, the State then becomes the patrimony of the bureaucratic class and then falls— or, if you will, rises—to the position of a machine. But in any case it is absolutely necessary for the salvation of the State that there should be some privileged class devoted to its preservation.[42]

But in the People's State of Marx there will be, we are told, no privileged class at all. All will be equal, not only from the juridical and political point of view but also from the economic point of view. At least this is what is promised, though I very much doubt whether that promise could ever be kept. There will therefore no longer be any privileged class, but there *will* be a government and, note this well, an extremely complex government. This government will not content itself with administering and governing the masses politically, as all governments do today. It will also administer the masses economically, concentrating in the hands of the State the production and division of wealth, the cultivation of land, the establishment and development of factories, the organization and direction of commerce, and finally the application of capital to production by the only banker—the State. All that will demand an immense knowledge and many heads "overflowing with brains" in this government. It will be the reign of *scientific intelligence*, the most aristocratic, despotic, arrogant, and elitist of all regimes. There will be a new class, a new hierarchy of real and counterfeit scientists and scholars, and the world will be divided into a minority ruling in the name of knowledge, and an immense ignorant majority. And then, woe unto the mass of ignorant ones!

Such a regime will not fail to arouse very considerable discontent in the masses of the people, and in order to keep them in check, the "enlightened" and "liberating" government of Mr. Marx will have need of a not less considerable armed force. For the government must be strong, says Engels, to maintain order among these millions of illiterates whose mighty uprising would be capable of destroying and overthrowing everything, even a government "overflowing with brains."

You can see quite well that behind all the democratic and socialistic phrases and promises in Marx's program for the State lies all that constitutes the true despotic and brutal nature of all states, regardless of their form of government. Moreover, in the final reckoning, the People's State of Marx and the aristocratic-monarchic state of Bismarck are completely identical in terms of their primary domestic and foreign objectives. In foreign affairs there is the same deployment of military force, that is to say, conquest. And in home affairs the same employment of armed force, the last argument of all threatened political leaders against the masses who, tired of always believing, hoping, submitting, and obeying, rise in revolt.

Let us now consider the real national policy of Marx himself. Like Bismarck, he is a German patriot. He desires the greatness and glory of Germany as a state. No one in any case will count it a crime for him to love his country and his people, and he is so profoundly convinced that the State is the condition *sine qua non* for the prosperity of his country and the emancipation of his people. Thus he naturally desires to see Germany organized into a very powerful state, since weak and small states always run the risk of being swallowed up. Therefore Marx, as a clear-sighted and ardent patriot, must wish for the power and expansion of Germany as a state.

But, on the other hand, Marx is a celebrated socialist and, what is more, one of the principal initiators of the International. He does not content himself with working only for the emancipation of the German proletariat. He feels honor bound to work at the same time for the emancipation of the proletariat of all countries. As a German patriot, he wants the power and glory, the domination by Germany; but as a socialist of the International he must wish for the emancipation of all the peoples of the world. How can this contradiction be resolved?

There is only one way—that is to proclaim that a great and powerful German state is an indispensable condition for the emancipation of the whole world; that the national and political triumph of Germany is the triumph of humanity.

This conviction, once vindicated, is not only permissible but, in the name of the most sacred of causes, mandatory, to make the International, and all the federations of other countries serve as a very powerful, effective, and, above all, popular means for establishing the great pan-Germanic state. And that is precisely what Marx tried at the London Conference in 1871 and with the resolutions passed by his German and French friends at the Hague Congress [1872]. If he did not succeed more fully, it is assuredly not for lack of zeal or great skill on his part, but probably because his fundamental idea was false and its realization impossible.

IV

Final
Years

1873

———————

Statism and Anarchy

Statism and Anarchy (1873) is the first completed volume of a larger projected work by Bakunin. Written in Russian, with special emphasis on Slavic problems, this work tremendously influenced Russian revolutionary thought. In the first extract, "Critique of the Marxist Theory of the State," Bakunin, without specifically naming Marx, nevertheless lays the groundwork for attacking his statism. "The theory of statism as well as that of so-called 'revolutionary dictatorship' is based on the idea that a 'privileged elite,' consisting of those scientists and 'doctrinaire revolutionists' who believe that 'theory is prior to social experience,' should impose their preconceived scheme of social organization on the people. The dictatorial power of this learned minority is concealed by the fiction of a pseudorepresentative government which presumes to express the will of the people."

Even many of Bakunin's critics concede that perhaps his most timely ideas are contained in the devastating "Critique of the Marxist Theory of the State."[1] For example, in the winter 1968 issue of New Politics, Burton Hall writes:

> . . . it is most uncomfortable for a devout socialist to look over the argument exchanged between Marx and Bakunin and reflect that maybe it was Bakunin who was right all the time . . . not only because of the accuracy of his predictions as to what socialism would look like, if it were ever to come into existence, but even more to the point, because the reasoning on which he based these predictions, reinforced by the historical evidence of the past half-century, seems almost unanswerably persuasive.

In this connection, Bakunin's predictions about state-dominated economy and regimentation of labor were based on measures advocated in the Communist Manifesto: centralization of credit and transportation by the State, obligatory work for all, the establishment of industrial armies, particularly in agriculture, etc.

The second excerpt, "Some Preconditions for a Social Revolution,"[2] discusses two main questions: the subjective (psychological) and the objective (material) preconditions for a social revolution, and whether the Slavic peoples can achieve the Social Revolution through the establishment of a pan-Slavic or any other form of state. This naturally leads to a discussion of the nature of the State; and Bakunin proceeds to expound his view that the State is more than just "the executive committee of the capitalist class." To this end he cites the example of the Serbia of his time, to show how the State can become a self-perpetuating dictatorship dominating both the people and the economy; how an immense army of government officials can create, under certain conditions, its own state, and "exploit the . . . people in order to provide the bureaucrats with all the comforts of life." This description will bring readily to mind the fate of various modern national minorities who have freed themselves from their colonial masters and established their own states.

The final excerpt, taken from the appendix to Statism and Anarchy, deals primarily with the preconditions for a social revolution in Russia.[3] Contrary to what is generally believed, Bakunin does not idolize the Russian peasant, nor does he, like so many of his contemporaries, uncritically accept the Mir (peasant community) as the ideal unit of the future society. In discussing the program of the moderate liberals and the Populists, Bakunin gives his views on the efficacy of cooperatives, and the establishment of colonies (communes) and other reformist measures to bring about fundamental social changes. He also outlines what intelligent and dedicated Russian youth from upper and middle classes could do to promote social revolution.

Statism and Anarchy represents among other things Bakunin's opposition to the argument of Auguste Comte (1798–1857), the founder of modern sociology, that social life must be regulated in accordance with the immutable laws of the physical sciences. In opposition to the Comtean positivists, Bakunin contended that the scientific laws governing inanimate objects could not apply to the behavior of living beings endowed with the faculty of choice and the ability to modify their conduct as the situation demanded. While he approved of Comte's effort to place the study of society on a materialistic basis, he objected to positivism as a "religion of humanity" under the aegis of a scientific church, and to any form of philosophic idealism or metaphysics, even if couched in scientific terms, as fundamentally reactionary because inclined "to force future generations into the narrow mold of . . . necessarily tentative theories."

Critique of the Marxist Theory of the State

There is no road leading from metaphysics to the realities of life. Theory and fact are separated by an abyss. It is impossible to leap across this abyss by what Hegel called a "qualitative jump" from the world of logic to the world of nature and of real life.

The road leading from concrete fact to theory and vice versa is the method of science and is the true road. In the practical world, it is the movement of society toward forms of organization that will to the greatest possible extent reflect life itself in all its aspects and complexity.

Such is the people's way to complete emancipation, accessible to all—the way of the anarchist social revolution, which will come from the people themselves, an elemental force sweeping away all obstacles. Later, from the depths of the popular soul, there will spontaneously emerge the new creative forms of social life.

The way of the gentlemen metaphysicians is completely different. Metaphysician is the term we use for the disciples of Hegel and for the positivists, and in general, for all the worshippers of science as a goddess, all those modern Procrusteans who, in one way or another, have created an ideal of social organization, a narrow mold into which they would force future generations, all those who, instead of seeing science as only one of the essential manifestations of natural and social life, insist that all of life is encompassed in their necessarily tentative scientific theories. Metaphysicians and positivists, all these gentlemen who consider it their mission to prescribe the laws of life in the name of science, are consciously or unconsciously reactionaries.

This is very easy to demonstrate.

Science in the true sense of that word, real science, is at this time within reach of only an insignificant minority. For example, among us in Russia, how many accomplished savants are there in a population of eighty million? Probably a thousand are engaged in science, but hardly more than a few hundred could be considered first-rate, serious scientists. If science were to dictate the laws, the overwhelming majority, many millions of men, would be ruled by one or two hundred experts. Actually it would be even fewer than that, because not all of science is concerned with the administration of society. This would be the task of sociology—the science of sciences—which presupposes in the case of a well-trained sociologist that he have an adequate knowledge of all the other sciences. How many such people are there in Russia—in all Europe? Twenty or thirty—and these twenty or thirty would rule the world? Can anyone imagine a more absurd and abject despotism?

It is almost certain that these twenty or thirty experts would quarrel among themselves, and if they did agree on common policies, it would be at the expense of mankind. The principal vice of the average specialist is his inclination to exaggerate his own knowledge and deprecate everyone else's. Give him control and he will become an insufferable tyrant. To be the slave of pedants—what a destiny for humanity! Give them full power and they will begin by performing on human beings the same experiments that the scientists are now performing on rabbits and dogs.

We must respect the scientists for their merits and achievements, but in order to prevent them from corrupting their own high moral and intellectual standards, they should be granted no special privileges and no rights other than those possessed by everyone—for example, the liberty to express their convictions, thought, and knowledge. Neither they nor any other special group should be given power over others. He who is given power will inevitably become an oppressor and exploiter of society.

But we are told: "Science will not always be the patrimony of a few. There will come a time when it will be accessible to all." Such a time is still far away and there will be many social upheavals before this dream will come true, and even then, who would want to put his fate in the hands of the priests of science?

It seems to us that anyone who thinks that after a social revolution everybody will be equally educated is very much mistaken. Science, then as now, will remain one of the many specialized fields, though it will cease to be accessible only to a very few of the privileged class. With the elimination of class distinctions, education will be within the reach of all those who will have the ability and the desire to pursue it, but not to the detriment of manual labor, which will be compulsory for all.

Available to everyone will be a general scientific education, especially the learning of the scientific method, the habit of correct thinking, the ability to generalize from facts and make more or less correct deductions. But of encyclopedic minds and advanced sociologists[4] there will be very few. It would be sad for mankind if at any time theoretical speculation became the only source of guidance for society, if science alone were in charge of all social administration. Life would wither, and human society would turn into a voiceless and servile herd. The domination of life by science can have no other result than the brutalization of mankind.

We, the revolutionary anarchists, are the advocates of education for all the people, of the emancipation and the widest possible expansion of social life. Therefore we are the enemies of the State and all forms of the statist principle. In opposition to the metaphysicians, the positivists, and all the worshippers of science, we declare that natural and social life always comes before theory, which is only one of its manifestations but never its creator. From out of its own inexhaustible depths, society develops through a series of events, but not by thought alone. Theory is always created by life, but never creates it; like mileposts and road signs, it only indicates the direction and the different stages of life's independent and unique development.

In accordance with this belief, we neither intend nor desire to thrust upon our own or any other people any scheme of social organization taken from books or concocted by ourselves. We are convinced that the masses of the people carry in themselves, in their instincts (more or less developed by history), in their daily necessities, and in their conscious or unconscious aspirations, all the elements of the future social organization. We seek this ideal in the people themselves. Every state power, every government, by its very nature places itself outside and over the people and inevitably subordinates them to an organization and to aims which are foreign to and opposed to the real needs and aspirations of the people. We declare ourselves the enemies of every government and every state power, and of governmental organization in general. We think that people can be free and happy only when organized from the bottom up in completely free and independent associations, without governmental paternalism though not without the influence of a variety of free individuals and parties.

Such are our ideas as social revolutionaries, and we are therefore called anarchists. We do not protest this name, for we are indeed the enemies of any governmental power, since we know that such a power depraves those who wear its mantle equally with those who are forced to submit to it. Under its pernicious influence the former become ambitious and greedy despots, exploiters of society in favor of their personal or class interests, while the latter become slaves.

Idealists of all kinds—metaphysicians, positivists, those who support the rule of science over life, doctrinaire revolutionists—all defend the idea of state and state power with equal eloquence, because they see in it, as a consequence of their own systems, the only salvation for society. Quite logically, since they have accepted the basic premise (which we consider completely mistaken) that thought precedes life, that theory is prior to social experience, and, therefore, that social science has to be the starting point for all social upheavals and reconstructions. They then arrive unavoidably at the conclusion that because thought, theory, and science, at least in our times, are in the possession of very few, these few ought to be the leaders of social life, not only the initiators, but also the leaders of all popular movements. On the day following the revolution the new social order should not be organized by the free association of people's organizations or unions, local and regional, from the bottom up, in accordance with the demands and instincts of the people, but only by the dictatorial power of this learned minority, which presumes to express the will of the people.

This fiction of a pseudorepresentative government serves to conceal the domination of the masses by a handful of privileged elite; an elite elected by hordes of people who are rounded up and do not know for whom or for what they vote. Upon this artificial and abstract expression of what they falsely imagine to be the will of the people and of which the real living people have not the least idea, they construct both the theory of statism as well as the theory of so-called revolutionary dictatorship.

The differences between revolutionary dictatorship and statism are superficial. Fundamentally they both represent the same principle of minority rule over the majority in the name of the alleged "stupidity" of the latter and the alleged "intelligence" of the former. Therefore they are both equally reactionary since both directly and inevitably must preserve and perpetuate the political and economic privileges of the ruling minority and the political and economic subjugation of the masses of the people.

Now it is clear why the dictatorial revolutionists, who aim to overthrow the existing powers and social structures in order to erect upon their ruins their own dictatorships, never were or will be the enemies of government, but, to the contrary, always will be the most ardent promoters of the government idea. They are the enemies only of contemporary governments, because they wish to replace them. They are the enemies of the present governmental structure, because it excludes the possibility of their dictatorship. At the same time they are the most devoted friends of governmental power. For if the revolution destroyed this power by actually freeing the masses, it would deprive this pseudorevolutionary minority of any hope to harness the masses in order to make them the beneficiaries of their own government policy.

We have already expressed several times our deep aversion to the theory of Lassalle and Marx, which recommends to the workers, if not as a final ideal at least as the next immediate goal, the *founding of a people's state*, which according to their interpretation will be nothing but "the proletariat elevated to the status of the governing class."

Let us ask, if the proletariat is to be the ruling class, over whom is it to rule? In short, there will remain another proletariat which will be subdued to this new rule, to this new state. For instance, the peasant "rabble" who, as it is known, does not enjoy the sympathy of the Marxists who consider it to represent a lower level of culture, will probably be ruled by the factory proletariat of the cities. Or, if this problem is to be approached nationalistically, the Slavs will be placed in the same subordinate relationship to the victorious German proletariat in which the latter now stands to the German bourgeoisie.

If there is a State, there must be domination of one class by another and, as a result, slavery; the State without slavery is unthinkable—and this is why we are the enemies of the State.

What does it mean that the proletariat will be elevated to a ruling class? Is it possible for the whole proletariat to stand at the head of the government? There are nearly forty million Germans. Can all forty million be members of the government? In such a case, there will be no government, no state, but, if there is to be a state there will be those who are ruled and those who are slaves.

The Marxist theory solves this dilemma very simply. By the people's rule, they mean the rule of a small number of representatives elected by the people. The general, and every man's, right to elect the representatives of the people and the rulers of the State is the latest word of the Marxists, as well as of the democrats. This is a lie, behind which lurks the despotism of the ruling minority, a lie all the more dangerous in that it appears to express the so-called will of the people.

Ultimately, from whatever point of view we look at this question, we come always to the same sad conclusion, the rule of the great masses of the people by a privileged minority. The

Marxists say that this minority will consist of workers. Yes, possibly of former workers, who, as soon as they become the rulers of the representatives of the people, will cease to be workers and will look down at the plain working masses from the governing heights of the State; they will no longer represent the people, but only themselves and their claims to rulership over the people. Those who doubt this know very little about human nature.

These elected representatives, say the Marxists, will be dedicated and learned socialists. The expressions "learned socialist," "scientific socialism," etc., which continuously appear in the speeches and writings of the followers of Lassalle and Marx, prove that the pseudo-People's State will be nothing but a despotic control of the populace by a new and not at all numerous aristocracy of real and pseudoscientists. The "uneducated" people will be totally relieved of the cares of administration, and will be treated as a regimented herd. A beautiful liberation, indeed!

The Marxists are aware of this contradiction and realize that a government of scientists will be a real dictatorship regardless of its democratic form. They console themselves with the idea that this rule will be temporary. They say that the only care and objective will be to educate and elevate the people economically and politically to such a degree that such a government will soon become unnecessary, and the State, after losing its political or coercive character, will automatically develop into a completely free organization of economic interests and communes.

There is a flagrant contradiction in this theory. If their state would be really of the people, why eliminate it? And if the State is needed to emancipate the workers, then the workers are not yet free, so why call it a People's State? By our polemic against them we have brought them to the realization that freedom or anarchism, which means a free organization of the working masses from the bottom up, is the final objective of social development, and that every state, not excepting their People's State, is a yoke, on the one hand giving rise to despotism and on the other to slavery. They say that such a yoke-dictatorship is a transitional step towards achieving full freedom for the people: anarchism or freedom is the aim, while state and dictatorship is the means, and so, in order to free the masses of people, they have first to be enslaved!

Upon this contradiction our polemic has come to a halt. They insist that only dictatorship (of course their own) can create freedom for the people. We reply that all dictatorship has no objective other than self-perpetuation, and that slavery is all it can generate and instill in the people who suffer it. Freedom can be created only by freedom, by a total rebellion of the people, and by a voluntary organization of the people from the bottom up.

The social theory of the antistate socialists or anarchists leads them directly and inevitably towards a break with all forms of the State, with all varieties of bourgeois politics, and leaves no choice except a social revolution. The opposite theory, state communism and the authority of the scientists, attracts and confuses its followers and, under the pretext of political tactics, makes continuous deals with the governments and various bourgeois political parties, and is directly pushed towards reaction.

The cardinal point of this program is that the State alone is to liberate the (pseudo-) proletariat. To achieve this, the State must agree to liberate the proletariat from the oppression of bourgeois capitalism. How is it possible to impart such a will to the State? The proletariat must take possession of the State by a revolution—an heroic undertaking. But once the proletariat seizes the State, it must move at once to abolish immediately this eternal prison of the people. But according to Mr. Marx, the people not only should not abolish the State, but, on the contrary, they must strengthen and enlarge it, and turn it over to the full disposition of their benefactors, guardians, and teachers —the leaders of the Communist party, meaning Mr. Marx and his friends—who will then liberate them in their own way. They will concentrate all administrative power in their own strong hands, because the ignorant people are in need of a strong guardianship; and they will create a central state bank, which will also control all the commerce, industry, agriculture, and even science. The mass of the people will be divided into two armies, the agricultural and the industrial, under the direct command of the state engineers, who will constitute the new privileged politi-cal-scientific class.

Some Preconditions
for a Social Revolution

The propaganda and organization of the International is directed exclusively to the working class, which in Italy, as in the rest of Europe, embodies all the life, power, and aspirations of the future society. The International attracted only a handful of adherents from the bourgeois world who, having learned to passionately hate the existing social order and all its false values, renounced their class and dedicated themselves body and soul to the cause of the people.

If they can root out the last vestiges of subjective loyalty to the bourgeois world, and those of personal vanity, these men, though few in number, could render priceless services to the revolutionary movement. They draw their inspiration from the movement of the people. But in exchange they can contribute expert knowledge, the capacity for abstract thought and gen-eralization, and the ability to organize and coordinate—qualities which constitute the creative force without which any victory is impossible. In Italy and Russia there are more such young men than there are in other countries. But what is a much more important asset for the Revolution is that there is in Italy an enormous proletariat, unusually intelligent by nature but very often lacking education and living in great poverty. This proletariat comprises two or three million urban workers, mainly in factories and small workshops, and approximately twenty mil-lion totally deprived peasants. This huge class has been reduced to such desperation that even the defenders of this terrible society are beginning to speak out openly in parliament and in the official press, admitting that things have reached the breaking point, and that something must immediately be done to avoid a popular holocaust which will destroy everything in its path.

Nowhere are there more favorable conditions for the Social Revolution than in Italy. There does not exist in Italy, as in most other European nations, a special category of relatively affluent workers, earning higher wages, boasting of their literary capacities, and so impregnated by a variety of bourgeois prejudices that, excepting income, they differ in no way from the bourgeoisie. This class of bourgeois workers is numerous in Germany and in Switzerland; but in Italy, on the contrary, they are insignificant in number and influence, a mere drop in the ocean. In Italy it is the extremely poor proletariat that predominates. Marx speaks disdainfully, but quite unjustly, of this *Lumpenproletariat*. For in them, and only in them, and not in the bourgeois strata of workers, are there crystallized the entire intelligence and power of the coming Social Revolution.

A popular insurrection, by its very nature, is instinctive, chaotic, and destructive, and always entails great personal sacrifice and an enormous loss of public and private property. The masses are always ready to sacrifice themselves; and this is what turns them into a brutal and savage horde, capable of performing heroic and apparently impossible exploits, and since they possess little or nothing, they are not demoralized by the responsibilities of property ownership. And in moments of crisis, for the sake of self-defense or victory, they will not hesitate to burn down their own houses and neighborhoods, and property being no deterrent, since it belongs to their oppressors, they develop a passion for destruction. This negative passion, it is true, is far from being sufficient to attain the heights of the revolutionary cause; but without it, revolution would be impossible. Revolution requires extensive and widespread destruction, a fecund and renovating destruction, since in this way and only this way are new worlds born. . . .

Not even the most terrible misery affecting millions of workers is in itself enough to spur them to revolution. Man is by nature endowed (or cursed) by marvelous patience, and only the devil knows how he can patiently endure unimaginable misery and even slow death by starvation; and even the impulse to give way to despair is smothered by a complete insensibility toward his own rights, and an imperturbable obedience. . . .

People in this condition are hopeless. They would rather die than rebel. But when a man can be driven to desperation, he is then more likely to rebel. Despair is a bitter, passionate feeling capable of rousing men from their semiconscious resignation if they already have an idea of a more desirable situation, even without much hope of achieving it. But it is impossible to remain too long in a state of absolute despair: one must give in, die, or do something about it—fight for a cause, but what cause? Obviously, to free oneself, to fight for a better life. . . .

But poverty and desperation are still not sufficient to generate the Social Revolution. They may be able to call forth intermittent local rebellions, but not great and widespread mass uprisings. To do this it is indispensable that the people be inspired by a universal ideal, historically developed from the instinctual depths of popular sentiments, amplified and clarified by a series of significant events and severe and bitter experiences. It is necessary that the populace have a general idea of their rights and a deep, passionate, quasi-religious belief in the validity of these rights. When this idea and this popular faith are joined to the kind of misery that leads to desperation, then the Social Revolution is near and inevitable, and no force on earth will be able to resist it.

This is exactly the situation of the Italian proletariat. The sufferings they are forced to endure are scarcely less terrible than the poverty and misery that overwhelm the Russian people. But the Italian proletariat is imbued with a greater degree of passionate revolutionary consciousness than are the Russian masses, a consciousness which daily becomes stronger and clearer. By nature intelligent and passionate, the Italian proletariat is at last beginning to understand what it wants and what must be done to achieve its complete emancipation. In this sense the propaganda of the International, energetically and widely diffused during the last two years, has been of great value. This profound sentiment, this universal ideal, without which (as we have already said) every mass insurrection, however great the sacrifices made, is absolutely impossible, has been stimulated by the International, which at the same time pointed out the road to emancipation and the means for the organization of the people's power.

At first this ideal naturally manifests itself in the passionate desire of the people to put an end to their poverty and misery and to satisfy all their material needs by collective labor, equally obligatory for all. Later it will come to include the abolition of all domination, and the free organization of the life of the country in accord with the needs of the people. This will mean the rejection of the State's form of control from the top in favor of organization from the bottom up, created by the people themselves, without governments and parliaments. This would be organization achieved by the free participation of associations, of the agricultural and industrial workers, of the communes and the provinces. Ultimately, in the more distant future, it would erect on the ruins of all states the fraternity of peoples.

It is worth noting that in Italy, as in Spain, the program of Marxist state communism has had absolutely no effect, while the program of the famous Alliance of revolutionary socialists [anarchist vanguard organization], which proclaimed uncompromising war against all domination, all tutelage and governmental authority, was overwhelmingly and enthusiastically accepted by the workers.

A people inspired with such ideas can always win its own freedom and ground its own life on the most ample freedom for everyone, while in no way threatening or infringing on the freedom of other nations. This is why neither Italy nor Spain will embark on a career of conquest but will, on the contrary, help all peoples to accomplish their own social revolutions. . . .

Modern capitalist production and bank speculation inexorably demand enormous centralization of the State, which alone can subject millions of workers to capitalist exploitation. Federalist organization from the bottom upward, of workers' associations, groups, communes, cantons [counties], regions, and finally whole peoples, is the sole condition for true, nonfictitious freedom, but such freedom violates the interests and convictions of the ruling classes, just as economic self-determination is incompatible with their methods of organization. *Representative democracy*, however, harmonizes marvelously with the capitalist economic system. This new statist system, basing itself on the alleged *sovereignty* of the so-called *will of the people*, as supposedly expressed by their alleged representatives in mock popular assemblies, incorporates the two principal and necessary conditions for the progress of capitalism: state centralization, and the actual submission of the sovereign people to the intellectual governing minority, who, while claiming to represent the people, unfailingly exploits them.

The exploitation of human labor cannot be sugar-coated even by the most democratic form of government . . . for the worker it will always be a bitter pill. It follows from this that no government, however paternalistic, however bent on avoiding friction, will tolerate any threat to its exploitative economic institutions or its political hegemony: unable to instill habitual obedience to its authority by cajolery and other peaceful methods, the government will then resort to unceasing coercion, to violence, i.e., to political control, and the ultimate weapon of political control is military power.

The modern State is by its very nature a military State; and every military State must of necessity become a conquering, invasive State; to survive it must conquer or be conquered, for the simple reason that accumulated military power will suffocate if it does not find an outlet. Therefore the modern State must strive to be a huge and powerful State: this is the indispensable precondition for its survival.

And just as capitalist production must, to avoid bankruptcy, continually expand by absorbing its weaker competitors and drive to monopolize all the other capitalist enterprises all over the world, so must the modern State inevitably drive to become the only universal State, since the coexistence of two universal states is by definition absolutely impossible. Sovereignty, the drive toward absolute domination, is inherent in every State; and the first prerequisite for this sovereignty is the comparative weakness, or at least the submission of neighboring states. . . .

A strong State can have only one solid foundation: military and bureaucratic centralization. The fundamental difference between a monarchy and even the most democratic republic is that in the monarchy, the bureaucrats oppress and rob the people for the benefit of the privileged in the name of the King, and to fill their own coffers; while in the republic the people are robbed and oppressed in the same way for the benefit of the same classes, in the name of "the will of the people" (and to fill the coffers of the democratic bureaucrats). In the republic the State, which is supposed to be the people, legally organized, stifles and will continue to stifle the real people. But the people will feel no better if the stick with which they are being beaten is labeled "the people's stick."

. . . No state, however democratic—not even the reddest republic—can ever give the people what they really want, i.e., the free self-organization and administration of their own affairs from the bottom upward, without any interference or violence from above, because every state, even the pseudo-People's State concocted by Mr. Marx, is in essence only a machine ruling the masses from above, through a privileged minority of conceited intellectuals, who imagine that they know what the people need and want better than do the people themselves. . . .

We are as unalterably opposed to any form of pan-Slavism as we are to any form of pan-Germanism. It is the sacred and urgent duty of the Russian revolutionary youth to counteract in every possible way the pan-Slavic propaganda inside Russia itself, and particularly that spread in other Slavic lands, officially and unofficially by government agents, and voluntarily by fanatical Slavophiles, which strives to convince the unfortunate Slavs that the Slavic Tsar deeply loves his Slavic brothers, and that the dastardly pan-Russian Empire, which throttled Poland and Little Russia [Ukrainia?] can, if only the Tsar wishes, free the Slavic lands from the German yoke. [Bakunin includes as Slavs those in the now defunct Austro-Hungarian Empire—Hungary, Austria, Bulgaria, Serbia, Yugoslavia, Czechoslovakia, etc.]

This illusion is widespread among Austrian Slavs. Their fanatical though understandable hatred of their oppressor has driven them to such a state of madness that, forgetting or ignoring the atrocities committed against Lithuania, Poland, Little Russia and even Great Russia by Tsarist despotism, they still await deliverance by our pan-Russian slave driver.

One should not be surprised that the Slavic masses harbor such illusions. They do not know history or the internal situation in Russia: all they are told is that an all-Slavic empire has been created to defy the Germans; an empire so mighty that the Germans tremble in fear . . . and what the Germans hate, the Slavs must love.

All this is to be expected. But what is sad, hard to understand, and inexcusable is that people who should know better, the educated Austrian Slavs, experienced, wise, and well informed, have organized a party that openly preaches pan-Slavism. According to some, this would involve the creation of *a great Slavic empire* under the domination of the Tsar, and according to others it would consist in the emancipation of the Slavic peoples by the Russian Empire. . . .

But what benefits would the Slavic people derive by the formation of a mighty Slavic empire? This would indeed be advantageous for the states [composing the empire] but not for the proletariat, only for the privileged minority—the clergy, the nobility, the bourgeoisie—and probably for some intellectuals, who because of their diplomas and their alleged mental superiority feel called upon to lead the masses. In short, there is an advantage for some thousands of oppressors, hangmen, and other exploiters of the proletariat. As far as the great masses of the people are concerned, the vaster the State, the heavier are the chains and the more crowded the prisons.

We have demonstrated that to exist, a state must become an invader of other states. Just as the competition which in the economic sphere destroys or absorbs small and even medium-sized enterprises—factories, landholdings, businesses—so does the immense State likewise devour small and medium-sized states. Therefore every state, to exist not on paper but in fact, and not at the mercy of neighboring states, and to be independent, must inevitably strive to become an invasive, aggressive, conquering state. This means that it must be ready to occupy a foreign country and hold many millions of people in subjection. For this it must exercise massive military power. But wherever military power prevails, it is goodbye to freedom! Farewell to the autonomy and well-being of the working people. It follows from this that the construction of a great Slavic empire means only the enslavement of the Slavic people.

Yet the Slavic statists tell us, "we don't want a single great

Slav state; we want only a number of middle-sized Slavic states, thereby assuring the independence of the Slavic peoples." But this viewpoint is contrary to logic and historic facts and to the very nature of things; no middle-sized state, in our times, can exist independently. There will therefore be either no state at all, or there will be a single giant state which will devour all the weaker states—a despotic, absolutist Russian state.

Could a smaller Slavic state defend itself against the new pan-Germanic empire, without itself becoming just as great and just as powerful? Could it depend upon the assistance of countries united by self-interest? In both cases the answer is no. In the first place, because an alliance of various smaller heterogeneous powers, even when equal or numerically superior, remains weaker because their enemy is consolidated, homogeneous, responsive to a single command, and therefore much stronger. Secondly, one cannot depend on the friendly cooperation of other states, even when their own interests are involved. Statesmen, like ordinary mortals, are often so preoccupied with momentary interests and passions that they cannot see when their vital interests are threatened. . . .

But could not the centralized pan-Germanic state be neutralized by a pan-Slavic federation, i.e., a union of independent Slavic nations patterned after Switzerland or North America? We reply in the negative. Because to form such a federation, it will first be absolutely necessary to break up the pan-Russian Empire into a number of separate, independent states, joined only by voluntary association, and because the coexistence of such independent federated and medium or small states, together with so great a centralized empire, is simply inconceivable. . . .

This federation of states could to some extent safeguard bourgeois freedom, but it could never become a military state for the simple reason that it *is* a federation. State power demands centralization. But it will be contended that the example of Switzerland and the United States refutes this assertion. But Switzerland, in order to increase its military power, tends toward centralization; and federation is possible in the United States only because it is not surrounded by highly centralized, mighty states like Russia, Germany, or France. Switzerland retains federation only because of the indifference of the great international powers, and because its people are roughly divided into three zones speaking the language of its neighboring states, France, Germany, and Italy. To resist triumphant pan-Germanism on the legalistic and statist field—by founding an equally powerful Slavic state—would be disastrous for the Slavs, because it would inevitably expose them to pan-Russian tyranny. . . .

The progressive Slavic people should realize by now that the time for flirting with Slavic ideology is over, and that there is nothing more absurd and harmful than to compress all the aspirations of the people into the narrow mold of a spurious nationalism. Nationality is not a humanitarian principle; it is an historical, local fact which should be generally tolerated along with other real and inoffensive facts.

Every people, however tiny, has its own specific character, style of life, speech, way of thinking and working; and precisely this character, this style of life, constitutes its nationality, which is the sum total of its historic life, aspirations, and circumstances. Every people, like every individual, are perforce what they are and have the incontestable right to be themselves. This constitutes the alleged national right. But if a people or an individual lives in a certain way, it does not by any means give them the right, nor would it be beneficial, to regard this nationality and individuality as absolute, exclusive principles, nor should they be obsessed by them. On the contrary, the less preoccupied they are with themselves and the more they are imbued by the general idea of humanity, the more life-giving, the more purposeful, and the more profound becomes the feeling of nationality and that of individuality.

The same applies to the Slavs. They will remain insignificant as long as they are obsessed with their narrow-minded, egotistical . . . Slavism, an obsession which by its very nature is contrary to the problems and the cause of humanity in general. They will attain their rightful place in the free fraternity of nations when, together with all other peoples, they are inspired by a wider, more universal interest. . . .

In all historical epochs we find one universal interest which transcends all exclusively national and purely local boundaries, and those nationalities who have sufficient understanding, passion, and strength to identify themselves wholeheartedly with this universal interest become historical peoples [play major historic roles]. The great revolution at the close of the eighteenth century again placed France in a preeminent place among the nations of the world. She created a new objective for all humanity —the ideal of absolute freedom for all men—but only in the exclusively political field. This ideal could never be realized because it was afflicted with an insoluble contradiction: political freedom despite economic servitude. Moreover, political freedom within the State is a fraud.

The French Revolution thus produced two diametrically opposed trends which finally coalesced into one—the systematic exploitation of the proletariat for the benefit of a diminishing and increasingly wealthy minority of monopolists. Upon this exploitation of the laboring masses, one party erects a democratic republic and the other, being more consistent, tries to erect a monarchistic, i.e., openly despotic, centralized, bureaucratic police State. In the latter, a dictatorship is thinly masked by innocuous constitutional forms.

From out of the depths of the proletariat there emerged a new and opposing tendency, a new universal objective: the abolition of all classes and their main base of support, the State, and the self-administration of all property by the workers. . . .

Such is the program of the Social Revolution. There is only one main question confronting all nations, one universal problem: how to achieve economic and political emancipation from the yoke of the State. And this problem cannot be solved without a bloody, terrifying struggle. . . .

Is it not evident that the Slavs can find their rightful place in the fraternal union of peoples only through the Social Revolution?

But a social revolution cannot be confined to a single isolated country. It is by its very nature international in scope. The Slavs must therefore link their aspirations and forces with the aspirations and forces of all other countries. The Slavic proletariat must join the International Workingmen's Association en masse. . . . After joining the International the Slavic proletariat must form factory, crafts, and agricultural sections, uniting these into local federations, and if expedient unite the local federations into an all-Slavic federation. In line with the principles of the International, and freed from the yoke of their respective states, the Slavic workers should and can—without in the least endangering their own independence—establish fraternal relations with the German workers, since an alliance with them on any other basis is entirely out of the question.

Such is the only road to the emancipation of the Slavs. But the path at present followed by the great majority of the young western and southern Slavs, under the influence of their respected and venerable patriots, is a statist path involving the establishment of separate Slavic states and entirely ruinous for the great masses of the people.

The Serbian people shed their blood in torrents and finally freed themselves from Turkish slavery, but no sooner did they become an independent principality than they were again and perhaps even more enslaved by what they thought was their own state, the Serbian nation. As soon as this part of Serbia took on all the features—laws, institutions, etc.—common to all states, the national vitality and heroism which had sustained them in their successful war against the Turks suddenly collapsed. The people, though ignorant and very poor, but passionate, vigorous, naturally intelligent, and freedom-loving, were suddenly transformed into a meek, apathetic herd, easy victims of bureaucratic plunder and despotism.

There are no nobles, no big landowners, no industrialists, and no very wealthy merchants in Turkish Serbia. Yet in spite of this there emerged a new bureaucratic aristocracy composed of young men educated, partly at state expense, in Odessa, Moscow, St. Petersburg, Vienna, Paris, Germany, and Switzerland. Before they were corrupted in the service of the State, these young men distinguished themselves by their love for their people, their liberalism, and lately by their democratic and socialistic inclinations. But no sooner did they enter the state's service than the iron logic of their situation, inherent in the exercise of certain hierarchical and politically advantageous prerogatives, took

its toll, and the young men became cynical bureaucratic mar-
tinets while still mouthing patriotic and liberal slogans. And, as
is well known, a liberal bureaucrat is incomparably worse than
any dyed-in-the-wool reactionary state official.

Moreover, the demands of certain positions are more compelling than noble sentiments and even the best intentions. Upon
returning home from abroad, the young Serbs are bound to pay
back the debt owed to the State for their education and maintenance; they feel that they are morally obliged to serve their
benefactor, the government. Since there is no other employment
for educated young men, they become state functionaries, and
become members of the only aristocracy in the country, the
bureaucratic class. Once integrated into this class, they inevitably
become enemies of the people. . . .

And then the most unscrupulous and the shrewdest manage
to gain control of the microscopic government of this microscopic state, and immediately begin to sell themselves to all
comers, at home to the reigning prince or a pretender to the
throne. In Serbia, the overthrow of one prince and the installa-
tion of another one is called a "revolution." Or they may peddle
their influence to one, several, or even all the great domineering
states—Russia, Austria, Turkey, etc.

One can easily imagine how the people live in such a state!
Ironically enough, the principality of Serbia is a constitutional
state, and all the legislators are elected by the people. It is worth
noting that Turkish Serbia differs from other states in this principal respect: there is only one class in control of the government,
the bureaucracy. The one and only function of the State, therefore, is to exploit the Serbian people in order to provide the
bureaucrats with all the comforts of life.

Preconditions for a
Social Revolution in Russia

Ways and means to make the Social Revolution can be of
two sorts: one purely revolutionary and leading directly to the
organization of a general uprising of the people; the other, more

peaceful, way leads to the emancipation of the people by a gradual, systematic, but at the same time radical transformation of the conditions of existence . . . it is the formation of associations of craftsmen and consumers and, above all, producers' cooperatives, because they lead more directly to the emancipation of labor from the domination of capitalism. . . . The experience of the last twenty years in different lands has shown conclusively that this is impossible.

For the last several years the question of cooperative associations has stirred lively debates in the International; based on numerous arguments, the International has come to the following conclusions, formulated at the Congress of Lausanne (1868) and adopted at the Congress of Brussels (1868).

The various forms of cooperation are incontestably one of the most equitable and rational ways of organizing the future system of production. But before it can realize its aim of emancipating the laboring masses so that they will receive the full product of their labor, the land and all forms of capital must be converted into collective property. As long as this is not accomplished, the cooperatives will be overwhelmed by the all-powerful competition of monopoly capital and vast landed property; . . . and even in the unlikely event that a small group of cooperatives should somehow surmount the competition, their success would only beget a new class of prosperous cooperators in the midst of a poverty-stricken mass of proletarians. While cooperatives cannot achieve the emancipation of the laboring masses under the present socioeconomic conditions, it nevertheless has this advantage, that cooperation can habituate the workers to organize themselves to conduct their own affairs (after the overthrow of the old society). . . .

The Russian people possess to a great extent two qualities which are in our opinion indispensable preconditions for the Social Revolution. . . . Their sufferings are infinite, but they do not patiently resign themselves to their misery and they react with an intense savage despair which twice in history produced such popular explosions as the revolts of Stenka Razin and Pugachev, and which even today expresses itself in continuous peasant outbreaks.

What then prevents them from making a successful revolution? It is the absence of a conscious common ideal capable of inspiring a genuine popular revolution. . . . [Fortunately,] there is no need for a profound analysis of the historic conscience of our people in order to define the fundamental traits which characterize the ideal of our people.

The first of these traits is the conviction, held by all the people, that the land rightfully belongs to them. The second trait is the belief that the right to benefit from the soil belongs not to an individual but to the rural community as a whole, to the *Mir* which assigns the temporary use of the land to the members of the community. The third trait is that even the minimal limitations placed by the State on the *Mir*'s autonomy arouse hostility on the part of the latter toward the State.

Nevertheless, the ideal of the Russian people is overshadowed by three other traits which denature and retard the realization of this ideal; traits which we must combat with all our energy. . . . These three traits are: 1) paternalism, 2) the absorption of the individual by the *Mir*, 3) confidence in the Tsar. . . . The last two, absorption of the individual by the *Mir* and the cult of the Tsar, are the natural and inevitable effects of the first, i.e., the paternalism ruling the people. This is a great historic evil, the worst of all. . . .

This evil deforms all Russian life, and indeed paralyzes it, with its crass family sluggishness, the chronic lying, the avid hypocrisy, and finally, the servility which renders life insupportable. The despotism of the husband, of the father, of the eldest brother over the family (already an immoral institution by virtue of its juridical-economic inequalities), the school of violence and triumphant bestiality, of the cowardice and the daily perversions of the family home. The expression "whitewashed graveyard" is a good description of the Russian family. . . .

[The family patriarch] is simultaneously a slave and a despot: a despot exerting his tyranny over all those under his roof and dependent on his will. The only masters he recognizes are the *Mir* and the Tsar. If he is the head of the family, he will behave like an absolute despot, but he will be the servant of the *Mir* and the slave of the Tsar. The rural community is his universe;

there is only his family and on a higher level the clan. This explains why the patriarchal principle dominates the *Mir*, an odious tyranny, a cowardly submission, and the absolute negation of all individual and family rights. The decisions of the *Mir*, however arbitrary, are law. "Who would dare defy the *Mir*!" exclaims the *muzhik*. But there are among the Russian people personages who have the courage to defy the *Mir*—the brigands. This is the reason brigandage is an important historical phenomenon in Russia; the first rebels, the first revolutionists in Russia, Pugachev and Stenka Razin, were brigands. . . .

One of the greatest misfortunes in Russia is that each community constitutes a closed circle. No community finds it necessary to have the least organic connection with other communities. They are linked by the intermediary of the Tsar, the "little father," and only by the supreme patriarchal power vested in him. It is clear that disunion paralyzes the people, condemns its almost always local revolts to certain defeat and at the same time consolidates the victory of despotism. Therefore, one of the main tasks of revolutionary youth is to establish at all costs and by every possible means a vital line of revolt between the isolated rural communities. This is a difficult, but by no means impossible, task.

The Russian rural community, already sufficiently weakened by patriarchalism, is hopelessly corrupted and crushed by the State. Under its yoke the communal elections are a mockery, and the persons elected by the people become the tools of the oppressors and the venal servants of the rich landlords. In such circumstances the last vestiges of justice, of truth, and of elemental humanity vanish from the rural community, ruined by the authorities. More than ever brigandage becomes the only way out for the individual, and a mass uprising—the revolution— for the populace.

Amid the general confusion of ideas, two diametrically opposed trends emerge. The first, of a more pacific character, inclines toward gradual action; the other, favoring insurrectionary movements, tends directly to prepare the people for revolutionary warfare. The partisans of the first trend do not believe that the revolution is really possible; but as they do not want to remain passive spectators of the misfortunes of the people, they are determined to go to the people, like brothers, suffer with them and at the same time teach and prepare them for action, not theoretically but practically, by example. They will go among the factory workers, and toiling side by side with them awaken in them the desire to organize.

Others try to found rural colonies where all will enjoy the land in common . . . in accordance with the principle that the product of collective labor shall be distributed on the basis of "from each according to his ability; to each according to his need." The same hope inspired Cabet, who, after the defeat of the 1848 revolution, left with his Icarians for America where he founded the colony of New Icaria, whose existence was brief. If this kind of experiment could not last very long in America, where the chances of success were much greater . . . it follows that it could never succeed in Russia.

But this does not discourage those who want to prepare the people for peaceful social change. By organizing their own domestic life on the basis of full liberty, they hope to combat the shameful patriarchal regime. . . . By their example they hope to imbue the people with practical ideas of justice, of liberty, and of the means of emancipating themselves. . . . All these plans are very fine, extremely magnanimous and noble, but are they realizable? It will be only a drop in the ocean . . . never sufficient to emancipate our people.

The other tendency is to fight, to revolt. We are confident that this alone will bring satisfactory results. Our people have shown that they need encouragement. Their situation is so desperate that they find themselves ready to revolt in every village. Every revolt, even if it fails, still has its value, yet isolated actions are insufficient. There must be a general uprising embracing the whole countryside. That this is possible has been demonstrated by the vast popular movements led by Stenka Razin and Pugachev.

The struggle against the patriarchal regime is at present raging in almost every village and in every family. In the rural community, the *Mir* has degenerated to the point where it has become an instrument of the State. The power and the arbitrary bureaucratic will of the State is hated by the people and the revolt against this power and this arbitrary will is at the same time a revolt against the despotism of the rural community and of the *Mir*.

But this is not all. The principal evil which paralyzes the Russian people, and has up till now made a general uprising impossible, is the closed rural community, its isolation and disunity. We must at all costs breach these hitherto impregnable communities and weld them together by the active current of thought, by the will, and by the revolutionary cause. We must contact and connect not only the most enlightened peasants in the villages, the districts, and the regions but also the most forward-looking revolutionary individuals naturally emerging from the rural Russian environment; and above all, wherever possible, we must establish the same vital connections between the factory workers and the peasants. These connections can be only between individuals. The most advanced and active peasants in each village, district, and region must be put in contact with like-minded peasants in other villages, districts, and regions, though obviously this must be done with extreme caution.

Above all, we must convince these advanced elements, and through them all, or at least the majority of, the most energetic people, that . . . all over Russia and outside its frontiers there exists a common evil and a common cause. We must convince the people that they are an invincible force . . . and that if this force has not yet freed the people, it is only because they have not acted in unison to achieve a common aim. . . . In order to achieve unity, the villages, districts, and regions must establish contact and organize according to an agreed and unified plan. . . . We must convince our peasant and our worker that they are not alone, that on the contrary there stand behind them, weighed down by the same yoke but animated by the same enthusiasm, the innumerable mass of proletarians all over the world who are also preparing a universal uprising. . . . Such is the main task of revolutionary propaganda. How this objective should be concretized by our youth will be discussed on another occasion. We may say here only that the Russian people will accept the revolutionary intellectual youth only if they share their life, their poverty, their cause, and their desperate revolt.

Henceforth this youth must be present not as witnesses but as active participants in the front ranks of action and in all popular movements, great or small, anytime, anywhere, and anyplace. The young revolutionist must act according to a plan rigorously and effectively conceived and accept strict discipline in all his acts in order to create that unanimity without which victory is impossible. . . . He must never under any circumstances lie to the people. This would not only be criminal, but also most disastrous for the revolutionary cause. . . . The individual is most eloquent when he defends a cause that he sincerely believes in and when he speaks according to his most cherished convictions. . . . If we try to emancipate the people by lies we will mislead not only them but ourselves as well, deviating from and losing sight of our true objective.

A word in conclusion: The class that we call our "intellectual proletariat,"[5] which in Russia is already in a social-revolutionary situation, i.e., in an impossible and desperate situation, must now be imbued with revolutionary ideas and the passion for the Social Revolution. If the intellectual proletariat does not want to surrender they face certain ruin; they must join and help organize the popular revolution.

Letter to the Comrades
of the Jura Federation

October 12, 1873

The two selections following belong to the twilight of Bakunin's career. The letter to the "Comrades of the Jura Federation"[6] is not to be judged by its optimistic tone. Bakunin knew his health was in decline, and he was becoming increasingly pessimistic about the possibilities for revolution, but he did not want to discourage his comrades. Between October 1873 and February 1875, when he wrote his letter to Élisée Reclus,[7] his health became even worse, and his pessimism found expression in this letter, which ends on a sad note. But the growing reaction then enveloping Europe together with the colossal indifference of the masses had indeed given Bakunin solid grounds for his despair.

I cannot retire from public life without addressing to you these few parting words of appreciation and sympathy.

. . . in spite of all the tricks of our enemies and the infamous slanders they have spread about me, your esteem, your friendship, and your confidence in me have never wavered. Nor have you allowed yourselves to be intimidated when they brazenly accused you of being "Bakuninists," hero-worshipers, mindless followers. . . .

You have to the highest degree always conscientiously maintained the independence of your opinions and the spontaneity of your acts; the perfidious plots of our adversaries were so transparent that you could regard their infamous insinuations only with the most profound disgust. . . .

Powerfully supported by your fellow workers of Italy, Spain, France, Belgium, Holland, and America, you have once again repulsed the dictatorial attempts of Mr. Marx and placed the great International Workingmen's Association back on the right road. . . .

Your victory, the victory of freedom and of the International against authoritarian intrigues, is complete. Yesterday, when victory seemed to hang in the balance—although I for my part never doubted it—it would have been impermissible for anyone to leave your ranks. But now that it is a *fait accompli*, everyone has the freedom to act according to his personal convenience.

I therefore take this opportunity, my dear comrades, to beg you to accept my resignation as a member of the Jura Federation and of the International.

. . . Do not believe that I resign mainly because of the personal disgust and disappointments that I have suffered during the last few years. Although I have not been altogether insensitive to these indignities, I would have continued to endure them if I thought that my participation in your struggles would help the cause of the proletariat. But I do not think so any longer.

By birth and personal status—though certainly not by sympathy or inclination—I am a bourgeois and, as such, the only useful work that I can do among you is propagandize. But I am now convinced that the time for grand theoretical discourses, written or spoken, is over. During the last nine years more than enough ideas for the salvation of the world have been developed in the International (if the world can be saved by ideas) and I defy anyone to come up with a new one.

This is the time not for ideas but for action, for deeds. Above all, now is the time for the organization of the forces of the proletariat. But this organization must be the task of the proletariat itself. If I were young, I would live among the workers and share their life of toil, would together with them participate in this necessary work of proletarian organization.

But neither my age nor my health allows this. I must, on the contrary, have privacy and repose. Any effort, even a short journey, becomes for me a very serious undertaking. I feel sufficiently strong morally, but physically I tire too quickly, and I no longer have the necessary strength for struggle. In the camp of the proletariat I can be only an obstacle, not a help.

You see then, my friends, that I am obliged to offer my resignation. Living far from you and from everyone, of what use would I be to the International in general and the Jura Federation in particular? Your great association in its militant and practical activities cannot permit sinecures or honorary positions.

I will retire then, dear comrades, full of gratitude to you and sympathy for your great and holy cause, the cause of humanity. With brotherly concern I will avidly watch your progress, and salute with joy each of your new triumphs. Until death I will be yours. . . .

But before parting, permit me again to add these few words. The battle that you will have to sustain will be terrible. But do not allow yourselves to be discouraged and know that in spite of the immense material resources of our adversaries, your final triumph is assured if you faithfully fulfill these two conditions: adhere firmly to the great and all-embracing principle of the people's liberty, without which equality and solidarity would be falsehoods. Organize ever more strongly the practical militant solidarity of the workers of all trades in all countries, and remember that infinitely weak as you may be as individuals in isolated localities or countries, you will constitute an immense irresistible force when organized and united in the universal collectivity.

Farewell,
your brother,
M. Bakunin

1875

Letter to Élisée Reclus

February 15, 1875

You are right, the revolutionary tide is receding and we are falling back into evolutionary periods—periods during which barely perceptible revolutions gradually germinate. . . . The time for revolution has passed not only because of the disastrous events of which we have been the victims (and for which we are to some extent responsible),[9] but because, to my intense despair, I have found and find more and more each day, that there is absolutely no revolutionary thought, hope, or passion left among the masses; and when these qualities are missing, even the most heroic efforts must fail and nothing can be accomplished.

I admire the valiant persistence of our Jura and Belgian comrades, those "Last Mohicans" of the International, who in spite of all the obstacles and in the midst of the general apathy, obstinately set themselves against the current of events and continue to act as they did before the catastrophes, when the movement was growing and even the least efforts brought results.

Their labor is all the more praiseworthy in that they will not see the fruits of their sacrifices; but they can be certain that their labor will not be wasted. Nothing in this world is ever lost; tiny drops of water form the ocean.

As for myself, my dear friend, I am too old, too sick, and—shall I confess it?—too disillusioned, to participate in this work. I have definitely retired from the struggle and shall pass the rest of my days in intense intellectual activity which I hope will prove useful.

One of the passions which now absorb me is an insatiable curiosity; having recognized that evil has triumphed and that I cannot prevent it, I am determined to study its development as objectively as possible. . . .

Poor humanity! It is evident that it can extricate itself from this cesspool only by an immense social revolution. But how can this revolution come about? Never was international reaction in Europe so formidably organized against any movement of the people. Repression has become a new science systematically taught in the military schools of all countries. And to breach this well-nigh impregnable fortress we have only the disorganized masses. But how to organize them, when they do not even care enough about their own fate to know or put into effect the only measures that can save them? There remains propaganda; though doubtlessly of some value, it can have very little effect [in the present circumstances] and if there were no other means of emancipation, humanity would rot ten times over before it could be saved.

There remains another hope: world war. These gigantic military states must sooner or later destroy each other. But what a prospect!

1876

On Building
the New Social Order

By James Guillaume

Bakunin was above all preoccupied with the theory and practice of revolution and wrote very little about how the everyday
practical problems of social reconstruction would be handled immediately following a successful revolution. Nevertheless, these
problems were intensively discussed in Bakunin's circle and
among the antiauthoritarian sections of the International. In
this selection (original title "Ideas on Social Organization") Guillaume discusses the transition from capitalism to anarchism—a
synthesis of "Bakuninist" ideas on how this transition could be
effected without the restoration of authoritarian institutions.[10]

Its value lies not in the specific recommendations (most of
them outdated, some rather naïve, although a number of them
are remarkably similar to measures adopted by anarchist collectives in Spain during the late thirties) but in its formulation of
the fundamental constructive principles of anarchist or free
socialism. It proves that the early anarchists were not merely
temperamental oppositionists to all and any order, but were
indeed concerned with making practical plans for a stable, free
society. Hence Guillaume's essay, written in 1874 and published
in 1876, the year of Bakunin's death, by a friend who was in

many respects an alter ego, is included here as the closest we can
come to a clear outline of Bakunin's own vision of the constructive tasks ahead after the Revolution. This is its first publication
in English.

I

The ideas outlined in the following pages can be effectively
achieved only by means of a revolutionary movement. It takes
more than a day for the great flood to break the dike; the flood-
waters mount slowly, imperceptibly. But once the crest of the
flood is reached, the collapse is sudden, the dike is washed away
in the winking of an eye. We can distinguish, then, two successive acts, the second being the necessary consequence of the first.
At first there is the slow transformation of ideas, of needs, of
the motives for action germinating in the womb of society; the
second begins when this transformation is sufficiently advanced
to pass into action. Then there is a brusque and decisive turning
point—the *revolution*—which is the culmination of a long process
of *evolution*, the sudden manifestation of a change long prepared for and therefore inevitable.

No serious-minded man would venture to predict exactly
how the Revolution, the indispensable condition for social reno-
vation, will come about. Revolution is a natural fact, and not
the act of a few persons; it does not take place according to a
preconceived plan but is produced by uncontrollable circumstances which no individual can command. We do not, therefore, intend to draw up a blueprint for the future revolutionary
campaign; we leave this childish task to those who believe in the
possibility and the efficacy of achieving the emancipation of
humanity through personal dictatorship. We will confine ourselves, on the contrary, to describing the kind of revolution
most attractive to us and the ways it can be freed from past
errors.

The character of the revolution must at first be negative,
destructive. Instead of modifying certain institutions of the

past, or adapting them to a new order, it will do away with them altogether. Therefore, the government will be uprooted, along with the Church, the army, the courts, the schools, the banks, and all their subservient institutions. At the same time the Revolution has a positive goal, that the workers take possession of all capital and the tools of production. Let us explain what is meant by the phrase "taking possession."

Let us begin with the peasants and problems concerning the land. In many countries, particularly in France, the priests and the bourgeoisie try to frighten the peasants by telling them that the Revolution will take their land away from them. This is an outrageous lie concocted by the enemies of the people. The Revolution would take an exactly opposite course: it would take the land from the bourgeoisie, the nobles, and the priests and give it to the landless peasants. If a piece of land belongs to a peasant who cultivates it himself, the Revolution would not touch it. On the contrary, it would guarantee free possession and liquidate all debts arising from the land. This land which once enriched the treasury and was overburdened with taxes and weighed down by mortgages would, like the peasant, be emancipated. No more taxes, no more mortgages; the land becomes free, just like the man!

As to the land owned by the bourgeoisie, the clergy, and the nobles—land hitherto cultivated by landless laborers for the benefit of their masters—the Revolution will return this stolen land to the rightful owners, the agricultural workers.

How will the Revolution take the land from the exploiters and give it to the peasants? Formerly, when the bourgeois made a political revolution, when they staged one of those movements which resulted only in a change of masters dominating the people, they usually printed decrees, proclaiming to the people the will of the new government. These decrees were posted in the communes and the courts, and the mayor, the gendarmes, and the prosecutors enforced them. The real people's revolution will not follow this model; it will not rule by decrees, it will not depend on the services of the police or the machinery of government. It is not with *decrees*, with words written on paper, that the Revolution will emancipate the people but with *deeds*.

II

We will now consider how the peasants will go about deriving the greatest possible benefit from their means of production, the land. Immediately after the Revolution the peasants will be faced with a mixed situation. Those who are already small proprietors will keep their plots of land and continue to cultivate it with the help of their families. The others, and they are by far the most numerous, who rented the land from the big landowners or were simply agricultural wage laborers employed by the owners, will take collective possession of the vast tracts of land and work them in common.

Which of these two systems is best?

It is not a matter of what is theoretically desirable but of starting with the facts and seeing what can be immediately achieved. From this point of view, we say first that in this mixed economy the main purpose of the Revolution has been achieved: the land is now the property of those who cultivate it, and the peasants no longer work for the profit of an idle exploiter who lives by their sweat. This great victory gained, the rest is of secondary importance. The peasants can, if they wish, divide the land into individual parcels and give each family a share. Or else, and this would be much better, they can institute common ownership and cooperative cultivation of the land. Although secondary to the main point, i.e., the emancipation of the peasant, this question of how best to work the land and what form of possession is best also warrants careful consideration.

In a region which had been populated before the Revolution by peasants owning small farms, where the nature of the soil is not very suitable for extensive, large-scale cultivation, where agriculture has been conducted in the same way for ages, where machinery is unknown or rarely used—in such a region the peasants will naturally conserve the form of ownership to which they are accustomed. Each peasant will continue to cultivate the land as he did in the past, with this single difference: his former hired hands, if he had any, will become his partners and share with him the products which their common labor extracts from the land.

It is possible that in a short time those peasants who remain small proprietors will find it advantageous to modify their traditional system of labor and production. If so, they will first associate to create a communal agency to sell or exchange their products; this first associated venture will encourage them to try others of a similar nature. They would then, in common, acquire various machines to facilitate their work; they would take turns to help each other perform certain laborious tasks which are better accomplished when they are done rapidly by a large team; and they would no doubt finally imitate their brothers, the industrial workers, and those working on big farms, and decide to pool their land and form an agricultural association. But even if they linger for some years in the same old routine, even if a whole generation should elapse before the peasants in some communes adopt the system of collective property, it would still not constitute a serious hindrance to the Revolution. The great achievements of the Revolution will not be affected; the Revolution will have abolished agricultural wage slavery and peonage and the agricultural proletariat will consist only of free workers living in peace and plenty, even in the midst of the few remaining backward areas.

On the other hand, in large-scale agricultural operations, where a great number of workers are needed to farm vast areas, where coordination and cooperation are absolutely essential, collective labor will naturally lead to collective property. An agricultural collective may embrace an entire commune [autonomous regional unit] and, if economically necessary for efficiency and greater production, many communes.

In these vast communities of agricultural workers, the land will not be worked as it is today, by small peasant owners trying without success to raise many different crops on tiny parcels of unsuitable land. There will not be growing side by side on one acre a little square of wheat, a little square of potatoes, another of grapes, another of fodder, another of fruit, etc. Each bit of land tends, by virtue of its physical properties, its location, its chemical composition, to be most suitable for the successful cultivation of certain specific crops. Wheat will not be planted on soil suitable for grapes, nor potatoes on soil that could best be used for pasture. The agricultural community, if it has only one type of soil, will confine itself to the cultivation of crops which can be produced in quantity and quality with less labor, and the community will prefer to exchange its products for those it lacks instead of trying to grow them in small quantity and poor quality on unsuitable land.

The internal organization of these agricultural communities need not necessarily be identical; organizational forms and procedures will vary greatly according to the preferences of the associated workers. So long as they conform to the principles of justice and equality, the administration of the community, elected by all the members, could be entrusted either to an individual or to a commission of many members. It will even be possible to separate the different administrative functions, assigning each function to a special commission. The hours of labor will be fixed not by a general law applicable to an entire country, but by the decision of the community itself; but as the community contracts relations with all the other agricultural workers of the region, an agreement covering uniform working hours will probably be reached. Whatever items are produced by collective labor will belong to the community, and each member will receive remuneration for his labor either in the form of commodities (subsistence, supplies, clothing, etc.) or in currency. In some communities remuneration will be in proportion to hours worked; in others payment will be measured by both the hours of work and the kind of work performed; still other systems will be experimented with to see how they work out.

The problem of property having been resolved, and there being no capitalists placing a tax on the labor of the masses, the question of types of distribution and remuneration become secondary. We should to the greatest possible extent institute and be guided by the principle *From each according to his ability, to each according to his need*. When, thanks to the progress of scientific industry and agriculture, production comes to outstrip consumption, and this will be attained some years after the Revolution, it will no longer be necessary to stingily dole out each worker's share of goods. Everyone will draw what he needs from the abundant social reserve of commodities, without fear of depletion; and the moral sentiment which will be more highly developed among free and equal workers will prevent, or greatly reduce, abuse and waste. In the meantime, each community will decide for itself during the transition period the method they deem best for the distribution of the products of associated labor.

III

We must distinguish different types of industrial workers, just as we distinguished different kinds of peasants. There are, first of all, those crafts in which the tools are simple, where the division of labor is almost nonexistent, and where the isolated worker could produce as much alone as he would by associated labor. These include, for example, tailors, shoemakers, barbers, upholsterers, and photographers. It must, however, be remarked that even in these trades, large-scale mass production can be applied to save time and labor. What we say, therefore, applies primarily to the transitional period.

Next in order are the trades requiring the collective labor of numerous workers using small hand-operated machinery and generally employed in workshops and foundries, printing plants, woodworking plants, brickworks, etc.

Finally, there is the third category of industries where the division of labor is much greater, where production is on a massive scale necessitating complicated and expensive machinery and the investment of considerable capital; for example, textile mills, steel mills, metallurgical plants, etc.

For workers operating within the first category of industry, collective work is not a necessity; and in many cases the tailor or the cobbler may prefer to work alone in his own small shop. It is quite natural that in every commune there will be one or perhaps several workers employed in each of these trades. Without, however, wishing to underestimate in any way the importance of individual independence, we think that wherever practical, collective labor is best; in a society of equals, emulation stimulates the worker to produce more and heightens morale; further, work in common permits each worker to learn from the experience and skill of the others and this redounds to the benefit of the unit as a whole.

As to the workers in the remaining two categories, it is evident that collective labor is imposed by the very nature of the work and, since the tools of labor are no longer simple individual tools but machines that must be tended by many workers, the machines must also be collectively owned.

Each workshop, each factory, will organize itself into an association of workers who will be free to administer production and organize their work as they think best, provided that the rights of each worker are safeguarded and the principles of equality and justice are observed. In the preceding chapter, while discussing the associations or communities of agricultural workers, we dealt with management, hours of labor, remuneration, and distribution of products. The same observations apply also to industrial labor, and it is therefore unnecessary to repeat them here. We have just said that particularly where an industry requires complicated machinery and collective labor, the ownership of the machinery of production should also be collective. But one point remains to be clarified. Will these tools belong to all the workers in each factory, or will they belong to the corporation comprising all the workers in each particular industry? [Corporation here is equivalent to industrial union.]

Our opinion is that the second of these alternatives is preferable. When, for example, on the day of the Revolution, the typographical workers of Rome take possession of all the print shops of Rome, they will call a general meeting and proclaim that all the printing plants in Rome are the property of the Roman printers. Since it will be entirely possible and necessary, they will go a step further and unite in a pact of solidarity with all the printing workers in every city of Italy. The result of this pact will be the organization of all the printing plants of Italy as the collective property of the typographical federation of Italy. In this way the Italian printers will be able to work in any city in their country and have full rights and full use of tools and facilities.

But when we say that ownership of the tools of production, including the factory itself, should revert to the corporation, we do not mean that the workers in the individual workshops will be ruled by any kind of industrial government having the power to do what it pleases with the tools of production. No, the workers in the various factories have not the slightest intention of handing over their hard-won control of the tools of production to a superior power calling itself the "corporation." What they will do is, under certain specified conditions, to guarantee reciprocal use of their tools of production and accord to their fellow workers in other factories the right to share their facilities, receiving in exchange the same right to share the facilities of the fellow workers with whom they have contracted the pact of solidarity.

IV

The commune consists of all the workers living in the same locality. Disregarding very few exceptions, the typical commune can be defined as the local federation of groups of producers. This local federation or commune is organized to provide certain services which are not within the exclusive jurisdiction or capacity of any particular corporation [industrial union] but which concerns all of them, and which for this reason are called *public services*. The communal public services can be enumerated as follows:

A. *Public works (housing and construction)*

All houses are the property of the commune. The Revolution made, everyone continues for the time being to live in the same quarters occupied by him before the Revolution, except for families which had been forced to live in very dilapidated or overcrowded dwellings. Such families will be immediately relocated at the expense of the commune in vacant apartments formerly occupied or owned by the rich.

The construction of new houses containing healthy, spacious rooms replacing the miserable slums of the old ghettos will be one of the first needs of the new society. The commune will immediately begin this construction in a way that will not only furnish work for the corporations of masons, carpenters, iron-workers, tilers, roofers, etc., but will also provide useful work for the mass of people who, having no trade, lived in idleness before the revolution. They would be employed as laborers in the immense construction and road-building and paving projects which will then be initiated everywhere, especially in the cities.

The new housing will be constructed at the expense of the commune, which means that in exchange for the work done by the various building corporations these corporations will receive from the commune vouchers enabling them to acquire all com-modities necessary for the decent maintenance and well-being of their members. And since the new housing has been con-structed at public expense, this system will enable and require free housing to be available for all.

Free housing might well cause serious disputes because people living in bad housing will compete with each other for the new accommodations. But we think that it would be a mistake to fear serious friction, and for the following reasons: First we must concede that the desire for new and better housing is a legitimate and just demand; and this just demand will stimulate the build-ing workers to make even greater efforts to speed construction of good housing.

But while awaiting new construction people will have to be patient and do the best they can with the existing facilities. The commune will, as we have said, attend to the most pressing needs of the poorest families, relocating them in the vast palaces of the rich; and as to the rest of the people, we believe that revolution-ary enthusiasm will stimulate and inspire them with the spirit of generosity and self-sacrifice, and that they will be glad to endure for a little longer the discomforts of poor housing; nor will they be inclined to quarrel with a neighbor who happens to have gotten a new apartment a little sooner. In a reasonably short time, thanks to the prodigious efforts of the building workers powerfully stimulated by the demand for new housing, there will be plenty of housing for all and everyone will be sure to find satisfactory accommodations.

All this may seem fantastic to those whose vision goes no

further than the horizon of bourgeois society; these measures are, on the contrary, so simple and practical that it will be humanly impossible for things to go otherwise. Will the legions of masons and other building workers be permanently and incessantly occupied with the construction of new housing worthy of a civilized society? Will it take many years of incessant labor to supply everyone with good housing? No, it will take a short time. And when they will have finished the main work, will they then fold their arms and do nothing? No, they will continue to work at a slower pace, remodeling existing housing; and little by little the old somber quarters, the crooked filthy streets, the miserable houses and alleys that now infest our cities will disappear and be replaced by mansions where the workers can live like human beings.

B. Exchange

In the new society there will no longer be *communes in the sense that this word is understood today*, as mere political-geographical entities. Every commune will establish a *Bank of Exchange* whose mechanics we will explain as clearly as possible.

The workers' association, as well as the individual producers (in the remaining privately owned portions of production), will deposit their unconsumed commodities in the facilities provided by the Bank of Exchange, the value of the commodities having been established in advance by a contractual agreement between the regional cooperative federations and the various communes, who will also furnish statistics to the Banks of Exchange. The Bank of Exchange will remit to the producers negotiable *vouchers* representing the value of their products; these vouchers will be accepted throughout the territory included in the federation of communes.

Goods of prime necessity, i.e., those essential to life and health, will be transported to the various communal markets which, pending new construction, will use the old stores and warehouses of the former merchants. Some of the markets will distribute foodstuffs, others clothes, others household goods, etc.

Goods destined for export will remain in the general warehouses until called for by the communes.

Among the commodities deposited in the facilities of the Bank of Exchange will be goods for consumption by the commune itself, such as food, lumber, clothes, etc., and goods to be exchanged for those produced by other communes.

At this point we anticipate an objection. We will probably be asked: "The Bank of Exchange in each commune will remit to the producers, by means of vouchers, the value of their products, before being sure that they are in demand; and if these products are not in demand, and pile up unused, what will be the position of the Bank of Exchange? Will it not risk losses, or even ruin, and in this kind of operation is there not always the risk that the vouchers will be overdrawn?"

We reply that each Bank of Exchange makes sure in advance that these products are in demand and, therefore, risks nothing by immediately issuing payment vouchers to the producers.

There will be, of course, certain categories of workers engaged in the construction or manufacture of immovable goods, goods which cannot be transported to the repositories of the Bank of Exchange, for example, buildings. In such cases the Bank of Exchange will serve as the intermediary; the workers will register the property with the Bank of Exchange. The value of the property will be agreed upon in advance, and the bank will deliver this value in exchange vouchers. The same procedure will be followed in dealing with the various workers employed by the administrative services of the communes; their work resulting not in manufactured products but in services rendered. These services will have to be priced in advance, and the Bank of Exchange will pay their value in vouchers.

The Bank of Exchange will not only receive products belonging to the workers of the commune; it will correspond with other communes and arrange to procure goods which the commune is obliged to get from outside sources, such as certain foodstuffs, fuels, manufactured products, etc. These outside products will be featured side by side with local goods. The consumers will pay for the commodities in the various markets with vouchers of different denominations, and all goods will be uniformly priced.

It is evident from our description that the operations of the Bank of Exchange do not differ essentially from the usual commercial procedures. These operations are in effect nothing but buying and selling; the bank buys from the producers and sells to the consumers. But we think that after a certain length of time the functions of the Banks of Exchange will be reduced without inconvenience and that a new system will gradually replace the old system: exchange in the traditional sense will give way to *distribution*, pure and simple. What do we mean by this?

As long as a product is in short supply it will to a certain extent have to be rationed. And the easiest way to do this would be to *sell* these scarce products at a price so high that only people who really need them would be willing to buy them. But when the prodigious growth of production, which will not fail to take place when work is rationally organized, produces an oversupply of this or that product, it will not be necessary to ration consumption. The practice of selling, which was adopted as a sort of deterrent to immoderate consumption, will be abolished; the communal banks will no longer *sell* commodities, they will distribute them in accordance with the needs of the consumers.

The replacement of exchange by distribution will first, and in a comparatively short time, be applied to articles of prime necessity, for the workers will concentrate all their efforts to produce these necessities in abundance. Other commodities, formerly scarce and today considered luxuries, will in a reasonable length of time be produced in great quantity and will no longer be rationed. On the other hand, rare and useless baubles, such as pearls, diamonds, certain precious metals, etc., will cease to have the value attributed to them by public opinion and will be used for research by scientific associations, as components of certain tools, e.g., industrial diamonds, or displayed as curios in museums of natural history.

C. *Food Supply*

The question of food supply is a sort of postscript to our discussion of exchange. What we said about the organization of the Bank of Exchange applies in general to all products, including foodstuffs. However, we think it useful to add in a special section a more detailed account of the measures dealing with distribution of the principal food products.

At present the bakeshops, meat stores, wine and liquor shops, imported food stores, etc., are all surrendered to private industry and to speculators and these, by all kinds of fraud, enrich themselves at the expense of the consumers. The new society must immediately try to correct this situation by placing under communal public service the distribution of all the most essential foodstuffs.

This must be borne in mind: we do not mean to imply that the commune will take possession of certain branches of *production*. No. Production in the true sense of the term will remain in the hands of the associations of producers. But, for example, what is involved in the production of bread? Nothing beyond the growing of wheat. The farmer sows and reaps the grain and transports it to the warehouses of the Bank of Exchange; his function as producer ends at this point. Grinding grain into flour or changing flour into bread is not production; it is work similar to that performed by various employees in the communal markets, work designed to put a food product, bread, at the disposal of the consumer. The same goes for meat, etc.

Thus viewed, it is only logical that the processing and distribution of foodstuffs—baking, slaughtering, winemaking, etc.— should be performed by the commune. Thus, wheat from the warehouses of the commune will be ground into flour in the communal flour mill (which will be shared with several communes); the flour will be transformed into bread in the communal bakeries and delivered to the consumers in the communal markets. It will be the same for meats: the animals will be slaughtered in the communal slaughterhouse and cut up in the communal butcher shops. Wines will be preserved in the communal wine cellars and bottled and distributed by special employees. Finally, all the other perishable food commodities will be kept fresh in communal warehouses and kept in glass enclosures in the communal markets.

Above all, immediate efforts must be made to institute the free distribution of certain essential foods, such as bread, meat, wine, dairy products, etc. When abundant food is available and free for all, civilization in general will have taken a giant step forward.

D. Statistics

The main function of the Communal Statistical Commission will be to gather and classify all statistical information pertaining to the commune. The various corporations or associations of production will constantly keep up-to-date records of membership and changes in personnel so that it will be possible to know instantly the number of employees in the various branches of production.

The Bank of Exchange will provide the Statistical Commission with the most complete figures and all other relevant facts on the production and consumption of goods. By means of statistics gathered from all the communes in a region, it will be possible to scientifically balance production and consumption. In line with these statistics, it will also be possible to add more help in industries where production is insufficient and reduce the number of men where there is a surplus of production. Statistics will also make it easy to fit working hours to the productive needs of society. It will be equally possible to estimate, not perfectly, but enough for practical purposes, the relative value of the labor time involved in the various products, which will serve as the criteria for the prices of the Banks of Exchange.

But this is not all. The Statistical Commission will be able to perform some of the functions that are today exercised by the civil state, for example, recording births and deaths. We do not include marriage because in a free society, the voluntary union of a man and a woman will no longer be an official but a purely personal matter, not subject to, or requiring, public sanction.

There are many other uses for statistics: in relation to diseases, weather phenomena, in short, all facts which regularly gathered and classified can serve as a guide to the development of science and learning in general.

E. Hygiene

Under the general heading Hygiene, we have assembled the various public services which are indispensable to the maintenance of public health. First, of course, are medical services, which will be free of charge to all the inhabitants of the commune. The doctors will not be like capitalists, trying to extract the greatest possible profits from their unfortunate patients. They will be employed by the commune and expected to treat all who need their services. But medical treatment is only the *curative* side of the science of health care; it is not enough to treat the sick, it is also necessary to prevent disease. This is the true function of hygiene. . . .

F. Security

This service embraces the necessary measures to guarantee to all inhabitants of the commune the security of their person and the protection of their homes, their possessions, etc., against deprivation and accident (fire, floods, etc.).

There will probably be very little brigandage and robbery in a society where each lives in full freedom to enjoy the fruits of his labor and where almost all his needs will be abundantly fulfilled. Material well-being, as well as the intellectual and moral progress which are the products of a truly humane education, available to all, will almost eliminate crimes due to perversion, brutality, and other infirmities. It will nevertheless still be necessary to take precautions for the security of persons. This service, which can be called (if the phrase has not too bad a connotation) the Communal Police, will not be entrusted, as it is today, to a special, official body; all able-bodied inhabitants will be called upon to take turns in the security measures instituted by the commune.

It will doubtless be asked how those committing murder and other violent crimes will be treated in the new equalization society. Obviously society cannot, on the pretext of respect for individual rights and the negation of authority, permit a murderer to run loose, or wait for a friend of the victim to avenge him. The murderer will have to be deprived of his liberty and confined to a special house until he can without danger be returned to society. How is the criminal to be treated during his confinement? And according to what principles should his term be fixed? These are delicate questions on which opinions vary widely. We must learn from experience, but this much we already know: that thanks to the beneficent effects of education (see below) crimes will be rare. Criminals being an exception, they will be treated like the sick and the deranged; the problem of crime which today gives so many jobs to judges, jailers, and police will lose its social importance and become simply a chapter in medical history.

G. Education

The first point to be considered is the question of child support (food, clothes, toys, etc.). Today parents not only support their children but also supervise their education. This is a custom based on a false principle, a principle that regards the child as the personal property of the parents. The child belongs to no one, he belongs only to himself; and during the period when he is unable to protect himself and is thereby exposed to exploitation, it is society that must protect him and guarantee his free development. It is also society that must support him and supervise his education. In supporting him and paying for his education, society is only making an advance "loan" which the child will repay when he becomes an adult producer.

It is society and not the parents who will be responsible for the upkeep of the child. This principle once established, we believe that we should abstain from specifying the exact manner in which this principle should be applied: to do otherwise would risk trying to achieve a Utopia. Therefore the application must be left to free experimentation and we must await the lessons of practical experience. We say only that vis-à-vis the child, society is represented by the commune, and that each commune will have to determine what would be best for the upbringing of the child; here they would have life in common, there they would leave children in care of the mother, at least up to a certain age, etc.

But this is only one aspect of the problem. The commune feeds, clothes, and lodges the children, but who will teach them, who will develop their best characteristics and train them as producers? According to what plan and principles will their education be conducted?

To these questions we reply: the education of children must be integrated; that is, it must at the same time develop both the physical and mental faculties and make the child into a whole man. This education must not be entrusted solely to a specialized caste of teachers; all those who know a science, an art, or a craft can and should be called upon to teach.

We must distinguish two stages in the education of children: the first stage, where the child of five or six is not yet old enough to study science, and where the emphasis is on the development of the physical faculties; and a second stage, where children twelve to sixteen years of age would be introduced to the various divisions of human knowledge while at the same time learning one or more crafts or trades through practice.

The first stage, as just mentioned, will be devoted to development of the physical faculties, to strengthening the body and exercising the senses. Today the powers of hearing, seeing, and manual dexterity are incompletely and haphazardly developed: a rational education, on the contrary, will by special systematic exercises develop these faculties to the highest possible degree. And as to hands, instead of making children only right-handed, attempts will be made to render children equally proficient in the use of the left hand.

And while the senses are developed and bodily vigor is enhanced by intelligent gymnastic exercises, the culture of the mind will begin, but in a spontaneous manner; the child will naturally and unconsciously absorb a store of scientific knowledge. Personal observation, practical experience, conversations between children, or with persons charged with teaching—these will be the only form of instruction children will receive during this first period.

No longer will there be schools, arbitrarily governed by a pedagogue, where the children wait impatiently for the moment of their deliverance when they can enjoy a little freedom outside.

In their gatherings the children will be entirely free. They will organize their own games, their talks, systematize their own work, arbitrate disputes, etc. They will then easily become accustomed to public life, to responsibility, to mutual trust and aid. The teacher whom they have themselves chosen to give them lessons will no longer be a detested tyrant but a friend to whom they will listen with pleasure.

During the second stage, the children, being ages twelve to sixteen, will successively study in a methodical manner the principal branches of human knowledge. They will not be taught by professional teachers but by lay teachers of this or that science, who are also part-time manual workers; and each branch of knowledge will be taught not by one but by many men, all from the commune, who have both the knowledge and the desire to teach. In addition, good books on the subject studied will be read together, and intelligent discussion will follow, thereby lessening the importance attached to the personality of the teacher.

While the child is developing his body and learning the sciences, he will begin apprenticeship as a producer. In the first stage of his education, the need to repair or modify toys will introduce the child to the use of simple tools. During the second stage, he will visit different factories and, stimulated by his liking for one or more trades, will soon finally choose the trade in which he will specialize. The apprentices will be taught by men who are themselves working in the factories, and this practical education will be supplemented by lessons dealing with theory.

In this way, by the time a young man reaches the age of sixteen or seventeen he will have been introduced to the range of human knowledge, learned a trade, and chosen the discipline he likes best. Thus he will be in a position to reimburse society for the expenses involved in his education, not in money but by useful work and respect for the rights of his fellow human beings.

In conclusion, we should make a few remarks on the relationship between the child and his family. There are people who assert that the program of placing the child in the custody of society means "the destruction of the family." This doctrine is devoid of sense. As long as the concurrence of two individuals of different sexes is necessary for procreation, as long as there are fathers and mothers, the natural connection between the parents and the child can never be obliterated by social relations.

Only the character of this connection will be modified. In antiquity the father was the absolute master of the child. He had the power of life and death over him. In modern times paternal authority has been subject to certain restrictions. What, then, could be more natural, than that a free egalitarian society should obliterate what still remains of this authority and replace it with relations of simple affection?

We do not claim that the child should be treated as an adult, that all his caprices should be respected, that when his childish will stubbornly flouts the elementary rules of science and common sense we should avoid making him feel that he is wrong. We say, on the contrary, that the child must be trained and guided, but that the direction of his first years must not be exclusively exercised by his parents, who are all too often incompetent and who generally abuse their authority. The aim of education is to develop the latent capacities of the child to the fullest possible extent and enable him to take care of himself as quickly as possible. It is painfully evident that authoritarianism is incompatible with an enlightened system of education. If the relations of father to son are no longer those of master to slave but those of teacher to student, of an older to a much younger friend, do you think that the reciprocal affection of parents and children would thereby be impaired? On the contrary, when intimate relations of these sorts cease, do not the discords so characteristic of modern families begin? Is not the family disintegrating into bitter frictions largely because of the tyranny exercised by parents over their children?

No one can therefore justly claim that a free and regenerated society will destroy the family. In such a society the father, the mother, and the children will learn to love each other and to respect their mutual rights; at the same time their love will be enriched as it transcends the narrow limits of family affection, thereby achieving a wider and nobler love: the love of the great human family.

V

Social organization cannot be restricted to the local commune or the local federation of producers' groups. We will see how social organization is expanded and completed, on the one hand by the establishment of *regional corporative federations* comprising all the groups of workers in the same industry; and on the other by the establishment of a federation of communes.

We have already indicated in Section III what a corporative federation is. Such organizations in a rudimentary form exist in present society. All workers in a given trade or craft belong to the same organization, for example, the federation of typographical workers. But these organizations are a very crude sketch of what they will become in the new society. The corporative federations will unite all workers in the same industry; they will no longer unite to protect their wages and working conditions against the onslaughts of their employers, but primarily to guarantee the mutual use of the tools of production which are the property of each of these groups and which will by a reciprocal contract become the collective property of the whole corporative federation. In this way, the federation of groups will be able to exercise constant control over production, and regulate the rate of production to meet the fluctuating consumer needs of society.

The corporative federation will operate in a very simple fashion. On the morrow of the revolution, the producers' groups [local unions] belonging to the same industry will find it necessary to send delegates from city to city to exchange information and learn from each other's experience. These partial conferences will prepare the way for a general congress of the corporative federation to be held at some central point. This congress will formulate a federative contract which will be submitted for the correction and approval of all the groups of the corporative federation. A permanent bureau, elected by the congress and responsible to it, will serve as the intermediary link between the groups of the federation and between the federation and all the other corporative federations.

When all the branches [industries], including the agricultural organizations, have been organized in this manner, they will constitute a vast federative network spanning the whole country and embracing all the producers, and therefore all the consumers. The statistics of production, coordinated by the statistical bureaus of every corporative federation, will permit the determination in a rational manner of the hours of labor, the cost price of products and their exchange value, and the quantities in which these products should be produced to meet the needs of the consumers.

People impressed by the hollow declamations of the so-called democrats will perhaps demand that all these details should be settled by a direct vote of all the members of the corporative federations. And when we reply in the negative they will accuse us of despotism; they will protest against what they consider to be the *authority* of the bureaus, arguing that the bureaus should not be invested with the exclusive power to deal with such grave problems and to make decisions of the greatest importance. Our answer will be that the tasks performed by the permanent bureaus do not involve the exercise of any authority whatsoever. They concern only the gathering and classification of information furnished by the producers' groups. Once this information is combined and *made public*, it will be used to help fix prices and costs, the hours of labor, etc.

Such operations involve simple mathematical calculations which can yield only one correct result, verifiable by all who have access to the figures. The permanent bureau is simply charged to ascertain and make the facts known to everyone. Even now, for example, the postal service performs a somewhat similar service to that which the bureaus of the corporative federations will render in the future; and we know of no person who complains that the post office abuses its authority because it collects, classifies, and delivers the mail without submitting every operation to universal suffrage.

Furthermore, the producers' groups forming the federation will intervene in the acts of the bureau in a far more effective and direct manner than simply by voting. For it is they who will furnish all the information and supply the statistics, which the bureau only coordinates. The bureau is merely the passive intermediary through which the groups communicate and publicly as ertain the results of their own activities. The vote is a device for settling questions which cannot be resolved by means of scientific data, problems which must be left to the arbitrary decision of numbers. But in questions susceptible to a precise scientific solution there is no need to vote. The truth cannot be decided by vote; it verifies and imposes itself by the mighty power of its own evidence.

But we have only dealt with one half of the extracommunal organization; the federative corporations will be paralleled by the establishment of the Federation of Communes.

VI

The revolution cannot be confined to a single country: it is obliged under pain of annihilation to spread, if not to the whole world, at least to a considerable number of civilized countries. In fact, no country today can be self-sufficient; international links and transactions are necessary for production and cannot be cut off. If a revolutionary country is blockaded by neighboring states the Revolution, remaining isolated, would be doomed. Just as we base ourselves on the hypothesis of the triumph of the Revolution in a given country, we must also assume that most other European countries will make their revolutions at the same time.

In countries where the proletariat has managed to free itself from the domination of the bourgeoisie, the newly initiated social organizations do not have to conform to a set pattern and may differ in many respects. To this day there are many disagreements between the socialists of the Germanic nations (Germany and England) and those of the Latin and Slavic countries (Italy, Spain, France, and Russia). Hence, it is probable that the social organization adopted by the German revolutionists, for example, will differ on some or many points from what is introduced by the Italian or French revolutionaries. But these differences are not important insofar as international relations are concerned; the fundamental principles of the Revolution (see Sections I and II above) being the same, friendly relations and solidarity will no doubt be established between the emancipated peoples of the various countries.

It goes without saying that artificial frontiers created by the present governments will be swept away by the Revolution. The communes will freely unite and organize themselves in accordance with their economic interests, their language affinities, and their geographic circumstances. And in certain countries like Italy and Spain, too vast for a single agglomeration of communes and divided by nature into many distinct regions, there will probably be established not one but many federations of communes. This will not be a rupture of unity, a return to the old fragmentation of petty, isolated, and warring political states. These diverse federations of communes, while maintaining their identity, will not be isolated. United by their intertwining interests, they will conclude a pact of solidarity, and this voluntary unity founded on common aims and common needs, on a constant exchange of informal, friendly contacts, will be much more intimate and much stronger than the artificial political centralization imposed by violence and having no other motive than the exploitation of peoples for the profit of privileged classes.

Notes

Preface

1. E. Lampert: *Studies in Rebellion* (London; 1957), p. 118.
2. E. H. Carr: *Michael Bakunin* (New York; 1961), p. 196.
3. Lampert: *Studies*, p. 138.
4. Eugene Pyziur: *The Doctrine of Anarchism of Michael A. Bakunin* (Milwaukee; 1955), p. 1.
5. Yu. M. Steklov: *Mikhail Aleksandrovich Bakunin* (Moscow; 1926–7), Vol. III, p. 112.
6. Carr: *Bakunin*, p. 175.
7. M. A. Bakunin: *Oeuvres* (Paris; 1895–1913), Vol. II, p. 399; Steklov, *Bakunin*, Vol. I, p. 189.
8. Peter Kropotkin: *Memoirs of a Revolutionist* (Boston; 1899), p. 288.
9. Pyziur: *Doctrine of Bakunin*, p. 10.
10. *Dissent*, January–February 1968, pp. 41–4.
11. George Woodcock: *Anarchism* (Cleveland; 1962), p. 155.
12. Frantz Fanon: *The Wretched of the Earth* (New York; 1966), p. 88.
13. Herbert Marcuse: *One Dimensional Man* (Boston; 1964), pp. 256–7.
14. Max Nomad: *Apostles of Revolution* (Boston; 1939), p. 127. Cf. Lewis Feuer: *Marx and the Intellectuals* (New York; 1969), pp. 216–28.
15. M. A. Bakunin: *Gesammelte Werke* (Berlin; 1921–4), Vol. III, pp. 120–1.
16. Régis Debray: *Revolution in the Revolution?* (New York; 1967), pp. 95–116.
17. Carr: *Bakunin*, p. 181.
18. Ibid.
19. Ibid., p. 411.
20. Paul Avrich: *The Russian Anarchists* (Princeton; 1967), p. 129.
21. Ibid., p. 128.
22. Steklov: *Bakunin*, Vol. I, pp. 343–5; Vol. III, pp. 118–27.
23. M. A. Bakunin: *Izbranniye sochineniya* (Petrograd; 1919–22), Vol. I, p. 237.
24. Bakunin: *Gesammelte Werke*, Vol. III, pp. 35–8, 82.
25. Nomad: *Apostles of Revolution*, pp. 227–33. The burden of

authorship seems to have been Nechaev's, but Bakunin probably did have a hand in it.

26. Eldridge Cleaver: *Soul on Ice* (New York; 1968), p. 12.
27. Avrich: *Russian Anarchists*, p. 200.
28. Ibid., p. 231.
29. Pyziur: *Doctrine of Bakunin*, p. 5.
30. Rudolf Rocker: *Anarcho-Syndicalism* (Indore; n.d.), p. 88.
31. Bakunin: *Oeuvres*, Vol. IV, p. 376.
32. Nomad: *Apostles of Revolution*, p. 206; K. J. Kenafick: *Michael Bakunin and Karl Marx* (Melbourne; 1948), p. 304.
33. G. P. Maximoff, ed.: *The Political Philosophy of Bakunin* (New York; 1953), p. 48.

Introduction

1. M. A. Bakunin: *Oeuvres* (Paris 1895–1913), Vol. I, p. 288.
2. Production of a massive fifteen-volume edition in French is now being carried out by the International Institute for Social History in Amsterdam, Holland. Only four volumes have been issued to date.
3. *Letter to La Démocratie, April 1868. Obras de Bakunin* (Barcelona: Tierra y Libertad; 1938), Vol. I, pp. 38–9.
4. Rudolf Hilferding, quoted by Sidney Hook: *Marx and the Marxists* (New York: Van Nostrand; 1955), p. 241.
5. Michael Bakunin, quoted by Henri Arvon: *L'Anarchisme* (Paris: Presses Universitaires; 1964), p. 53.
6. See "God and the State."
7. Herbert Marcuse: Foreword to Raya Donayevskaya, *Marxism and Freedom* (New York: Bookman Associates; 1958).
8. *Philosophical Considerations* in Gaston Leval's *La Falacia del Marxismo* (Mexico City: Editores Mexicanos; 1967), p. 63.
9. Karl Marx, quoted from *Civil War in France*, by Erich Fromm: *The Sane Society* (New York: Fawcett; 1955), p. 266.
10. Bakunin, quoted by Eugene Pyziur: *The Doctrine of Anarchism of Michael A. Bakunin*, 2nd ed. (Chicago: Henry Regnery; 1968), p. 129.
11. See Letter to *La Liberté* of Brussels, 1872.
12. See "The Commune of Paris and the Idea of the State."
13. Franco Venturi: *Roots of Revolution* (New York: Grosset & Dunlap; 1966), p. 62.
14. Isaiah Berlin: Introduction to Venturi: *Roots of Revolution*, p. xxix.
15. G. D. H. Cole: *A History of Socialist Thought* (London: Mac-

millan; 1954), Vol. II, pp. 121, 117.

16. Bakunin, quoted in James Joll: *The Anarchists* (Boston: Little, Brown; 1964), pp. 109–10.
17. See "Program of the International Brotherhood."
18. See Extract II of *Statism and Anarchy*.
19. See "The Program of the Alliance."
20. See Extract II of *Statism and Anarchy*.
21. Bakunin, quoted in Max Nettlau: *Der Anarchismus von Proudhon zu Kropotkin* (Berlin: Der Syndikalist; 1927), p. 46.
22. See *Letters to a Frenchman on the Present Crisis*.
23. See "Program of the International Brotherhood."
24. See *Letters to a Frenchman on the Present Crisis* for a full discussion of this whole subject.
25. See Letter to Albert Richard.
26. See "The International and Karl Marx"; "The Policy of the International"; "The Program of the Alliance."
27. *The IWW: A Study in American Syndicalism* (New York: Columbia University Press; 1920), pp. 36–7.
28. Michel Collinet: "Le Centennaire de l'Internationale," *Le Contrat Sociale* (Paris, January–February 1964).
29. Ibid.
30. Ibid.
31. Nettlau: *Der Anarchismus*, p. 133.
32. Geoffrey Osterrgard: "The Relevance of Syndicalism," *Anarchy* (London), No. 38.
33. Ibid.

Michael Bakunin: A Biographical Sketch

(All notes, unless otherwise specified, are the translator's.)

1. May 18 by the Russian calendar; May 30 by our own.
2. The Decembrists formed a movement for constitutional monarchy which in December 1825 staged a revolt of officers and nobles against the tsarist autocracy. The movement was ruthlessly suppressed, with its ringleaders executed and many others imprisoned.
3. Nicholas Stankevich was a teacher of philosophy, Vissarion Belinsky a renowned literary critic.
4. Arnold Ruge (1802–1880) was a leading radical Hegelian who for some time influenced both Marx and Bakunin.
5. Wilhelm Weitling, a self-educated German tailor, settled in Switzerland and also lived for a time in Paris. He founded the Communist Workers' Clubs, and wrote such works as *Humanity*

As It Ought to Be and *Guarantees of Human Freedom*. His ideas were largely derived from Fourier and Saint-Simon; he eventually emigrated to the United States, where he tried to set up utopian communities. Bakunin rejected Weitling's primitive Christianity and his authoritarian form of communism—his conception of a State ruled by scientists, technologists, and intellectuals who would exercise a benevolent despotism over the workers. Nonetheless, he was deeply impressed by Weitling's insistence on the class struggle, the violent overthrow of the State, and the abolition of a money economy, and above all by his dictum, which Bakunin was fond of quoting, that "The perfect society has no government, but only an administration; no laws, only obligations; no punishment, only means of correction."

6. Bakunin had good grounds for this accusation. The article quoted above (actually written by Engels and approved by Marx) was particularly hostile to the Czechs, and went so far as to say:

This "nation," which historically does not exist at all, seeks restoration of its independence. The stubborn Czechs and the Slovaks should be grateful to the Germans, who have taken the trouble to civilize them by introducing them to commerce, industry, agricultural science, and education. . . . To the sentimental phrases about fraternity which we are here offered [in Bakunin's article] in the name or defense of the counter-revolutionary nations of Europe, we reply: that hatred of the Russians was and remains the primary revolutionary passion of the Germans; that since the revolution it extends to the Czechs and the Croatians and that we together with the Poles and the Magyars can safeguard the revolution only by the most determined terrorism against these Slavic peoples. (Quoted in H. Kaminski: *Bakunin* [Paris: Aubier; 1938], pp. 120–1)

7. From Herzen's posthumously published works—summary of a letter from Bakunin dated December 8, 1860.

8. James Guillaume: In *Bulletin de la Fédération Jurassienne de l'Internationale*, Suppl. of July 9, 1876.

9. The meaning of Bakunin's title can be put in the form of a question: Who is to be preferred as the leader of the Revolution —Nicholas Romanov, the Tsar; Pugachev, the peasant rebel leader; or Pestel, chief of the Decembrist conspiracy?

Emelyan Pugachev was an eighteenth-century Russian peasant revolutionist who, during the reign of Catherine the Great, led armed peasant bands in burning and looting property, killing landlords, seizing "their" holdings, and fighting guerrilla battles against the army. Pavel Ivanovich Pestel, colonel in the Russian army, son of the

Governor General of Siberia, was one of the outstanding leaders of the Decembrist movement of 1825. He was far more radical than his comrades, believing that a constitutional monarchy should ultimately be supplanted by a republic with a socialistic program. When asked by his father on the eve of his execution what he would do if victorious, he replied that first "We would free Russia from monsters like you!"

Bakunin's political differences with the editors of *Kolokol* and his ideas as expressed in the two pamphlets are clarified in Kaminski's *Bakunin*, pp. 190–2, of which the following is a summary:

After the Crimean War, the situation in Russia changed profoundly. Bakunin, imprisoned in Siberia, and cut off from outside contact, instinctively grasped the situation better than Herzen, despite the fact that the latter was free in London (and was in constant communication with Russians in Russia and newly escaped activists). The Russian aristocrats who read *Kolokol* enjoyed posing as liberals only as long as their opposition went no further than polite drawing-room conversation. Only some of the nobility remained true to Decembrist ideals. Alexander II thought he had made enough concessions when he liberated the serfs (without giving them the land on which they had toiled for centuries); he had, in fact, made a few petty reforms which in no way affected the basic structure of the absolutist regime. He even rejected the moderate program of the aristocratic reformers, and when the representatives of the Tver nobility begged him to grant a constitution to his subjects, they were arrested and sent to Siberia. Among them were two of Bakunin's brothers.

Under Alexander II, as under Nicholas I, Russia remained a country without liberty. But the time when Bakunin was the only Revolutionist had passed. A new generation had arisen which, under the influence of Chernichevski, declared war to the death on Tsarism and placed their hopes on the Russian people, who demanded "Land and Liberty"—the rallying cry which was adopted as the name of the first Russian revolutionary organization. Herzen, who felt that the opposition between the Tsar and his people could be resolved, was inclined towards the reformism of the liberal aristocracy. Bakunin, on the contrary, showed himself in perfect accord with the policy of "Land and Liberty" when he declared: "Any reconciliation is impossible."

At the time of Bakunin's collaboration on *Kolokol*, Herzen did not try to impose his ideas upon him. Herzen was not entirely immune to Bakunin's influence, but while he was not fully taken in by the Tsar's promises, he still thought that the reforms were not mere palliatives and that much more could be gained by appeals to the goodwill of the Tsar. Bakunin, in a pamphlet (*Romanov, Pugachev, Pestel?*) also appealed to the Tsar. In demanding that the Tsar repudiate the ruling class and become the Tsar of the people, he was deliberately asking him to commit political suicide. The difference between Bakunin and Herzen was precisely that Herzen was sincere in his appeals to the Tsar, while Bakunin regarded his appeal as a mere propaganda device.

In the pamphlet *To My Russian, Polish and Slav Friends* Bakunin dispenses with the formality of addressing himself to the Tsar and the other rulers. Speaking directly to the people, he declares, "Out of the ruins of the Russian Empire the people will spring to new life." He demanded that the nobles surrender all their privileges and even their titles; that the nobles give the people the land and full freedom; that the only living force must be the people, and that finally there will be only two classes, the peasants and the workers! Here Bakunin already foreshadows his later ideas when he declares that the new society will eventually be based upon the autonomy of the communes, federated throughout the entire country and crowned by the federation of all countries.

In a third pamphlet, *The People's Cause*, he goes even further. The signs of impending revolution seem to him to be multiplying. The peasants, dissatisfied that the so-called "liberation" robs them of their land, burn the palaces of their lords. Bakunin's program becomes more and more anarchistic and he cries, "If blood is necessary for the realization of freedom, blood will flow!"

10. See "Program of the International Brotherhood" in this volume.

11. Nicholas Utin, 1845–1883, was the son of a wealthy Russian liquor merchant. He fled Russia to Switzerland, and was later pardoned by the Tsar and allowed to return to Russia, where he made a fortune as a war profiteer. A strong partisan of Marx, who engineered his appointment to the General Council of the International as Corresponding Secretary for Russia, he was entrusted by the Marxists with the task of gathering (or manufacturing) "information" for their campaign against Bakunin. For details of his dishonest and unprincipled methods, see Franz Mehring's *Karl Marx*, pages 474, 475, and 498 in the Ann Arbor paperback edition, 1962.

12. Caesar de Paepe, 1842–1890, was a printer who later became a physician and a founder of the Belgian section of the International. He fought the dictatorship of Marx and the General Council's efforts to capture the International. Eugene Varlin, 1839–1871, was a bookbinder and a left-wing Proudhonist. A prominent activist in the French section of the International, he opened a cooperative kitchen for workers and their families, fought on the barricades of the Paris Commune in 1871, and was shot to death by reactionaries on May 28, 1871.

13. Bakunin was to receive nine hundred rubles for the translation,

and was paid three hundred rubles in advance. Thinking that the translation would be finished by Zhukovsky, Bakunin thought that he could settle the matter in friendly fashion, and Nechaev promised to arrange the settlement. But instead Nechaev wrote a letter in Bakunin's name to the publisher, D. Poliakov, stating that Bakunin was so greatly needed by the "Revolutionary Committee" (which existed only in Nechaev's imagination) that he could not finish the translation; this letter ended with threats against the publisher if he protested or did anything about the matter. When Bakunin learned of this, he was outraged by Nechaev's duplicity and presumption; it was one of the reasons for Bakunin's break with him [Guillaume's note]. The letter was sent to the publisher's agent, Lyubovin.

14. Sergei Nechaev, 1847–1882, was the son of a serf and did not learn to read until he was sixteen. He taught at a religious school while studying at the University of St. Petersburg. Nechaev united various leftist student groups into a secret revolutionary organization which was soon suppressed, a number of its members being arrested. He escaped to Switzerland, where he concocted a story that he had been arrested but had escaped. Nechaev's ideas are outlined in his *Rules That Must Inspire the Revolutionist*, which is better known as the *Revolutionary Catechism*. This document must not be confused with Bakunin's *Revolutionary Catechism* (see selection in this volume), which was written in Italy in 1866. The Nechaev *Catechism* was written in 1869 in Switzerland. Bakunin's alleged collaboration is now firmly disproved, but its worst portions were, in any case, always credited to Nechaev. It elevates lying and treachery, even to one's friends, into a principle to guide one's actions. The Revolution, Nechaev claimed, must be directed by a Machiavellian dictatorship, and the Jesuits of the Revolution must be absolutely unscrupulous and devoid of all moral feelings and ethical obligations. To exert pressure on a man with power, the revolutionist should seduce his wife. To find money for the organization, revolutionists must cooperate with prostitutes, pimps, murderers, and other criminals. Fellow revolutionaries were not exempt from victimization if necessary.

Nechaev practiced what he preached. He stole documents which would have endangered the lives of Bakunin and others had they reached the authorities. He tried to seduce Herzen's daughter in order to extort money from Herzen. He told Bakunin, in the presence of friends, that ". . . it is sometimes useful to betray to the secret police a member or sympathizer of the organization!" Because of these and similar acts, Bakunin wrote letters warning friends to whom he had recommended Nechaev. Bakunin's objective estimation of Nechaev's complex personality was tempered by compassion. The following excerpts from Bakunin's letter to his friend Talandier also reveal a good deal about Bakunin's character:

> It is perfectly true that Nechaev is the man most persecuted by the Russian government, that all its spies on the continent of Europe are trying to trap him, and that they have demanded his extradition from Germany and Switzerland should he be found there. It is also true that Nechaev is one of the most active and energetic men I have ever known. To serve what he calls the "cause" he will stop at nothing, and will be just as ruthless to himself as he is to others. This is the principal quality which attracted me to him; his only excuse is his fanatical devotion. He does not realize that he is a terrible egocentric who winds up confusing his own person with the revolution. But he is not an egoist in the vulgar sense of that term, for he recklessly risks his own safety, and lives the life of a martyr, enduring unheard-of privations. His fanaticism has made him a perfect Jesuit. He relishes Jesuitism as others relish revolution. Despite his relative naiveté, he is very dangerous, and daily commits the most flagrant betrayals and abuses of confidence. All of this is very sad and humiliating for us who recommend him to you, but the truth is still the best way and the best remedy for our mistakes. . . .
>
> Seeing himself unmasked, this poor Nechaev remained so naïve and childish, despite his systematic perversity, that he believed it possible to convert me. He even went so far as to beg me to agree to develop his theory in a Russian paper which he proposed that I set up. He has betrayed the confidence of us all, he has stolen our letters, he has horribly compromised us all—in a word, he has behaved like a scoundrel. After exhausting all means of argument, I have been forced to dissociate myself from him, and since then I have had to fight him to the death.

Even before the recent work of Michael Confino (*Cahiers du Monde Russe*, Oct.–Dec. 1966) decisively settled the issue, it should have been plain that Bakunin would hardly have been guilty of advocating precisely the tactics for which he denounced Nechaev.

Bakunin's pamphlet *Some Words to My Young Brothers in Russia* reveals how deep was the gap between him and Nechaev. In it Bakunin provided the watchword for the *Narodniki*, the populist movement calling upon intellectuals and the upper classes to live with the people and struggle with them for their liberation. Bakunin wrote:

> So, young friends, leave this dying world—these universities, academies, and schools in which you are now locked, and where you are permanently separated from the people. *Go to the people!* This is your field, your life, your science. *Learn from the people how best to serve their cause!* Remember, friends, that educated youth must be neither the teacher, the paternalistic benefactor, nor the dictatorial leader of the people, but only the midwife for their self-liberation, inspiring them

to increase their power by acting together and coordinating their efforts!

After wandering from one European country to another, Nechaev made the mistake of reentering Switzerland. According to a prior agreement, the Swiss government handed him back to the Russian authorities. Bakunin knew of this agreement and had sent a warning to Nechaev, but the latter refused to take heed and was arrested in October 1872. On November 2, 1872, Bakunin wrote to Ogarev:

I pity him deeply. No one ever did me, and intentionally, as much harm as he did, but I pity him all the same. He was a man of rare energy and when we met there burned in him a very ardent and very pure flame for our poor, oppressed people; our historical and current national misery caused him real suffering. At that time his external behavior was unsavory enough, but his inner self had not been soiled. It was his authoritarianism and his unbridled willfulness which very regrettably and through his ignorance together with his Machiavellian and Jesuitical methods, finally plunged him irretrievably into the mire.
. . .
However, an inner voice tells me that Nechaev, who is lost forever and certainly knows that he is lost, will now call forth from the depths of his being, warped and soiled, but far from being base or common, all his primitive energy and courage. He will perish like a hero and this time he will betray nothing and no one. Such is my belief. We shall see if I am right. (Translated by K. J. Kenafick in *Karl Marx and Michael Bakunin*, Melbourne, 1948, pages 132-3)

Kenafick remarks that

Bakunin was right in every particular. This time he was not mistaken about Nechaev. The prisoner was condemned to hard labor for life and died in 1882 in that same fortress of St. Peter and St. Paul where Bakunin himself had passed so many terrible years. Nechaev displayed to the end the same fanatical courage and hatred of tyranny which, though they did not excuse his treachery to those who trusted him, yet make us feel that, as Bakunin remarked, here was a warped mind, but by no means a vulgar one. (page 133)

15. Louis Auguste Blanqui, 1805–1881, was a French socialist who advocated seizure of political power by a handful of revolutionary plotters who would then direct and control the State and the populace by authoritarian methods.

16. Guillaume quotes only one paragraph, the last of those which follow. Because of the importance of the circular for an understanding of the conflict within the International, we have supplied additional paragraphs.

17. Peter Lavrov was a professor of mathematics in a military academy at St. Petersburg. A colonel in the Russian Army, he was a leader of the moderate wing of the Russian populist movement,

and for this he was forced to emigrate to Western Europe. He lived in France, and then in Switzerland, where he met Bakunin. His conflict with Bakunin had its source not merely in their divergent views, but in Lavrov's refusal to allow any Bakuninist representatives on the editorial board of the paper he and his followers controlled.

18. Of the five members of the Commission of Inquiry, one, Walter, whose real name was Von Heddeghem, was a Bonapartist police spy. In March of 1873, about twenty members of the International were tried in France on the evidence he supplied. Another member of this commission, Roch Splingard, submitted a minority report contending that Bakunin was being indicted on insufficient evidence. He declared that "I am resolved to fight the decision before the Congress." (See *The First International: Minutes of the Hague Congress*, Madison, The University of Wisconsin Press, 1958, pages 226–7, 312.)

19. The Blanquists split away from Marx on September 6, 1872, at the Hague Congress, accusing the Marxists of betraying the coalition between these two antilibertarian groups. On the split, see Miklos Molnar's *Le Declin de la Première Internationale: Le Conference de Londres de 1871*, Geneva, 1963.

20. Both Guillaume and Bakunin attended the St.-Imier Congress. The third resolution, not included in this text, was written by Bakunin. It reads as follows:

Considering that the wish to impose upon the proletariat a single course of action or uniform political program as the only way to achieve its social emancipation is a pretension as absurd as it is reactionary; That no one can legitimately deprive the sections and autonomous federations of the incontestable right to determine and carry out whatever political policies they deem best, and that all such attempts must inevitably lead to the most revolting dogmatism; That the economic aspirations of the proletariat can have no other aim than the establishment of absolutely free organizations and federations based on the labor equally of all and absolutely separate and independent from every political state government; and that these organizations and federations can be created only by the spontaneous action of the proletariat itself, [that is, by] the trade bodies and the autonomous communes; That every political state can be nothing but organized domination for the benefit of one class, to the detriment of the masses, and that should the proletariat itself seize power, it would in its turn become a new dominating and exploiting class; For these reasons, the Congress of St.-Imier declares:

1. That the destruction of all political power is the first task of the proletariat;
2. That the establishment of a so-called "provisional" (temporary)

revolutionary authority to achieve this destruction can be nothing
but a new deception and would be just as dangerous for the proletariat as any existing government;
3. That the proletariat of all lands, absolutely rejecting all compromise in order that the Social Revolution be attained, must create
the solidarity of revolutionary action; this is to be done independently
of and in opposition to all forms of bourgeois politics.

(Taken from Max Nettlau's Der Anarchismus von Proudhon zu Kropotkin, Verlag Der Syndikalist, Berlin, 1927, page 199.)

21. This opinion of Guillaume's is shared by many responsible
historians and biographers, e.g., Franz Mehring and Otto Rühle.

22. Carlo Cafiero, 1846–1892, was the son of a very wealthy family,
and seemed destined for a diplomatic career. While in London,
he became a socialist, and developed an almost lifelong friendship with Friedrich Engels, with whom he carried on an extensive correspondence. While Cafiero, who was a pioneer in the
Italian Labor movement, was engaged in organizing for the
Marxists in Italy, Engels sent him letters filled with invectives
against Bakunin. This aroused Cafiero's curiosity and, upon
meeting Bakunin, he became an enthusiastic and dedicated
anarchist and helped found the International in Italy. The fortune Cafiero inherited was spent for the cause of the revolutionary movement. When, later in life, he became penniless, he
worked as a photographer. In 1881 he was confined to a mental
hospital, where he passed the rest of his days. His distracted
ramblings were often touching: he insisted on closed windows
so as not to appropriate the light that belonged to all.

I The Pre-Anarchist Period: Revolutionary Pan-Slavism

1. Translated by Mary-Barbara Zeldin: Russian Philosophy, Vol. I
(Chicago: Quadrangle Press; 1965), pp. 389, 393, 394, 400, 404,
405, 406.
2. Daniel Guérin, ed.: Ni Dieu, Ni Maître (Paris; 1965), p. 185.
3. Appeal to the Slavs, pp. 190–3. Added section by H. E. Kaminski: Bakounine: La Vie d'un Révolutionnaire (Paris; 1938), pp.
118–19.
4. In the early part of December 1847, the French newspapers
reported the condemnation to death on the guillotine of Louis
Meroslavsky and seven of his companions, accused of high treason in a royal Prussian court of justice. Eighty-two other accused
men received severe prison sentences.
5. E. H. Carr: Michael Bakunin (New York: Vintage; 1961), p.
178.

6. Ibid., p. 183.
7. Eugene Pyziur: *The Doctrine of Anarchism of Michael A. Bakunin* (Milwaukee; 1955), p. 96.
8. Franco Venturi: *Roots of Revolution* (New York: Grosset & Dunlap; 1966), pp. 58, 62.
9. Osmanlis (or Ottomans): Turks of the Western branch of the Turkish peoples (Bakunin calls them "Osmantis"). [Translator's note]

II The Anarchism of Michael Bakunin

1. Daniel Guérin, ed.: *Ni Dieu, Ni Maître* (Paris; 1965), pp. 203–15.
2. Ibid., pp. 201–3.
3. H. E. Kaminski: *Bakounine: La Vie d'un Révolutionnaire* (Paris; 1938), pp. 213–14.
4. Guérin: *Ni Dieu, Ni Maître*, pp. 197–215.
5. The issue of secession is not explicitly treated by Bakunin in the *Revolutionary Catechism*. We have supplied some of his thoughts on the issue in this paragraph, at a point where they seem relevant. The first two sentences here are from the *National Catechism*, the rest from the *Organization of the International Revolutionary Fraternity*. Both of these pieces were written within a year of the *Revolutionary Catechism*.
6. Who will recognize these associations? In subsequent paragraphs, Bakunin describes each of the organizations which, on many levels, collaborate to form the Federation.
7. Bakunin: *Oeuvres* (Paris: Stock; 1895), Vol. I, pp. 14–35.
8. The illustrious Italian patriarch Giuseppe Mazzini, whose ideal of a republic is none other than the French Republic of 1793 recast according to the poetic traditions of Dante and ambitious reminiscences of ancient Rome as sovereign of the world, later again reexamined and corrected to comply with a new theology, half rational and half mystical—this eminent, ambitious patriarch, so ardent and always so arbitrary in his views, always preferring, in spite of all his efforts to rise to heights of international justice, the grandeur and power of his country to its real welfare and its liberty—Mazzini has always been a bitter enemy of the autonomy of provinces, which would naturally interfere with his great Italian State. He claims that the autonomy of the communes would be sufficient to counterbalance the omnipotence of the strongly constituted republic. He is mistaken. No isolated commune would be able to resist the power of this formidable

centralization; it would be crushed by it. In order not to succumb in this struggle the commune would have to federate, for purposes of a joint resistance, with all the neighboring communes; that is, it would have to form an autonomous province with them. Also, if the provinces are not completely autonomous, they will have to be governed by the functionaries of the State. There is no middle ground between a rigorously organized federalism and a bureaucratic regime. Thus it follows that the republic which Mazzini desires would be a bureaucratic, and hence a military, State, founded for the purposes of external power and not for international justice or external liberty. In 1793, under the Terror, the communes of France were recognized as autonomous, which did not prevent them from being crushed by the revolutionaries of the Convention or rather by the despotism of the Commune of Paris, which Napoleon naturally inherited. [Bakunin's note]

9. It is a well-known fact that in America it is the supporters of the interests of the South as against the North, i.e., of slavery as against the emancipation of the slaves, who call themselves "democrats" exclusively. [Bakunin's note]

10. Such a bourgeois education, backed by the solidarity which links all the members of the bourgeois world, assures everyone who has obtained it an enormously privileged remuneration for his work. The most ordinary work done by the bourgeois is paid at three or four times the rate received by the most intelligent worker. [Bakunin's note]

11. Bakunin: *Oeuvres* (Paris: Stock; 1895), Vol. I, pp. 36–59.

12. In this respect, the science of jurisprudence offers a perfect resemblance to theology. Both these sciences start equally: one, from a real but iniquitous fact—appropriation by force, conquest; the other, from a fictitious and absurd fact—divine revelation as an absolute principle. On the basis of this absurdity and this iniquity, both resort to the most rigorous logic to erect a theological system on the one hand and a juridical system on the other. [Bakunin's note]

13. These interrelationships, which, incidentally, could never have existed among primitive men, because social life preceded the awakening of individual conscience and of intelligent will among men, and because, outside society, no human individual had ever been able to have any liberty, absolute or even relative—these interrelationships are precisely the same as those now in existence between modern states. Each one of them considers itself invested with a liberty of power and of absolute right, to the exclusion of all other states, and therefore, in its relations with all the other states, is guided only by such considerations as are

commanded by its own interests. All of this necessarily involves a state of permanent or latent war between all of them. [Bakunin's note]

14. Quoted by E. H. Carr: *Michael Bakunin* (London: Macmillan; 1937), p. 421.
15. Guérin: *Ni Dieu, Ni Maître*, pp. 228–31.
16. Paul Brissenden: *The I.W.W.: A Study in American Syndicalism* (New York: Columbia University Press; 1920), pp. 36–7.
17. François Muñoz, ed.: *Bakounine et la Liberté* (Paris; 1965), pp. 195–6.
18. Bakunin: *Politique de l'Internationale* (Paris: Stock; 1911), Vol. V, pp. 169–99.
19. This paragraph is taken from *Double Strike in Geneva* (1869), and is inserted here to further illustrate Bakunin's concern with practical measures.

III The Franco-Prussian War and the Paris Commune

1. Quoted by Max Nettlau in *Der Anarchismus von Proudhon zu Kropotkin* (Berlin: Der Syndikalist; 1927), pp. 148–51.
2. Franz Mehring: *Karl Marx: The Story of His Life* (Ann Arbor; 1962), p. 467.
3. G. D. H. Cole: *A History of Socialist Thought* (London: Macmillan; 1954), Vol. II, p. 121.
4. Max Nettlau, ed.: *Gesammelte Werke Bakunins* (Berlin; 1921–4), Vol. II, p. 62.
5. Bakunin: *Lettres à un Français* (Paris: Stock; 1907), Vol. II, pp. 160–73, 213–48.
6. Ibid., Vol. IV, pp. 16–23, 28–31.
7. The year before, 1869, at the Basel Congress of the International, Bakunin, in contradistinction to the traditional conception of the State which is necessarily national, had called for the establishment of the International State, saying: "[Our] mission is to destroy all national territorial states and erect on their ruins the International State of all the millions of workers." To call for the building of the International State over the ruins of national states was, for Bakunin, the equivalent of demanding the destruction of the State in every form. [Note by James Guillaume]
8. This extremely important question of representative government and universal suffrage is dealt with by Bakunin in a separate selection.
9. Bakunin: *Oeuvres: Les Ours de Berne et l'Ours de Saint Petersbourg* (1907), Vol. II, pp. 35–43.

10. Quoted in François Muñoz: *Bakounine et la Liberté* (Paris: Pauvert; 1965), p. 226.
11. Ibid., p. 175.
12. Bakunin: *Oeuvres* (1871), Part Two, Vol. III, pp. 18–132.
13. Bakunin: *Oeuvres* (Paris; 1895), Vol. I, pp. 264–7, 273–5, 277–85, 288–96.
14. Bakunin: *God and the State*. Trans. by Benjamin R. Tucker (New York: Mother Earth Edition; 1915?), pp. 28–35, 60–4.
15. Bakunin: *Oeuvres* (Paris; 1913), Vol. VI, pp. 15–28, 55–91.
16. This paragraph, not included in the standard text, was found in a fragment of the original reprinted in Max Nettlau's *Der Anarchismus von Proudhon zu Kropotkin* (Berlin: Der Syndikalist; 1927), p. 133.
17. Bakunin: *Oeuvres* (Paris: Stock; 1910), Vol. IV, pp. 245–75.
18. Quoted by Daniel Guérin, ed.: *Ni Dieu, Ni Maître* (Paris; 1965), pp. 262–3.
19. Mehring: *Karl Marx*, pp. 452–3.
20. Louis Charles Delescluze (1809–1871) was a French political journalist. A participant in the revolutions of 1830 and 1848, he was a member of the National Assembly of 1871 and a military delegate of the Paris Commune. He was killed while fighting on the barricades, May 1871.
21. See Note 12 to "Michael Bakunin: A Biographical Sketch."
22. Bakunin: *Oeuvres* (1910), Vol. IV, pp. 339–50.
23. Ibid., pp. 373–87.
24. Bakunin uses "political" here in a broad sense, embracing not merely the government or the State, but any area or problem in community life other than those dealing with wages and subsistence.
25. Practical, in the sense that its realization will be much less difficult than that of the Marxian idea, which, in addition to the paltriness of its program, has the serious drawback of being absolutely impractical. It will not be the first time that clever and rational men, advocates of things possible and practical, will be called "utopians," and those who are today called "utopians" will be acknowledged as the practical men of tomorrow. The absurdity of the Marxist system consists precisely in the vain hope that by inordinately narrowing down the socialist program to make it acceptable to the bourgeois radicals [liberals] it will transform the latter into unwitting and involuntary servants of the Social Revolution. This is a great error. All the experience of history demonstrates that an alliance concluded between different parties always turns to the advantage of the more reactionary party; this alliance necessarily enfeebles the more progressive party by diminishing and distorting its program, by undermining

its moral strength and self-confidence; while a reactionary party, when guilty of falsehood, is acting normally and merely being true to itself, and even manages to recover its undeserved reputation for veracity. One should never forget the example of Mazzini, who, in spite of his rigid republicanism, passed his whole life in transactions with the monarchy, and ended always by being its dupe. I also do not hesitate to say that all the Marxist flirtations with the radical bourgeoisie, whether reformist or "revolutionary," can result only in the demoralization and disorganization of the nascent power of the proletariat, and consequently in a new consolidation of the established power of the bourgeois rulers.

The communalist insurrection of the Paris Commune of March 1871 inaugurated the Social Revolution. The importance of this revolution lies not in the very feeble attempts which the Commune had the time and the opportunity to make, but rather in the ideas stirred up, the glaring light which it has cast upon the true nature and goal of the Revolution, and the hopes which have been awakened everywhere. It generated tremendous power among the masses of all countries, especially in Italy, where the popular awakening dates from this insurrection against the State.

The effect of this revolt has been so powerful that the Marxists themselves, whose ideas were completely refuted by it, have been forced to doff their hats to it. They have indeed done more: against the most elementary logic and their own real sentiments, they proclaim that its program and cause are also theirs. . . . They have seen the power of the passion which this revolution has sparked in everyone. [Bakunin's note]

26. Bakunin: *L'Empire Knouto-Germanique et La Révolution Sociale, Oeuvres* (Paris; 1910), pp. 393–480.

27. This refers to the "Address of the International Workingmen's Association" written in 1864, and translated in 1865 into French by Charles Longuet under the title "Manifeste de l'Association Internationale des Travailleurs."

28. Written by Marx and adopted without change by the Geneva Congress.

29. The "Considerations" was adopted in its French and German versions, together with the English text, by the Geneva Congress of 1866.

30. "The International Alliance of Social Democracy," founded by Bakunin and others in 1868. Its program was the ideological base of the libertarian wing of the First International.

31. Bakunin meant that the Marxists had abstained from presenting a positive program proposing to the proletariat "The Conquest of Political Power." (James Guillaume)

32. This was written November 4, 1872.

33. Words used by Engels in a letter to Cafiero.

34. The Hague Congress resolutions.

35. Sedan was the decisive French defeat in the Franco-Prussian War of 1870–1.

36. Bakunin here refers to a remark by Sorge, a delegate from America to the Hague Congress: "The partisans of autonomy say that our association has no need of a head. We, on the contrary, think that we *must* have one, with a lot of brains inside." (J.G.)

37. The phrase "Proudhon, whom he loved so much" is an ironic allusion to Marx's well-known detestation of Proudhon. (J.G.)

38. "The unfortunate pamphlet" is probably *Si les traités de 1815 ont cessé d'exister* (1864), in which Proudhon opposed the reestablishment of Poland as an independent state. (J.G.)

39. The crime of Proudhon consisted in ignoring two truths. The first was that the old Polish republic was based on the enslavement of the rural population by the institutions of the nobility. The second was that since the insurrection of 1863, like each of the preceding uprisings, was inspired by an ardent, exclusively political patriotism, devoid of socialist ideals, any reestablishment of the great Polish state within its old limits was doomed to fail. It was perhaps cruel to tell these truths to an unfortunate nation at the very moment when it was succumbing to the foremost of its assassins. But at least it was the truth, and it had to be told. Proudhon's guilt was that his opposition to the Polish patriots led him to picture the troops, the functionaries, the savage hordes of the Tsar as the socialist emancipators of the Polish peasants from their treacherous Polish masters. Proudhon, like most of his compatriots, was as profoundly ignorant of Poland as they were of Russia, but even so his revolutionary instinct should have guarded him against advancing a monstrous distortion which earned him the gratitude of our patriotic Moscow pan-Slavists. These patriots, furthermore, were at that very moment confiscating the property of the insurgent Polish landlords—not for distribution to the peasants, but to share the loot with the Russian Imperialists in Poland. That the Russian Empire might emancipate anyone—what a revolting absurdity! An absurdity which certainly is not to the honor, the judgment, or the revolutionary instinct of Proudhon. [Note by Bakunin]

40. At this point Bakunin should have given us his promised explanation of Marx's reason for condemning the partition of Poland, while Bismarck approved the partition and wished to keep the Polish nation in servitude. But Bakunin forgot his promise. Nevertheless it is not difficult to divine his thought. Bakunin

reasoned that Marx, seeing in the Russian Empire the future enemy of his great German republic, was amenable to the restoration of an independent Poland which would serve as a buffer between Russia and Germany, and would thereby safeguard the eastern frontier of the (future) German republic. (J.G.)

41. Louis Adolphe Thiers (1797–1877) was president of the Third Republic, 1871–3, and responsible for the suppression of the Paris Commune (1871).

42. This paragraph does not appear in the original text but has been added because it clarifies and summarizes Bakunin's point. It comes from Volume 1, page 227, of *Oeuvres*; more specifically, from the "Letter to the Internationalists of the Jura-Switzerland," dated April 28, 1869.

IV Final Years

1. Bakunin: *Gosudarstvennost i Anarkhiya (State and Anarchy)*, *Archives Bakounine*; International Institute for Social History, E. J. Brill, Leiden, Holland; 1st edition, 1873. Reprinted in the original Russian with French translation by Marcel Brody 1967, pp. 209–16, 273–6, 278–81, 283.

2. Ibid., pp. 7–8, 17–19, 34–5, 42, 47–8, 56–7, 63–7, 69–83.

3. Ibid., Appendix A, pp. 4–7, 10–11, 13–19, 20–2.

4. By sociologists Bakunin means those we nowadays call generalists, men who know enough of all special fields to deal with the entire range of intellectual endeavor.

5. People from various strata of Russian society, of various degrees of education, but alienated from the "establishment," in a rebellious mood, and seeking an outlet for their frustrations.

6. *Obras de Miguel Bakunin* (Barcelona: Editorial Tierra y Libertad; 1938), Vol. VI, pp. 245–8.

7. Élisée Reclus (1830–1905) was a famous geographer and scientist, a close friend of Bakunin, and a leading member of the vanguard anarchist organization, the Alliance.

8. K. J. Kenafick: *Marx and Bakunin* (Melbourne; 1948), pp. 303–6.

9. "The disastrous events for which we are to some extent responsible" were the victory of the Prussian armies in the Franco-Prussian War, and the defeat of the Lyons uprising of September 1870, of the Paris Commune (March–May 1871), and of uprisings in Spain and Italy, followed by the victory of the reactionary forces that dominated continental Europe. Bakunin felt that the revolutionary movement was partly responsible for these

setbacks because it was ideologically and tactically unprepared to take advantage of favorable revolutionary situations.

10. "Idées sur l'organisation sociale," in Daniel Guérin, ed.: *Ni Dieu, Ni Maître* (Paris; 1965), pp. 299–323.

Selected Bibliography

With the exception of *Statism and Anarchy* which was written in Russian, Bakunin wrote his major works in French. The best source, available only in large public and some university libraries, is *Oeuvres* (collected works in six volumes), published by P. V. Stock-Paris from 1895 to 1913. Volume I was arranged with an introduction and notes by the greatest historian of anarchism, Dr. Max Nettlau. Volumes II-VI were arranged with introduction and notes by Bakunin's friend and coworker, James Guillaume. Volume II contains Guillaume's *Biographical Sketch* of Bakunin (rendered into English in this anthology). All writings are reproduced as originally written by Bakunin, except *Response à l'Unità Italiana* and the *Circulaire à Mes Amis d'Italie*, Volume VI (the original French manuscript was lost and was retranslated from the Italian by Guillaume).

Oeuvres

Volume I (1895)
  Federalism, Socialism, Anti-Theologism (1867)
  Letters on Patriotism (1869), a series of ten articles written for
    Progrès de Genève.
  Dieu et l'État (title given by Nettlau to a fragment of *L'Empire
    Knouto-Germanique et la Révolution Sociale*).

Volume II (1907)
  Les Ours de Bern et l'Ours de Saint Petersburg (1870).
  Lettres à un Français sur la Crise Actuelle (an abridged and severely
    edited text by Guillaume followed by the exact text as originally
    written by Bakunin).
  L'Empire Knouto-Germanique et la Révolution Sociale (first edi-
    tion, 1870–71).

Volume III (1908)
  L'Empire Knouto-Germanique et la Révolution Sociale (second edi-
    tion, 1871). Part of this work was published as a pamphlet entitled
    God and the State with numerous alterations by Carlo Cafiero
    and Élisée Reclus, two of Bakunin's friends. Translated into many
    languages, including English, and not to be confused with the
    selection under the same title in Volume I.

L'Empire Knouto-Germanique et la Révolution Sociale (appendix to first edition of 1870).

Considérations Philosophiques sur le Fantôme Divin, sur le Monde Réel et sur l'Homme (1870).

Volume IV (1910)

Lettres à un Français sur la Crise Actuelle (continuation, 1870).

Manuscrit écrit à Marseille (1870).

Lettre à Esquiros (1870).

Préambule pour la seconde livraison de *L'Empire Knouto-Germanique et la Révolution Sociale* (1871).

Avertissement pour *L'Empire Knouto-Germanique et la Révolution Sociale* (1871).

Lettre au journal *La Liberté de Bruxelles* (1872).

Fragment formant une suite à *L'Empire Knouto-Germanique et la Révolution Sociale* (1871).

Volume V (1911)

The following articles were written for the journal *L'Égalité* during the years 1868 and 1869:

Lettre à Commission du journal L'Égalité de Genève.

Le Journal Fraternité.

Mme. André Leo et L'Égalité.

La Double Grève de Genève.

Le Mouvement Internationale des Travailleurs.

L'Agitation du Parti Démocratie Socialiste en Autriche.

La Montagne et M. Coullery.

Les Endormeurs.

L'Instruction Intégrale.

Politique de l'Internationale.

Rapport de la Commission sur la Question l'Héritage.

Lettre Addressée aux Citoyens Redacteurs du Reveil à Paris (1869).

Trois Conférences Faites aux Ouvriers du Val de Saint-Imier (1871).

Volume VI (1913)

Protestation de l'Alliance.

Réponse d'un International à Mazzini (1871).

Lettre de Bakounine à la Section de l'Alliance de Genève (1871).

Rapport sur l'Alliance (1871).

Circulaire à Mes Amis d'Italie (1871).

The German, Russian, and Spanish editions generally follow the French, with certain significant differences (the Spanish edition includes *Statism and Anarchy*).

German: *Gesammelte Werke*, edited with an introduction and notes by Max Nettlau. Volume I (1921), Volume II (1923), Volume III (1924), Der Syndikalist, Berlin.

Russian: Volume I (1919). Volume II (1919). Volume III (1920). Volume IV (1920). Volume V (1922). *Golos Truda*, Leningrad and Moscow.

A four-volume biography of Bakunin was published by the historian Yuri M. Steklov, Moscow, 1926. Steklov also edited a four-volume collection of letters and other writings by Bakunin, not going beyond 1861; this appeared in Moscow, 1934. The publication of further volumes was suspended, because of controversy surrounding the differences between Bakunin and Marx. Special mention must be made of Dr. Max Nettlau's monumental *Michael Bakunin: Eine Biographie*, which consists of three parts totaling 1,282 pages. Most of the material by and about Bakunin contained in this biography was never published. It contains hundreds of notes and is the indispensable sourcebook for almost all the works and biographies of Bakunin. All the writings of Bakunin included in this work are reproduced in the original (i.e., not translated). Nettlau made fifty copies which he distributed to the principal libraries of the world. This work was completed between 1896 and 1900.

There are two Spanish editions of Bakunin's works. The five volumes published by Editorial La Protesta Buenos Aires, Argentina, with introduction by Max Nettlau, were completed in 1929. Volume V, translated from the original Russian, is titled *Statism and Anarchy*. The other Spanish edition of *Obras de Bakunin* consists of six volumes with prologue by Max Nettlau and was published in 1938 by Editorial Tierra y Libertad, Barcelona, Spain.

As noted above, all these works are out of print and extremely difficult to obtain and none of them is complete. For these reasons The International Institute of Social History of Amsterdam, Holland, is now in the process of publishing in French the complete works of Bakunin in fifteen large volumes, together with introductions and copious notes, under the title *Archives Bakounine* (publiées pour International Instituut voor sociale gescheidnis, Amsterdam, par E. J. Brill, Leiden, Holland; arranged and edited by A. Lehning, A. J. C. Rüter, and P. Scheibert). At this writing, the following volumes have been published:

Volume I. *Michel Bakounine et Italie*, 1871–72. Première partie: *La Polémique avec Mazzini*. Ecrits et Materiaux. 1961.

Volume I. *Michel Bakounine et Italie*, 1871–72. Deuxième partie: *La Première Internationale en Italie et le Conflit avec Marx*. 1963.

Volume II. *Michel Bakounine et les Conflits dans l'Internationale*, 1872. *La Question Germano-Slave*. *La Commune d'État*. 1965.

Volume III. *Étatisme et Anarchie*, 1873. Translated from the Russian by Marcel Brody. The original Russian text is published together with the French translation. All these volumes are accompanied by extensive notes and hitherto unobtainable documents are reproduced.

In addition to the collected works, the following materials are particularly useful:

L'Internationale, documents et souvenirs by James Guillaume. 4 vols. E. J. Stock, Paris, 1905–10.

Correspondence de Michel Bakounine. Lettres à Herzen et à Ogareff, 1860–74. Published with a preface and annotations by M. Dragamanoff; translated from the Russian by Marie Stromberg. Perrins et cie, Paris, 1896.

Confession de Michel Bakounine. Translated from the Russian by Paulette Brupbacher; introduction and notes by Max Nettlau. Éditions Rieder, Paris, 1932.

Aufruf an die Slaven ("Appeal to the Slavs"). Köthen, 1848.

La Cause Populaire: Romanoff, Pugachev, ou Pestel? London, 1861.

A Mes Amis Russes et Polonais. Translated from the Russian. Leipzig, 1862.

Lettre inédite à Celso Cerretti. Vol. 1, Société Nouvelle, Paris, 1896.

The following writings of Bakunin are published in the outstanding anthology of the anarchist movement, *Ni Dieu, Ni Maître,* edited by Daniel Guérin. Éditions de Delphes, Paris, 1965:

La Commune de Paris et la Notion de l'État.

Programme et Objet de l'Organisation de Fréres Internationals.

Points essential de Catéchisme Révolutionnaire.

Catéchisme Révolutionnaire.

Organisation de la Fraternité Internationale Révolutionnaire.

Marx et Bakounine by Fritz Brupbacher. French edition, De La Baconniere, Neuchatel, Switzerland, 1955.

Bakounine: La Liberté, edited with notes by François Muñoz. Jacques Pauvert, Paris, 1965.

Bakounine, ou La Vie Contre la Science by Henry Arvon. Seghers, Paris, 1966.

Bakounine: La Vie d'un Révolutionnaire by H. E. Kaminski. Editions Montaigne, Paris, 1938.

The following works are in English:

Kenafick, K. J., trans. and ed. *Marxism, Freedom and the State.* Freedom Press, London, 1950.

Kenafick, K. J. *Karl Marx and Michael Bakunin.* Melbourne, 1948.

Maximoff, G. P., comp. and ed. *The Political Philosophy of Bakunin.* The Free Press, Glencoe, Illinois, 1953.

Pyziur, Eugene. *The Doctrine of Anarchism of Michael A. Bakunin.* 2d ed., Henry Regnery, Chicago, 1968.

God and the State, with a preface by Carlo Cafiero and Élisée Reclus. Translated from the French by Benjamin Tucker. Mother Earth Publishing Company, 1915. New edition with an introduction by Paul Avrich, 1970.

Index

VINTAGE HISTORY—WORLD

LE ROUGE IDÉAL

DU MÊME AUTEUR

Les Montagnes russes. Roman.
   Montréal : VLB, 1988.
Les Tours de Londres. Roman.
   Montréal : VLB, 1991.
Les Amitiés inachevées. Roman.
   Montréal : Québec/Amérique, coll. Littérature
   d'Amérique, 1994.

Le Docteur Wilfrid Derome. Biographie.
   Montréal : Boréal, 2003. (À paraître)

Nébulosité croissante en fin de journée. Roman.
   Beauport : Alire, Romans 034, 2000.
Le Rouge idéal. Roman.
   Lévis : Alire, Romans 063, 2002.

LE ROUGE IDÉAL

JACQUES CÔTÉ

ALIRE

Illustration de couverture
BERNARD DUCHESNE

Photographie
VALÉRIE ST-MARTIN

Diffusion et distribution pour le Canada
Québec Livres
2185, autoroute des Laurentides, Laval (Québec) H7S 1Z6
Tél.: 450-687-1210   Fax: 450-687-1331

Diffusion et distribution pour la France
D.E.Q.   (Diffusion de l'Édition Québécoise)
30, rue Gay Lussac, 75005 Paris
Tél. : 01.43.54.49.02   Fax: 01.43.54.39.15
Courriel : liquebec@noos.fr

Pour toute information supplémentaire
LES ÉDITIONS ALIRE INC.
C. P. 67, Succ. B, Québec (Qc) Canada G1K 7A1
Tél.: 418-835-4441   Fax : 418-838-4443
Courriel : alire@alire.com
Internet : www.alire.com

Les Éditions Alire inc. bénéficient des programmes d'aide à l'édition
de la Société de développement des entreprises culturelles du Québec
(SODEC), du Conseil des Arts du Canada (CAC) et reconnaissent l'aide
financière du gouvernement du Canada par l'entremise du
Programme d'aide au développement de l'industrie de l'édition
(PADIÉ) pour leurs activités d'édition.
Les Éditions Alire inc. ont aussi droit au Programme de crédit d'impôt
pour l'édition de livres du gouvernement du Québec.

1er dépôt légal : 4e trimestre 2002
Bibliothèque nationale du Québec
Bibliothèque nationale du Canada

À Marc et Martine

Toute ressemblance entre des personnages
et des personnes réelles ne serait que pure coïncidence.

TABLE DES MATIÈRES

Vous avez chu dans l'aube aux sillons des chemins
Vous pleurez de mes yeux, vous pleurez de mes mains

Émile Nelligan

Car je ne puis trouver parmi ces pâles roses
Une fleur qui ressemble à mon rouge idéal

Charles Baudelaire

PREMIÈRE PARTIE

PORTRAIT DE NUIT
DU LIEUTENANT

1

Le téléphone retentit trois fois. Un bras frissonnant s'extirpa des couvertures et cueillit à tâtons le récepteur sur la table de chevet. Le courant d'air s'infiltra dans les draps, glaçant l'échine de l'homme. Peu importait la saison, il dormait à la fraîcheur. Le cadran marquait minuit douze. Il décrocha à la quatrième sonnerie. Pour le commun des mortels, le timbre d'un appel nocturne est angoissant. Penser au pire est alors la norme. Son réveil à lui annonçait le cauchemar des autres. La mort au programme. La mort à la petite semaine. Ces appels de routine pour le lieutenant Duval, enquêteur à l'Escouade des crimes contre la personne de la SQ, avaient l'inconvénient de réveiller toute la maisonnée, en l'occurrence sa fille Mimi, qui dormait à l'étage. Sa conjointe, Laurence, travaillait de nuit cette semaine-là à l'Hôtel-Dieu.

Duval marmotta l'adresse et les indications du standardiste : 30, chemin du Tour-du-Lac, Lac-Beauport. Il éloigna le récepteur à deux pieds de son oreille. La voix forte du répartiteur dans le silence de la nuit se répercutait à dix pieds.

— Le chimiste du labo est là.

Duval raccrocha, s'arracha du lit dans un froissement de couette. Le halo du lampadaire au bord de la falaise tachait de lumière les stores vénitiens : assez pour distinguer l'éclatant saxophone de John Coltrane sur fond indigo, un tableau que lui avait acheté Laurence pour son anniversaire.

Il alluma la lampe de chevet, s'assit sur le bord du lit, bâilla, s'étira les bras à s'en décrocher les trapèzes. Saisi de froid, il ramassa à tâtons son pantalon qui reposait sur un valet de nuit. Mais il l'empoigna par l'ourlet et une pluie de monnaie tomba sur le plancher. Comme de raison, une pièce de 25 cents roula sous le lit dans un mouvement giratoire exaspérant qui ne voulait plus finir. Il ramasserait le tout plus tard. Pas de chemise ni de cravate à cette heure, mais un lainage noir. Il bâilla à nouveau, se frotta le cuir chevelu, regarda à gauche et à droite en cherchant ce qu'il oubliait. Il détestait remonter à l'étage dans ces cas-là. Il jeta un coup d'œil dans le miroir pour replacer une mèche rebelle et constater *de visu* le poids de la nuit dans son regard.

Il referma la porte de la chambre de Mimi, qui ne s'était jamais habituée à ces appels nocturnes.

— C'est qui ?

— Rien de grave. C'est le bureau, répondit laconiquement Duval. Rendors-toi.

Mimi avait perdu très jeune sa mère – une policière qui était morte dans une collision alors qu'elle répondait à un appel d'urgence. Elle craignait pour la vie de son père, c'était un réel tourment. Rarement parvenait-elle à se rendormir. L'affaire Hurtubise[1], dans laquelle son père avait failli laisser sa peau en 1976, n'avait fait qu'accroître son anxiété et ses cauchemars.

---

[1]   Voir *Nébulosité croissante en fin de journée*, Éditions Alire, coll. Romans 034, 2000.

Duval se laissa guider par la veilleuse du passage en forme de grenouille. Après s'être brossé les dents, il descendit au rez-de-chaussée. Les vieilles marches de l'escalier craquaient et il se promettait depuis bien des samedis de les réparer en enfonçant des intercalaires dessous. Mais l'amour récent pour une femme l'avait éloigné du bricolage, goût qu'il avait développé pendant son veuvage.

Il prit son coupe-vent et tiqua ; il n'avait pas ses clés et il lui fallait retourner à l'étage.

2

Par cette nuit fraîche d'octobre, le souffle se condensait en vapeur blanche. Le mercure avoisinait le point de congélation. Le siège froid de la voiture faisait regretter la chaleur du lit et le volant glaçait les doigts. Duval aurait dû prendre ses gants. Il oubliait toujours quelque chose.

Lorsqu'il actionna le démarreur, le rugissement de son 4 X 4 fit contrepoint à la *Symphonie inachevée* que diffusait la radio d'État.

Il descendit la longue côte Saint-Sacrement, chemin qu'il empruntait souvent pour se rendre au Laboratoire de sciences judiciaires et de médecine légale. La désolation du parc industriel, succession de manufactures en brique et d'entrepôts, le dégoûta. Il tourna sur le boulevard Charest en brûlant prudemment le feu rouge.

La route était à peu près libre de circulation à cette heure. Du boulevard Laurentien jusqu'à la Montée du Lac, les lampadaires filèrent derrière lui et Schubert déchaîna toute sa fureur romantique. La flèche de l'indicateur de température commençait à peine à monter. Il actionna la commande de chauffage et l'air chaud se répandit dans l'habitacle. Le ciel d'automne, d'un noir bleuté, s'étirait comme un grand écran piqué d'étoiles. Plus il avançait vers le Relais, plus la forêt se densifiait. Il bifurqua à gauche à la hauteur du centre de ski et roula en suivant les indications que lui avait fournies le bureau. Il pensa à Laurence, sa copine, qui travaillait de nuit à l'urgence et se sentit moins seul.

La vue d'un panneau du gouvernement, *À la chasse, on est prudent*, lui arracha un sourire. Il souhaita du temps doux pour sa partie de chasse. Son collègue Francis l'attendait à son chalet de Charlevoix pour le long congé de l'Action de grâces.

Une brume légère se mouvait alors qu'il gagnait en altitude. En arrivant au sommet du vallon, il vit cette nuée s'allumer de bleu, de rouge et de blanc au bas d'une côte fortement inclinée : les couleurs sinistres de sa profession, celles des gyrophares. Les camions du Laboratoire de sciences judiciaires et de médecine légale ainsi que deux voitures de patrouille étaient rangés sur l'accotement.

Duval tiqua lorsqu'il aperçut le car de reportage. Les journalistes judiciaires sont aux policiers ce que les hyènes sont aux grands fauves. Toujours là, dents carnassières, à arracher des morceaux d'intimité. Et ils appelaient leurs papiers de l'information. Voilà ce qu'il avait toujours pensé des scribes. Quelques curieux, des voisins probablement, observaient la scène en grillant des cigarettes.

Un cordon de sécurité, sur lequel on lisait en grosses lettres «ACCÈS INTERDIT / SÛRETÉ DU QUÉBEC /

SCÈNE DE CRIME », délimitait les lieux. Les gars de l'Identité, lampe de poche à la main, cherchaient des empreintes de pieds et autres indices. Mais avec tous ces véhicules d'incendie devant la maison, les traces seraient difficiles à déceler.

3

La victime habitait une maison de style chalet suisse construite sur un coteau. La maison triangulaire en stuc blanc comportait à l'étage un grand balcon brun et un toit en pignon. Un long chemin asphalté en forme de fer à cheval menait à la résidence entourée de conifères géants. Sur un mât, un drapeau du Québec tout effiloché se laissait fouetter par le vent. Des fenêtres à carreaux aux verres fracassés s'échappait une fumée noire. Les pompiers vêtus de cirés jaunes s'affairaient à rouler les tuyaux. L'eau s'écoulait du talus jusqu'au chemin.

Duval stationna sa voiture en bordure du fossé, derrière celle de Rivard, le chimiste judiciaire, et marcha entre l'ambulance et un véhicule d'incendie. Saisi aux os par l'air humide, il pressa le pas. Le vent s'était levé, faisant bruisser les feuillus. Il flaira une nuit de première neige.

Dans le vestibule, il fut salué par Marceau, un technicien en identité qui, bouteille de poudre et pinceau à la main, relevait les empreintes sur la poignée de la porte intérieure.

— Bonjour, lieutenant. Mon défunt père, pendant des années, me disait d'étudier pour être bien dans la vie. Des soirs comme ça, je lui donne raison.

— Si tu gagnes ton ciel, tu pourras toujours lui dire.

D'un signe de tête, Marceau indiqua à Duval, qui s'en doutait bien, que toute la ribambelle de la police scientifique l'attendait à l'étage.

Le lieutenant, les mains sur les hanches, jeta un coup d'œil au salon et fut dégoûté par le rideau de style bonne femme et la cantonnière boursouflée jaune ocre qui ornaient la grande baie vitrée. Dans un coin, l'eau pissait du plafond à travers le gypse en cloques. Un canapé capitonné, coquille d'œuf, à grosses volutes, reposait sur un tapis de type « shag ». Duval pensait qu'il y avait des scènes de crime qu'annonçait la décoration. Quand il magasinait son mobilier, il pouvait associer des objets à ceux de scènes de crime où il avait joué un rôle. Il replongeait dans de mauvais souvenirs. Il se rappela avoir vu un lit exactement comme celui de Mimi et dans lequel gisait un enfant qu'on avait secoué à mort.

En haut, la lourdeur des pas des différentes équipes donnait une idée de l'activité qui régnait. Dans l'escalier qui ruisselait d'eau, un technicien monta à la course avec sa scie à chaîne.

L'odeur de carbonisé fit toussoter Duval. Seul l'étage du haut avait subi des dommages importants. En entrant dans la chambre, il regarda aussitôt le plafond et les murs. Cette méthode amusait ses collègues, mais donnait des résultats. Que ce soit dans les cas de meurtre ou de suicide, « les murs parlent », comme le lui avait fait remarquer un jour, lors d'un colloque, le docteur Noguchi du Laboratoire de médecine légale de Los Angeles. Avant de regarder le ou les corps, il examinait toujours le « décor ». Les traînées de sang et les giclées artérielles, les traces de poudre, les objets renversés, les meubles déplacés et les sacs d'épicerie abandonnés sur un comptoir devenaient la mémoire matérielle du crime. Dans le cas présent, il y avait beaucoup de suie, contrecoup particulier du feu de matelas. Puis, Duval nota des effets brisants sur la tête du lit, une gerbe de carbone, résultat d'une déflagration. La tête de lit en plastique avait fondu et pris la forme étrange d'un coquillage ramolli avec une Vénus carbonisée en son centre.

Un jeune agent aux yeux bleus et aux joues rosées comme celles d'un poupon procédait à un relevé des lieux. Il réalisait minutieusement son croquis avec la méthode des coordonnées. Duval constata qu'il utilisait celle de l'horloge et qu'il avait encore deux heures à couvrir sur son graphique. Duval alla quérir auprès de lui les premières informations.

— Bonne nuit, lieutenant! dit le jeunot, tout sourire. La dame était morte à notre arrivée.

— C'est une vérité de la police, répondit un technicien à la blague.

Duval eut envie de les reprendre. Il détestait les blagues des jeunes policiers sur le lieu d'un homicide. Qu'est-ce que ce serait à quarante ans?

Un technicien de l'Identité prenait des photos en faisant attention de ne pas contaminer la scène du crime.

Rivard, le chimiste judiciaire, qui se trouvait accroupi près du lit, avait maintes fois travaillé avec Duval. Celui-ci le salua. L'autre se releva, retroussa ses manches et marcha vers le lieutenant. Tout était bois et arêtes sur ce corps, à commencer par le long nez affûté.

— Pas même besoin du chien pour découvrir ce qui s'est passé ici.

Rivard avait un pif incroyable pour sentir les accélérants et les explosifs de toutes sortes. Avant toute analyse chromatographique, c'était le nez qui inter-venait dans un premier temps et ensuite la vue. Il était à la criminalistique ce qu'est l'œnologue à la dégustation du vin : si ce dernier percevait cuir, vanille, réglisse et cerise dans le verre, l'organe olfactif de Rivard détectait les combustibles tous azimuts. À la blague, on disait qu'il faisait une rude compétition à Sneak, le berger allemand de Madden, le maître-chien. Rivard faisait partie des vingt pour cent de la population qui reconnaissaient l'odeur d'amande dégagée par le cyanure.

— À première vue, un feu de matelas. Elle s'est endormie en fumant. C'est une voisine qui habite plus haut sur le coteau qui a vu la fumée s'échapper. Les pompiers sont arrivés très rapidement pour sauver les meubles… mais pas l'occupante. Une grosse fumeuse, semble-t-il. On a trouvé un *cartoon* dans le garde-manger.

Duval, qui détestait la cigarette, ne pouvait comprendre cette absence de volonté des fumeurs face à ce fléau qui les dominait. Dans ce cas-ci, songeait-il, elle mettait le feu à un matelas, du moins selon les apparences. Pas assez de se tuer à petit feu, elle transformait son lit en rôtissoire.

Sur le matelas reposaient les restes d'une femme couchée sur le dos. La contraction des muscles avait figé les membres dans une pose insolite. Au bout des bras tendus vers le ciel, écartés du cadavre, les poings s'étaient refermés, comme pour maudire le destin. La suie dégagée par le matelas avait noirci le corps. Le volume de ce dernier, sous l'effet de la chaleur intense, avait diminué substantiellement. La peau avait séché et durci, prenant l'aspect du cuir. Le feu avait ravagé inégalement la surface antérieure, sur laquelle on décelait différents types de brûlures. La peau présentait par endroits des bulles sèches, soit des brûlures du troisième degré. La couche de graisse avait été touchée sous le derme au niveau du ventre et de la taille, surtout du côté droit. Des bulles humides, des cloques, signes de brûlures du second degré, couvraient les jambes. Il y avait des zones rouges et jaunes où l'on voyait le derme à nu et aussi les vaisseaux sanguins.

Sur le mur au-dessus de la tête du lit, une reproduction à moitié calcinée montrait des jeunes filles aux seins nus dans un paysage brumeux.

Rivard pointa le cendrier en verre sur le matelas, à la hauteur de l'abdomen. Duval se pencha. À voir les bouts filtres et unis des mégots calcinés qui flottaient dans l'eau, on distinguait deux sortes différentes de cigarettes. Il regarda la femme.

— Il semble qu'elle n'ait jamais su que le feu était pris, dit Rivard.

— C'est bizarre, car elle aurait dû se rendre compte à un moment que ça brûlait ou qu'elle étouffait. On aurait dû la retrouver près d'une fenêtre ou recroquevillée par terre. Avez-vous découvert des accélérants dans la maison ?

— Ça sent encore l'essence à briquet.

— On voit les effets brisants, la gerbe de la déflagration est évidente.

— Jusqu'en haut du mur.

Puisque tous les relevés de la police avaient été effectués, Rivard indiqua au technicien à quel endroit découper le plancher avec sa scie. En raison des fentes dans les lattes de bois franc, l'essence avait dû s'infiltrer dans le sous-plancher.

Duval intercepta un gars de l'Identité.

— Installez-moi une grande bâche en plastique au plafond, en bas, question de ne pas perdre des indices quand il va scier le plancher.

Le jeune homme opina du chef et descendit les marches en courant.

Duval plongea son regard par la fenêtre, et la vue de la forêt lui rappela qu'il serait crevé pour filer sur les routes de Charlevoix. Là, il avait les pieds sur la catalogne mouillée, respirait de la suie et s'infligeait la mort la plus horrible qui soit. Il ne s'y était jamais habitué. Le feu lui faisait peur. L'explication lui était venue de son père. Ses parents l'avaient un jour surpris à l'âge de quatre ans, debout sur le poêle, avec tous les ronds allumés à feu vif, alors qu'il fouillait dans l'armoire au-dessus de la hotte. La correction infligée et l'explication des dangers qu'il avait courus avaient laissé des traces. De six à dix ans, il avait exigé de ses parents, au moment d'aller dormir, de vérifier si les ronds de poêle étaient éteints. Cela avait fini par amuser la parenté et devenir un objet de taquinerie. «La rengaine à Daniel», disait-on.

Duval observa le cadavre, perplexe.

— Elle était peut-être dopée? conjectura-t-il.

Il demanda aux policiers s'ils avaient vérifié la pharmacie de la dame.

— Non. Pas encore. On n'est pas rendus là, répondit Bégin.

— J'y vais.

— Peux-tu ramasser les draps dans le panier de linge sale? Envoie-les au labo pour expertise.

Duval fit signe aux deux employés de la morgue de transporter le corps au laboratoire.

La salle de bains était décorée d'un papier peint miroitant avec de grosses fleurs psychédéliques orange et roses. Le lieutenant enfila ses gants de latex, ouvrit l'armoire de la pharmacie. La dame devait souffrir de dépression. Il y trouva du lithium, du Demerol, des Ativan et du Nembutal. «Beau cocktail!» pensa l'enquêteur.

Il lut la date de prescription sur l'une des bouteilles: 15 août. Il en déduisit, après un calcul sommaire, que la victime n'avait fait que suivre la posologie. Pas de suicide au Nembutal cette fois-ci. Sur une tablette se dressait une bombe de crème à raser pour homme et des rasoirs jetables. Il referma l'armoire et rejoignit Rivard, qu'il voyait de dos dans l'embrasure de la chambre. Les gars de la morgue, qu'on appelait amicalement Laurel et Hardy à cause de leur physique respectif, tournaient avec la civière dans le haut de l'escalier.

— Bonne nuit, lieutenant.

— Salut, les gars !

La scie à chaîne faisait un boucan d'enfer dans la maison. Rivard donnait des indications à un employé du labo pour qu'il prépare le transport du matelas et d'une section du plancher. Il allait leur faire subir un examen au chromatographe afin de prouver la présence de l'accélérant.

Duval s'adressa à Rivard, penché sur l'échantillon de plancher.

— Sa pharmacie est remplie d'antidépresseurs.

— Une fumeuse obsessive. On a trouvé des paquets dans toutes les pièces.

Rares étaient les suicidaires qui s'immolaient par le feu. L'autopsie allait révéler d'autres indices très rapidement. Duval prit quelques notes et s'assura que toutes les pièces à conviction soient apportées au labo.

Il descendit au salon et fouilla dans un cendrier sur pied, surmonté d'un DC 3, qui avait été protégé de l'eau. Il découvrit encore des mégots appartenant à deux marques différentes : des Mark Ten couronnées de rouge à lèvres et des Export'A. Il se pencha pour les examiner et constata que les cigarettes avaient été fumées récemment. Il demanda à un technicien de l'Identité d'emporter les mégots.

Un expert en Identité plaça devant le cendrier un carton qui comportait les renseignements sur l'objet saisi. Appareil photo à la main, un technicien se pencha, focalisa, photographia l'objet, puis son collègue enfouit ce dernier dans un sac d'épicerie.

Le lieutenant marcha vers une étagère en mélamine. Il examina des photos de la disparue, à qui il donna entre cinquante-cinq et soixante ans. L'une d'elles avait été prise à Terre des Hommes devant le géodôme du pavillon américain. La femme était blonde, mais pas d'un blond naturel, ce que révélaient ses larges sourcils noirs. Elle était accompagnée d'un homme beaucoup plus jeune. « Son mari », pensa Duval. Il y avait aussi dans un cadre la photo d'un enfant qui devait être son fils.

Sur le secrétaire Louis XVI dans le vestibule, Duval examina le courrier de la dame. Elle devait vivre seule puisque tout était à son nom : madame Eugénie Fournier. À en juger par les meubles et la décoration, elle semblait à l'aise financièrement. Duval sortit respirer une bouffée d'air frais. Les lieux empestaient le gaz carbonique dégagé par la scie à chaîne.

À l'extérieur, une femme aux cheveux blancs observait la scène. Elle s'avança vers Duval.

— C'est moi qui ai appelé les pompiers.

Encore sous le choc, la femme était prise d'un léger tremblement. Elle avait revêtu une canadienne beige.

— Est-ce… qu'elle est morte, inspecteur ?

— Oui, madame.

Elle claquait des dents à présent.

Duval allait en profiter pour tirer quelques informations de cette voisine.

— Vous connaissiez madame Fournier ?

— C'est ma voisine depuis vingt ans.

Puisqu'elle avait froid, Duval l'invita à monter dans sa voiture. Il ouvrit la portière et la referma avec sa galanterie habituelle. Il démarra la voiture pour chauffer l'habitacle. Elle tira la fermeture éclair de son sac à main pour en sortir un paquet de cigarettes. Duval soupira :

— Je vous demanderais de ne pas fumer dans la voiture.

— Oui. Pas de problème.

Elle remit le paquet au fond de son sac. Duval ajusta la commande du chauffage.

— Est-ce que madame Fournier était mariée ?

— Non, elle ne s'est jamais mariée.

— Avait-elle un conjoint ?

— Oui, un homme qu'elle avait rencontré depuis peu.

La femme donna l'impression qu'elle avait déjà trop parlé.

— Vous le connaissiez ?

— On se croisait de temps à autre.

— Comment s'appelle cet homme ? On va devoir appeler un proche pour l'identification.

Le mot identification accentua les tremblements de la voisine.

— Jean-Pierre Émond. Ils avaient l'air de bien s'entendre.

— Avaient l'air ?

— Ils semblaient heureux.

— La question que je vais vous poser est très importante. Avez-vous été témoin de chicanes de couple entre eux ?

Elle réfléchit, mais ne voulut pas répondre.

— Je ne peux pas vous dire. Je suis juste sa voisine. On se parle de jardinage, de température, mais on n'entre jamais dans les détails.

— Jean-Pierre Émond : qu'est-ce qu'il fait dans la vie ?

— Il travaille dans une coop de taxis à Québec.

— Savez-vous s'il est venu au cours de la soirée ?

— Je ne l'ai pas vu. Je travaillais.

— Avez-vous vu ou entendu quelque chose de suspect au moment où vous êtes arrivée ? Une voiture ?

— Non.

— Savez-vous si madame Fournier avait des problèmes psychologiques ?

Elle hésita à répondre à cette question, probablement par respect pour la disparue.

— C'était une femme un peu déprimée. Elle n'a pas eu une vie facile. Son fils unique est mort dans un accident de voiture, il y a deux ans.

Sous le porche d'entrée, les techniciens de l'Identité sortaient avec le matelas et, juste derrière, les deux employés de la morgue suivaient avec la civière. Les rafales collaient les vêtements aux corps.

Les hommes se dirigèrent vers leur camion respectif. Duval baissa sa vitre et demanda à Rivard, qui fermait la sinistre procession, s'il serait possible de procéder à l'autopsie dans l'avant-midi.

— C'est que je pars à la chasse en fin d'après-midi.

— Je ne sais pas, Daniel. Les corps s'empilent. Je vais demander au stagiaire du docteur Villemure.

La dame posa une main sur sa bouche et murmura : « Mon Dieu. » Ces paroles avaient été dites avec une telle désinvolture…

Rivard s'informa sur ce que Duval allait chasser et lui envoya un salut de la main.

Duval prit le nom, l'adresse et le numéro de téléphone de la femme et lui annonça qu'il la rappellerait si nécessaire dans les prochaines heures.

4

Duval se rendit sans perdre un instant à la bicoque de la coopérative de taxis, rue Crémazie. Deux chauffeurs attendaient, assis sur un banc, en lisant le *Journal de Québec* de la veille. Le répartiteur appela un chauffeur pour lui dire de se rendre à l'hôpital Saint-François-d'Assise. L'autre répondit « 10-4 » dans un chuintement de bruits parasites. L'homme aux gros sourcils touffus, penché sur ses mots cachés, redressa la tête en ajustant ses lunettes à monture dorée, style aviateur.

— Je voudrais parler à Jean-Pierre Émond.

— Djé-Pi est sur un *call*, dit l'autre d'un ton baveux.

— Appelez-le, je voudrais lui parler.

— Pourquoi ? demanda l'homme, suspicieux.

Duval montra sa carte d'enquêteur.

— Sa conjointe est décédée, ce soir.

Le visage consterné, le répartiteur toussa et, d'une voix rauque, invita Émond à se pointer à la coop.

— C'est urgent, ajouta-t-il sur un ton compassé. Non, prends pas de *call* en revenant.

Quinze minutes plus tard, un homme dans la trentaine avancée, celui que Duval avait vu sur la photo, entra. Il portait un veston de cuir noir, une casquette écossaise et arborait de longs favoris, une moustache et une permanente. À première vue, une vingtaine d'années séparaient Émond de madame Fournier. Un écart significatif.

Nonchalamment, le répartiteur désigna Duval.

— Djé-Pi, monsieur a affaire à toi.

— Je suis le lieutenant Duval.

Il observa attentivement la réaction du chauffeur de taxi. Celui-ci ne broncha pas.

— J'ai une mauvaise nouvelle. Votre conjointe, madame Fournier, est morte dans un incendie à sa résidence, ce soir.

L'homme demeura figé un instant et regarda le répartiteur.

— Comment c'est arrivé ?

— On ne le sait pas encore.

L'homme s'assit et grimaça, l'œil aussi sec que le Mojave. Son visage se tordit de douleur comme un ver coupé en deux. Le répartiteur s'approcha pour le consoler par une tape virile sur l'épaule. Duval observa de près le comportement de l'homme. Les collègues semblaient plus affectés qu'Émond.

— On est avec toi, mon Djé-Pi.

— Ça se peut pas ! Pas ça !

Après quelques instants, Duval demanda avec délicatesse à Émond s'il pouvait lui poser des questions. Le chauffeur, dépité, le corps prostré, hocha la tête.

Afin de ne pas le braquer immédiatement en le désignant comme un suspect, Duval voulut savoir si Eugénie Fournier fumait au lit.

Émond glapit un « Tabarnak ! », suivi d'un « Pas ça ! ».

Il sortit son paquet et s'alluma une cigarette. Duval trouva le réflexe étrange et paradoxal. Les fumeurs le décourageraient toujours autant.

— Je le savais. Je lui ai dit tellement souvent de ne pas fumer au lit. Elle faisait toujours à sa tête.

Duval nota qu'il fumait des cigarettes à bout uni comme celles dont les mégots avaient été trouvés dans les cendriers. Des Export'A. Duval examina les mains de l'homme, mais ne vit nulle trace de brûlure, ce qui arrivait parfois aux incendiaires. Mais là, rien, à part ces gros doigts boudinés, jaunis par la nicotine.

Un chauffeur entra dans le bâtiment et le répartiteur l'avisa d'aller dans l'autre pièce.

Duval, que la fatigue envahissait, regarda l'heure sur l'horloge à l'effigie du chevalier O'Keefe.

— Monsieur Émond, quand avez-vous vu Eugénie Fournier pour la dernière fois?

— Hier. On a soupé ensemble vers 5 h et ensuite je suis venu travailler.

— Hier, vous voulez dire mercredi?

— Non, mardi.

— Vous ne l'aviez pas vue depuis plus de trente heures?

— C'est ça.

— Vous ne viviez pas ensemble?

— Non. Parfois elle venait coucher chez moi, d'autres fois je restais chez elle. On s'était entendus comme ça.

— Combien de paquets fumait-elle par jour?

— Au moins trois. Une grosse fumeuse.

— Et vous?

— Près de deux paquets. Pourquoi?

Son organe vocal sonnait comme un râle de gramophone à l'aube des 78 tours.

Une pensée chicotait Duval: comment une fumeuse industrielle, qui n'avait pas vu son conjoint depuis vingt-quatre heures, avait-elle pu laisser ses mégots et ceux de son ami dans son cendrier? Normalement, elle aurait dû vider le cendrier qui contenait les mégots d'Émond.

— Vous êtes sûr que vous ne l'avez pas vue depuis mardi soir?

— C'est bien ça.

— C'est quand la dernière fois qu'elle a couché chez vous?

— Dans la nuit de samedi.

— Pourriez-vous me dire où vous étiez entre 11 h et minuit?

Le visage d'Émond vira rubicond. Il n'appréciait pas le sous-entendu. Mais Duval ne broncha pas, flegmatique devant ce regard qui simulait la peine.

— Écoutez, je vis un drame et vous…

— Je suis là pour éclaircir ce qui est arrivé à votre amie.

— Demandez au répartiteur, il vous dira où je me trouvais.

Le répartiteur acquiesça et parcourut du bout de son stylo la liste des appels de la soirée.

— Vers 10 h 40, continua Émond, j'ai été reconduire un homme à Cap-Rouge et ensuite je me suis rendu à l'aéroport pour prendre un client.

Le répartiteur, d'un signe de tête, confirma les dires de son chauffeur.

— Vous étiez à l'aéroport à quelle heure ?

D'une voix exaspérée, le répartiteur lança d'un ton sec : « 11 h 10 ».

Avec des yeux de fauve, Duval se tourna vers lui et pointa un index menaçant.

— Si j'ai des questions à vous poser, je vous ferai signe.

L'homme marmonna quelques mots et ouvrit son journal.

Duval nota l'information dans son calepin : 23 h 10. Il calcula mentalement qu'il fallait une vingtaine de minutes pour rallier Lac-Beauport à partir de L'Ancienne-Lorette. Les chauffeurs de taxi ont le pied pesant et connaissent les raccourcis.

— Pouvez-vous me dire où vous avez déposé votre client à Cap-Rouge ?

Soit que les murs aient des oreilles, soit que le répartiteur ait fait part aux collègues de la torture mentale qu'infligeait Duval à leur confrère, car dans l'encadrement qui séparait les deux pièces, quatre hommes dévisageaient Duval, les bras croisés. Émond lança sans hésiter :

— Rue Bertrand.

— Un homme ou une femme ?

— Une femme.

— Où avez-vous déposé votre client de l'aéroport ?

— Au Château Frontenac.

— Vers quelle heure ?

— 11 h 50.

— Vous avez mis tout ce temps !

— Vous savez, on fait parfois des détours avec les touristes pour rendre la course plus payante. Tout le monde fait ça.

Duval connaissait cette pratique et elle indiquait que Jean-Pierre Émond était quelque peu malhonnête. Il détestait ce genre de justification : « Tout le monde le fait, alors moi aussi ». Combien de fois, quand il était patrouilleur, avait-il entendu : tout le monde roule à cent vingt kilomètres à l'heure, ici. Pour Duval, cette attitude était un symptôme du cancer civique qui rongeait la société.

— Qu'est-ce qui vous dit que c'était un étranger ?

— Il venait pour un meeting.

— Quel genre de meeting ?

Émond haussa le ton.

— Je ne lui ai pas demandé. Il parlait pas français. C'était un étranger.

— À quelle heure avez-vous pris le client suivant ?

Un cri retentit alors dans la pièce.

— Arrêtez de le harceler, hurlait un grand blond au teint rougeaud et à la peau luisante de sébum.

Duval le dévisagea et martela chaque syllabe.

— Un mot de plus et je vous fais arrêter pour entrave au travail d'un policier.

L'homme se calma et ses confrères l'entraînèrent à l'extérieur.

Duval poussa un long soupir et se tourna vers le chauffeur.

— À quelle heure avez-vous pris le client suivant ?

— À minuit et dix.

Cette précision dans l'horaire laissa Duval perplexe. Habituellement, les suspects étaient évasifs et celui-ci semblait avoir appris ses allées et venues par cœur.

Duval referma son calepin et demanda au répartiteur s'il pouvait faire un appel en privé. L'autre se hâta de lui montrer la cabine téléphonique à l'extérieur. Cet excès de courtoisie redoubla l'ardeur du lieutenant à régler l'affaire. Il n'avait pas envie de manquer sa partie de chasse pour une enquête qui l'obséderait.

Duval sortit, monta la fermeture éclair de son coupe-vent. Ses doigts raidis par le froid feuilletaient le bottin. Mais les pages qui l'intéressaient avaient été arrachées. Il composa le 0 et la téléphoniste le transféra à l'aéroport. Il tomba sur un préposé affable.

— Un avion d'Air Canada en provenance de Toronto vers 19 h, l'autre de Montréal a atterri à 20 h.

Mais pourquoi le client avait-il mis tout ce temps avant de prendre un taxi ? Duval raccrocha, songeur. D'un pas déterminé, il retourna dans la coop, prêt à coincer Émond qui s'enfonçait dans le mensonge.

Il s'approcha du suspect, qui discutait avec des collègues aux regards compatissants.

— J'ai une dernière question à vous poser.

Duval l'entraîna dans un coin.

— Comment expliquez-vous que le dernier avion en provenance de Toronto a atterri à 19 h et que l'homme est monté après 23 h dans votre voiture ?

— Je vous ai pas dit qu'il venait de Toronto, et je vous ferais remarquer que les voyageurs vont souvent manger au restaurant après un vol. Et puis, il y avait aussi un avion en provenance de Montréal à 18 h, et il y a des Anglais à Montréal.

— Habituellement, ils mangent dans l'avion, répliqua Duval.

— Pas sur des vols aussi courts.

Duval attacha son manteau et invita Émond à passer à la centrale, avant 8 h, pour sa déposition. Avant de le laisser à son deuil, il lui demanda son adresse. Décidément, il n'aimait pas la bouille de cet homme, mais jamais dans le passé il n'avait fait fi de la présomption d'innocence.

Il lui fallait attendre les résultats de l'autopsie pratiquée par Maher et ceux de la chromatographie de Rivard. Ensuite, il faudrait prouver que ce combustible avait bel et bien été versé par Émond.

5

Duval rentra se coucher. Sa résidence, à deux kilomètres de là, surplombait la falaise au-dessus de la Basse-Ville : un cottage aux impostes composées de magnifiques vitraux ambre et blancs représentant des motifs floraux. Il entra sans faire de bruit, mais buta contre un barrage de chaussures de sport. Duval, en marathonien accompli, effectuait ses quatre-vingts kilomètres de jogging hebdomadaire pour goûter à la plénitude d'un corps sain.

L'odeur familière, la chaleur des lieux l'apaisa.

La fringale le prit, mais il s'interdit le sandwich tant désiré, sachant qu'il mettrait son sommeil en péril. Il consulta l'horloge : 3 h 28. Il actionna doucement le robinet et remplit un verre d'eau qu'il but d'un trait. Il ouvrit la dépense et fouilla dans la boîte de biscuits Ritz. Accoudé contre le comptoir, il avala ses craquelins en réfléchissant à la mort d'Eugénie Fournier.

Son regard se posa sur le vitrail de la cuisine que la lanterne murale extérieure avivait. Ces ambres, ces blancs et ces verts le calmaient. Sur le tableau noir de la cuisine, Mimi avait adressé un énième message à son paternel sur la cruauté de chasser les animaux :

> « Si une espèce venait une fois par année
> chasser l'humain et que tu perdais un ami,
> qu'en penserais-tu ? Je suis convaincue que
> les animaux ont une âme. Je suis l'élan que
> tu chasseras… »

Mimi ne cessait depuis une semaine de lui faire des remontrances sur la chasse. Il avait beau lui répéter que la chasse à l'arc était noble, elle se fâchait. Inutile de lui servir l'argument de l'alimentation puisque Mimi était végétarienne. Les charges morales avaient commencé à l'ébranler et Laurence, sa copine, participait aussi à la « démonisation » de la chasse.

Il effaça le tableau et inscrivit :

> « Tes flèches me font mal…
> Je t'aime. Papa. »

Il éteignit la lumière et monta à l'étage en se rappelant tout ce qu'il lui restait à faire en prévision de la chasse. Il avait hâte de s'enfoncer avec les copains au fond de la forêt boréale, loin de la criminalité et des tribunaux.

Le drap était glacial. Il ramena la couette sur lui et éteignit la lampe de chevet. Au bout de dix minutes, sa conscience plongea dans un gouffre noir.

6

Quand Duval se pointa devant la centrale du boulevard Saint-Cyrille, il aperçut à cinq mètres de l'entrée Madden qui posait pour les journalistes avec Sneak, la vedette de l'escouade canine. Sneak allait bientôt être intronisé au Temple de la renommée des animaux de Toronto. Il était certes le membre le plus décoré de la centrale et le moins bien payé. La veille, le lieutenant-gouverneur en avait profité pour dresser le panégyrique du berger allemand, notamment le nombre de kilos de drogue qu'il avait flairés et tous les truands qu'il avait envoyés en taule, sans compter les cas d'agression où son nez avait conduit à des condamnations. En page trois, tout de suite après l'incendie de Lac-Beauport, les journaux montraient Sneak, fier, la bouche ouverte, médaille au cou. Tous les collègues savaient que le berger allemand faisait de l'ombre à son maître. On n'en avait que pour Sneak. Si bien que Madden se contentait de palabrer sur son toutou, comme toujours, comme si lui n'existait pas. Ses collègues adoraient l'entendre causer à son chien. On ne pouvait imaginer Madden sans son compagnon.

Son père était un Québécois d'origine irlandaise et sa mère une Juive américaine rencontrée lors d'un salon canin à New York. Tous deux étaient éleveurs de chiens. Chez les Madden, on avait la passion des chiens de père en fils. L'arrière-grand-père avait fait beaucoup d'argent dans les courses de lévriers à Dublin. Le grand-père de Samuel avait été vétérinaire à Québec.

Lorsque Sneak aperçut le lieutenant, il se lança vers lui à grandes foulées pataudes pour sa ration de câlins. Duval, Sneak et Madden faisaient souvent équipe. Duval se pencha et reçut une grosse léchée matinale peu ragoûtante. Un photographe s'approcha pour croquer la scène. Madden ramena à l'ordre son cerbère.

— Sneak ! Ici !

Le chien se dressa et obtempéra tout de go.

Samuel salua Daniel et lui confia :

— Je ne serais pas surpris qu'on lui mette un jour un micro devant la gueule.

Cette boutade plut à Duval.

— Puis, l'incendie de Lac-Beauport ? reprit le maître-chien.

— On ne devrait pas jouer avec le feu. On se brûle !

Madden venait d'avoir trente-deux ans. Tout était sombre chez lui, si bien qu'il ressemblait plus à l'idée qu'on se fait d'un Espagnol qu'à un Québécois aux racines franco-judéo-irlandaises. Alors que son père était surnommé Ginger à cause de la couleur de ses cheveux, Samuel avait hérité de la chevelure noir corbeau de sa mère, ses yeux étaient une paire de billes charbonneuses et ses sourcils en accent circonflexe aggravaient ce faciès étonnant tout en longueur, aux lèvres charnues.

Son pessimisme, pour ne pas dire son fatalisme, était légendaire : il avait la poisse. « Les bons finissent trop souvent derniers et les crapules s'en tirent trop bien », disait Madden. Maxime assez paradoxale pour un policier.

L'appel nocturne l'avait épuisé et il affichait les marques d'une nuit troublée par le boulot. Une autre. Samuel travaillait énormément, car il était l'un des rares maîtres-chiens de la région. Dans les cas de disparition d'enfants, on faisait toujours appel à lui ; c'était certainement la tâche qu'il trouvait la plus difficile. Ces interminables battues finissaient trop souvent mal, avec des parents brisés, inconsolables.

Madden salua nonchalamment les photographes et se tourna vers Duval.

— Daniel, je peux toujours te voir pour mon grade ?

— Mon horaire est serré, mais passe à mon bureau vers 13 h.

— En passant, j'ai ça à t'offrir.

Il sortit une enveloppe qu'il remit à son ami. Duval l'ouvrit et y découvrit des billets de spectacle.

— Frankie m'a dit que tu aimais le jazz et j'ai su que Dave Brubeck venait jouer au Grand Théâtre avec ses fils.

— C'était pas nécessaire !

— Non, mais c'est juste pour te remercier du temps que t'as pris depuis deux semaines.

Madden préparait pour la seconde fois son examen en vue de l'obtention du grade de caporal. Il avait échoué la première fois, ce qui lui avait grandement miné le moral. Depuis deux semaines, Duval le « coachait » en lui prodiguant des conseils. Il appréciait ce garçon qui, malgré la trentaine, avait conservé une mine de gamin.

L'épreuve aurait lieu le mardi matin et, mauvaise nouvelle, Pouliot et Malo seraient les examinateurs, ce qui constituait un obstacle majeur. La mauvaise foi de Pouliot, l'adjoint du chef, était bien connue et Duval avait eu sa part d'ennuis avec celui qu'on appelait « le boffeur » ou, pire encore, « le crosseur ».

Avant d'entrer dans son bureau, Duval fut intercepté par l'aumônier, Émile Dion. Le bon père mesurait cinq pieds et on l'avait baptisé Spike tellement il était droit et trapu. Il portait de grosses lunettes noires et souriait tout le temps. Tous les policiers l'adoraient et il servait de confident à nombre d'entre eux.

— Puis, mon Daniel, je compte sur toi pour la messe des policiers ? Loulou serait pas content que son vieux chum l'oublie.

— Loulou peut compter sur moi.

— Tu vas me préparer un discours ?

Duval hésita, haussa les épaules.

— Vous savez, je ne suis pas porté sur les discours. Un discours sur quoi ?

— Sur le pardon. T'es capable, mon p'tit gars, dit Spike en regardant en contre-plongée.

Duval, qui était croyant mais non pratiquant, se gratta le front.

— Le pardon ?

Il trouvait le sujet ambitieux mais pertinent dans l'optique de son métier. Fallait maintenant qu'il trouve quelque chose d'intelligent à dire.

— C'est d'accord ?

Duval hocha la tête, incapable comme toujours de dire non à l'aumônier.

— Pas plus de cinq minutes.

— Merci, Danny. Sois prudent à la chasse. Je prie saint Hubert.

— Pourquoi ?

— C'est le saint patron des chasseurs.

— Ah !

Il se dirigea vers le bureau de Dallaire pour faire le point sur l'enquête de la nuit. Dans le cas d'Émond, il souhaitait que saint Michel, le patron des policiers, lui permette de ne pas manquer sa partie de chasse.

Le capitaine Dallaire, grand manitou de la Section des crimes contre la personne, était le chef idéal. Il ne gueulait jamais, n'abusait pas de son pouvoir et avait l'estime de son escouade. Sa recette s'avérait fort simple : le respect envers ses employés, la discrétion

absolue, l'art de prendre les bonnes décisions et de sti-
muler ses troupes au moment opportun. La fête qu'il
avait organisée pour Louis avait été grandement ap-
préciée et témoignait de son dévouement envers son
escouade. Tout le contraire de Pouliot, qui avait fait
baver tout le monde, en 1976, quand la SQ avait prêté
Dallaire à la Ville de Montréal pour les Olympiques.
« Pouvait-on pardonner à des idiots pareils ? » se demanda Duval.

Le capitaine avait les cheveux d'un blanc immaculé,
coupés très ras sur un crâne d'une belle rondeur. Son
visage gardait à l'année un léger hâle. Ses yeux bleus
baignaient dans une vaporeuse tendresse avec ses
amis et devenaient acier tranchant devant la bêtise et
les criminels. Son nez légèrement aquilin donnait un
aspect sculptural à son profil.

Il était si calme qu'on se demandait quel sang
coulait dans ses veines. Dès son arrivée, il s'était avéré
une inspiration pour le lieutenant, qui se remettait alors
d'une dépression. Son éloquence faisait de lui un porte-
parole exemplaire auprès des médias. Par contre, il
aimait se sucrer le bec alors qu'il souffrait de diabète et
il devait s'injecter des doses d'insuline pour compenser
ses excès caloriques. Une bonbonnière remplie de petits
poissons rouges et blancs à la menthe se vidait et s'em-
plissait régulièrement.

Les photos de sa femme, de ses enfants et de ses
petits-enfants trônaient à côté de celles des criminels
les plus recherchés du pays. Enfoncé dans son fauteuil
pivotant, il écouta les conjectures de Duval au sujet
de l'incendie de la nuit.

— Rivard va analyser ce qui reste des draps et du
matelas. J'ai aussi envoyé au labo des draps de la
dame.

— Est-ce qu'on a des doutes suffisants pour aller
aussi loin ?

Duval expira.

— Émond a déjà été arrêté pour avoir falsifié ses rapports d'impôt.

Duval prit le journal sur le bureau et regarda la photo de Sneak à la une. C'est à peine si l'on distinguait Madden.

— Pourrais-tu demander qu'on fasse un article sur Madden dans la revue *Sûreté* et que, pour une fois, ce soit lui qu'on voie sur la photo ?

— Pourquoi ?

— Je crois que Madden le mérite bien et tout le monde sait qu'il traverse une période difficile.

— Il n'a pas l'air dans son assiette.

— Il faudrait un deuxième maître-chien. Il est débordé et angoisse pour son grade.

Dallaire inscrivit la requête à son agenda.

— En passant, reprit Duval, depuis quand Pouliot est autorisé à faire partie d'un comité d'examen ?

— Je dois m'absenter à cette heure-là et j'ai le droit de le déléguer.

Duval hocha la tête, sceptique, prêt à croire à la poisse légendaire de son copain Madden.

Le capitaine pivota sur sa chaise et agita son index devant son lieutenant.

— Daniel, est-ce que tu veux te joindre à notre chorale pour la messe à Loulou ?

— Moi ? Chanter ? Je veux bien parler, mais pas chanter. L'aumônier m'a demandé de faire un discours.

— Au train où vont les choses, Loulou va nous transformer en une bande de mormons… On va être la risée des autres corps policiers quand on va reprendre notre saison de hockey.

Duval se leva, l'avisa qu'il procédait immédiatement dans le cas Fournier. Dallaire, qui trouvait l'affaire puante, allait s'occuper des mandats de perquisition.

Daniel se dirigea d'un pas vif vers son bureau. Le café matinal répandait ses effluves à travers les cagibis. Le soleil bombardait de lumière chromes et verres, qu'il fragmentait et reflétait sur les murs. Du haut d'une tablette, les bégonias coulaient en une cascade de verdure.

Vers 11 h, Duval reçut un appel de Villemure, le médecin-chef du labo.

— Prêt pour la chasse ?

— Laquelle ? La chasse à l'homme ou à l'orignal ?

Le docteur Villemure s'esclaffa. Duval poursuivit :

— François, si je veux être aussi en forme que vous autres en fin de semaine, il me faut des nouvelles du cas Fournier le plus tôt possible. Sinon, je ne suis pas rendu à l'auberge.

— Maher me fait signe qu'il ne peut pas avant 16 h. Passe vers 14 h 30. Je m'en occupe.

Alors que Duval allait sortir, il reçut un message de Claudette, la blonde de Loulou, qu'il devait prendre devant l'entrée du centre d'emploi à Place Laurier. Duval se demanda comment il allait faire pour tout régler à temps. La course contre la montre était lancée. Au pire, il demanderait à François Villemure de jouer les taxis pour Claudette et Laurence.

Il traversa la pièce de bout en bout jusqu'au bureau de Bernard Prince pour lui expliquer son plan de match.

Bernard, assis derrière son bureau, lisait des renseignements au sujet d'une fugueuse. Barbe de trois jours, cheveux en brosse, visage anguleux, Prince avait pris le relais de Louis dans l'équipe de Duval. Sa discrétion et son savoir-vivre en faisaient un collègue idéal pour Duval. Bien sûr, l'humour, le cabotinage et les crises de rage de Louis lui manquaient, mais il valait mieux être avec Prince le taciturne qu'avec un imbécile comme Malo ou un panier percé comme Méthot. Les langues sales l'horripilaient comme une mouche dans un verre de bière.

Prince se remettait tant bien que mal de la maladie mentale de sa fille, diagnostiquée schizophrène. Les médecins lui avaient dit qu'il n'y avait rien à espérer, qu'il fallait la calmer avec des médicaments. Prince était persuadé que la consommation de drogue était à la base du drame de sa fille. Aujourd'hui, elle se prenait pour un ange et croyait qu'elle pouvait voler, ce qui avait obligé Prince à vendre sa maison à deux étages pour se reloger dans un bungalow. Toute la peine qu'il parvenait mal à dissimuler avait pour origine cette maladie.

— Salut, Daniel. Tu dois avoir hâte de partir ?

— La question est de savoir si on va me laisser partir.

— Le capitaine m'a appris pour l'incendie du chalet.

— Je voudrais que tu vérifies les alibis d'Émond, celui du passager mystérieux de l'aéroport et celui de la rue Bertrand. Demande au répartiteur de la coop de te donner les adresses.

◆

À 13 h, on frappa sur la fenêtre de la porte dont le store était baissé. Duval écarta les lames d'une main et entrevit Madden. Celui-ci entra avec nonchalance et s'assit. Souffrant d'une migraine, il se frotta les tempes. Duval sentit aussitôt l'angoisse qui le tenaillait. Le jeune policier ne dormait plus depuis deux nuits. Cet examen le torturait mentalement. Sa mine sombre et ses yeux cernés montraient son anxiété. Il posa des questions sur des points techniques et juridiques à Duval et conclut en disant :

— Ils vont encore me recaler.

Duval détestait cette attitude de Madden. Tête basse, ce dernier reprenait son laïus sur le mauvais sort qui s'acharnait contre lui. Quand il choisissait une file dans une épicerie, il prenait toujours la plus lente. Le même phénomène se produisait dans le trafic. Il avait raté 200 000 $ à l'Inter Loto par un seul chiffre. Le lamento continuait ainsi par des « Si j'avais, je… ». Duval le coupa sec et se leva pour en imposer davantage.

— Comme tu le sais, j'ai perdu ma femme dans un accident de voiture alors qu'elle répondait à un appel d'urgence. Trente autres policiers étaient de service ce matin-là et l'appel est tombé sur elle. Alors ne me fais pas pleurer avec la fatalité, ce discours, je n'y crois pas. La fatalité, c'est une excuse pour justifier un échec.

— T'as raison, excuse-moi.

Décidément, la dépression couvait dans cette sombre caboche. Duval laissa tomber un bouquin devant lui.

— Révise le gros livre bleu et ça ira.

— Et Pouliot ? Il me déteste !

Duval eut envie de lancer qu'il touchait là la vérité.

— Pouliot ne sera pas le seul examinateur. Et pourquoi il te recalerait ?

Vers 13 h 30, Madden partit chercher son chien pour une saisie de drogue à Stoneham.

7

Duval se dirigea vers le Laboratoire de sciences judiciaires et de médecine légale de la rue Semple. Il hésita entre le chemin Sainte-Foy et le boulevard Charest, et opta pour la première solution ; quelques

minutes plus tard il pensa à Madden, car ce choix
s'avéra lamentable : des employés de la voirie réparaient
une conduite. Il prit son mal en patience en écoutant
Dixie d'Harmonium qui passait à la radio. Après dix
minutes, il descendit la côte Saint-Sacrement, puis
croisa le boulevard Charest et tourna à gauche dans
la rue Semple. Le bâtiment à l'architecture moderne
voisinait des entreprises d'alimentation et de transport.
Une morgue dans un parc industriel avait de quoi faire
sourire, mais pour les spécialistes de la police scientifique et les médecins légistes, la compétence et la
haute technologie étaient ce qu'ils avaient à offrir à la
société. Curiosité, ingéniosité et instinct s'avéraient des
qualités essentielles pour ces experts judiciaires qui
donnaient une identité à la mort, faisant parler l'invisible.

Duval entra en saluant d'anciens collègues de la
centrale. Il marcha jusqu'à la première salle d'autopsie
où trois corps attendaient de livrer leurs réponses aux
regards des médecins légistes. Le pathologiste judiciaire Fabien Maher s'y trouvait en compagnie de
François Villemure. Le jeune docteur Maher, disciple de
Villemure, suggéra à Duval de se munir d'un masque,
ce qui arrivait rarement. Duval préféra étaler un peu
de Vicks sous ses narines.

Le corps boursouflé d'un noyé, retiré de l'eau après
trois mois, gisait sur la table en inox. Sous la lumière, le
corps graisseux et bleu en état d'adipocire ressemblait
à un croisement de loup-marin et d'homo sapiens.

— Un motard…

— Les cimenteries font de bonnes affaires… lança
Duval, ce qui déclencha un éclat de rire.

Duval se demandait bien comment les pathologistes
faisaient pour tenir dans ces conditions. Le docteur
Maher lui avait un jour confié que l'horreur avait l'imagination constante dans son métier. C'était toujours

aussi brutal. Contrairement à Villemure, et aux idées reçues, il ne s'y habituait pas. Au dire de ses collègues, le métier ne payait pas assez pour les onze années d'étude et de spécialisation : médecine générale, pathologie et médecine légale. Et toutes ces heures perdues, une sur cinq, dans l'antichambre des tribunaux, pendant que le boulot s'accumulait, les rendaient fous. Les effectifs étaient toujours insuffisants et la relève se comptait sur la main d'un amputé. Qui voulait pratiquer dans des conditions pareilles alors que la pathologie hospitalière s'avérait plus payante, plus valorisée et, surtout, moins pénible ? Le soir après une dure journée de travail, la femme de François lui intimait d'aller immédiatement se doucher, car il sentait le cadavre. Mais éclairer la justice représentait un idéal que peu de métiers pouvaient offrir. La pathologie ne ramenait jamais les victimes à la vie, mais elle fournissait les preuves qui inculpaient leurs assassins et les empêchaient de récidiver. Une satisfaction indescriptible pour François Villemure.

Villemure retira ses gants de latex, se lava les mains et fit signe à Duval de le suivre dans la salle de radio qui séparait les deux salles d'autopsie.

Il retira son masque, replaça une mèche blanche de son toupet. Il portait des verres à demi-foyer retenus par une chaînette en or.

— Il n'y a pas de fumée sans feu.

Villemure sortit une radiographie d'une enveloppe et l'agrafa au négatoscope lumineux au-dessus de lui.

— Le petit os en forme de fer à cheval, l'os hyoïde, qui jouxte la mandibule, était cassé, ce qui arrive souvent dans une strangulation. À moins de trouver un avocat qui dira que la victime s'est étranglée elle-même. On finit par tout entendre…

Villemure sortit ensuite des photos qu'il avait prises de la trachée.

— On n'a noté aucune trace de suie dans les voies respiratoires, ce qui signifie qu'elle était morte avant que le feu soit allumé. Elle ne pouvait pas inhaler de suie.

— Ce qui confirme aussi la thèse du meurtre qu'on a essayé de camoufler en incendie.

— Comme je ne crois pas à la combustion spontanée – Villemure sourit d'un air moqueur –, ça veut dire que la dernière personne qui se trouvait avec elle est son meurtrier. C'est aussi simple que ça : meurtre prémédité.

Le regard satisfait, Villemure remit les documents dans l'enveloppe. Ce moment était celui qu'il préférait dans son travail. Sans même avoir assisté au meurtre, il avait établi la preuve hors de tout doute qu'il y avait eu homicide. Une conviction telle qu'elle permet de dormir sur ses deux oreilles la nuit avant de se présenter en cour. Maintenant, c'était à Duval de débusquer le meurtrier et tous les soupçons pesaient sur Jean-Pierre Émond.

La tête d'une secrétaire apparut dans la porte entrebâillée.

— Un policier de Sainte-Foy veut vous voir, docteur Villemure. Ils ont ramassé un chien mort.

Villemure afficha une gueule sûre.

— Écoutez, dites-leur que les cadavres d'animaux ne sont pas de mon ressort mais de celui de la SPCA, lança le médecin d'un ton cinglant.

Il remit les documents à Duval et le salua.

En passant devant le labo, Duval s'arrêta devant le bureau de la biologiste. Le sarrau lui allait si bien ! Bel ange blanc aux cheveux de blé, Mireille était penchée sur la lunette de son microscope où elle examinait des fibres synthétiques. Ses cheveux étaient ramenés vers l'arrière et retenus par une barrette sertie de lapis-lazuli. Ses petites lunettes rondes en écaille lui donnaient

l'allure d'une intellectuelle. Sa peau était satinée et cou-
verte d'un fin duvet blond. Duval se plaisait à penser
qu'elle avait une ossature de moineau et des seins
comme des pommettes. Elle sentit la présence du lieutenant et redressa la tête. Avant de rencontrer Laurence,
Duval avait été happé par les charmes de la jeune
femme. Mais il s'était toujours refusé à lui faire des
avances. Son regard bleu le glaçait littéralement, au
point qu'il en perdait ses moyens.

— Bonjour, lieutenant. Beau travail !

— Mauvais boulot du meurtrier qui nous rend la
vie facile.

— Vous êtes trop modeste !

Elle l'avait toujours vouvoyé et il avait constamment
résisté à l'idée de la reprendre. Cette marque de respect
avait fini par lui plaire. Il jeta un coup d'œil dans le
microscope : du sang.

— Ça va ?

— On ne chôme pas. Il y a des malades partout pour
nous faire gagner notre croûte. On vient de recevoir
un échantillon de sang qui a servi à écrire un graffiti
misogyne sur un mur à l'Université Laval. On craignait
que ce soit du sang humain – il y en avait une telle
quantité qu'on redoutait le pire. Finalement, je viens
d'effectuer le test d'Uhlenhuth et ouf, ou plutôt wouf…
il s'agit de sang animal. Mais le message est effrayant :
« Au bout de ton sang, femelle ».

Connaissant les convictions féministes de Mireille,
Duval se doutait bien de la hargne qui l'animait.

— La police de Sainte-Foy s'occupe de l'affaire,
ajouta-t-elle.

— Aussi rassurant que de confier l'enquête à Mutt
et Jeff…

Elle s'esclaffa dans une petite cascade de rires cris-
tallins et hocha la tête.

— Vous êtes trop sévère, lieutenant.

Duval connaissait les problèmes de discipline et de corruption qui sévissaient dans le corps policier de la Ville de Sainte-Foy.

— Qu'est-ce que t'as à raconter dans le dossier Fournier ?

— Je viens de finir.

D'une poussée, elle se propulsa sur sa chaise jusqu'au bout de la table où était rangé le dossier et se donna un élan pour revenir au point initial.

— On a examiné le drap sale et on n'a découvert aucune fibre de tabac. Il semble donc qu'elle ne fumait pas au lit. On a prélevé assez de salive sur le mégot à bout uni pour établir un profil sanguin de type B.

— Émond fume des Export'A, l'avisa Duval. Je ne veux pas être sexiste, mais c'est une cigarette d'homme. Il faudra vérifier le profil sanguin d'Émond.

De l'autre côté du corridor, à travers la vitre de la section Chimie, Daniel aperçut Rivard qui lui faisait des signes à la manière d'un sémaphore.

Mireille lui remit le dossier.

— Tenez, lieutenant.

Duval demeura rivé un instant à ce regard.

— Je vais aller chercher ma dernière preuve. C'est comme avoir une flush royale en cour.

— Bonne fin de journée, lieutenant. Si je peux faire autre chose, n'hésitez surtout pas.

Ces paroles et ce regard suspendu n'avaient rien d'innocent. Autant de sensualité dans un lieu aussi sinistre ! Qu'est-ce que ce serait dans l'intimité d'une chambre ? « Il faudrait lui présenter Frankie, notre célibataire endurci », pensa Duval.

Duval passa de l'autre côté du corridor où se trouvait le labo de chimie.

— Salut !

Dans un seau s'entassaient des morceaux de tissu et du rembourrage de matelas. Rivard sortit le graphique tracé par le stylet du chromatographe et dont les crêtes indiquaient le type de combustible.

— L'appareil m'indique que de l'essence à briquet, du butane, a été utilisée comme accélérant, triompha Rivard.

— Il ne reste plus qu'à aller cueillir l'incendiaire.

8

En entrant dans le vestibule de la centrale, Duval hésita entre le bel escalier de marbre et l'ascenseur. La nuit courte lui fit opter pour la solution paresseuse.

Sur son bureau, il trouva une note de Bernard Prince :

Me suis rendu au Château Frontenac. Aucun anglophone ne s'est inscrit à l'heure mentionnée. Pensé que le gars avait peut-être décidé d'aller au bar avant de s'inscrire. Non. Un couple d'Anglos s'est enregistré vers minuit trente : des Américains.

Ensuite me suis rendu à l'adresse de la rue Bertrand et la personne a bien pris un taxi, mais il était conduit par une femme rousse. Quelqu'un ment. Émond n'est pas venu déposer.

Bernard

Duval téléphona d'abord au domicile de Jean-Pierre Émond. Pas de réponse. À la coop de taxis, le répartiteur annonça qu'Émond « était sur un *call* ». Duval resta stupéfait. Comment le gars pouvait-il travailler le lendemain de la mort de sa conjointe, à moins d'être coupable ? Duval eut alors l'idée de se faire passer pour un client et de demander la voiture d'Émond devant le Grand Théâtre. L'homme se livrerait de lui-même et le lieutenant gagnerait un temps précieux. Mais les risques étaient élevés si Émond flairait l'astuce. La fatigue qui lui sciait le corps lui enlevait toute envie de conduire à la noirceur sur les routes sinueuses de Charlevoix. Le téléphone sonna. Dallaire lui annonçait que les mandats étaient prêts et qu'il pouvait perquisitionner chez Émond. Mais il se rendit d'abord, avec deux patrouilleurs et un membre de l'Identité, à la coop de la rue Crémazie.

Tout prouvait qu'Eugénie Fournier avait été tuée, mais encore fallait-il démontrer qu'Émond se trouvait bien sur les lieux du crime.

◆

Le répartiteur faisait une patience en écoutant le plus idiot des animateurs de tribune téléphonique cracher sa haine contre ses auditeurs. Duval frappa sur le comptoir pour arracher l'homme à son jeu de cartes. Il lui ordonna d'appeler Émond pour qu'il se présente tout de suite à la coop. Il ne lui en précisa pas la raison.

Il regarda l'heure. Aurait-il le temps d'interroger Émond avant d'aller chercher la copine de Louis ? Émond arriva quinze minutes plus tard. Duval confisqua ses clés. Il lui montra les mandats de perquisition et d'arrestation.

Émond, les yeux pochés, semblait ne pas avoir dormi.

— Vous êtes malades. Ma blonde vient de mourir et…

— Écoutez, vous m'avez menti, hier, avec vos mystérieux passagers.

Les policiers procédèrent à l'arrestation d'Émond en lui lisant les droits que lui conférait la justice. Un agent lui passa les menottes et le suspect ne protesta pas.

◆

Émond habitait dans un immeuble de la rue Canardière à Limoilou : un gros sarcophage en brique brune aux fenêtres en aluminium. Duval frappa, mais n'obtint pas de réponse. Il saisit la poignée. Étrangement, la porte n'était pas verrouillée. En pénétrant dans l'appartement, Duval entendit le bruit de la douche.

— Il y a quelqu'un ?

Une voix apeurée, de toute évidence féminine, lui répondit.

— Qui est là ?

On ferma le robinet.

— Police !

Au bout du corridor, la tête d'une femme aux cheveux auburn apparut dans l'embrasure de la porte. Une large repousse noire rayait son cuir chevelu. Serviette enroulée autour du corps, la femme sortit, auréolée de vapeur. L'eau s'égouttait de ses longues couettes frisées.

— Minute. Je m'habille, dit-elle en s'avançant vers Duval à pas rapides dans le passage pour tourner dans la première chambre à droite.

Les gars de la police scientifique derrière Duval s'étaient tous postés pour la voir sortir mais n'avaient pas été comblés comme ils l'avaient espéré. C'était une petite boulotte aux cuisses criblées de cellulite et au dos zébré de vergetures.

Duval ordonna aux deux policiers à l'affût derrière ses épaules de fouiller l'appartement au lieu de jouer les voyeurs.

Les méninges du lieutenant n'eurent pas à s'activer très longtemps. Et si c'était elle qui avait conduit le taxi ?

Duval arpenta le corridor et le travelling avant s'avéra lamentable. L'endroit sentait le gras de cuisson imprégné jusque dans les murs. L'appartement, un cinq et demie, affichait un désordre complet. Au salon, deux des trois coussins du canapé reposaient sur le plancher. Des sacs de croustilles vides, des bretzels et trois grosses bouteilles de bière attendaient d'être ramassés sur une table en similibois. Le *TV Hebdo* gisait en deux parties, une sur la chaîne stéréo et l'autre par terre. Un cadre était retourné à l'envers sur l'élément mural. Duval le releva. Étrange ironie ! Une photo d'Eugénie Fournier en compagnie d'Émond en des jours plus heureux.

Des piles de vaisselle s'entassaient sur le comptoir et les cendriers débordaient de mégots. La table n'avait pas été débarrassée et des chaudrons traînaient au centre.

Aucun rideau aux fenêtres, sauf dans la chambre. Émond n'avait pas les moyens financiers d'Eugénie Fournier.

Duval s'inquiéta du temps que la femme mettait à sortir de la chambre. Elle réapparut cinq minutes plus tard toute maquillée. C'était le genre de fille incapable de faire un pas le matin sans ses poudres, ses fards et son mascara. Elle portait un jean trop collant et un chandail à col roulé en mohair. Ses talons hauts blancs claquaient sur le plancher de merisier tout marqué.

— Vous êtes l'amie de Jean-Pierre Émond ?

— Je suis une amie. Je suis venue consoler Jean-Pierre aussitôt que j'ai su ce qui lui est arrivé.

— Votre nom ?

— Cindy Rinfret.

Ses longs faux cils encrassés de rimmel battaient nerveusement. Duval y alla d'abord d'une question suggestive.

— Madame Rinfret, j'ai des raisons de croire que vous vous êtes rendue dans la rue Bertrand à Cap-Rouge, hier.

Elle hésita à répondre, parut complètement désemparée comme une élève soupçonnée d'avoir triché et qui le sait trop bien.

— Bin non, j'ai passé la nuit icitte.

Duval s'étira le cou pour examiner l'état du lit.

— Si je comprends bien, Jean-Pierre Émond vous a téléphoné pour vous dire de venir le rejoindre avant ou après le meurtre ?

— Djé-Pi m'a appelée vers 2 h en pleurant.

Il soupira d'impatience.

— Écoutez, madame Rinfret, je ne sais pas si vous comprenez, mais la complicité dans une affaire d'homicide risque de vous mener à la prison des femmes.

Elle sortit son paquet de Caméo. Ses doigts rougis, pris de tremblements, peinèrent à saisir le bout d'une cigarette.

— Je vous ai dit ce que je savais.

— Vous connaissiez madame Fournier ?

— Oui, on sortait parfois ensemble.

— Tous les trois ?

— Oui.

— Êtes-vous mariée ?

— Je suis divorcée.

— Depuis quand ?

— Six mois.

— Est-ce que monsieur Émond connaissait votre ex-mari ?

— Non.

— Donc, vous avez rencontré Émond après votre divorce ?

— C'est ça.

Duval la sentit sur le bord de craquer. Jamais dans sa carrière il n'avait reconstitué un casse-tête avec des pièces aussi grosses. Même un aveugle aurait pu le faire. C'était un jeu d'enfant avec ces adultes qui, heureusement, n'avaient pas le sens du crime parfait.

— Je vous annonce que votre ami est dans de beaux draps et que vous êtes en train de le rejoindre.

— Voyons, j'ai rien faite.

— Madame Rinfret, je sais que vous avez conduit le taxi d'Émond pendant qu'il assassinait Eugénie Fournier. J'ai des preuves directes. Des témoins.

Elle expira longuement de la fumée et parut réfléchir. Ses yeux fixaient le bout incandescent de sa cigarette comme s'il pouvait l'éclairer. Duval sut qu'elle cherchait un moyen de sauver sa peau.

Il sentit une présence derrière lui.

— Lieutenant, j'ai trouvé ce que vous cherchiez.

Un policier lui tendit le mobile : la photocopie d'une police d'assurance Allstate.

— C'était entre le sommier et le matelas.

Le sourire de Duval contrastait avec le désarroi de la fille, qui avait tout compris.

Sur le document, daté du 17 août de l'année courante, Eugénie Fournier avait désigné Jean-Pierre Émond comme son bénéficiaire : 200 000 $ advenant une mort accidentelle. Assez pour vendre son taxi.

— C'est normal, y sortaient ensemble, argua Rinfret.

La rouquine, dont les propos paraissaient aussi faux que la couleur de ses cheveux, essaya jusqu'à la fin de protéger Émond, mais en vain.

— Je vous arrête pour meurtre prémédité, incendie criminel et fraude.

— Heille, cé pas moé !

Elle eut beau monter sur ses ergots, Duval fit signe aux policiers de l'embarquer. Quant à lui, il regagna la centrale pour entendre la déposition d'Émond.

9

Les murs en contreplaqué de la salle de déposition n'avaient rien d'inspirant pour un suspect. Bernard installait la bobine pendant que Duval lisait au chauffeur de taxi ses droits. Daniel fit signe à Bernard qu'il était prêt et ce dernier appuya sur la touche d'enregistrement. Le lieutenant s'assit sur le coin du bureau en toisant Émond. Une longue pause s'ensuivit, puis la voix assurée de Duval brisa le silence.

— Monsieur Émond, je vais être direct avec vous. Votre conjointe a été assassinée.

— Non…

— Oui, et je vais être encore plus direct en vous accusant de ce meurtre.

Les poings d'Émond s'abattirent sur la table.

— Vous délirez.

— Monsieur Émond, je vous prie d'être poli avec le détective Duval et de vous tranquilliser, dit Prince.

— Montrez-moi vos mains, monsieur Émond.

Émond leva timidement ses mains en montrant ses paumes. C'est fou ce qu'on peut faire de mal avec deux mains.

— Des mains d'étrangleur, d'incendiaire et de fraudeur.

— Vous n'avez pas le droit, argua Émond en s'agitant.

— Vous dites être allé reconduire un client dans la rue Bertrand, hier.

— Oui.

— Eh bien, j'ai appris que c'est une femme qui conduisait : une rousse. À moins que vous n'ayez le don d'ubiquité ou du travestissement, je ne comprends pas.

— Je vais vous expliquer…

— Pas nécessaire, votre amie l'a fait, dit Duval en exerçant davantage de pression. Cindy Rinfret correspond exactement à la description de la personne qui conduisait le taxi. Et comment expliquez-vous que mon collègue Prince n'ait pu retrouver la trace de votre client supposémment amené au Château Frontenac ?

Émond ne disait plus un mot, figé de stupeur. Duval le savait traqué, pris dans une embuscade de preuves.

— Il y a autre chose qui me chicote, poursuivit le lieutenant. Vous avez vu pour la dernière fois Eugénie Fournier une trentaine d'heures avant son décès. Cette femme fumait près de trois paquets par jour. Alors pourquoi a-t-on retrouvé vos cigarettes dans deux cendriers qui auraient dû être vidés ?

— Elle les éteignait parfois dans le bol des toilettes.

— C'est pas sérieux, ça, monsieur Émond, lança Duval. Le labo a démontré que vous étiez présent bien après ces trente heures. En fait, vous avez rendu visite à madame Fournier le soir même de sa mort. Votre salive a été prélevée sur des mégots fraîchement fumés.

— Ça se peut pas ! Vous me contez n'importe quoi !

— Et ce document ?

Duval sortit le contrat d'assurance.

— J'ai fait un peu de ménage dans vos affaires.

Prince s'inquiéta en voyant Duval étaler toute la preuve, mais elle était si blindée qu'Émond pouvait déjà déchirer son permis de conduire et envisager une longue retraite au pénitencier.

Émond mit ses grosses mains sur son visage. Il pencha la tête et pleura comme un gamin pris en fla-grant délit. Les larmes qu'il aurait bien voulu extraire la veille coulaient à flots. Après une ultime saccade de sanglots, il se mit à table.

— Oui, je l'ai tuée.

Vers 16 h 38, Émond avait tout avoué et fut incar-céré en attente de sa comparution du mardi.

Devant l'ascenseur, Prince salua Duval et lui sou-haita une bonne fin de semaine.

— T'es sûr que tu ne veux pas venir, Bernard ?

— Non. J'aime pas le bois. Je préfère le football ! Mais tu diras à Loulou que j'irai à sa messe de la police ; pas question de retraite charismatique, par exemple.

Prince s'isolait de plus en plus, refusant les activités à l'extérieur avec les collègues. Il avait déserté le club de hockey, lui dont les mises en échec faisaient si mal aux autres équipes. Pas pour rien qu'on l'appelait le policier du club. La maladie de sa fille l'avait ravagé, il ne serait plus jamais le même. Il se sentait respon-sable du mal qui arrivait à son enfant. La culpabilité l'avait fait sombrer dans l'alcoolisme, sa vie de couple connaissait aussi des ratés. Au bureau, il avait récem-ment confié à Duval qu'il avait l'impression de lire sur tous les visages des collègues qu'il était le père d'une folle. Désormais, Dallaire refusait de lui confier des enquêtes impliquant des motards : l'été précédent, Prince avait pété les plombs… et le crâne d'un Outlaws, qui s'était retrouvé alité pour deux mois à l'hôpital Saint-François-d'Assise.

Duval serra la pince de son collègue.

10

Assis derrière son bureau, Daniel Duval tapa le point final à son dossier, le signa et l'adressa au substitut du procureur. La semaine était complète : un trafiquant de PCP écroué pour six ans, la fugue d'un mineur élucidée et des retrouvailles pleines de larmes, un cas de violence conjugale et une fille de plus dans un centre pour femmes battues, et pour finir une tentative d'extorsion avec meurtre prémédité suivi d'un incendie criminel.

Il recouvrit sa machine à écrire de sa housse noire. L'horloge marquait 17 h 07. Le concert de frappes des machines à écrire s'estompait peu à peu tout autour. Le concierge écoutait *Staying alive* à la radio, chanson au titre pertinent dans son métier. Duval se leva, se planta devant la fenêtre en frottant son visage fatigué et apprécia le coucher de soleil automnal.

Trois jours dans la nature avec ses amis lui feraient le plus grand bien. Francis, qui avait pris un congé d'une semaine pour profiter de la chasse, les attendait à son chalet près de Baie-Sainte-Catherine. Le chouenneux, comme on l'appelait, ne tenait plus en place l'automne venu.

En apercevant un musicien qui montait la rue Turnbull avec un étui à guitare, il songea à Mimi, qui s'était fait un copain, un étudiant du Conservatoire, et avait refusé l'invitation, trop prise par l'amour. Daniel, qui ne pouvait blairer ce chevelu de la classe de percussion, craignait qu'il ne couche à la maison. La vie n'était-elle qu'une suite de préoccupations ? Tout lui parut un jeu d'addition et de soustraction d'ennuis. De la fenêtre, il contempla les Laurentides qui rougeoyaient comme des oranges sanguines.

Le téléphone sonna : sans doute Laurence qui voulait lui rappeler d'acheter du vin et des provisions. Il prit une voix lascive qu'il n'utilisait jamais.

— Salut, mon chou… J'enquête et j'encaisse pour vous…

Une voix de stentor s'esclaffa à l'autre bout. C'était le capitaine Dallaire. Duval, qu'on n'associait à aucune fantaisie, était pris en flagrant délit.

— Tu me dragues ou quoi ?

Duval bredouilla que sa conjointe devait l'appeler à cette heure.

— Félicitations pour la belle prise ! Je ne pensais jamais que ça se réglerait aujourd'hui.

— Tout de suite en le voyant, j'ai su qu'on avait affaire à un crosseur.

— Je te souhaite une autre belle prise en fin de semaine. Salue les gars et encore une fois je te remercie pour la grosse journée. Je te donne congé lundi. Ah ! ah !

Le lundi s'avérait un jour férié. Duval pouvait aller rejoindre les amis. Un saut à la maison, un autre au centre commercial et il débarquerait au chalet de Francis vers 21 h.

En route vers la maison, il entendit à la radio un porte-parole de la SPCA qualifier « d'odieux et de cruel » le geste qu'on avait fait. Un chien éventré avait été retrouvé dans le boisé de l'Université Laval. Duval pensa tout de suite à ce graffiti sanguin qu'avait laissé un malade sur les murs d'un couloir souterrain de l'université.

LA CHASSE DE
L'ACTION DE GRÂCES

11

Il stationna sa Jeep derrière la Datsun 240 Z de Laurence. Devant la maison, la plate-bande offrait sa dernière vague de couleurs : beaucoup de mauve, comme si la nature annonçait son deuil automnal. Il adorait l'horticulture et connaissait le nom des fleurs de son jardin. Une fois la main dans la terre, il oubliait toutes ses préoccupations. Il constata que les cosmos, les asters, les mauves et les orpins résistaient bravement à la froidure nocturne. Seuls les tournesols et les rosiers chinois ajoutaient des touches de couleurs chaudes et semblaient défier les intempéries à venir.

Le vieil orme dont l'écorce s'était torsadée en un siècle se délestait de ses feuilles. Elles planaient, accompagnées par les samares qui virevoltaient et recouvraient le sentier de pierres plates. La cime des arbres chapeautait le toit en pignon qui servait de grenier. Son cottage, une maison étroite tout en hauteur et recouverte de bardeaux de cèdre, paraissait minuscule à côté du vénérable géant.

Il était attendu puisqu'on lui ouvrit toute grande la porte, un bras l'invitant à entrer, et surtout ce magnifique

sourire étalé, celui de Laurence, la compagne qui partageait sa vie. Il l'avait rencontrée l'année des Olympiques
dans un club d'entraînement de course à pied. Tous
deux pratiquaient la longue distance.

Elle s'accrocha à son cou et remarqua la fatigue qui
assombrissait le visage de son conjoint.

— Ça va ?

Il l'embrassa.

— Mimi m'a dit que tu as été réveillé, la nuit dernière.

— Puis il a échappé toute sa monnaie, lança du
salon la voix moqueuse de sa fille.

— Nuit courte. Grosse journée. Je viens de coffrer
quelqu'un pour meurtre, l'histoire du chalet incendié.

— Ils en ont parlé à la radio.

Duval frotta ses yeux brumeux de fatigue et bâilla.

— Je vais conduire, suggéra sa compagne.

— Non, ça va aller.

Duval tenait à conduire, sinon il lui faudrait causer
tout au long du voyage alors qu'il n'en avait pas le goût
après cette journée harassante.

En glissant un œil au salon, Duval constata qu'il
était là, avachi, le grand échalas chevelu aux petites
lunettes d'intello qui fréquentait Mimi. Le garçon le
regarda à peine. Il osait fumer dans sa maison et appuyer ses longues cannes sur la table en chêne. Mimi
courut vers son père tout enchantée, se mit sur le bout
de ses souliers Mao pour l'embrasser, mais elle tenait
surtout à le féliciter pour sa décision de ne pas chasser.

— Tu me fais plaisir !

Mimi afficha sa satisfaction quand le paternel ramassa son arc et son carquois pour les redescendre au
sous-sol. Longiligne adolescente à l'allure hippie, elle
avait de grands yeux aux iris bleu clair et de longs cheveux châtains qu'elle nattait en tresses indiennes. Rien
à voir avec la tenue de son père, qu'elle jugeait *clean cut*

au possible. Ce n'était pourtant pas une adolescente révoltée. Duval trouvait sa fille équilibrée et adorable. Une jeune fille enjouée au sourire craquant comme celui de sa mère.

Après toutes ces années à pester contre le costume des Ursulines, elle voulait des vêtements dans lesquels elle se sentait flotter. Elle portait souvent, presque toujours, des salopettes en jean et de vieilles chemises qu'elle piquait à son paternel, ne lui extorquant son accord qu'une fois le délit commis. Dans son cou, elle affichait la chaînette en or que son père avait offerte un jour à sa mère.

En le voyant passer avec les armes, Frédéric le dévisagea comme s'il faisait partie d'un club de fascistes : celui de la police, « les traîtres de la crise d'Octobre », aimait-il à répéter.

Par un signe de tête, Duval amena Mimi à l'écart et lui demanda de respecter les règles du contrat.

— Je veux bien me payer un safari-photo, mais toi, tu me promets qu'en fin de semaine tu…

— Oui, oui, oui. Promis, promis. C'est clair.

— Et comment ça, il fume en dedans ?

— Plus tard, je vais lui dire. Y veut arrêter.

— En tout cas, y va arrêter ici !

Mimi roula des yeux, se rembrunit et s'éloigna.

Duval avait échangé la chasse contre la certitude que sa fille n'amènerait pas son percussionniste dans la chambre à coucher. Et Mimi, connaissant l'efficacité légendaire de l'enquêteur Duval, savait que, si elle rompait sa promesse, son père aurait tôt fait d'établir des preuves accablantes contre elle. Il était vraiment vieux jeu, c'était le seul reproche qu'elle pouvait formuler à son endroit.

Duval ouvrit le réfrigérateur et se déboucha une bière. Il repassa devant le salon en déboutonnant sa chemise, qu'il retira. À son grand plaisir, il surprit Fred à toiser la crosse du Smith & Wesson qui sortait de l'étui au-dessus de la camisole blanche. En voyant saillir les puissants pectoraux du lieutenant, le garçon sourit. Laurence, qui bouclait ses valises, eut connaissance de ce tournoi de virilité. Elle n'en revenait pas, d'autant plus que cette attitude ne correspondait en rien aux habitudes de Daniel. Elle comprenait qu'il avait éduqué seul sa fille et qu'il y était grandement attaché. Père et fille lisaient la pensée l'un de l'autre. Souvent, ils s'étonnaient de songer à la même chose au même instant. Mimi l'avait aidé à se relever de sa dépression après la mort de Marie-Claude.

— Je vais me doucher.

— Je vais ranger les sacs dans la voiture.

À travers les barreaux de la rampe, il aperçut les bas de bûcheron étalés sur la table et le jean rapiécé. Comment pouvait-il se permettre un tel laisser-aller? Mimi était trop bien pour ce hippie à gogo. Elle méritait autre chose qu'un arlequin chevelu qui piochait sur des tambours.

12

Duval roula dans le trafic de consommateurs qui se dirigeaient vers les centres commerciaux du boulevard Laurier. Les feux de circulation non synchronisés, à une époque où l'on déployait des sondes qui ricochaient d'un système gravitationnel à l'autre à la seconde près, le rendaient maboul.

Duval devait passer prendre la copine de Louis, Claudette, bénévole d'une communauté religieuse qui avait aidé Loulou durant sa convalescence. Elle avait veillé et prié pour lui tout au long de son voyage entre la vie et la mort. Par la suite, elle avait ramené Loulou dans le giron divin. Elle s'en était occupée comme une nurse et tous deux s'étaient liés d'amitié. Louis ne voulait pas que la relation aille plus loin, mais il avait fini par craquer.

Claudette attendait avec ses deux valises devant l'entrée du Towers. Elle travaillait comme fonctionnaire au centre d'emploi. Elle avait une carrure masculine et, dans son blouson de cuir, elle avait plus l'air d'une rockeuse que d'une prédicatrice. Elle faisait de la moto avec un groupe de motards appelé *The Love Supreme Angels*. Ils sillonnaient la Belle Province et les États-Unis, s'arrêtant dans des patelins pour échanger avec d'autres motards affiliés à la cause de Dieu. Question beauté, on était loin de Sandra, la strip-teaseuse qui arrachait des convulsions de plaisir à Loulou. Claudette avait un nez proéminent et crochu, des yeux rapprochés. Mais son sourire radieux et le pétillement de ses yeux noirs donnaient à cette femme un charme qui forçait à regarder autre chose que ses défauts physiques. Elle était spontanée et «pas barrée à quarante», comme disait Louis. Duval descendit, l'embrassa et déposa ses valises dans le coffre.

— Tu pars pour un siège ou quoi ?

— Nous autres, les poupounes, on a besoin d'nos patentes.

Claudette était une vraie réclame de produits de beauté : fond de teint, mascara, fard à paupières, rouge à lèvres, anti-cernes, teinture, fixatif et parfum capiteux. Les effluves de cette chimie cosmétique se mélangeaient et levaient le cœur de Duval qui aurait à rouler deux cent cinquante kilomètres dans ces conditions. Et elle fumait en plus.

Duval lui ouvrit la portière arrière.

— Salut, ma petite fille, ça va? dit Claudette en s'avançant pour embrasser Laurence, assise à l'avant.

Son rouge à lèvres macula la joue de la jeune femme.

— Salut, Claudette.

Claudette avait beaucoup donné à Louis depuis le jour où elle l'avait vu sur ce lit d'hôpital. Cette fusillade avait à jamais transformé leur vie. Paraplégique, Louis avait dû renoncer aux avantages d'une totale mobilité, quoiqu'il eût réappris à se déplacer avec des béquilles sur de courtes distances. Heureusement, disait-il, ses capacités érectiles avaient été conservées.

Louis travaillait comme analyste et s'occupait de la pastorale avec l'aumônier du poste de police. Il avait dû renoncer jusqu'à nouvel ordre à son statut d'enquêteur, même s'il agissait à titre de consultant, ce qui faisait bien rire les collègues, le gros Louis également. Quand on connaissait ses méthodes, il valait mieux le consulter sur les paris à l'hippodrome ou sur les chances des Expos d'atteindre les séries mondiales.

La paralysie de Louis avait aussi eu des conséquences pour le lieutenant Duval. Celui-ci avait perdu son vieux confrère, le détestable cabotin, l'irascible macho, le batailleur si inefficace dans ses enquêtes. Louis ne faisait pas l'unanimité à la SQ, mais Duval, un as-détective, ne s'était jamais ennuyé en sa compagnie. Dans les moments de crise, Louis possédait le don de dérider tout le monde avec une bonne grosse blague. Son inconscient était une véritable passoire et son manque de tact, mémorable. Comme Loulou avait parrainé Duval à son arrivée à Québec et qu'il l'avait initié à la ville, Duval l'avait tout de suite apprécié.

Dans son rapport sur l'affaire Hurtubise, Duval avait précisé que, sans les risques pris par Louis, Hurtubise n'aurait pas été abattu ce soir-là. Il avait fait cavalier seul, ce qu'on lui reprochait – et il en avait payé le prix – mais il fallait lui pardonner. Loulou traversait à cette époque une période difficile et il essuyait les quolibets des collègues. Sans parler du cahier de charges de sa belle-mère qui lui menait la vie dure. Charlène, sa femme, avait demandé le divorce lorsqu'elle avait appris l'aventure de Louis et de Sandra. Louis fréquentait alors cette effeuilleuse de la pègre et elle l'avait aussi laissé tomber avant même qu'il sorte du coma.

Le voyage se déroula tout en montées et en descentes au cœur du massif laurentien. De grands gouffres sombres avalaient la Jeep puis la relançaient au sommet des collines traversées de villages, de clochers et de pâturages avant qu'elle disparaisse de nouveau dans la marée de feuillus et de résineux. De temps à autre perçaient des points lumineux à l'est, des navires qui sillonnaient le fleuve, comme un *lite bright* dépouillé de lumière. Des camions à remorque passaient en coup de vent, exigeant une attention de tous les instants.

Après une halte à La Malbaie, Claudette et Laurence s'installèrent toutes deux sur la banquette arrière. La discussion s'enclencha sur le marché immobilier et les taux d'intérêt insensés des banques. Laurence avait sa maison dans la tête.

Au bulletin de nouvelles, le chef d'antenne annonça qu'on avait retrouvé une main empalée sur un poteau d'une cour d'école de Sillery. Duval et Laurence se regardèrent dans le rétroviseur. L'imagination de Duval se mit aussitôt en branle. Il pensa à ce que lui avait dit Mireille, le matin, au labo. Avait-on affaire à un sadique qui allait livrer les morceaux un par un ? Il songea à l'affiche posée dans son bureau avec les photos des enfants disparus.

Duval savait que Laurence avait hâte de reprendre la discussion sur le moment approprié pour emménager ensemble. Elle aurait voulu que ce soit avant les fêtes et désirait lui en parler. Mimi s'entendait très bien avec Laurence, ce qui n'avait pas été le cas au début. Daniel, lui, aurait souhaité entretenir Laurence de ce garçon qu'il ne pouvait blairer et qui allait sûrement dévergonder sa fille. En attendant, il l'écoutait causer avec Claudette de la situation dans les urgences, du départ des missions vers le tiers-monde, de l'économie et du phytothérapeute de Loulou qui était un homosexuel. La conversation ricochait sans cesse. Louis appelait ça des conversations de bonne femme. Duval fut heureux d'entendre l'indicatif de l'émission *Jazz Soliloque* et une énième version de *Solitude*.

Il plissa les yeux, aveuglé par les phares de nuit d'un automobiliste qui approchait. La voiture le croisa à plus de cent quarante kilomètres à l'heure dans un violent froissement de vent. Un train routier, rempli de billots de bois, passa immédiatement après en vrombissant.

Quinze kilomètres après Saint-Siméon, un panneau lui indiqua la route qui menait au chalet de Francis.

Duval sentait la fatigue surfer sur son corps. Elle lui taraudait les muscles et il ne pensait plus qu'à prendre une bière avec les copains.

La Jeep s'enfonça dans le bois par un petit chemin sinueux où l'on ne pouvait dépasser les trente kilomètres à l'heure. Des ravins et des massifs rocheux donnaient le vertige. Par cette nuit claire, l'endroit respirait le calme alors que, quelques heures plus tard, les détonations résonneraient à travers les montagnes qui bordent le Saguenay. À vingt kilomètres de la route 138, il repéra enfin, sur un bouleau, le geai bleu sculpté dans un panneau de bois et, en dessous, l'écriteau au nom de la famille Tremblay. La Jeep s'engagea à petite vitesse dans un chemin pentu et bosselé. À travers les arbres, des lumières scintillaient.

Puis il discerna les fenêtres lumineuses et des ombres qui se mouvaient derrière. Il se réjouit en apercevant les voitures de ses amis et collègues. Il se stationna entre la Mercedes de Villemure et l'Econoline de Louis.

Il sortit et s'étira. Le labrador de Francis jappa.

— Hé qu'y fait noir icitte, dit Claudette d'une voix inquiète.

Tout près mais invisible à cette heure, la rivière répandait son mugissement. Devant le chalet, l'eau du grand lac Noir clapotait sur le quai et seuls les flancs des montagnes se découpaient encore à travers la nuée d'étoiles. De la cheminée s'échappaient une longue volute et la bonne odeur d'un feu de bois.

Duval bomba le torse en respirant une première bouffée d'air épicé aux odeurs de résineux.

— Regardez, c'est la Voie lactée. On ne voit pas ça en ville !

Claudette leva les yeux au ciel et parut émerveillée.

La nuit était douce. Duval fit quelques pas et s'étira tout en contemplant le petit paradis de son collègue.

Sur le devant du chalet, la fenestration abondante offrait des levers de soleil et une vue panoramique sur le lac et les montagnes.

Duval ouvrit le hayon de la Jeep et donna congé aux dames.

Le chien sortit devant Francis par la porte de côté et se rua vers les invités. Francis, lampe de poche à la main, les accueillit avec ce rictus qu'il ne perdait jamais, au point que certains collègues à son arrivée avaient cru que le jeunot se moquait d'eux en permanence.

— Salut, la visite !

Il tenait une bière à la main et ressemblait, avec sa veste bleue à carreaux, à un roi du Nord, à un fils de

Menaud. Charlevoix, son royaume ! Il s'avança avec la démarche tout en souplesse du champion d'aïkido qu'il était. À l'intérieur, le rire gras de Louis perçait les murs.

Francis tapota amicalement l'épaule de son lieutenant.

— Ça s'est bien passé ?

Le gaillard fit la bise à Claudette, qu'il avait rencontrée au réveillon du capitaine Dallaire.

— Claudette, ton chum est en train de me vider les poches aux cartes. Arrête-le ! Y plume le docteur aussi.

— Y joue à l'argent, lui ? Y me semblait qu'y avait arrêté, le torvis !

Francis se tourna ensuite vers Laurence, qu'il trouvait belle à en faire parfois l'éloge à son lieutenant, mais avec le plus grand respect. Rien à voir avec les commentaires machistes de Louis quand Duval avait commencé à la fréquenter.

Francis aida Daniel à rentrer l'équipement et remarqua aussitôt qu'il n'avait emporté ni son arc ni son carquois.

— Où est ton *longbow* ?

— Je t'expliquerai. Longue histoire.

13

Dans le chalet, Louis et Villemure s'étaient retirés devant le feu de foyer, laissant la table recouverte de cartes et de verres vides. Le fauteuil roulant de Louis pivota à cent quatre-vingts degrés et se mit aussitôt en troisième vitesse quand sa copine et ses amis entrèrent. Loulou devint tout enjoué, ses joues et son crâne rougis par la chaleur du feu et de l'alcool.

Claudette se pencha pour l'embrasser.

— Tu joues aux cartes, mon maudit ?

— Pis je gagne !

À travers de longues exclamations, les copains se saluaient en se taquinant.

Une odeur irrésistible de gibier, mélangée à celle du bois qui chauffait le poêle à deux ponts, flottait dans la pièce.

Les lampes au gaz se reflétaient dans les grandes baies de la façade qui donnait sur le lac.

Lorsque Villemure et Laurence se donnèrent la bise, Francis, en décapsulant une bière, lança une boutade :

— En tout cas, si on a des problèmes de santé, on est gréyés : un médecin pour nous soigner et un médecin légiste pour nous expédier à la morgue avec certificat de décès écrit sur une feuille d'écorce…

— Et trois bouseux pour arrêter le meurtrier… ajouta aussitôt Louis.

L'humour noir de Francis et de Loulou fit s'esclaffer Laurence et Duval, mais ramena ce dernier à cette main découverte tôt en soirée et qui le taraudait.

Louis, tout guilleret, ressemblait plus à un monarque sur son trône qu'à un handicapé. Étrangement, cette épreuve lui avait redonné le goût de vivre. Il fallait chercher la raison de cette paix dans la croix d'argent qu'il portait au cou. Louis avait juré avoir vu, pendant son coma, une croix argentée qui flottait fiévreusement devant lui. Ses copains lui avaient rétorqué qu'il s'agissait sans doute du crucifix d'argent que portait la sœur qui le soignait en compagnie de Claudette. Mais il ne voulait rien entendre. Louis avait interprété cette croix et la présence de Claudette comme des signes de Dieu qui allaient transformer sa vie et ses rapports avec les autres. Sa messe de la police et ses fins de semaine à Jésus-Ouvrier lui donnaient des allures de prêcheur protestant. Ses amis, qu'il tentait d'entraîner, résistaient par maintes astuces à ces injonctions de se joindre à lui pour des assemblées charismatiques.

Les désirs compulsifs qui l'amenaient jadis à boire, courailler et s'empiffrer s'étaient transposés dans la sphère de la croyance religieuse et Dieu pouvait compter sur un fort en gueule.

Sa grosse tête chauve, d'une rondeur parfaite – il avait perdu ses derniers cheveux durant son coma –, contrastait avec la carrure de son visage. Ses yeux bleus ressemblaient à ceux d'un poupon et son menton était une structure à angles droits. Il avait perdu les cinquante livres en trop accumulées avant son séjour prolongé à l'hôpital et il se battait contre sa gourmandise pour ne pas les reprendre.

L'équipe qu'il formait avec Duval avait été rudement mise à l'épreuve en 1976. Tous avaient été marqués par l'affaire Hurtubise. Duval avait failli y laisser sa peau, Louis avait perdu l'usage de ses jambes et Francis, tireur d'élite, avait abattu le meurtrier sadique qui canardait les automobilistes sur l'autoroute Duplessis. On ne tue pas sans que le geste laisse des traces. Il ne manquait que Prince, prisonnier de ses angoisses, qui déclinait toute invitation, car il préférait noyer sa peine dans l'alcool et la solitude. Un quatuor imparfait.

Francis décapsula une bière qu'il remit à Daniel.

Son labrador brun, la queue tout agitée et la langue pendante, circulait entre les jambes des invités.

Duval tendit la main à Louis, qui accueillit son ancien chef d'équipe.

— Salut, mon vieux !

Louis savait qu'il devait la vie à Daniel, mais ce dernier se culpabilisait en se rappelant qu'il aurait pu devancer l'arrivée d'Hurtubise sur les lieux du dépotoir. Cette idée fixe continuait de le miner. Quelques minutes à peine et Louis aurait encore l'usage de ses jambes. Mais Louis répétait à tous qu'il n'aurait rien changé à sa condition, qu'il avait vécu son chemin de Damas.

Voyant que Daniel prenait un air songeur, Louis l'apostropha à sa manière :

— T'as don' l'air constipé, Danny ?

— Ils ont retrouvé une main sur une clôture.

— Y passera la r'prendre demain ! lança Loulou en gloussant, ce qui sema l'hilarité.

Villemure, vêtu comme un mannequin de Christian Dior, se joignit à eux, posa une main sur l'épaule de Daniel.

— On oublie le boulot pour les trois prochains jours. Laissons les cadavres à la morgue !

— Et ta femme à la maison ! expédia Louis dans un torrent de rires.

Le docteur Villemure expliqua que sa femme était « sourisphobe » et qu'elle lui avait jadis fait vivre une nuit d'enfer dans un chalet en raison des souris. Il avait dû tout remballer à 2 h du matin.

Il se tourna de nouveau vers Duval.

— On n'est plus en service.

Duval sourit en acquiesçant de la tête. Il avala une gorgée puis une main lui agrippa le bras, celle de Francis qui l'entraîna vers le poêle en fonte. Il souleva le couvercle de la casserole sur le poêle et lui montra les perdrix qu'il avait chassées à l'arc de trente livres et qui mijotaient à feu doux.

— Sens-moi ce festin ! Des perdrix flambées au calvados et au cidre de pommes. Ça me donne le goût de revoir ma Normandie !

Duval ferma les yeux et huma profondément.

— Demain, j'ai du canard ou du faisan. Sinon, j'ai mes lièvres.

Claudette prit une photo d'eux à leur insu avec son Instamatic et le flash laissa Duval avec des éclairs lumineux dans son champ de vision.

Francis, toujours célibataire, attendait désespérément qu'une femme entre dans sa vie. Il s'en confiait parfois à son lieutenant, qui l'encourageait à la patience. Pour Francis, il était plus facile de lire les indices d'une scène de crime que d'interpréter ceux d'une femme qui pouvait s'intéresser à lui. Par chance, il chassait, trappait et aurait pu vivre en autarcie au milieu de son domaine. Son chalet, hérité de son père, était décoré de vieux objets qu'il avait ramassés dans des bric-à-brac ou qu'il avait reçus de ses parents. Un gramophone RCA dans un coin du salon reposait sur une table ronde ; accroché sur le mur, juste au-dessus, un agrandissement d'une photo noir et blanc d'une voiture d'eau. Sur le mur opposé, dans deux cadres ovales, les portraits de ses grands-parents, Elzéar et Alice, « les Tremblay du rang croche » comme on les appelait. De vieilles cannes à pêche et une collection de vieux moules en bois servant à fabriquer des personnages en sucre d'érable étaient suspendus un peu partout, de même que des scies de bûcheron. Francis tenait à ce patrimoine tout autant qu'à l'indépendance de sa province, mais il n'en discutait que très rarement avec ses collègues.

Sur le comptoir, les bouteilles de vin s'alignaient comme de belles quilles vertes.

C'était une première d'accueillir l'équipe chez lui. Il ne manquait que Bernard.

— Il faudra que je lui parle, argua Louis.

Claudette s'était déjà mise à l'ouvrage en dressant la table, ce qui incita Laurence à lui donner un coup de main. Duval remarqua que Claudette paraissait mal à l'aise avec le docteur Villemure. Il se demanda si c'était à cause de son métier, de sa tenue vestimentaire ou de sa prestance – Villemure avait l'air d'un grand seigneur de la Renaissance. Ou était-ce la renommée du médecin légiste, dont le nom apparaissait souvent à la une ?

Francis piqua les perdrix pour constater qu'elles étaient prêtes. Il ne lui restait plus qu'à délayer la crème et le jaune d'œuf, à napper les oiseaux et à les décorer avec du persil. Il invita les copains rassemblés devant le feu à passer à table. Tablier de cuistot autour de la taille, il remplissait les assiettes, aidé par Claudette et Laurence.

Louis lança une prière improvisée et chacun se signa. Pendant le souper, prélude à la partie de chasse qui allait se dérouler le lendemain à la première heure, chacun y alla d'anecdotes et de projections quant à celui qui tuerait la bête.

La chair des perdrix abattues tôt à l'automne et qui s'étaient nourries de petits fruits sauvages était exquise. Villemure, bon buveur, avait sorti de sa cave un Château Kirwan 1975 Margaux et un Pouillac Baron de Rothschild 1972. Il porta un toast à la santé de Francis et tous les verres tintèrent au-dessus du gibier.

◆

Verre de Grand Marnier à la main, le ventre repu, les invités se déplacèrent au salon pendant que Francis, tisonnier au bout du bras, alimentait le foyer de grosses bûches qui étincelaient au contact de la braise. Louis effectua assez péniblement la courte distance avec ses béquilles, mais il s'améliorait de semaine en semaine et Laurence le félicita.

— Avec la moumoune qui me soigne, j'ai intérêt à réapprendre à marcher vite, lança Louis dans une grande saccade de rire contagieux.

Claudette réclama le silence et leur demanda de raconter, à tour de rôle, la situation la plus inusitée à laquelle leur métier les avait conviés.

Tous se tournèrent vers Duval, qui esquissa un sourire éloquent :

— J'hésite à vous la conter, parce que…

Un tollé de « oui » martelés s'ensuivit et il dut aller de l'avant avec son histoire. Il avala une gorgée de Grand Marnier, sourit et s'exécuta.

— Un jour, je me présente dans un appartement où un homme, un étudiant, si je me rappelle bien, venait de se suicider. Des traces de brûlure apparentes et de poudre ainsi que la position de l'arme indiquaient clairement qu'il s'était tiré une balle à bout portant. Période critique de l'année : une semaine avant Noël. Un lugubre classique. Il y avait un livre à ses côtés, près d'une causeuse. Je me suis penché et j'ai lu le titre : c'était écrit… laissez-moi me rappeler, oui, voilà, *Prolégomènes à toute métaphysique future*. Pas besoin de vous dire que j'ai failli inculper l'auteur d'homicide involontaire…

Tous s'esclaffèrent à l'exception de Duval, qui revoyait la tête éclatée du jeune homme.

Villemure, qui avait fait son cours classique, leva son verre en direction du lieutenant.

— T'aurais eu un problème dans ton enquête, car le philosophe en question est mort depuis un siècle.

— Bonne affaire ! conclut Louis.

Le feu crépitait, les braises éclataient et sifflaient dans le foyer. La chaleur se répandait devant les vieux canapés des années quarante. Le feu se reflétait sur le chrome de la roue du fauteuil roulant de Louis. Sur le tapis tressé, devant le feu, le labrador dormait, couché sur le flanc.

— À toi, François, dit Francis.

Villemure but une gorgée, réfléchit quelques instants.

— Ce sera bref et pathétique. Un lundi matin, j'entre dans la salle d'autopsie. Pas besoin de lire l'étiquette qui pend au gros orteil de la victime, je reconnais tout de suite la personne sur la table en inox : Andrée, une fille à qui j'avais fait la cour quand j'étais au collège et qui m'avait laissé sécher. Le type de jeune fille dont la beauté vous glace les sens et empêche toute tentative d'approche intelligente. Elle était étendue là, toujours aussi belle et blanche, et je la voyais nue pour la première fois. Elle avait été assassinée par son mari jaloux. Il l'avait tuée dans son bain en lui écrasant l'abdomen contre le rail de la douche, pour simuler une mort accidentelle par submersion. Les lésions étaient encore visibles sur le thorax.

— Tu vois, t'as même pas eu besoin de la déshabiller ! s'esclaffa Louis.

Duval tiqua. Religion, morale et décence, rien ne pouvait venir à bout du Gros quand il avait envie de jeter une vanne bien salée.

— Louis ! Quand même ! Un peu de respect, est morte, dit Claudette en expirant la fumée de sa cigarette.

— Bin, justement ! Elle peut rien entendre ! répliqua le Gros.

— Hé qu'y me décourage, lui, des fois… maugréa Claudette.

— Toi, Francis ? lança Laurence.

— Et une petite vite ! En ti-gars de Charlevoix, j'ai été élevé à manger des bourgaux, ce mollusque délicieux qui peuple les eaux salées du coin. J'en raffolais. Je patrouillais à Baie-Sainte-Catherine quand je suis appelé pour aller repêcher un cadavre sur le quai. Imaginez ma surprise quand j'ai aperçu le corps décomposé parasité par les bourgaux. Le médecin légiste m'a dit que ce mollusque était un vidangeur friand de cadavres. Ç'a été la fin des bourgaux pour moi.

— Frankie, c'est dégueulasse ! dit Louis.

Francis se tourna vers lui.

— Moi, dit Louis, je pourrais vous en compter pendant des heures.

— Ça, on le sait ! lança Duval en déclenchant de grands éclats de rire.

— Je commençais ma carrière, raconta Louis, j'étais patrouilleur à Sorel. J'ai pris mon beau-père sur le radar à cent quarante kilomètres sur l'autoroute et il s'est mis à m'engueuler. J'avais beau lui dire que tout était enregistré, y avait rien à faire. J'étais pas digne de sa fille, et j'étais un maudit beu comme les autres. Un crisse de beu ! Un hostie de beu sale ! Je l'ai salué. Il m'a répondu : « Va chier. » Il a été un mois sans me parler, le temps de régler sa contravention. Ah ! ah ! ah !

— Toi, Laurence ? demanda Claudette.

— C'est la nuit où j'ai vu arriver mon nouveau chum – elle le montra du menton – mordu par des rats dans un égout, transporté par ambulance, et à qui j'ai dû administrer une piqûre antirabique alors que je ne lui avais jamais vu les fesses. On commençait à sortir ensemble.

Des « hou » intéressés retentirent.

— Et t'as piqué Sherlock ou Holmes ? lança Louis.

— J'ai piqué Holmes et j'ai gardé Sherlock pour l'autre main.

Elle le regarda, les yeux dans les vapes, et Duval l'embrassa.

Peu après minuit, Francis proposa à tout le monde d'aller se coucher. Les corps éméchés et fourbus s'extirpèrent avec peine des vieux coussins.

Francis, en hôte distingué, distribua à chacun sa chambre. Louis – parce qu'il ronflait et se déplaçait difficilement – et Claudette couchèrent au rez-de-chaussée dans l'une des deux chambres. Intimité oblige, Francis offrit l'autre à Duval et à Laurence. Villemure et Francis montèrent sur la mezzanine où s'alignaient les vieux lits de camp.

Duval croulait de sommeil, mais la chaleur du poêle rendait l'air sec et la gorge pareille à du papier-émeri. Il se leva discrètement pour ouvrir la fenêtre. Laurence vint se blottir contre lui. Elle avait envie de faire l'amour, mais la proximité des pièces l'en dissuada. Comme elle avait travaillé de nuit la veille et s'était levée dans l'après-midi, elle ne s'endormait pas. Elle aurait voulu jaser avec Daniel, mais ce dernier passa vite au pays de Morphée.

Un cauchemar emporta rapidement Duval. Un chien aboyait. Le lieutenant entrait dans une maison, montait à l'étage. Les jappements s'intensifiaient. Il apercevait le bord d'une baignoire éclairé par une chandelle rouge. Une main décomposée, bleuâtre et pleine de lésions, l'invitait à s'approcher : le visage flou, submergé d'une jeune fille en robe de nuit, couchée dans son bain, les cheveux flottants, ses yeux grands ouverts et injectés de sang, le fixait. Et toujours cette main l'appelait. La bouche ronde criait, mais n'émettait aucun son, que des bulles qui émergeaient à la surface. Il s'approcha et finit par lire sur les lèvres : « Ma main ! Ma main ! » Il lui manquait la main gauche. Lorsqu'il s'avança pour aider la jeune femme, elle l'agrippa et l'attira vers elle.

Le corps de Duval devint un réseau de tics et Laurence sut qu'il faisait un cauchemar et le secoua. Il se réveilla en nage et se redressa.

— Ça va ?

— Un mauvais rêve.

Il préféra taire l'appréhension qui le gagnait. Mais il pensait à ce graffiti, à cette main et à ce chien éventré. Apaisé par le bruissement des feuilles et le chuchotement de la rivière, il replongea dans un sommeil corrompu par de mauvais pressentiments.

14

À pas feutrés, Francis alla réveiller chacun de ses compagnons emmitouflés dans leurs couvertures.

Il chauffa le poêle avec du bouleau, ravivant du tisonnier la braise de la veille, et déposa la bouilloire sur la plaque. Le soleil n'était pas encore levé, mais on distinguait le lac par la fenêtre panoramique et les montagnes rougeoyantes sur l'autre rive. Les colverts filaient en rase-mottes au-dessus de l'eau.

La caisse roulante de Louis bringuebala par à-coups, passa juste dans l'embrasure de la porte et déboucha dans la cuisine. Tous étaient frigorifiés.

— Ça va chauffer, les rassura Francis en se frottant les mains.

Le chouenneux ne tenait plus en place, une vraie queue de veau. Une tâche n'attendait pas l'autre : préparer le déjeuner, emplir les thermos de café, ranger la bière dans la glacière. C'était sa vie, la chasse. Ce jour-là, il n'avait plus d'âge. Qu'il adorait ce moment ! Il renvoya son toupet vers l'arrière. Il portait un vieux pantalon noir de la SQ transformé en pyjama et un vieux t-shirt FBI offert lors de son stage à Quantico en Virginie.

— Viens manger, dit Louis en le voyant s'agiter.

— Non, j'ai jamais faim le matin de la chasse.

La bouilloire siffla. Le grille-pain catapulta toast après toast. Le poêle répandait sa chaleur toujours un peu plus loin.

Sur la table, pots de confitures, beurre d'arachide et Corn Flakes passaient de main en main.

À l'est, dans un ciel bleu, le soleil se hissait sur les montagnes.

Laurence et Claudette ne s'étaient pas levées. Elles préféraient rester au chalet pour se reposer. Francis leur écrivit un mot pour les aviser qu'elles pouvaient marcher sans danger sur le chemin, que la chasse avec des armes à feu ne commençait que le lendemain.

L'équipement les attendait près de la porte. Francis avait passé une heure à affûter ses flèches avec une lime douce et une pierre. Il avait préparé des sandwichs en quantité industrielle. Il ne restait plus qu'à empiler les bagages.

À l'extérieur, le froid du matin glaçait la colonne. Duval se dressa pour respirer les odeurs de feuillus et de résineux. De main à main, on se passa les objets que Francis rangea dans la vieille familiale.

Villemure et Duval se demandaient bien comment Louis allait pouvoir atteindre la cache. La réponse se trouvait sur le toit de la Ford. Francis avait construit une litière avec des deux par quatre et un panneau de contreplaqué. Deux poignées dépassaient aux extrémités. À la blague, il montra le montant transversal qui servait de renfort.

— C'est solide !

On transporterait Loulou sur ce brancard de fortune jusqu'au site et quelqu'un se chargerait du fauteuil roulant. Villemure hocha la tête et afficha un sourire sardonique.

— Louis, tu vas ressembler à une princesse égyptienne !

— Vous avez besoin de pas m'échapper !

Mais lorsque Francis apparut, en tenue de camouflage, avec un arc et des flèches, la stupeur sur le visage de Loulou se révéla totale. Francis avait beau être tireur d'élite à la SQ, il fallait être fou pour utiliser un arc contre un orignal. Louis réclamait des canons.

— Cou'don, Frankie, tu te prends pour Robin des Bois ou quoi ? On n'est plus au Moyen Âge. Pour le petit gibier, je peux comprendre, mais devant un animal de mille livres ! Amène la 303, je vais me sentir plus rassuré !

— Louis, t'en fais pas. C'est un arc avec soixante-quinze livres de puissance. Je peux coucher un bison avec ça.

Mais le Gros, qui allait se retrouver sur le plancher des vaches avec Francis, continua de s'inquiéter. Bien qu'il ne possédât pas de permis de chasse, il réclama de nouveau une carabine.

Francis, qui tenait à respecter les règlements du ministère de la Chasse et de la Pêche, lui opposa un non catégorique. La chasse à l'arc se terminait aujourd'hui. Demain, on sortirait les carabines.

Louis, terrifié, se tourna vers Duval.

— Et toi, tu chasses pas ? Tu changes pas d'idée ?

— Non.

Francis déposa dans le coffre son petit arc de trente livres au cas où il apercevrait des perdrix sur le bord de la route.

— Tiens, Loulou. Pour te rassurer, je prends mon arc à deux poulies Browning au cas où Daniel changerait d'idée.

Louis n'était pas dupe de l'astuce.

— Tu chatouillerais même pas ta belle-mère avec cette corde à linge-là.

— De toute façon, je suis célibataire.

Une nuée de condensation s'éleva dans l'air froid.

Francis referma le hayon. Les premiers jours de la chasse à l'arc avaient été infructueux. Depuis qu'il avait découvert cette méthode de chasse ancestrale, il ne voulait plus rien savoir des armes à feu pour tuer son gibier. Duval comprenait bien Francis. Quel mérite avait un tireur d'élite, embusqué derrière des buissons ou dans une cache, à tirer un orignal ?

Louis qui, après des mois de physiothérapie, avait gagné des forces dans les bras et quelque peu dans les jambes, s'appuya sur le rebord avec une main et se glissa sur le siège avant. Duval plia le fauteuil roulant et le déposa dans le coffre du véhicule.

Louis bougonna et ne porta aucune attention au spectacle du jour qui se levait ni au martin-pêcheur que leur montra Francis. L'inquiétude le taraudait.

Francis avait préparé cette chasse dès la fin du mois d'août. Les orignaux étant friands de pommes et de sel, il était venu en déposer à proximité du lac aux Castors. Il avait ensuite recouvert ses traces avec de l'urine de mouffette. Dans les jours qui avaient suivi, les empreintes de sabots s'étaient multipliées autour de la saline.

— Ça me rassure pas, dit Louis.

Ils croisèrent un rondelet *pick-up* Fargo d'une autre époque transportant deux gardes-chasse qui les saluèrent.

La journée allait être splendide, le soleil s'élevait dans la « turbulente musique de la forêt toute bruissante », comme le disait Félix-Antoine Savard, ce poète qu'adorait Francis depuis qu'il l'avait découvert au cégep. La fraîcheur du petit matin l'obligea à allumer la chaufferette pour désembuer le pare-brise. La voiture montait et descendait les chemins de terre cabossés. Les montagnes rouges et jaunes semblaient embrasées par ces lumières végétales que sont les feuilles à l'automne.

Duval se sentait bien malgré la fatigue qui lui vrillait les épaules. La main énigmatique avait perturbé son sommeil.

À six kilomètres du Saguenay et de Baie-Sainte-Catherine, Francis rangea la Ford Country Squire.

— On y est ! La chasse commence !

◆

Immédiatement en descendant de la voiture, Francis chercha des pistes. L'empreinte des sabots d'un orignal, en forme de deux grosses gouttes, était fraîche de la nuit. Le chouenneux se pencha :

— On n'est pas tout seuls à matin !

Villemure détacha les liens de la litière. Francis et Daniel empoignèrent chacun une extrémité. Louis s'y assit. À la blague, Francis fit chanceler le brancard.

— Hé ! Allez-y mollo !

Ils se trouvaient à moins d'un demi-kilomètre de la cache. Le docteur Villemure ouvrait la marche et écartait les branches qui obstruaient le sentier. Le moelleux couvert de feuilles mortes bruissait sous les pas.

— Une chance que t'as maigri, mon gros, chuchota Francis, parce que tu serais resté avec les femmes.

— Là, la chasse aurait été dangereuse pour vous autres, les gars ! lança le docteur Villemure.

Le raidillon qui menait au lac fut la section la plus périlleuse à parcourir. Le terrain était pentu et vaseux, il leur fallait maintenir le ballant et regarder où ils mettaient les pieds, enjamber des troncs et de grosses branches mortes. Le bois craquait sous les pieds. Une dizaine de blocs erratiques moussus, disposés en cercle et creusés de cavités, ressemblaient à un temple dédié à la nature par elle-même. Des viornes à feuilles d'aulnes – le bois d'orignal – bordaient le chemin.

Ils entraient dans la pinède au sol couvert d'aiguilles. Le lac, cintré par les montagnes de l'autre côté, miroitait à travers les branches. À cinquante mètres à droite s'élevait un arbre dans lequel une cache en bois rond, à une vingtaine de pieds du sol, pouvait accueillir jusqu'à six personnes. Une échelle de fortune permettait d'y accéder. Francis avait prospecté les lieux et jeté son dévolu sur cet endroit. À sa base, il avait construit un imposant affût avec des branches de sapin.

— C'est là qu'on s'installe, Loulou. Vous autres, vous montez et vous faites la vigie.

Du doigt, il indiqua à ses amis l'emplacement du dépôt de sel et de pommes, tout près du lac. De nombreuses pistes d'orignaux y marquaient les lieux.

Voulant tester l'écho, Louis se mit à chanter *Ton amoouur… a changééé… maaa viiee.*

— Louis, la ferme ! Il faut garder le silence, ordonna Francis.

— Je me sens pas rassuré ici.

Pour taquiner Louis, au grand amusement de Duval et de Villemure, Francis recouvrit les roues du fauteuil avec des branches de sapin.

— T'es camouflé, Louis. Y te verront pas…

— J'aime pas ça. J'ai pas envie d'être chargé par un orignal.

Louis savait que la charge d'un orignal parvenait à briser de jeunes arbres, à casser des branches de fort diamètre. Le fauteuil roulant ne résisterait pas, lui encore moins.

— Louis, la bête la plus dangereuse dans le bois, c'est toi, lui lança Francis avec un sourire éclatant. Y a pas un orignal qui va vouloir t'affronter ! s'esclaffa-t-il sous le regard amusé des copains.

Francis enfila son gant de tir en peau de cerf et son brassard.

Duval et Villemure grimpèrent jusque dans la cache par les barreaux de fortune plantés dans l'écorce. Le plafond consistait en une bâche militaire qui, en raison de l'humidité, sentait la poudre de Jell-O. Deux bancs faits de rondins de bouleau permettaient de s'asseoir.

Par-devant et sur le côté droit de leur cabane suspendue s'ouvrait une vaste perspective sur le lac et le versant nord-est de la montagne.

Des canards survolaient le lac à fleur d'eau.

Duval ouvrit le thermos à café et en versa deux tasses. À ses côtés se trouvait l'arc à poulies de Francis, telle une véritable tentation.

Une violente éclaboussure brisa la tranquillité. Un castor, dont seule la tête émergeait, donnait l'alerte en tapant l'eau de sa queue. Il plongea et remonta quinze mètres plus loin, tout près de son barrage.

Duval s'avança pour jeter un coup d'œil en bas. Le gros Louis, bonnet de laine sur la tête, café fumant dans une main, regardait par la meurtrière de sapin.

Francis marcha en direction du lac avec une boîte de conserve dans la main. Il fit quelques pas dans la vase, laissant échapper des bruits de succion, et entra dans l'eau en la faisant gicler pour lancer le rituel appel de l'orignal. Il se pencha, remplit le contenant, et le versa afin d'imiter la bête qui urine dans le lac. Il sortit de l'eau, fit craquer des branches avec ses doigts. Puis, utilisant ses mains comme porte-voix, il « calla » l'orignal comme le lui avait appris son père. Le langoureux appel porta loin et se répercuta en écho.

Louis leva la tête en direction de la cache et leva le pouce. Daniel craignit qu'il se mette à cabotiner, mais le Gros respecta la consigne du silence.

Francis répéta à quelques reprises l'appel et il revint vers son embuscade. Le regard perçant du docteur Villemure épiait au loin. Tous ses sens semblaient allumés, alors que Duval fermait les yeux et basculait de sommeil en réveil.

Le temps fila. Vers midi, le temps se réchauffa et ils avalèrent quelques sandwichs. La tête de Francis apparut dans l'ouverture de la cache.

— Ça va, ici ?

Le docteur décapsula une bière qu'il offrit à Francis.

— Je redescends, Louis veut pas rester seul.

En bas, Louis lisait la biographie de Cassius Clay tout en avalant des sandwichs.

◆

Francis répéta son rituel à maintes reprises, mais rien à l'horizon. De temps à autre, la détonation sinistre d'un braconnier venait rompre la paix relative qui régnait dans la forêt. Francis détestait les pilleurs de son royaume.

Villemure tapa sur l'épaule de Duval pour lui montrer un aigle pêcheur. Le balbuzard traça une ellipse dans le ciel, plia ses ailes vers l'arrière pour faire du surplace, observa le lac et plongea dans l'eau pour cueillir son poisson.

Vers 15 h, le son d'une éclaboussure fit sursauter les chasseurs. Là, il ne s'agissait ni d'un castor ni d'un balbuzard ! Une grosse bête en rut venait de se jeter à l'eau. Duval prit les longues-vues.

Francis se dressa et agita un bras vers la cime de l'arbre pour leur demander ce qu'ils voyaient. Villemure acquiesça du bonnet et mit une main de chaque côté de sa tête pour imiter les bois imposants. Francis imita le cri plaintif de la femelle. L'orignal traversait l'extrémité nord du lac avec le tiers de la distance à parcourir.

D'un geste, Villemure signala à Francis que l'orignal s'approchait lentement, la tête et l'imposant panache hors de l'eau. Francis fit craquer quelques branches et appela l'animal. La bête émergea de l'eau et se secoua en bramant. De nouveau elle n'était plus visible. Puis, on entendit des craquements dans le sous-bois à l'extrémité du lac. Francis répéta le cri langoureux de la femelle. La ramure gigantesque émergea à l'orée des feuillus. L'animal s'avança lentement vers le dépôt de sel, à moins de quarante mètres de l'embuscade qu'on lui tendait. C'était fascinant. Francis sortit du carquois une flèche monolame, l'encocha. Il mit son index sur sa bouche pour signaler à Louis de se taire. L'orignal poursuivit son avancée, cherchant cette femelle qui l'appelait. À trente-cinq mètres, il se trouvait encore trop loin. Pour Francis, c'était le moment le plus excitant. Il sentait son cœur battre la chamade. Quand la bête fut à trente mètres, il s'approcha très lentement. Il ressemblait à un G.I. américain dans sa tenue de camouflage.

Son père lui avait appris que l'orignal est un animal favorisé par tous les sens à l'exception de la vue. Heureusement, un vent léger soufflait dans leur direction, aidant l'homme au détriment de l'animal. Puis la bête se déplaça vers l'appât de pommes. Ses bois enchevêtrés mesuraient bien un mètre d'envergure. Francis, dans sa tenue de camouflage, lui faisait face à quinze mètres. Heureusement, le Charlevoisien ne ressentait pas la *buck fever*. Il ne pouvait tirer dans cette position. Un archer consciencieux répugne à blesser un animal à la tête. Ce dernier aurait la vie sauve, mais conserverait d'affreuses séquelles. Avec un tel gibier, on ne gaspillait pas ses munitions. La pointe de la flèche devait pénétrer le plus loin possible, couper les organes dans sa traversée, déclencher une hémorragie importante et rendre ainsi le pistage aisé. L'orignal se tourna, hésitant, fixa devant lui, flaira le danger, le museau aux aguets.

Louis gesticulait, paniquait à l'idée d'être estropié par le cervidé.

L'archer avança encore d'un mètre. Le majeur et l'annulaire sous l'encoche, l'index au-dessus, Francis se concentra sur la cible tout en focalisant en arrière-plan la pointe de la flèche. Il banda la corde à pleine allonge, décocha la flèche qui siffla et s'enfonça sous l'épaule, au-dessus de la cuisse. La bête tendit le cou, la tête bien haute, cherchant de l'air. Touché !

Duval descendit en trombe, suivi de Villemure.

L'animal, avec l'énergie du désespoir, s'enfonça dans le bois dans un bruit fracassant. Rien ne lui résistait.

Francis entreprit le pistage. La traînée de sang s'avérait abondante. Il avait frappé au bon endroit. Villemure aperçut l'empennage en plume jaune de la flèche sur le sol. Un tir parfait. Elle avait traversé le corps. Il la ramassa. En voyant les bulles de sang sur la flèche et sur la piste, le docteur avisa Duval qu'une artère importante et les poumons avaient été atteints.

La bête gisait dans un fourré, une large blessure visible à son flanc. Elle n'avait pas franchi cent cinquante mètres avant de s'écrouler. Heureusement, Francis n'aurait pas à utiliser sa dague pour achever l'animal.

— Je l'ai eu ! cria Francis, qui sautillait, les bras levés, en voyant apparaître Villemure et Duval.

Francis, en s'enfonçant comme un fou dans le bois, s'était entaillé le visage, mais dans l'excitation, il ne semblait pas s'en rendre compte. L'orignal était gigantesque. Il devait peser plus de cinq cents kilos et faire deux mètres cinquante dans sa longueur.

De la blessure s'écoulait abondamment le sang. Villemure constata que la flèche, tranchante comme une lame de rasoir, avait creusé un orifice de quatre centimètres.

Duval vivait une expérience paradoxale. À la fois fier de son copain Francis, il était aussi peiné pour le roi de la forêt qui n'avait eu qu'un but en ce jour : se reproduire en paix. Il ressentait toujours des émotions contradictoires.

Villemure tapa sur l'épaule de Francis pour le féliciter.

La scène rappela à Francis une légende amérindienne que son père lui avait racontée très jeune et qui l'avait impressionné, à savoir qu'il fallait boire une tasse du sang de l'orignal ou manger son cœur en guise de rituel.

— On mange le cœur ? demanda-t-il.

— On te le laisse, répondit Duval.

Le chouenneux rayonnait comme un gamin.

— Il est mort rapidement, sans trop souffrir…

Francis était encore tout essoufflé.

Un coup de feu sinistre tonna au loin en écho. Francis releva la tête.

— Des hosties de braconniers !

Il pensa de nouveau à son père. Il soupçonnait depuis toujours que son paternel, garde-chasse, avait été abattu par des braconniers. Un jour, il en aurait le cœur net.

Pour que la viande animale ne soit pas souillée au contact du sol, il fallait se hâter de la déposer sur des rondins de bois.

— Comment on va faire pour le sortir de là ? demanda le docteur.

— Je vais aller chercher mes cordes, mes scies et mes couteaux. On va le soulever au palan et l'éviscérer sur place…

Avec des poulies et beaucoup de sueur, l'orignal fut suspendu par les bois à une branche d'arbre.

Puisque l'opération serait longue, on rapatria Louis.

Villemure, expert dans les coupes, fut mis à contribution, ce qui amusa tout le monde sauf Louis, qui éprouva un fort dédain en voyant le médecin légiste éviscérer cette carcasse animale qu'il allait manger, alors que, depuis quinze ans, il observait Villemure dépecer hommes et femmes. Regarder le docteur débiter des coupes de viande, ronde, croupe, surlonge et palette, le répugnait.

Deux heures plus tard, les morceaux de la carcasse avaient été transportés dans la remorque. L'imposant panache avait été conservé.

Louis eut le temps de terminer son livre.

Au chalet, la fête se prolongea tard dans la nuit.

Francis fit un feu devant le lac et, les yeux fixés sur la flamme, raconta des souvenirs de chasse et de pêche. Vers minuit, il essaya l'appel des loups, ce qui énerva Claudette et amusa Louis. Mais lorsque la meute répondit, Louis intima à Francis de cesser ses folies.

RETOUR À L'ANORMAL

15

Mardi matin. L'asile sur quatre roues. Le trafic se densifiait alors que les fonctionnaires assaillaient la colline parlementaire. Sur le boulevard Saint-Cyrille, la lenteur de la circulation rendait les automobilistes impatients et enclins à défier les feux rouges, ce que venaient de faire deux conducteurs. Duval les retrouva bloqués cinq cents mètres plus loin à la hauteur de la rue Cartier.

La radio matinale déversait les immondices de la veille, sa canonnade de commerciaux agressants et l'imbuvable chanson disco du jour. Duval l'éteignit et amorça son virage dans la rue Turnbull.

Quand il passa devant la réception, le répartiteur avisa Duval qu'il était attendu dans le bureau du capitaine. Le lieutenant alla quérir son courrier et tomba sur Samuel, pour qui c'était jour d'examen.

Le maître-chien, qui ne tenait plus en place, croisa les doigts au-dessus de son visage anxieux et froissé par une nuit blanche. Couché dans son lit, il avait passé le temps à ressasser des réponses toutes faites.

— À quelle heure ?

— 9 h.

— Je te dis merde ! lui lança Duval.

Duval éplucha rapidement son courrier, regarda la photo du juge Dutil sur la couverture du magazine *Sûreté* et se dirigea vers le bureau du capitaine.

Tous les journaux du matin s'étalaient devant Dallaire, qui parlait au téléphone avec son fils d'une voix toute paternelle. Le bambin avait contracté la varicelle et le capitaine le consolait. Sourire aux lèvres, il invita Duval à s'asseoir et du doigt lui indiqua qu'il n'en avait que pour une minute. «Oui, papa te promet que ça va partir. Papa l'a eue quand il était petit. » Dallaire cligna d'un œil. «C'est pas dangereux. Tu dois te reposer », dit le capitaine d'une voix que Duval ne lui connaissait pas. Tout en poursuivant l'appel, il désigna à Duval le pot de café sur la console, du Nescafé instantané avec du lait en poudre. Le chef n'utilisait jamais son percolateur. Duval déclina. « Passe-moi maman, maintenant. Papa a du travail. » Les plantes que Pouliot avait si mal entretenues alors qu'il remplaçait Dallaire avaient reverdi. Le capitaine annonça à sa femme qu'il ne rentrerait pas à la maison pour dîner et raccrocha.

— Loulou m'a raconté votre partie de chasse. Belle prise !

— Faudra penser à ajouter un échelon salarial pour les tireurs d'élite qui sont archers…

— Le pire, c'est que le syndicat vous soutiendrait… Si votre chasse a été bonne, ici, on a un drôle d'animal qui s'est lancé dans une traque morbide. On est inquiets.

La voix enrhumée de Dallaire ne parvenait pas à camoufler l'angoisse qui le tenaillait. Il sortit d'une enveloppe des photos qu'il passa à Duval.

Duval grimaça en voyant la main livide d'une femme, à côté de laquelle se trouvait une règle à mesurer. Le capitaine avala une gorgée de café.

— Normalement, ce n'est pas de notre juridiction, mais comme on craint d'avoir affaire à un type dérangé et que l'expert en sciences comportementales, c'est toi, les policiers de Sillery et de Sainte-Foy, à la demande du coroner, acceptent de nous laisser enquêter.

Duval avait bien su qu'il serait rattrapé par cette main.

— Vendredi, on a trouvé, dans un boisé à l'université, un caniche dépecé et cette main plantée sur un piquet d'une clôture du collège Jésus-Marie. La veille, quelqu'un avait tracé sur un mur à l'université un message haineux avec du sang : *Au bout de ton sang, femelle.* Dans une poubelle près du Grand Séminaire, on a aussi trouvé une éponge sanguinolente qui aurait servi à écrire le message. Au labo, on précise qu'il s'agit du sang du caniche. Un scalpel aurait servi à éviscérer le chien et une scie de chirurgie à couper la main. Un message avait été enroulé autour de l'index de la main. La main d'une femme assez jeune, d'après le docteur Villemure. Il était écrit, avec des lettres découpées dans des journaux : *Mes amours décomposés.* Méchant malade ! Tu peux t'imaginer la panique qui règne dans le coin. Surtout les parents des enfants qui fréquentent l'école Jésus-Marie. Les bonnes sœurs doivent s'user les doigts à égrener leurs chapelets. Il y a de la psychose dans l'air.

— Tout ça près des écoles.

— Et c'est aussi ce qui me fait peur. Le plus bizarre, c'est que la main, d'après le rapport de Villemure, appartient à une personne décédée depuis quelque temps.

Duval fronça les sourcils. Dallaire prit le rapport du pathologiste judiciaire, ajusta ses lunettes et le paraphrasa :

— On a décelé dans les tissus des traces de formaldéhyde, des muscles raidis sous l'action du formol et du maquillage qui avait coulé à cause de la pluie.

S'agit-il de quelqu'un qui a maquillé la main après avoir tué sa victime ou est-ce le travail du croque-mort ? On penche pour la seconde solution. On est à peu près sûrs que ce n'est pas un meurtre. À qui appartient cette main ? C'est ce qu'il faut savoir au plus vite.

— On a affaire à un nécrophile, conjectura Duval.

— Je le crains… On ne sait jamais quand ça s'arrête, avec eux…

Absorbé, Duval laissait filer le train de paroles que prononçait Dallaire. Il spéculait, supposait, repensait à des délits semblables commis aux États-Unis ou en Angleterre. Quelqu'un dans la ville s'amusait à jouer une farce macabre. On dénombrait de nombreux gestes semblables dans les annales judiciaires. Depuis le célèbre cas du sergent Bertrand, nécrophile parisien, qui vidait les tombeaux du cimetière du Père-Lachaise, les actes de nécrophilie et de vampirisme alimentaient les études criminelles et psychiatriques : les vampires de Highgate à Londres et celui de Dusseldorf en Allemagne se révélaient des cas classiques. Toutefois, contrairement à Bertrand qui ne tuait pas, mais se contentait de déterrer ses cadavres et de se livrer à des attouchements, allant jusqu'à éjaculer dans les organes putréfiés des cadavres, les deux autres psychopathes abattaient leurs victimes avant de se repaître de leur sang. Aux États-Unis, Albert Fish, un sadique-anthropophage, était devenu un objet d'étude pour les criminologues et les psychiatres. Duval lui avait consacré un chapitre de son mémoire de maîtrise. Ce vieillard, qu'on surnommait l'homme gris, avait le visage émacié, longiligne, les pommettes saillantes, les oreilles proéminentes et le nez crochu, interminable. Il ressemblait à un ogre de conte de fées, sauf que son histoire était bien réelle et cauchemardesque. En 1928, il s'était présenté sous le nom de Frank Howard dans une famille, les Budd, afin d'offrir du travail à l'aîné. La vue de la sœur du gamin, Grace, une jeune beauté, le renversa. Comme Fish possédait la faculté de créer un climat de confiance entre lui et ceux qu'il rencontrait pour la première fois, les parents l'apprécièrent immédiatement. Howard combla les Budd de cadeaux et proposa à la mère de faire visiter New York à Grace. Les parents acquiescèrent. Après tout, il s'était montré si généreux. Le vieillard partit avec Grace, mais ne revint pas le soir comme il l'avait promis. La famille, morte d'inquiétude, appela la police et il se révéla que l'adresse donnée par Fish n'existait pas. Une dizaine de jours plus tard, la famille reçut une lettre horrible dans laquelle Fish racontait comment il avait dépecé puis cuisiné Grace. Il y avait consigné toutes sortes de détails morbides : la réaction de Grace quand elle s'était sentie piégée, les instruments qu'il avait pris pour la découper, les ingrédients qu'il avait utilisés et les recettes qu'il avait préparées, le temps qu'il lui avait fallu pour la manger au complet, soit neuf jours. Les confessions de Fish lors de son interrogatoire et de son procès représentent un sommet dans l'art du sadomasochisme et de la déviance. Il avoua avoir tué un enfant dans au moins vingt-trois États et en avoir mutilé plusieurs autres. La défense eut beau plaider l'aliénation, la Couronne rejeta le diagnostic et il fut exécuté par électrocution en 1938. Étrangement, Fish, père de six enfants et séparé de sa femme, n'avait jamais manifesté de brutalité envers eux. Par contre, lors de son procès, Fish admit qu'il aimait se faire souffrir et qu'il avait pris l'habitude de s'enfoncer des aiguilles dans le rectum, ce que révélèrent des radiographies à la stupéfaction de la cour.

Plus récemment, on avait appris que le sanguinaire dictateur Idi Amin Dada, le président de l'Ouganda, cannibale notoire, conservait dans un congélateur les corps de ses victimes, souvent des ministres, afin de les apprêter au repas. La nouvelle avait secoué la communauté internationale.

Mais dans le cas de la main empalée, qui pouvait jouir à réaliser un acte aussi dément, sinon un nécrophile ou un mauvais plaisant ? Duval souhaita que ce soit l'œuvre d'un farceur, mais il n'aimait pas la connotation misogyne des messages sanglants. Heureusement, la plupart des nécrophiles ne commettaient pas de meurtres pour satisfaire leur étrange pulsion.

— Daniel, tu m'écoutes ?

Duval releva la tête. Le cauchemar de Charlevoix, cette jeune fille qui l'appelait, repassait dans sa tête.

— Oui, excuse-moi.

— Je te refile un autre enquêteur dans ton équipe.

— Je voudrais Louis.

— Louis ? Pourquoi ? Il n'a pas enquêté depuis longtemps.

— Justement. Louis va coordonner les renseignements. Et il sait détendre l'atmosphère quand ça devient trop tendu.

— Es-tu sûr que ça l'intéresse ?

— Oui, il brûle de revenir, même en fauteuil roulant, dit Duval.

— Parfait. On aura notre Perry Mason. Tu lui annonces la nouvelle ?

Tout heureux, Duval gratifia Dallaire d'un salut militaire et se hâta d'aller convaincre Louis de se jeter dans la mêlée.

16

Louis accueillit d'abord la nouvelle comme une blague, éclata de rire, puis se rembrunit.

— Comment je pourrai suivre le bal dans ma caisse roulante ? J'ai de la misère à faire dix pieds en béquilles.

Il replongea ses doigts dans sa boîte de Cracker Jack, l'air faussement bourru.

Debout devant lui, Duval leva les mains comme un prêcheur l'exhortant à le suivre.

— On fera comme avant. Parfois tu iras de ton côté à ton rythme et à d'autres moments tu suivras le mien. Tu vas faire aussi de la recherche au bureau.

Louis sortit le sachet de la boîte de Cracker Jack et du maïs roula sur les statistiques des pages sportives. Il observa un instant le sachet contenant le cadeau-jouet de la boîte de friandises – une catapulte miniature en plastique. Il avala une poignée de maïs soufflé et parla la bouche pleine.

— T'es sûr ?

— Dallaire est même enthousiaste, mentit Duval.

Louis grimaça, balança la tête.

— Claudette aimera pas ça. Je sais déjà ce qu'elle va me dire. Danny, j'ai la chienne de recommencer…

— C'est normal.

De l'index, Loulou se cura une molaire où s'était coincé un grain de maïs, clappa de la langue sur son palais avant de se lécher l'arcade dentaire supérieure. Ses grosses pattes d'ours aplatirent le contenant de friandises, qui plana d'un jet dans la corbeille. Il marmonna quelques mots incompréhensibles, ouvrit le tiroir de son bureau où une Bible et un calibre .38 dans un étui formaient un couple insolite. Il sortit d'abord la Bible, puis son arme. Duval se dit qu'il n'y avait que Louis pour ranger la parole de Dieu et celle de Smith & Wesson côte à côte. Tout comme il n'y avait que lui

pour passer d'une strip-teaseuse à une fervente charismatique. Il ouvrit le Livre au hasard et pointa son gros
index sur la page tout aussi aléatoirement. Il tomba
sur un passage du Psaume 18 et son visage irradia, en
proie à l'illumination.

— C'est fantastique, écoute-Le, écoute-Le me parler.
C'est le passage de l'Action de grâces… On vient juste
de la passer ensemble.

*Tu élargis le chemin sous mes pas, de sorte que
mes pieds ne chancellent jamais. Quand je poursuis
mes ennemis, je les atteins, et ne reviens pas que je
ne les ai anéantis.*

— C'est pas beau, ça ?

Long silence. Louis referma le Livre. Duval, par
respect, maintint sa position de recueillement, mais il
avait envie d'éclater de rire.

— J'arrive, reprit Louis. Mais à une condition.

— Laquelle ?

— Tu fais un *speech* sur la nécessité du pardon à la
messe de la police.

Duval n'allait pas dire qu'il avait déjà accepté la
proposition de l'aumônier.

— Louis, j'ai jamais senti le besoin de réfléchir là-
dessus.

— Eh bien, c'est le temps !

Duval roula des yeux, sourit et hocha la tête.

Louis referma la Bible, la déposa avec respect dans
le tiroir et accrocha son étui à la patère. Méchant Louis
était de retour.

17

La présence de Loulou dans leurs rangs combla d'enthousiasme les collègues. Quelques blagues fusèrent pour accueillir le Gros après cette longue absence. Duval expédia la meilleure vanne.

— Le retour de Louis devrait éviter la faillite des Marie-Antoinette en banlieue.

Frankie eut envie de lancer : «Loulou, tu ne tueras point», mais il craignit que Louis ne l'encaisse mal. Dans le passé, l'humour noir de Francis lui avait valu des remontrances de la part du Gros.

Duval ferma les rideaux et les lumières, alluma le rétroprojecteur et y déposa l'acétate. Les photos étaient choquantes. Autour d'un café et d'un beignet, chacun y allait de son hypothèse. La chasse au dément était lancée.

— Aucune empreinte. Le type utilise des gants, dit Daniel.

Louis se gratta le crâne et communiqua son idée.

— Ça pourrait pas avoir été fait dans le cadre de la chasse aux exploits des étudiants de l'Université Laval ?

Louis amorçait de piètre façon son retour. Duval, découragé, se prit la tête entre les mains.

— Louis, un peu de sérieux ! Qui voudrait revendiquer un geste pareil ? Une chienne éventrée, une main dérobée… C'est pas le festival des horreurs !

— Oui, mais aujourd'hui, les jeunes ne respectent plus rien. Puis l'Halloween s'en vient.

Francis leva l'index. La lampe du projecteur accentuait la longue éraflure qu'il avait au visage.

— Si la main a baigné dans le formol, on a peut-être affaire à un étudiant en médecine ou encore à un thanatologue…

— Pourquoi ? demanda Prince en expirant longuement sa fumée de cigarette.

— En médecine, les étudiants ont à travailler sur des cadavres, pas toujours récents, en thanato aussi. Il se peut que quelqu'un ait coupé la main d'un cadavre, d'autant plus qu'il semble utiliser des instruments de précision. Faudrait demander au docteur Villemure à qui il donne des cours de pathologie. Je sais que des thanatologues font aussi des stages au laboratoire de médecine légale.

Duval nota cette conjecture et se gratta nerveusement le cuir chevelu.

— Intéressant, Francis. Tu te rends à l'Université Laval. Tu rencontres le directeur de la Faculté de médecine. Prince s'occupera de la morgue.

— T'en profiteras pour demander à François de t'apporter un rôti d'orignal… gloussa Loulou. Ses coupes sont extra.

Prince écrasa sa cigarette et une épaisse fumée s'échappa de ses narines :

— Où vont les restes des corps donnés à la science ?

Duval laissa glisser une main sur son visage.

— Dans une fosse commune du cimetière de la Côte.

— Et les déchets biomédicaux ?

— Je crois qu'une compagnie les incinère. Il faudrait que je demande à Laurence.

— Quelqu'un aurait pu prendre une main et la maquiller pour faire une mauvaise blague.

— C'était un travail de professionnel.

Francis tambourina des doigts sur la table, se berça sur les deux pattes arrière de sa chaise, son visage passa de l'ombre à la lumière.

— Voilà deux premières pistes. Mais tant qu'on ne saura pas à qui appartient la main, on reste dans la grande noirceur. Les agents de sécurité à l'université sont comme nous, dans le noir.

— Le ou les propriétaires du chien disparu doivent être retracés, signala Louis.

— Oui. Pourrais-tu vérifier si on a relevé à la SPCA un avis de disparition pour un caniche ? lui demanda Duval.

— Je peux bien m'occuper de la chronique vétérinaire.

— Prince va te seconder. Rendez-vous à l'endroit où on a découvert l'animal. Ensuite, promenez-vous dans les rues de Sillery, faites une enquête de voisinage et cherchez des photos de toutous disparus. Je m'occupe du cimetière.

Duval déplaça l'acétate sur le plateau du projecteur et ajusta le foyer. En bon maître d'école, il se leva et pointa sa baguette sur l'écran.

— Voilà ce que nous avons :

1. *Une main de femme*
2. *Une chienne dépecée*
3. *Des messages misogynes (dont un écrit avec le sang du chien) : « Au bout de ton sang, femelle » et « Mes amours décomposés » (message enroulé autour d'un doigt)*
4. *Une éponge ensanglantée.*

Duval passa devant l'écran en frappant la paume de sa main avec la baguette.

— Plusieurs de ces éléments, qui semblent disparates, convergent. La main d'une femme, un animal femelle dépecé dont le sang a servi à inscrire un graffiti haineux. La femme est associée à l'animal, à la chienne de surcroît.

Le bout de la baguette martela le point trois :

— Le message vient d'un individu qui s'identifie à une souffrance, à la mort : psychose ? névrose ? Les deux messages allient amour et haine, mort et vengeance. À mon avis, on a affaire à un gars qui a de la suite dans les idées. Obsession marquée pour les cadavres, ce qui devrait nous inquiéter, et aversion pour les femmes, ce qui doit nous préoccuper encore davantage. Ce qui me dérange également, c'est ce chien étripé. On a remarqué chez plusieurs psychopathes qu'ils commencent par faire souffrir et par tuer des animaux. Ces types-là ont des pulsions sadiques extrêmement fortes. Ils prennent plaisir à la souffrance des autres et à s'infliger des sévices. Ils laissent également une signature. Son of Sam, il y a deux ans à New York, a expédié des lettres, dont certaines adressées directement à l'enquêteur Borelli, qui menait l'enquête.

— À une certaine période de ma vie, j'aurais aimé qu'une nymphomane m'écrive des messages cochons! gloussa Louis, qui communiqua son rire à tout le monde sauf à Daniel, qui avait toujours exécré ce type de quiproquo.

Prince allait parler quand Duval reçut un appel du standardiste. Un chroniqueur judiciaire voulait lui poser des questions sur l'affaire Fournier-Émond qui avait fait la une du *Journal de Québec*. Duval regarda son horaire.

— J'ai dix minutes à 16 h. À mon bureau.

Il raccrocha.

— On se revoit à 13 h pour faire le point à mon bureau. Bonne cueillette!

Alors que Louis ouvrait la porte de la salle de conférences, une engueulade retentit à l'autre bout du corridor. C'était Madden qui disait sa façon de penser à Pouliot, le sergent-adjoint. La tension grimpait comme un crescendo qui éclate dans un fracas de cymbales et de cuivres. Duval regarda Louis.

— L'examen s'est mal déroulé.

Madden bouillait, ses bras traçaient d'étranges arabesques dans les airs.

— Non, Pouliot ! T'as rien compris, crisse ! Comme d'habitude ! Tu vois juste ce que tu veux voir. Vous autres, tout ce que vous regardez, c'est la petite crotte dans mon dossier. Qu'est-ce que vous faites des vies que j'ai sauvées ? Des risques que j'ai pris pour aller aider quelqu'un en danger ? Après les battues, les familles que je dois réconforter ? Où est-ce que c'est dans mon dossier ? Non, vous revenez toujours à cette hostie d'histoire de citoyen que j'ai tabassé. Pouliot, t'es juste un enfant de chienne et toi, Malo, son lèche-cul, c'est connu.

La tension monta d'un autre cran. Madden empoigna Pouliot et le secoua comme un pommetier. Malo sauta alors dans le dos du maître-chien, ce qui ne surprit pas Duval. À grandes enjambées, le lieutenant et ses collègues se lancèrent à l'assaut du corridor avant que l'altercation dégénère : vingt mètres à faire claquer les talons sur le linoléum ciré.

À un mètre derrière, Louis, les bras comme les bielles d'une vieille locomotive, fonçait droit devant dans son fauteuil.

Duval arracha sans ménagement Malo à Madden, tandis que Prince s'interposait entre Pouliot et Madden, qui le fustigeait en postillonnant.

— Du calme, ici ! lança Duval.

Pouliot reçut l'injonction de Duval comme celle d'un colporteur qu'on n'attend pas après une querelle de ménage.

— Toi, mêle-toi pas de ça.

Samuel essaya d'atteindre Pouliot d'une droite. Le mal était fait. Louis, en bon pacificateur qu'il était devenu, s'interposa.

— Viens, Sammy.

— Non.

— Qu'est-ce qui se passe ?

— On me recale pour une crisse de niaiserie, une question piège. Ça se peut pas, dit le jeune homme en criant.

Louis fustigea du regard Pouliot et Malo. Il ne les aurait jamais cru assez culottés pour recaler Madden, dont le travail exemplaire avait été maintes fois remarqué. Ne venait-on pas de saluer son efficacité comme maître-chien ?

— Pourquoi vous lui donnez pas, son sacrament de grade ? lança Louis.

— Harel, ça dépasse tes compétences, lui balança Malo comme un crachat au visage.

Louis, qui avait souvent eu à en découdre avec Malo et Pouliot dans le passé, vira écarlate. Il avait beau prêcher la tolérance, il ne fallait pas le chercher, même en fauteuil roulant.

— Toi, Pouliot, et toi, Malo, vous êtes deux maudits pharisiens, deux hypocrites. Vous voyez la paille dans l'œil de votre prochain alors que vous avez un poteau de téléphone qui vous barre les deux yeux.

— Toi, Harel, viens pas nous écœurer avec la relish… Laisse ton tit-Jésus au ciel.

Une rotation d'épaules et Louis s'avança, écrasant, par inadvertance ou non, le pied de Malo sous la roue arrière de son fauteuil. Le grand blond poussa une plainte.

— Tasse ton crisse de fauteuil de su' mon pied !

— Excuse. Je t'avais pas vu.

Trois ans plus tôt, Louis avait asséné un violent coup de poing sur la gueule de Malo après que ce dernier l'eut traité de pédale, ce qui avait déclenché les hostilités.

Au cours de la mêlée, Madden pénétra dans un bureau, verrouilla la porte et se mit à briser le mobilier : éclats de verre, étagère renversée, bruits de fureur, craquements du bois qu'on fend dans la rage. Sidérés, les policiers ne savaient pas comment intervenir. Le charivari dura au moins une minute.

Essoufflement. Plus un mot ni un bruit.

— Sam, ouvre, demanda Louis. Ouvre-moi. On va jaser.

— ...

Louis se tourna vers Malo et Pouliot, qui restaient là comme deux imbéciles prêts à procéder à une arrestation. Duval s'interposa :

— Vous autres, allez-vous-en. Vous en avez assez fait comme ça. Votre journée est remplie encore une fois... Sacrez votre camp !

— Je m'en vais te faire un rapport.

Duval se plaça à six pouces du visage de Malo, son ennemi juré, avec vue sur les crevasses de sa peau de vipère.

— Malo, si jamais tu fais un rapport, je coule aux médias toutes les erreurs que vous avez commises quand toi et Pouliot avez pris en main l'affaire Hurtubise, le temps qu'on a perdu, l'histoire de l'épouvantail assassiné... Vous allez vivre l'enfer. Tu m'entends : y a rien qui va sortir d'ici. Toi aussi, Pouliot, tu comprends le message ?

— Tu parles à un supérieur, Duval.

— Ça, c'est une question de perception.

Venant de Duval, cette apostrophe était exceptionnelle. Mais de vieilles rancunes pourrissaient à l'Escouade des crimes contre la personne.

Malo, dont l'épiderme rubicond et poinçonné d'acné pissait de sueur, se banda comme un arc à l'idée que les journalistes se délectent de ses gaffes. Malo et Pouliot s'éloignèrent comme deux chiens battus qui faisaient une fois de plus l'unanimité contre eux.

Louis avisa Duval qu'il allait rester auprès de Madden. Dans la pièce, on entendit le maître-chien se mettre à marteler fébrilement la machine à écrire, ce qui inquiéta tout le monde.

— Sammy, ouvre, c'est Louis.

Mais son nez demeura longtemps contre la porte.

18

La journée lumineuse se réchauffait peu à peu. L'été des Indiens promis se poursuivait.

Monette, le directeur-général du cimetière de la Côte, accueillit Duval avec une certaine méfiance. Cette histoire ne pouvait que faire une mauvaise publicité à son cimetière. L'homme portait un complet vert lime, une cravate brune et ses cheveux gommés, parsemés de pellicules, semblaient avoir été peignés avec un râteau tellement les sillons étaient larges. La forme de son visage ressemblait à une poire renversée avec des yeux aussi petits qu'une olive et des lèvres totalement absentes. L'homme ne lui apprit rien de neuf. Duval savait qu'au printemps, avec le dégel qui remuait la terre, il arrivait que des morceaux de cercueils, poignées, bout de satin, vêtements, chaussures, restes humains et autres objets morbides remontent à la surface, ce qui rendait certains médias avides de photos et de commentaires salés : une belle première page pas chère et facile à vendre. *Mère Nature rapatrie ses morts*. Mais ce phénomène ne se produisait jamais à l'automne.

— Pouvez-vous me parler de votre personnel ?

— Irréprochable. Mes employés font leur travail avec professionnalisme.

— Dans le passé, rien à signaler ?

— Non plus.

Duval demanda à voir l'emplacement de la fosse commune.

La marche dans les allées paisibles du cimetière l'apaisa. Les arbres laissaient pleuvoir leurs grosses feuilles. Le soleil d'automne coulait sa lumière à travers le feuillage jaune et rouge. Des écureuils, funambules du règne animal, couraient sur les écorces et sautaient de branche en branche, en quête de provisions. D'imposants mausolées et des statues impressionnantes jetaient de l'ombre sur les pierres tombales plus modestes. Même dans la mort, les différences de classe s'affichaient au grand jour, songea Duval.

Une excavatrice jaune les dépassa, suivie d'un camion dans lequel des hommes d'entretien étaient assis. Monette les salua et des mains nonchalantes lui répondirent.

Ils passèrent dans la partie déclive du cimetière où se dressaient de petites croix de fer rouillées : dernier reposoir des pauvres. Le directeur lui expliqua qu'il s'agissait de familles qui ne pouvaient se payer un lot pour une longue période. Une sorte de location pour dix ans.

La fosse commune était située près de la pente, dans un boisé qui menait au boulevard Charest. Horrible endroit pour faire reposer des restes. Le vrombissement des véhicules en contrebas envahissait cette partie du cimetière.

Le directeur sortit son mouchoir en tissu et déboucha son nez enchifrené. Il stoppa devant le charnier, un carré qui faisait environ trente mètres de côté.

— C'est ici.

— Comment se déroule l'enfouissement ?

— On reçoit le matériel de l'université ou de la morgue. L'excavatrice creuse et on ensevelit les morceaux de corps, les corps ou les organes.

— Vous voulez dire que cette terre est fréquemment retournée et que tout est mélangé ?

— Oui. On est tenus de creuser au minimum à un mètre pour des raisons d'hygiène, mais il arrive, avec l'excavatrice, que les restes soient revirés.

— Donc, il serait possible pour quelqu'un de repartir avec un trophée ?

— Voyons, inspecteur ! Pensez-vous que mes gars feraient une chose pareille ?

Le directeur avait la susceptibilité à fleur de peau. « Vous connaissez mal la nature humaine », aurait voulu lui rétorquer le lieutenant.

— Est-ce possible pour quiconque de venir chercher ce qu'il veut ?

— Il n'y a pas de surveillance la nuit. Mais qui connaît l'existence de cette fosse commune et voudrait y déterrer des restes ?

— Vous creusez donc au moins quatre pieds ?

— Oui.

— Moi, je trouve que c'est assez facile pour quelqu'un de prendre un souvenir…

— Mais on s'en rendrait compte : on replace de la tourbe après avoir remblayé.

Duval marcha sur le site et l'examina attentivement. Il avait peine à croire qu'en dessous se dissimulait une morgue de corps sans identité, de cobayes anonymes. En bon jardinier, Duval remarqua la qualité de la pelouse. « Pas étonnant, avec un compost organique de première qualité », pensa-t-il, mais il préféra garder ses considérations horticoles pour lui. La nature tirait profit même de la pourriture humaine.

Duval se redressa et tourna le dos à l'affreuse nécropole.

19

Duval s'était habitué, au fil des ans, à tolérer l'odeur de formaldéhyde. Il entendit crier son nom au bout du corridor blanc de néons. Quand il mettait les pieds au laboratoire de la rue Semple, il revoyait les collègues du boulevard Saint-Cyrille.

La préposée à l'accueil l'avisa que le docteur Villemure l'attendait dans son bureau.

Debout derrière un comptoir, François procédait à un examen microscopique. Sur la lame se trouvait un prélèvement de foie. Grossi des centaines de fois, l'échantillon ressemblait à une tranche de salami. Sur le moniteur, on voyait un « foie gras », comme il les appelait. Le cytoplasme des hépatocytes était gorgé de bulles de gras, maladie dégénérative entraînant une formation excessive de tissus conjonctifs qui contractaient l'organe. Villemure inscrivit la cause de la mort sur son rapport : « Cirrhose du foie » et « Hémorragie de l'estomac ». Puis il le signa.

Duval posa un doigt sur l'épaule du docteur et s'assit sur une chaise.

— Salut, François. Ça va ?

Villemure tourna la tête, fixa Duval de ses yeux bleus glacés.

— Après cette fin de semaine-là, c'est dur de se remettre au travail. Avec plus de vingt ans de métier, je peux dire qu'il est plus agréable de congeler un orignal que tous ces corps avec des points d'interrogation.

Le bureau de Villemure se voulait un modèle d'ordre, tout était à sa place. Sur l'étagère s'alignaient les ouvrages importants de pathologie et de médecine légale avec des titres tout aussi inspirants les uns que les autres : *The Pathology of Trauma, Craniofacial Identification in Forensic Medicine, Wounds* et ses propres manuels, ceux qu'il utilisait dans ses cours : *Morts suspectes et Scènes de crimes* et son *Précis de médecine légale*, son best-seller, s'amusait-il à dire. Mais à cent dollars l'unité, les étudiants en pathologie trouvaient la blague moins drôle. Sur un lutrin trônait une édition originale des *Expertises en armes à feu* de Wilfrid Derome, un livre de collection. Son diplôme en pathologie de l'Université de Montréal et de nombreux certificats amassés partout dans le monde étaient affichés. Il avait accroché la photo de son maître, le docteur Rosario Fontaine, celui qui avait remplacé le docteur Wilfrid Derome, le fondateur de l'Institut de recherches médico-légales et de police technique de Montréal. François avait le sens des traditions et savait que le labo de Montréal avait été le premier en Amérique. Vingt ans avant la création du labo du FBI, celui de Montréal avait ouvert la voie dans les sciences judiciaires partout en Amérique. Dans les colloques aux États-Unis, il ne manquait jamais l'occasion de le mentionner, même si le fait heurtait le chauvinisme de ses collègues américains.

Sur le mur derrière son bureau en acajou était accrochée une reproduction du célèbre tableau de Rembrandt, *La leçon d'anatomie du docteur Tulp,* qu'il avait fait encadrer. Quelques dessins réalisés par des enfants rendaient les lieux plus joyeux.

Duval pivota sur sa chaise :

— Crois-tu que la main retrouvée puisse appartenir à quelqu'un qui se trouve parmi les corps non réclamés ?

— Tu sais bien qu'on a vérifié. Et, comme je l'ai écrit dans le rapport, cette main avait été traitée et maquillée de façon professionnelle. Par qui d'autre que par un thanatologue ?

— D'après toi, est-ce qu'un étudiant en médecine aurait pu s'emparer de cette main pour faire une farce ?

— Tu sais, j'ai tout vu, et plus rien ne m'étonne en crimino. Mais j'aurais des réserves, parce que cette main a été coupée avec une certaine minutie. J'ai l'impression que celui que tu cherches connaît quelques principes chirurgicaux. C'est ce que j'ai pu constater en me rendant à la SPCA pour examiner le chien.

— Un étudiant en médecine vétérinaire ?

Villemure pinça les lèvres.

— Non. Ces gens-là aiment trop les animaux.

Le médecin légiste cacheta l'enveloppe adressée au coroner. Cartier, un anthropologue légiste, apparut dans l'embrasure de la porte.

— Docteur Villemure, j'ai une question à vous poser : je travaille sur un noyé qui a été repêché dans une étrange position.

L'homme prit une pose qui rappelait celle du pugiliste : les bras parallèles, presque coude à coude, et les poings à la hauteur du visage.

Villemure sourcilla.

— Ce n'est pas normal. Habituellement, les corps se détendent dans l'eau, les bras s'écartent, dit Villemure en mimant la position du corps. Il n'était pas attaché ?

— On s'est peut-être débarrassé de la corde avant de le jeter à l'eau alors qu'il était déjà dans un état de raideur cadavérique, intervint Duval.

— J'irai voir ça tout à l'heure, dit Villemure en roulant des yeux.

L'homme le remercia et regagna sa table de travail.

— En passant, François, c'est toi qui as poussé pour que j'obtienne l'affaire ?

— Oui, c'est moi qui ai fait des pressions.

— Pourquoi ?

— Parce qu'on a toutes les raisons de craindre le pire…

20

Devant la centrale, il aperçut des punks et un dalmatien qui sautillait autour d'eux. Les punks se donnaient des coups de pied en riant. Drôle de jeu, pensa Duval.

En voyant sortir du Grand Théâtre une musicienne avec son étui à violon, il pensa à Mimi qui étudiait au Conservatoire.

Sa fille voulait inviter son barbu à souper, encouragée par Laurence, qui poussait pour que le repas ait lieu. Duval avait autant envie de le rencontrer que d'avoir un tête-à-tête avec Charles Manson, si bien qu'il avançait des dates hypothétiques constamment reportées.

Il avait sur le cœur la question que lui avait posée Mimi la veille. Elle lui trottait encore dans la tête : « Papa, est-ce que t'as participé aux rafles de la SQ pendant la crise d'Octobre ? On habitait Montréal, à l'époque. »

Il ne l'avait pas encore digérée, sachant que cette question était celle de ce petit gauchiste pouilleux qui l'adressait par l'entremise de Mimi. Mimi n'était pas politisée, la question ne pouvait venir que de lui.

Duval entra à la centrale et grimpa deux à deux les marches du grand escalier qui menait à l'étage. Au bout du corridor, un groupuscule s'était formé autour de Louis. Madden n'était pas encore sorti de son repaire. Le lieutenant s'approcha de l'attroupement. Louis, penché, le visage collé sur la porte, reprit pour la énième fois son laïus.

— J'ai l'assurance de Dallaire qu'il ne t'arrivera rien, Samuel. Ouvre, dit Louis d'une voix douce. On passe l'éponge. Le syndicat est derrière toi.

L'autre ne soufflait mot et continuait de faire crépiter les touches de sa machine à écrire. Louis roula des yeux, expira, leva la tête vers Duval.

— En tout cas, si c'est une lettre de démission, le gamin en a long sur le cœur. As-tu une idée ? Parce que moi, j'ai tout épuisé…

Duval réfléchit un instant, massa avec le pouce et l'index ses paupières.

— Samuel, c'est Daniel. Ouvre-moi. J'aimerais qu'on parle… Allez.

Mais aucun signal de la part de Madden, hormis cette furie de frappes. Dallaire s'amena d'un pas lourd et, d'un signe de tête, demanda à Louis s'il y avait du nouveau.

— Non, il continue de faire du boudin.

Duval mit une main sur l'épaule de Louis.

— Sneak est au chenil ?

Louis acquiesça de la tête. Duval leva l'index.

— J'ai une idée.

Il s'élança à la course et disparut dans le grand escalier. Il revint deux minutes plus tard avec Sneak qui tirait sur sa laisse. Lorsque le berger tourna le coin du corridor et qu'il sentit l'odeur de son maître, il se rua vers le bureau. Duval fut incapable de le retenir. Sneak arriva à la hauteur du fauteuil roulant de Louis, jappant, geignant. Il flairait quelque chose de bizarre. Il glapit de nouveau, la langue pendante, le museau collé contre la poignée, puis il se cambra et renifla le seuil et parvint à insérer l'extrémité de ses pattes sous la porte. Les geignements et les jappements se firent plus insistants.

— Ça veut dire : « Ouvre, Sam, j'ai un boulot à faire », cabotina Louis.

Dallaire sourit. Puis la frénésie de frappes cessa. On entendit le recul de la chaise sur le linoléum. Duval suggéra aux collègues de s'éloigner. Trente secondes plus tard, la porte s'entrebâilla lentement, comme si un mystérieux fantôme l'avait ouverte. Sneak se faufila et se jeta sur Madden. Louis se donna deux bonnes poussées et aperçut le chien debout sur ses pattes de derrière, enlacé par Madden. Loulou se tourna et leva le pouce pour signifier que tout allait bien. Chien et maître réunis, le premier consolant l'autre. Louis signala par un geste de la main que Madden pleurait et leur fit signe de s'éloigner. Il allait intervenir. La pièce était sens dessus dessous.

Dallaire, appuyé contre le mur de biais à la porte, s'avança.

— Je vais aller le voir.

— Non, je m'en occupe, dit Louis.

La porte se referma lentement derrière lui.

21

Derrière la table de travail croulant sous les documents, Louis et Francis consultaient des dossiers judiciaires. On n'apercevait que leurs visages derrière les monticules de papier.

Duval entra dans la pièce, tira sur un verre conique en carton. Il se pencha et appuya sur le bouton de la fontaine, qui implosa d'une grosse bulle pendant que son verre se remplissait.

— C'est sérieux, ici !

— La récolte est amaigrissante.

— Prince est dans les parages ?

— Non, il lui restait des vérifications à faire, dit Louis.

Duval se tourna vers Francis.

— Qu'est-ce que t'as trouvé ?

— *Niet*. Pas de Mister Hyde à l'université. Aucun étudiant suspect. On a vérifié les corps dans le formol et tous ont leurs mains. Rien d'anormal.

— Louis ?

— Avec l'histoire de Madden, j'ai juste eu le temps d'apprendre qu'aucun caniche disparu n'avait été signalé à la SPCA.

— En ce qui me concerne, rien de concluant au cimetière de la Côte. Par contre, je viens de recevoir un rapport de la section Documents du labo et on y fait remarquer que tous les textes sont écrits sans faute, ce qui me laisse croire que le type est instruit, qu'il éprouve sans doute un faible pour les lettres.

Prince arriva tout en sueur, hors d'haleine, avec du neuf. Cigarette au coin des lèvres, le colosse alla à la fontaine et remplit son verre, qu'il cala d'un trait pour l'emplir de nouveau et le boire cul sec. Il s'épongea le front avec la manche de sa chemise, dénoua sa cravate.

— J'ai ratissé le secteur avec deux gars de l'Identité et on a trouvé ça.

Il déposa un sac de papier sur la table et en sortit une laisse à laquelle une médaille était accrochée.

— La chienne s'appelait Doric. On a découvert le collier au fond d'une poubelle près du pavillon Pouliot.

Le visage de Duval s'illumina, car il s'agissait d'un indice important.

— D'autres indices ?

— J'ai l'adresse de la maîtresse : une veuve, retraitée, une dame Turner. Elle n'avait pas avisé la SPCA, persuadée que son chien allait revenir. Pour le reste, je n'ai pu me rendre au collège Jésus-Marie, on a mis beaucoup de temps à fouiller le secteur du boisé de l'Université Laval.

Duval se frotta les mains.

— Parfait, je m'en occupe avec Louis. Vous allez de votre côté éplucher les dossiers de cas bizarres, les maniaques sexuels qui ont été libérés récemment, de même que les déficients mentaux en circulation. Vérifiez aussi si on n'aurait pas des cas de profanation de cimetière dans nos archives.

Prince afficha une moue découragée.

— Aussi bien brûler la botte de foin pour trouver l'aiguille.

22

Madame Turner habitait une grande maison de plain-pied ultramoderne juchée sur un talus : une forteresse de granit généreusement fenestrée. La maison était entourée de peupliers de Lombardie, de longues fusées végétales. Dans l'entrée du garage, une Cadillac rouge et blanche décapotable des années cinquante, avec ses grandes ailes futuristes, ajoutait excentricité et luxe.

Pour une première enquête sur le terrain depuis son accident, Louis était mal tombé. Il fallait monter une quinzaine de marches avant d'atteindre le heurtoir en cuivre.

Malgré les progrès de sa physiothérapie, Louis n'était pas encore prêt à recourir uniquement à des béquilles. Ses jambes lui semblaient comme des chiffes molles tenues par des baguettes chinoises.

— Tu vas devoir y aller en poussant par-derrière.

Duval fit pivoter le fauteuil à cent quatre-vingts degrés.

— Maudite maison de péteux ! pesta Louis. On dirait que toutes ces marches-là, c'est juste pour qu'on regarde la maison plus longtemps.

— Allez, on y va.

Le heurtoir à tête de lion s'abattit trois fois avec force sur la porte noire.

Une main tremblante rabattit le rideau en dentelle de Bruges du salon. La vieille dame jeta un coup d'œil sur les colporteurs.

La première porte s'ouvrit lentement. Une ombre longiligne se mut derrière la vitre givrée au jet de sable de l'autre porte. La vieille dame se montra d'abord méfiante mais retrouva confiance quand Duval tendit ses papiers. L'index rougi, rachitique et ridé de la femme se posa sur un bouton posé dans sa gorge qui lui permettait de parler.

— Bonjour, messieurs.

Sa voix, ainsi amplifiée, retentit comme dans un ampli agonisant qui sonne la tôle froissée. Son français était correct malgré un accent anglais très prononcé. En voilà une autre qui avait trop fumé, pensa Duval. La voix caverneuse, ébréchée, les cordes vocales toutes de crin faisaient mal à entendre. Le son semblait sortir d'une radio des années trente.

La dame portait une barrette en cuir qui retenait son chignon gris. Elle était le portrait type de la vieille Anglaise pleine de dignité qui prend d'assaut sa coiffeuse dès 7 h du matin pour se maquiller, même si elle ne verra personne de la journée. Son cardigan vert pomme et sa jupe noire lui donnaient l'air d'une ancienne maîtresse d'école austère qu'on n'oublie jamais.

— Entrez. *Come in.*

Duval manœuvra le fauteuil avec délicatesse pour ne rien heurter.

Heureusement, la porte était large.

Des miroirs étaient accrochés partout dans la maison, qui sentait le bouilli et le chou, ce qui leva le cœur de Duval et mit Louis en appétit.

— Voulez-vous du thé ou du café ?

— Non, merci, répondit Duval, tandis que Louis déclinait l'offre avec dépit d'un signe de tête.

D'un geste de la main, elle les invita à passer au salon. Elle s'assit dans une bergère rouge, se croisa les jambes.

— Madame Turner, vous savez ce qui est arrivé à votre chien ?

La vieille dame se rembrunit.

— *Poor* Doric… dit-elle en saisissant une photo encadrée du caniche.

Duval craignit qu'elle se mette à pleurer et il ne lui laissa pas un espace de silence.

— Avait-il l'habitude de fuguer ?

— Oui, mais il revenait tout le temps.

— À quel moment y'a décampé ? demanda Louis.

Elle eut du mal à comprendre son accent et grimaça.

— *What ?*

— *When did he vanished ?* reprit Duval.

— Il a disparaître depuis jeudi matin.

Duval, le dos penché en avant, colla ses mains comme pour une prière. Ses index frappaient l'arc dentaire supérieur.

— Soupçonnez-vous quelqu'un dans le quartier ?

— Certainement, les jeunes.

Duval, pour qui l'usage de l'article indéfini ou défini faisait toute une différence dans son travail, l'interrompit.

— Vous voulez dire quelqu'un en particulier ?

— *No.*

— Avez-vous été victime d'intimidation ?

— *No.*

— Est-ce que votre chien jappait ou faisait ses besoins sur le terrain d'un propriétaire qui aurait voulu se venger ? s'enquit Louis.

— *No*, je ne pense pas. *He never barked* et il était *very clean.*

— Avait-il peur des étrangers ?

— Non, il va devant le monde et se montrait beaucoup affectueux.

Duval regarda Louis. C'était là sans doute le drame de Doric. Duval ne pourrait rien tirer de plus de madame Turner.

— Il faut poursuivre l'enquête de voisinage, dit Louis en se tournant vers Duval. Notre gars habite à proximité.

— *Oh ! My God !*

Elle afficha un rictus qui déplissa son visage. Celui-ci ressemblait à un masque de cire. Duval tenta de la rassurer, mais les dommages étaient faits.

— Pas nécessairement. Il peut travailler de jour et rentrer chez lui, loin d'ici, après le boulot.

Duval referma son calepin noir et se leva en remerciant madame Turner. Louis, qui ne cessait de reluquer la belle bonbonnière, demanda s'il pouvait se servir avant de partir et la vieille dame lui en donna une poignée en riant.

— Oui ! Tenez ! Prenez ça ! Vous donnez ça à vos enfants.

23

Puisqu'ils étaient à proximité du poste de police de Sillery, Duval décida d'aller poser des questions aux policiers. Ils en profiteraient pour casser la croûte dans la rue Maguire. L'enquêteur qui s'était d'abord rendu sur les lieux, le capitaine Plante, les accueillit sans enthousiasme.

Plante, bien empâté sous la ceinture, teignait ses cheveux avec Gracian Formula et entretenait mal sa moustache, dont les poils envahissaient sa lèvre supérieure et s'emmêlaient à ceux des narines. Son nez ressemblait à une coquille Saint-Jacques tellement il était aplati, « forcément de se l'être trop décrotté », pensa Louis.

Plante semblait écroué et cimenté dans son fauteuil tandis qu'il écoutait Duval.

— Avez-vous eu récemment des cas de cruauté animale sur votre territoire ?

Le policier posa une main sur son menton et réfléchit.

— Non, pas récemment.

— Dans le passé ? dit Louis.

— Oui, mais il s'agissait de mineurs et leurs dossiers ont été retirés des classeurs à leur majorité.

— Des cas qui vous reviennent en mémoire ?

— Non.

L'air bête et peu avenant de Plante souleva l'ire de Loulou.

— Perdons pas notre temps, Daniel, on va avoir plus de chance en interrogeant la clôture du collège Jésus-Marie. En tout cas, si j'entends des citoyens inquiets se plaindre de l'enquête, je leur rappellerai votre collaboration… Viens, dit Louis.

Duval, qui n'avait pourtant pas d'ordre à recevoir de Louis, se plia naturellement à l'injonction. Il tourna les talons, saisit les guidons du fauteuil et poussa Louis vers la sortie. Quel drôle de couple ils devaient former maintenant, songea le lieutenant.

Ils arrêtèrent au restaurant Saint-Germain. Loulou avala un club sandwich avec des frites et Duval prit une salade César et une soupe en entrée.

Louis, qui ne confiait presque jamais ses sentiments, avoua qu'il se sentait heureux.

— C'est bon d'être de retour. La paperasse, je commençais…

— T'es un gars de terrain.

— Je sais que ça va faire jaser. Je suis en chaise roulante.

— C'est mieux que de ne plus avoir sa tête. On s'en sacre de ce que les autres pensent. On va mener nos enquêtes comme avant et on prendra un peu plus de temps pour le transport.

Louis télescopa une cuillerée de pouding au riz dans sa bouche.

— Mais quand on va enquêter dans un champ, dans le bois, dans des endroits inaccessibles ? Je vais être aussi efficace que Doug Jarvis sur l'attaque à cinq du Canadien.

— On s'arrangera. Frankie ou Bernard prendront la relève.

24

La vieille école centenaire d'inspiration néoclassique couronnait la falaise qui dominait le fleuve. Le bâtiment de quatre étages en vieilles pierres avait été construit au siècle dernier : une impressionnante muraille percée de fenêtres cintrées aux arcs surbaissés. Sur le toit mansardé en tôle de baguettes se dressait un superbe dôme argenté qui servait de puits de lumière.

Le chemin large qui menait à l'entrée, entouré d'arbres et de verdure, finissait en rond-point devant la porte d'entrée. Duval y stationna la Chevrolet. Le portique, surmonté d'un balcon aux balustrades ouvragées, était soutenu par des colonnes.

Heureusement, une rampe permettait aux gens en fauteuil roulant d'accéder à l'entrée principale. Les religieuses pensaient à tout.

À l'intérieur de l'établissement, Duval fut saisi par la beauté des lieux et l'atmosphère toute monacale qui y régnait : boiseries, vitraux, planchers de bois franc étincelaient.

Une statue de la Vierge dans sa robe turquoise foulant du pied un serpent accueillait les visiteurs. Une étudiante en retard courait dans un corridor avec ses livres sous le bras et sa queue de cheval se balançait à chaque enjambée. L'ombre de Duval et du fauteuil roulant de Louis se projetait loin devant eux en une étrange composition de lignes. De longues épées de lumière perçaient en oblique le sombre corridor. Une voix résonna :

— Mademoiselle, vous n'avez pas le droit de courir.

Un voile noir apparut à l'extérieur d'une salle de classe. La sœur s'attarda un instant à examiner les deux hommes, présence qui ne manquait jamais d'impressionner les jeunes filles en ce lieu où l'on matait momentanément les désirs féminins. Duval s'en rendait bien compte désormais. Sa fille Mimi, dont l'*alma mater* était l'école des Ursulines, avait eu trois copains en un an.

Au milieu du corridor, un superbe escalier en chêne foncé et à la rampe ouvragée s'élevait gracieusement vers l'étage.

Ils s'approchèrent de la religieuse, qui leur rendit un regard méfiant.

— Bonjour, ma sœur, dit Louis, on voudrait parler à la directrice.

— Vous la trouverez à son bureau, suivez le corridor jusqu'au bout.

Duval se demanda comment ces sœurs cloîtrées avaient pu survivre derrière ces murs, une prison avec Dieu comme seule consolation et seul amant.

Le lieutenant frappa sur la porte identifiée au nom de sœur Laurette Pineau.

Elle accueillit Duval avec courtoisie et lui serra la main d'une poigne qui justifiait son titre de Mère supérieure et de directrice générale. Une main veineuse et osseuse pareille à une serre. Duval, forte stature, cachait Louis et la sœur écarquilla les yeux en l'apercevant dans son fauteuil.

— Excusez-moi, à cause de ce gaillard-là, je ne vous avais pas vu, dit-elle, enjouée.

— Je suis habitué, ma sœur. Ça fait dix ans que je suis dans l'ombre de monsieur.

— Je ne vous crois pas, mais là pas du tout, répondit-elle en riant.

Elle portait de petites lunettes à monture bon marché en plastique. Les verres épais créaient, selon un certain angle, des effets de loupe qui rendaient ses yeux bleus menaçants.

— Vous êtes détectives ?

— Vous avez deviné ? dit Louis.

— Vous avez l'air d'une police ! s'exclama-t-elle.

Duval prit la remarque avec le sourire.

— Vous êtes messieurs…

— Je vous présente mon collègue Louis Harel, et moi, c'est Daniel Duval.

— Monsieur Duval, je vous replace, je vous ai vu dans le journal l'autre jour : le meurtre de la pauvre dame de Lac-Beauport. C'est terrible, cette histoire !

Duval hocha la tête affirmativement, même s'il n'avait pas envie de s'étendre là-dessus. Les affaires classées ont du bon, dans la mesure justement où elles sont classées.

— Vous venez pour la main ?

— Oui. On m'a confié l'enquête.

— Dieu soit loué. Les parents sont très inquiets. On organise une neuvaine, ce soir…

« J'espère qu'elle ne s'attend pas à ce que j'y aille et que Louis ne proposera pas qu'on s'y rende », pensa Duval.

— Heureusement, c'est le jardinier qui a trouvé la main et non une étudiante. Imaginez le choc pour nos petites filles !

La veine saillante et tortueuse de sa tempe droite battait à la cadence de son pouls. Elle parlait avec un accent suave et un véritable plaisir à mordre dans les mots, à en faire gicler toutes les harmoniques possibles. Mais le ton laissait percevoir la gravité de la situation. Dans la pièce du haut résonnait le piano d'une sœur musicienne qui répandait ses gammes en triolets sur plusieurs octaves. Dans une autre pièce, une chanteuse soprano poussait ses arpèges toujours plus haut.

— Est-ce que des étudiantes se sont plaintes de quelque chose, d'un rôdeur, de quelqu'un de bizarre ?

Les yeux de sœur Pineau s'écarquillèrent comme de gros bulbes bleus et blancs aux mots « rôdeur » et « bizarre ».

— On a déjà épinglé des voyeurs dans le passé, mais pas récemment.

— Les étudiantes auraient-elles aperçu un individu suspect ?

Le visage de la directrice affichait un air dévasté. Elle plissait les yeux en s'imaginant les pires horreurs.

— Arrêtez, lieutenant, vous me faites peur.

— Ma sœur, je dois vous poser toutes ces questions.

— Voulez-vous visiter notre chapelle ?

— Non, merci. Nous avons beaucoup de travail.

Louis regardait la photo agrandie en noir et blanc d'une jeune femme.

— C'est Dina Bélanger, notre inspiration, l'informa la sœur.

Soudainement, la tête de Louis glissa de la sœur à la grande fenêtre qui donnait sur la partie est de la cour. Il roula son fauteuil jusqu'à la fenêtre et y plongea un regard trouble. Les yeux tourmentés de la religieuse auraient bien voulu savoir ce que l'enquêteur Harel avait vu dans le cimetière qui jouxtait la façade est du bâtiment. La communauté y enterrait ses sœurs depuis le siècle dernier. Duval s'approcha à son tour. Il sut tout de suite ce que Louis pensait. Devant eux se dressait un petit charnier en pierre des champs au toit en pignon et surmonté d'une croix argentée.

— Vous avez l'air inquiet ? dit la directrice en appuyant sur chaque syllabe. Est-ce que je me trompe ?

— Excusez-moi, ma sœur. Mais je veux parler à mon collègue.

— Vous m'angoissez, là ! lança la directrice générale.

— Ce ne sera pas long.

Louis entraîna Duval au fond du bureau près de la seconde fenêtre en ogive.

— Louis, tu vas lui causer une syncope avec tes manières, murmura Duval dans la grosse oreille de Loulou.

Louis chuchota à son tour son hypothèse à l'oreille du lieutenant.

— Écoute-moi, la main était piquée sur la clôture. Comme tu remarques, à cet endroit, il y a un boisé. Où a-t-il pu se procurer cette main sinon dans le charnier qui s'y trouve ? Il entre par effraction, ce n'est pas surveillé, coupe la main, zling zling…

Duval afficha une moue sceptique.

— Il s'agit d'une main ayant appartenu à une jeune femme. Excuse-moi de briser tes fantasmes, mais des sœurs jeunes, il y en a de moins en moins…

— Toi ! dit Louis en pouffant de rire comme un gamin mal élevé.

Il n'était pas habitué à ce type d'humour de la part de son partenaire.

L'hypothèse offrait un certain intérêt et Duval s'informa aussitôt auprès de sœur Pineau qui était demeurée là à se faire du mauvais sang.

— Est-ce que le charnier est encore utilisé ?

— Comme nous enterrons nos religieuses dans notre cimetière, nous utilisons le charnier pour conserver les corps durant l'hiver, et au dégel nous inhumons nos disparues.

— Est-ce qu'une jeune sœur y aurait été entre-posée… Pardon, reprit Louis, conservée ?

La sœur pinça les lèvres. Duval aurait voulu s'arra-cher les cheveux. Quand Louis prenait les commandes d'un interrogatoire, les lapsus les plus idiots fusaient.

— La dernière avait soixante-cinq ans. C'était l'hiver dernier.

Pour Duval, l'hypothèse de Louis était morte et enterrée. Il regarda l'heure.

— Allons voir ce que Francis et Bernard ont trouvé.

Ils la remercièrent avant de tourner les talons.

— Vous nous tenez au courant ?

— Oui, ne craignez rien, ma sœur.

De grands rais de lumière sortaient des endroits où les portes de classes étaient ouvertes. La poussière dansait à travers la lumière. Duval et Louis passèrent en silence de l'ombre à la lumière jusqu'à la grande porte.

25

— Puis, ça avance, ici ? demanda Duval.

Francis et Bernard épluchaient des dossiers à la recherche d'individus arrêtés pour des actes de perver-sion dans les dernières années. Duval s'approcha, se pencha sur un document que parcourait Prince.

La nuque carrée de Bernard, entre ses larges épaules, glissait lentement d'une marge à l'autre d'un dossier. Il avait rempli une page de notes.

Prince laissa rouler son stylo devant lui.

— Du neuf ? répéta Duval.

— Non, rien de nouveau. On trouve rien dans les archives. Il y a bien ce maniaque qui entrait par effraction chez les gonzesses pour leur sucer le gros orteil mais rien d'autre.

— J'ai parlé à un responsable de la gestion des déchets médicaux dans un hôpital, dit Francis, mais rien d'intéressant. Ah oui ! Miljours, de la section Documents, a appelé pour dire que le gars lit des *comics*, des bandes dessinées de superhéros. C'est là qu'il aurait découpé les lettres pour écrire le message attaché à la main.

— Intéressant, conclut Duval. Est-ce qu'il existe des abonnements à ces magazines ou il faut les acheter dans les comptoirs de revues ?

— Les deux sont possibles, dit Francis. On vérifie les abonnements.

— Vous autres ? demanda Bernard.

Duval expira. Une journée à oublier.

— Rien.

Louis entra dans la pièce. Le lieutenant flaira qu'il continuait de fumer en catimini, lui qui avait juré de mettre fin à son vice. Ses vêtements froissés sentaient la fumée. Il avait beau mâcher de la Dentyne rouge, avaler du Listerine et sucer des menthes, Duval n'était pas dupe : le Gros s'était trouvé un coin dans la centrale où griller en paix des cigarettes.

— Qu'est-ce qu'on fait ? demanda Louis.

Duval ramena ses cheveux vers l'arrière, mais une couette rebelle retomba sur son front. Puis il regarda l'heure. La trotteuse rouge de l'horloge Westclock semblait retenue par une force invisible. Il décréta la journée de travail terminée.

— Je vais aller faire mon rapport au capitaine. On se remet à l'ouvrage demain. Pour l'instant on est crevés. On ferme la boutique !

26

En sueur, Duval se laissa choir sur le banc du vestibule, délaça ses chaussures de sport. Il consulta sa montre et calcula avoir maintenu une moyenne de quatre minutes et quinze secondes au kilomètre, ce qui lui donnerait un temps respectable au marathon de Washington.

Un coup de semelle sur le renfort et il envoya valser la première chaussure sur une circulaire et fit pareil avec l'autre. Il sentit toute la chaleur enfermée dans la chaussure se dissiper. Couché sur le plancher de bois franc, il effectua plusieurs étirements musculaires. Il apprécia la fraîcheur du merisier. La sueur collait au plancher et créait un effet de succion. Duval se redressa en nage, alla à la cuisine et étancha sa soif avec un grand verre d'eau qui ruissela dans sa gorge.

À l'étage, Mimi et Frédéric discutaient dans la chambre, la porte fermée. La voix traînante du garçon, qui semblait avaler les syllabes, allait avec sa dégaine je-m'en-foutiste, se dit-il. Il n'avait pas appris à sa fille à parler par ellipses et le joual l'horripilait.

Mimi se mit à jouer le morceau de Debussy qu'elle préparait pour son examen de flûte traversière.

Sur le tableau de la cuisine, elle avait écrit à la craie un message annonçant que Laurence venait souper. Duval avala un autre verre d'eau et monta se doucher.

En passant devant la porte de la chambre de sa fille, il sentit une odeur qu'il prit pour du pot. Il faillit sortir de ses gonds et vider le garçon de la maison. Mais, après moult frétillements de narines, il s'aperçut qu'il s'agissait de tabac Drum, le même que fumait un ami d'enfance. Il pensa à la question embarrassante de Mimi. Ces allusions à son rôle dans la crise d'Octobre ne passaient toujours pas.

Devant la glace, il s'observa et parut satisfait de la forme qu'il maintenait à son âge. Malheureusement, cette masse de muscles à traîner avait toujours représenté un handicap pour lui qui espérait devenir un grand marathonien. Trop lourd, trop osseux. Un gabarit de coureur de courte distance. « Tu te rendras même pas aux jeux du Commonwealth », lui avait dit un jour en toute franchise l'entraîneur du centre Claude-Robillard.

Il fila sous la douche et fredonna une chanson de Chet Baker. Puis il entendit *Si doucement* d'Harmonium qui jouait dans la chambre de Mimi.

Il se savonna amplement avec un gel de corps et émergea de la nuée de vapeur l'esprit et le corps reposés.

Laurence entra tout en liesse vers 18 h. Elle avait réussi à réanimer un enfant alors que toute l'équipe médicale s'apprêtait à lancer la serviette.

Duval la prit par la taille, la blottit contre lui et l'embrassa.

Il lui caressa le visage.

— Ma blonde fait des miracles, dit Daniel.

— Et toi, tu es mon dieu !

Il la souleva et la serra contre lui à lui en faire craquer les vertèbres.

— Belle journée ? lui demanda Laurence en se déchaussant.

— Un concentré de merde en canne. On piétine.

Le solo de clarinette de *Dixie* enjouait toute la maisonnée. Duval pointa le menton vers l'étage.

— Lazare est ici… Tu pourrais peut-être refaire un miracle !

Laurence roula des yeux en hochant la tête.

— Écoute, Daniel. Arrête, parce que tu vas te mettre ta fille à dos. Rappelle-toi qu'elle m'a acceptée assez rapidement quand je suis entrée dans ta vie.

— Superbe collision… parodia Duval en se frappant contre elle.

— Un flic poète…

Duval voulut l'embrasser, mais elle l'éloigna avant de lancer sur un ton ferme :

— C'est ce soir qu'on fait un souper de couples.

— Quoi ?

— Je vais aller voir Mimi pour les inviter.

— Y sont végétariens !

— Toi aussi, tu manges peu de viande, lui rappela Laurence.

— Mais ce soir, j'en ai envie.

Il se rappela que le rôti d'orignal offert par Francis faisandait dans le frigo.

— On fera un spag aux courges pour les granos et on mangera de l'orignal.

Duval et Laurence prirent l'apéro au salon.

Les pieds traînants de Mimi dans ses bas de bûcheron glissaient avec nonchalance sur le plancher. Elle tenait un sac de biscuits Oréo et deux verres de lait vides.

Laurence se leva et l'intercepta.

— On se fait un souper d'amoureux ce soir, Mimi. Qu'est-ce que t'en dis ?

— Là, là ?

— Oui.

— Hey ! C'est cool au boutte ! Donnez-moi trente secondes. J'en parle à Fred.

Stupéfaite, elle afficha un sourire malicieux et remonta l'escalier à grandes enjambées.

Duval regarda l'heure. Deux minutes s'étaient écoulées.

— La négociation s'éternise. On ne veut pas souper à la table de la méchante police fasciste… ricana Duval à l'oreille de Laurence.

— Arrête…

Duval se levait pour aller chercher des croustilles quand un oui retentissant se fraya un passage à travers la musique.

27

« Non, je n'aime pas ce garçon », songea Duval. Sa manière de se tenir : une amibe ! Sa chemise à carreaux puait le tabac et ses cheveux blonds, longs, pas lavés, lui répugnaient. Derrière ses petites lunettes à monture ronde, comme celles de Mimi, ses yeux semblaient mijoter dans la friture. Un regard de merlan frit. Et quelle dégaine ! Jamais lui-même n'aurait osé adopter une telle attitude quand il était l'invité des parents de

Marie-Claude, son premier amour, sa première femme. Fred se tenait mal à table, n'avait pas de bonnes manières, et il était peu loquace. Il ne respectait aucun protocole : son coude gauche était appuyé sur la table et il sapait légèrement en avalant ses pâtes. Atteint du syndrome aigu de la « patte folle », il donnait l'impression de vouloir faire un solo de batterie à tout moment avec la coutellerie et son pied gauche battait la mesure sous la table.

Duval en profita pour faire l'éloge de ce rôti d'orignal.

— Ça fond dans la bouche !

Le garçon le dévisagea comme s'il était un barbare des temps modernes.

— Moé, j'préfère les voir se fondre dans la nature…

La bouchée passa de travers. Heureusement que la chair était tendre. Duval ressentit une poussée d'adrénaline. La petite lumière rouge de son taux de patience hormonal clignotait.

Il aurait voulu raconter son voyage de chasse, mais cela aurait été interprété comme de la provocation.

Duval mit un disque de Chet Baker, mais le percussionniste se plaignit que le jazz traditionnel était devenu « trop pépère », il aimait mieux les « structures complexes » de Zappa. Duval mastiqua longuement avant d'avaler pour ne pas s'étouffer.

Laurence posa doucement une main sur sa cuisse. Duval la caressa. Mimi parla du concert de l'orchestre qui aurait lieu dans dix jours.

— Vous allez venir ?

— Sauf si vous faites de la musique de fanfare trop contemporaine, dit le détective.

— C'est ce qu'on disait de la musique de Beethoven à l'époque. Les gens n'étaient pas prêts, c'était trop avancé, répliqua le chevelu.

Si l'autre disait «pas assez évolué», Duval le sortait à coups de pied au cul.

— Tu sais, entre les percussions des tribus primitives et ce qui se fait aujourd'hui, les pulsions primaires semblent être les mêmes. On en reste au stade du boum boum originel. Comme si le darwinisme ne touchait pas l'évolution musicale.

Fier de lui, Duval venait de rembarrer le jeune prétentieux. Il prit son couteau et se trancha un gros morceau de viande qu'il mastiqua avec jouissance. Mimi le regarda d'un air mauvais. Ses yeux donnaient l'impression de vouloir lancer un rayon qui aurait pulvérisé son père en cendres.

— On annonce de la neige cette nuit, dit Laurence pour meubler le silence désagréable.

Duval versa du vin à ses convives et se leva pour changer la musique. Il sortit le disque de Félix Leclerc que lui avait offert Laurence. *L'Alouette en colère* allait enfoncer le clou de la question nationale. Le vilain flic de la SQ, qui arrête des indépendantistes sans mandat, pouvait-il écouter les chants patriotiques du chantre national?

Laurence écarquilla les yeux.

La discussion se termina sur la première moitié du mandat du Parti québécois. Duval fut étonné d'apprendre que le jeunot n'était pas péquiste, mais appartenait à un groupe marxiste opposé à l'indépendance pour l'indépendance.

— L'indépendance oui, mais pour un État vraiment socialiste.

— Bin oui, avec des Ladas pour tout le monde! dit Duval en éclatant de rire. Les garagistes vont devenir les nouveaux riches!

Mimi le foudroya du regard.

LES FLEURS MORTES

28

Avant de partir à l'école, Mimi, toujours en pyjama dans son lit, écoutait une sonate de Telemann interprétée par Jean-Pierre Rampal, qu'elle devait apprendre pour son examen final. Après la cadence, elle se leva, prit son instrument et déchiffra la partition. Le tic-tac mécanique du métronome l'aidait à en maîtriser le rythme complexe.

Devant le miroir de la salle de bains, Duval agita son blaireau dans le moussoir et, d'un geste énergique, savonna son visage tout en regardant par la fenêtre. Un duvet de neige recouvrait la ruelle que les feuilles déjà commençaient à tapisser. L'été des Indiens cassait sec comme les mottes de barbe qui tombaient dans le lavabo. Le téléphone sonna.

Les cris perçants de Mimi confirmaient qu'il y avait urgence.

— Papa ! C'est pour toi ! Vite ! C'est pressant !

À demi rasé, une serviette autour du cou, il marcha jusqu'à son bureau. Mimi passa devant lui comme un coup de vent. Duval saisit le récepteur et marcha vers la fenêtre qui surplombait la Basse-Ville. Quelques flocons voletaient dans l'air gris.

Dallaire lui demandait de se rendre au cimetière de Sillery immédiatement :

— On pense que c'est en lien avec les événements des derniers jours. Pas beau à voir, y paraît.

Dans le jargon, il s'agissait d'un meurtre ignoble, probablement à caractère sexuel.

— Je m'y rends tout de suite.

— Louis et Francis sont en route.

Pressé, il retira une Pop Tarts de la boîte que tenait Mimi, ce qu'il ne faisait jamais, et s'élança vers son véhicule en ouvrant le sachet. Il avait oublié son balai à neige au sous-sol. Il pinça la tartelette givrée de sucre multicolore entre ses dents et d'une main balaya la fine pellicule de neige sur le pare-brise. Le temps frisquet lui fit échapper ses clés. Il jura, les ramassa et s'engouffra à l'abri du vent. Lorsqu'il démarra la voiture, une chanson de Joe Dassin acheva de le déprimer. Il fit le tour des stations, mais on ne parlait pas encore du meurtre. Bonne affaire, il n'aurait pas les mouches dans les pattes.

Il passa par Holland et se retrouva rapidement sur le chemin Saint-Louis. La grisaille contrastait avec les ciels azurés des jours précédents. Les pneus chuintaient sur le pavé humide et la condensation embuait les vitres. La voiture roula dans la sinueuse partie commerciale du chemin Saint-Louis. Duval se buta à l'imposante grille du cimetière. Les portes ressemblaient à des harpes en fer forgé. Un patrouilleur s'avança et le dévisagea d'un air suspicieux. Duval allongea le bras pour montrer sa carte. En s'ouvrant, les grilles laissèrent échapper un affreux grincement.

Duval n'avait qu'à suivre le va-et-vient des experts pour savoir où s'était déroulé le drame.

Près d'un mausolée, un cordon jaune encadrait la scène du crime. Duval sentit un nœud à l'estomac, appréhendant ce qu'il allait voir. Les feuilles tombaient et s'envolaient, balayées par les rafales de pluie. Duval sortit de son véhicule, inspirant une bonne bouffée d'air frais. Un policier de Sillery s'avança pour l'empêcher d'aller plus loin et Duval sortit sa carte.

Le lieutenant-détective passa sous le cordon jaune. Un expert de la police technique qu'il connaissait marcha vers lui :

— C'est un joggeur qui l'a découverte ce matin. Le gars est sous le choc. Il la connaissait. Elle habite près d'ici. Les parents avaient signalé sa disparition vers 3 h du matin. Une étudiante de l'université, Rosalie Nantel.

Duval passa à côté du rectangle blanc formé par le drap. Il avait affronté le cynisme des meurtriers dans sa vie mais rarement à cet extrême. Jamais autant de mépris contre l'innocence. Elle avait l'âge de Mimi, à qui elle ressemblait : grande et élancée comme sa fille adorée. Des cristaux de neige scintillaient dans ses cheveux.

Il dut surmonter son indignation et retrouver vite sa concentration. Reprendre froidement le contrôle. Le photographe de la police prenait des photos sous tous les angles avec un flash. En raison de la grisaille, les techniciens avaient installé de puissants projecteurs pour les aider à chercher des preuves.

Le meurtrier avait ligoté les poignets de sa victime à la croix d'une pierre tombale en granit. Une image de crucifixion, pensa Duval. Ses jambes reposaient vulgairement, comme si l'assassin les avait placées délibérément dans cette position grotesque : la jambe gauche repliée sous la cuisse et la droite étendue et bien écartée. Derrière la victime, une Vierge blanche en marbre priait, le regard implorant son fils, comme si elle avait tout vu, tout entendu et qu'elle appelait à l'aide. Devant, un ange noir déployait ses ailes, la trompette pointée vers le ciel, mais n'avait jamais volé à son secours.

La tête de la jeune fille était ployée, le menton appuyé contre la poitrine. Elle avait saigné du nez et des oreilles. Ses longs cheveux noirs, ondulés, donnaient l'impression de vouloir cacher son visage. La chemise sous son blouson noir avait été déchirée et un sein était découvert, marqué par des lésions, probablement une morsure. Le jean était déboutonné et baissé à mi-cuisse, le capucin de son ceinturon reposant le long de la cuisse droite. Duval remarqua des traces de sperme sur les poils du vagin et sur le jean.

Le docteur Villemure s'activait autour du corps de la victime.

— Salut, Daniel. C'est ce que je craignais ! J'ai jamais vu quelque chose de pareil.

Penché près du corps, il appliquait le protocole médico-légal dans le cas d'agression sexuelle.

Il enveloppa délicatement les mains de la jeune fille dans des sacs de plastique retenus par des élastiques aux poignets afin de préserver les micro-indices – peau, cheveux, fibres – qui se seraient fixés sous les ongles et que l'on chercherait à reconnaître au labo.

Duval se pencha sur le corps de la jeune fille pendant que les experts de l'Identité s'affairaient tout autour. Puisque le couvert de feuilles n'avait cessé de s'accroître depuis le décès, les membres de la police scientifique, truelle et pinceau à la main, recherchaient tout indice qui aurait pu se trouver caché dans le tapis de végétaux.

Villemure enregistra ses premières conclusions dans son magnétophone portatif. Duval, à ses côtés, obtiendrait déjà des informations pour procéder à son enquête.

— Sillons multiples autour du cou au niveau du larynx. Direction du lien horizontal. Elle a été étranglée avec une corde très mince. La pression locale semble avoir été très forte. La surface de contact entre le lien et la peau est très étroite : sans doute une chaînette ou un fil très rigide. Des traces de lutte démontrent que la personne s'est débattue alors qu'on tentait de la contrôler. Je note des dépressions profondes dans la peau, des entailles. Son visage est congestionné, bleui. J'observe des pétéchies dans les conjonctives oculaires, les paupières, les blancs de l'œil et les muqueuses. Du sang également au niveau du nez et des narines.

— Le nez a été cassé? demanda Duval.

— Non, c'est le résultat de la strangulation. Dans les cas extrêmes, il se produit une hémorragie.

Le corps n'avait aucune rigidité, ce qui laissait supposer que la mort était survenue dans la nuit. L'atteinte du point de congélation, une fois la nuit tombée, avait fait baisser rapidement la température du corps et il devenait inutile de prendre celle-ci pour connaître l'heure du décès.

Comme il y avait eu éjaculation et que le sperme sèche et meurt à l'air libre, Villemure voulait procéder le plus rapidement possible. Au pire, il serait toujours possible d'identifier les spermatozoïdes séchés au microscope par leur morphologie et leur double coloration. L'analyse permettrait de déterminer le groupe sanguin de l'individu et ainsi d'éliminer des suspects potentiels et de fournir une preuve supplémentaire.

Après avoir examiné l'environnement autour du corps, un technicien en identité recueillait avec un aspirateur industriel des indices potentiels qui seraient passés au peigne fin. Qui sait ce que révéleraient ces feuilles mortes?

Villemure, gant de latex à la main, releva doucement la tête de la jeune fille pour observer les lésions. Statue de marbre bleu au visage lisse et beau. Du sang avait séché sur la lèvre inférieure jusqu'au bout du menton. À travers le sang coagulé, Villemure repéra une lésion.

— Elle s'est mordue ou encore l'agresseur l'a fait.

Les traces de morsures s'avéreraient éventuellement d'un grand secours pour la section d'odontologie, qui aurait à comparer les fiches dentaires de suspects.

Le médecin légiste observa les griffures sur un sein.

Duval fut interpellé par un policier.

— Lieutenant, venez voir.

Madden avait été forcé à un congé, le syndicat ayant pu éviter la suspension ; on avait donc fait appel à Jobin, le maître-chien du corps policier de Charny. Le policier récompensait son berger allemand, toujours assis à un mètre de sa découverte. Duval se pencha.

— Un gant de latex.

Après l'avoir photographié, l'expert le ramassa avec sa pince et le déposa dans un sac.

— Le gant nous donne une idée de l'endroit par où l'agresseur a pris la fuite : côté sud du cimetière, vers le fleuve. Peut-être a-t-il été surpris par quelque chose. S'est-il rendu compte qu'il perdait le gant ou était-il trop pressé pour faire demi-tour ?

Francis se joignit à eux en compagnie de Louis. Le parapluie du grand blond protégeait son comparse contre les averses qui formaient un rideau autour du fauteuil.

Louis, qui avait vu des meurtres sadiques dans sa carrière, afficha une mine sombre. Francis avait aussi un air grave. Des gouttes de pluie ruisselaient sur ses lunettes. Ses cheveux blonds détrempés étaient parfaitement lisses sur sa tête. Il avait abandonné son parapluie à Louis qui, avec son Stetson brun sur la tête, ressemblait à un policier d'une autre époque.

Duval s'en voulait. Le meurtrier leur avait laissé une marge de manœuvre dont il n'avait pas su profiter.

— Nous avons deux meurtres sur le dos, dit Louis.

Duval se plaça sous la branche d'un orme qui faisait office d'abri.

— Non, rappelle-toi : l'autre main appartient à une femme déjà embaumée. Et comme on se retrouve ce matin avec un meurtre commis dans un cimetière, on peut conjecturer que le meurtrier a une passion morbide pour ces lieux.

— Écoute, Daniel, j'ai l'impression qu'en identifiant la personne à qui appartient cette main, on en saura un peu plus sur le meurtrier. C'est le premier morceau du casse-tête.

Duval acquiesça.

— Les policiers de Sainte-Foy interrogent des étudiants et des employés qui circulaient près du boisé de l'université, ajouta Francis. Ici, les policiers de Sillery ont commencé une enquête de voisinage.

— Tu te mets là-dessus. Va voir ce qu'ils ont. Bernard et toi, vous allez rencontrer les parents de la jeune fille et vous interrogerez les gens des alentours.

— Le grognon de la police de Sillery a déjà avisé les parents, dit Louis.

Duval parut soulagé. Il se demandait comment il aurait fait pour se présenter devant la famille. Au début de sa carrière, quand il était patrouilleur, il avait toujours eu horreur d'annoncer à des parents la mort de leur enfant.

Le camion bourgogne de la morgue recula. Des journalistes, derrière la barrière, interpellèrent Duval.

— Un crime sexuel, lieutenant ? A-t-elle été violée ?

« Non, un crime économique », avait-il envie de lancer.

Duval demeura sourd aux abois des scribes. Il ne se sentait pas bien dans cette affaire.

Les experts en identité détachèrent avec précaution les cordes jaunes en nylon qui retenaient le corps de la jeune fille à la croix. On l'étendit de tout son long et on l'enveloppa dans un sac pour préserver d'autres indices. Au labo, on chercherait avec plus de précision des fibres, des poils pubiens, des cheveux, de la salive. Duval remarqua que les cordes de nylon, d'un jaune lustré, semblaient neuves.

L'employé tendit la sangle de cuir de la civière, qui glissa sur le rail du fourgon.

Duval s'adressa à un membre de la police technique.

— Des empreintes de pieds ?

— Non. Le couvert de feuilles et la neige ne nous favorisent pas.

— Aurait-il pu venir avec un véhicule jusqu'ici ?

— Je ne pense pas. Mais on va vérifier. Il y a effectivement des traces d'ornières, lieutenant.

À cent mètres de là, le maître-chien avait fini son boulot. Il ouvrit le hayon de son camion et l'animal monta d'un bond joyeux puis se coucha.

Le docteur Villemure avait un air grave. Il était père d'une adolescente. Pour les policiers et les experts légistes, il devenait difficile de ne pas faire de projection.

— Je fais immédiatement l'autopsie. Rappelle-moi en fin d'avant-midi.

Daniel salua François et se dirigea vers son véhicule, près duquel attendaient Louis et Francis.

Francis sortit son carnet noir et repéra l'adresse des parents de la jeune fille que lui avait refilée le policier de Sillery.

— J'aimerais interroger le joggeur, leur dit Duval.

29

Dans le vieux poste de police et d'incendie de la rue Maguire, les pompiers profitaient du mauvais temps pour astiquer les rutilants camions Thibault.

Dans son bureau, Plante, dont l'imperméable détrempé reposait sur la patère, annonça qu'on avait interrogé brièvement le coureur, puis qu'on l'avait relâché. L'homme, un avocat, s'en allait plaider une cause au Palais de justice. Duval lut les informations qu'il avait laissées et aucune ne lui parut utile.

Il déposa le document sur le bureau du chef.

— Avez-vous d'autres informations ? Des témoins qui auraient vu quelque chose ?

— Non.

— Qui habite la maison blanche dans le cimetière ?

— D'après vous ? Le comte Dracula… Le gardien, c't'affaire…

Duval n'apprécia pas le sarcasme.

— Je vous demande son nom !

— Il s'appelle Roger McClean et tout le monde le connaît.

— Eh bien pas nous ! On ne fréquente pas les fossoyeurs ! largua Louis.

Duval, heureux de la répartie de son copain, déposa une carte professionnelle devant le chef.

— Aussitôt que vous avez des informations supplémentaires, appelez-moi à mon bureau.

Duval se rendait bien compte que le capitaine Plante n'avait aucune considération à son endroit. Il lui faudrait constamment lui tirer les vers du nez.

◆

Le gardien habitait effectivement un petit cottage à l'intérieur du cimetière, en bordure du chemin Saint-

Louis, seul vivant à dormir parmi les morts. La maison était recouverte de bardeaux de cèdre.

Duval frappa trois coups vigoureux. À travers la dentelle, il entrevit un homme plutôt malingre, dans la cinquantaine. Le gardien tira le rideau puis, après inspection, ouvrit la porte.

— Bonjour, monsieur McClean, je suis le lieutenant-détective Daniel Duval, enquêteur, et voici mon collègue, Louis Harel.

L'homme hochait nerveusement la tête. Le mouvement semblait incontrôlable.

— On est chargés de l'enquête.

Il les pria d'entrer. Du piano classique jouait en sourdine à la radio.

L'homme aux cheveux poivre et sel avait un visage longiligne, presque chevalin, et ses yeux gris-bleu dégageaient un magnétisme inquiétant. De longues rides couraient à la verticale sur fond de cernes. Le lobe de son nez servait de terreau à une dizaine de poils hirsutes. Ses sourcils fusaient comme de la laine folle.

— Venez vous asseoir, dit-il sans se rendre compte de sa bourde.

Les roues du fauteuil roulant de Louis laissèrent de la boue sur le linoléum et le Gros s'en excusa.

— Pas de problème, dit l'homme.

La maison était meublée avec sobriété. Les électroménagers, tout en rondeur, étaient d'une autre époque, et les meubles du salon, que Duval voyait à travers les portes françaises, avaient aussi des courbes toutes victoriennes. Des fenêtres on voyait l'alignement des tombes multipliées à l'infini. « Comment pouvait-on vivre au milieu des morts toute sa vie ? » se demanda Duval. Mais, après tout, n'était-ce pas aussi une partie de son existence ?

Duval, qui faisait tourner son stylo entre ses doigts, fixa ses yeux sur le gardien.

— Avez-vous vu ou entendu quelque chose cette nuit ?

— Comme vous l'avez constaté, c'est arrivé assez loin de la maison. J'ai entendu des voix qui chantaient, des voix de jeunes sur le party, comme il arrive fréquemment.

— Combien de temps ?

— Quelques secondes.

— Vous n'êtes pas allé voir ?

— J'étais couché.

— Quelle heure était-il ?

— Aux alentours de 1 h. Je m'étais assoupi vers minuit trente et j'ai souvent de la difficulté à dormir.

— D'après vous, ils étaient combien ?

— Deux, trois. Je ne peux vous dire.

— Et vous avez dit des cris de jeunes qui semblaient sur le party ?

— Oui.

— Et qu'est-ce qui vous fait croire qu'ils étaient en train de faire la fête ?

Son expression faciale se figea. Il dodelina de la tête.

— Je ne sais pas, monsieur Duval. J'ai entendu ce qui me paraissait être des cris de gens en boisson.

— Et ce n'étaient pas les hurlements de quelqu'un qui souffre ?

Duval crut que le gardien allait être emporté par une embolie. Sa pression dut baisser subitement. Il s'adossa en expirant, le teint livide. McClean se culpabilisait-il ? Payé pour veiller sur le cimetière, il n'avait su lire la détresse dans les cris entendus.

— Écoutez, si quelqu'un avait appelé au secours, je serais intervenu. Les cris ont presque aussitôt cessé.

— À quelle heure ?

— Tout de suite après.

— Oui, mais à quelle heure ? reprit Louis.

— 1 h 15, 1 h 30.

— Et vous vous êtes endormi…

Duval se dit qu'il fallait cesser de taper sur ce clou. La culpabilité ne ferait pas revenir la victime. Il jeta un coup d'œil aux bottes noires du gardien, boueuses, qui reposaient dans le vestibule.

— Est-ce que des incidents se sont produits au cimetière dans les dernières semaines ?

L'homme hocha la tête et parut terrifié.

— Il y a trois semaines, des pierres ont été renversées par des vandales. Puis, ce qui est plus grave, un caveau a été vandalisé.

Duval écarquilla les yeux, incrédule.

— Un caveau, vous dites ?

— Quel type de vandalisme ? demanda Louis.

— On s'est introduit dans un mausolée en brisant la serrure et on a écrit un graffiti obscène sur le mur.

Duval regarda Louis, les yeux pleins de stupeur. Ils détenaient maintenant la clé de l'une des portes closes de leur enquête. Il invita McClean à lui montrer immédiatement l'emplacement.

La pluie s'était intensifiée. Il tombait des trombes d'eau et l'homme se para d'un imper et de bottes en caoutchouc. McClean était fort, il avait les muscles d'un gaillard qui travaille de ses bras depuis longtemps.

Il mit une main sur la poignée et invita Duval à le précéder.

À travers la grisaille de pluie et de feuilles, le lieutenant observa au loin les hommes de l'Identité qui s'activaient sur la scène du crime. Francis venait vers lui.

— Puis ?

— Les commerces étaient tous fermés.

— Il faudrait aussi interroger les chauffeurs d'autobus, ceux de la ligne 25 qui ont circulé hier entre minuit et 1 h 45, se rappela Duval.

Le sentier sinueux et incliné les mena dans la partie sud-est du cimetière. Les semelles des chaussures s'enfonçaient dans la boue. Les arbres traçaient de sombres artères dans le ciel. L'eau zébrait l'écorce lisse des hêtres. La pluie tombait alors si dru qu'il devenait difficile de se comprendre. À trois mètres des lieux, McClean pointa le doigt vers le mausolée, qui en imposait par ses pierres grises, ses deux colonnes en granit et les chérubins qui veillaient au-dessus d'un portail de fer noir. Un vitrail magnifique présentant un ange émergeant de l'eau ornait l'imposte. L'inscription *Lacrimarum valle* avait été gravée sur le linteau.

— À qui appartient ce mausolée ? s'enquit Duval.

— Au docteur Fraser, un chirurgien qui habite Sillery.

— Je suppose qu'il a porté plainte ?

— Non, justement. Quand la police a contacté la famille, c'est monsieur Fraser qui a répondu, et comme sa femme n'est toujours pas remise de la mort de sa fille, il a fait en sorte qu'elle n'en sache rien. Monsieur Fraser m'a payé pour tout nettoyer et nous avons gardé ça mort.

Duval sourit, car l'homme ne s'était pas rendu compte de son jeu de mots.

— Vous avez les clés ?

— Je les avais. C'est monsieur Fraser qui les a maintenant. Ne parlez pas à sa femme, surtout.

La pluie ruisselait au bout du long nez de McClean transformé en chantepleure.

Heureusement, le vieil Écossais avait rabattu son capuchon, ce qui n'était pas le cas des enquêteurs, à l'exception de Louis, qui tenait son Stetson tout détrempé d'une main pour qu'il ne s'envole pas au vent.

— Savez-vous quel âge avait la fille de monsieur Fraser ?

— Angélique n'avait pas vingt ans.

— Vous avez nettoyé le graffiti. Vous devez vous rappeler ce qui était écrit.

— Comment l'oublier ?

L'homme prononça les mots comme si du pus sortait de sa bouche : *Un trou… dans la boue. C'est… ce qu'il faut à un tel hôte !*

Ce message, dans l'esprit du précédent, marquait davantage de cynisme et une idée de vengeance, se dit Duval qui nota la phrase dans son calepin noir.

— C'était tout ? Rien d'autre ? demanda Duval.

— C'est tout ce qu'il y avait d'écrit.

— Avez-vous trouvé des objets suspects ?

— Non.

— Avez-vous nettoyé, ramassé ?

— Oui…

— Parlez !

— J'ai trouvé un préservatif que j'ai jeté.

Duval et Francis s'observèrent, consternés.

— Avait-il été utilisé ?

L'homme hocha la tête affirmativement.

— Je l'ai ramassé. J'ai rien dit à monsieur Fraser. C'était déjà tellement horrible pour lui. Imaginez !

Puisque Fraser n'avait pas porté plainte, McClean ne pouvait être accusé d'avoir fait disparaître une preuve, mais il n'en demeurait pas moins que le gardien avait caché une information importante au père de la défunte.

— Écoutez, monsieur McClean, il va falloir qu'on vous pose d'autres questions. Cela risque d'être long. On reviendra. Pour l'instant, vous allez nous donner les coordonnées du docteur Fraser.

— Je ne sais pas où il demeure, mais il travaille au CHUL.

◆

Tout en retraitant vers la voiture, Duval avisa Francis qu'il était l'heure d'aller rencontrer les parents de la jeune victime. Il sentit la gorge de son partenaire se comprimer.

— Tu veux vraiment que j'y aille ?

Duval hocha la tête.

— Pendant ce temps, j'irai au CHUL rencontrer le docteur Fraser.

La mort dans l'âme, Francis se résigna à subir l'avalanche d'émotions et de rage. Jamais il n'avait affronté directement ce genre de crime auparavant. Il avait enquêté sur des cas de viols très durs mais jamais sur une agression sexuelle suivie d'un homicide.

Pendant ce temps, à la centrale, Louis établirait les contacts avec un responsable du Service des transports en commun de Québec.

30

Les rafales de pluie lessivaient le pare-brise. Les essuie-glaces parvenaient à peine à maintenir une visibilité minimale. La tôle de la voiture crépitait. Duval mit le chauffage pour désembuer les vitres. Ses os étaient sciés par l'humidité.

Il se gara devant l'entrée du CHUL. À la réception, il demanda où se trouvait le département de cardiologie.

— Vous voulez voir qui ?

— Le docteur Fraser.

La dame écrivit sur un bout de papier le numéro du local et lui indiqua la direction à suivre.

À la réception du département de cardiologie, la secrétaire lui annonça qu'il ne pourrait pas voir le docteur, qui recevait ses patients. Duval sortit sa carte de la SQ et ajouta deux mots.

— C'est urgent.

La préposée s'extirpa enfin de son coma bureaucratique.

— Pas son épouse ?

— Non.

— Je vais voir ce que je peux faire.

Elle revint une minute plus tard en priant Duval de prendre un siège : « Le docteur Fraser va vous recevoir. »

Duval prit une vieille revue avec Gilles Villeneuve à la une et se rappela que les vacances avaient passé trop vite. La vie se déroulait à la vitesse d'un ragtime qui file sur un vieux piano. Il lui semblait que le marathon de Boston, c'était hier. Avril : la fonte des neiges ; mai et ses lilas. Bientôt, l'hiver allait refermer son étau blanc sur la ville.

Deux minutes plus tard, une voix grave appela Duval. Le lieutenant croisa le patient du médecin qui paraissait avoir toute une pente à remonter.

Le docteur Fraser, vêtu de sa blouse verte de chirurgien, stéthoscope autour du cou, salua Duval. Il le pria d'entrer, il serait à lui dans quelques instants. Les murs du bureau étaient tapissés d'affiches illustrant les méandres du système cardiovasculaire. Bien en évidence sur le bureau du médecin reposait un cœur en plastique avec son réseau inextricable d'artères, d'oreillettes, de veines et de valves. Tout près se trouvaient les photos de ses enfants : deux filles et un garçon. L'une de ses deux filles, il devina laquelle à son âge, reposait dans son mausolée. Elle portait les cheveux longs et avait un regard sombre. Elle souriait sans montrer ses dents – sans doute à cause de broches, car les autres enfants avaient le sourire accroché aux oreilles.

Fraser entra. C'était un homme svelte, dans la mi-quarantaine, plein d'assurance. Ses cheveux châtains grisonnaient, mais son visage tanné par le soleil avait conservé des traits jeunes. Ses mains, comme celles d'un virtuose, étaient effilées et délicates. Son timbre avait un grain poreux et les graves de quelqu'un qui a suivi des cours de pose de voix.

— Je ne peux pas vous parler longtemps, je suis en salle d'op dans trente minutes et il me faut aller rassurer mon patient dans dix minutes. Que puis-je pour vous ?

— Il y a eu un meurtre sordide au cimetière de Sillery, cette nuit. Je vous fais grâce des détails. En interrogeant le gardien, j'ai appris qu'on avait profané la tombe de votre fille.

Le visage du médecin fut paralysé de stupeur.

— Lieutenant Duval, je voudrais que tout ça reste entre nous. Ma femme est en pleine dépression et je veux lui épargner tous les détails que vous savez.

— Parlez-moi de votre fille.

— Angélique avait dix-neuf ans. Comme bien des jeunes de son âge, elle a décidé que c'était assez.

— Pourquoi ?

— Beaucoup de pression, mais, d'après moi, le cours de philo qu'elle a suivi au cégep l'a encouragée dans cette idée.

— Expliquez-moi.

— Le cours s'intitulait *Philosophie de la mort*. Il était donné par un être dégénéré, sordide. Dire qu'à l'époque où j'ai étudié au Séminaire, on ne pouvait même pas lire Camus ! Le professeur drainait toute une clique de disciples, dont Angélique. Son cours était couru et apprécié. Ma fille l'aimait beaucoup. Les

jeunes sont fascinés par la mort et l'horreur. Lui, il en
avait, des histoires à raconter.

— En quoi consistait le cours, docteur Fraser ?

Les yeux du médecin montrèrent une hargne qu'il
n'avait sans doute jamais cessé d'entretenir.

— Je pourrais vous faire voir les notes de cours
d'Angélique. Ce pervers se complaisait dans la morbi-
dité au point de les emmener en promenade au cimetière
à l'Halloween.

— Comment s'appelle-t-il ?

— Victor Déziel. Vous devriez enquêter sur le passé
de cet homme. Il n'était pas directement mêlé à la mort
de ma fille, quoique nous ayons su qu'Angélique avait
eu une relation intime avec lui. Elle en était amoureuse.
C'était comme un gourou. Puis il n'en a plus voulu,
sans doute accroché à une autre. Nous avons porté
plainte à la direction du Séminaire, deux autres parents
également, mais nous n'avons pas obtenu ce que nous
désirions : le renvoi de ce pervers.

— Vous n'avez jamais établi de lien entre ce qui est
arrivé par la suite dans le mausolée de votre fille et
ce professeur ?

— Comme je ne voulais pas que ma femme
apprenne ce qui s'était passé, j'ai décidé de ne pas
enquêter. Bien sûr, je me suis fait aller la cervelle,
mais je n'ai rien appris de plus que ce que je savais
déjà.

— Peut-être que nous pourrions…

— Écoutez, ma femme est dans une profonde dépression. C'est elle qui a découvert Angélique dans
son bain.

— Je peux vous demander comment est morte votre
fille ?

— Elle s'est tailladé les veines. Ce dégénéré leur
avait dit que les Romains se saignaient sans douleur
dans leur bain.

Le cardiologue regarda sa montre et leva les mains pour signifier que c'était tout le temps dont il disposait pour l'instant.

Duval se leva et lui posa directement la question.

— Me permettez-vous, docteur, d'aller inspecter l'intérieur du mausolée ?

Le médecin se rembrunit, expira, puis fixa Duval droit dans les yeux.

— Pourquoi ?

— La semaine dernière, nous avons découvert une main près de l'école Jésus-Marie. Il est possible, et je dis cela sous toute réserve, que cette main soit celle d'Angélique.

Le médecin dévisagea Duval avec des yeux sidérés.

— Qu'est-ce que vous me dites là ? Avez-vous d'autres raisons de croire à cette thèse farfelue ?

— Le docteur Villemure, du laboratoire de médecine légale, a écrit dans son rapport qu'il s'agissait d'une main déjà embaumée.

— François, je le connais bien. Il fait de la pathologie hospitalière pour nous de temps à autre. Sur quoi se base-t-il pour arriver à cette conclusion ?

— Le maquillage. Les muscles avaient aussi une teinte, une coloration et une texture particulières. Des produits chimiques servant à assoupir l'effet du formaldéhyde ont été retrouvés dans les tissus. La taille et la calcification des os correspondent à la main d'une femme âgée approximativement de quinze à vingt-cinq ans.

Le chirurgien devint exsangue. Duval n'aurait pas voulu se retrouver à la place du patient que le docteur allait opérer. Fraser se leva, appuya ses pouces contre son bureau, regarda la photo d'Angélique.

— Docteur, vous devez nous laisser enquêter à l'intérieur du mausolée.

— Vous voulez dire qu'un individu aurait profané le corps de mon ange chéri ?

Les muscles de son visage étaient tendus comme des élastiques qui allaient faire éclater la peau. Il regarda de nouveau la photo de son enfant, serra la mâchoire, hocha la tête, déterminé.

— On suit présentement la piste de ce qu'on croit être un nécrophile, qui, en plus de troubler le sommeil des disparus, tue pour apaiser ses pulsions morbides.

— Et si c'était lui ?

— Lui ?

— Déziel. Je sais que rien n'arrête ce genre d'individu. Pourquoi amener des jeunes à des lectures aussi troublantes ?

— Si vous nous permettez d'ouvrir une enquête, on en saura davantage sur ce qui s'est passé. J'irai rencontrer Déziel. Mais vous devez nous autoriser à exhumer le corps de votre fille.

Le docteur soupira et donna son accord, mais à une condition.

— Vous n'en parlez pas à ma femme et je ne veux rien voir dans les journaux.

— Je vais tout faire pour…

Le médecin pointa vers Duval un doigt menaçant.

— Non, vous n'avez pas compris. Vous devez vous y engager. Ma femme ne doit rien apprendre de cette histoire. Pas dans son état. Si jamais c'était le cas, je ne sais pas ce qui lui arriverait.

— Je vous le promets.

Duval tapota sa lèvre avec son index comme s'il ne voulait pas oublier ce qu'il allait dire.

— Est-ce que je pourrais voir la chambre d'Angélique, ses notes de cours ?

— On pourra s'arranger, mais vous ne passez jamais par ma femme. Vous appelez à l'hôpital.

Duval lui serra la main. Sa poigne était la serre d'un homme en colère.

— Je vous appellerai pour la signature des formulaires. Vous devrez désigner un avocat pour assister à l'exhumation.

— Vous comptez procéder quand ?

— Demain matin. Le temps est un facteur important dans une enquête.

Fraser consulta sa montre et frotta ses yeux gorgés de fatigue. L'opération serait plus difficile que prévu.

31

Duval regagna son quartier général. Pendant qu'il roulait sur le boulevard Laurier en direction de Québec, il mémorisa tout ce qu'il devait faire par ordre de priorité : se rendre au labo dans l'après-midi, s'assurer pour le lendemain des services de l'Identité judiciaire afin de relever les indices éventuels dans le mausolée d'Angélique Fraser, exhumer le corps, rencontrer la direction du Séminaire, interroger Victor Déziel, le professeur de philo… et ne pas oublier d'acheter des rasoirs.

Il vit apparaître une masse noire dans son rétroviseur. Un chauffeur jouait aux autos tamponneuses à quelques pouces de son pare-chocs, la manœuvre dangereuse qu'il détestait le plus sur la route. Duval, qui roulait déjà à soixante-dix kilomètres à l'heure, resta dans sa voie. Il prit sa radio et lança un appel au répartiteur, lequel avisa un collègue qui patrouillait dans les parages.

La voix du patrouilleur Bédard grésilla dans le récepteur.

— Salut, Paul, c'est Daniel Duval. Je suis dans la rue Saint-Louis à la hauteur de Bougainville et un fou dans une Toronado veut enculer ma voiture.

— Là tu me fais plaisir ! Je m'en occupe ! Je suis à la hauteur de Holland. J'arrive en cinquième…

Duval l'entendit actionner la sirène.

Un feu rouge immobilisa les deux voitures mais pas longtemps. L'homme aux lunettes fumées continuait d'intimider Duval en donnant des coups d'accélérateur suivis de coups de frein secs.

Duval reçut un message de Bédard.

— Daniel, je suis caché au coin de la rue Bourla-maque.

— Merci, Paul. Je te remettrai ça.

— En passant, Louis m'a demandé de jouer de la basse et de chanter *Love me tender* pour sa damnée messe.

— Moi, je fais un sermon…

Le feu passa au vert.

— Tiens, je vous vois. Attache ta tuque. Hésite pas à prendre de la vitesse, pèse sur la suce, recommanda Bédard. Je le prends en chasse.

— N'oublie pas le constat également pour conduite dangereuse…

— Non. Et je vois aussi que le feu arrière est brûlé… Et avec les résonateurs qu'il a installés, il dépasse le contrôle de décibels permis. Un petit quarante-huit heures pour une inspection complète me sécuriserait.

Duval accéléra jusqu'à quatre-vingts kilomètres à l'heure. Le fou continua de lui coller au derrière. Soudain, comme sorti de nulle part, le gyrophare de la voiture de patrouille annonça que la récréation était terminée.

Daniel regarda avec contentement dans ses rétroviseurs. L'énorme Toronado se rangeait au coin de la rue Cartier.

— Merci !

— Bonne journée, lieutenant !

Duval se gara à la centrale avec des images horribles en tête. La mise en scène macabre sur le corps de la victime annonçait le pire s'il ne mettait pas la main rapidement au collet de ce maniaque. Il se demanda ce que sa fille, Mimi, apprenait dans son cours de philosophie.

Francis aussi parut ébranlé après avoir passé un rude moment à interroger les parents de Rosalie Nantel.

— C'était affreux, Daniel.

Il avait le visage complètement délavé.

— J'ai fait de mon mieux. Madame Nantel est dans un état qui ne me permettait pas d'aller au fond des choses. Son mari avait fait venir un médecin et il m'a prié de revenir plus tard. J'ai insisté en lui expliquant l'urgence d'en savoir le plus possible le plus rapidement. Et là, le mari a parlé et la femme également.

— Et puis ?

— Ils accusent déjà l'ancien petit ami de leur fille, un dénommé Michaël Mathieu : un gars pas très apprécié dont les Nantel sont sans nouvelles. Rosalie est sortie, hier, au Fuzz, un bar punk de Québec. Elle était accompagnée d'un ami, son cousin en fait, car elle craignait de rencontrer son ex qui lui a mené la vie dure après leur séparation.

— La vie dure, qu'est-ce que ça veut dire ?

— Il lui téléphonait, piquait des crises au téléphone, manifestait de l'hostilité.

— Des menaces directes ?

— Les parents ne savent pas, mais hier Rosalie a insisté pour que son cousin l'escorte.

— Tu as le numéro de téléphone du cousin ?

— Oui, il s'appelle Sébastien Poirier. J'ai aussi son adresse. Il habite Lévis. Vers 2 h, les parents de Rosalie ont appelé chez lui et Poirier leur a dit qu'elle était sortie en même temps que lui pour prendre l'autobus. Il a ajouté que l'ex-copain de Rosalie se trouvait au Fuzz et qu'il lui avait lancé de mauvais regards. Peut-être s'étaient-ils parlés et qu'elle s'était rendue chez lui après une ultime réconciliation ? Autre événement troublant : samedi dernier, au dire des parents, il s'est passé quelque chose de bizarre avec des punks au restaurant Le Laurentien. C'est du moins ce que Rosalie aurait raconté à son père.

— Des témoins ?

— Oui, toujours cet ami qui l'accompagnait, Sébastien.

— On va vérifier tout ça.

Duval aperçut Louis et Bernard qui retraitaient vers le bureau.

— Il va falloir prendre les bouchées doubles. Un monstre est en liberté.

— Vous autres ? demanda Prince.

— Beaucoup de travail. Un paquet de pistes.

Duval invita ses amis à dîner. La Pop Tarts était loin. Il leur donnerait les instructions au restaurant. Louis proposa à ses collègues d'aller Chez Diana, au coin de la rue Saint-Jean, et la réponse fut unanimement enthousiaste.

◆

Duval adorait ce resto qui affichait encore son mobilier des années quarante : le juke-box défilait du bon vieux swing. Tout étincelait. Le vieux comptoir en

Arborite blanc aux pigments dorés et les bancs aux appliques chromées recouverts de cuirette rouge replongeaient Duval dans son enfance. Ses parents l'emmenaient à la fin des années trente dans ces restos aux enseignes éclatantes de l'avenue du Mont-Royal.

Louis immobilisa son fauteuil près de la banquette, abaissa son accoudoir et se glissa jusqu'au bout de la table. Il salua de la main la vieille gérante, qui appréciait que l'équipe de gaillards protège son établissement.

Une jeune noiraude à chignon rouge et lèvres écarlates s'empressa de prendre les commandes.

Louis en profita pour lancer ses sempiternels jeux de mots à la serveuse. Comme celle-ci était nouvelle et surtout très jolie, Duval sut que Loulou la taquinerait.

— Pour moi, ce sera un *hot chicken*… J'ai beau perdre des plumes – il frotta son cuir chevelu – rappelle-toi, beauté, qu'on peut pas refroidir un vieux poulet comme moi !

Elle sourit et, lorsqu'elle vit le fauteuil roulant, elle se souvint d'avoir lu dans les journaux un article sur Louis.

— C'est vous, ça, le Perry Mason de Québec ?

— Oui, ma poulette. En plus beau ! Et voici ma basse-cour.

Elle rougit, mais ne le prit pas mal. Derrière le comptoir, la patronne, madame Leclerc, cessa d'égoutter les frites dans leur panier ; elle avait écouté le cabotinage du Gros. Elle se tourna et lança :

— Fais attention à lui, Maryse, c't'un enfirouapeux de la pire espèce. Y chante la pomme à toutes les filles depuis vingt ans. Y a pas une serveuse à qui y a pas faite une déclaration d'amour !

Louis éclata de rire, fier de lui. Sa réputation s'étendait à tous les restos de Québec.

— Maryse, c't'un beau nom, conclut Francis.

Duval voyait bien qu'elle lui plaisait. Le chouenneux avait hâte de rencontrer « la femme », comme il le disait. Il aurait bien aimé emmener cette fille à son chalet pour la fin de semaine.

Finalement, l'exiguïté des lieux, le grand nombre de clients, la verve de Loulou, excité par la serveuse, et le sujet macabre dont ils devaient discuter incitèrent Duval à reporter la séance de travail à l'après-midi au bureau.

De retour à la centrale, le répartiteur lui remit un mémo lui enjoignant de se rendre au laboratoire.

32

Duval glissa sa carte magnétique dans le senseur et la porte battante s'ouvrit. L'entrée de Louis, qui l'accompagnait au Laboratoire de sciences judiciaires et de médecine légale, fut remarquée. Immédiatement, ses anciens collègues, qui occupaient auparavant le sous-sol du boulevard Saint-Cyrille, se regroupèrent autour de lui. Il n'avait pas remis les pieds au labo depuis l'affaire Hurtubise. Les hommes en blouse blanche, les techniciens de la morgue et le vieux docteur O'Neil se pressaient autour du fauteuil roulant. Les blagues fusaient en dépit des circonstances graves qui les amenaient au labo. Il fallait rigoler dans ce métier, sinon on ne tenait pas le coup. Étrangement, c'est dans ces cas de meurtres sauvages, ceux d'enfants ou de jeunes femmes, que l'humour et le rire devenaient salvateurs. Une bouée de sauvetage. La pilule de survie. Mais jamais d'humour cynique avec le cadavre comme objet de dérision.

O'Neil s'approcha.

Louis récoltait la bonne humeur qu'il avait toujours semée, et ce, en dépit des crises de rage célèbres qu'il avait piquées au fil des ans.

— Tu reprends du service, mon Louis ?

— Oui, ma blonde n'en peut plus de me voir assis à rien faire, gloussa Loulou.

C'était ça, Louis, le gros macho plein de paradoxes, tendre et dur, bourru et sympathique, que l'on avait acculé au pied du mur au point qu'il s'était senti obligé de prouver à tous qu'il avait encore de la valeur. Résultat : un soir, il était parti seul à la poursuite d'Hurtubise.

Deux techniciens qui faisaient rouler une civière brinquebalante sur laquelle reposait un corps destiné à la section Anthropologie s'arrêtèrent pour contempler le survivant.

Le vieux docteur O'Neil, qui avait été recommandé par le célèbre docteur Derome, demanda à Louis comment il avait fait pour survivre à autant de balles. La réponse fut cinglante et instantanée :

— Quand t'as un sergent-adjoint comme Pouliot, tu survis à tout. Tu deviens blindé contre n'importe quoi. Même les balles *dum dum*.

Les rires gras fusèrent dans la pièce blanche au carrelage rouge et luisant. C'était surréaliste, tous ces rires avec le macchabée dans son sac.

— Et puis je connais le docteur Villemure, il aurait consolé tout le monde en disant que de toute façon mon alimentation et mes poumons me condamnaient à court terme…

Duval aperçut juste à ce moment Villemure qui sortait de la salle de radio avec des documents. Le médecin lui fit signe de venir. Daniel s'excusa et se dirigea vers lui. Louis salua ses amis et suivit le lieutenant.

— Salut, messieurs, c'est affreux ce qu'on a sur les bras, dit le docteur.

— Je n'en reviens pas d'une telle charge de sauvagerie, ajouta Duval.

La cadence rapide des pas sur le carrelage était sinistre.

Jamais Duval n'avait vu Villemure aussi sombre dans la pratique de son métier. Ses yeux bleus glacés qui, croyait-on, avaient tout vu au cours de sa longue carrière, témoignaient d'une réelle angoisse. L'appréhension du pire ne venait pas tellement des violences perpétrées sur le corps que du cérémonial macabre du meurtrier.

— Alors que j'effectuais un frottis pour recueillir du sperme, j'ai ramené avec mon coton-tige un bout de papier.

— Un autre message?

Villemure avait aussitôt acheminé le billet à Miljours, de la section Documents.

— On l'a déchiffré. Suivez-moi.

Il ouvrit la porte de la salle d'autopsie. Maher, l'assistant, indiquait au technicien où photographier. La table en inox occupait le centre de la pièce.

De son fauteuil, Louis se trouvait à la hauteur du corps. Il serra les lèvres. Jamais il n'avait vu une morte aussi belle. Il l'avait pourtant regardée au cimetière. Était-ce parce qu'il la voyait nue?

Elle semblait si paisible, songea Duval. Et ce léger sourire qu'elle avait. La vie avait tellement d'ironie, pensa-t-il. À côté d'elle, s'entassaient dans un bac les organes qui avaient été examinés et retirés de son corps.

Villemure prit le rapport que lui avait remis Miljours.

— Le message est dans le genre des précédents : on dirait la prose d'un croque-mort, dit Villemure. *Et faire à ton flanc étonné une blessure large et creuse.*

— Il est complètement malade ! s'offusqua Louis.

— Ça, on le sait déjà, lança le jeune Maher.

— Écrit à la main ou au lettrage ? demanda Duval.

— Des lettres découpées dans des revues. Miljours affirme que c'est le même gars qui a laissé le message sur la carcasse du chien, sur le mur de l'université et sur la main.

Duval fixa la dalle blanche où il restait, autour du pied de la table, quelques vestiges du linoléum rouge qui donnaient l'impression d'une tache de sang. On avait dû recouvrir l'ancien plancher, car l'usage du flash sur fond rouge donnait des photos d'une couleur bizarre qui induisait en erreur.

Villemure baissa son masque.

— On sait maintenant comment il s'y est pris : il l'a étranglée. Les traces de strangulation sont apparentes et les lésions profondes. La surface du lien de constriction est étroite. Pendant que la victime agonisait, ou après sa mort, le meurtrier s'est livré à des agressions qui ont été jusqu'à la pénétration et l'éjaculation. Les lésions et les blessures *post mortem* dans le vagin sont nombreuses. J'ai envoyé les échantillons de sperme au biologiste. Étrangement, il y avait une très grande quantité de spermatozoïdes, ce qui pourrait signifier que le coït a eu lieu *post mortem*. Je ne suis pas tout à fait d'accord avec Fabien, mais c'est ce qu'il croit.

Le docteur Maher intervint tout en étiquetant une fiole :

— Des études récentes montrent que le sperme se détériore plus rapidement dans un corps vivant que dans l'utérus d'une femme décédée. Les tissus vivants détruisent le sperme plus facilement. On ne sait pas pourquoi, mais c'est ainsi.

— Du fait qu'il a laissé toutes ces traces, j'ai l'impression qu'on a affaire à quelqu'un qui joue son va-tout, dit Duval en hochant la tête.

— Ils pouvaient être deux ? demanda Louis.

— Non. Mireille vous confirmera la chose.

Les déclics de l'appareil photo cessèrent. Villemure s'appuya contre le comptoir en inox, retira ses gants et son masque vert, révélant ses traits tirés :

— J'ai procédé à une coupe de son estomac et elle avait mangé environ quatre-vingt-dix minutes avant d'être tuée. D'après l'analyse des aliments – un hamburger et des frites –, le meurtre s'est produit quarante-cinq minutes à une heure après sa sortie du restaurant. On a retrouvé dans son sang du phénobarbital, qu'elle avait déjà assimilé, et un taux d'alcool de .09. C'était assez pour la rendre amorphe.

Duval, qui observait Villemure inscrire des données dans son rapport, marcha autour de la table.

— On l'aurait auparavant droguée ? Il faudra demander à Poirier comment elle se sentait avant qu'il la quitte. Elle et son cousin sont, semble-t-il, allés manger chez Popeye. Quarante minutes, c'est le temps qu'il faut pour quitter le carré D'Youville et se rendre à Sillery en autobus. Dix minutes en voiture. L'effet du barbiturique a dû taper au maximum au restaurant.

— Aurait-elle pu repartir avec le garçon qui l'accompagnait ?

Louis prit la parole.

— Elle est repartie seule, car il habite Lévis et elle, Sillery. Elle devait prendre l'autobus 25. Cependant, Poirier est sur notre liste. Il aurait pu utiliser la voiture de sa mère, aller reconduire Rosalie et s'en prendre à elle.

Villemure, qui ressemblait à un phénix dans son sarrau blanc et avec sa chevelure abondante, intervint.

— On a prélevé quelques fibres beiges sous ses bottes, ce qui veut dire qu'elle est montée dans une voiture. Il faudra vérifier chez Poirier si elles peuvent provenir de la voiture de ses parents.

— Et l'autre, Michaël Mathieu, où habite-t-il ? s'enquit Louis.

— Québec. Mais on ne sait pas où pour l'instant. On cherche encore. Il serait squatter.

Villemure les avisa qu'on avait relevé des cheveux sur le corps de la jeune fille.

— À première vue, l'examen des cheveux, la présence de la racine, laisse croire qu'ils ont été arrachés. Mireille vous en dira plus. Et pour ce qui est de la morsure, elle correspond à l'arc dentaire supérieur de Rosalie. Elle s'est mordue elle-même, sans doute en se débattant.

— Les marques sur le sein ? demanda Duval.

— Ce sont les ongles de l'assassin, qu'il semble porter assez longs.

Le technicien, scie à la main, attendait pour effectuer la coupe de la calotte crânienne. Il abaissa sa visière protectrice, actionna l'appareil. Le son strident de l'engin incita Duval et Louis à sortir.

Ils passèrent ensuite à la section Biologie du labo. Mireille, derrière son microscope, examinait justement des échantillons de cheveux. Louis savait que Duval avait longtemps été possédé par le charme de la jeune femme. Il parla assez fort pour être compris de Mireille.

— Cette fille-là pourrait être Miss Univers et elle réserve ses beaux yeux pour la lunette de son microscope. Si j'étais pas aussi vieux, fêlé et mal emmanché, je la draguerais.

Elle fit pivoter sa chaise et toisa Loulou du regard.

— Je ne suis pas sûre que ta femme aimerait ça.

Huit ans plus tôt, les propos machistes de Louis auraient déplu à Mireille, mais elle s'était vite rendu compte qu'il la taquinait et prenait plaisir à la voir grimper dans les rideaux. Elle avait fini par le relancer du tac au tac ; il n'y avait rien d'autre à opposer à cet irréductible.

— Louis, on m'a dit que tu es de retour.

— Eh oui ! Il fallait bien que Batman retrouve Robin. Qu'est-ce que tu fais dimanche matin prochain ?

— Le dimanche matin, je dors après avoir veillé tard.

— Eh bien, tu veilleras tard, mais tu viendras à la messe de la police que j'organise. On a un *band*, une chorale, et un petit buffet après.

Daniel ricana.

— Je ne suis pas pratiquante, Louis.

— La religion, c'est comme un virus, ça fermente en dedans. Ça finit toujours par remonter.

— C'est aussi ce qui se produit au moment d'une indigestion…

— Ça, c'est quand tu manges trop.

Elle afficha un sourire plein de fraîcheur.

— On verra, Louis. Je ne te promets rien.

Duval aperçut le dossier qu'elle remplissait et lui demanda ce qu'elle avait à lui dire sur les preuves accumulées.

— D'abord, en ce qui concerne le sperme, je peux confirmer que le gars était seul. Son sang est du groupe O. Je complète l'examen des cheveux.

Duval se pencha pour regarder dans la lunette du microscope et il apprécia le parfum d'agrumes qui émanait de Mireille. L'examen visuel offrait déjà une idée de la longueur des cheveux du suspect et de la teinte de ceux-ci.

Un examen microscopique plus poussé, ce qu'elle était en train d'effectuer, permit d'établir le diamètre du cheveu, sa couleur exacte et les couleurs secondaires, car il n'est pas rare qu'un individu ayant un cheveu de couleur X possède aussi en petit nombre des cheveux de couleur Y ou Z. Elle détermina aussi le type de racine, les caractéristiques du canal médullaire, du cortex, de l'épidermicule et la forme de l'extrémité du cheveu.

— On est chanceux d'avoir ces éléments-là. La victime, même amorphe, a résisté au début. Elle a eu le temps de redouter ce qui allait suivre. Pauvre petite femme… Je devrais avoir terminé l'examen complet du cheveu d'ici vingt minutes. Pour l'instant, on peut déterminer qu'il a les cheveux brun clair – on en a trouvé en plus grand nombre – mais il y a aussi deux cheveux noirs et un cheveu blanc, ce qui ne veut pas dire qu'il soit vieux pour autant. À partir de déductions statistiques, je dirais qu'il a les cheveux d'un brun assez foncé. La racine du cheveu est creuse, mais j'ai relevé un aspect bizarre : l'angle de l'extrémité du cheveu est plus arrondi sur certains cheveux, surtout les bruns, et d'autres sont coupés en biseau, ce qui me fait dire que la coupe est récente à ces endroits alors qu'elle serait plus vieille pour les cheveux plus longs. J'ai l'impression que ses cheveux sont coupés d'une façon inhabituelle. Pour les poils pubiens, j'aurai fini de les analyser vers la fin de l'après-midi.

— Une coupe bizarre, dit Duval.

— Les jeunes ont tous des coupes de dégénérés, conclut Louis. On n'a pas fini de chercher…

Duval se demanda s'il était possible d'imaginer la coupe du suspect à partir de ces quelques indices.

Louis ne put s'empêcher de lancer une boutade à Mireille.

— Je voudrais pas être ton mari.

— Pourquoi ?

— Je me méfierais des cheveux que tu pourrais trouver sur mon veston…

Son petit rire cristallin, haut perché, tout pétillant de malice, emplit le labo d'une gaieté qui tranchait sur la lourdeur de l'enquête.

— Cré Louis, tu changes pas.

— Et le gant de latex ? demanda Duval.

— Quelques poils. C'est tout.

— Où est-ce qu'on se procure ces gants-là ? interrogea Louis.

— Il y a des fournisseurs comme Johnson et Johnson. On les trouve aussi en pharmacie.

Daniel avait tout pris en note, ce que Louis ne faisait plus depuis longtemps. Tous deux remercièrent Mireille et Louis lui rappela de venir à la messe de la police. Daniel, qui n'en pouvait plus d'entendre parler religion, pointa un doigt sur Louis.

— On sanctifiera le beu à la place de l'agneau.

Mireille éclata de rire, ce qui amena Marcel Rivard, le chimiste, à s'en mêler. Louis joua les vierges offensées, mais personne ne fut dupe.

— On s'amuse ferme, ici ! dit Rivard.

— C'est Mireille qui nous inspire. Toi, l'expert en incendie, tu devrais comprendre ça : elle nous enflamme, dit Louis.

— Il n'y a pas un accélérant plus puissant que Mireille, conclut le chimiste.

— Bande de vieux machos, soupira la biologiste. J'aimerais vous entendre répéter ces paroles-là devant vos femmes.

— On aurait droit à des effets repoussants, railla le chimiste.

33

La salle de conférences du dernier étage, près de la coupole, avait été réservée pour la réunion. Alignées sur un mur, les photos de tous les capitaines de l'ancienne Sûreté provinciale et de la SQ vous fixaient de leurs regards tranchants. Sur la grande table d'acajou, Duval avait déposé des photocopies du rapport encore partiel de l'autopsie. Dallaire entra, salua ses hommes et s'assit à droite de Duval, face à Louis, qui piqua un crayon à Francis. Duval révisa les notes qu'il avait prises. Prince, lui, la tête comme un bloc de granit, épluchait le rapport et le soulignait à plusieurs endroits.

Duval, qui avait étudié la question du jeu dans les meurtres en série, en s'attardant au fétichisme, allait sortir de la théorie pour passer à la pratique. Le lieutenant était reconnu comme un spécialiste de la question et il avait fait ses preuves dans l'affaire Hurtubise. Cependant, l'enquête immédiate n'était pas de la juridiction de la SQ et les critiques ne tarderaient pas si les choses traînaient en longueur.

— J'ai peur que nous ayons affaire à un tueur en série. Mais je n'en suis pas sûr à cent pour cent. Heureusement, nous n'avons qu'un cadavre, il est donc tôt pour se prononcer là-dessus. Mais je n'aime pas du tout ce qui se trouve en périphérie : les messages, les objets trouvés et la régularité des manifestations. Si c'est le cas, le tueur voudra faire sa loi dans les parages et même nous narguer.

Sans s'en rendre compte, Duval faisait tournoyer son stylo sur la table.

— L'affaire a commencé par un jeu, un jeu macabre qui s'est poursuivi par un homicide. Ce qu'on craint est arrivé et pourrait encore se reproduire. Ce genre d'individu ne ressent aucune autre émotion que le plaisir de dominer et de tuer. La souffrance de la victime constitue sa récompense. Il en jouit. Le rapport de l'autopsie pratiquée sur la jeune Nantel nous force à envisager cette perspective, car le meurtrier a l'imagination morbide, scabreuse.

Remarquant la moue de Louis, qui détestait ce jargon, Duval montra le dictionnaire et reprit.

— La puissance qu'il ressent au moment de perpétrer son crime, aussi vicieux soit-il, est une drogue. Présentement, il mijote sans doute le scénario de son prochain meurtre. Rappelez-vous le Fils de Sam, qui sévissait à New York il y a deux ans.

Le portrait alarmant peint par Duval avait de quoi inquiéter Dallaire, qui leva la main.

— Peux-tu nous faire un portrait de l'agresseur ?

— J'ai l'impression que notre type est beaucoup plus intelligent que Sam Berkowitz. Jeune, probablement très instruit, il est assez inspiré, compte tenu des messages qu'il laisse : des vers au vocabulaire élaboré et sans faute. Je veux aussi vous souligner une donnée troublante.

Duval se leva, ferma les lumières et actionna le rétroprojecteur. La poussière se mouvait à travers le faisceau lumineux. Un graphique dessiné à la va-vite apparut sur l'écran.

— Le chien mort a été abandonné près d'une école, de même que la main. Un graffiti obscène a été écrit sur le mur d'un tunnel à l'université. Aujourd'hui, on découvre un cadavre dans un cimetière et le gardien nous apprend qu'un mausolée a été profané et qu'on y a découvert un graffiti dont la teneur ressemble à ce qu'on a trouvé sur les autres scènes de crime.

Prince intervint avec sa grosse voix atone.

— Tout se passe dans un secteur très restreint, d'environ deux kilomètres carrés.

— Oui, c'est exact, et ça devrait nous servir de balise, répondit Duval.

Louis intervint :

— La bonne vieille madame Turner, dont les bonbons sont excellents, habite aussi très près.

— Oui, Louis. Et tu aurais dû lui demander où elle les achète, railla Duval.

— J'ai rien dit de déplacé !

Duval soupira, puis pointa sa baguette sur l'écran.

— Notez que le cimetière est situé près d'une école privée : Jésus-Marie, une institution qui reçoit des filles. Juste à côté, le Séminaire des Pères Maristes accueille des garçons. Fraser nous a dit que sa fille fréquentait le Petit Séminaire.

Francis coupa Daniel.

— Et si on avait affaire à quelqu'un qui en veut aux bourgeois ? Ou encore à un bourgeois qui sévit dans son milieu ?

— C'est une hypothèse parmi d'autres, affirma Duval. Mais je crois qu'on a affaire à quelqu'un qui tue pour un autre motif.

Le lieutenant observa dans la semi-obscurité ses collègues qui prenaient des notes.

— Rosalie Nantel est passée par Jésus-Marie, dit Dallaire. Elle a poursuivi ses études collégiales à Mérici, une école privée.

Duval hocha la tête.

— C'est ce que Prince m'a appris tout à l'heure. Ce qui me trouble aussi, ajouté à la teneur du message, c'est la présence d'éléments profanes et sacrés sur la scène du crime. Tout tourne autour d'une même haine, celle des femmes. Ce matin, le corps se trouvait disposé entre deux monuments : le premier montrant un ange et le second représentant une Vierge. Le maniaque a choisi le lieu en fonction d'un effet.

Francis se pencha et leva l'index.

— Des messages non verbaux ?

— Mais très explicites. En tout cas, la position des jambes, la manière dont elles étaient écartées, m'apparaît comme un message. Il n'a pas pu pénétrer la fille dans cette position. En laissant la victime dans cette posture grotesque, il veut premièrement narguer ceux qui arrivent sur la scène du crime et, deuxièmement, signer son meurtre. C'est ça aussi son jeu, le plaisir qu'il prend à marquer son passage. Comme une bête. Dans le mausolée, c'est pareil, il y avait un graffiti.

— C'est tiré de son imagination ? demanda Francis en se cachant les yeux de la lumière vive.

— Aucune idée, Frankie. Il va falloir travailler la question.

— C'est un cas patent de nécrophilie, conclut Dallaire.

— Plus récemment, on a appris qu'Idi Amin Dada, le président de l'Ouganda, était un anthropophage.

Francis ne put s'empêcher d'interrompre son chef.

— Ici, on a Pierre Elliot Trudeau qui bouffe du Québécois, lança-t-il en pouffant de rire.

La blague entraîna de larges sourires, sauf chez Prince, membre du Parti libéral et grand admirateur de Trudeau.

— Toi, on le sait, le chouenneux, t'es un maudit séparatiste.

— Idi Amin, il les mange saignants ou bien cuits ? demanda Louis pour détendre l'atmosphère.

Après quelques éclats de rire, Duval, qui avait l'impression d'être devant des élèves turbulents mais n'avait pas le goût de la rigolade ni d'une échauffourée politique, reprit son laïus comme s'il n'avait pas été interrompu.

— On peut déjà penser qu'il existait un lien entre cette jeune fille qui s'est suicidée et le meurtrier de Rosalie Nantel. Des amis communs ? Il faut chercher. La main découverte pourrait être celle d'Angélique Fraser. J'ai su aussi qu'elle avait suivi un cours intitulé *Philosophie de la mort* au Séminaire de Québec, titre qui peut laisser songeur. Le père en veut au professeur, un certain Déziel, avec qui elle aurait brièvement entretenu une relation amoureuse. Il croit que ce cours a poussé sa fille au suicide. Il faut interroger ce professeur. Savoir s'il a déjà été le sujet de plaintes de la part de ses étudiants.

Il se tourna vers Prince.

— Je vais te demander de t'occuper de toutes les dispositions pour exhumer le corps d'Angélique Fraser. Interroge encore le gardien. Puis informe-toi à la STCUQ pour savoir qui étaient les chauffeurs d'autobus à cette heure-là. On n'a toujours pas cette information. Les parents ont remis une photo de Rosalie à Francis. Je l'ai jointe au dossier. Fais circuler.

Louis leva la main.

— Bernard et moi, on a appris qu'un employé du cimetière de la Côte a été renvoyé pour avoir profané un lot qu'il s'apprêtait à déplacer. C'est arrivé il y a un an. On a reçu cette information de façon anonyme, ce matin. Une voix de femme. L'affaire avait alimenté la tribune téléphonique de l'idiot national.

— Mais le directeur du cimetière m'a affirmé que ses hommes avaient toute sa confiance, argua Duval.

— Ceux d'aujourd'hui peut-être, mais y paraît que ce gars-là a été renvoyé à la demande de ses collègues fossoyeurs, qui l'appelaient le Corbeau. La personne a refusé de s'identifier, répondit Bernard.

— Il faut suivre cette piste également. Francis, tu vas interroger les anciens collègues de Corbeau et tu cuisines le directeur, qui m'avait tu cette information.

Ensuite, tu iras rencontrer Miljours pour voir ce qu'ils ont trouvé. Louis et moi, on va s'occuper de l'ami de Rosalie Nantel. Il est le dernier à l'avoir vue en vie. Puis on ira au collège rencontrer le prof de philo.

Finalement, il y avait assez de travail pour foutre en l'air la fin de semaine, pensa Duval.

Dallaire prit le relais.

— Je vais faire surveiller de plus près les cimetières et les écoles. Je m'occupe du suivi avec le capitaine Plante, de la police de Sillery. Je vais mettre plus d'hommes sur les enquêtes de voisinage.

Duval demanda l'attention de tous ses collègues.

— Un dernier mot avant qu'on se quitte : je voudrais qu'aucune information ne coule dans les médias. On ne mentionne pas les messages. Ces débiles-là ont la passion des albums sanglants relatant leurs exploits. Et les rédacteurs de certains journaux salivent au goût du sang qui tache les premières pages. Faites attention.

34

Sébastien Poirier habitait rue Wolfe, à Lévis. Duval regarda l'heure à son poignet et conclut qu'il parviendrait à temps à la traverse de Québec-Lévis si les feux de circulation voulaient coopérer. Il éviterait ainsi les ponts et le trafic de 16 h. Il aimait prendre le traversier, cela lui permettait de s'arrêter un instant tout en continuant d'avancer.

Duval roula en jonglant avec la circulation pour éviter les bouchons et les arrêts. Il connaissait la ville par cœur et tous les trucs qui font gagner du temps. La voiture arriva à la hauteur de Place-Royale.

La passerelle du traversier était toujours abaissée et les pneus ronronnaient contre le grillage gaufré du tablier du pont.

D'un mouvement de bras répétitif, le préposé lui indiqua la queue qu'il devait suivre. Comme d'habitude, peu de voitures empruntaient le traversier. Trois minutes plus tard, un matelot à quai largua les amarres sur le pont. Dans une traînée d'écume, les puissants moteurs du Radisson le propulsèrent loin de la rive.

Compte tenu du peu de temps dont ils disposaient et de sa mobilité réduite, Louis resta dans la voiture et Daniel lui tint compagnie.

Il aurait voulu dire à Louis qu'il était content de se retrouver de nouveau sur le terrain en sa compagnie. Mais il savait que Loulou n'aimait pas trop parler de sentiments.

Dans le rétroviseur, la ville de Québec s'éloignait, toute de gris, alors que les gratte-ciel poussaient dans le ciel à mesure que la rive de Lévis se rapprochait. Daniel pensa à Laurence. La date à laquelle ils emménageraient ensemble n'avait toujours pas été déterminée. Peu à peu, le cap et la terrasse de Lévis envahissaient son champ de vision.

◆

Duval gara son véhicule dans l'entrée d'une vaste résidence victorienne aux volets noirs. La maison de trois étages, en brique rouille, méritait bien la rue du général Wolfe. Une imposante haie de cèdres, digne d'un rempart, camouflait tout le premier étage. Devant la demeure, un jardinier installait des cônes aux rosiers.

Duval sortit le fauteuil roulant du coffre. Quand il voulut aider Louis à s'extraire de l'habitacle, ce dernier refusa en pestant contre ce monde qui faisait des handicapés des êtres dépendants d'une main secourable. Duval lui suggéra de se calmer pendant qu'il dépliait le fauteuil roulant. Louis jaugea le terrain. Il était plat du stationnement jusqu'à la porte.

— Laisse faire le fauteuil. Passe-moi les béquilles.

Pendant que Louis se tenait contre la voiture, Duval ouvrit le coffre et en sortit les béquilles en aluminium. Après les avoir glissées sous ses aisselles, Loulou soupira :

— Enwoye, Lazare, marche !

Il avança prudemment en s'appuyant uniquement sur sa jambe droite, qui avait conservé une certaine sensibilité. Sa masse corporelle était lourde à déplacer.

Duval le surveillait de près.

— Regarde-moi pas de même, ça me gêne. J'ai l'impression d'être enceinte.

— Mais c'est super ! Tu te déplaces assez rapidement.

Toutefois, le Gros parut vite à court de souffle. Il dut s'arrêter à deux mètres de la porte. Puis, il s'activa de nouveau et se rendit jusqu'au seuil.

Duval l'observait comme un père fier de son fiston.

Louis appuya même sur le bouton de la sonnette. Un carillon prétentieux de type Westminster retentit. Une dame distinguée, dans la cinquantaine, apparut dans l'embrasure de la porte. Son regard indisposé glissa de haut en bas, de Duval à Harel, comme s'ils étaient des colporteurs.

— Lieutenant Duval et caporal Harel.

Elle esquissa un vague sourire aussi pâlot que son teint. Les taches brunes sur ses mains annonçaient des problèmes à la vésicule biliaire, ce que confirmait l'odeur âcre de foie malade qu'elle dégageait.

— Entrez, messieurs. Sébastien est à l'étage. C'est affreux ce qui est arrivé à ma nièce. Sébastien et Rosalie étaient inséparables.

Duval saisit le coude de Louis pour l'aider à franchir le seuil.

La mère appela son fils.

— Il corrige pour un professeur.

Elle hocha la tête, consternée.

— J'ai pu parler une dizaine de minutes avec ma sœur et elle est complètement démolie. C'est atroce. Elle qui était tellement près de Rosalie.

L'intérieur était décoré de meubles antiques et tous les murs étaient couverts de papier peint. Une bonne odeur de feu de foyer planait dans l'air et les flammes se reflétaient sur le plancher de bois franc. La pièce était séparée de la salle à manger par des portes en chêne au verre ciselé. Par une baie vitrée on voyait le Château Frontenac juché au sommet du cap Diamant, sur lequel s'étirait la Citadelle.

Poirier apparut dans le tournant de l'escalier et descendit sans se presser. Il portait des bottillons bruns en cuir italien, un pantalon en velours côtelé beige et un col roulé noir en laine. Il avait une allure nettement androgyne. Duval ne lui donnait pas plus de vingt ans. Sa peau était légèrement acnéique, mais la délicatesse de ses traits, ses lèvres pulpeuses et ses yeux vifs rachetaient cette tare. Ses cheveux bruns étaient rasés sur le côté et hérissés sur le dessus du crâne.

Duval lui serra la main. Une main rougie par l'encre. D'un geste mollasson, le jeune homme invita les enquêteurs à passer au salon et à prendre place sur le canapé. Louis s'appuya contre un accoudoir et se laissa choir dans le Chesterfield rouge.

Ils échangèrent quelques politesses. Le jeune homme étudiait à l'université, mais il avait manqué ses cours depuis qu'il avait appris la nouvelle. À voir ses yeux cernés et rougis, Duval sut qu'il avait pleuré une partie de la journée. À moins que ce ne soit le manque de sommeil.

— Mon petit gars est fatigué, dit la mère. Il lui faut corriger cent dissertations d'ici deux jours.

Elle posa une main tendre sur l'épaule de son fils, qui rejeta cette marque d'affection par une rotation d'épaule et une moue embarrassée.

— Après l'appel de ma tante, j'ai été incapable de me rendormir.

Sa voix sonnait fêlée, peut-être à force de répéter ce qui s'était passé. Il se cala dans un fauteuil, de biais à Duval. Le lieutenant amorça l'interrogatoire avec une voix douce, avenante.

— Vous vous doutiez de quelque chose ?

— On n'a jamais de bonnes ondes quand on est encore debout à 3 h du matin. Ma tante m'a dit qu'elle n'était pas rentrée. J'ai pensé qu'elle était allée coucher chez son ex-chum, ce qui m'étonnait d'ailleurs, car ils s'étaient laissés après une grosse chicane. Elle le craignait. Rosalie avait coupé le contact avec lui.

La mère se retira dans la cuisine, mais sans doute écoutait-elle tout ce qui se disait au salon. Louis fixait l'encre rouge qui tachait les doigts du garçon. Le calepin ouvert, il était disposé pour une fois à prendre des notes et attendait le déluge d'informations.

— Sébastien, les parents de Rosalie ont avisé mon collègue, l'enquêteur Tremblay, que vous êtes sorti avec elle à sa demande. Pouvez-vous me rappeler la conversation que vous avez eue et à quelle heure ?

— Elle m'a téléphoné vers 19 h. Elle voulait se rendre au Fuzz.

— C'est quoi au juste, le Fuzz ?

— Une discothèque.

— Je le sais. Mais de quel genre ?

— C'est plutôt punk.

Duval avait vu au téléjournal un reportage sur le phénomène punk. On y montrait comment les Sex Pistols avaient perturbé le jubilé de la reine Élisabeth. Ils avaient loué un bateau et craché, la nuit tombée, leurs décibels haineux aux environs de Buckingham Palace et St. John's Wood. « Une belle bande de tarés », s'était-il dit. Et on les avait arrêtés au retour de leur virée.

— On nous a dit qu'elle avait une raison précise de vous demander de l'accompagner ?

Poirier parut surpris. L'information circulait déjà.

— Elle avait peur de son ex.

— Comment s'appelle-t-il ?

— Michaël Mathieu.

— Quel âge a-t-il ?

— Vingt.

— Il habite où ? On ne parvient pas à lui mettre la main dessus.

— Il habitait dans la rue d'Aiguillon. Mais il est parti sans payer son loyer. Il squatterait quelque part dans la côte d'Abraham, près de la Procure générale de musique.

— Rosalie connaissait son adresse ?

— Oui, je crois.

— Les parents de Mathieu ne savaient pas où il logeait. Étaient-ils brouillés ?

— Oui, Michaël avait une relation orageuse avec eux, comme avec bien du monde.

— Rosalie avait-elle lieu de le craindre ?

— Oui, il l'avait menacée.

— Quel genre de menaces ?

— Il voulait lui faire du mal.

Avec maniérisme, Poirier sortit une Du Maurier d'un porte-cigarettes en argent et l'alluma avec un briquet plaqué or.

— Le mal peut prendre bien des formes : il voulait lui faire mal physiquement ou moralement ?

— Autant l'un que l'autre ; Michaël ne pouvait accepter qu'elle lui échappe. Il en était amoureux depuis plusieurs années. Elle était tout ce qu'il lui restait. Rosalie était une fille superbe, très belle et spirituelle, courtisée par plein de gars. Michaël, lui, avait décidé de mener une vie de parfait nihiliste. Il dénigrait tout, ne croyait en rien, bafouait toutes les conventions alors que Rosalie voulait mener une vie normale, devenir médecin. Il n'acceptait pas qu'elle ne le suive pas dans sa doctrine. Rosalie m'a confié qu'elle ne pouvait plus lui dire « Je t'aime » sans être ridiculisée. Tous nos gestes, d'après lui, étaient motivés par notre déterminisme biologique. C'était sa nouvelle philosophie. Elle le voyait dépérir et ça l'inquiétait. Mais qu'est-ce qu'elle pouvait y faire ?

Louis écarquilla les yeux et grogna. L'odeur des tartes qui émanait du four lui infligeait le supplice de Tantale.

— Mathieu n'étudiait pas ?

— Non, il a tout abandonné après trois semaines. Autant il était bolé au Séminaire, autant la philo à l'université l'a dégoûté au point qu'il a tout rejeté. Il a décidé de vivre avec le moins de biens matériels possible pour faire un pied de nez à la société. Toutes ses privations ont fini par affecter sa santé physique et, je crois bien, mentale.

— Mathieu est-il d'une famille aisée ?

— Ses parents sont riches.

— Je reviens sur ses menaces. Avait-il essayé de la faire souffrir ?

— Elle m'a dit qu'il l'intimidait au téléphone et à la sortie des classes.

— Quel genre d'intimidation ?

— Il disait qu'il se tuerait. D'ailleurs, il a déjà fait une tentative de suicide. L'histoire est connue.

— Connue ?

— L'affaire a circulé.

— Où étudiait Rosalie ?

— En médecine à l'Université Laval.

Poirier inhala longuement sa cigarette, en tapota le filtre avec son pouce.

— Est-ce que Mathieu est venu au Fuzz, hier ?

— Oui, mais pas longtemps. Il a fait le tour et il est ressorti.

— Comment a-t-elle réagi ?

— Elle ne l'a pas regardé.

— A-t-il tenté de lui parler ?

— Non, pas à ma connaissance.

— À quelle heure avez-vous quitté le Fuzz ?

— Autour de minuit. On est allés manger un morceau au Popeye.

— Vous y êtes restés combien de temps ?

— Moins d'une heure.

— Plus précisément ?

Tout en estimant le temps, son visage se contorsionna.

— Disons quarante-cinq minutes.

— Avez-vous remarqué quelque chose de spécial ? Auriez-vous été observés ?

— Non.

— Mathieu ne se trouvait pas à l'extérieur ?

— Non.

— Avez-vous quitté ensemble le restaurant ?

Ses yeux s'embuèrent et sa voix chevrota. Il revivait ces derniers moments qui repassaient dans sa tête. Il essuya une larme au coin de l'œil.

Il écrasa sa cigarette et Duval fixa cette main rougie par l'encre.

— Oui, comme je ne voulais pas manquer mon traversier, je l'ai accompagnée à l'arrêt de la 25.

— Au carré D'Youville ?

— Oui.

— Puis ?

— On s'est fait la bise, et ce matin j'ai appris ce qui s'était passé.

— Vous l'avez vue monter dans l'autobus ?

— Non, je suis parti avant.

— Vous rappelez-vous avoir vu à l'arrêt d'autobus quelqu'un qui aurait pu engager la conversation avec Rosalie ?

— Non. À cette heure-là, je crois qu'elle était seule.

— Comment était-elle ?

Il hésita à répondre.

— Elle avait terriblement sommeil. Elle n'arrêtait pas de dire qu'elle avait un gros coup de barre. Elle se sentait lourde.

— Qu'est-ce qu'elle a bu ce soir-là ?

— Un piña colada et une margarita.

— Avez-vous laissé vos verres sans surveillance ?

— On est allés danser deux fois. Vous voulez dire…

— On vérifie toutes sortes d'hypothèses. Sébastien, vous savez que dans mon métier il faut tout vérifier. Avez-vous encore votre ticket de traversier ?

— J'ai un laissez-passer mensuel.

Il sortit son portefeuille et leur montra sa carte de la Société des traversiers.

Duval observa l'objet attentivement. Ce laissez-passer ne prouvait rien. Il aurait pu prendre le bateau à n'importe quelle heure ou revenir à Lévis avec la voiture de sa mère.

— Je ne veux rien insinuer, mais qu'est-ce qui me certifie que vous avez pris le bateau à l'heure que vous me dites ?

Le jeune homme roula les yeux, mais ne manifesta aucun signe d'agressivité.

— Écoutez, j'ai rien d'autre à vous montrer. Demandez à ma mère, j'étais couché depuis une heure quand ma tante a téléphoné.

— Avez-vous parlé à quelqu'un sur le traversier ?

— À cette heure, le traversier est désert. Et je ne suis pas du genre sociable.

— Le préposé au guichet vous reconnaîtrait-il ?

— Sans doute.

Duval tourna quelques pages de son carnet.

— Le père de Rosalie nous a dit qu'il s'est passé un incident, samedi soir dernier au Laurentien, à la sortie des bars. Un acte de grossière indécence.

— J'allais vous en parler. C'est d'ailleurs pour cette raison qu'on n'est pas retournés au Laurentien. Ce sont des punks de la Basse-Ville qui font des cochonneries sous les tables du restaurant. Ils avaient pris la gageure de se masturber. Et c'était au premier qui éjaculerait. Rosalie s'était sentie observée par un des gars. Puis la serveuse s'est finalement rendu compte de leur pari stupide. Ils se sont fait virer ou plutôt ils se sont enfuis. La serveuse était hors d'elle-même et la nouvelle a vite fait le tour des tables.

Duval glissa un regard vers la baie vitrée de la salle à manger. La noirceur tombait sur la ville que découpaient les lumières des tours à bureaux et des immeubles d'habitation. La mère préparait le souper. Une odeur de poulet mêlée à celle des tartes aux pommes gagnait peu à peu la pièce et titillait les papilles gustatives de Louis, qui salivait déjà en songeant au repas que lui réservait Claudette.

— Pouvez-vous m'indiquer le nom et l'adresse de la meilleure amie de Rosalie ?

— C'est Andréanne Marceau ; elle habite rue du Parc à Québec. Je sais comment m'y rendre, mais je ne connais pas l'adresse exacte. Par contre, j'ai son numéro.

Il sortit son agenda de poche et donna le numéro de téléphone de la jeune femme à Duval, qui le nota.

Le lieutenant se leva et signala à Sébastien qu'il aurait encore besoin de lui.

— Est-ce aussi affreux qu'on semble le dire ? Qu'est-ce qu'on lui a fait ?

Duval serra les lèvres et hocha la tête, autant de dépit que pour dire oui.

— C'est le meurtre d'un être dérangé. J'ai une dernière question, Sébastien. Est-ce que Mathieu aurait pu aller jusqu'à tuer Rosalie ?

— Il y a six mois, je vous aurais dit : impossible. Mais dans l'état où il se trouve présentement et sans chercher à l'accuser, loin de là, je dirais que tout est possible. Ce gars-là traverse une saison en enfer.

Duval croyait avoir déjà entendu cette phrase quelque part.

— Michaël Mathieu avait-il un penchant morbide ?

— Oh oui ! Absolument.

La mère, qui avait sans doute compris que l'entretien tirait à sa fin, s'approcha. Elle serra son fils par la taille, mais celui-ci, une fois de plus, se raidit comme une barre, puis s'écarta brusquement. Décidément, les marques d'attention de cette mère poule l'horripilaient. Elle détacha son tablier.

— Avez-vous des suspects ?

Duval craignait que Louis ne réponde : « Oui, madame, votre fils. » Tous ceux qui avaient gravité autour de Rosalie étaient suspects.

— On a quelques pistes.

Daniel donna un appui à Louis pour l'aider à se relever du fauteuil. Il consulta sa montre et constata qu'ils devaient patienter trente minutes avant le prochain traversier. À son grand déplaisir, un détour par les ponts s'avérait inévitable. Il détestait parcourir autre chose qu'une ligne droite pour se rendre à son but, quel qu'il soit. Le cercle était une figure géométrique maudite pour Duval : il signifiait tourner en rond.

Il déposa Louis dans le stationnement de la centrale, sortit le fauteuil roulant du coffre arrière, et donna congé à son acolyte pour la soirée. Avant de partir, il lui confia qu'il était content de retravailler en sa compagnie.

Louis parut heureux.

— J'ai deux couples qui marchent dans ma vie : le premier avec Claudette et l'autre avec toi. Mais toi, je te baiserais pas !

Daniel s'esclaffa et souhaita une bonne soirée à son copain, qui allait assister à un match de la LNH ; les Nordiques jouaient contre les Oilers d'Edmonton.

35

Duval se doutait bien que Francis était au boulot. De l'extérieur, la fenêtre de son bureau était la seule allumée.

Il marcha rapidement dans le corridor, tourna dans la pièce où s'alignaient les cagibis vitrés. Les leurs étaient près d'une fenêtre avec une vue au nord. Penché sur un bloc-notes, Francis rédigeait son rapport de la journée. Une fine mèche blonde tombait dans ses lunettes. Une pile de mouchoirs s'accumulait devant lui.

Il éternua, une fois, deux fois, trois fois. Il leva la tête en entendant les bruits de pas de son collègue. Il recula sa chaise et posa ses pieds sur son bureau. La journée avait été longue. Il avait les traits tirés et le nez rougi, congestionné. Son rhume allait sûrement faire ricochet et se transmettre à toute l'équipe.

— Du nouveau, Francis ?

Il renifla deux coups secs.

— On cherche Mathieu, mais on ne le trouve pas. C'est une question d'heures. Prince a pu parler aux chauffeurs d'autobus de la 25. L'un d'eux affirme avoir fait monter en début de soirée la jeune fille, qu'il voit fréquemment sur ce parcours, mais les autres ne se rappellent pas l'avoir vue par la suite.

— Est-elle montée ou descendue avec quelqu'un qu'elle aurait rencontré ?

— Le chauffeur ne s'en souvient pas. Pour ce qui est de l'exhumation du corps, Prince a obtenu l'autorisation du coroner et celle de monsieur Fraser, mais le docteur demeure inquiet pour sa femme si elle apprend ça.

— Et toi ?

— Une histoire d'horreur. Je t'attendais pour en avoir le cœur net.

— Quoi ?

Francis ferma les yeux. Il appréhendait un éternuement. Il éternua fortement dans ses mains, arracha deux Kleenex de la boîte et trompeta pendant dix secondes.

— Tu veux savoir, pour Corbeau ?

Duval pencha la tête, anxieux de découvrir l'horreur se cachant derrière Corbeau.

— J'ai rencontré les ex-collègues de Corbeau et ils ont esquissé un portrait épouvantable du gars. À vrai dire, le portrait d'un dégénéré. Corbeau a travaillé huit ans au cimetière comme fossoyeur et *foreman*. Il manœuvrait aussi la pépine. L'une de ses perversions préférées, une fois que les proches d'une disparue avaient quitté le cimetière – tu devrais t'asseoir, Dan, c'est épouvantable, tu vas vouloir te faire incinérer après ça – était d'ouvrir le cercueil pour contempler le corps des femmes. On m'a dit qu'il leur baissait la jupe, regardait les organes génitaux ou retirait le soutien-gorge pour contempler les seins. Ensuite seulement on la portait en terre.

— Est-ce que les autres fossoyeurs participaient ?

— Non. Ils ont été catégoriques. Ils avaient beau tenter de le dissuader, rien n'y faisait. C'était lui le chef d'équipe. Mais les pires profanations se produisaient lorsque Corbeau devait replacer un lot.

— Explique. Je ne te suis pas.

— Un lot, c'est toute une famille qui est enterrée ensemble. Comme l'espace dans un cimetière coûte cher, les cercueils sont empilés les uns par-dessus les autres. Dans certains cas, tu as jusqu'à cinq ou six cercueils superposés. Si bien que le cercueil du fond peut être là depuis cent ou cent trente ans, celui du milieu depuis cinquante ans. Et comme le bois finit par pourrir, il arrive parfois que le sol s'affaisse légèrement. Lorsqu'il n'y a plus de place et qu'une famille veut réunir les proches, ils achètent un autre lot. Tu me vois venir. Il faut alors exhumer les cercueils un à un. Toute l'opération se fait à la pelle et les cercueils sont dans un état pitoyable. Malgré toutes les précautions, ils se brisent sous le poids des fossoyeurs et l'action de la pelle. Un fossoyeur m'a dit, et ç'a été confirmé par deux autres gars, que Corbeau s'amusait à défigurer des cadavres qui avaient été remarquablement conservés à cause de l'absence d'humidité qui prévaut à certains endroits. Il lui arrivait d'enfoncer les yeux de cadavres avec son pic. Des histoires dégueulasses ! J'en avais la chair de poule. Finalement, un travailleur a dénoncé

Corbeau. Le directeur général, Monette, pour ne pas ternir la réputation de son cimetière, n'a pas porté plainte à la police, mais il a congédié Corbeau. Celui-ci n'avait aucun respect et aucun scrupule à agir ainsi, m'a-t-on dit. «Y sont morts, bande de crétins», répétait-il à ses collègues, qui en avaient peur. C'est un gros gars agressif, d'après le portrait qu'on m'en a brossé.

Duval écarquilla les yeux.

— T'as essayé d'aller l'interroger ?

— Oui, mais il n'y avait pas de réponse.

— Où habite-t-il ?

— Rue Laforest. C'est près de l'aquarium.

— C'est aussi près du chemin Saint-Louis.

— Autre élément intéressant : lorsque Corbeau voyait dans la rue une femme qui l'excitait, ou encore le Rayon matinal[2] dans le *Journal de Québec*, il passait des commentaires haineux et à connotation sexuelle. Ou encore lorsqu'il apercevait une jolie défunte photographiée dans la notice nécrologique, et constatait qu'elle serait inhumée au cimetière de la Côte, il disait aux gars qu'elle serait là tel jour à telle heure.

Duval écarquilla les yeux de stupeur.

— As-tu pensé à leur demander s'ils croyaient Corbeau capable de se livrer à des attouchements sexuels sur des corps en dehors de son travail ? Revenir le soir sur place ?

— Non, j'y ai pas pensé.

— Quand a-t-il été congédié ?

— Il y a environ un an.

— Le portrait qu'ils t'ont fait est celui d'un nécrophile. Ce gars-là devait éprouver une grande satisfaction à effectuer ce boulot. Privé de son travail, il pourrait être sevré de cette jouissance-là. Le plaisir de ces types peut ressembler à celui que je prends à faire de la course

---

2 Nom de la section où des starlettes apparaissaient à demi nues dans le *Journal de Québec* au cours des années soixante-dix.

à pied et toi de l'aïkido ou de la chasse, ça devient un besoin. Sauf que, dans notre cas, ces activités sont permises.

— Encore pire, j'ai appris qu'il avait postulé pour travailler au cimetière de Sillery et qu'on lui a refusé l'emploi. Sa réputation était connue. Aurait-il voulu se venger?

— A-t-il un casier judiciaire? demanda Duval.

— Oui, pour voies de fait.

— T'as envie d'aller interroger le Corbeau?

— On n'a pas de mandat.

— On peut essayer quand même.

— Ça me va.

— Zut, il est déjà 18 h 30. Je passe un coup de fil à la maison.

Duval avisa Mimi qu'il rentrerait tard et de ne pas l'attendre pour souper.

— La fille assassinée, ce matin?

— Oui, répondit laconiquement le père.

— J'ai deux amies au Conservatoire qui la connaissaient. Elles sont traumatisées.

— On se reparle peut-être tout à l'heure. Je t'embrasse.

Laurence, qui bénéficierait de cinq jours de congé après son horaire de nuit, pesterait un peu, mais elle comprendrait la situation.

36

Corbeau habitait un modeste appartement situé à Pointe-Sainte-Foy. L'immeuble de trois étages, un monstre de l'architecture résidentielle des années soixante, jouxtait le chemin Saint-Louis. Des piles de circulaires jonchaient l'entrée sous les casiers postaux. Un pot-pourri d'odeurs de repas flottait dans le vestibule. Les voix des locataires, des télévisions et des radios dialoguaient en cacophonie. Francis frappa deux coups. Quelqu'un s'y trouvait, car une musique *hard rock* jouée à fort volume faisait trembler les murs.

Francis frappa plus fort avec le revers du poing. On baissa le volume de la musique. Un gros rot perça à travers les cloisons.

Un homme dont la tignasse sombre avait une texture de laine d'acier ouvrit la porte, sa bedaine à l'air soumise à la gravité, selon la théorie de Newton. Ses yeux vitreux, trop écartés, petites fentes sans humanité, vous dévisageaient froidement comme ceux d'un reptile. Duval lut aussitôt toute la démence de ce regard. Le nez bosselé de Corbeau affichait une vilaine fracture qui n'avait jamais été opérée. Ses bras étaient un canevas pour tatoueur en herbe où il fallait chercher la peau non altérée.

— Vous êtes monsieur…

Duval faillit dire « monsieur Corbeau » mais il se ravisa.

— … Barbeau ?

— Ouan ? Quesse vous voulez ?

Ses dents bleuies ressemblaient à un fromage stilton craquelé.

— Nous sommes de la police et nous avons des questions à vous poser.

— Pourquoi ?

— Un meurtre a été commis dans un cimetière.

— Hé ! menute. Où cé que tu vas, toé ? C'est quoi c't'affaire-là. Avez-vous un mandat, d'abord ?

Francis s'avança à deux centimètres de son visage.

— Non, mais j'ai la possibilité d'ouvrir une enquête sur les corps que t'as profanés. Avec les témoins que j'ai entendus, tu vas prendre tes vacances à Bordeaux et tu vas marcher le cul serré.

L'homme soupira, se rembrunit. Une épaisse fumée de cigarette se mouvait au plafond. Le monstre jaune sur l'affiche d'Iron Maiden semblait sortir du brouillard.

— Tout ça a été réglé avec Monette, le d.-g. du cimetière. J'ai rien à vous dire.

Il commença à refermer la porte, mais Francis l'obstrua du pied.

— Ils sont prêts à rouvrir une enquête si on démontre qu'on a des raisons de te soupçonner. Et laisse-moi te dire que tu vas passer un mauvais quart d'heure à raconter au juge les atrocités faites à ces corps. J'aimerais pas que ta mère lise ça dans les journaux.

— C'est que…

On entendit d'abord une voix éraillée, brisée par l'alcool et la nicotine.

— Cé qui, Doris ?

Puis elle apparut, toute de noir vêtue, haute comme trois pommes, les cheveux noirs, hirsutes, avec des filaments argentés, le visage potelé et bouffi, les hanches larges et les épaules rondes. Elle devait peser plus de cent kilos, évalua Duval. On aurait dit une lutteuse naine. Ses jambes pleines de varices ressemblaient à une carte routière.

— Je suis prêt à vous parler, mais je veux qu'elle parte.

Il se tourna vers elle.

— Je vas aller te rejoindre au Kentucky dans une vingtaine de menutes. Commande un baril.

— Pourquoé tu veux pas que j'reste ? Qu'est-ce qui te veulent, eux autres ?

Son regard heurta celui de Duval, qui afficha un sourire malicieux. Elle pointa ensuite son triple menton vers Francis.

— Y sont don bin *clean cut*, té chums.

— Mona, je te l'dirai pas deux fois, câlice, va au Kentucky, j'vas te r'joindre. C'est t'y assez clair ?

— Ockaye ! Ockaye !

Elle ouvrit la penderie, enfila son coupe-vent des Expos et sortit en tenant son paquet d'Export'A dans une main.

Corbeau ferma la porte.

Doris Barbeau était à la fin de la trentaine. Ses doigts jaunes donnaient l'impression qu'il avait mangé des crottes au fromage toute sa vie, mais il s'agissait bien de nicotine.

Même l'Armée du Salut aurait refusé les meubles du salon tellement ils étaient moches. Les coussins du canapé en faux cuir noir étaient couverts de longues lacérations. La table basse et l'étagère avaient été repeintes avec de la peinture à l'huile orangée lustrée. Seul objet de valeur, une imposante chaîne stéréo dont les haut-parleurs faisaient un mètre de hauteur. De quoi pulvériser le plancher du voisin à l'étage. Il n'y avait aucun livre dans la pièce alors que Duval recherchait un homme cultivé. Le demi-sous-sol empestait une odeur rance de vêtements non lavés imprégnés de senteur de friture.

Duval remarqua sur la table un crâne, un vrai, qui servait de cendrier, la gueule servant d'appui à la cigarette et la cendre tombant dans une assiette.

Barbeau leur offrit de s'asseoir. Duval aurait préféré ne pas avoir à le faire tellement la propreté des lieux laissait à désirer. Finalement, il prit place sur le bout du canapé, qui s'enfonça au point qu'il avait les genoux en pente.

— Où étiez-vous, hier, entre minuit et 3 h du matin?

— L'autre bord.

— Ça veut dire quoi, ça, l'autre bord?

— Dans ma chambre.

— Quelqu'un pour confirmer?

— Oui, le petit Jésus à qui j'ai fait ma prière!

Francis ne la trouva pas drôle.

— Écoute, Barbeau… si tu veux jouer aux épais, on va t'amener faire un petit tour quelque part où tu vas prier le bon Dieu… Contente-toi de répondre précisément aux questions.

Duval reprit.

— Quelqu'un pour confirmer?

— Non.

— Qu'est-ce qui vous amenait à mutiler des cadavres?

— Écoutez, j'me suis arrangé avec Monette là-dessus. Quelqu'un voulait mon poste. Les gars ont voulu me faire sauter et ils en ont inventé des bouts.

— Et ça?

Duval pointa le menton vers le crâne. Barbeau esquissa un sourire.

— Un vieux souvenir que j'ai ramassé dans la fosse commune. Faites le tour des cimetières, les fossoyeurs ont tous des petits trophées du genre.

Francis, perplexe, regarda son collègue.

— Avez-vous une voiture?

— Oui.

— La marque?

— Un GTO.

— Et vous n'êtes pas sorti, hier?

— Non.

Duval observa ses cheveux à la lumière et ils ne correspondaient pas à ceux qu'avait analysés Mireille.

Ceux de Barbeau étaient noir de jais avec un peu de gris.

Le lieutenant lui passa un crayon, déchira une feuille de son carnet :

— Tu vas écrire la phrase suivante : *Et faire à ton flanc étonné une blessure large et creuse.*

— C'est quoé ça ?

— Écris !

Il griffonna les mots en marmonnant comme un demeuré chaque syllabe. D'emblée, Duval vit qu'il ne savait pas écrire, qu'il avait devant lui un illettré qui peinait à former les lettres.

— La dictée est finie. On la corrige maintenant.

Duval reprit la feuille et comprit pourquoi Barbeau avait opté pour le métier de fossoyeur à dix-sept ans : *Et fair a ton flan étoné une blessur large et proffonde.* Jamais une telle phrase n'aurait pu jaillir d'un cerveau aussi démuni d'intelligence.

— Heureusement que la dictée n'avait que onze mots, dit Francis.

— J'ai toujours hagui l'école.

Duval fit signe à Francis qu'ils perdaient leur temps. Mais, avant de partir, il demanda à Barbeau s'il pouvait utiliser la salle de bains. D'un signe de tête, l'homme lui indiqua la porte rouge dans le coin de l'appartement. En s'y engageant, Duval sentit son cœur se hisser au bord des lèvres. Il lui fallut retenir sa respiration. Le bain était cerné d'une bande de crasse stratifiée, le bol semblait teint d'urine. Il chercha à tâtons dans la pharmacie une brosse à cheveux et un peigne desquels il arracha des cheveux, qu'il déposa dans un sac.

Duval sortit prestement de la salle de bains et se dirigea vers la porte de sortie où l'attendait Francis. Tous deux avaient envie de grand air. Duval pointa le doigt vers Corbeau.

— Si jamais j'apprends que tu t'es trouvé un job dans un cimetière, tu vas jouer avec des poignées de cercueil en prison.

Corbeau enfila sa veste à carreaux rouge et noire.

Duval se sentait comme un enfant qui n'a pas envie de rentrer à la maison. Il croyait qu'un squat près de la Procure générale de musique ne devait pas être si difficile à découvrir. Il éprouvait une irrésistible envie de surprendre l'ex-petit ami de Rosalie Nantel. Francis, qui s'en allait à un entraînement d'aïkido, déclina l'offre et conseilla à Duval de rentrer au bercail.

— Tu ne tiens plus debout.

— Mais je veux en avoir le cœur net.

— La police de Québec l'a cherché, il est introuvable.

— C'était avant qu'on rencontre Sébastien Poirier, le cousin de Rosalie. Mathieu habiterait un squat près de la Procure de musique.

Duval avait faim, mal à la tête, mais il lui fallait procéder sans attendre. Il déposa Francis dans le stationnement de la centrale. Avant de s'éloigner, Francis lui tapa amicalement sur l'épaule.

— Va manger une bouchée quand même.

— Là tu parles !

Avant de tenter de débusquer Mathieu, il suivit le conseil de son collègue et arrêta chez J.A. Moisan cueillir un sandwich et un jus.

37

Le stationnement était interdit à cet endroit, mais Duval actionna ses feux de détresse. Devant lui, en bas du cap, l'édifice du journal *Le Soleil,* tout de brique orangée, avec sa grosse enseigne rouge. Le ciel partiellement nuageux laissait entrevoir par moments la lune.

Si Mathieu squattait apparemment un immeuble situé près du magasin de musique, il fallait que ce soit dans le bas de la côte d'Abraham. Et comme l'imprimerie jouxtait la Procure, il fallait que le bâtiment soit celui à la peinture pelée couvert de graffitis. Le manque d'entretien trahit aussitôt l'existence du squat. La vitre de la porte d'entrée était souillée par les éclaboussures. Duval l'ouvrit. L'obscurité l'enveloppa. Il chercha à tâtons l'interrupteur. Il sentit ses doigts effleurer le bouton, l'actionna, mais celui-ci ne fonctionnait pas. La cage d'escalier puait l'humidité et les excréments d'animaux.

Duval rouvrit la porte extérieure et les phares d'un autobus lui permirent de voir une ampoule au-dessus des casiers postaux déglingués. Il vissa l'ampoule, mais pas de lumière. Hydro-Québec avait coupé l'alimentation en électricité. Il retourna à son véhicule et revint avec une lampe de poche.

Sur le mur d'entrée, on avait peint une murale sur un fond orange et mauve : une sorte de monstre, comme sur les couvertures des revues psychédéliques. Duval examina avec attention les détails de cette fresque hallucinée. Un diable enfilait avec sa corne et sa queue deux femmes à la fois. Il lut des graffitis d'un goût douteux :

« *Fuck* », « *Suck forever* », « *Never trust a hippie* ».

Duval avait l'impression que personne n'habitait le taudis. Il avança dans le petit couloir qui menait à l'appartement du rez-de-chaussée. À gauche, un escalier, d'où montait une odeur de cave mal drainée, menait au sous-sol. Le rayon de la lampe ne révéla rien d'autre que des dessins obscènes et plutôt sinistres. Les grosses blattes d'un brun huileux grouillaient sur le béton de la cave. Un chat miaulait sans arrêt dans un des appartements à l'étage.

La porte du premier logement n'était pas verrouillée et elle grinça en s'ouvrant. Le plancher était jonché de déchets : des boîtes de pizza, des paquets de cigarettes vides et des bouteilles de bière. Un sofa-lit était déplié. L'endroit puait l'urine. De vieux matelas et un sommier s'empilaient dans un coin. Duval arpenta le corridor. Il fit rapidement le tour de la pièce et ne vit rien. L'ampoule de la lampe de poche faiblissait de minute en minute. Les piles, qui n'avaient pas été remplacées depuis des lustres, n'en avaient plus pour très longtemps.

Il monta l'escalier avec précaution car la rampe reposait par terre. La porte de l'appartement de l'étage était verrouillée. Derrière, le miaulement obsessif du chat redoubla d'ardeur. Duval frappa pour la forme. Pas de réponse. Le chat gratta frénétiquement. Daniel retira un trombone qui retenait les pages de son calepin, le déplia et en un tournemain déverrouilla. Un chaton noir et blanc se frotta contre lui et poursuivit ses appels. Duval le ramassa d'une main et le caressa. L'animal ronronnait. Il le déposa sur le plancher.

Il balaya la pièce d'un faisceau lumineux. Ce n'était guère mieux qu'à l'autre appartement ; là aussi les conditions d'hygiène laissaient à désirer. Le froid et l'humidité rongeaient les os. Les plafonds étaient lézardés. Des dessins comme ceux du vestibule décoraient l'appartement. Il lut en grosses lettres rouges : *Comment survivre…* Son sang fit un tour et il sentit un engourdissement chatouiller son cuir chevelu. Le message, en lettres rouges stylisées, se poursuivait sur le mur : *aux décombres de nos amours ?* Duval continua d'avancer jusqu'au fond du corridor, où se trouvait une autre pièce. Le chat suivait Duval en se frottant contre lui et poussait une plainte de temps à autre. La lampe de poche agonisait. Le lieutenant avait peine à lire le message. Duval ouvrit la porte au bout du couloir, la lumière s'éteignit ; il secoua la torche électrique, fit quelques pas et cogna un objet en suspension. Il recula, repoussa la chose, qui ballotta au loin. La lumière s'allumait par intermittence. Noir, blanc. Noir, horreur. Duval ressentit une forte accélération cardiaque en voyant revenir vers lui le cadavre au bout de sa corde. Il se tassa sur la droite. Le corps poursuivit son sinistre mouvement pendulaire. Le chat se frotta contre sa cheville puis contre le tabouret renversé qui avait servi de gibet de fortune. L'animal se remit à miauler et Duval le prit dans ses bras, ce qui le calma.

Il aperçut une chandelle à moitié consumée et l'alluma, répéta le geste avec trois lampions d'église qu'il repéra près de la fenêtre. Une fois assuré de ne pas contaminer la scène du crime, il répartit çà et là les lampions pour y voir plus clair.

Un frisson glaça son échine.

Le garçon avait dessiné avec un rouge à lèvres un sourire de clown autour de sa bouche. Son visage, beau mais congestionné, était bleu par la strangulation. Il avait des cheveux brun foncé – une coupe mohawk. Il s'était pendu vêtu d'un blouson de cuir clouté. Ses pieds, nus et rougis, se balançaient à trois pieds du sol.

Duval s'approcha avec la chandelle, ses yeux à la hauteur de la taille du corps, et tourna autour. La corde passait sous le menton et remontait au milieu des joues : une corde en nylon identique à celle qui liait les poignets de Rosalie. Le malheureux l'avait attachée à un gros tuyau en fonte.

Un rubis au bout d'une chaîne sortait de la poche arrière de son jean noir. N'ayant pas de gants de latex sur lui, Duval coinça la pierre précieuse entre deux stylos, retira l'objet lentement et le déposa sur une table. C'était un pendentif typiquement féminin. Duval remarqua aussitôt l'absence de l'agrafe et de l'anneau. L'enquête qui s'annonçait si longue tirait déjà à sa fin.

◆

Il se demanda s'il devait appeler la police de Québec ou la SQ. La juridiction n'était pas la sienne, mais son enquête l'avait mené là. De sa voiture, il prit contact avec son patron, qui lui recommanda de transmettre l'affaire aux policiers de Québec.

Duval eut le temps de vérifier l'identité du garçon. Il s'agissait bel et bien de Michaël Mathieu, s'il se fiait aux enveloppes disposées çà et là qui lui étaient adressées. Sur un calorifère traînait le journal de Mathieu, à la couverture noire avec une reliure rouge, et Duval s'en empara. Pas question de le laisser à l'enquêteur qui se pointerait. Il chercha un carnet d'adresses mais en vain.

La lueur des chandelles rendait la pièce sinistre et macabre. Le corps qu'il avait auparavant secoué reposait immobile dans les airs. Par les odeurs qui s'en dégageaient, les lividités qui s'étaient fixées, Duval supposa que la mort remontait à une vingtaine d'heures.

Les bruits de pas d'une armada retentirent dans l'escalier.

Heureusement, Duval n'eut pas à tout expliquer à Granger, l'enquêteur de la Ville de Québec, le patron s'en était chargé. Il espérait maintenant ne pas avoir l'autre dans les jambes. Duval était avisé. De réputation, Granger n'était pas très bavard et peu avenant. Sa seule qualité : ne pas travailler pour la police de Sainte-Foy. Il répondait laconiquement aux questions. Un gars au bord de la retraite, à voir sa peau épaisse, tannée par le soleil de la Floride et la multitude de rides. Sa mâchoire à quatre-vingt-dix degrés, son nez camus et son front haut avaient quelque chose d'une sculpture antique. Ses cheveux gris étaient coupés en brosse et on aurait voulu y passer la main pour tester la raideur de ce crin argenté. Granger portait un complet d'une génération en retard, sans doute un deux pour un de St. Lawrence Clothing. Il ne serra pas la main de Duval et distribua aussitôt ses ordres. Il écouta ce que le lieutenant de la SQ avait à dire et déploya ses effectifs.

— Il faudra d'abord démontrer que le bijou appartenait bien à Rosalie Nantel.

Duval s'approcha du docteur Villemure, qu'on avait dépêché sur les lieux. La présence de pétéchies surprenait l'expert légiste.

— C'est une pendaison complète, mais on observe rarement ce genre d'hémorragie dans ces circonstances.

— Est-ce que c'est assez pour briser la colonne cervicale ?

Villemure jaugea la hauteur.

— Non, pas assez haut. On trouve ce type de fracture uniquement dans les pendaisons judiciaires. Le corps avec tout le poids du lien de strangulation doit faire une chute d'environ dix pieds pour qu'il y ait fracture de la colonne cervicale. Mais dans ce cas-ci, non. Ce sont surtout les lésions qui me laissent songeur. Ce pendu est un paradoxe. Il y a un sillon complet, comme c'est le cas pour une strangulation commise par derrière, et un sillon incomplet et oblique, qui part au-dessous du menton et monte vers la haut de la joue.

Duval réfléchit :

— Il a pu essayer d'abord une pendaison incomplète en fixant le lien de strangulation contre une poignée de porte pour ensuite opter, voyant que la première méthode ne fonctionnait pas, pour une pendaison complète.

— C'est possible… Les pendaisons incomplètes ne sont pas rares. On s'en reparle, dit Villemure, qui voulait poursuivre son travail seul.

Granger écoutait tout ce que racontait François à Duval, qui prenait des notes. Pendant que les hommes de Granger et ceux de la police technique déployaient des lampes sur pied et quadrillaient les lieux, Duval circulait, calepin à la main, pour que rien ne lui échappe au cas où le lieutenant-détective de Québec voudrait faire cavalier seul. Duval sentait bien que les emmerdes allaient se poursuivre sur un autre front : la juridiction. Granger semblait exaspéré de le voir glaner des informations autour du cadavre. Comme si la compétition venait de commencer.

Granger lui demanda s'il croyait Mathieu coupable du meurtre de sa petite amie.

— À première vue, on pourrait le penser. L'amant jaloux tue son ancienne petite amie et se suicide.

— C'est clair pour moi.

La thèse du meurtre sadique suivi d'un suicide lui paraissait évidente. De plus, la découverte du pendentif lui donnait toutes les raisons de croire que l'affaire était classée. Granger restait là, devant Duval, à attendre la suite de la réponse. Duval se rappela ce que lui avait dit le cousin de Rosalie.

— J'ai su que Mathieu avait déjà essayé de se suicider.

— Voilà !

Un technicien de l'Identité poussa un cri. Il venait de découvrir un message coincé entre le cylindre et le presse-papier de la machine à écrire.

Il n'y a qu'un problème philosophique vraiment sérieux, c'est le suicide. Juger que la vie vaut ou ne vaut pas la peine d'être vécue, c'est répondre à la question fondamentale de la philosophie.

AC

— On ne peut pas lui reprocher de ne pas avoir répondu à la question, conclut Villemure, pince-sans-rire.

— Il étudiait la philosophie, rappela Duval.

— Il aurait pas dû, maugréa Granger.

Duval se frotta la barbe à la hauteur du menton.

— Il y avait des messages sur les autres scènes de crime, plus violents que celui-ci. Mais comme ce message d'adieu s'adressait à celle qu'il aimait, il est peut-être normal qu'il en soit ainsi.

Le regard de Duval se posa sur un livre placé au-dessus d'une pile d'ouvrages philosophiques. Un format poche à la couverture rouge : *Le Mythe de Sisyphe*.

— On tient notre auteur. C'est Albert Camus. AC, ironisa Duval.

— «Assez», vous voulez dire, pesta Granger dont la racine du nez bougeait quand il parlait, remarqua Duval.

Le jeu de mots ne fit rire personne.

— Les autres graffitis n'étaient pas signés, fit remarquer Duval à Granger.

— Est-ce que ça pourrait être du même auteur?

— Je ne sais pas.

— Ma culture littéraire s'arrête à la famille Plouffe.

Un technicien déposa le livre dans un sac de papier.

Le chat talonnait Duval où qu'il se déplaçât dans l'appartement. Le lieutenant se pencha pour regarder les livres dans une bibliothèque de fortune en briques et en planches de pin : Artaud, Bakounine, Heidegger, Schopenhauer, Platon, Cioran, Baudelaire, Sénèque, Cicéron, Rimbaud, Cendrars, Freud, Ducharme, Nietzsche, Céline.

Sur un mur, quelqu'un avait inscrit en lettres noires sur fond rose : *Never mind the bollock's*. Duval se demanda ce que signifiait cette phrase. Un jeune policier qui passait par là lui apprit qu'il s'agissait du titre de l'album des Sex Pistols. Il le savait parce que son frère écoutait cette musique.

Duval salua le docteur et s'éclipsa. En descendant l'escalier, il croisa deux employés de la morgue avec une civière. Derrière lui tambourinaient de petits pas. Il se retourna, le chaton miaulait à ses pieds.

38

Fourbu, esquinté de sa journée, Duval regagna la maison. Le train du labeur avait roulé sur son corps. La pluie crépitait sur le toit de la voiture. Sans doute allait-elle se changer en neige. Dans la côte Saint-Sacrement, le véhicule d'un idiot qui roulait avec ses feux de route l'aveugla. Qu'allait-il faire de cette soirée ? Il hésitait à aller courir malgré cette fatigue qui le taraudait de partout. Il décida de remettre l'entraînement au lendemain, trop épuisé, trop éreinté.

Il s'arrêta au dépanneur et considéra que c'était sa dernière corvée.

La chaleur de la maison réchauffa ses os transis. Mimi, flûte à la main, s'assit sur la marche du haut.

— Grosse journée ?

— Tu parles ! Un meurtre, un suicide, peut-être le meurtrier, et une main qu'on n'arrive pas à identifier.

— Tout le monde en parle aux nouvelles.

Sauf que Duval, lui, ne voulait pas causer d'homicide devant sa fille. Il s'assit à son tour dans l'escalier, délaça ses chaussures, passa ses mains sur son visage fatigué.

— J'ai mangé avec Laurence, reprit Mimi, puis comme tu venais pas souper, elle est sortie au cinéma. Il reste de la lasagne au four.

Le regard de Mimi glissa du visage de son père à la poche de son imperméable. Un bruit étrange s'échappait de là. Daniel se tourna vers elle.

— J'ai une surprise pour toi.

Duval sortit de la poche de son imperméable le chaton blanc et noir, dont les yeux nécessitaient un bon décrottage.

Le visage de Mimi devint extatique. Elle se rua vers lui du haut de l'escalier et le prit dans ses bras. Le chaton miaulait et ronronnait. Mimi le blottit contre elle.

Elle embrassa son père, qu'elle remercia.

— Papa ! Pourquoi ? T'as jamais voulu…

— Il me suivait partout alors que j'enquêtais dans un lieu abandonné.

— T'es super *blood* !

Il détestait ce vocabulaire. Pour Duval, il n'était pas question de dire à sa fille que ce chat était le compagnon du pendu. Il n'aimait pas ses réflexes de mère poule, mais il ne voulait pas non plus que Mimi associe l'animal à une autre sale affaire qui allait s'étaler dans les journaux.

— Vous le gardez pas comme pièce à conviction ? interrogea-t-elle à la blague.

— Pas nécessaire, mais on peut lui trouver un nom de circonstance.

— Que penserais-tu de Suspect ?

— C'est trop négatif.

— Alibi ?

— Oui, c'est bien. Alibi !

Duval tira de sa poche des boîtes de nourriture pour chats. Il les tendit à Mimi.

— Tiens, donne-lui à manger. Je crois qu'il est vraiment affamé.

— Et la litière ?

Duval n'en avait pas trouvé au dépanneur du coin.

— Pour ce soir, on prendra du carton et du papier journal.

Duval marcha vers la cuisine, tiraillé entre l'envie d'une bière et celle d'une aspirine. Il ouvrit le réfrigérateur, mais la pression qui lui comprimait le lobe frontal alors qu'il penchait la tête lui fit refermer la porte. Il valait mieux se soigner. Il regarda le dessus de la lasagne qui avait croûté et alluma le four. Tout près, Alibi, le museau plongé dans l'écuelle, dévorait sa pâtée au poisson.

Duval monta prendre une douche. Avant de se sécher les cheveux, il avala deux cachets d'aspirine.

En passant devant la chambre de Mimi, il s'arrêta pour observer les jeux d'Alibi. Mimi faisait rouler son crayon sur le plancher et le chaton se livrait à toutes sortes d'acrobaties. Daniel redescendit au rez-de-chaussée.

Trente minutes plus tard, Alibi s'était endormi au pied du lit et Mimi put reprendre l'étude de son examen d'histoire de la musique.

Pendant que la lasagne gratinait, Duval sortit son carnet pour voir où il en était dans son enquête.

Il tomba sur le message trouvé à l'intérieur du corps de la jeune fille. Il prit la craie du tableau accroché au mur et inscrivit les mots suivants : *Et faire à ton flanc étonné une blessure large et creuse.*

Il considéra longuement la pensée de ce détraqué. Il souhaita que Rosalie Nantel règle ses comptes au paradis et que cette enquête ne soit plus que formalité administrative. L'ange assassiné et le démon meurtrier de nouveau face à face. Au tribunal céleste d'engager ses procureurs dans la cause. Plus de problème de juridiction et de crise d'ego. La tranquillité d'esprit recouvrée.

Et, surtout, pas de Granger dans les jambes pendant son enquête.

Il retira la lasagne du fourneau et ne résista pas à une bonne rasade de bière.

Sur la table de la salle à manger s'étalaient des revues de courtiers en immeubles. Laurence avait souligné l'adresse d'un domaine à l'île d'Orléans. Il prit la revue et jeta un coup d'œil sur les choix de sa concubine. Dans les 120 000 $! Il lui faudrait bien s'asseoir avec elle et régler cette question.

LE CERCLE THANATOS

39

Les vibrisses du chaton lui chatouillaient le menton, ses petites pattes blanc et noir s'enfonçant dans sa poitrine. Puis ce furent des coups de tête entrecoupés de nombreux miaulements. Duval battit des paupières, tourna la tête et aperçut en gros plan, à travers la brume matinale de ses yeux, la boule de poils hirsutes qu'il avait rescapée. Le réveil marquait 6 h. Duval regretta presque d'avoir adopté le chaton. Chat rimerait avec achat de litière, bouffe et portes qu'il faudrait ouvrir, selon les caprices saisonniers du félin. Il s'assit sur le bord du lit, laissa lentement glisser ses mains sur son visage. Il se leva et Alibi louvoya entre ses pieds, plongeant la tête la première dans l'escalier et passant à un cheveu de lui faire perdre l'équilibre. L'écuelle était vide. Il la remplit de nourriture et le ronronnement du chat marqua toute sa gratitude. Sans bruit – Mimi ne commençait ses cours qu'à 11 h – Duval monta sur la pointe des pieds accomplir ses ablutions matinales.

Il déposséda le valet de nuit en cuivre de ses vêtements. Il regarda Laurence qui dormait. Ils avaient échangé quelques mots doux – dont plusieurs pour lui faire accepter l'idée de garder le chat du pendu – et s'étaient endormis dans la position de la cuillère.

Il retourna au rez-de-chaussée en bâillant. Il secoua la pinte de lait, un peu trop légère pour les besoins de la famille. Il dut calculer la quantité nécessaire tant pour le café de Laurence que pour les céréales de Mimi et le boire du chat. Il déposa son bol de Croque Nature sur la table, retourna à la cuisine pour mettre de l'eau dans la cafetière. Lorsqu'il revint, Alibi avait la tête plongée dans son bol de céréales. Duval claqua des mains pour le chasser et le réprimanda. Le chat fila comme un missile à l'étage.

◆

Les tasses de café chaud fumaient sur la table de réunion. Deux mains s'agitaient devant le tableau noir pour témoigner de l'étrange face-à-face de la veille. Duval racontait à son équipe ce qui s'était passé dans l'appartement de la côte d'Abraham. Plusieurs personnes avaient téléphoné pour dénoncer Michaël Mathieu, que l'on accusait des pires vices. Cependant, les journaux n'avaient pu dévoiler le nom du jeune homme en raison de l'identification tardive du cadavre.

Le téléphone sonna. Bernard répondit. Sa voix éraillée par deux paquets quotidiens de nicotine sonnait creux.

— C'est le patron. Il demande qu'on se rende tous au labo. Du nouveau. Villemure veut nous rencontrer.

Loulou ramassa sa tasse.

— Apportez votre café, là-bas ils le servent froid !

◆

Alors que les détectives de l'escouade, tirés à quatre épingles, passaient devant la baie vitrée de la section Biologie, Mireille s'étira le cou et les invita à entrer. Avec Louis en tête dans son fauteuil et les trois costauds qui suivaient derrière, Duval imagina les trois mousquetaires et demi.

— Salut, Mireille !

Les gaillards en complets-cravates l'entouraient comme un rempart impénétrable.

— Bonjour, messieurs. Je viens de terminer mon analyse des cheveux de Michaël Mathieu. Ils ont la racine pleine, le canal médullaire est discontinu et l'extrémité pointue. Ce ne sont pas ceux qui viennent de la scène du crime. Son groupe sanguin est de type B. De plus, ce ne sont pas ses spermatozoïdes qu'on a trouvés dans le vagin de Rosalie. Par ailleurs, le docteur Villemure étudie une autre hypothèse qui va peut-être vous jeter par terre.

Louis, qui avait toujours aimé la décontenancer, répliqua.

— Tu sais, je suis pas mal bas déjà. J'aurais besoin de ton soutien.

— Louis, tu es incorrigible !

Le téléphone sonna et elle les chassa à la blague d'un geste de la main.

— François vous attend.

L'équipe se déplaça dans la salle d'autopsie numéro 2 où l'éclairage aux néons donnait déjà aux cadavres un affreux teint. Un technicien nettoyait une table en inox avec la douche téléphone tandis que le docteur Maher marquait un bocal contenant un rein.

— Le docteur Villemure ne va pas tarder.

Fabien Maher était le protégé de Villemure. Ce dernier avait donné l'ordre qu'on bichonne le stagiaire pour qu'il ne soit pas récupéré par le CHUL, qui se cherchait un pathologiste hospitalier. Puisque les mé-

decins légistes étaient une denrée rare – les horaires
ingrats et l'ampleur de la tâche y faisaient pour beaucoup –, Villemure souhaitait que toute l'expérience
qu'il partageait avec Maher ne soit pas à recommencer
comme il arrivait trop souvent, surtout que le stagiaire
était le meilleur candidat à avoir été formé. Il avait la
médecine légale infuse, s'amusait à lui répéter Villemure. Devant une cour de justice, ses exposés précis
et imagés en faisaient un atout indispensable pour la
Couronne.

Sur la troisième table reposait le corps de Mathieu,
vidé de ses entrailles : un corps osseux blanc comme
de la chaux, la tête appuyée sur un bloc de bois qui
semblait affreusement inconfortable, même pour un
mort. Les cheveux du gamin, tout en fardoches, donnaient l'impression qu'il allait se lever après une
mauvaise nuit. Mais ce ne serait pas le cas. Son visage
bleui, congestionné, marqué d'hémorragies pétéchiales,
ne mentait pas. Les lividités s'étaient fixées dans les
parties déclives, des genoux aux orteils, des coudes aux
doigts.

— Nous avons des surprises pour vous, messieurs,
lança Maher.

Louis s'avança vers Maher et le nargua.

— Vous autres, les médecins légistes, vous savez
toujours tout, mais vingt-quatre heures trop tard.

Ricanements.

— Et vous autres, vous ne savez jamais rien, riposta
Fabien avec un rire sardonique.

Le jeune Maher avait l'humour et la réplique redou-
tables, prisés par les juges qui ne détestaient pas être
déridés.

À ce moment, le docteur Villemure, dans sa blouse
verte, les yeux au-dessus de ses demi-lunettes à double
foyer retenues par une chaînette, entra dans la pièce,

rapport entre les mains, accompagné du lieutenant Granger et de Landry, son collègue.

— Salut ! Comme je le croyais, ça se complique, dit le docteur en déposant sa planchette à pince sur le comptoir.

Les deux équipes se saluèrent du bout des lèvres. Duval retourna à Granger son salut imperceptible par un froncement de menton tout aussi discret.

Villemure s'approcha.

— Il est rare, dans le cas d'une pendaison complète, que la langue soit expulsée, serrée entre les dents. C'est ce que nous avions, hier. D'ordinaire, le sang est très noir, et les poumons comportent des taches de Tardieu : des bulles violacées. Non, Louis, ça ne se nettoie pas avec du Spic n' Span ! Dans le cas qui nous intéresse : *niet*. Ni sang noir ni taches de Tardieu. Il y a des sillons horizontaux et un sillon oblique. Le cou présente clairement la striction d'un lien autre que celui de la corde qui aurait servi à pendre le garçon au départ. Pour les sillons horizontaux dans les parties médianes du cou, j'ai pensé qu'il avait d'abord essayé une pendaison incomplète, c'est-à-dire en se pendant à une poignée de porte, un coin de table ou un coin de lit, le corps se trouvant à l'horizontale. Des cas qu'on rencontre assez souvent. La surface de contact entre le lien et le cou était plus large que celle remarquée chez Rosalie Nantel. Des traces d'asphyxie et de congestion prouvent que la victime a fourni des efforts considérables pour inspirer et expirer. J'ai noté à plusieurs endroits des brûlures causées par les frottements de la corde pendant que la victime se débattait. Mathieu avait de petites ecchymoses aux doigts. J'ai noté une hémorragie auriculaire avec éclatement des tympans. On ne peut pas s'infliger de telles blessures. Ce garçon faisait cent trente-huit livres et je n'ai pas vu le type de lésions qu'aurait causées la chute d'un corps de ce poids d'une hauteur d'environ quatre pieds, soit celle du tabouret sur lequel il est monté pour se jeter dans le vide avec ce lien au cou. Le corps a dû reposer quelque temps sur le dos, car on a trouvé des micro-indices sur les vêtements qui se trouvaient aussi sur le plancher : poussières, sable, poils, pollen, etc. On n'a pas trouvé par contre le rouge à lèvres qui a servi à dessiner cet affreux sourire. À première vue, la corde jaune en nylon qui a permis de hisser le corps de Mathieu est la même qui aurait servi à lier les poignets de Rosalie. Le chimiste va pouvoir confirmer ça d'ici quelques heures. On connaîtra peut-être même le fabricant et le détaillant qui vend ce produit. La corde était pratiquement neuve.

Les détectives se regardèrent, incrédules.

— De plus, je crois que le collier qui a servi à étrangler Rosalie Nantel est celui qu'on a trouvé dans la poche de Michaël Mathieu. Les marques de striction dans le cou de Rosalie correspondent à la surface de contact de la chaînette. Ce qui me fait dire qu'il s'agit d'un homicide, c'est aussi la présence de gardénal dans l'estomac. J'ai découvert également des traces de cocaïne dans l'estomac et dans les muqueuses de Mathieu. C'était un gros consommateur.

Ça démangeait à Duval de poser des questions au docteur.

— La mort de Mathieu remonte à quand ?

— Il a été tué après Rosalie, deux ou trois heures plus tard.

— C'est donc quelqu'un qui les connaissait ? demanda Bernard.

Villemure acquiesça.

— Fort possible. Quelqu'un qui les connaissait ou qui s'en prend aux couples.

Louis coupa la parole au docteur.

— Peut-être a-t-il cherché à le mettre en confiance en lui offrant de la cocaïne pour ensuite l'abrutir avec un tranquillisant et l'étrangler ?

— Berkowitz s'en prenait lui aussi aux jeunes couples. On ne pourrait pas être aux prises avec un émule du Fils de Sam ? suggéra Francis.

— Ou encore avec un malade qui veut semer les fausses pistes et faire passer ses meurtres sur le dos d'un autre, avança Duval.

— Il y a tentative de simulation, c'est clair, argua Granger qui se réveillait enfin.

— Le suspect jalousait peut-être Rosalie et Michaël, lança Duval. Il faut prouver que le bijou appartenait bel et bien à Rosalie.

Francis sortit la photo que lui avait remise la famille Nantel et la déposa sur le corps de Mathieu qu'on avait grossièrement recousu.

— Tu as ta réponse.

Le rubis en forme de scarabée parait le cou de Rosalie sur son portrait de finissante.

Granger jeta un coup d'œil.

Miljours, de la section Documents, s'amena avec un rapport.

— La lettre retrouvée sur la machine à écrire de Mathieu n'a pas pu être tapée sur celle-ci, une Smith-Corona mécanique, car on a ici les caractères d'une IBM électrique.

— Il nous prend pour des cons ou quoi ? s'insurgea Francis.

Ou peut-être était-il assez brillant pour faire tomber quelqu'un dans un piège à cons, pensa Duval.

— À part le message citant Albert Camus, savez-vous si les autres textes proviennent d'auteurs connus ? demanda le rouquin Landry.

— On n'en a aucune idée pour l'instant, répliqua Miljours.

Puisque Duval avait la responsabilité de l'enquête, il demanda à Granger de chercher dans le squat des indices qui pourraient prouver qu'une personne avait hissé le corps de Mathieu jusqu'au tuyau.

L'autre essaya de ne pas s'étouffer de rire. Recevoir un ordre d'un bonhomme vert – référence aux couleurs des patrouilleurs de la SQ – n'avait jamais fait partie de sa tâche.

— Pour le tuyau, appelez le plombier…

Et le vieux masque de granit tourna les talons. Duval sut dès lors que le limier agirait seul.

Bernard agrippa le bras de son lieutenant d'une poigne ferme pour éviter un esclandre. De toute manière, ils possédaient un kilomètre d'avance sur l'équipe de Granger, qui allait s'essouffler à courir derrière eux, se dit Duval.

Ce dernier enfonça son calepin dans la poche de son veston.

— L'enquête reste ouverte.

Il remercia Villemure et Maher et dénicha une salle de conférences près du labo.

Il vit, aux visages consternés de ses collègues, que cette affaire écœurait tout le monde. Il effleura du coude le tableau noir et tacha son veston, qu'il épousseta. Il prit une craie et inscrivit en grosses lettres rondes les corvées à accomplir.

— Demain matin, on se rend aux funérailles de Rosalie. On se fait discrets, mais on ouvre l'œil, surtout au cimetière. Un gars de l'Identité va filmer la cérémonie. On fera pareil aux funérailles de Mathieu.

Louis intervint.

— En passant, le prof de philo, Déziel, reçoit ses élèves à son bureau jusqu'à 10 h, ce matin.

— On s'y rend tout de suite, annonça Duval.

Il se tourna de nouveau vers le tableau et inscrivit «AMIS ?».

— Bernard et Frankie, vous vous informez auprès des parents pour savoir qui aurait pu en vouloir à Rosalie et à Michaël. Quelque chose me chicote aussi : Sébastien Poirier. À quelle heure est-il rentré ce soir-là ? Il a beau avoir un laissez-passer de la Société des traversiers, cela ne nous dit pas à quelle heure précise il s'est embarqué. On n'a jamais vérifié si Poirier avait un dossier. Il étudie la philo et Mathieu avait commencé son cours en philosophie à Laval. Poirier a une très mauvaise opinion de Mathieu et il est notre principal témoin et la dernière personne qui a été vue avec Rosalie.

— Mais c'est son cousin ! argua Louis.

— Il existe beaucoup d'histoires d'amour à l'intérieur des familles. Rappelle-toi ! T'as dû un jour fantasmer sur une de tes cousines…

— On s'est même embrassés.

— Je le savais ! dit Francis en roulant les yeux.

— À 15 h, on se rejoint au cimetière de Sillery pour l'exhumation du corps d'Angélique Fraser. Je vous répète qu'il faut être discrets. Je l'ai promis à Fraser, car sa femme est au bord de la crise de nerfs.

— Est-ce que l'enterrement de Rosalie a lieu dans le cimetière où on l'a retrouvée morte ? demanda Louis.

Bernard Prince lança un coup d'œil complice en direction de Francis. Duval eut une mine atterrée. Question psychologie, avec Louis, on avait beau repasser, on trouvait toujours la case vide.

Duval jongla avec la craie et transperça le Gros du regard.

— Mets-toi à la place des parents. Penses-tu un instant qu'ils auraient accepté qu'elle soit inhumée à Sillery après ce qui s'est passé ?

Loulou leva les bras d'impuissance. Duval retrouva le fil conducteur de son agenda mental. Il sortit de son sac un livre noir à la reliure rouge.

— C'est le livre de Mathieu. Je l'ai piqué avant que les hommes de Granger mettent la main dessus.

— Vol de pièce à conviction… Tu risques combien ? dit Louis à la blague.

— J'ai l'impression que Granger n'aime pas assez la poésie pour s'y intéresser…

— Qu'est-ce que t'as découvert dedans ? demanda Francis.

— Je compte l'examiner plus à fond aujourd'hui. À première vue, il semble y avoir des écrits bizarres, des dessins, des réflexions. Bref, messieurs, beaucoup de travail.

Prince leva la main.

— Avec la description que les serveuses du Laurentien et les employés du Fuzz nous ont faite, on devrait retrouver assez facilement le punk qui a commis des actes de grossière indécence devant Rosalie Nantel.

Il sortit de sa mallette le portrait-robot du punk. La police s'était lancée à sa recherche et le filet se resserrait de plus en plus. Louis s'esclaffa devant le portrait.

— Cou'don, qu'est-ce qu'ils ont tous à s'attriquer comme des Bobino sur l'acide !

Duval examina le dessin de Badeau, l'artiste judiciaire.

— Michaël Mathieu aussi était punk. Cherchons à savoir s'il n'y aurait pas un lien entre eux. Le cercle des punks doit être assez restreint à Québec. Qui fréquentait-il ? Ils se tiennent tous au même endroit : le Fuzz. Mathieu aussi écrivait des textes bizarres.

40

Après avoir fait trois tours de montagnes russes pour dégoter un stationnement et avoir pesté contre le quartier latin, Duval se rua vers un espace qui se libérait dans la rue des Remparts.

La rue de l'Université se terminait par une porte cochère. C'est là que la première université canadienne-française, Laval, avait été érigée. Les cours du secteur collégial du Petit Séminaire de Québec se donnaient dans cet édifice remarquable qui surplombait le cap Diamant.

Le clocheton de l'édifice brillait dans la grisaille. La rue était bordée d'imposants bâtiments de pierres grises salies par le temps. L'administration occupait un édifice sis de l'autre côté de l'immeuble où étaient dispensés les cours.

Heureusement, le lieu était aménagé pour recevoir des handicapés. Louis, qui avait les yeux tout le tour de la tête, n'avait rien d'un handicapé visuel.

— T'as vu ce repaire de beautés ?

— Elles pourraient être tes filles, lui lança froidement Duval.

L'administration était située tout de suite à gauche de la porte d'entrée.

Il leur aurait fallu chanter *En revenant de Rigaud* pour que la secrétaire daigne lever son chignon blanc au-dessus de sa machine à écrire. Elle finit par leur jeter un œil derrière ses lunettes de vieille fille. Elle ne tenait pas à déranger le directeur des études, car il attendait d'un instant à l'autre un fonctionnaire du ministère de l'Éducation. Comme Ali Baba, qui n'avait qu'à lancer sa célèbre formule, Duval, lui, allongea sa carte de la SQ pour que toutes les portes s'ouvrent devant lui. Par téléphone, elle avisa son patron de la présence des détectives.

Boutin, un homme dans la cinquantaine, portait des lunettes rectangulaires en métal, une barbe épaisse et aussi bouclée que sa coupe afro, et quinze kilos de trop autour de la taille. Du fourneau de sa pipe, qu'il gardait constamment au coin des lèvres, s'échappaient de graciles volutes de tabac Old Rhum.

Duval se chargea des présentations.

Boutin invita les enquêteurs à s'asseoir. Un porte-pipes en bois trônait sur son bureau avec toute une kyrielle de pipes.

— Qu'est-ce que je peux faire pour vous, messieurs ?

Duval le regarda droit dans les yeux.

— Monsieur Boutin, une étudiante du nom d'Angélique Fraser s'est suicidée l'an dernier après avoir suivi le cours de philosophie de Victor Déziel.

Le directeur l'interrompit sur-le-champ.

— Un instant ! Elle n'était déjà plus au collège quand elle a mis fin à ses jours. Il n'y a aucun lien de cause à effet.

— Ce n'est pas ce que pense le père d'Angélique.

— C'est facile de chercher un bouc émissaire. Déziel est un professeur controversé mais apprécié. Plusieurs élèves ont changé d'orientation après avoir suivi un cours avec lui.

— En dépit des plaintes…

— Il a reçu des plaintes, c'est vrai. Vous savez, Déziel enseigne dans un nouveau programme d'élite qui regroupe la crème des élèves. Les étudiants proviennent d'un milieu privilégié. Il faut une moyenne de quatre-vingts pour cent dans toutes les matières au secondaire pour accéder à ce programme collégial. Les parents suivent de très près le cheminement scolaire de leurs enfants. Les méthodes pédagogiques et le contenu des cours de Déziel déplaisaient à certains d'entre eux. On a rencontré les parents et tout s'est réglé à l'amiable. D'ailleurs, les étudiants ne voulaient pas porter plainte. Ce sont deux parents qui ont insisté.

— Pourquoi ?

— Ils disaient que l'enseignement de Déziel avait influencé le comportement de leurs enfants.

— De quelle manière ?

Boutin aspira trois fois au bout de sa pipe et expira un long nuage de fumée qui piqua les yeux du lieutenant.

— Ils avaient développé une fascination pour le morbide. Vous savez, à cet âge, et même après, nous sommes fascinés par la mort.

— Quel type de comportements face à la mort ?

— Comme les étudiants forment un groupe homogène et qu'il se crée des liens privilégiés entre eux, certains se réunissaient pour faire des expériences bizarres : défis et jeux avec la mort. Ils portaient des vêtements sombres, avaient leur cercle littéraire… Donc, ils se sont constitué un petit cénacle. Ils se donnaient aussi des surnoms étranges reliés d'une manière ou d'une autre à la mort. On le sait parce qu'un professeur de français a intercepté un texte anonyme qui parlait du cercle Thanatos, et qu'on y trouvait ces surnoms.

— Pourriez-vous me retrouver ce texte ?

— Il n'existe plus, heureusement.

— Pourquoi heureusement ?

— C'était un texte troublant.

— Pourquoi ?

— Parce que terriblement violent, ce qui ne reflète pas la culture de notre école.

— Des menaces ?

— Voilées sous le couvert de la fiction.

— Des soupçons sur l'auteur ?

— Non. Tous les suspects ont nié.

Duval notait tout dans son calepin.

— Savez-vous si ce « cénacle » existe encore ?

— Il aurait disparu à la fin de l'année dernière. La nuit du bal des finissants, un grave accident de voiture a tué un des jeunes tout en en laissant un autre gravement handicapé. Ils avaient fumé et bu. Il semble que quelqu'un soit allé trop loin.

— Et de qui tenez-vous cette information ?

— Comme je vous l'ai dit, c'est une rumeur.

— Est-il possible de savoir qui était membre de ce groupe ?

— C'était un cercle fermé. Tout est demeuré anonyme. Bien sûr, on connaît nos ouailles et on soupçonnait des étudiants d'en faire partie, car c'était lié à une forme de prestige.

— Vous avez des noms à me donner ?

— Non, c'est vague dans ma tête.

— Et comment avez-vous traité l'affaire Angélique Fraser ?

— Angélique devait être admise en médecine. Son père voulait qu'elle suive ses traces. Ses notes durant sa première année ont été exceptionnelles – elle a remporté le mérite étudiant – et par la suite, étrangement, elles ont baissé ; son comportement aussi a changé, juste assez pour qu'elle soit refusée dans son programme. Elle s'est alors inscrite en biologie ; elle croyait qu'en performant au cours de sa première année on l'accepterait en médecine, mais en vain. Les parents ont pensé que le cours de Déziel, *Philosophie de la mort*, avait pu distraire Angélique de ses études et, plus tard, l'avoir incitée à se tuer. C'est complètement farfelu. On cherche souvent des excuses pour les rêves qu'on projette sur nos enfants et qui ne se sont pas réalisés. Les parents ont beaucoup d'ambition pour leurs enfants. Il ne faut pas oublier que ces enfants appartiennent à la crème de la crème.

— Et la crème a tourné ! lança Louis qui, jusque-là, écoutait attentivement.

Boutin n'apprécia pas la remarque. Il tourna sa grosse face barbue vers Louis et dévisagea le malotru. Duval replaça rapidement la conversation sur ses rails.

— Vous me parliez de son comportement…

— Elle a commencé à se rebeller, à s'habiller bizarrement.

— Est-il possible qu'elle ait eu à en découdre avec Déziel ?

— Non, rien de tel.

— On m'a dit qu'elle entretenait une relation étroite avec Déziel.

— Vous me l'apprenez.

— Monsieur Boutin, pourrions-nous examiner le dossier de Déziel ?

— Non, c'est confidentiel. À ce que je sache, il n'a pas commis d'actes criminels.

— Mais il semble que d'autres parents aient porté plainte. Pourquoi ?

— Comme je vous l'ai dit, on remettait en question les méthodes pédagogiques du professeur.

— Pourquoi le gardez-vous dans vos rangs ?

— Vous savez, aujourd'hui, les emplois sont bétonnés contre le licenciement. De toute manière, en dépit de ses méthodes controversées, Déziel demeure un professeur très apprécié. Les élèves l'adorent.

— Et ce cours, il le donne encore ?

— Non. Après la mort d'Angélique Fraser, on lui a demandé de ne plus le donner. Du moins, il a changé l'intitulé. On ne peut certes pas l'empêcher d'enseigner ce qui fait l'essence de la philosophie en Occident : la vie, la mort, où je vais, d'où je viens. Ce serait une atteinte à la liberté d'expression.

— Monsieur Boutin, nous sommes en train d'enquêter sur un meurtre, celui d'hier au cimetière de Sillery, et sur une affaire de profanation de tombeau qui pourraient être liés à Déziel.

Boutin se figea comme une statue de cire. Daniel poursuivit :

— Pourriez-vous nous remettre la liste des étudiants qui ont suivi les cours de Déziel ? La cohorte de 78-79.

— Ceux du programme enrichi, pas de problème.

— Nous voudrions aussi parler à monsieur Déziel, demanda Louis.

— Vous le trouverez dans l'autre bâtiment. En raison du programme, il fait bande à part. Son bureau est au cinquième, dans l'école.

Il remit à Duval un billet avec le numéro du bureau.

— Pourrions-nous avoir cette liste avant de partir ?

— J'appelle l'organisation scolaire et vous pourrez passer la prendre au bureau de la secrétaire d'ici quinze minutes. Moi, je dois vous laisser, j'ai une rencontre.

Il se leva, frappa sa pipe contre le cendrier pour vider le fourneau et les accompagna jusqu'à la porte.

41

Au rez-de-chaussée du collège, un tableau de Monseigneur de Laval revêtu de sa soutane écarlate rappelait la contribution du fondateur de la première université française en Amérique. Dans le vestibule, on butait contre trois portes closes en bois foncé. Duval regarda Louis, sceptique.

Un jeune handicapé traversa la pièce et Louis roula vers lui.

— Excuse-moi, jeune homme, peux-tu me dire où se trouve la catapulte ?

L'étudiant, lourdement handicapé par la paralysie cérébrale, explosa de rire. Dans un ballet de contorsions, il indiqua à Louis avec moult gestes et paroles l'emplacement de l'ascenseur. Louis le remercia chaudement.

— Tu vois, Daniel, je n'ai rien. Je ne suis pas handicapé comparé à ce garçon. Pourquoi je me plains toujours ? Dieu est bon pour moi !

Immédiatement à gauche, un vieil écriteau délavé annonçait le *Laboratoire de chimie Lavoisier*. Dans l'aile sud, d'imposantes étagères en acajou étaient garnies de fioles, d'éprouvettes, de vases, de pipettes et de brûleurs.

Les plafonds étaient si hauts qu'il eût été possible de construire un étage supplémentaire. Autre époque, autres mœurs architecturales. Aujourd'hui, rien ne se perd, et rien ne se crée sans que le moindre pouce carré soit exploité, pensa Duval en jouant sur la devise de Lavoisier. Un vaste corridor ponctué d'arches tous les six mètres créait un effet de plénitude. Les classes dans lesquelles s'élevaient des colonnes de soutènement s'apparentaient à des salons de cour.

Le bureau de Déziel était perché au dernier étage. Pour y accéder, il fallait tourner à droite et suivre un long corridor qui offrait une vue imprenable sur le Château Frontenac, le fleuve et Lévis. Le vieux plancher de linoléum qui avait été foulé par l'élite québécoise dessinait un mandala de carreaux. Les oreillons et les saillies de maçonnerie des linteaux de porte ressemblaient à d'appétissantes meringues.

Sur la porte du bureau de Déziel se trouvait accrochée une photo d'un type appelé Cioran, une affiche promotionnelle avec le titre de l'œuvre, *Précis de décomposition,* ce qui intrigua Duval. La porte était entrebâillée. Ils entendaient le professeur qui discutait avec un étudiant ou, plutôt, le réconfortait. Le jeune parlait d'une voix atone. Seule la voix grave de Déziel était audible : « Courage, tu vas passer à travers. Je ne peux rien y faire. De toute façon, c'est temporaire… Ils ne pourront pas te garder sans réévaluer ton dossier… Écoute, on s'en reparle… Je dois te laisser, j'ai beaucoup de corrections ! »

Le professeur souhaita au jeune homme une bonne fin d'après-midi.

La porte s'ouvrit brusquement. L'élève, un costaud à l'allure rebelle, fila en frôlant le fauteuil de Louis.

D'un air suffisant, Déziel les dévisagea de pied en cap.

— Oui, messieurs, qu'est-ce qu'on peut faire pour vous ? Mes impôts ?

— Nous devons vous parler, monsieur Déziel.

— Vous êtes huissiers ?

— Non, détectives.

Déziel grimaça.

— Entrez.

Le professeur affichait les traits d'un éternel jeunot au sommet de la trentaine. Il paraissait bien et, contrairement à ce que s'était imaginé Duval, qui s'attendait à voir un maigrichon décomposé, il donnait l'impression d'un homme solide comme le roc, à la stature de coureur de 400 mètres. Son visage semblait une sculpture de marbre blanc percée d'yeux bleus, plutôt inquiétants, des yeux d'hypnotiseur. Il portait un bouc et un filin de moustache taillé à la manière asiatique. Une courte couette qu'il attachait avec un élastique longeait la nuque. De longs filaments gris sillonnaient cette chevelure lustrée, aussi aplatie qu'un bonnet de bain. Il portait une ample chemise blanche, un nœud papillon et un gilet en velours noir.

La pièce empestait les cigarettes françaises. Duval faillit avoir le réflexe d'entrouvrir la fenêtre. Sur le bureau de Déziel, *Le Devoir* faisait sa une avec une photo de l'ayatollah Khomeyni.

— Alors de quel crime s'agit-il ? lança Déziel avec désinvolture tout en fermant la porte.

— On ne vous accuse de rien. On veut juste vous poser des questions.

— Comme Socrate. Eh bien, allez-y ! Habituellement, c'est moi qui les pose.

— Vous vous rappelez Angélique Fraser ?

À la mention de ce nom, Déziel eut une grimace comme s'il venait d'avaler la ciguë.

— Pourquoi venir m'interroger là-dessus ? Toute la lumière a été faite à ce sujet. Je n'ai pas de temps à perdre avec ça.

— Peut-être, mais le mausolée où est Angélique a été profané et un meurtre a été commis à quelques mètres d'où elle repose.

— Écoutez, je suis peiné pour la famille d'Angélique, mais je ne suis pas responsable ni de près ni de loin pour ce qui s'est produit et je ne suis pas la chronique judiciaire. Si vous posiez plus de questions à monsieur Fraser, il vous dirait que sa fille vivait une peine d'amour.

— Pour qui ?

Il hésita longuement.

— Pour moi.

— Avez-vous eu des relations intimes ?

— Ça ne vous regarde pas. D'abord, avez-vous un mandat ?

— Non, mais je peux m'en procurer un aussi facilement qu'un sac de chips.

Déziel, qui montrait de l'agressivité, se calma et parut plus disposé à répondre aux questions.

Une étudiante frappa à la porte afin de lui remettre un travail en retard. La voix paniquée, elle s'excusa en prétextant qu'elle avait fait une gastro et demanda si elle allait perdre des points. Déziel répondit non de la tête et la jeune fille lui décocha un sourire de grâce. Duval observa la pièce et aperçut au mur une autre photo de Cioran ainsi qu'une affiche de Nietzsche.

La jeune femme salua Déziel et il referma la porte en accrochant à l'extérieur un écriteau priant de « Ne pas déranger ».

— C'est vous qui avez mis sur pied « Le cercle Thanatos » ?

— Je l'ai encouragé. Une fois rodé, j'ai laissé les élèves s'occuper de leur créature. À tour de rôle les élèves devaient animer des ateliers de discussion. Les choses se déroulaient très bien. Le cercle de lecture est devenu prestigieux, une sorte de mythe s'est créé autour de ses membres. Ils faisaient paraître leur revue qui circulait sous le manteau : *Éros et Thanatos*. Mais, dès le départ, le groupe est resté, à de rares exceptions, fermé aux autres étudiants, alors que plusieurs auraient voulu accéder à ce petit cénacle.

— Vous ne pouviez pas intervenir ?

— Non, car je voulais les laisser régler seuls leurs conflits.

— Comment se comportaient-ils ?

— Ils se faisaient un malin plaisir d'entretenir le mystère autour d'eux. Ils cultivaient leur snobisme. Imaginez ce que ce doit être, pour des snobs, d'être snobés par d'autres snobs ! dit Déziel en éclatant de rire. Ça n'allait pas sans créer des frictions. Ils ont commencé à faire des initiations, et là les choses se sont gâtées. C'est à ce moment que j'ai cessé de les voir en dehors des cours.

— Pourquoi ?

— On m'invitait trop souvent dans des partys et je me retrouvais dans des situations délicates. Ces fêtes se passaient chez mes élèves. C'est un collège très prestigieux et tout finit par se savoir.

— Comment se faisait le recrutement ?

— Il y avait une initiation. Certains se côtoyaient depuis le secondaire. Ils avaient étudié ensemble au Petit Séminaire, au Collège des Jésuites, chez les Pères Maristes, les Ursulines, à Jésus-Marie et aussi dans certaines écoles publiques. Mais la plupart provenaient d'écoles privées. Après avoir été bridés pendant autant d'années, ils étaient enivrés par la vie au collège. Et ils vivaient à 200 à l'heure.

— Combien étaient-ils ?

— Une douzaine, peut-être plus.

— Est-ce vrai qu'ils se donnaient des surnoms ?

— Comme des scouts, ils avaient des *bush soul* ou des noms qui convenaient à leur personnalité, le plus souvent liés à la mort.

— Vous vous rappelez certains d'entre eux ?

Déziel sourit en se frottant la barbichette, pencha la tête pour mieux replonger dans ses souvenirs.

— Je me rappelle Spectre, Black, Styx, Tod, Cobra et il y en avait d'autres.

— Le nom Thanatos était connu ?

— Évidemment.

— Thanatos signifie relatif à la mort.

— Vous faites des mots croisés…

Duval n'apprécia pas le sarcasme.

— Thanatos est le dieu de la mort dans la mythologie grecque.

Duval posa l'extrémité du crayon sur son menton avant de poser l'autre question. Il fixa Déziel droit dans les yeux.

— Il semble que certains d'entre eux soient allés trop loin.

— C'est ce qu'on dit.

Déziel continua de se ronger l'ongle du pouce.

— Professeur Déziel, on a un cas de meurtre horrible perpétré dans un cimetière, et tout près de là, le tombeau de l'une de vos anciennes étudiantes, Angélique Fraser, a été profané. Le père est prêt à faire rouvrir l'enquête, dit Duval en exagérant juste ce qu'il fallait.

— Je ne peux pas dévoiler de noms. Je dois respecter la confidentialité des élèves. Et de toute façon, je ne suis pas au courant de tous les noms.

— Avez-vous assisté à l'une de ces initiations? demanda Duval.

— Non.

— Quelles formes prenaient-elles?

Il haussa les épaules.

— Sincèrement, aucune idée. Probablement un calque des initiations francs-maçonniques ou rosicruciennes. Ou quelque chose de plus dionysiaque.

— Racontez-moi ce qui s'est passé pour que cessent leurs activités.

— Cette histoire n'est qu'une rumeur parmi tant d'autres. Quelqu'un avait organisé une initiation bidon chez lui et il semble que l'on ait poussé trop loin la farce.

— Jusqu'où?

— Je ne sais pas.

— Et cet événement a mis fin au cercle?

— Du moins, il l'a scindé.

— Vous venez de me dire qu'il n'existe plus.

— Scindé jusqu'à ne plus exister.

— Et vous les revoyez, ces élèves?

— Il m'arrive de les croiser.

— Avez-vous de nouveau un cercle de discussion?

— J'ai repris un cercle de discussion avec de nouveaux élèves, mais les activités se déroulent au collège et je les dirige.

Duval se rappela que, quand il fréquentait le collège, les livres intéressants étaient à l'Index, et que l'enfer, l'endroit où l'on conservait les lectures interdites, attirait les élèves.

— Croyez-vous l'un de ces individus assez timbré pour commettre un meurtre ? lança Louis avec ses gros sabots.

— D'abord, je n'aime pas le mot « timbré », mais je vous dirais qu'à cette époque je les croyais capables de faire une grosse connerie uniquement par défi. Ces étudiants m'apparaissaient dans un état second. Des êtres exaltés comme jamais je n'en avais vu dans ma carrière. Il y avait une grande émulation entre eux. Ils se stimulaient. Certains se prenaient pour Zarathoustra. La lecture de Nietzsche avait laissé un goût de surhomme à plusieurs. Nietzsche, dit le professeur en se tournant vers la photo du philosophe affichée au mur, est à consommer avec modération.

Les deux enquêteurs regardaient l'affiche montrant Nietzsche de profil. Sa moustache épaisse faisait penser à celle de certains collègues, pensa Duval. Il ne lui manquait que la casquette, la matraque, l'insigne et le .38 spécial. En se retournant vers Déziel, Duval s'inquiéta soudainement de ce qu'on enseignait à sa fille dans ses cours de formation générale.

— Avaient-ils un talent pour l'écriture ? demanda le lieutenant.

— Ils avaient pour la plupart une belle culture littéraire, mais s'intéressaient surtout à la philosophie.

On frappa de nouveau à la porte. Une tête chauve avec un visage totalement glabre s'infiltra dans l'embrasure. On eût dit Monsieur Net en plus maigre. Le collègue lui demanda s'il venait jouer au squash après son cours.

— Attends-moi, j'en ai pour une minute. Il me faut vous quitter, messieurs, je dois revoir mon cours.

— Connaissez-vous Rosalie Nantel ?

Déziel réfléchit tout en ramassant ses effets personnels, qu'il glissa dans sa mallette.

— Vous savez, on voit tellement d'élèves… Non. Ce nom ne me dit rien.

Duval, pas rassasié, aurait aimé poursuivre, mais le collègue l'attendait à l'extérieur.

— J'ai d'autres questions.

— Vous n'avez qu'à faire comme mes élèves et à prendre rendez-vous, monsieur l'enquêteur.

— Simple formalité : où étiez-vous avant-hier entre minuit et 2 h du matin ?

— J'étais dans les bras de Morphée.

— Et elle pourra confirmer ? demanda Louis.

Le professeur de philosophie éructa à plein gosier un rire gras.

— Ah non ! C'est la meilleure ! Morphée est un dieu et non une déesse !

Louis, conscient de sa méprise, affirma qu'il avait compris Murphy. Mais le professeur continua de rire comme un dément. D'un coup sec, Louis avança son fauteuil vers Déziel. Il aurait aimé se lever comme Lazare et foutre une claque sur la gueule à ce monstre d'arrogance.

— Écoute, espèce de bousier idéologique, tu vas pas te payer ma gueule comme ça.

Duval intervint pour calmer Louis.

— OK. On s'en va, Louis, mais on va revenir.

Déziel devança les policiers pour leur ouvrir la porte et leur souhaiter une bonne fin de journée. Après avoir refermé la porte, le professeur siffla un thème connu de Mozart. Louis serra la mâchoire, mais se sentit vengé

en refilant à Duval un plan de cours qu'il avait piqué
sur une tablette.

— C'est pour une bonne cause.

— Je le *truste* pas.

— T'as vu ce regard ? On dirait un hypnotiseur de
foire avec sa coupe à la Shogun.

Pour Duval, la récolte était bonne. Il ne restait plus
qu'à mettre tous les éléments en place. Ils passèrent
par le bureau du directeur des études et la secrétaire
leur remit les listes d'étudiants.

Dans la voiture, Duval téléphona à Dallaire. Ce dernier lui mentionna que Bernard avait déniché l'adresse
du punk exhibitionniste, un certain Lizotte, qui squattait
au coin de la rue MacMahon et de la côte du Palais,
dans un taudis aux fenêtres placardées, près de l'arsenal.
« On est à deux pas. On y va », lui dit Duval. Louis
rappela à son collègue qu'il avait faim et que le punk
pouvait attendre. Daniel lui proposa de calmer sa faim
en arrêtant chercher des sandwiches chez Bardou dans
le quartier latin. Louis acquiesça à la suggestion. Il
avait toujours un creux.

42

Pendant que Duval conduisait, Louis examina les
listes de noms. Il alla immédiatement à la lettre M sur
la première liste qui comptait vingt-huit élèves, classe
5512. Rien. Dans le groupe 5513, le nom d'Angélique
Fraser lui sauta en plein visage. Liste suivante, groupe

5514, Lemieux, Maranda, Matteau, Mathieu Michaël.
Il ressentit une poussée d'adrénaline.

— Déziel nous cache quelque chose.

À la défense de Déziel, Duval rétorqua que le nom
de Mathieu n'avait pas été révélé dans les journaux,
mais que celui de Rosalie l'avait été et qu'elle était la
copine de son ex-élève. Son silence trahissait-il sa
culpabilité ? Mais la mémoire d'un professeur – Duval
le savait bien, lui qui avait été chargé de cours – ne
peut retenir tous les noms des étudiants qu'il croise
dans une carrière. La mémoire à court terme semble
faire d'elle-même un tri à partir d'un certain âge.

Duval se gara dans la côte du Palais, face à l'Armée
du Salut. Le punk habitait un pitoyable galetas à l'ombre
de l'Hôtel-Dieu, un de ces immeubles désaffectés qui
deviennent objets de spéculations. Deux fenêtres au
rez-de-chaussée avaient été recouvertes de panneaux
en contreplaqué peints de graffitis anti-américains. Louis
estima la hauteur de la marche, grimaça, la trouvant
trop abrupte.

— Tu vas te faire chier à me hisser partout où on va ?
Je peux pas prendre mes béquilles. Je vais piquer un
petit somme. Laisse-moi le chauffage.

Louis, qui avait détesté son sandwich à la morta-
delle, était de mauvaise humeur. Duval insista.

— Viens-t'en, je vais vais te monter. J'ai l'impression que tu vas aimer rencontrer Lizotte.

Louis roula des yeux excédés et expira, prêt à faire
face à un nouveau cas de dépravation humaine.

— Bon, allons-y.

La peinture écaillée n'avait pas été rafraîchie depuis
le premier mandat de Duplessis, pensa Duval qui craignait que la structure ne s'effondre. L'escalier, très à
pic, n'avait rien de rassurant avec ses marches arrachées. Les deuxième et troisième étages étaient con-
damnés ; l'édifice avait été la proie des flammes.

Duval eut besoin de toutes ses forces pour soulever les quatre-vingt-dix kilos de Loulou. Franchir le
seuil et lever l'arrière du fauteuil exigea un difficile
arraché.

À voir les bottes, les sacs de déchets et la tourelle
de caisses de bière qui gisaient pêle-mêle à l'extrémité du vestibule, la porte de l'appartement ne devait
pas se trouver bien loin.

— J'ai l'impression que l'inspecteur sanitaire n'est
pas venu ici depuis longtemps, râla Louis.

Le fauteuil passait à peine dans le corridor étroit.
Les murs défoncés laissaient apparaître les lattes de
bois sous le plâtre.

Duval frappa. Sur la porte rouge, on avait inscrit
en lettres jaunes «*Fuck you!*» en guise de bienvenue.
Un chien jappa en se ruant vers l'entrée puis grogna.
Le maître poussa un cri et entrouvrit la porte que retenaient au moins deux chaînes. Une face javellisée,
criblée de boutons jaunes, rouges et blancs, les observait
avec un regard d'animal fou tandis que le chien se
remettait à japper, la gueule ouverte, les crocs menaçants.

Les cheveux peroxydés, en bataille, marinaient dans
un gras visqueux. Du jaune partout. Il aurait fallu un
marteau-piqueur pour détartrer ses dents.

— Police, ouvre !

— Et si j'ouvre pas… fanfaronna-t-il.

— Tu vas embrasser la porte, fiston, répliqua Louis.

Duval colla sa carte d'identification devant le nez
du punk, qu'il avait tout irrité à force de consommer de
la poudre.

— Qu'est-ce que j'ai fait ?

Duval lança d'une voix sans émotion les charges
retenues contre Lizotte.

— Grossière indécence dans un lieu public, bris de
mobilier, violation de résidence et autres méfaits.

Louis sortit sa grosse voix.

— T'as intérêt à ouvrir, Bobinette, parce que ma patience est limitée aujourd'hui.

Il ouvrit et le rottweiler se braqua. Loulou dégaina son .38 et menaça d'abattre le chien.

— Tire pas !

Lizotte en avait plein ses petits bras de poulet à tirer sur la laisse. Louis avança le canon du .38 à dix centimètres du museau.

— Tu l'enlèves de ma vue, sinon j'en fais des Gaines Burger.

— Sade ! Ta gueule !

Le punk enferma son molosse dans une pièce. Duval fit quelques pas dans le passage, précédé de Louis qui s'immobilisa devant l'arche du salon. Le Gros fronça les sourcils. Duval s'approcha. Une fille à demi habillée était couchée sur un vieux sofa. Elle semblait complètement dopée, au point qu'elle était sourde à tout ce qui se passait autour d'elle. Elle faisait penser à une poupée de chiffon malade avec ses cheveux orange, ses yeux peinturlurés, son visage blême, sa bouche écrasée comme une grosse fraise contre le coussin jaune sur lequel elle bavait. Totalement étiolée. Les lieux étaient tout aussi bordéliques que les squats de la côte d'Abraham. Une odeur de colle époxy flottait dans l'air, certes pas pour assembler des modèles réduits.

Lizotte leur demanda de le suivre à la cuisine. Là s'étalait un désordre, une scène de désolation totale : l'antichambre de la vermine, Dresde en microcosme après un bombardement. L'hygiène avait laissé place aux germes, l'effort à la paresse. Le plancher en linoléum noir et blanc était un damier à tout foutre, une macédoine d'écœuranteries : taches, pelures de patates, croûtes de pizzas, sauce tomate, mégots. Duval s'assit derrière une vieille table ovale. Son revêtement d'Arborite, couvert de brûlures de cigarette, taches de Ketchup, de moutarde et de mélasse séchées, ressemblait à un tableau abstrait de Jackson Pollock. Avec une précision toute mécanique, Louis manœuvra son fauteuil à travers le capharnaüm pour se trouver à proximité de Lizotte, qu'il ne pouvait déjà pas blairer.

Duval avait dans sa poche la photo de Rosalie, qu'il sortit et déposa à l'envers sur la table.

— Des serveuses du Laurentien nous ont dit que tu prends plaisir à faire gicler ton sperme sous les tables du resto.

— Cé jusse un pari qu'on a faite avec mé chums. Jusse pour le fun.

En écoutant Lizotte massacrer sa syntaxe, Duval sut qu'il n'avait pas fréquenté l'école très longtemps.

— J'étudie les déviances de toutes sortes et j'aimerais savoir quel plaisir on y prend.

— Veux-tu que je le r'fasse devant toé ?…

Duval prit une longue respiration par le nez tandis que Louis agrippait ses accoudoirs pour ne pas écraser son poing dans le visage de cet idiot. Duval s'avança à quelques centimètres de cette face lunaire.

— Écoute, Lizotte, si mes fréquences cardiaques montent à plus de soixante-dix, je te fais arrêter.

— Je vous l'ai dit, c'tait un pari.

Duval retourna la photo de Rosalie.

— Un témoin nous a affirmé que tu avais dragué cette fille – et même que tu lui aurais tiré la langue. C'est vrai ?

— Quand vous sortez dans les bars, c'est pas pour draguer ? Quand j'ai vu cette petite plotte-là, elle m'a allumé avec ses bottes.

Duval se sentit piqué au vif. Louis, qui s'était toujours chargé du boulot d'intimidation, n'en pouvait plus. D'une main, il saisit Lizotte par la nuque et ce dernier dut se lever tellement il avait mal. Louis l'entraîna vers lui et l'assit sur ses genoux comme un père Noël en colère.

— Tiens, assis-toi sur mon'oncle Louis, martela le Gros en lui tapotant la cuisse.

— Lâche-moé, hostie !

Louis resserra davantage les ouïes du punk qui hurla. Le chien se remit à aboyer. Duval incita discrètement Louis à relâcher la pression avant que Lizotte ne pète tous ses boutons.

— Écoute, Fanfreluche, dit Louis en postillonnant de colère, si t'as de quoi à voir dans la mort de Rosalie Nantel, t'as intérêt à attacher ton savon à ton poignet parce que je connais des gars en dedans qui vont se faire un plaisir de mousser ton petit cul plein de crotte. Et moi, je vais te crisser un set carré de taloches qui va te faire regretter les danses en ligne de ton grand-père. Rosalie Nantel est morte assassinée et je n'accepte pas qu'un peigne-cul comme toi, un taré de l'évolution animale, déshonore la mémoire d'une jeune fille bien. Alors tu réponds convenablement à nos questions. Je te le dis, j'ai faim, et quand je suis affamé, je perds patience. Ne retarde pas mon dîner. J'ai l'estomac dans les talons.

Louis le repoussa vers sa chaise. Le punk, tout rembruni, se massa la nuque. Duval appréciait et se demandait comment il avait fait pour travailler sans Louis au cours des dernières années. Il reprit son interrogatoire.

— Des témoins t'ont vu sortir du restaurant peu de temps après elle. Tu l'as suivie ? inventa Louis de toutes pièces.

L'autre gesticula, protesta énergiquement.

— Je me suis en venu icitte. J'ai même pas vu quand elle est sortie. Je savais même pas qu'elle avait été tuée ! J'vous l'dis !

— Tu lui as tiré la langue ?

— C'est vrai ! J'la trouva *cute*. Mais ça c'était l'autre soir.

— Depuis quand tu te teins les cheveux comme une madame ? intervint Louis.

— J'me *bleache* depuis un an. Regarde, *man*, ça m'brûle les cheveux au point que je les perds.

— Bin, crisse d'innocent, qu'est-ce que t'attends pour arrêter ! s'exclama Louis.

Le punk serra les lèvres devant le sarcasme du détective.

Duval lança une autre salve de questions.

— T'étais *bleaché* le soir du meurtre de Rosalie ?

— Oui, tu demanderas au barman.

Duval voyait bien que ses cheveux n'avaient rien de commun avec ceux trouvés sur le corps de Rosalie.

— Est-ce que t'as quelqu'un pour confirmer ta version ?

— Oui, ma copine a fait une overdose vers 2 h du matin et je suis allé à l'Hôtel-Dieu la reconduire.

— On va vérifier. Comment elle s'appelle ?

— Lyne Lortie.

— T'es pas retourné au Fuzz ?

— Non.

Duval sortit une photo de Mathieu.

— Tu le connais ?

— Lui, c'est Lethal. Enfin, c'est ce qui est écrit sur sa froc.

— Tu l'as vu au bar ?

— Non, je l'ai pas vu. Mais ça veut pas dire qu'il était pas là. On le voit moins qu'avant.

— Ce matin, Mathieu, alias Lethal, est à la morgue.

— *Gosh* ! Lui'si.

Le visage du punk marqua un total étonnement.

— T'es sûr que t'aurais pas vu Mathieu en compagnie de quelqu'un ?

Il réfléchit un instant.

— Non.

— Tu le connais, ce gars-là ?

— De vue seulement. Et ça me suffit. Je me tiens pas avec des petits frappés de bourges de la haute qui crachent sur du prolo.

— Frappés ?

— C'est facile de jouer les décadents quand on roule dans la BMW à papa. Ça me fait rire leur révolte. Je les encule tous. Y sont fendants, et quand je peux en cogner un sur la piste de danse du Fuzz, j'le manque pas. Leur vieux décadent aussi.

Duval eut un mouvement de recul.

— Le vieux décadent ?

— Le prof. L'Hercule à la queue de cheval. Il danse avec un t-shirt de Karl Marx. C'est la meilleure.

— Déziel ?

— Il est dur à manquer avec son look et sa petite bande de frais chiés qui le suivent depuis des années. Enfin, on les voit moins qu'avant et c'est juste bon pour l'air qu'on respire.

Il s'arrêta, regarda Louis, inquiet de sa réaction, puis continua :

— Faut dire qu'eux aussi se gênent pas pour nous frapper. Eux autres, y sentent ça à distance, du pauvre.

— Pour en revenir à Déziel, était-il là le soir du meurtre ?

— Comme à toué soirs.

— À quelle heure tu l'as vu ?

— Je sais pas, 11 h, 11 h 30.

Louis jeta un regard étonné vers son collègue.

— Comment se comporte Déziel au Fuzz ?

— En tout cas, pas comme on imagine un prof. Y danse comme un malade ! On dirait un pogo ! Y *cruise* les petites jeunes, y pogne pas mal avec sa tite couette

LA MOISSON FRATERNELLE

64

La chapelle de la rue Sainte-Ursule se remplissait peu à peu. Les vitraux irradiaient, attisés par le soleil qu'accentuait le tapis de neige déroulé durant la nuit. Niché dans le jubé ouvragé de boiseries, d'anges et de rosettes, Duval observait les gens entrer et prendre un siège. Il n'était pas allé dans une église depuis la mort d'un collègue en service. Il appréciait le calme après la tempête. Toute cette lumière et cette chaleur étaient nécessaires en ce dimanche.

En arrivant, il s'était aussitôt réfugié dans les hauteurs par l'escalier en colimaçon, au-dessus des nuages d'encens, pour écrire son texte en paix. À proximité, les immenses tuyaux d'orgue déversaient leurs puissants accords. Une vieille organiste maigrichonne au chignon gris se contorsionnait sur le clavier. Ses longues jambes, habillées d'un collant en tissu de couleur chair, se tordaient sur le pédalier.

Le lieutenant avait choisi la solidarité et la camaraderie particulières qui le liaient à Loulou et à ses collègues, sauf qu'il peinait à coucher trois mots sous le titre. Le sommeil l'avait déserté la veille, après la mort de Maranda.

Il mâchonna son stylo en fixant le Christ en croix.

À travers la balustrade, son regard plongea vers Louis. Près du bénitier, le Gros, vêtu de son complet à carreaux et d'une cravate bariolée, accueillait « ses chums ». Il se tenait fièrement debout à l'aide de ses béquilles. L'aumônier, Spike, l'assistait à l'accueil. À ses côtés, Claudette le secondait avec ses airs de rockeuse convertie. Elle distribuait avec entrain la propagande de Jésus-Ouvrier.

Se trouvait rassemblée dans l'église une faune bigarrée que seul Louis pouvait réunir. Beaucoup de policiers endimanchés avec leurs épouses et leurs enfants, des employés du labo, des membres du Club Lions, des charismatiques, le Cercle des fermières de Beauport…

Des sœurs hospitalières entrèrent comme une nuée d'oiseaux rares avec leurs cornettes. La sœur-infirmière de l'hôpital Saint-Sacrement, qui avait veillé sur Loulou, le salua par un bec sonore sur chaque joue. Louis multipliait les « ma sœur » par-ci et les « ma sœur » par-là de sa grosse voix qui résonnait dans la nef.

Le docteur Villemure apparut à son tour dignement en compagnie de sa femme habillée comme la duchesse de Windsor. Le docteur pointa les jambes de Louis et applaudit discrètement.

Puis ce fut au tour du grand Francis de faire son entrée, avec à son bras Adèle Marino, vêtue d'un tailleur rose. Les blessures du détective ne paraissaient pas à cette distance, ni les sucettes.

Louis, fatigué, regagna son fauteuil et roula à grandes épaulées vers Francis.

Une clameur se répandit. Duval écarquilla les yeux. Une batterie de talons aiguilles claquèrent sur le linoléum. Se trouvait là un bataillon de prostituées qui semblait avoir confondu la chapelle et le Red Light.

Louis s'agita, ne sachant plus où donner de la tête. Un coup de roue sec vers la droite. Le Gros était aux anges. Les consœurs de Layla avaient entendu son invitation. Elles étaient venues prier la disparue. Une dizaine de péripatéticiennes plutôt délurées firent cercle autour du fauteuil: *brushing*, franges, minijupes, jeans serrés, cuissardes. Loulou et l'aumônier les reçurent avec gentillesse. Certaines se penchaient pour embrasser Louis, qui jubilait. Le Gros en profita pour tapoter quelques hanches au passage. L'aumônier conduisit les filles dans l'allée jusqu'à leurs bancs. Leur démarche chaloupée et ces talons percutants avaient de quoi faire retourner toute l'assemblée. Duval regardait le Gros gesticuler, ses mains pleines d'amour s'agitaient au-dessus de son immobilité. Un rire gras éructait après l'autre. Ses copains lui donnaient des tapes dans le dos.

Pouliot et Malo, ennemis jurés de Louis et de Duval, s'amenèrent en dignes bouffons de la centrale. Pouliot portait une chemise brune imprimée avec un long collet. Que seraient les départements sans les paniers percés de service? Louis s'avança pour les recevoir et leur offrit une franche poignée de main. Son accueil contrastait avec les coups de gueule qu'ils s'étaient infligés quelques jours plus tôt.

Une ombre passa. Madden, un peu perdu mais escorté d'une superbe Noire, vint serrer la pince à Loulou. À cette distance, il était difficile de juger du moral du maître-chien. Gros éclats de rire. Duval suspecta une blague cochonne, du genre «Je te comprends d'avoir donné congé à Sneak.»

Louis s'écria, en voyant Mireille, la biologiste: «Ah toi! Ma fausse athée! Je savais que tu viendrais.»

Il fit ensuite une provision de baisers.

— Je ne suis pas venue pour Dieu mais pour toi, lui annonça-t-elle. On parle de toi à pleines pages dans le journal.

Duval remarqua qu'elle fréquentait le docteur Maher, le stagiaire. Stage fructueux ! Anatomie du plaisir !

— Venir pour moi, c'est pardonnable ! rétorqua Louis.

Duval entendit un tonitruant « Bernie » ! Bernard assistait à la messe avec toute sa famille et sa fille malade. Duval n'en revenait pas.

Il étira le cou, surpris d'apercevoir Mimi et Frédéric, main dans la main, arpentant l'allée centrale de la chapelle. Il fallait que ce dimanche soit magique. Le garçon avait attaché ses cheveux, mais il avait oublié de les glisser sous sa veste à carreaux. L'arche de Noé était bondée de spécimens. Tout de suite, Frédéric se rendit examiner la batterie du percussionniste, un agent de la SQ qui avait fait un DEC en musique. Sans doute lui trouvait-il des défauts, pensa Duval.

Le regard en plongée du lieutenant sur l'assemblée l'inspira. Il griffonna des mots simples. Les mots du cœur. Les siens. Il n'avait rien d'un littéraire, même s'il écrivait des rapports sans fautes qui lui valaient les compliments du substitut du procureur.

Louis monta à son tour l'allée. Duval se rappela les événements de la veille, Louis lui prêtant main-forte, pressentant le danger imminent qu'il courait. Duval avait apprécié la témérité de son collègue alors qu'il se trouvait dans le pétrin, désarmé, en territoire hostile.

Malgré le succès de la cérémonie, Duval était déçu pour son ami. Il savait que Loulou aurait souhaité y voir ses enfants et Charlène, son ex, mais qu'ils manqueraient au rendez-vous. Le pardon, thème de la messe, ne trouvait pas encore chez elle une oreille conciliante. Le pardon ne se commandait pas. La rédemption était difficile. Le lieutenant savait que Louis y pensait et qu'il continuait d'espérer que sa famille se présente, sinon tout serait à recommencer.

Devant le retable, les musiciens de la SQ accordaient leurs instruments. Le patrouilleur et bassiste Paul Bédard ouvrit sa partition. Louis leur avait demandé d'interpréter des chansons en compagnie d'un animateur de pastorale.

En bas, Laurence l'attendait au tout premier rang. Le capitaine Dallaire, sa femme et ses sept enfants occupaient presque toute la rangée à eux seuls.

Duval poursuivit son texte, une lettre écrite à la deuxième personne. Le ton était loin des rédactions ennuyeuses qu'il devait composer après une journée de travail devant sa machine à écrire. C'était pour lui un vrai moment de libération.

Puis le chanteur, un charismatique policier de Val-Bélair, entonna *La Ballade des gens heureux* et invita l'assemblée à chanter le refrain. Duval sourit et chanta du bout des lèvres. L'enceinte était remplie à pleine capacité et le chœur résonna.

Duval plia sa lettre et la déposa dans la poche de son veston. Il descendit l'escalier en colimaçon et gagna sa place. Au passage, il expédia un clin d'œil à Francis, qui n'osait pas chanter.

Le prêtre s'approcha de l'autel avec deux servants de messe. Il bénit l'assemblée. Louis, assis en retrait près du lutrin, s'avança. Le chanteur lui passa un micro. Loulou sortit ses grosses lunettes et livra son message avec entrain.

— Chers amis, chers collègues, voilà des semaines que je prépare cette messe. J'avais hâte de vous retrouver. C'est mon party avec Lui – il leva les mains – et vous. Je remercie tous ceux qui m'ont aidé, de même que le groupe qui a préparé toutes les chansons pour l'occasion. Un merci tout spécial à ma Claudette, sans qui rien ne se ferait. Il y a trois ans, j'ai failli mourir, tiré à bout portant par Donald, un garçon dont j'avais tué le frère, Paul. Je ne savais pas que cet événement allait être le plus important de ma vie. Quand je me suis réveillé à l'hôpital, j'ai constaté que les collègues ne m'avaient pas abandonné ; Danny, Bernie, Frankie, sœur Paula et Claudette aussi veillaient sur moi, et surtout Lui, le Tout-Puissant. Lui était là et Il m'a donné une nouvelle chance. Des mauvaises langues disent qu'Il ne me voulait pas au paradis pour y mettre la foire. Je le crois !

L'assemblée s'esclaffa.

— Tout le monde connaît la vie dissipée que j'ai menée… Bon, je suis dur à vivre ! Même moi, je m'endure pas !

La foule rigola.

— Mais j'ai appris à respecter ceux qui m'entourent. Je me suis aperçu que toute la haine accumulée en moi s'exprimait contre mes proches, mais aussi contre ceux que j'arrêtais. Le 7 juin 1976, ma vie allait être complètement bouleversée. Pendant que mon ami, le lieutenant Duval, s'apprêtait à remettre Donald Hurtubise entre les mains de la justice divine, moi, je gisais dans un dépotoir, presque au bout de mon sang. Au bout du rouleau… Étrangement, c'est un peu comme ça que je me sentais dans les heures qui ont précédé : un déchet, un bon à rien. Quand je me suis réveillé, j'ai appris que je serais en fauteuil roulant. Mais je revenais à la vie et à sa dure réalité : ma femme demandait le divorce, ma maîtresse me laissait tomber, ça vous coupe les jambes, ça aussi…

Le Gros gloussa alors que l'assemblée était visiblement émue. Duval vit Laurence sortir un mouchoir pour absorber les grosses larmes qui roulaient sur ses joues.

— Mais je me réveillais aussi à la vie… Puis Il est venu comme un vent de soleil, sous la forme d'une lumière, et j'ai marché vers Lui ou plutôt roulé sur son chemin. Aujourd'hui, c'est une date importante. J'ai pis ses lunettes d'intello. Y a du cash, de la dope, yé *cool*.

— De la dope ?

— *You name it, man* : speed, coke, hasch.

— Écoute, Lizotte, je suis prêt à diluer les accusations de grossière indécence si tu collabores à notre enquête comme tu sembles vouloir le faire.

Le type réfléchit et déclina l'offre d'un rictus et d'un signe de tête négatif.

— Dans ce cas, je rajoute possession de drogue, dit Louis.

— Où vous avez vu ça ?

Le Gros zieuta tout autour.

— Ça prendra pas deux minutes que je te coffre pour un an à Orsainville. Puis qu'est-ce que tu fais ici ? C'est une propriété privée et non pas publique… Es-tu sûr que la jeune fille dans le salon a dix-huit ans ? Et les sorties de secours sont bouchées. Ton chien présente les blessures d'un animal de combat, c'est illégal.

Lizotte grimaça, serra le poing et fixa Duval droit dans les yeux. Il s'alluma une cigarette et aspira intensément avant d'expirer à s'envelopper la tête dans un cocon de fumée.

— Bon, OK, je vais répondre aux questions. *Shoot* !

— Qu'est-ce que tu sais d'autre sur Déziel et sa gang ?

— Comme tout le monde se *spotte* et s'étiquette, eux autres, on les appelle les croque-morts. Y sont toutes habillés en noir.

— Les jeunes qui tournaient autour de Déziel, tu les connais de nom ?

— Y se donnent des surnoms bizarres. Y en avait un qui se teignait les cheveux vert vomi et qui était pas mal sauté. Y était toujours en délire. Ses yeux, c'taient des braises. Y me faisait peur. Mes copines l'aimaient pas. Y dansait et avait tendance à faire bin d'l'air autour de lui. T'as pas intérêt à danser trop près quand y *slamme*. Y regardait personne, même pas ses p'tits amis. Y semblait toujours dans sa bulle.

— Son nom ?

— Je sais pas son nom, mais y se faisait appeler… Je crois que c'était quelque chose comme Spin. Un soir, y a sorti un revolver au bar. Je l'ai vu.

Duval prenait des notes : Lizotte s'avérait un excellent placement. Il devenait la mémoire vivante de ce qui s'était passé le soir du meurtre.

— Un revolver ? reprit Duval.

— Oui.

La jeune fille traversa la pièce comme une somnambule sans regarder personne, les cheveux hirsutes. Elle marchait en traînant ses pieds nus sur le plancher, une coulissure de bave séchée sur le menton. Elle se rendit jusqu'au frigo sans se soucier des policiers. Elle ouvrit la porte, prit le litre de jus de raisin et le vida en échappant quelques gouttelettes rouge grenat sur son menton.

Duval se tourna vers Lizotte.

— Tu as déjà parlé à Lethal ?

— Une fois, dans les toilettes, pour lui acheter de la coke pis du speed. Il est parti à rire de moi. Un rire hystérique. J'ai décrissé.

Le punk écrasa son mégot dans une soucoupe, ce qui horripila Duval.

— Comment était Déziel, l'autre soir ?

— J'sais pas. J'passe pas mes soirées à le regarder.

— A-t-il commis des gestes déplacés à l'endroit de cette fille ?

Duval lui montra la photo de Rosalie Nantel.

— Non. Elle dansait avec un grand fif maigrichon.

— Sébastien Poirier ?

— Je sais pas. Y fait tapette.

— Tu les as vus ensemble, récemment, Mathieu et elle ?

— Y sortaient pus ensemble, c'est ce que j'avais constaté.

— Pourquoi t'avais remarqué ça ? demanda Louis.

— Un pétard comme elle, on *spotte* ça tout de suite. Enfin, moi, j'avais vu qui dansaient pus ensemble.

— Et les autres membres du groupe ?

— Des hosties de poseurs de faces à claques ! On les voit moins, comme je vous dis, pis c'est parfait de même !

Le regard de Duval dévia vers une grande affiche rose et jaune des Sex Pistols accrochée au mur de la cuisine, juste au-dessus de la tête de Louis. Le lieutenant n'aimait pas la connotation violente du message.

— En tout cas, merci pour l'initiation au monde punk.

— Vous devriez essayer ça.

— Je préfère les danses en ligne, marmonna Louis.

Pendant qu'il poussait le fauteuil de Louis, Duval ne pensait qu'à Déziel, la clé de l'énigme. Il ne lui avait pas tout dit et Daniel comptait reprendre l'interrogatoire. Il allait sortir le professeur de sa caverne.

Duval plia et rangea le fauteuil de Louis dans le coffre de la voiture.

— Il est suspect ? demanda Louis en attachant sa ceinture.

— Non, je ne pense pas, dit Duval. Quoique son agressivité envers les bourgeois puisse paraître suspecte. On a essayé de faire de Mathieu l'assassin de Rosalie. Quelqu'un en voulait au jeune couple. Pourtant, ils ne se fréquentaient plus. Ils étaient même brouillés au point que Rosalie se sente menacée par Mathieu.

— C'est ce que Poirier nous a dit.

— Oui. Le mobile pourrait être la vengeance. À moins que ce soit un jeu sadique. Par contre, Déziel me doit des explications. Il ne nous a pas tout raconté. Il se tenait avec eux au Fuzz et a tout de la pharmacie ambulante.

En démarrant, Duval aperçut de l'autre côté, face au Cercle électrique, deux motards qui portaient leurs couleurs. Un rictus dégoûté s'imprima sur son visage.

— Regarde-moi les crottés…

— La ville est devenue un véritable asile.

Louis ne les lâchait plus du regard.

— Des tarés. Finalement, Lombroso avait raison, malgré tout le mal qu'on a dit de l'anthropologie criminelle. Certains sont nés avec la tête de l'emploi.

— Tu dis n'importe quoi !

Loulou savait qu'il ne devait pas s'aventurer sur ce terrain glissant avec Duval.

La faim le rappelant à d'autres sentiments, le Gros sortit un coupon-rabais de quinze pour cent sur le buffet à volonté d'un restaurant chinois du Vieux-Québec.

— C'est *all you can eat*. Claudette m'a dit que c'était pas pire.

— Je préfère qu'on mange tous ensemble à la cafétéria. Après, on fera le *debriefing*.

Louis marmonna son dégoût.

43

Duval déposa les listes d'étudiants de Déziel sur le mica vert de son bureau. Il en survola les noms. Il sortit de son sac le journal de Mathieu, qui allait peut-être lui révéler quelques secrets.

Le téléphone sonna.

— Es-tu bien assis, Daniel? dit le capitaine Dallaire.

Duval avala sa salive de travers. Il craignait un autre homicide.

— Rivard vient d'analyser le rouge à lèvres dont s'est servi le meurtrier de Mathieu pour le peinturlurer et c'est le même que celui de Rosalie. C'est donc dire que le meurtrier a conservé certains objets appartenant à la jeune fille. Le pendentif a bel et bien servi à tuer Rosalie Nantel. Les gars de l'Identité judiciaire ont retrouvé le fermoir du collier dans l'aspirateur à travers les feuilles mortes. Il correspond à la pièce manquante du collier. Finalement, il y avait aussi du gardénal dans un verre de bière chez Mathieu. Rivard en a décelé une dose importante. Sans doute lui a-t-il été administré par son assassin.

— Quelqu'un qu'il connaissait, alors.

— Oui.

— Contrairement au corps de Rosalie, celui de Mathieu n'a pas été mutilé sexuellement. Les seuls actes de ritualisation et marques *post mortem* seraient cette pendaison et surtout ce sourire triste dessiné avec le rouge à lèvres. Le tueur est un fétichiste, ce qui n'a rien de rassurant.

— Il a sans doute voulu brouiller les pistes ou nous défier. Il s'amuse à nos dépens.

— À la section Documents, Miljours confirme que le texte est de Robert Camus.

— Albert!

— Oui! Albert Camus, excuse-moi. Le livre appartenait bel et bien à Mathieu, il avait signé son nom à l'intérieur, ce qui indique que le suspect a des points communs avec lui. Il connaissait ce roman.

— C'est un texte philosophique.

— Mais Camus est un romancier?

— Et un philosophe, si je me fie au dictionnaire. Je crois qu'on est face à quelqu'un qui joue son va-tout. Un impulsif sadique, sexuellement frustré, qui veut faire le plus de dommages en un minimum de temps et narguer l'autorité en prenant des risques et en brouillant les pistes. Je t'annonce que Mathieu et Angélique ont tous les deux étudié au Séminaire. L'assassin les a probablement connus là ou au Fuzz. Le professeur Déziel a enseigné à Mathieu et à Angélique et un témoin l'a vu au Fuzz vers 11 h, le soir du meurtre. Si le meurtrier connaissait Mathieu, Rosalie lui était sans doute familière. Ce qui fait de Déziel un témoin important, d'autant plus qu'il a eu des mœurs troubles dans le passé.

— Ce sont des pistes intéressantes, Daniel. En passant, je n'assisterai pas à l'exhumation. J'ai toujours haï ça.

◆

Dans le décor monotone de la cafétéria, le dîner fut englouti à la va-vite. Devant des boîtes de sandwiches vides et des verres de styromousse émiettés, Duval raconta où il en était rendu. Francis et Prince n'avaient pas grand-chose à rapporter sinon que Sébastien Poirier leur avait remis une photo pour justifier son alibi. Il ne restait qu'à retracer le préposé qui se trouvait derrière le comptoir de la traverse de Lévis cette nuit-là. D'ailleurs, un appel anonyme laissait sous-entendre que Sébastien Poirier était frustré sexuellement. La personne n'avait rien voulu ajouter et avait raccroché. La meilleure amie de Rosalie, Andréanne, suspectait Mathieu du meurtre. Elle ignorait que les preuves n'incriminaient pas Mathieu. Ce genre de messages anonymes et de rumeurs étaient fréquents dans ces enquêtes.

— Les amis vous poignardent dans le dos même après votre mort, conclut Louis.

— Écoutez, il est possible que le meurtrier de Nantel et de Mathieu assiste aux funérailles de Rosalie qui auront lieu demain.

Duval eut droit à des regards sceptiques.

— Qu'est-ce qu'il irait faire là ? demanda Francis en déchiquetant un peu plus son verre de styromousse.

— Voyeurisme. Défi. Assister à la finale de son œuvre. Éprouver même de la compassion. S'il a une double personnalité, il ne ressentira aucun remords. Enfin, les annales judiciaires comportent un lot de voyeurs-meurtriers.

— Tu ne crois pas qu'il aurait pu agir par vengeance plutôt que d'une façon hasardeuse ? lança Francis tout en érigeant un monticule de pièces de styromousse.

— Ce qui est clair, c'est que les trois morts, deux meurtres et un suicide, nous ramènent à Déziel. Il a enseigné à Angélique Fraser, à Michaël Mathieu et connaissait sans doute Rosalie Nantel, même s'il ne l'a pas eue comme élève. Quelqu'un dans son entourage tue. Déziel donne un cours intitulé *Philosophie de la mort*. Soit qu'il ait pété les plombs, soit qu'un idiot ait décidé de concrétiser son cours et de faire de sa vie une philosophie pratique de la mort.

Cette dernière pensée lui glaça le sang.

Louis hocha la tête.

— Moi, je serais de l'avis du docteur Fraser, Déziel est un pervers. Je le *truste* pas.

Duval pianota sur la table.

— S'il n'est pas capable de fournir un alibi pour la nuit des meurtres de Rosalie et de Michaël, je demande un mandat d'arrêt contre lui.

Daniel regarda la première page du *Journal de Québec* exhibant une photo du cimetière et, en médaillon, une autre de Rosalie. Déziel aurait dû savoir que l'amie de son ex-élève était décédée, d'autant plus qu'ils semblaient tous se connaître. Mais un intellectuel lisait-il le *Journal de Québec* ? Le lieutenant se rappelait avoir vu *Le Devoir* sur le coin de son bureau.

44

Vers 13 h 50, l'escouade du lieutenant Duval prit la direction du cimetière de Sillery. Le soleil faisait briller l'écorce argentée des hêtres. Les feuilles jaunes des bouleaux blancs, plus résistantes aux assauts de l'automne, frémissaient dans un flou impressionniste. Au sol, le feuillage brun en décomposition dégageait une agréable odeur de tabac. Des chandelles, des couronnes et des bouquets de fleurs avaient été déposés à l'endroit où Rosalie était décédée. Duval pensa qu'il faudrait vérifier les messages envoyés avec les fleurs. La nécropole grise baignait dans le calme jusqu'au moment où Duval aperçut les deux individus. Un journaliste avait dû capter l'information sur la bande-radio réservée à la police. On allait exhumer un macchabée, et cette perspective suffisait à exciter les scribes qui spéculaient sur les événements sadiques et bizarres des derniers jours.

— Il y a un photographe, pesta Duval. J'avais promis à Fraser que l'exhumation resterait privée.

Déjà, le photographe criblait de flashes le mausolée dans lequel reposait Angélique Fraser. Le journaliste, lui, attendait de pouvoir décrire le spectacle sanglant à son public. Duval eut l'impression d'avoir manqué à sa parole. Il fallait s'occuper d'eux pour qu'on ne publie jamais ces clichés.

— Je m'en occupe, dit Louis avant de s'élancer.

— Louis ! Non !

Sans écouter, le Gros fonça vers le photographe avec la force d'un bélier mécanique. La pente aidant, son fauteuil prit de la vélocité au point que la course du bolide instable inquiéta Duval. Comment s'arrêteraient ces kilos de muscles et d'acier en perte de contrôle volontaire ?

La grosse tête chauve de Louis ressemblait à un boulet de canon. Il freina son élan sur le gars, qui chuta. L'appareil photo cogna l'asphalte. Faisant demi-tour pour s'excuser, Louis roula sur le Nikon 35 millimètres, écrasant la lentille et le boîtier, qui s'ouvrit et exposa ainsi le film à la lumière. « Mais qui oserait s'en prendre à un handicapé ? » se dit Duval en regardant Louis jouer les innocents. Le Gros se confondait en excuses et pestait contre ce fauteuil bas de gamme.

L'avocat de Fraser, vêtu d'un complet bleu, attendait près du mausolée en grillant une cigarette. Le gardien du cimetière, le vieux McClean, passa près de lui et le salua. Il sortit la clé et le mausolée frais répandit toute son humidité. On remarquait les traces de nettoyage à l'acide muriatique, une bande grise plus pâle, afin d'effacer le graffiti obscène.

Les techniciens du labo investirent la sépulture. Ils installaient déjà des projecteurs afin de recueillir fibres, poils, cheveux et autres indices. Un spécialiste en scène de crime agitait son pinceau de poudre pour relever les empreintes digitales. Le camion rouge de la morgue annonçait bien ce qui allait suivre, de même que l'arrivée des enquêteurs. Il fallait prendre des précautions pour exhumer un cadavre, procéder dans un lieu bien aéré. Les gaz délétères dégagés par un corps en décomposition étaient combustibles.

Villemure se trouvait aussi dans le mausolée. Il portait ses grosses lunettes fumées Christian Dior et, dans sa main droite, sa valise en cuir italien. Dans ce décor, il ressemblait plus à un vieil aristocrate italien qui médite ses aphorismes qu'à un médecin légiste. Il accueillit les enquêteurs avec un salut discret.

— Du neuf ? demanda-t-il à Duval.

— Rien d'autre.

Duval se pencha, plissa les yeux et eut l'impression que la lourde stèle ne reposait pas entièrement sur le coffre de granit. Il ne faisait aucun doute que la pierre plate avait été déplacée. Des iris avaient été sculptés sur le cippe et les mots latins *Lacrimarum valle* y avaient été gravés.

Il fallait beaucoup de force pour déplacer la pierre, comme il en avait fallu pour hisser le corps de Mathieu.

— Pouvaient-ils être deux ? envisagea Francis en se tournant vers le lieutenant.

— Je ne crois pas, dit Duval.

Le lieutenant appuya une main sur la pierre froide et réfléchit à voix haute.

— Quelle serait la position idéale pour y parvenir seul ?

— Laisse-moi te montrer, dit Francis.

Alors qu'il ne risquait plus de contaminer la sépulture, Francis s'agrippa à la stèle pour suggérer une position ergonomique favorable. Une main de chaque côté de l'angle droit. La bordure arrondie du couvercle excédait de dix centimètres et offrait une prise valable.

— Ensuite, on pousse.

Le visage de Francis prit la couleur d'un poivron. La pierre plate bougea de quelques centimètres.

— Puis on recommence. S'il y est arrivé seul, il est costaud.

Sous la poussée de Duval et de Francis, la pierre plate glissa lentement. On laissa s'échapper les gaz pendant quelques minutes. L'odeur pestilentielle imprima des grimaces sur les visages. Il fallut quatre hommes pour soulever la stèle et la déposer contre le mur. Le bois poli du cercueil en chêne brillait sous les projecteurs. Pinceau et poudre à la main, l'expert de l'Identité judiciaire releva les empreintes. Si quatre hommes avaient été nécessaires pour lever la stèle, Duval comprit que, en raison du couvercle en deux parties du cercueil, le profanateur n'avait eu qu'à glisser la pierre vers la partie qui était demeurée rabattue. Cinq minutes plus tard, on put ouvrir le demi-couvercle qui allait de la taille à la tête. Passant de l'ombre à la lumière, le visage d'Angélique apparut, entièrement caché par sa longue chevelure bouclée qui cascadait sur sa poitrine.

Villemure, l'air grave, se tourna vers Duval en hochant la tête. La tension monta d'un cran.

— Ce n'est pas normal.

Le médecin légiste s'éloigna pour que le photographe prenne des photos.

La robe blanche d'Angélique, toute jaunie par l'humidité, s'harmonisait avec les ancolies séchées dispersées sur sa poitrine. Le corps dégageait une affreuse odeur de putréfaction. Villemure distribua des masques chirurgicaux aux enquêteurs.

Tous les regards se fixèrent au même endroit. L'une des mains, en effet, manquait. Une fois de plus, on laissa agir le technicien qui cherchait indices et micro-indices. Une carte de souhaits était insérée parmi les tiges d'ancolies. Duval, qui avait enfilé des gants de latex, demanda à la voir et lut à haute voix le contenu du message : « Le ver rongera ta peau comme un remords. » Le texte, en caractères imprimés sur du papier de piètre qualité, avait été découpé dans un livre.

La voix grave de Francis résonna dans le caveau humide.

— C'est dans l'esprit de ce qui avait été inscrit sur le mur.

Le lieutenant déposa la pièce à conviction dans un sac. Il se demandait comment on s'y était pris pour trancher la main, mais finit par comprendre. Pour commettre son acte dément, le nécrophile avait ramené la main au-dessus de la tête. À cet endroit, des marques de stries dans le satin du cercueil étaient apparentes. Autre objet de profanation et de ritualisation, le crucifix avait été placé à l'envers.

Villemure découvrit le visage de la morte comme on ouvre un rideau et la stupéfaction se lut sur tous les visages. L'avocat poussa un râle et sortit en vitesse pour vomir sur les feuilles mortes. Le vieux McClean, les yeux exorbités, ne broncha point. François, qui avait presque tout vu dans sa carrière, se raidit.

— Espèce de salaud !

Un filin d'acier paré de lames de rasoir entourait le cou de la morte. Les lames étaient enfoncées à égale distance dans la chair. Étrange collier qui rappelait le suicide de la jeune fille. Le corps éclairé par des lampes très puissantes était spectral : une Ophélie décomposée.

Le pathologiste judiciaire observa les marques qu'avait pratiquées le boucher à la hauteur du poignet.

— On a vraiment affaire à un nécrophile. Dans le cas de Rosalie, on comptait une dizaine de signes *post mortem* : mutilations du cadavre, positionnement des jambes, éjaculation, signature. Ici, c'est pareil, sauf qu'il n'a pas tué sa victime.

Duval se rappela que Fraser était chirurgien. Mais un père pouvait-il faire une chose pareille à sa fille ?

Francis ne voulut plus rentrer à l'intérieur du mausolée et resta à causer avec Louis qui protégeait la scène des curieux.

Villemure prenait des notes et observait le cadavre, tout en écoutant Duval livrer ses conjectures.

— Elle s'est tailladé les veines. Le profanateur le savait sans doute.

— Il faudra revoir le rapport d'autopsie après ce qui s'est passé avec Mathieu.

— Quelqu'un qui commet un tel acte nous dit clairement qu'on n'en a pas fini avec lui, répliqua Duval.

Villemure le regarda, consterné.

— Daniel, ce tueur est compulsif. Il faut absolument le contrer parce que la fréquence de ses délits est très serrée. Il en éprouve le besoin.

Duval se refusait à penser à la suite. Il avait lu l'histoire de cas du genre dans des revues spécialisées. Les annales judiciaires foisonnaient en récits d'horreur. Les tueurs en série s'étaient multipliés au cours des dernières années aux États-Unis et même au Québec. Aujourd'hui, la Couronne le mandatait pour interrompre le festin d'un ogre sexuel et nécrophile qui s'en prenait à des êtres dont il connaissait le passé.

45

Duval retourna au Petit Séminaire de Québec pour rencontrer de nouveau le professeur de philosophie, mais ce dernier n'était pas à son bureau et son horaire indiquait qu'il était en classe. Duval mémorisa le numéro du local, qui se trouvait au bout du corridor.

Cependant, la vaste salle était vide. Sur le tableau noir, un membre de la direction avait inscrit un message annonçant que Victor Déziel avait dû s'absenter. Quelqu'un avait écrit en dessous avec de grosses lettres jaunes : « Semaine de lecture. Il reste encore deux places pour le voyage à Boston. Renseignements à l'Asso. » De grosses fleurs roses avaient été dessinées à la fin du message. Il se rappela que le numéro de téléphone de Déziel était noté sur le plan de cours. Avait-il peur ? Se terrait-il ?

Duval retourna à la centrale, préoccupé par toutes les tâches qui l'attendaient. Il fila vers son bureau. Il sortit le plan de cours de son classeur. Le récepteur appuyé contre son épaule, il composa le numéro mais, après cinq sonneries, il renonça. Son regard dévia vers le livre de Michaël Mathieu, mais avant de s'y plonger il se rappela qu'il devait contacter le docteur Fraser.

Il composa le numéro du département de cardiologie du CHUL et demanda à la secrétaire de lui passer d'urgence le docteur Fraser. Sans aucune politesse, elle le mit en attente avec une horrible version musak de la *Vie en rose*.

— Le docteur Fraser doit sortir de la salle de réanimation d'ici trente minutes. Il peut vous rappeler ?

— Oui, dites-lui d'appeler le lieutenant Duval.

Il retéléphona à la résidence de Déziel, mais n'obtint pas plus de réponse.

Il laissa un message au répartiteur à l'intention de Bernard. Il demandait à ce dernier de rencontrer la famille de Michaël Mathieu pour en savoir davantage sur la vie et les fréquentations de leur fils.

Trois messages identiques du lieutenant Granger s'entassaient sur la bande de son répondeur : « Lieutenant Duval, veuillez me rappeler… » Duval décida de ne pas leur donner suite immédiatement. Il sentait l'urgence de la situation. Il prit une grande respiration, pivota nerveusement sur sa chaise. Le détective se rappela qu'on lui avait confié cette enquête, qui ne relevait pas de sa juridiction, surtout parce qu'il était expert en psychologie criminelle, une discipline relativement nouvelle, et ce, même aux États-Unis.

Avant de se retirer pour parcourir le livre de Mathieu, il passa par les locaux du capitaine afin de lui relater les derniers événements.

À peine 16 h 30 et le jour tombait. Le bureau de Dallaire semblait un petit îlot de lumière perdu dans l'obscurité. Seul le verre de l'abat-jour en laiton luisait sur le bureau du patron. Derrière lui, dans l'ombre, le drapeau de la SQ et celui du Québec paraissaient former une haie d'honneur. Un coupe-papier plaqué or reposait sur une pile d'enveloppes. La tête grisonnante et fatiguée du capitaine était penchée sur ses rapports. Il apposa sa signature à une série de lettres tout en engageant la conversation.

— J'ai croisé Louis. C'est effrayant !

— La signature du meurtrier est la même. On sait qu'il aime les lieux sordides.

— Pourquoi se manifeste-t-il dans des lieux aussi risqués ? demanda le chef.

— Probablement parce qu'il aime défier la peur et qu'il adore effrayer ses victimes. Il prend plaisir à les savoir terrorisées. Il éprouve certainement une déviance sexuelle quelconque. C'est un frustré. Il existe des récurrences dans le *modus operandi*. Dans le cas de Rosalie, il l'a violée et mutilée après la mort. Il l'a étranglée, puis s'est livré à des actes *post mortem* sur le corps. Dans le cas d'Angélique, il s'est masturbé devant son corps, ce qui montre peut-être qu'il est embarrassé de se montrer nu parce qu'il a déjà subi les sarcasmes des filles. La mutilation du corps, la mise en scène, font ressortir un besoin de puissance et l'envie de narguer l'autorité. Il est atteint d'une pathologie de cet ordre. Avec Angélique, il n'a pas eu à tuer et pouvait se livrer à sa perversion. Du moins, il faut attendre un réexamen de l'autopsie initiale. Le suspect a peut-être des personnalités multiples.

— Tu crois à ça, que quelqu'un prend plaisir à se masturber devant un cadavre ?

— On est dans le domaine de la maladie mentale. C'est connu dans les annales criminelles. Même le docteur Derome, dans son *Précis de médecine légale* qui date pourtant de 1920, associe nécrophilie et masturbation. Le cas Bertrand en France, dont je t'ai déjà parlé, n'est pas une fiction non plus. Il éjaculait dans les organes décomposés des cadavres.

Dallaire expira, passa sa main dans ses cheveux gris.

— Et pourquoi s'en prendre aussi à Mathieu ?

Duval hocha la tête.

— Il a voulu brouiller les pistes, nous faire croire que Mathieu était l'auteur du meurtre, rire de nous pendant quelques heures. Les psychopathes sont manipulateurs.

— Et Déziel ? Tout nous ramène à lui. Il les connaissait tous les trois. Il fallait de la force pour hisser le corps de Mathieu jusqu'au tuyau. Déziel est un colosse.

— Il s'est absenté du travail cet après-midi.

— Tu veux un mandat d'arrêt ? Je te l'obtiens pour demain matin. Déziel est le seul suspect qui pourrait coller au type qu'on cherche.

— Oui, je veux un mandat. Déziel donne un cours à 8 h demain matin et j'espère bien le cueillir avant qu'il entre en classe.

Dallaire gratta sa joue rugueuse comme du papier-émeri et une longue strie rouge marqua son visage. Il inspira longuement et fixa son lieutenant d'un regard inquiet.

— Daniel, j'aimerais que tu collabores mieux avec Granger et le chef de la police de Sillery, sinon tu risques de te retrouver dans une mauvaise position. Moi, je te fais totalement confiance, mais eux, ils vont bientôt rugir. Tu t'imagines l'état dans lequel se trouvent les parents ? Tu sais comment ça se passe : ils vont bientôt se mettre à appeler pour savoir ce qu'on fait. Mets-toi à leur place. Eux, ils exigent des résultats, d'autant plus qu'on leur a dit que tu étais le meilleur. Les journalistes ne feraient qu'une bouchée de toi si Granger, un vieux routier, décidait de jouer les rivaux.

Duval pianota nerveusement sur le bureau du chef.

— Donne-moi encore vingt-quatre heures. Le gars laisse beaucoup de pistes, et normalement on devrait pouvoir l'arrêter d'ici peu. C'est un être compulsif, complètement halluciné. Il va commettre des erreurs. Il en commet déjà. On va l'avoir.

En sortant du bureau, il aperçut Pouliot et Malo, les Mutt et Jeff de l'escouade, qui causaient en buvant un coke. Ils semblaient se réjouir du fait qu'il en avait plein les bras avec son enquête.

Duval avisa le répartiteur de lui transférer tout appel dans la salle de conférences. Là, il ne serait pas dérangé par le va-et-vient des collègues. Il plaça devant lui une tablette de papier, le livre de Mathieu et les listes d'élèves. Le manuscrit ressemblait à l'ébauche d'un roman. Mathieu avait dessiné des motifs étranges sur la couverture. Le texte était écrit à la première personne.

D'une journée à l'autre, l'état d'esprit de Mathieu semblait déteindre sur la qualité graphique de l'écriture. Sur une échelle de 0 à 10, où 0 voulait dire illisible et 10 très lisible, elle se situait dans une fenêtre de 0 à 7. Par contre, Mathieu dessinait très bien et Duval reconnut le visage de Rosalie esquissé en quelques traits. D'autres visages, sans doute ceux de ses amis, complétaient la galerie de portraits. Michaël ne semblait pas s'attacher à un stylo particulier, à voir toutes les couleurs qu'il avait utilisées. Sans doute perdait-il ses crayons. Il y avait une rature par phrase. Duval finit par s'y habituer. Mathieu écrivait aussi beaucoup par notations télégraphiques, sans doute des aide-mémoire afin de réaliser un roman ou autre chose. Des titres de romans, justement, avaient été ébauchés : *L'Exécuteur, Cyanure*.

Mais l'histoire comportait une dimension symbolique qui donnait du fil à retordre à Duval sans rien apporter à l'enquête. C'était brouillon à la manière de l'écrivain en herbe qui se cherche. Mathieu lui-même se décrivait sous les traits d'un personnage appelé Lethal, le nom qu'il affichait sur son blouson. Certains surnoms que Duval avait entendus de la bouche du professeur servaient à identifier les autres protagonistes : Cobra, Spectre, Tod. Duval aurait aimé savoir si *l'Éminence* désignait Déziel. Si c'était le cas, celui-ci manquait d'éthique professionnelle, car il baisait tout ce qui bougeait, garçons et filles. Un des personnages était appelé tout simplement S.

Mathieu relatait certains partys en termes très explicites : « Nuit d'enfer à renifler de la coke, à boire, danser et baiser. » Il décrivait en détail ses « baises avec Érosalie », sans doute le surnom de Rosalie. Parfois, il glissait un peu de poésie inspirée de sa muse : *Rosalie petits bosquets d'épines, laisse-moi humer tes roses. J'aime que tu me fasses mal.* Le Fuzz semblait son lieu de prédilection.

Çà et là apparaissaient des citations de philosophes grecs et allemands et des références à Baudelaire, Rimbaud et Cioran. Duval se rappelait avoir vu ce dernier nom sur la porte du bureau de Déziel. Mathieu se risquait aussi à des paroles de chansons en anglais dont le contenu s'avérait fort violent. Y figurait également une liste de disques à acheter: Clash, Stranglers, Ramones, Damned.

Dans une section rédigée au stylo vert, Mathieu abordait la question de l'initiation de S, intitulée *Le Martyr de saint Sébastien*: un exercice humiliant et dégradant. Duval ouvrit le *Petit Robert des noms propres* et apprit que saint Sébastien avait été bâtonné à mort. Des icônes le montraient aussi crucifié. Duval soupira. Il lui faudrait apporter le document au labo. L'initié dans le livre de Mathieu paraissait avoir été ridiculisé. Se pouvait-il que la mort de Rosalie, les bras en croix sur la pierre tombale, et cette scène de crucifixion aient un lien avec l'initiation? Et ce S? S'agissait-il de Sébastien Poirier?

Plus loin dans le carnet, il était question d'un bain de minuit sur l'acide qui se terminait par un *bad trip*. Une balade à deux cent cinquante kilomètres dans la Porsche 911, celle du père de Tod, s'était achevée dans le fossé: un mort et un blessé grave nommé Styx. Le même Tod avait juré de ne pas vivre au-delà de vingt-cinq ans. «Il a gagné ce pari à défaut de terminer son bac en droit», écrivait Mathieu. «Quant à Styx, il n'était plus que l'ombre de lui-même», notait-il. Grâce à la date, Duval trouverait l'identité réelle des victimes.

L'appel de la mort semblait une constante dans les textes de Mathieu. Datura, une fille plantureuse, avait succombé à un cocktail de cocaïne et d'alcool. «La Grande Faux ne chôme pas dans le cercle Thanatos, rasant tout ce qu'elle peut», écrivait-il.

Duval demeura perplexe. Paroles prophétiques? Depuis, Michaël et Rosalie avaient rejoint leurs amis. Angélique Fraser s'était apparemment suicidée et son mausolée avait été profané. Duval avait l'impression de jouer avec un cube Rubik sans jamais atteindre la solution. S semblait un personnage très controversé dans l'histoire et Duval aurait aimé savoir s'il s'agissait de l'individu que craignait Lizotte. À première vue, l'énergie folle et la démence du personnage renvoyaient étrangement à la description faite par le punk.

Le téléphone sonna. Duval referma le journal. C'était le docteur Fraser. Longue inspiration du médecin.

— La sépulture a été profanée, lieutenant?

— Oui.

Duval, qui ne tenait pas à l'informer des derniers développements par téléphone, lui demanda s'il pouvait dès le soir examiner la chambre d'Angélique.

— Ensuite, je vous donne rendez-vous quelque part où nous pourrons discuter de vive voix.

— D'accord, lieutenant, je vais trouver un prétexte pour sortir avec ma femme et vous trouverez la clé dans la boîte aux lettres. Soyez là à 20 h. La chambre est la dernière à l'est, avec une vue sur le fleuve. Vous aurez une heure. Si jamais il y a du changement, je vous rappelle.

— Bien, je serai là. Pour le rendez-vous?

— À 21 h 30, au Shamrock?

— Ça me va. Angélique avait-elle un carnet d'adresses?

— Oui. Mais est-il encore là? Vous trouverez les notes de son cours de philo sous le lit.

— D'accord. En passant, tenait-elle un journal?

— Oui, mais ma femme, ne pouvant supporter ce qui y était écrit, l'a jeté.

— Vous a-t-elle fait part du contenu avant?

— Non, jamais. Je ne voulais pas savoir que ma fille avait souffert. Je croyais lui avoir donné ce qu'il y avait de mieux.

— Serait-il possible de vous informer sur le contenu du journal?

— Je peux essayer.

— On se voit plus tard, docteur. Je veux en discuter avec vous en personne.

Ses yeux fatigués fixèrent de trop près l'ampoule de la lampe et des zébrures lumineuses fusèrent sous ses paupières.

Duval appela ensuite à la section Documents du labo pour requérir une expertise du carnet de Michaël Mathieu. Les spécialistes pourraient lire, après un certain nombre de manipulations, les noms cachés sous les biffures.

Duval téléphona de nouveau chez Déziel et n'obtint aucune réponse. Il réessaya cinq minutes plus tard et toujours pas de Déziel en ligne. Il contacta le service du personnel du Petit Séminaire, qui refusa de lui donner l'adresse du professeur. Il prit le bottin et chercha sans succès un Victor Déziel.

Laurence, qui travaillait de nuit, lui manquait et il irait coucher dans son appartement de la rue des Remparts s'il ne revenait pas trop crevé de sa rencontre avec Fraser.

Duval photocopia le carnet de Mathieu. Il passerait déposer l'original au labo avant de rentrer chez lui.

Il éteignit la lampe métallique, glissa les documents dans sa mallette, décrocha son imperméable de la patère.

Le téléphone retentit et Duval sursauta. C'était Francis. Les parents de Mathieu ne voulaient pas parler avant les funérailles.

Alors qu'il s'apprêtait à sortir, Dallaire se pointa.

— Salut, Danny, je viens de recevoir un appel de Granger. Il a interrogé le père de Mathieu et ce dernier lui a mentionné que son fils tenait un journal. Il a toutes les raisons de croire que celui-ci a disparu. Tu ne l'aurais pas vu, par hasard ?

Duval le prit aux mots : après tout, n'était-ce pas plus un roman qu'un journal ?

— Non, il n'y avait pas de journal.

— Les parents sont catégoriques.

Duval se gratta une oreille et prétexta la rédaction d'un rapport pour ne pas étirer la conversation.

46

Duval rentra après quarante-cinq minutes de jogging dans le quartier, à traîner la patte. Il s'assit dans l'escalier et retira ses chaussures de sport. Coup d'œil à sa montre : une heure de répit avant d'aller chez Fraser. Couvert de sueur, il monta à l'étage, s'étira en s'appuyant contre le chambranle de la salle de bains. Il actionna la douche. Le jet de chaleur massait ses muscles et il se sentait bien. Mais sa vie marquée par le diktat de l'horaire le ramena à la raison. Il s'extirpa de la douche, se sécha et enfila son peignoir.

Il s'arrêta devant la porte de chambre de Mimi, qui étudiait en écoutant de la musique classique. Il frappa.

— Oui, entre.

Couchée sur son lit, elle lisait une sonate de Beethoven pour son cours d'harmonie. Avec des crayons de couleur, elle disséquait l'œuvre jusqu'à la faire ressembler à un bouquet de fleurs tellement les flèches fusaient en tous sens. Alibi était enroulé sur son ventre. Duval se laissa choir sur le lit et sa fille l'embrassa sur la joue. Alibi se réveilla, s'étira et s'approcha pour sentir son libérateur.

— Salut, t'as l'air crevé. T'as eu une bonne journée ?

— Oui, mais je repars dans une heure.

— Il reste de la quiche au frigo.

— Merci. Toi, t'as eu une journée intéressante ?

— Oui, j'ai eu dix sur dix dans mon devoir de contrepoint.

Duval, fier de sa fille, replaça la tresse de Mimi derrière son oreille.

— Tu tiens le don de la musique de ta mère. Moi, je suis incapable de jouer un accord de guitare. Il est possible que j'aille coucher chez Laurence ce soir.

Il descendit en pensant à la bière froide qui l'attendait. Il ouvrit la porte du réfrigérateur et faillit échapper sa bouteille quand il aperçut sur le tableau les vers que Mimi avait écrits sous le sien, celui trouvé sur la première victime.

Et faire à ton flanc étonné
une blessure large et creuse

Et, vertigineuse douceur !
À travers ces lèvres nouvelles,
Plus éclatantes et plus belles,
T'infuser mon venin ma sœur

Baudelaire

Duval grimpa l'escalier en troisième vitesse, le pas si lourd qu'il fit sauter le disque.

— Tu marches trop fort ! Tu brises mon disque, cria Mimi.

— Excuse, mais il faut que j'te parle. C'est urgent !

— Qu'est-ce que t'as ? Tu m'inquiètes.

Duval baissa le volume de la chaîne stéréo, s'assit sur le bout du lit de Mimi.

— Tu connaissais l'auteur du texte que j'avais inscrit sur le tableau ?

— Bin oui. Tout le monde connaît ça ! On étudie *Les Fleurs du mal* en français au cégep.

Mimi était stupéfaite de la réaction de son père. Pourquoi *bad tripait*-il sur ce poème ?

Elle déposa l'édition complète des sonates de Beethoven. *L'Appassionata*, tout en sourdine, passa au mouvement lent.

— Mais pourquoi tu veux savoir ça ?

— Je te le dirai plus tard. D'abord, parle-moi de ce recueil et de Baudelaire.

— Tu veux que je sorte mes notes de cours ?

— Dis-moi tout ce que tu peux en vrac.

— Papa... T'es drôle... Tu connaissais pas ça ?

Duval roula des yeux impatients.

— Non. Je ne connaissais pas ça...

Elle se leva et sortit sa copie des *Fleurs du mal* de sa bibliothèque.

— Tu connais Baudelaire de nom, au moins ?

— Oui, mais je ne pourrais pas te dire ce qu'il a écrit.

Elle lui remit le livre. Sur la couverture, une tête humaine farcie de fleurs et de légumes illustrait le recueil : étrange nature morte.

— C'est un tableau d'Arcimboldo. Le titre du recueil te dit quelque chose ?

— Je ne suis pas idiot, quand même !

Mimi lui montra la photo du poète qu'on trouvait derrière la page de garde.

— Les vers du poème que tu as transcrits font partie, si je me rappelle bien, des *Épaves*. Ces poèmes ont valu à Baudelaire un procès et il a dû les retirer des *Fleurs du mal* à l'époque. Il lui a fallu les publier séparément quelques années plus tard.

— Pourquoi ?

— On les jugeait obscènes et Baudelaire s'adressait en plus à une grande dame de Paris à qui il reprochait d'être trop gaie.

— Pourquoi les blessures ? On dirait une scène de crime.

— D'après notre professeur, certains experts croient que Baudelaire suggérait, sur le plan symbolique, la transmission volontaire de la syphilis à cette femme.

— Mais il était complètement malade !

— C'est ça que je te dis. Il avait la syphilis et souffrait d'aphasie.

— Et ses poèmes sont toujours aussi morbides ?

— C'est un univers peuplé de tombeaux, de cimetières, de caveaux, de cloches funèbres et de corbillards.

— Et son rapport avec les femmes ?

— Vraiment misogyne. Il les aime au début, puis les démolit par la suite dans ses poèmes. C'est un cycle destructeur, obsessif.

Duval parcourut frénétiquement les pages de son carnet de notes pour retrouver le message laissé près du chien.

— Et ça : *Mes amours décomposés...*

— Super connu. C'est tiré d'un poème intitulé *Une charogne,* un poème archiconnu.

Duval passait pour un ignare, lui qui avait consacré douze ans à aider sa fille à faire ses devoirs. Elle lui arracha le livre des mains, alla à la table des matières et lut les dernières strophes à son père.

> — Et pourtant vous serez semblable à cette ordure,
> À cette horrible infection,
> Étoile de mes yeux, soleil de ma nature
> Vous, mon ange et ma passion !
>
> Oui ! telle vous serez, ô reine des grâces,
> Après les derniers sacrements,
> Quand vous irez, sous l'herbe et les floraisons
>   grasses,
> Moisir parmi les ossements.

Alors, ô ma beauté ! dites à la vermine
Qui vous mangera de baisers,
Que j'ai gardé la forme et l'essence divine
De mes amours décomposés !

Duval afficha une mine aussi sombre que le poème récité par sa fille. Le meurtrier signait ses crimes avec des textes littéraires. Il se rappela que Mathieu possédait un livre de Baudelaire dans sa bibliothèque et qu'il avait noté quelque part les noms des ouvrages. Il devrait vérifier si le livre se trouvait dans le plan de cours de Déziel.

Voyant qu'il réfléchissait en silence, Mimi, par une chiquenaude devant ses yeux, le ramena à la réalité.

— Papa !

— Oui.

— Tu es absent !

— Mais c'est écœurant tout ça. C'est ce qu'on vous enseigne au cégep ?

Mimi afficha une moue découragée devant le conservatisme du paternel.

— Tu veux le retour de l'Index ? Ce livre-là était interdit au Québec jusque dans les années soixante.

Elle voulut savoir pourquoi son père tenait tant à ce cours de poésie 101 improvisé. Habituellement, c'était lui qui l'aidait à faire ses devoirs et là, il prenait tout en note. Son père ne pouvait être devenu un amateur de poésie entre 6 h et 19 h. Ce n'était pas dans ses cordes. À part le jazz, aucune forme d'expression artistique ne le rejoignait.

— Et Baudelaire ? Parle-moi de lui.

— Il a perdu son père assez jeune et il détestait son beau-père, qui était militaire. Il a hérité d'une fortune qu'il a dilapidée au point que sa mère l'a fait mettre sous tutelle, ce qui l'a rendu hargneux. Très à la mode, un vrai dandy, il dépensait son argent chez les couturiers, s'achetait de beaux costumes et des bijoux. Il consommait aussi beaucoup de drogue. Il a écrit des textes là-dessus. Je te répète à peu près mes notes de cours. Il a aussi connu une période dite satanique.

Duval laissa vibrer ses lèvres de stupeur en soupirant. Il repensa aux vers inscrits dans le mausolée d'Angélique Fraser. Il ouvrit son carnet et les lut à Mimi.

— Et ça : *Le ver rongera ta peau comme un remords*?

Elle lui arracha presque le carnet des mains, se concentra, plissa le front.

— Je ne suis pas sûre, mais le mot «remords» m'indique qu'il s'agirait peut-être d'un des «Spleen».

— Tu as dit «Spleen»? J'ai vu ce mot quelque part, précisa Duval en se rappelant le dénommé Spin mentionné par Lizotte. Le punk, un ignare, avait pu déformer le nom. Duval établit un lien avec le personnage appelé S dans le journal de Mathieu.

— Oui, c'est une forme de déprime, d'état langoureux : le mal du siècle.

— Pourquoi un auteur décide-t-il de nommer un personnage par une lettre de l'alphabet?

— Kafka l'a fait souvent avec son personnage K. Je ne sais pas. Peut-être pour montrer le caractère anonyme du personnage ou pour brouiller les pistes.

Mimi feuilleta le recueil, mais sans dénicher le poème en question. Puis, elle leva l'index en criant eurêka.

— C'est «Remords posthume»!

— Ça raconte quoi?

— Le poème évoque une belle ténébreuse au fond d'un monument en marbre noir. Car c'est tout ce qui lui reste, un caveau pluvieux et une fosse creuse.

Duval avala de travers sa salive.

— Baudelaire dit que le tombeau comprend le poète et dans cette grande nuit le cercueil dit...

Duval roula des yeux étonnés :

— Le cercueil parle !

— Bin oui, c'est de la poésie… Écoute-moi au lieu de m'interrompre. Le cercueil dit : « "Que vous sert, courtisane imparfaite / De n'avoir pas connu ce que pleurent les morts ?" » – Et le ver rongera ta peau comme un remords ».

Il saisit avec tendresse les poignets de Mimi et la regarda dans les yeux.

— Mimi, tu m'es d'une aide extrêmement précieuse.

— Pourquoi ?

Il hésita à lui répondre, mais finit par s'y résoudre.

— Le tueur laisse des messages empruntés à la littérature.

Mimi écarquilla les yeux. Duval pointa son index devant le visage de Mimi.

— Promets-moi de n'en parler à personne.

Il n'avait pas voulu que les messages soient divulgués à la presse de manière à écarter les imitateurs.

Il prit le livre des mains de Mimi.

— Je te l'emprunte.

— Oui, mais j'en ai besoin.

Duval sortit un billet de dix dollars.

— Tu t'en achèteras un autre.

— Papa, il y a plein de commentaires…

— Excellent, je vais m'instruire. Je te le rapporte demain soir. Je le fais photocopier.

Le lieutenant se leva et s'appuya contre le chambranle.

— Que veut dire ce titre : *Les Fleurs du mal* ?

— Ce sont des femmes.

Il expira et sut que le danger planait sur la ville.

— Cioran, ça te dit quelque chose ?

— Juste de nom.

Prévoyant qu'il lui faudrait en savoir davantage sur Baudelaire, il demanda à Mimi de lui fournir le nom de son professeur de lettres.

— C'est madame Marino, Adèle de son prénom.
Elle est très bonne.

— Avec la leçon que j'ai reçue, je vois ça.

— Avant de sortir, pourrais-tu remettre le premier
mouvement ? J'ai un examen d'harmonie demain.

Duval déposa le diamant sur la platine. Il regarda
l'heure au cadran de Mimi. La quiche devrait attendre
à plus tard. Il descendit à la cuisine, ouvrit le réfrigérateur, mais ne vit rien d'inspirant pour apaiser sa faim
entre-temps.

47

Duval ouvrit la boîte aux lettres et s'empara de la
clé. La longue maison rectangulaire en bois, située
dans la rue de La Promenade, faisait face au fleuve.
Elle comportait de grandes surfaces vitrées à la manière de Frank Lloyd Wright.

Duval entra et se dirigea tout de suite vers la
chambre d'Angélique en suivant le plan. Avant de pénétrer dans la pièce, il sortit de son sac des gants de
latex. La chambre de la jeune Fraser n'avait rien d'angélique. Une affiche de Nelligan avait été épinglée sur
un mur. La photo de la jeune fille, mortier sur la tête
et diplôme collégial à la main, vous regardait sans
sourire, la mort dans l'âme : elle n'entrerait pas en médecine. Difficile de croire qu'il avait vu cette jeune

fille dans un état de décomposition avancé, le corps mutilé par un pervers. Le lit en acajou était recouvert d'une courtepointe en damier rouge et blanc.

L'espace de travail d'Angélique consistait en un vieux bureau à cylindre. Duval l'enroula. Dans les compartiments du haut étaient classés des papiers, mais c'est un album de photos miniatures qui piqua sa curiosité. Il s'installa sur le lit. Toutefois sa déception fut grande. L'album avait été dégarni de la plupart de ses photos. Sans doute que la mère ne pouvait supporter de voir sa fille avec Déziel ou avec cette bande de malotrus, d'aussi bonnes familles fussent-ils. Il ne restait que des photos d'Angélique avec des amies. Aucun garçon sur ces photos.

Il prit une photo où l'on voyait Angélique avec un groupe de copines. Dans la belle bibliothèque vitrée, Duval repéra plusieurs livres qu'il avait aperçus chez Mathieu. Il tira sur le bouton cuivré pour ouvrir le panneau de verre. Il crut reconnaître des titres qu'il avait vus dans le plan de cours de Déziel. Angélique avait beaucoup d'ordre, car chaque tablette était consacrée à un genre ou à un sujet, et les auteurs étaient classés par ordre alphabétique. La philosophie comprenait des titres de Camus, Cioran, Nietzsche, Platon, Sartre, Schopenhauer, Sénèque. Duval nota la présence d'une bonne centaine de romans et d'ouvrages scientifiques, dont *La Flore laurentienne*. Des livres d'art remplissaient toute la tablette inférieure. À elle seule, la poésie occupait la moitié de la section supérieure. En passant son index d'un dos à l'autre, il aperçut *Les Fleurs du mal*. Il souleva le rabat vitré et retira le livre. Cette édition devait coûter assez cher, à en juger par l'enluminure. Lorsqu'il l'ouvrit, un frisson lui glaça l'échine. Sur la page de garde, une dédicace mystérieuse en lettres mauves :

Sanguine ancolie que flaire le vice
Sa corolle à celle d'un pendu
Et l'autre qui s'abîme
Dans la fureur

I. A. M.

Le texte avait été écrit en lettres attachées. « Dédicace récente », pensa Duval en raison de la couleur de l'encre d'un stylo-feutre. Le livre, lui, devait avoir une cinquantaine d'années ou plus à en juger par l'odeur âcre et poussiéreuse qu'il dégageait. Dans le coin écorné de la page, un nom avait été biffé, sans doute celui de l'ancien possesseur.

La référence à la pendaison était pour le moins étrange. Avait-elle tenté une fois, avant son suicide, de mettre fin à ses jours par la pendaison ? Le pendu pouvait-il parler de Mathieu dans une sorte de pacte à venir ? Quant aux ancolies, il en avait vu sur la poitrine d'Angélique, de cette espèce indigène qu'il avait un jour plantée dans son jardin. Le réfrigérateur redémarra et l'éclairage chancela. Il feuilleta les pages. Plusieurs textes étaient soulignés. Sur l'avant-dernière page, Duval écarquilla les yeux en voyant le tampon du Petit Séminaire de Québec. Le temps n'était pas venu de spéculer mais de cueillir les indices, se rappela-t-il.

Duval ne pouvait concevoir que des livres aient causé cette hécatombe. Les livres, aussi maudits soient-ils, ne tuent pas, croyait-il. Mais ce livre se trouvait tant chez Mathieu que chez Fraser. Sans doute verrait-il le même chez Rosalie Nantel.

Il se pencha et aperçut sous le lit un cahier noir à reliure spirale sur lequel on pouvait lire *Philosophie*. Il découvrit également un court billet d'un certain V. D. qui était adressé à Angélique. Il laissa choir le tout dans le sac. Duval était pressé de les lire, mais il lui fallait sortir.

Les autres reliures s'empilaient sur une tablette du secrétaire, les titres des cours bien indiqués sur chacune.

Il ne disposait plus que de dix minutes. Il souleva le matelas, mais ne trouva rien.

Dans la penderie qui sentait le cèdre rouge, il ne vit rien d'autre que les vêtements d'Angélique. Mais en farfouillant dans l'impressionnante collection de chaussures sur le plancher, il aperçut un sac d'école en cuir. Il inspecta son contenu mais rien d'intéressant : des livres de biologie et les notes d'un cours d'histoire de l'art, sans doute un cours facultatif. Coup d'œil à sa montre : à peine cinq minutes. Il fallait déguerpir.

◆

— Oui, la main manquait et il avait caché son visage avec ses longs cheveux. Des lames de rasoir avaient été enfoncées dans son cou.

— Mais qu'est-ce qu'il lui veut, ce malade ? Profaner, c'est violer ! lança le docteur d'une voix désespérée.

— J'en conviens parfaitement.

Duval n'avait pas cherché à épargner le docteur Fraser.

Accoudé au bar du Shamrock, le visage consterné, le chirurgien enfilait les scotchs. Les détails l'avaient assommé.

— Votre fille a-t-elle fréquenté Michaël Mathieu ?

— Je le connaissais de nom, car c'était un jeune homme très populaire.

— Avez-vous déposé des ancolies dans la tombe d'Angélique ?

— Non. Il n'y avait pas de fleurs.

Après un silence qui s'éternisa, la question du médecin trancha comme un couperet.

— Aurait-elle été tuée, lieutenant ?

— Je ne crois pas, répondit Duval pour éviter que le doute ronge la nuit du médecin.

Duval lui demanda s'il avait des photos des funérailles d'Angélique. Fraser allait vérifier.

Duval lui montra le vieux livre des *Fleurs du mal*.

— Je ne sais pas d'où il provient. Ce livre ne fait pas partie du patrimoine familial. Comme j'aime les livres anciens, je l'avais bien sûr remarqué.

Il ne se rappelait pas qui l'avait offert à Angélique, mais il suspectait Déziel. Il allait le demander à sa femme, à qui sa fille se confiait davantage.

— Vous trouverez dans ses notes un cours sur les philosophes stoïciens, dont certains approuvaient le suicide. Il est question aussi d'un club de suicide qui existait à Berlin au début du siècle. Six membres se sont donné la mort.

— Saviez-vous qu'elle et ses amis vouaient un culte à la mort ?

— Oui. C'était leur manière de se donner un genre. Je m'en suis inquiété et elle m'a dit de la laisser tranquille.

Duval, que cette longue journée avait claqué, pivota sur le tabouret.

— Je vous appelle aussitôt que j'ai du neuf.

Il posa une main sur l'épaule du cardiologue.

— Bonsoir, docteur.

L'autre répondit par un signe de tête.

48

Debout dans la cuisine, Duval parcourut le plan de cours de Déziel que Louis avait piqué et constata que *Les Fleurs du mal* faisaient partie des ouvrages de référence. Shakespeare et son *Hamlet* avaient droit au même honneur. Les livres trouvés chez Mathieu et Fraser figuraient sur la liste des ouvrages obligatoires ou à consulter. Deux cours portaient en effet sur le suicide en Occident et en Orient. Les étudiants devaient faire un exposé oral sur le concept de la mort en philosophie. Quarante-cinq heures à digérer un tel menu avait de quoi vous rendre suicidaire, pensa Duval. Lui-même, qui avait la mort dans son contrat chaque fois qu'il allait travailler, plaignit les élèves de Déziel.

Après avoir fait chauffer la quiche dix minutes – de toute évidence elle serait tiède, trop pressé qu'il était de faire le point sur les derniers indices –, il monta avec son assiette et alla s'asseoir dans le fauteuil rouge devant la fenêtre en saillie. Lui qui avait plutôt prévu de remiser sa moto pour l'hiver, devait se taper l'œuvre d'un poète maudit. Carnet de notes sur la cuisse gauche et recueil à la main, il reconnut aussitôt dans Baudelaire l'univers profane et sacré qui plaisait tant au meurtrier : des anges, des tombeaux, des croix, des vierges, des sorcières et des corps. Un poème où il était question de planche anatomique le laissa pantois.

Il enfourna une bouchée de la quiche humide et infecte. Les brocolis étaient ratatinés.

Les lumières de la ville pétillaient à travers les branches des arbres du coteau Sainte-Geneviève. Il traça un nouveau portrait du meurtrier à la lumière de ce qu'il venait d'apprendre. Le temps passa jusqu'à ce que la voix chaude de Gilles Archambault à la radio le sorte de ses réflexions. L'animateur de *Jazz Soliloque* annonça Monk en concert. Le pianiste interpréta *Well you needn't* en dribblant sur les touches du piano de belles notes qui semblaient rebondir, blues et rondes. Duval ressentait une telle fatigue que ses paupières tombaient d'elles-mêmes. Il téléphona à l'hôpital dans l'intention de dire à Laurence qu'il la verrait le lendemain soir et qu'il avait hâte de la prendre dans ses bras. Mais il dut laisser un message, car Laurence était dans une situation d'intervention.

Brosse à dents à la main, il alla souhaiter bonne nuit à Mimi. Il lui demanda quel était son poème préféré dans l'œuvre de Baudelaire.

— *À une passante*, répondit-elle.

Curieux, il retourna au salon. Les tercets du sonnet avaient de quoi inquiéter.

> *Un éclair... puis la nuit ! – Fugitive beauté*
> *Dont le regard m'a fait soudainement renaître,*
> *Ne te verrai-je plus que dans l'éternité ?*
>
> *Ailleurs, bien loin d'ici ! trop tard ! jamais peut-*
> *être !*
> *Car j'ignore où tu fuis, tu ne sais où je vais,*
> *Ô toi que j'eusse aimée, ô toi qui le savais !*

Un psychopathe pouvait trouver dans ces textes une nourriture malsaine à ses fantasmes, un prétexte fraternel entre lui et une confrérie d'auteurs pour aller au-delà des mots. Il savait qu'un pervers sadique projetant ses fixations sur une idole pouvait jouir à passer de la théorie à la pratique. Il existait mille et une façons pour ces désaxés de signer leurs œuvres. Hurtubise, un être intelligent dans le vice, laissait des cartes de Mille Bornes sur l'autoroute ; celui-ci marquait ses crimes de messages littéraires. Quelle différence ?

Le portrait qu'il ébaucha en quatre points mettait en évidence l'intelligence du meurtrier :

> *Milieu bourgeois, jeune vingtaine, cultivé, l'esprit*
> *cynique.*

*Il méprise tout sauf lui-même et quelques idoles.
Tout comme Baudelaire, il déteste probablement
son père.*

*Parents divorcés. Très près de sa mère. Il ne dé-
teste pas les femmes à ce point sans être atteint
d'une démence quelconque.*

*Beau et charmeur au point de créer un rapport de
confiance avec ses victimes. Fort physiquement.*

La trompette de Bix Beiderbecke conclut l'émission
par *In the mist*. Duval se laissa couler dans la tendresse
mélodique du jeune trompettiste mort d'alcoolisme au
seuil de la trentaine.

Il inscrivit dans son carnet les tâches à faire pour
le lendemain.

Spleen for murder, écrivit-il en anglais. Spleen, un
assassin qui aimait Baudelaire et compagnie. Spleen
avait gravité autour du cercle Thanatos. Déziel allait
avoir une visite pas très courtoise qui lui délierait la
langue.

Le souffle du vent l'apaisa, les petits bruits rassurants
de la maison aussi ; même le chat qui jouait avec sa
pelote de laine.

Au bout de dix minutes, alors qu'il commençait à
s'assoupir, le téléphone sonna. Il décrocha le récepteur.
C'était le docteur Fraser.

— Excusez-moi, lieutenant, mais je viens de discuter
avec mon épouse.

Fraser parlait à voix basse pour ne pas être entendu
de sa femme.

— Ce n'est rien, docteur Fraser, vous pouvez m'appeler à l'heure que vous voulez.

— Elle connaît l'histoire du livre, qui a été livré par
la poste. Angélique ne lui a jamais avoué qui le lui
avait expédié. D'ailleurs, il semble que la livraison de
ce colis avait troublé ma fille. Elle avait cru à ce

moment-là à un admirateur secret. Déziel avait nié être celui qui le lui avait envoyé.

— Savez-vous à quel moment elle a reçu le livre ?

— Environ un mois avant de mourir.

— Aimait-elle la poésie ?

— Oui, elle adorait la poésie. D'ailleurs, elle participait à des récitals. Ma fille avait un tempérament d'artiste… comme bien des médecins.

Il y eut un long silence.

— Autre chose. Nous avons reçu sporadiquement des appels anonymes un mois avant sa mort.

— Ont-ils cessé à sa mort ?

— Oui… Mais je dois vous laisser, ma femme se lève. Je vous souhaite bonne nuit, monsieur Duval.

— Vous pareillement, docteur.

Un coup de vent fouetta les rideaux, les feuilles bruissaient dans la tourmente. Duval chercha de nouveau à détendre son corps, mais son cerveau fonctionnait trop pour qu'il puisse dormir. Il ne pensait qu'à aller quérir le mandat d'arrêt contre Déziel. Incapable de fermer le contact de sa conscience, sa pensée oscilla de l'enquête en cours à la communication qu'il devait donner sur le docteur Wilfrid Derome à la fin de novembre à l'Université de Montréal. Tout comme lui, le vieux limier affrontait l'horreur : les corps défaits et humiliés.

Vers minuit, ne tenant plus en place, il appela Dallaire et les membres de son équipe et convoqua une réunion pour 6 h le lendemain matin. Et il ajouta :

— Je ne veux pas de retard.

DANSER AVEC LE DIABLE

49

Duval, craignant de voir sourdre à la réunion des spectres en colère tout fripés de sommeil, avait prévu le coup, s'arrêtant acheter beignes et muffins, préparant du café au percolateur. Au bureau dès 5 h 30, il avait photocopié tous les documents nécessaires à l'intention des collègues : les textes laissés par le meurtrier ainsi que des extraits du carnet de Mathieu qui s'avéraient significatifs pour l'enquête, de même que le plan de cours de Déziel et le billet adressé par le professeur à Angélique. À sa droite se trouvaient l'exemplaire des *Fleurs du mal* ainsi qu'une photocopie de la version saisie chez Angélique. À tour de rôle, Dallaire, Bernard, Francis et Louis entraient avec des faces à ne pas embêter, des saluts et des bonjours secs. Francis, qui avait un œil au beurre noir, résultat d'un coup reçu la veille dans un combat d'aïkido, ressemblait à un raton laveur enrhumé. Son nez coulait et il vida ses poches d'un monticule de mouchoirs qu'il déposa devant lui, l'air de se dire : « J'étais si bien dans mon lit. » Heureusement, les douceurs sucrées du matin et l'arôme du café colombien soulevèrent un peu de sympathie. Personne ne passait de commentaire sur le zèle de Duval, le sujet étant tabou. Faire partie de son équipe signifiait travailler tôt et tard quand le feu devenait trop chaud.

Le lieutenant avait noirci à la craie le tableau noir de la première maxime bidon qui lui était venue en tête : *L'avenir appartient au lève-tôt*, ce à quoi Louis répliqua :

— Et le présent aux imbéciles qui ne font que travailler…

Baguette à la main, Duval déposa l'acétate sur le rétroprojecteur et le texte suivant apparut :

1- *Le meurtrier cite un auteur appelé Baudelaire (voir vos photocopies). Le texte d'un autre écrivain, Camus, servait à brouiller les pistes dans le cas du suicide de Mathieu.*

2- *Carnet de Mathieu et dédicace dans le livre expédié à Angélique.*

3- *Référence à la mort d'Angélique. Appels anonymes.*

4- *Sceau du Séminaire sur l'avant-dernière page de garde du recueil.*

5- *Association de noms fictifs et de certains noms sur la liste de Déziel. Qui est S ?*

6- *Billet de Déziel qui écrit à Angélique que tout rentrera bientôt dans l'ordre : « Tu ne dois pas te torturer pour ça. La réaction au changement de médication s'avère toujours un choc. »*
Signé V. D.

7- *Autopsie sommaire d'Angélique.*

Duval étira ses trapèzes et salua ses collègues, puisant dans ses réserves d'amabilité en ce matin où la fatigue lui vrillait les os.

— Vous vous doutez bien que je ne vous ai pas fait venir ici pour rien.

— Non, c'est parce que je prends ma retraite !

— Tu sais où est le bureau du personnel, Louis, répliqua Duval.

Louis grimaça comme un écolier dont la blague ne passe pas.

— Il y a du neuf. À défaut d'un coupable, on peut identifier l'auteur fétiche sur lequel le meurtrier a une fixation. Il s'agit d'un poète appelé Baudelaire. Mimi, ma fille, l'étudie au cégep. C'est elle qui m'a mis sur la piste.

Louis lut à voix haute un extrait avec tout le mépris qu'il avait pour la culture autre que celle de la masse.

— C'est quoi ce charabia incompréhensible ?

— C'est ce qu'on retrouve sur les scènes de crime : sur le chien, dans la main, sur les cadavres et dans leur environnement.

Bernard parcourut rapidement les textes en attendant les explications. Le capitaine Dallaire sortit ses grosses lunettes à monture noire. Il paraissait plein d'appréhension.

— En cherchant un individu, reprit Duval, qui voue un culte à cet auteur dans un milieu restreint comme celui qui nous concerne, il est possible de découvrir le suspect. Notre homme a une fixation morbide et un *alter ego* auquel s'identifier. Baudelaire, dans son livre, se complaît dans un univers funèbre en racontant ses fantasmes alors que notre pervers semble réaliser tous les siens. Ce qui m'inquiète, c'est que les *Fleurs* du titre en question correspondent à des femmes. Étrangement, ce recueil revient autant chez Fraser que chez Mathieu et Nantel. Il est aussi mentionné dans le plan de cours de Déziel.

— Si ta fille l'étudie, c'est un ouvrage obligatoire, non ? On n'est pas sortis du bois, dit Francis.

— Pas dans tous les établissements.

Les découvertes que Duval avait faites la veille, grâce à Mimi et aux documents perquisitionnés chez

Fraser, apportaient un éclairage nouveau, tous en convenaient.

— Le billet laissé à Angélique par V. D., sans doute Victor Déziel, sous-entend que l'un d'eux, Mathieu, Déziel, Poirier ou un autre compère dans leur entourage, ferait usage de neuroleptiques. Qui est souffrant ? Déziel ? Une connaissance commune ? Et de quoi souffre-t-il ? Schizophrénie ? Maniaco-dépression ? Le message reflète un changement de caractère dans la personnalité de quelqu'un. Ça ne permet pas de savoir si Déziel parle de lui-même ou de quelqu'un d'autre. Mais Déziel aura beau dire qu'il ne lit pas le *Journal de Québec*, il devait bien savoir que Rosalie avait été tuée la veille. Elle gravitait autour du cercle Thanatos. Quand on l'a interrogé, hier, jamais il n'a fait mention de ce qui venait d'arriver à la copine de son ancien élève. Pourtant, rappelle-toi, Loulou, argua Duval, quelqu'un pleurait dans son bureau.

— Il s'agit peut-être d'un schizophrène paranoïaque ? déduisit Francis.

Duval n'aimait pas aborder le sujet de la schizophrénie devant Bernard, car la fille de ce dernier souffrait de cette maladie mentale.

— Le Fils de Sam entendait des voix qui lui disaient de tuer, rappela Dallaire.

Duval approuva.

— Le docteur Fraser m'a affirmé avoir reçu plusieurs appels anonymes un mois avant la mort d'Angélique et ils n'ont cessé qu'après le décès de sa fille, ce qui signifie qu'elle était victime de harcèlement. Dans l'exemplaire d'Angélique, portant le sceau du Séminaire de Québec, se trouve un poème très morbide signé par un certain I. A. M. Dans cette dédicace, il est question d'ancolies et d'un pendu. C'est une fleur dont la corolle inclinée peut suggérer un cou cassé. Rappelez-vous que des ancolies paraient la poitrine d'Angélique lors de l'exhumation. Mais le docteur Fraser m'a affirmé qu'il n'y avait pas de fleurs quand ils ont refermé le cercueil. Dans le livre de Mathieu, poursuivit Duval, il est question d'expériences bizarres. Les surnoms que lui et ses amis se donnent évoquent la mort. Le cercle Thanatos est un nom qui prend tout son sens.

Francis se plongea dans le rapport d'autopsie d'Angélique.

— Une morsure dans le cou ? Y se prend pour Dracula ou quoi ?

Duval commenta ce nouvel indice :

— L'odontologiste affirme que notre suspect a des incisives centrales inférieures qui se chevauchent et que celles du haut démontrent un diasthème, une légère fente entre les palettes.

Louis afficha un affreux rictus de révulsion.

Duval sortit son agenda.

— Les funérailles de Rosalie ont lieu ce matin à 11 h. On se rend à l'église et ensuite au cimetière. On photographie à distance tout le monde. J'ai la permission des parents. Je ne serais pas étonné que le meurtrier soit affligé de la jouissance du voyeur et qu'il se rende aux obsèques.

Louis rompit l'explication.

— Dans ce cas, vous auriez vu ma belle-mère au cimetière si H m'avait eu…

Le rire libérateur s'éleva dans la pièce. Louis était rouge de plaisir.

Bernard intervint.

— Et le père d'Angélique Fraser ? Moi, comme j'ai dit à Loulou, je le *truste* pas une minute. Comment se fait-il qu'il cache tout ça à sa femme depuis le début ?

— Après l'avoir rencontré, hier, je l'écarterais de la liste. Sa femme est P.M.D.

Louis, qui détestait le jargon et les abréviations, coupa son patron.

— Qu'est-ce que ça veut dire : petite, mince et délurée ?

Duval sentit sa main serrer fortement la craie.

— Louis, je comprends pourquoi un professeur t'a garroché un jour sa craie à deux pouces des oreilles.

— Parle pour qu'on comprenne !

— Elle est psycho-maniaco-dépressive. Elle remonte d'une dépression.

— Expression de lologue ! marmonna Louis.

— Bernard, occupe-toi du résultat de l'autopsie d'Angélique. Quand tu iras au labo, demande à Miljours d'accoucher au plus vite des expertises sur le recueil qu'on a remis à Angélique et sur le carnet de Mathieu. Il faut savoir qui est le mystérieux S…

— OK. Je peux aussi m'occuper de vérifier les dossiers médicaux de Victor Déziel et de Sébastien Poirier.

Duval acquiesça d'un signe de tête.

— Ce matin, je m'occupe d'aller cueillir Déziel avec les mandats, se délecta Duval.

Le lieutenant se tourna vers Francis et lui remit sur un bout de papier le nom de la professeure de littérature de Mimi.

— Tu n'as qu'à traverser la rue. Tu la trouveras au Conservatoire.

Francis grimaça.

— Mais je ne connais rien à la littérature !

— C'est l'occasion. Il n'y a pas que Tintin et Astérix !

Duval se pencha vers Louis et lui glissa la liste des étudiants de Déziel. Le cégep n'avait pas le droit de fournir les numéros de téléphone.

— Tu me repères des noms d'élèves dont le numéro de téléphone pourrait être dans le bottin et qui sauraient des choses.

L'équipe allait se mettre en branle lorsque Dallaire demanda à tout le monde de se rasseoir.

— Moi, je voudrais qu'il y ait une meilleure coordination entre la police de Sillery, celle de Québec et la nôtre. Il faudrait former un groupe d'intervention.

On entendit des grognements dans la salle.

— J'ai reçu des appels du commandant de la police de Sillery. Les parents sont inquiets et ils trouvent que l'enquête ne progresse pas assez vite.

Duval, qui était fier des progrès accomplis, se rembrunit.

— Mais qu'est-ce qu'ils veulent de plus ? Qu'on l'attire avec des morceaux de cadavre ?

Le capitaine calma son lieutenant.

— Je sais que vous faites du beau boulot. Mais si ça se met à chauffer, on va en prendre plein la gueule.

Duval pinça les lèvres et acquiesça de la tête.

— Donne-nous la journée avant d'envisager cette possibilité. S'il ne s'est rien passé aujourd'hui, on va modifier notre approche.

Duval éteignit le rétroprojecteur et on se dispersa.

50

Duval fulmina lorsqu'il se présenta devant la porte du bureau de Déziel. Ce dernier avait laissé une note disant qu'il était parti à New York pour la semaine de relâche. Le lieutenant n'avait pas prévu ce congé, un

beau prétexte pour prendre la poudre d'escampette.
Une relâche de dix jours en comptant les fins de
semaine. Il jeta un coup d'œil sur l'horaire de Déziel
et se rendit compte que le professeur avait encore fait
l'école buissonnière en ce vendredi où il devait enseigner de 8 h à 10 h. *Cours annulé*, avait-il inscrit sur sa
porte. « Et ensuite, pensa Duval, les enseignants se
plaignent d'exercer une des professions les plus dé-
préciées. »

Peu après 8 h, quand la fébrilité estudiantine diminua
dans les couloirs, Duval sortit un trombone, regarda à
gauche et à droite, puis en un tournemain déverrouilla
la porte. Il pénétra en vitesse dans le bureau, ferma à
clé, tira le loquet. Devant lui, le fleuve gris happa son
regard : les deux traversiers se croisaient au milieu du
Saint-Laurent.

La pièce empestait les cigarettes françaises et un
cœur de pomme pourrissait dans la poubelle en ré-
pandant son odeur pénétrante. Duval inspecta le bureau
de Déziel où s'amoncelaient des piles de travaux non
corrigés. Il s'approcha du babillard accroché devant
le poste de travail pour observer une photo. On y voyait
Déziel avec des élèves durant une fête quelconque. Il
reconnut sur l'une d'elles Michaël Mathieu, Angélique
et Rosalie. Il la connaissait. Duval retira la punaise
pour prendre la photo. Il regarda au verso et n'y vit
aucune information. Qui étaient les autres jeunes en
compagnie de Déziel ? Il glissa la photo dans la poche
de son veston.

Puis il porta son regard sur la bibliothèque bien
garnie de Déziel. Il s'agissait d'un vieux meuble vitré
ressemblant à ceux qu'on trouvait chez les apothicaires.
Du feutre rouge recouvrait les tablettes. Un cliché
montrant sir Laurence Olivier récitant le monologue de
Hamlet, crâne à la main, était appuyé contre un livre.
Il s'agissait d'un souvenir acheté à Stanford-on-Avon.

La bibliothèque contenait surtout des ouvrages de philosophie, mais, fait troublant, il lut sur le dos d'un gros bouquin un titre étrange : *De corporis humani fabrica libri septem*[3]. Il sortit le livre et se rendit compte qu'il s'agissait d'un traité d'anatomie écrit à la Renaissance par un médecin du nom d'André Vésale. Les dessins qu'on y montrait faisaient peur : des hommes écorchés dans des postures étranges ainsi que le nom des parties du corps. La gorge de Duval se serra. Puis il se rappela que les collèges classiques offraient jadis des cours d'anatomie et que des prix, comme pour les cours de grec et de latin, étaient décernés.

Quand il jeta un coup d'œil dans le premier rayon, la présence du livre maudit le troubla. Il le feuilleta et constata qu'il était amplement commenté. C'était un exemplaire récent. Les poèmes des scènes de crime étaient annotés. En fait, tous les textes étaient abondamment commentés. Un signet avait été inséré à la page 93 et le titre du poème, *Le Squelette laboureur*, intrigua Duval.

> *Dans les planches d'anatomie*
> *Qui traînent sur ces quais poudreux*
> *Où maint livre cadavéreux*
> *Dort comme une antique momie,*
>
> *[...]*
>
> *On voit, ce qui rend plus complètes*
> *Ces mystérieuses horreurs,*
> *Bêchant comme des laboureurs*
> *Des Écorchés et des Squelettes.*
>
> *[...]*
>
> *Dites, quelle moisson étrange,*
> *Forçats arrachés au charnier,*

───────────────

[3]   *La Fabrique du corps humain.*

> *Tirez-vous, et de quel fermier*
> *Avez-vous à remplir la grange ?*
>
> *[...]*
>
> *Dans quelque pays inconnu*
> *Écorcher la terre revêche*
> *Et pousser une lourde bêche*
> *Sous notre pied sanglant et nu ?*

Quelqu'un s'immobilisa derrière la porte. Duval entendit le tintement d'un porte-clés. Une clé glissa dans la serrure. Duval se catapulta dans le placard. À travers une mince ouverture, il aperçut de dos un jeune adulte, sans doute un étudiant, tout vêtu de noir, plutôt svelte, les cheveux bruns. Le garçon se tourna pour accéder au classeur et le lieutenant reconnut Sébastien Poirier, le cousin de Rosalie. Le jeune homme ouvrit le classeur en bois, y déposa un document, éplucha des dossiers et s'empara de l'un d'eux.

Puis, il alla au bureau de Déziel, vérifia le contenu du tiroir et s'empara d'un autre dossier. Duval remarqua ses yeux étranges, tracés au crayon, comme ceux d'un oiseau. Sébastien Poirier repartit aussi vite qu'il était venu. Mais que faisait-il dans le bureau de Déziel ? Pourquoi en possédait-il la clé ?

Duval s'extirpa de sa cachette et fouilla à son tour dans le classeur. Il contenait des travaux corrigés d'années antérieures : des dissertations de fin de session que les étudiants n'avaient jamais réclamées, des notes de cours, des lettres d'étudiants, des procès verbaux de réunions.

Avant de tourner les talons, il téléphona à Dallaire pour lui signaler l'entrée de Poirier dans le bureau de Déziel.

— Faites-le surveiller.

— Je m'en occupe, répondit le chef.

Il avisa aussi le patron du départ de Déziel à New York. Dallaire mettait tout de suite la GRC et le service des Douanes sur l'affaire. Déziel ne passerait pas la frontière, à moins que ce ne soit déjà fait.

Duval entrouvrit la porte, jeta un coup d'œil à gauche et à droite, et s'éloigna en coup de vent. Ensuite, il se dirigea vers le bureau du directeur des études. Il lui fallait les noms des étudiants renvoyés au cours des dernières années ainsi que de ceux qui avaient eu un comportement jugé déviant.

Il avait suffisamment d'éléments pour justifier une perquisition chez Déziel, qui allait passer un mauvais quart d'heure.

La secrétaire lui annonça que Boutin assistait à une réunion.

— Dites-lui de m'appeler au bureau. C'est urgent, insista Duval en déposant sa carte de visite sous le nez de la femme.

◆

Lorsque Duval arriva au poste, il trouva Louis et Francis en train de comparer des documents.

— Du nouveau, dit Duval en accrochant son coupe-vent à la patère. Déziel s'est enfui à New York.

— Le patron nous a déjà avisés. Le barbu sent la soupe chaude, conclut Louis.

— En tout cas, sa bibliothèque est un musée de la mort.

— T'es entré ? s'enquit Francis, étonné.

— Oui, et la visite en valait la peine, dit Duval en décrivant l'univers morbide dans lequel baignait le bureau de Déziel.

À l'évocation des lieux, Francis eut un rictus dégoûté. Il éternua une fois, deux fois, et garda la bouche grande ouverte, en attente du troisième éternuement qui tardait et explosa enfin. Il se moucha en maugréant. Duval avait envie de le renvoyer à la maison pour qu'il se soigne, mais il aurait besoin de tous ses effectifs.

— Pendant que j'étais là, Sébastien Poirier est entré. Et pas par effraction, il avait la clé.

Duval se tourna vers Francis, qui avait en plus une vilaine coupure à la racine du nez.

— Et toi, avec la prof de lettres ?

— Elle était en cours. Elle me reçoit dans vingt minutes. Je lui ai laissé les textes découverts jusqu'à maintenant.

Louis regarda Francis avec une moue pleine d'ironie.

— Le chouenneux la trouve *cute*. C'est une Française. Y paraît qu'elle ressemble à Françoise Hardy et qu'elle a des totons comme des boules de quille…

Duval roula des yeux furibonds et Francis se prit la tête entre les mains.

— Et ça se dit prêcheur de la Bonne Parole !

Duval, qui n'entendait pas rigoler en cette journée où chaque minute comptait, remit les pendules à l'heure.

— C'est pas une partie de drague et cette femme est une ressource pour comprendre ce qui se passe dans la tête du fou.

Louis tourna son fauteuil roulant vers son collègue.

— Voyons, Danny, calme-toi. On détend l'atmosphère.

Duval toisa Louis avec un regard de fauve. Il n'aimait pas qu'on rajoute le « y » à son nom et tout le monde en avait pris l'habitude. Louis avait le même réflexe que Sandra, l'effeuilleuse qu'il avait fréquentée, il accolait le suffixe « y » ou « ie » à tous les noms. Francis devenait Frankie, Bernard Bernie, Charlène Charlie, Claudette Claudie, Samuel Sammy…

— Et toi avec la liste ? ronchonna Duval.

— Quelle liste ? cabotina le Gros.

— Niaise-moi pas !

— J'ai joint les parents d'un étudiant qui s'appelle Todorovsky, alias « Tod » dans le livre de Mathieu. Facile, il n'y en avait que deux dans le bottin. La mère Todorovsky m'a refilé des informations et les numéros de certains amis de son fils. Le sien est décédé dans un accident de voiture. J'ai appris que son compagnon Gabriel Cantin, alias Styx, le conducteur de la voiture, souffre de graves lésions à la tête depuis cet accident. J'ai parlé au père de Martineau. Son fils étudie en droit à McGill. Pas de réponse chez Cantin. Il me reste encore d'autres contacts à établir.

— Des nouvelles de Bernard ?

— Non, répondit Louis. Il est parti avec des agents pour interroger des proches des victimes.

Bernard entra à ce moment, les yeux cernés de fatigue, un millefeuille dans la main droite.

— Quand on parle du diable, le diable apparaît, lança Louis.

Bernard parla la bouche pleine.

— Le frère de Mathieu m'a dit que Michaël n'avait pas d'ennemis mais qu'il filait un mauvais coton et qu'il ne voyait plus ses connaissances. Rosalie, elle, filait le parfait bonheur. Personne ne mentionne le nom de Déziel. Pour ce qui est de Poirier, je n'ai rien su de plus. Sa mère, qui semblait insultée, ne voulait rien dire. Le préposé de la gare maritime ne se rappelle pas avoir vu Poirier franchir le tourniquet à l'heure précisée. Aurait-il pris un autre moyen de transport ? Si c'est le cas, il nous a menti.

— Eh bien ! Il faudra que Sébastien nous explique ce qu'il faisait dans le bureau de Déziel.

Duval décida d'accompagner Francis à son rendez-vous littéraire. Il voulait en savoir plus sur l'auteur et, par ricochet, sur le meurtrier.

— Mais il n'a pas besoin de chaperon, cabotina Louis.

51

Dans les cubicules de pratique, les sons des divers instruments se mélangeaient en une épaisse fricassée sonore : sons filés des vents, arpèges des violons, cadences diaboliques et gammes en séries donnaient l'impression d'un grand orchestre cacophonique ; une sorte de rhapsodie du chaos. Duval chercha Mimi du regard à travers les petits carreaux vitrés, mais ne la trouva pas. C'était la première fois qu'il visitait la nouvelle école de sa fille et il examinait le tout avec curiosité. Mais quand il s'engagea dans une autre aile, le tintamarre des percussions et les roulements sourds des timbales lui rappelèrent que Fred n'était pas loin. Il se raisonna. Puisque Mimi avait accepté la présence de Laurence dans sa vie, il se devait d'accueillir son batteur à gogo.

— J'aurais aimé ça te présenter ma fille.

— Ce sera pour une prochaine fois. As-tu déjà joué d'un instrument ?

— En amateur, mais je suis nul. Mimi ne tient pas de son père pour la musique. J'adore la musique, mais je suis incapable de jouer un morceau. Je n'ai aucun sens artistique alors que la famille de Marie-Claude, ma première femme, regorgeait de musiciens.

Duval remarqua que Francis était tendu comme une barre.

— Qu'est-ce qui se passe ? T'es nerveux ?

— Elle s'appelle Adèle, comme dans la vieille série télévisée… Elle est superbe. Son regard est un .44 Magnum pointé sur le cœur. Et moi, regarde comment je suis arrangé. Ma cicatrice de la chasse et le coup que j'ai mangé hier donnent l'impression qu'on m'a crissé une volée. En plus, j'ai le nez tout rouge à force de morver !

Duval se contenta de sourire.

Francis lui indiqua du doigt la salle de cours et s'immobilisa devant la porte. Mademoiselle Adèle Marino rappelait aux étudiants de préparer le plan de dissertation sur Maupassant pour la semaine suivante.

Rapidement, sans attendre qu'elle ait dit « Bonjour, à la prochaine », les élèves prirent d'assaut le couloir.

Adèle Marino ramassa la brosse et effaça le tableau. Elle portait un tailleur bleu et une chemise blanche. Elle avait les jambes bien galbées et des seins aussi généreux qu'annoncés. Un pan de chemisier, soulevé sous l'action du bras tendu, afficha l'épiderme cuivré de ses hanches. Elle avait quelque part entre vingt-cinq et trente ans. Elle portait de petites lunettes à monture ovale et attachait ses cheveux blonds, mi-longs, avec une barrette en cuir. Son nez légèrement retroussé faisait penser à celui d'Élisabeth Montgomery, la sorcière bien-aimée. Duval remarqua qu'elle avait transpiré.

Elle se retourna et rassembla ses documents sur le bureau quand elle aperçut Francis et Duval.

— Ah ! bonjour ! Entrez, messieurs. Entrez !

— Rebonjour, je vous présente mon collègue, le lieutenant Daniel Duval.

Elle allongea le bras et Duval apprécia sa poigne ferme et sympathique. Elle était pétulante, toute souriante, pleine d'assurance.

— Vous êtes le père de Mimi ?

— Oui, répondit Duval avec une fierté toute paternelle.

— Mimi est une fille vraiment super. Tout le monde l'aime. Et elle excelle dans toutes les matières.

Il n'en fallait pas plus pour que Duval dégaine un sourire éclatant d'orgueil.

— Merci. Elle aime tellement la musique.

— Il n'y a pas de cours après celui-ci, on peut rester ici, si vous voulez.

Elle s'assit sur le coin de son bureau alors qu'ils s'installaient sur le banc de piano près du tableau. Duval la regarda droit dans les yeux.

— Nous sommes sur une affaire de meurtre dans laquelle le tueur a une fixation sur certains poèmes, dont ceux de Baudelaire, le seul auteur qu'on a pu identifier avec certitude.

— Oui, l'inspecteur Tremblay m'en a glissé quelques mots. C'est épouvantable.

Francis avait l'impression qu'elle regardait uniquement ses plaies quand elle se tournait vers lui.

— Qu'est-ce qui vous est arrivé ? Avez-vous été blessé par ce criminel ? demanda Adèle.

Francis éclata de rire.

— Oh non ! C'est une longue histoire : deux blessures stupides.

Puisqu'il n'osait pas se vanter, Duval en profita pour raconter la mésaventure de la veille tout en vantant son collègue.

— Mon collègue Francis est ceinture noire d'aïkido, deuxième dan.

Francis devint tout rougeoyant.

— Hier, dans un combat, il a reçu un coup de coude sur le nez.

— Comme ça, vous pratiquez les arts martiaux ?

Francis hocha la tête.

— Ça vous donne un petit côté raton laveur. Vous ne trouvez pas ?

— On peut se tutoyer, si vous voulez, demanda Francis en rougissant de plus belle.

— Pas de problème !

Francis se leva pour écrire le nom du poète maudit au tableau.

— Vous faites une faute que commettent souvent les élèves. Baudelaire ne s'écrit pas « B-e-a-u » mais « B-a-u ».

Francis se confondit en excuses, corrigea son erreur et se rassit. Duval vint à la rescousse de son ami en s'étonnant de cette erreur, puisque d'ordinaire il avait une plume remarquable.

— Mimi m'a dit que les « fleurs », pour Baudelaire, pouvaient symboliser les femmes.

— C'est vrai. Il fait cette correspondance.

— Quel rapport avait-il avec ces dernières ?

— Très ambivalent. À l'image de ses poèmes. Il pouvait les considérer comme des vierges ou comme des putains.

— Donc, avec un regard parfois sacré, parfois profane.

Le visage d'Adèle s'éclaira de bonheur comme celui d'un professeur gratifié par la réponse inattendue d'un élève.

— C'est en plein ça. Vous avez fait vos lettres ?

— Non. C'est ce que j'ai observé sur les scènes de crime.

Adèle parut surprise de cette réponse. Elle ramena une mèche derrière une oreille dans un geste plein d'élégance. Sa voix était douce et son phrasé, musical.

— Par exemple, dans le cycle *Spleen et Idéal*, Baudelaire fait d'abord l'éloge des femmes comme l'amant tout feu tout flamme au début d'une relation. Par la suite, quand les choses se gâtent – et c'est toujours le cas –, il les démolit dans un jeu de massacre verbal et symbolique. Il peut même se montrer sadique à leur endroit. Dans une lettre, il écrivait : « Engendrer est la seule chose qui donne à la femelle l'intelligence morale. » Dans un essai intitulé *Mon cœur mis à nu*, Baudelaire dit aussi que la femme « doit faire horreur » : « La femme a faim et elle veut manger. Soif, elle veut boire. Elle est en rut et elle veut être foutue. La femme est naturelle, c'est-à-dire abominable. Aussi est-elle toujours vulgaire. » Imaginez si un meurtrier adopte cette vision à la lettre.

Duval siffla d'étonnement en écarquillant les yeux, content que Louis ne soit pas là pour commenter. Francis, totalement ignare en lettres, écoutait sans rien dire, essayant de prendre un peu d'espace pour intervenir au besoin. Il la trouvait belle et intelligente. Et que dire de ce corps si rond sous le tailleur moulant ?

— D'où vient cette fascination morbide ? demanda-t-il, à demi paralysé.

— Baudelaire est un héritier du romantisme et le thème de la mort constitue un élément marquant chez les romantiques.

Duval feuilleta son carnet noir.

— Vous avez eu le temps d'identifier les autres messages ? À part la citation de Camus, les autres sont-elles toutes de Baudelaire ?

— Pas toutes. Pour ce qui est d'*Un trou... dans la boue, c'est... ce qu'il faut à un tel hôte !* je ne sais pas. Je vais demander à des collègues. Même chose pour le premier message : *Au bout de ton sang, femelle*. Ce n'est pas la manière de Baudelaire. Quant au poème qui parle des ancolies, on dirait un pastiche. Je suis une spécialiste de la poésie et je n'ai jamais lu ce texte auparavant. Je ne reconnais pas non plus *Comment survivre aux décombres de notre amour*, mais je vais m'informer.

Duval remarqua que Francis cherchait à prendre la parole, mais que les mots ne sortaient pas. Tant bien que mal, il finit par articuler une suite intelligible de phonèmes.

— Oui, mais… ce Baudelaire, est-ce qu'il souffrait d'un dérangement mental ?

— À la fin de sa vie, la syphilis a affecté ses facultés mentales. Il était aphasique. Baudelaire parlait souvent du *Spleen* pour décrire cet état léthargique qui le rongeait.

— Est-ce que ça s'apparente à une forme d'état dépressif ? demanda Duval.

Elle hocha la tête, enthousiaste, étonnée de la réponse du détective.

— Oui, c'est un état d'abattement et de tristesse très lourd à supporter. On considérait même qu'il s'agissait d'une maladie. La maladie du siècle.

Francis, qui n'avait rien compris et ignorait tout de l'aphasie et du spleen, opinait de la tête en élève docile et intéressé.

— Ce n'est pas lui qui a tiré sur un ami poète ? renchérit-il en se rappelant son cours de lettres au cégep.

— Non, c'est Verlaine sur Rimbaud durant leur aventure londonienne.

Décidément, Francis faisait piètre figure, pensa son collègue qui referma son carnet. Il revint alors sur le strict plan professionnel.

— Mademoiselle Marino, nous cherchons à prévoir qui pourraient être les prochaines victimes. Pouvez-vous nous parler du genre de femmes que Baudelaire aimait ?

— Cela allait de la prostituée à la grande dame des salons parisiens, en passant par une mulâtre appelée Jeanne Duval qui savait, semble-t-il, attiser les fantaisies sexuelles de Baudelaire. Autant chez Baudelaire la femme est un corps qui pousse au vice et à la luxure, autant il peut la considérer comme une muse pleine de spiritualité qui l'inspire.

Duval observa Francis. Le jeune limier succombait, littéralement subjugué par la jeune femme au parfum léger d'agrumes.

— Est-ce qu'il avait des manies ? demanda Duval.

— Il aimait l'opium, le hasch et le vin.

Après de longues minutes à écouter ce concentré de cours sur la vie de Baudelaire, Duval jugea qu'il en savait assez pour continuer son enquête. Il regarda sa montre, il devait se rendre aux obsèques de Rosalie Nantel. Mais Francis, hors du temps, se mit alors à poser des questions. Il prétextait l'enquête pour draguer, ce que Duval ne pouvait tolérer très longtemps. Finalement, cette bande sombre qui ombrageait son regard devait plaire à la jeune professeure de lettres. Adèle excitait de plus en plus Francis, qui montrait des dispositions soudaines pour la littérature même s'il n'y comprenait pas grand-chose.

— Lorsque tu dis… – Duval maugréa en sourdine : Francis la tutoyait maintenant – « la beauté ne peut exister sans douleur chez Baudelaire », est-ce qu'on peut associer la chose à une forme de sadomasochisme ? demanda Francis.

— Justement…

Et Adèle repartit dans de longues explications. Ses petites mains gesticulaient, aussi emportées que ses paroles. Un étudiant passa dans le corridor. Duval jeta un coup d'œil, souhaitant voir Mimi.

Heureusement que le professeur de théorie musicale entra dans la classe, car Francis semblait disposé à écouter une leçon intensive.

Les salutations s'éternisaient et Francis demanda si elle était prête à collaborer de nouveau si c'était nécessaire. Elle acquiesça avec empressement.

— Je vais m'informer auprès d'autres professeurs au sujet des autres textes.

Ses yeux tout pétillants, son sourire avenant, venaient d'assassiner Francis.

Une fois à l'extérieur du Grand Théâtre, Duval se tourna avec un sourire moqueur. Francis semblait figé dans ses impressions et n'entendait plus rien.

— Hé ! Un peu plus et tu demandais à t'inscrire au Conservatoire.

— Tu sais, je joue de l'accordéon.

— Pour utiliser le langage musical, elle t'a presque fait faire une syncope…

— Daniel, je sens que cette fois c'est la bonne. Tu la trouves pas intéressante, toi ?

— C'est sûr ! Mais crois-tu qu'une artiste peut vivre avec un détective de la SQ ?

Duval lui recommanda de bien regarder en traversant le boulevard Saint-Cyrille.

— Et moi, l'imbécile, qui écris Baudelaire « B-e-a-u », dit Francis en montant sur le terre-plein.

— Vous autres, les jeunes policiers, vous faites autant de fautes que les criminels que vous interrogez.

— T'as vu cette beauté ? J'ai besoin d'une petite femme comme elle. Et moi qui n'ai jamais été aussi moche depuis longtemps… T'as vu ma gueule ? Y manque juste le numéro et le *Wanted*. D'après toi, qu'est-ce qu'elle a pensé de moi ?

— Elle aurait bien aimé te sauter dessus !

Duval posa un bras devant Francis pour l'empêcher de traverser le boulevard sans regarder. Le vieil autobus jaune et vert d'une autre époque, tout en rondeurs, vrombit devant eux en crachant un nuage de diesel.

— L'amour rend aveugle ! conclut Duval.

◆

Duval se pencha au-dessus de l'épaule de Louis qui compilait des informations, poursuivant son travail d'association de noms et d'adresses à partir de la liste d'étudiants. Les narines de Duval ne mentaient pas : le costard bleu de Louis dégageait l'odeur âcre et prenante de la fumée de cigarette. Le Gros ne pourrait plus se vanter très longtemps de faire partie de la secte des non-fumeurs. La boîte de TicTac à moitié remplie de ce matin avait été complètement vidée. À la radio, un imbécile d'animateur de tribune téléphonique commentait une nouvelle selon laquelle Elvis, toujours vivant, se terrait sur une île déserte.

— Puis, Loulou ? dit Francis d'une voix chantante.

— Depuis qu'Elvis est mort, le monde va mal.

— Quel est le rapport ? rétorqua Francis.

— Je réfléchissais sur ce qu'a dit Chose à la radio sur le King.

Chose était le surnom de l'idiot qui abreuvait d'insultes ses auditeurs, lesquels en redemandaient. Duval observa Louis avec un mélange d'amusement et d'exaspération.

— Vous autres ? Comment vous l'avez trouvée ?

Francis roula des yeux extasiés de sainte Vierge.

— Francis a été poignardé où ça fait du bien, dit Duval.

— La p'tite Française ! Tu lui as chanté la pomme ?

— Tout le bol à fruits, tu veux dire ! répliqua Duval.

Le rire de Louis emplit la pièce.

Bernard s'amena de sa démarche d'ailier défensif, une enveloppe du labo à la main. La section Documents apportait un nouvel éclairage à l'enquête.

— Miljours partage ton avis. Celui qui a écrit la dédicace inscrite sur la page de garde du livre d'Angélique est le même que celui qui a laissé des messages sur les murs de l'université.

L'expertise faite sur la mensuration des lettres et de ses ligatures était absolument affirmative. Miljours avait pu lire le nom inscrit sous la rature de la page de garde : Victor Déziel, à qui avait appartenu le livre. Quelqu'un avait pris la peine de rayer le nom de Déziel avant de remettre le livre à Angélique. Pourquoi ? Duval en perdait son alphabet. Par contre, l'écriture du nom qu'on avait biffé ne coïncidait pas avec celle de la dédicace poétique. « Qui est I. A. M. ? » s'interrogeait encore Miljours. Un acronyme ou un message pour dire « Je suis », « J'existe » ?

La section Documents confirmait aussi que Michaël Mathieu était bel et bien l'auteur du carnet noir, ce dont personne ne doutait, et qu'il avait écrit le graffiti *Comment survivre aux décombres de nos amours* sur le mur du squat.

— Une énigme de moins ! s'exclama Duval, réjoui.

— Pour le carnet de Mathieu, reprit Bernard, Miljours a fait une découverte intéressante. Il a remarqué que Mathieu, dans son récit de l'initiation bizarre, remplace dans quelques paragraphes de la fin la lettre S par un terme bizarre : Spleen. Puis il revient ensuite à la lettre S.

Duval, radieux, claqua des doigts.

— C'est ce que Lizotte avait cru entendre : Splinne.

— C'est ce dont nous parlait Adèle, reprit Francis. Le type s'identifie à Baudelaire.

— Qui est Adèle ?

— Longue histoire, Bernard. Mais le spleen, c'est une sorte d'état léthargique. Baudelaire utilise le mot dans ses textes.

Bernard, qui préparait toujours ses lunchs pour économiser, ouvrit son tiroir avec nonchalance, peu intéressé par la littérature. Il en retira un sandwich et un petit feuilleté Vachon qu'il enfourna en trois bouchées dans une averse de miettes.

La longue aiguille de l'horloge dépassait de trente minutes la dixième heure quand Dallaire pénétra dans la pièce.

— Où est le livre de Mathieu ?

— Ici, répondit Duval.

Dallaire le saisit. Son flegme légendaire était sur le point de céder à la colère.

— Granger est en crisse. Il a appris du labo qu'on avait ce document et il se demande pourquoi il n'en a pas été informé.

— Tout simplement parce qu'on attendait les analyses, mentit Duval.

— C'est toi qui l'as pris. Tu ne l'as pas avisé ? C'était pas notre juridiction.

— Parce que je savais que j'en ferais un meilleur usage que lui. À preuve, toutes les informations qu'on vient d'obtenir. Et côté juridiction, c'est assez confus, de toute manière.

Dallaire se montra découragé. Il avait déjà bien du mal à répondre aux doléances de la police de Sillery, qui trouvait que le lieutenant Duval poireautait dans cette affaire, il lui faudrait maintenant mentir à Granger.

— En passant, dit Louis pour faire diversion, je viens de recevoir un appel de la GRC. Toujours rien sur Déziel.

Dallaire se tourna vers ses hommes. Sa moustache argentée semblait constituée de fibres en acier inoxydable.

— Et on vient d'obtenir le mandat d'arrêt et de perquisition contre Déziel. Mais il y a un hic…

— Lequel ? s'enquit Duval.

— On a appris que Déziel ne vit plus avec sa deuxième femme depuis plusieurs mois.

— À qui tu as parlé ?

— J'ai téléphoné au directeur du personnel pour obtenir son adresse et il m'en a donné trois : celle des deux premières femmes de Déziel et son adresse actuelle. Il vit dans un hôtel du Vieux-Québec avec pas grand-chose.

— Qu'est-ce qu'on fait ? demanda Francis.

— On se rend d'abord à l'hôtel et ensuite on perquisitionne chez sa deuxième femme, trancha Duval.

— Il y a un problème, déplora Dallaire. Chez sa dernière femme, ce n'est plus chez lui. J'ai envoyé un agent vérifier et on a confirmé ses dires. Son ex l'a sacré à la porte. Déziel courait un peu trop les petites filles à son goût. En tout cas, il avait sans doute à se faire pardonner, car il lui a abandonné tous ses biens matériels.

— Une façon polie de dire qu'elle lui a tout pris, philosopha Louis.

— Non, il lui devait de l'argent, répliqua Dallaire.

Duval lança son trousseau de clés d'une main et le rattrapa de l'autre.

— Je me rends à l'hôtel et vous allez aux funérailles de Rosalie, ensuite je vais chez la première femme de Déziel. J'essaierai d'obtenir sa collaboration.

Duval était encore une fois pressé par les événements : une journée qui ne respirait pas, comme il aimait à dire.

52

Déziel logeait dans la rue de la Porte, en plein cœur du quartier latin, à l'ombre des tourelles du Château Frontenac et des ormes centenaires. Son hôtel faisait face à l'obélisque du général Wolfe planté au bout du parc Montmorency. Un peu plus bas s'étalait la terrasse Dufferin qui épousait le cap Diamant, surplombant le fleuve.

Déziel ne se privait pas de luxe. L'hôtel affichait ses quatre étoiles bien en vue. Un gros manoir anglais à trois étages en grosses pierres carrées noircies par la pollution urbaine. L'endroit était si capitonné que l'éclairage semblait absorbé par le moelleux tapis rouge ponctué de fleurs de lys. De vieux luminaires sur pied, chapeautés d'abat-jour de verre, servaient de sentinelles à tous les étages. On avait pris soin de bien entretenir les plafonniers, aussi dorés que des ostensoirs, ainsi que les moulures et les appliques en bois naturel qui n'avaient jamais été encroûtées par des couches de peinture. Les murs avaient aussi été peints en rouge. À voir toutes les distinctions reçues, l'hôtel avait acquis une bonne réputation. La réceptionniste semblait s'ennuyer à faire ses mots-mystères. Elle crut au départ que ces messieurs avaient réservé une chambre et leur demanda leur numéro de réservation.

Duval déroula le mandat de perquisition.

— On vient perquisitionner la chambre de monsieur Déziel.

Elle afficha une moue dévastée, posa sa main sur sa bouche plissée de rides. Elle ressemblait à une vieille maîtresse d'école avec ses cheveux blancs en chignon et sa verrue au coin du nez.

— Il ne lui est rien arrivé, toujours ?

— Non.

— Monsieur Déziel a quitté sa chambre ce matin. Il est parti en voyage pour la semaine de relâche.

— Vers quelle heure ?

— 8 h.

— On peut voir la chambre ?

Elle se leva avec la lenteur des aînés pour qui chaque mouvement semble représenter une épreuve. Ses os ténus se révélaient d'une étonnante fragilité.

En bas, dans le vestibule, les gars de l'Identité judiciaire débarquèrent avec leurs coffres en plastique.

Elle remit la clé de la chambre 7 à Duval. Son regard traduisait toute son inquiétude.

— Est-ce que ce sera long ? J'ai d'autres clients qui doivent arriver.

— Non.

— Vous briserez rien, j'espère.

— Non, madame, et si c'était le cas on réparerait tout à nos frais.

La chambre était située dans les combles. Une fenêtre triangulaire donnait une vue sur le fleuve. Sous la fenêtre, un grand lit à baldaquin occupait la moitié de la pièce. À un mètre devant le pied de lit, un meuble de rangement du siècle dernier, au vantail ouvragé, donnait du cachet à la pièce. Le lieu empestait la même odeur de tabac français que le bureau. Mais Duval percevait un léger parfum qu'il n'avait pas remarqué là-bas. Il flaira l'odeur du savon industriel de quelques frétillements de narines. Comme on avait nettoyé la chambre, la perquisition fut lamentable. L'avant-midi tournait en queue de poisson, sauf que Déziel devenait le suspect numéro un dans cette affaire. Un technicien de l'Identité demanda à madame Généreux, la réceptionniste, de sortir l'aspirateur qu'on avait utilisé, pour recueillir des indices matériels qui pourraient être utiles à l'enquête.

Duval en profita pour lui poser des questions, mais elle l'interrompit aussitôt pour répondre au téléphone. Des touristes anglais faisaient une réservation. Le lieutenant s'assit et feuilleta distraitement une revue dont l'ayatollah Khomeiny illustrait la première page. Duval observa les lieux. Il devenait impossible de déterminer l'heure du jour dans un endroit pareil. La lampe de bureau auréolait et marquait les traits de madame Généreux, ouvragés par les rides, maçonnerie du temps. Une musique classique, en sourdine, s'échappait de la radio.

Lorsqu'elle raccrocha, Duval se leva et se posta devant le comptoir avec son calepin.

Madame Généreux déposa sa plume dans un bocal de moutarde de Meaux qu'elle avait récupéré.

— Venez vous asseoir ici, je vais mieux vous comprendre. J'ai des problèmes auditifs, dit-elle en montrant sa prothèse en forme d'escargot.

Duval s'enfonça dans un vieux fauteuil aux ressorts fatigués.

— Madame Généreux, lorsqu'on perquisitionne chez un individu, c'est que des soupçons solides pèsent sur lui.

Elle eut un rictus inquiet.

— Monsieur Déziel est suspect dans une affaire… criminelle.

Duval avait failli dire « meurtre » mais il s'était retenu, craignant qu'elle ne succombe à son tour.

— Pas de meurtre, j'espère ? s'exclama-t-elle.

— Madame Généreux, est-ce que monsieur Déziel vous paraissait bizarre, anxieux ?

— Vous savez, c'est un artiste, un philosophe, et souvent ces gens-là sont assez spéciaux.

— Est-ce que des jeunes venaient le rencontrer ici ?

— Il est arrivé à quelques reprises que des jeunes lui rendent visite.

— Quel âge avaient-ils ?

— Dix-huit, dix-neuf, vingt ans.

— Ses étudiants ?

— Le Petit Séminaire est juste à côté. Il a des relations très étroites avec ses élèves. Son fils venait parfois le voir.

— Son fils ?

— Oui, mais ils ne s'entendaient pas très bien. C'est un jeune qui a des problèmes. Il vit chez son beau-père. Monsieur Déziel m'a dit qu'il n'était pas le père biologique de l'enfant. Comprenez ce que vous voulez.

Elle donna l'impression qu'elle avait trop parlé et se refusa à en révéler davantage sur cette relation père-fils.

— Aviez-vous l'impression qu'il…

— Une fois que la porte est fermée, je n'entends plus rien.

— À quoi ressemble son fils ?

— C'est un grand gaillard au regard fuyant.

Duval demanda à voir le registre. Elle le lui montra et il la questionna sur les allées et venues de Déziel le soir du meurtre.

— Je ne tiens pas un registre des entrées et des sorties. Ils sont enregistrés à l'arrivée et au départ. Mes clients ont leur clé et leur vie privée.

Duval sortit une photo de Michaël Mathieu et elle faillit tomber dans les pommes.

— Connaissez-vous ce garçon ?

— Oui, il m'est arrivé de le voir.

— Et cette jeune fille ?

Elle posa une main anxieuse sur sa bouche à la vue du cliché de Rosalie. Duval crut qu'elle allait défaillir.

— Oui, je la connais. C'est elle qui a été tuée. L'étudiante en médecine…

— Est-elle venue ici ?

— Non, je ne l'ai jamais vue ici. Mais j'ai vu sa photo dans le journal.

— Qui était à la réception dans la nuit de mardi ?

— C'est monsieur Labonté.

— Pourrais-je lui parler ?

Elle prit une carte professionnelle et la remit à Duval.

— Il sera ici à 20 h. Vous pouvez le joindre à ce numéro.

Duval se leva et rangea la carte dans la poche de son veston. Madame Généreux se redressa lentement. On aurait dit un frêle févier écrasé sous un chêne massif.

— Merci, madame.

Duval salua les gars de l'Identité aux prises avec les sacs de déchets de madame Généreux.

◆

Mariette Dagenais avait été la première femme de Déziel. L'Identité judiciaire avait confirmé à Duval qu'elle avait eu un fils avec le professeur et qu'elle s'était remariée. Son deuxième mari était propriétaire d'un grand magasin de fourrures et de chapeaux qu'il avait hérité de ses parents, magasin de prestige qui avait pignon sur rue à Québec depuis cinquante ans. Cependant, Mariette Dagenais était décédée un an plus tôt du cancer. Le fils de Déziel vivait avec son beau-père dans un impressionnant domaine aux limites de Sainte-Foy et de Sillery. Duval souhaitait discuter avec le fils, qui savait peut-être où se trouvait son père. Peut-être découvrirait-il Déziel à cette adresse.

Duval frappa à plusieurs reprises, mais n'obtint pas de réponse. Une Mercedes-Benz noire était stationnée sous un saule. Plusieurs sacs d'ordures s'entassaient près de la porte. Tous les rideaux étaient clos, pas de courrier dans la boîte aux lettres. Il rebroussa chemin,

s'arrêta devant une cabine téléphonique pour parler à
Boutin, le directeur des études. La secrétaire le mit en
attente et la communication fut coupée. La machine
digéra la pièce. Duval tiqua, fouilla le fond de sa poche
mais n'y dénicha aucune pièce de monnaie. Puis il
inséra un doigt dans la glissière à monnaie de l'appareil
mais en vain. Il se pencha, jeta un coup d'œil par terre
et ne vit rien. Une dame attendait pour téléphoner.
Apercevant Duval dans cette position, elle lui demanda
s'il avait perdu quelque chose.

— Je cherche une pièce de dix cents.

— Pauvre vous. Attendez.

La vieille dame poudrée sourit, fourragea dans son
sac à main blanc et offrit avec gentillesse une pièce à
Duval.

— Merci infiniment, madame.

Duval recomposa et, avant qu'on le remette en
attente, réussit à placer quelques mots.

— Lieutenant Duval de la Sûreté, je voudrais parler
à monsieur Boutin immédiatement.

— Il est parti pour la fin de semaine.

— Et est-ce qu'il m'a laissé la liste des cas…

— Non, je n'ai rien pour vous.

Duval voulut frapper le bottin avec le récepteur
mais se retint, car la charmante octogénaire patientait
derrière la porte.

— Écoutez, madame, si vous voulez rendre service
à monsieur Boutin, vous allez lui téléphoner et l'aviser
que faire obstruction à la justice constitue un acte criminel et que je commence à m'impatienter dans cette
histoire. Il sait où me joindre. Je veux une rencontre
avec lui ou le préfet de discipline dans les prochaines
heures, c'est clair?

Il raccrocha et sourit dans sa colère à la vieille
dame. Puisqu'il n'était pas très loin du cimetière de
la Côte et que la cérémonie devait tirer à sa fin, il alla
rejoindre ses compagnons.

53

Le ciel était partiellement couvert. Par moments, des tranches acérées de soleil perçaient à travers les nuages qui filaient à grande vitesse. La luminosité variait d'un instant à l'autre. Les branches fouettaient le ciel comme si la nature manifestait sa peine.

Duval entra dans le sentier boisé du cimetière, les feuilles bruissant sous ses pas. Le meurtre d'un innocent avait toujours représenté pour lui l'ultime affront commis envers la nature humaine. Il compatissait à la peine des parents. Il détestait avoir à faire face aux familles des victimes, pour qui l'enquête n'allait jamais assez vite. L'impression d'incompétence qu'elles lui renvoyaient lui avait toujours paru insoutenable.

Ses collègues se tenaient à une dizaine de mètres de la fosse où allait être inhumée Rosalie Nantel. Une superbe pleureuse avait été coulée dans le bronze, agenouillée, un bras levé portant la croix. Le flot d'amis et de parents s'approchait lentement, se soutenant les uns les autres. Duval pouvait entendre des gémissements. Le corbillard roulait lentement dans les ornières tapissées de feuilles brunes.

Beaucoup de jeunes de l'âge de Rosalie s'enlaçaient. Il reconnut Sébastien Poirier près de la famille. Ses amis, discrètement, lui envoyèrent la main. Duval balaya des yeux les alentours. Bien sûr, incapables de respecter l'intimité du deuil, les médias avaient envahi les lieux, faisant du sensationnalisme une affaire publique. Cameramen et photographes cultivaient la vigne du tragique pour l'offrir à boire au souper.

Il aperçut près d'un orme le cameraman de la SQ. Francis et Bernard ressemblaient à deux sentinelles postées aux côtés de Louis. Bernard lança au loin sa cigarette, qui étincela en touchant le sol. Ses compères examinaient les visages éplorés.

— Puis ? demanda Duval.

— Rien de neuf à l'exception d'un incident bizarre. Alors qu'on chantait *The Sound of Silence*, un type assez jeune est sorti en sanglots. C'est vrai que le moment était émouvant mais… Enfin, on l'a photographié, raconta Bernard.

— Il est retourné ?

— Non.

— Semblait-il connu de la famille ?

— On le sait pas, Daniel. C'était pas le moment de poser des questions.

— Déziel n'est pas là ? ironisa Duval.

Le curé récita à haute voix le *Pater Noster* avant l'inhumation. Louis se signa. Les pleurs gagnaient en intensité. L'employé du cimetière actionna le treuil et le cercueil argenté sombra lentement dans la fosse. À tour de rôle, parents et amis lancèrent des fleurs ou de la terre. Sébastien Poirier, tout compassé, droit et noir comme un pic, s'approcha et laissa tomber une rose d'un geste maniéré.

Francis se tourna et vit un jeune homme qui regardait la scène de loin.

— Hé ! Les gars ! C'est lui, là-bas, qui est sorti en larmes.

Discrètement, Francis sortit son walkie-talkie et demanda à Boivert de filmer le jeune homme. Duval observa l'individu. Il prit les lunettes d'approche :

— Je le connais. Où est-ce que je l'ai vu, lui ?

Le jeune homme portait un costume digne d'un dandy anglais et une rose à la boutonnière. Duval se creusa les méninges et la réponse le frappa de plein fouet. Puis il se rappela l'hypothèse de Mireille au sujet d'une coiffure bizarre. Le gars avait les cheveux assez ras sur les côtés de la tête et plus longs au-dessus, avec des mèches vertes, qu'il n'avait pas la dernière fois. Ces mèches devaient être récentes.

— C'est lui !

— Qui ? demanda Francis.

— Louis, rappelle-toi, le gars qui pleurait dans le bureau de Déziel quand on s'est rendus la première fois au Séminaire. Le costaud tout en noir.

— Oui ! Je le replace.

— Je veux qu'on le fasse suivre.

Francis lança aussitôt un message par walkie-talkie à l'agent Perreault, qui attendait dans une voiture banalisée.

— Vous voyez le gars qui traverse la rue Chapdelaine ? Ne le perdez pas.

À travers la friture d'ondes, Perreault marmonna un « Rodgers ».

D'un coup sec du menton, Francis désigna Granger qui s'était planté de l'autre côté.

Alors que le prêtre aspergeait de son goupillon le cercueil, les amis de Rosalie entonnèrent un hymne d'adieu. Duval serra les dents. Francis pencha la tête. Louis, à ce moment, sortit trois images qu'il remit à chacun de ses collègues. On y voyait la célèbre sculpture d'Alfred Laliberté : l'archange Michel terrassant le dragon.

— Écoutez, les gars, vous êtes libres de la prendre ou non. Je l'ai fait bénir par le cardinal Roy. Il nous faut absolument arrêter le monstre qui a fait ça.

Duval lança un sourire en coin à Loulou en glissant l'image dans une poche de son veston. La vue de l'archange Michel enfonçant sa lance dans le cœur de la bête qui se tordait de douleur redoubla l'ardeur du lieutenant à en finir avec ce désaxé. Duval s'imaginait en train d'écraser du pied ce malade. Francis, lui, était non croyant et cette image lui rappela celles que lui donnaient les frères au collège de Chicoutimi. Mais il apprécia la force et la vigueur de l'archange foulant du talon le monstre : exactement comme dans la pratique des arts martiaux.

Duval vit le jeune homme qui piquait à travers le stationnement du motel Universel. Duval se tourna vers Louis.

— Tu dis qu'il pleurait ?

— Oui. Il avait le visage comme une betterave. Avec ses mèches vertes, ça faisait une belle ratatouille.

— Demain, on remet ça aux funérailles de Mathieu.

◆

Après le dîner, Duval trouva sur son bureau une note lui disant que Déziel aurait pu passer les douanes avant qu'on mette en place le système de surveillance. La police de New York prenait l'affaire en main et des recherches étaient lancées.

Un second mémo concernait la filature du gars aux cheveux verts : il avait réussi à semer Perreault, qui n'avait ni mandat ni appui pour filer convenablement le suspect. Plusieurs voitures étaient nécessaires pour mener efficacement ce genre d'opération. Il aurait été mal avisé d'intercepter le jeune homme au cimetière et les policiers n'auraient eu aucun motif raisonnable de le faire. La note mentionnait seulement que le jeune homme avait pénétré dans le pavillon des sports de l'Université Laval et n'en était pas ressorti. Mais avec la complexité du réseau de tunnels de l'université, n'importe qui pouvait y semer un régiment au complet.

Puis Duval chercha, autant sur son répondeur que parmi ses mémos, un message de Boutin mais en vain. Il se voyait maintenant débarquer chez le directeur des études à 2 h du matin et, s'il le fallait, le prendre à partie tel un élève récalcitrant.

54

Retrouver Laurence s'avéra le meilleur moment de la semaine. Il lui semblait qu'il ne l'avait pas vue depuis des lunes. Étendue sur le canapé, elle feuilletait la revue d'agents d'immeubles. Vêtue d'un survêtement de sport bleu, elle revenait de faire de la course à pied. Elle jeta la revue par terre, se releva et lui ouvrit les bras. L'accolade s'éternisa. Duval la serra à lui faire craquer les os. Les yeux de Laurence annonçaient tous les plaisirs à venir.

À l'étage, Mimi pratiquait son instrument et Duval sut à l'absence d'odeur de tabac que son copain avait eu la bonne idée de ne pas venir.

Laurence se hissa sur le bout des pieds pour l'embrasser sur le front et lui annonça :

— Je suis en congé pour trois jours.

— On va en profiter.

Une mèche de cheveux glissa sur le front de la jeune femme et le lieutenant la replaça avec délicatesse derrière son oreille.

— Qu'est-ce que t'as envie de faire, ce soir ?

Il se demanda comment il allait lui proposer de joindre l'utile à l'agréable sans être taxé de zèle.

— As-tu envie de venir danser au Fuzz ?

Elle étala un sourire stupéfait.

— C'est un bar punk !

— …

— Tu me caches quelque chose.

— On est sur une série de pistes intéressantes. Je veux aller observer la faune qui se démène là, particulièrement les disciples de Déziel. Appelons ça une étude sociologique…

Duval souriait à pleines dents. Laurence afficha une moue teintée d'ironie.

— Qu'est-ce que tu dirais si je t'invitais à la cafétéria de l'hôpital pour m'assurer que tel ou tel patient cancéreux ne fume pas ?

— T'as raison. Sauf que l'hôpital n'est pas un endroit où veiller… On va aller ailleurs, si tu veux.

Elle leva l'index, fit non énergiquement de la tête.

— Sais-tu, ce serait drôle finalement de se retrouver là !

Mimi descendit l'escalier, suivie d'Alibi accroché à ses talons.

— Mimi, ton père m'emmène au Fuzz !

— Non ! Pas vrai ! Je rêve ! Papa au Fuzz !

Tout le corps de Mimi était secoué de rire. Elle n'arrivait pas à imaginer son paternel parmi les adeptes de la mode punk, qu'elle jugeait horrible et ridicule.

— Au moins, t'as les cheveux courts… Un peu de pommade et un trait de crayon noir autour des yeux et tu vas avoir l'air d'un rebelle.

— Ou plutôt du grand-père punk ! s'esclaffa Laurence.

— Un peu de respect, j'ai pas encore quarante ans.

— Pourquoi vous allez là ? demanda Mimi, sidérée.

Duval, qui ne parlait que très rarement de son travail devant sa fille, resta vague quant à ses motivations.

— T'as rencontré mon professeur, mademoiselle Marino ?

— Oui, elle est très gentille et je crois qu'elle a bien aimé Francis. Qui t'a dit que j'étais allé au Conservatoire ?

— Fred t'a aperçu.

Duval afficha un sourire en coin, plein de malice.

— Pas de danger qu'il soit venu saluer la grosse police…

Mimi grimaça et marmonna son mécontentement.

— Tu l'intimides…

Duval décida de ne pas en remettre. Pour l'instant…

— Et si on se préparait à souper ? demanda-t-il.

Laurence s'approcha, lui glissa quelques mots à l'oreille. Il l'enserra par la taille et l'embrassa.

— Pour donner l'appétit, rien de tel.

Elle s'engouffra dans la salle de bains, ouvrit les robinets, lança une bulle rouge d'huile parfumée qui roula sur l'émail.

◆

Devant le miroir, Mimi conseillait à son père de se vêtir de noir de pied en cap : pantalon coupe fuseau, col roulé et veston noir. Ainsi, il ne trancherait pas trop sur les hurluberlus qui se tenaient là.

— Ferme les yeux, lui dit Mimi.

— Pourquoi ?

— Tu vas voir. Fais-moi confiance.

Elle plongea sa main dans le bol de gel Dip et répandit toute cette moelle sur la chevelure sombre de son père.

— Hé ! Tu en mets trop, dit Duval en rouvrant les yeux.

Il se planta devant le miroir pour admirer sa métamorphose. Laurence riait à en avoir des contractions à l'estomac.

— Comme ça, tu vas pouvoir te confondre…

— Avec Elvis, ouais !

Laurence portait un jean bleu assez moulé et un débardeur blanc. Il se blottit derrière elle et la serra contre lui. Elle lui lança un regard lubrique.

— T'as l'air de mon garde du corps, habillé comme ça.

Il glissa sa bouche sur son cou gracile et long.

Pendant que Laurence allait dans la salle de bains, Duval enfila son étui, le dissimula sous son veston et ajusta le col de son pull. Il avait appris sa leçon depuis ce soir où il avait failli mourir. Il n'oublierait plus son .38 à la maison. Comme il s'agissait d'un modèle léger à cinq coups, il s'avérait peu incommodant à porter.

55

Un long escalier mal éclairé menait au Fuzz. Sur le coup de 23 h, Duval et Laurence entrèrent dans le repaire aux murs noirs que les punks bariolés coloraient de mouvements agités et spasmodiques. Sur la piste de danse, on eût dit des tubes de peinture qui dansaient en faisant gicler les couleurs de la mode. Duval ricana en apercevant des coupes mohawks. Comment pouvait-on se promener dans un tel accoutrement sans perdre la face ?

— Tiens, la statue de la Liberté ! dit Duval en montrant discrètement à Laurence un punk avec de longs pics de cheveux mauves englués de fixatif.

À travers les odeurs de patchouli, de pommade et d'aisselles en nage, Duval fraya un passage à Laurence jusqu'à une table près du mur noir et face au bar. De là, il pourrait observer la piste de danse et ses alentours.

Anarchy in the UK jouait à sept à l'échelle de Richter et les punks faisaient la danse du pogo, complètement disjonctés. Duval s'amusa à les regarder bondir comme des fusées qui ne décollaient pas.

Il reconnut dans un coin, debout près de la piste de danse, Punk Lizotte, enfoui dans son blouson de cuir couvert de pièces de métal. Son visage suintant et rougeaud semblait allumé comme une lanterne. Il jasait avec une fille au visage enfariné encadré par des cheveux raides, plats et lisses, une face de sorcière dont les yeux étaient pareils à des braises calcinées. Elle avait des mains griffues aux ongles vernis en rouge. Près d'eux se démenait un type bizarre aux cheveux verts zébrés de jaune pipi. Il semblait parti pour la quatrième dimension. Il dansait complètement dans les vapes et ne se gênait pas pour bousculer les autres danseurs. Une fille aux cheveux roses, attachés avec un bandeau blanc, dansait près de lui en le regardant. Le cœur de Duval pulsa aussi lourdement que la grosse caisse dans les haut-parleurs : c'était le gars en pleurs entrevu le matin même au cimetière, mais avec encore plus de coloris. Quel était le lien entre ce géant vert et Rosalie ?

Duval se positionna afin d'avoir un œil sur la piste de danse. La hauteur du tabouret était parfaite pour une vigie de fortune. Le serveur s'amena et Duval commanda une bière et un kir pour Laurence, qui rayonnait. La musique assourdissante rendait difficile toute ébauche de conversation. Duval avança son banc. Ils parlaient presque bouche à oreille. Naturellement, la conversation s'engagea sur la date idéale pour emménager ensemble. Duval aperçut alors le géant vert se pencher à l'oreille de la jeune femme. Elle répondit non de la tête. Duval fixa de nouveau Laurence. Le bail de Laurence ne prenait fin qu'en juin, mais Duval souhaitait qu'elle déménage chez lui avant Noël. Le géant vert toucha la fille, qui se laissa faire un instant.

— Qu'est-ce que tu en penses ?

— C'est ce que je souhaitais.

En arrière-plan, Duval aperçut, à sa grande surprise, Sébastien Poirier qui faisait son jars sur la piste de danse. Vêtu d'une chemise en soie rouge et d'un pantalon noir, il posait pour la galerie. Il se trémoussait avec un nain blond en smoking blanc. N'était-il pas en deuil ? Quelques heures après les funérailles de son amie, il s'éclatait sur la piste de danse ? Là, Duval ne comprenait plus. Il invita Laurence à danser. Elle pouffa de rire.

— Pourquoi tu ris ?

— Qu'est-ce que tu ne ferais pas pour ton boulot, hein ? Jamais t'as voulu danser auparavant !

— Mais ce soir la police danse...

Duval lui tendit la main et l'attira vers la marée de membres agités. Un excès de galanterie complètement déplacé en un tel lieu. Un punk à la coiffe porc-épic le toisa.

Sous les projecteurs qui dardaient leurs lumières agressives, Duval s'immisça dans le fouillis de corps sautillants. On lança des regards suspects à ce gaillard aux tempes grisonnantes qui affichait une telle assurance.

Une chanson du groupe The Clash, *I'm So Bored With the USA,* jouait et le lieutenant se risqua à effectuer quelques pas ridicules et incertains. Qu'il devait avoir l'air fou! Mais il ne s'en formalisait pas. Laurence, qui avait fréquenté les discothèques au début de sa jeune vingtaine, était manifestement plus à l'aise. Elle souriait de la maladresse de son partenaire. À travers bras et têtes, Duval repéra Sébastien qui dansait près du colosse aux cheveux citron-menthe. La fille aux cheveux roses l'avait momentanément quitté. On eût dit que Poirier était irrésistiblement attiré vers le monstre aux yeux captivants, qui semblait sur une autre planète. Duval fixa son regard sur Poirier. Finirait-il par l'apercevoir? Non, il ne comprenait pas ce que Poirier faisait là alors que les cendres de Rosalie étaient encore chaudes. Toute la crasse humaine, comme il l'appelait, rampait son chemin sur terre et rien ne viendrait à bout de celle-ci.

Le D.J. rata son *mix* et Poirier vit Duval alors qu'une chanson des Stranglers remettait le chaos de corps en marche, étrange mécanique de membres désarticulés par cette musique nouvelle. On eût dit une rixe de hooligans. On était loin des *ballrooms* que fréquentait Duval dans son adolescence. Le visage de Poirier pissait de sueur, laquelle traçait des rigoles dans son fond de teint. Duval crut que le garçon allait fondre sur la piste de danse. Poirier se détourna et chercha à attirer l'attention d'un ami. À la fin de la chanson, il se laissa dériver lentement jusqu'au bord de la piste de danse. Il cueillit sa bière qui reposait sur le comptoir. Duval souhaitait interroger Poirier qui passait en quelques heures du désespoir total à l'euphorie. Puis il observa Lizotte, ce punk roturier qui faisait son entrée sur la piste de danse, les bras mous, aériens, les yeux dans le vague. De la moutarde en état d'apesanteur. Duval le salua alors qu'il passait près de lui, mais le punk l'ignora, sans doute gêné de cette affabilité policière. Et si Lizotte, ce vicieux petit pervers, lui avait raconté une histoire ? Il passa devant des jumeaux aux yeux bridés qui ressemblaient à des Chinois. Il reconnut une fille qui avait aussi assisté aux funérailles. D'autres pleureurs et pleureuses du matin brillaient par leur présence. Sans doute voulaient-ils faire la fête en mémoire de leurs amis ?

Duval se tourna pour mieux observer le colosse fou, qui semblait maintenant aux tréfonds de la quatrième dimension. Ses doigts bougeaient frénétiquement devant son visage. *I Stab Your Back*, martelait le chanteur dans les enceintes acoustiques. Le titre de cette chanson édifiante glaça l'échine du lieutenant. Comment pouvait-on s'emballer pour une chanson qui glorifiait le meurtre ? Le monstre vert commença à *slammer*, à bousculer tout ce qui gravitait autour de lui. Cette pièce le galvanisait. Il rappela à Duval la sculpture romaine d'un satyre conservée au Louvre. Son visage prenait un relief granitique et ses joues, la finesse du marbre.

Duval vit l'énergumène progresser chaotiquement vers Laurence et il pesta. Il changea de place avec elle pour être dans la mire de l'abominable mister Vomit, le surnom qu'il lui avait donné spontanément. Le colosse, tout spasmodique, se collait peu à peu à lui et Duval se sentit bousculé, puis littéralement tassé, ce qu'il ne put tolérer. Voilà un tango qui se dansait à deux. Le punk le regarda avec des yeux sauvages et Duval le darda dans les hanches. Ce regard avait du pus. Duval ramena son poing vers lui et enfonça son coude dans le plexus solaire du garçon, qui se plia en deux, le souffle coupé.

Le punk, tête renversée, le toisa avec un sourire dément. Duval, d'un regard, indiqua à Laurence de le suivre hors de la piste de danse.

— Qu'est-ce qui t'arrive ? lui demanda-t-elle.

— T'as vu le ravage qu'il faisait ?

— C'est pas une raison pour le frapper.

En retournant à leur table, Duval se rendit compte qu'ils s'étaient fait piquer leurs verres. Il recommanda une bière et un kir.

— Laurence, sais-tu si la teinture qu'il a dans les cheveux dure longtemps ?

— Ce sont habituellement des teintures qui se décolorent aussitôt sous la douche.

- Une pièce des B-52's avec ses guitares tout en réverbération ramena un lot de danseurs sur la piste de danse.

Le serveur revint avec le plateau et Laurence sortit son porte-monnaie, et une carte professionnelle brochée à une feuille tomba par terre. Duval se pencha pour la ramasser : c'était un papier d'un agent d'immeubles. Il eut un sourire ironique en voyant le domaine choisi par Laurence.

— Je regarde des maisons à l'île.

— Tu veux dire des châteaux…

— Tant qu'à déménager, t'aurais pas envie qu'on reparte en neuf dans un endroit qu'on aurait choisi ensemble ?

Duval savait bien que la question de la maison allait venir sur le tapis tôt ou tard dans la soirée. Il savait que Laurence épluchait les revues d'agents immobiliers depuis des mois et que les maisons se chiffraient dans les 200 000 $. La plupart étaient situées sur l'île d'Orléans : des maisons bicentenaires, patrimoniales et parfois même des manoirs. Lui qui adorait la ville ne s'imaginait pas la quitter pour les pâturages de la campagne. Il était né à Montréal et ne comprenait pas cet engouement récent des Québécois pour le terroir. Des bouchons de circulation le matin pour gagner la colline parlementaire ? Le pont de l'île engorgé ? L'odeur du lisier ? Non, il devait tuer la poule dans l'œuf avant que le poussin ne devienne trop gros.

Duval passa une main dans ses cheveux et une mèche rétive se dressa à cause du gel, ce qui amusa Laurence.

Duval la regarda droit dans les yeux :

— Tu n'aimes pas ma maison ?

— Non, ce n'est pas la question. Mais ce serait bien d'habiter un endroit qui nous appartiendrait en propre.

Duval sentit qu'il faudrait en arriver à un compromis. Il avala une gorgée de bière.

— Moi, je suis prêt à faire un bout de chemin. On cherche une nouvelle maison, mais en ville.

Laurence sourit, acquiesça.

— Ça m'apparaît un excellent compromis. Quand commence-t-on ?

Mais le regard de Duval dévia vers la gauche. Il n'entendait plus ce que disait Laurence. Elle se demanda si son regard n'avait pas été capté par une fille qu'il trouvait jolie.

— Qu'est-ce qui se passe, Daniel ?

— Il est là.

— Qui ?

T-shirt et veston noirs, Déziel se pavanait aux abords de la piste de danse en compagnie d'un jeunot, tout vêtu de cuir. Pourquoi Déziel ne s'était-il pas rendu aux obsèques de Rosalie s'il était en ville ? se demandait le lieutenant.

— C'est qui ?

— Déziel, c'est lui qui est recherché. On devait perquisitionner où il habitait et il avait vidé la place.

Mister Vomit, après s'être extrait de la piste de danse, passa devant Déziel, qu'il matraqua d'un regard étrange.

Déziel prit d'assaut le plancher de danse, emporté par une énergie démentielle, comme s'il avait le diable au corps, foudroyé par une étrange folie.

Duval s'excusa auprès de Laurence. Il lui fallait téléphoner à Granger, de la police de Québec. Mais, tout bien considéré, Duval se dit qu'il pourrait procéder lui-même à l'arrestation de Déziel, même s'il n'avait pas le mandat sur lui. Après tout, le mandat existait bel et bien et Déziel devait se savoir recherché.

Déziel continuait à se déhancher, complètement décadent. Son corps se mouvait au ralenti. Laurence n'apprécia pas d'être plongée au cœur de l'enquête.

— Appelle tes collègues !

— Essaie de comprendre ! Si quelqu'un avait un malaise dans un endroit public, ton devoir de médecin te ferait intervenir. C'est pareil pour moi ! On a un fou qui charcute et tripote des corps et ce gars-là est notre suspect numéro un.

Laurence parut sceptique.

— Pendant que tu fais ton boulot, je vais aller danser.

— Laurence…

Elle louvoya en vitesse parmi la foule.

Duval se fraya un chemin jusqu'au bar sans perdre de vue Déziel. Son élégance anachronique dans un tel lieu attira aussitôt l'attention du barman, qui semblait s'être peigné avec une brosse magnétique. Duval lui demanda où se trouvait le téléphone le plus près.

L'employé lui indiqua de se rendre au carré D'Youville. Mais Duval se refusa à laisser ses proies sans surveillance, ne serait-ce qu'un instant. Son regard effectua un travelling vers la piste de danse. L'agité aux cheveux verts dansait au fond en se contemplant dans le miroir avec une complaisance toute narcissique. Laurence se trouvait à un mètre de lui. Au centre, Lizotte faisait la fusée en compagnie des punks prolos.

La silhouette émaciée de Sébastien Poirier n'était plus dans le décor. Sur le cercle de corps en nage, Déziel s'activait, tout convulsif, en compagnie d'une jeune fille en tenue d'amazone.

Duval obliqua lentement vers la piste de danse. Sans mandat, il se demandait comment Déziel réagirait à son arrestation. Le lieutenant, qui ressemblait plus à un mannequin de *G-Q* qu'à un disciple de Sid Vicious, faisait tourner la tête des punks, qui auraient aimé savoir ce qu'un « straight » du genre faisait dans leur galère.

Duval se fraya un chemin et se posta derrière Déziel. *Rock Lobster* des B-52's faisait vibrer le plancher de danse. Duval, gauchement, se déplaça jusqu'à s'immiscer entre Déziel et la fille qui lui faisait face. Mais il n'apprécia pas ce qu'il vit près du miroir. Le géant vert examinait Laurence, la déshabillant des yeux tout en essayant d'attirer son attention par sa danse lascive.

Déziel gesticulait comme un grand guignol en hurlant le refrain *Rock Lobster*. Duval le fixait dans les yeux et l'autre finit par mordre au regard du lieutenant. Il feignit d'abord de ne pas l'avoir vu et il effectua un demi-tour. Partagé entre deux cibles, Duval remarqua que la chose verte parlait à Laurence, qui l'ignorait dans toute sa superbe. Elle s'était déplacée vers la gauche et il l'avait suivie. Duval bougea de cent quatre-vingts degrés et lança un sourire satisfait en direction de Déziel. L'autre le lui rendit avec un soupçon de cynisme. Duval lui cria à l'oreille :

— Déziel, vous êtes en état d'arrestation.

L'autre éclata d'un rire sardonique sans cesser de bouger.

— Vous avez un mandat, lieutenant qui déjà ?

— Ce matin, nous avons perquisitionné chez vous, à votre ex-hôtel et à votre bureau.

— Et qu'avez-vous trouvé ? Des livres de philosophie…

— Nous avons de fortes raisons de croire que vous êtes impliqué de près ou de loin dans les meurtres qui ont eu lieu.

Déziel éructa un rire dément qui se maria à la musique décadente qui arrachait les tympans.

— C'est pas sérieux !

— Je vous arrête, Déziel.

— Monsieur Duval, pour la seconde fois, avez-vous un mandat ? hurla le philosophe.

Duval entrevit Laurence écoutant les propos du débile vert sur le bord de la piste de danse. Duval colla son visage à un centimètre de l'oreille qui portait un rubis. Il fallait s'époumoner pour être compris. Déziel, à la demande du lieutenant, accepta de poursuivre la conversation près du bar où il leur serait possible de discuter sans crier.

— Vous deviez être à New York. C'est ce qui était écrit sur la porte de votre bureau.

— Je ne suis pas parti, finalement.

— Pourquoi ?

— En quoi ça vous regarde ?…

— Déziel, si je vous interroge à la centrale, vous allez vous ennuyer des dialogues de Platon.

— Vous vous surestimez, lieutenant. Platon était un sage.

— Et vous n'êtes pas sorti de la caverne.

— Bravo, vous êtes capable de faire de l'esprit. Je ne croyais pas cela possible d'un flic.

— Assez d'esprit pour avoir coffré des crapules qui totalisent près de deux mille ans de prison.

— Vingt siècles ! Bravo ! La répression a ses chiffres…

Duval le dévisagea.

— Vous n'étiez pas aux funérailles de Rosalie ?

— Je vous rappelle qu'elle n'était pas mon élève mais la petite amie d'un de mes élèves.

— Lorsque je vous ai rencontré l'autre jour, vous n'avez fait aucune mention du décès de Rosalie ni de celui de Michaël. C'est étrange, car sur votre babillard il y a une photo d'étudiants sur laquelle Rosalie apparaît alors que vous disiez ne pas la connaître.

— Monsieur Duval, je ne lis pas les notices nécrologiques. Elles ne m'intéressent pas. Quant aux pages judiciaires, opium du peuple, pas pour moi ! Rosalie était l'amie de Michaël et il est possible que je sois allé à une fête où ils se trouvaient.

Duval, à distance, ne perdait rien de la scène entre Laurence et Vert-de-gris. Elle avait cessé de danser et s'était installée au comptoir qui jouxtait la piste, toujours escortée du punk.

— Pourquoi enseignez-vous à vos élèves qu'il existe des clubs de suicide et des philosophes qui justifient le suicide ?

— Parce que c'est un fait. Monsieur Duval, j'enseigne à mes étudiants les grands principes qui régissent la vie en société : comment fonctionne la *Polis,* l'organisation d'une société démocratique et idéale.

Duval lui lança un rire narquois.

— Je crois que vous leur enseignez un paquet de saloperies. Michaël pourrait en témoigner, Angélique Fraser également.

— Pauvre Angie… dit Déziel en chantant les paroles de la chanson.

C'était trop de cynisme. Duval saisit le poignet de Déziel et le pressa jusqu'à ce que l'autre pousse un cri qui aspira tous les regards.

— Laissez-moi !

Duval relâcha son étreinte et cria à l'oreille du philosophe.

— Aujourd'hui, je suis allé à votre bureau et un gars y est entré. Il avait la clé. Il a pris des documents dans votre classeur et dans votre bureau.

Déziel arbora un large sourire sur son visage.

— Et puis ? C'est interdit par le code criminel ? Je donne ma clé à qui je veux.

Duval voulut tester l'honnêteté de son interlocuteur sur une question dont il connaissait la réponse.

— Qui était ce gars ?

— C'est Sébastien Poirier, un étudiant en philosophie. Il est ici ce soir. Un ancien élève, brillant comme tout, qui est devenu mon correcteur. Il venait porter des copies et en reprendre d'autres.

Le visage de Duval se rembrunit. Déziel avait réponse à tout et affichait une morgue totale.

— Et que faisiez-vous dans mon bureau ? Entrée par effraction ?

— J'avais un mandat.

Duval pointa son doigt en direction du comptoir près de la piste de danse.

— Qui est le jeune homme là-bas que…

— Lequel ?

Le visage de Duval marqua une soudaine détresse. Voyant l'air désemparé du détective, Déziel en profita pour le déstabiliser davantage.

— Tous ces gamins sont un peu mes enfants illégitimes.

Duval eut l'impression que le plancher glissait sous lui. Il se rendit compte que Laurence n'était plus là ni l'homme vert.

Il pivota sur lui-même pour jeter un coup d'œil vers la table qu'ils occupaient un instant auparavant, mais deux filles s'y étaient installées. Son cœur battait la chamade. Le lieutenant balaya du regard la pièce. Ne distinguant ni Laurence ni le punk dans la masse de coiffures colorées, il plaqua Déziel, se tailla un chemin non sans bousculer quelques clients. Où était-elle ?

Duval se rua jusqu'au vestiaire, mais ne vit personne. Il descendit au rez-de-chaussée et questionna le portier.

— Avez-vous vu un gars aux cheveux verts, assez costaud, sortir à l'instant ?

L'autre se paya sa tête.

— Vous savez, ici, les cheveux verts, c'est comme les cheveux gris chez les fonctionnaires.

Duval sortit sa carte d'enquêteur et la lui mit sous le nez, puis il saisit le *bouncer* par le collet et le poussa dans un coin en donnant l'impression qu'il allait dévisser la tête de ce Monsieur Net qui puait l'ail et lui rappelait le lutteur Hans Schmitt.

— Écoute, bonhomme, vous outrepassez votre capacité d'accueil, les sorties de sécurité ne sont pas conformes, j'ai repéré des mineurs et il y a une tempête de coke dans les toilettes des femmes. Je vide la place dans cinq minutes si j'ai envie.

— Le grand punk avec un imper noir vient juste de sortir, ça fait environ trois minutes.

— Il était seul ?

— Non. Avec une fille.

— Dans quelle direction ?

— Vers le parking du carré D'Youville.

Duval courut vers le stationnement souterrain à l'ombre du Palais Montcalm. Il s'arrêta brusquement devant la cabine vitrée du préposé.

— Avez-vous vu un gars, un punk avec des cheveux verts, accompagné d'une jeune femme ?

Le vieux à la bouche pâteuse plissa le visage et fit signe que non de la tête.

— J'ai pas vu ça, monsieur.

Duval tourna les talons, s'engouffra dans l'escalier du souterrain humide, dégaina son arme. Il entendit des cris sinistres, repris en écho, et dévala un étage. C'étaient des jeunes qui s'en allaient fêter.

Duval ne distingua aucun mouvement suspect.

Des bruits de pas retentirent et une porte claqua lourdement un étage plus bas. Duval descendit en vitesse dans le soubassement du stationnement. Une voiture démarra. Il courut vers le véhicule qui reculait. Aveuglé par les phares, il utilisa son avant-bras comme visière. Mais l'homme derrière le pare-brise n'était pas le type qu'il cherchait.

Il parcourut du regard le trou gris, vaste et humide. L'eau suintait des murs fissurés. Deux claquements de porte se répercutèrent au fond du garage. Puis le son d'une radio s'éteignit presque immédiatement. Duval s'avança, la main serrée sur la crosse de son .38. Il compta dix espaces libres jusqu'à une BMW cachée partiellement par une poutrelle de ciment.

— Laurence, tu es là ? Réponds-moi.

Il se pencha au cas où quelqu'un se serait caché sous la voiture. Personne. La vitre du côté passager était au quart baissée. La voiture lui parut vide. Pourtant, il avait perçu deux claquements de porte et des bruits de pas. Derrière la colonne de béton, il jeta un coup d'œil de plus près. Un cri de femme. Une ombre remua. Il crut apercevoir un homme qui frappait sa passagère. Il s'approcha rapidement mais, près de la portière, un jet de poivre de Cayenne l'aveugla. Il se courba et la portière s'abattit lourdement sur sa tête. Il s'affaissa. La voiture démarra dans un crissement de caoutchouc brûlé.

Il entendit de nouveau hurler dans la voiture et, avant de perdre conscience, il crut reconnaître la voix de Laurence.

Quand il reprit conscience, des Samaritains étaient à ses côtés. Était-ce quelques instants ou quelques heures plus tard, il ne pouvait le dire. Un foret creusait des cylindres dans sa calotte crânienne. Des voix évanescentes et des corps flottaient autour de lui. Il ne distinguait que des contours flous. On commentait sa déveine : « Il a été attaqué. » « On l'a volé. » « Il

saigne. » «Appelez une ambulance. » « Il est armé. »
«C'est peut-être un bandit. »

Une jeune fille qui revenait de veiller manqua
défaillir à la vue du sang qui ruisselait encore sur son
visage. Duval toucha sa joue ensanglantée. Ses doigts
maculés ne mentaient pas. Sans doute souffrait-il
d'une légère commotion cérébrale. Lorsqu'une voix
suggéra d'appeler la police, il refusa net. « Je suis
policier», grommela-t-il sans convaincre personne.

Il se releva avec la lenteur d'un ivrogne. Du revers
de la main, il essuya la bave et le sang au coin de sa
bouche. Chancelant, il gagna le Fuzz aussi rapidement
qu'il put, les réflexes émoussés, sans coordination.
De ses glandes lacrymales s'écoulaient des chapelets
de larmes. Il ne cessait de se maudire, se traitant de
toutes les calamités.

Il avait bel et bien entendu une voix de fille. Laurence ? Il n'avait que son nom en tête et la hâte de
regagner la discothèque pour en avoir le cœur net.
Avant de quitter le garage, il s'arrêta devant le guichet
vitré du préposé au stationnement. En le voyant dans
cet état, l'homme, effrayé, sursauta. Duval frappa à la
vitre, mais l'homme hésita avant d'ouvrir la trappe.

— Qu'est-ce qui vous arrive ?

— Une BMW noire vient de sortir, vous avez vu
la personne qui la conduisait ?

— Non.

— La couleur de ses cheveux ?

— Non.

— Y avait-il une fille dans la voiture ?

— J'ai rien remarqué. Il a garroché l'argent et a
décollé en malade. Ça se passe vite ici.

— Dans quelle direction est-il allé ?

— Par là, mais après, aucune idée.

Duval retourna en direction du Fuzz, défia l'autobus
numéro 7 qui passa près de l'écrabouiller.

Devant la discothèque, il contourna la file d'attente et le portier chauve à la physionomie de lutteur l'intercepta. Duval, à bout de forces et de patience, le repoussa en exerçant une pression sur la carotide du type, imprimant une grande main rouge dans son cou. Puis il grimpa péniblement les marches du Fuzz. Une punk, genre fée des étoiles de l'apocalypse, se tordit le visage en le voyant. Les yeux rouges de Duval chauffaient comme s'ils marinaient dans le chili con carne.

Il sentit une main s'accrocher à son épaule. Il se retourna brusquement, prêt à se battre. C'était Laurence. Elle ne comprit pas sur le coup ce qui se passait.

— Comme ça, tu pars sans m'avertir ! lui reprocha-t-elle.

— Je t'ai cherchée partout.

Dans la semi-obscurité, elle constata alors l'ampleur de ses blessures. Sa colère s'apaisa.

— Hé ! Mais qu'est-ce qui t'arrive ?

Il la ramena vers lui pour la serrer. Il chercha ses mots, complètement dépité.

— Il faut que je t'explique…

— Tes yeux ?

— J'ai reçu du poivre de Cayenne du gars qui te draguait…

— Lui ! Pourquoi ? Viens, je vais te soigner.

Duval balaya la salle du regard pour repérer Déziel, qui avait sans doute déguerpi.

— Qu'est-ce qu'il te disait ?

— Il a essayé de me charmer par de belles paroles. Il avait de l'esprit mais utilisé à de mauvaises fins. Un dragueur spirituel.

— Tu te rappelles ce qu'il t'a raconté ?

— Il m'a récité quelque chose d'enflammé qui sonnait faux.

— Quoi ? Tu répètes ?

— Il semblait dire un texte du genre : « À voir ta cadence, ton abandon, on dirait un serpent qui danse au bout de son bâton. »

Duval repéra aussitôt les rimes alternées. Il s'agissait bel et bien d'un poème.

— Quoi encore ?

— Il m'a demandé si je voulais goûter à ses frissons chauds. Il a insisté pour me payer un verre.

— Où est-il, ton verre ?

— J'ai refusé. Pourquoi ?

— Il aurait pu y mettre un barbiturique. C'est ce que le meurtrier a fait avec les autres victimes.

Laurence écarquilla les yeux de stupeur.

— Ensuite, il a rencontré une fille qu'il semblait attendre et il est parti en la prenant par le bras, une fille qui ressemblait à la mère de la famille Adams. Une face de morte avec des cheveux roses. Elle était complètement gelée.

Duval se rappela le cri de la femme. Mais l'avait-il vraiment entendu ?

— Il t'a dit où il habitait ?

— Non.

— Et tu te laisses aborder par des gars comme ça…

— Je voulais t'aider dans ton enquête.

— …

— Et qui t'a frappé ?

— Je crois que c'est lui. C'est le gars louche qu'on a vu quitter le cimetière avant tout le monde.

Le visage de Laurence trahissait son anxiété.

Duval chercha Déziel des yeux, mais le philosophe s'était volatilisé. Il inspecta les toilettes, où il ne traînait qu'une bande de *cokés* qui faisaient la file pour se poudrer. Et si c'était Déziel et un complice qui lui avaient infligé ce coup ? Déziel aurait-il pu le suivre ? Pouvaient-ils faire équipe ? Duval soupira. Toutes ses proies lui échappaient. Voilà ce que ça donnait de courir tous ces lièvres à la fois. Seul Lizotte continuait de se défoncer avec ses copains.

— Il faut que j'appelle au poste pour lancer un avis de recherche.

— On rentre. Tu dois te soigner.

— D'accord.

Dans les oreilles de Duval résonnait un gros bourdon sonore, insupportable grondement de décibels.

Devant le vestiaire, Laurence l'aida à enfiler son manteau. Les regards antipathiques du portier étaient fixés sur lui. Une fois à l'extérieur, il repéra une cabine téléphonique. Question de juridiction, il téléphona à la police de Québec pour signaler la présence de Déziel en ville. Il se sentait comme un amateur, un incompétent. Il détestait saborder le déroulement logique de l'enquête. Malgré tout, l'envie de retracer Déziel était plus forte que sa honte.

Dans la cabine téléphonique, Duval, complètement groggy, s'embourba au point d'avoir l'air ridicule.

— Où est-il passé ? demanda le policier.

— Je ne sais pas.

— Sa voiture ?

— Aucune idée. Oui, une petite BMW.

— Couleur ?

— Blanche. Non, noire…

— Le modèle ?

— Je ne sais pas. La petite BM…

— Comment voulez-vous qu'on le file si on n'a aucun indice ?

— C'est pas fini. Je crois avoir été agressé par le type qu'on cherche. Il a assisté aux funérailles de Rosalie Nantel.

— Vous l'avez clairement aperçu ?

— À la discothèque, mais pas au moment de l'agression.

Duval entendit un long soupir.

— Je pense qu'il est sorti avec une fille aux cheveux roses, précisa le lieutenant. J'ai cru le voir assommer la fille assise dans le siège du passager.

Une expiration encore plus exaspérée siffla au bout du fil.

— Cou'don, vous êtes sûr de rien !

Duval s'irrita.

— Allez chier !

Laurence fut sidérée de sa répartie.

Il regarda l'heure. Sa montre marquait 1 h 45.

Le cou engoncé dans son coupe-vent, Duval conserva le silence durant le trajet. Plusieurs fois, il se sentit près de défaillir, la bile au bord des lèvres, la colère aussi. C'était noble en soi de sacrifier son vendredi soir pour se faufiler dans un trou pareil, mais encore fallait-il être efficace ! « Ne jamais plus impliquer Laurence de près ou de loin dans une enquête », ronchonnait-il. C'était stupide et dangereux. Mais il n'avait pas prévu rencontrer Déziel et il avait eu un mauvais pressenti-ment au sujet du type bizarre. Il aurait dû sortir seul pour travailler à l'aise. Il se sentait dans le même état d'esprit qu'à l'époque de l'enquête sur le meurtrier de l'autoroute : désemparé.

Laurence captait toute sa détresse. Son regard de chien battu se perdait dans les voyants lumineux du tableau de bord.

— Je vais mal dormir.

— Pourquoi ?

— Je suis dépassé par mon enquête. Les indices ne manquent pas, mais on glisse de l'un à l'autre. Mon flair me disait d'aller au Fuzz et j'ai tout raté ce soir.

Duval caressa le visage de Laurence, qu'éclairaient les phares des voitures venant en sens inverse.

— Je ne devrais pas mêler mon travail et nos loisirs, mais je pensais que ce serait amusant de le faire.

— …

— Je vais retourner au bureau et appeler les gars de l'escouade.

— Tu ne peux pas y aller comme ça. Je vais d'abord nettoyer ta plaie et la désinfecter. Je dois vérifier si tu n'as pas une commotion.

Duval maugréa. Il se recroquevilla, prit sa tête entre ses mains, en proie à une atroce migraine.

À la maison, il monta aussitôt se coucher. Sa voix pâteuse réclama un bassin. Laurence déposa le récipient en grès près du lit. Elle ferma la lumière et ne laissa que la veilleuse allumée. Assise au bord du lit, elle nettoya les plaies encroûtées de sang et appliqua une pommade antibactérienne. Elle retourna à la salle de bains, fit couler l'eau du robinet. Elle rappliqua avec une compresse d'eau froide avec laquelle elle épongea les yeux de Daniel. Celui-ci se déplia comme un jouet à ressort et vomit dans la cuvette. Il se redressa. Il avait l'impression qu'une turbine essorait son cerveau. Le plafond se mit à tourner. Il essaya de parler, mais il n'avait plus de voix.

Il ne pourrait pas aller travailler dans ces conditions. Laurence décida de prendre contact avec le capitaine Dallaire pour l'aviser des derniers événements.

Elle éteignit la veilleuse.

DANS LA LIGNE DE MIRE

56

Duval se réveilla vers 5 h et paniqua en constatant qu'il végétait dans son lit. Combien d'heures avaient passé ? D'un geste brusque, il retira la couverture. Quand il se redressa, une vive douleur lézarda sa tête. Des lignes fractales pleuvaient sous ses paupières. Une pulsation martelait sa calotte crânienne. Il marmonna son dépit : sa voix était voilée. Il puait la cigarette. Laurence n'était plus à ses côtés. Il traversa en chancelant le corridor et la trouva couchée sur le lit simple dans la chambre des invités. Il se blottit contre elle. Après quelques frémissements de paupières, elle fixa ses yeux sur lui. Il caressa son visage et chuchota :

— Qu'est-ce que tu fais couchée ici ?

— Tu ronflais, tu rêvais et tu étais secoué de tics. Je ne pouvais pas dormir.

— Je devais aller au bureau.

— Ton corps disait non, tu t'es endormi immédiatement. J'ai appelé à la centrale. J'ai raconté ce qui s'était passé au capitaine.

Il bâilla, se colla davantage contre elle et s'endormit de nouveau.

Vers 8 h, la flûte de Mimi le réveilla en douceur avec une suite de Bach. De belles cascades harmoniques ruisselaient sur plusieurs octaves. Entretemps, Laurence était descendue préparer le petit-déjeuner pour tout le monde.

La pensée du lieutenant émergeait de la brume. Il tentait d'y voir clair. Un procès avait lieu dans sa tête et certains passaient un mauvais quart d'heure. Des visages défilaient devant lui : le punk aux cheveux verts ; Sébastien Poirier se déhanchant sur la piste de danse ; Boutin, le directeur des études, qui ne collaborait qu'à moitié. Son entrave au travail des policiers le rendait furieux. Et Déziel : une présomption de meurtres pesait sur lui. Les heures avant son arrestation étaient comptées.

L'odeur des œufs et du bacon gagnait l'étage lorsque le téléphone sonna.

— Papa, c'est pour toi, cria Mimi.

Daniel se leva en s'enveloppant dans la couverture, recru de fatigue, les jambes molles.

— Oui, Duval.

C'était Dallaire.

— Granger vient de m'appeler. Une prostituée a été assassinée dans la rue Notre-Dame-des-Anges. Les policiers de Québec viennent d'arriver sur place. D'après Granger, c'est probablement le même meurtrier. J'ai su ce qui s'est passé pour toi, hier. T'es *poqué* ?

— Oui.

— Je peux te remplacer.

— Non, surtout pas, j'arrive.

— T'as pas réussi à lui mettre la main dessus ?

Il détestait ce genre de question, car la réponse était d'ores et déjà connue. Dans son for intérieur, Duval s'impatienta, mais en surface il garda son calme.

— Déziel connaît ses droits juridiques et je ne pouvais pas téléphoner du Fuzz. Et la musique, de toute façon, était si forte que je n'aurais pas pu parler.

— À partir de ce matin, on forme une escouade commune... Granger est en beau fusil parce que tu lui as caché de l'information. Je te le dis, ça risque de brasser. Granger, toi et l'espèce de sans-génie de Sillery qui se prend pour un chef de police, vous allez vous rencontrer pour élaborer un plan d'intervention.

Duval écouta sans broncher les directives du chef et le salua laconiquement.

Il descendit, la mort dans l'âme. Des mouches à feu dansaient devant ses yeux. Il n'arrivait pas à y croire : s'il fallait que par sa négligence une femme ait été tuée, il lui faudrait abandonner la crimino. De toute manière, il n'avait pas besoin de ce travail pour vivre. L'indemnisation des assurances reçue après la mort de sa femme suffisait à assurer son avenir financier.

Laurence sut tout de suite à sa mine qu'une mauvaise nouvelle s'ajoutait à celle de la veille. Duval lui annonça d'une voix atone qu'une femme avait été tuée dans la Basse-Ville.

Le meurtrier élargissait son territoire, ce qui n'avait rien de rassurant. Pourtant, Duval trouva étrange qu'il s'en prenne à une prostituée, les victimes ayant appartenu au même milieu jusqu'alors.

— Tu veux déjeuner ?

— Non, merci. J'ai aucun appétit.

Elle s'approcha et grimaça en constatant l'état de son hématome. L'enflure s'était accentuée.

— Tu devrais mettre un peu de glace.

— J'ai pas le temps.

Il l'embrassa. Elle se blottit contre lui. Il enfonça son portefeuille dans sa poche arrière. Il ne s'était pas rendu compte qu'il portait le jean noir de la veille. Quand elle le lui fit remarquer, il hocha la tête, prit son veston et sortit. Au diable la tenue vestimentaire.

57

Rue Notre-Dame-des-Anges : nom de circonstance. Duval aurait eu besoin des grâces de tous les anges et bienheureux de ce monde. Il trouva cynique que les prostituées pratiquent leur art dans une rue dédiée à la Vierge Marie. Puis il repensa à l'une des obsessions du meurtrier : le couplage d'éléments profanes et sacrés. Et Baudelaire aimait les prostituées, lui avait signalé Adèle Marino.

Le soleil ne suffisait jamais à rendre le quartier Saint-Roch enjoué et chaleureux. La grisaille ajoutait à la lourdeur de la misère. Un ciel tuberculeux. Les poches de pauvreté se fichent des bienfaits de mère Nature.

Les camions de l'Identité judiciaire et le fourgon bourgogne du coroner étaient garés devant un stationnement en béton, la Mercedes noire de Villemure également.

Trois filles bien grimées, aux jambes longues et bottées de talons aiguilles, faisaient le pied de grue devant un immeuble. Elles se tenaient par la taille, le mouchoir pendant à la main, le maquillage dégoulinant.

Duval se sentit soulagé lorsqu'il aperçut le fauteuil de Louis entouré de ces longues jambes féminines. Le gros Loulou leur parlait. Il avait fait jadis craquer le cœur d'une effeuilleuse et avait en haute estime les filles de la nuit, ces Marie-Madeleine d'aujourd'hui.

Lorsque Duval entra dans le champ de vision du Gros, ce dernier leva les bras et s'adressa aux filles en montrant le lieutenant.

— Voilà le meilleur enquêteur au Québec. Je vous le garantis. Il va retrouver l'écœurant qui a fait ça et j'aime mieux pas être à la place du gars.

Duval salua les prostituées et attira Louis à l'écart. Loulou grimaça en voyant la blessure subie par son ami.

— Y t'a pas manqué !

— C'est le type qui est parti avant tout le monde, hier, aux funérailles. Il m'a filé entre les mains. Il est pas clair avec moi !

— Le patron me l'a dit. On le recherche lui aussi.

Duval s'enquit alors du meurtre. Louis, qui n'avait pu voir la scène du crime, se contenta de répéter ce qu'on lui avait dit.

— C'est pas beau du tout, y paraît.

— Qui a découvert le corps ?

— C'est la grande Noire.

Duval s'approcha de la jeune fille au visage souligné par de généreuses lèvres rouges, craquelées par les gerçures comme le vernis d'un vieux tableau. Elle s'appelait Marie et elle était d'origine haïtienne. Elle avait une abondante coiffure afro. Elle portait de gros pendentifs aux oreilles, un collier en bois et une croix en or. Elle pleurait sans arrêt, ne cessant de dire que « c'était d'sa faute câlice ». Elle était tellement secouée que Duval voulut la faire hospitaliser. Elle souffrait d'un violent choc nerveux. Ses longues jambes flageolaient comme de jeunes trembles.

Duval, à qui il tardait d'aller examiner la scène du crime – il craignait que Granger ne procède sans lui –, demanda à la jeune fille pourquoi elle s'accusait ainsi.

— Marie, racontez-moi ce qui s'est passé.

Elle essuya ses yeux.

— J'ai reçu un *call* vers 3 h. Un gars qui voulait coucher avec une fille exotique, c'est le mot qu'il utilisait. Comme j'avais deux clients prévus pour la nuit, de trois heures trente à cinq heures, je lui ai refilé l'adresse d'une amie asiatique nouvellement arrivée. Elle et moi, on s'était donné rendez-vous au Dunkin Donuts, à 6 h ; comme elle n'est pas venue, je suis allée à sa chambre en pensant qu'elle s'était peut-être endormie. Je suis entrée et je l'ai vue. Il l'a…

Elle éclata en sanglots.

Duval n'avait pas besoin d'en entendre davantage.

— Marie, pouvez-vous me dire à quoi ressemblait la voix de l'homme ?

— …

— Une voix vieille ou jeune ?

— Je ne sais pas.

— Il s'exprimait avec un accent ?

— Non, il parlait comme tout le monde. Je trouvais qu'il avait l'air distingué. Quand je lui ai dit mon nom – enfin, celui de mon amie – il a fait un commentaire.

— Comment s'appelle-t-elle ?

— Layla.

— Et puis ?

— Il a dit que ce nom lui plaisait beaucoup.

— Qu'est-ce qui vous fait croire, Marie, que c'est ce client-là qui l'a tuée ?

— Layla m'a dit que ce serait son dernier. Pourquoi, mon Dieu ? Pourquoi ? Je suis punie. C'est ma faute !

La quincaillerie de bijoux tressautait à chaque sanglot. Duval lui demanda de l'attendre, il voulait encore lui parler.

— L'aut' aussi, le vieux, y veut me parler.

L'autre, le vieux, c'était Granger. Duval se tourna vers Louis.

— Louis, pourrais-tu faire les démarches pour connaître la provenance de l'appel?

— Oui, je m'en occupe.

Louis s'enquit auprès des jeunes filles où il pouvait téléphoner. La petite blonde teinte à la large repousse noire lui offrit d'utiliser son téléphone, mais sa chambre était située au troisième étage et hors d'atteinte pour Louis. Il se dirigea donc vers une boîte téléphonique au coin de la rue Dorchester.

Duval croisa un photographe du service de l'Identité judiciaire.

— Je te le dis, c'est franchement dégueulasse.

— T'as trouvé quelque chose?

— Il y a une belle empreinte de pied dans le sang.

Duval grimpa l'escalier d'un pas rapide. Mais lorsqu'il aperçut les gars de la morgue qui tournaient le coin avec la civière, il sentit une rage intense l'envahir. Le couloir était si étroit qu'il dut redescendre pour les laisser passer. Il leur ouvrit la porte. Une fois la civière derrière lui, il se catapulta au troisième. Il entra dans la pièce et se dirigea droit sur Granger, qui s'entretenait avec un policier en uniforme.

Il enfonça son index à plusieurs reprises dans l'épaule du détective.

— Qu'est-ce que ça veut dire? Pourquoi ne pas m'avoir attendu?

— Vous avez décidé de ne pas partager votre information? Je fais pareil.

Granger lui tourna les talons. Duval sentit que les plombs chauffaient et que son cœur s'emballait.

— Va dire ça aux filles qui sont en bas! Écoute, Granger, j'ai des informations de premier ordre. J'ai parcouru des kilomètres dans cette enquête alors que vous autres, vous faites vos premiers pas.

Granger lui tourna de nouveau le dos.

Duval aperçut le docteur Villemure et s'empressa de lui demander ce qui s'était passé.

— Elle a été poignardée. Il semble qu'elle se soit étouffée dans son sang.

Duval s'avança pour examiner les giclées artérielles. Une artère avait été touchée, ce qui avait projeté le sang. Dans le cas des meurtres précédents, les victimes avaient été étranglées. Ici, la prostituée avait tenté de fuir. Les marques de sang racontaient sa fuite interrompue près de la porte.

— Des messages ?

— Aucun message.

— Pourquoi Granger s'emballe ?

L'expert légiste répondit à voix basse.

— Il pense qu'en raison du livre trouvé sur la table de chevet, *Les Oiseaux se cachent pour mourir*, il s'agit du même meurtrier.

— Idiot ! Ce n'est pas lui. C'est confondre des pommes avec des oranges.

— C'est ce que je crois. En plus, regarde.

Villemure sortit un sachet contenant des cheveux.

— Le suspect a les cheveux longs. La couleur, châtain, est différente de celle des cheveux découverts sur les autres scènes de crime. Aucune ritualisation ou atteinte *post mortem* au corps de la victime.

De plus, pensa Duval, il aurait été inhabituel que le meurtrier change ainsi de catégorie sociale et de race dans le choix de ses victimes, mais il est vrai que Baudelaire, comme sa fille et mademoiselle Marino le lui avaient appris, frayait autant avec les grandes dames qu'avec les putains.

— A-t-elle été agressée sexuellement ?

— Elle avait du sperme dans le vagin, mais comme elle recevait plusieurs clients dans une nuit, cela pose un problème. Peut-être une histoire de « stup », comme c'est souvent le cas dans ce milieu.

— Ce n'est pas lui, c'est clair, ajouta Duval. On a le couteau ?

— Les gars de l'Identité l'ont emporté.

Granger, qui avait entendu l'opinion du lieutenant, l'interrogea.

— Qu'est-ce qui te fait dire ça, Duval ?

— Tu n'as qu'à revoir l'abc de la crimino, lui envoya Duval en souhaitant que la logique du meurtrier ait été respectée.

— Va dire ça aux filles en bas ! lui expédia Granger du tac au tac.

Duval s'avança à un pouce de son visage. Le vieux buste ridé faisait peur à voir à cette distance.

— Va te faire…

Villemure, sidéré, s'immisça entre eux comme un arbitre à la lutte.

— Hé ! vous deux ! Vous allez arrêter ça. Il faut travailler ensemble. On n'arrivera jamais à de bons résultats si vous continuez.

Duval annonça que son patron et le capitaine Beaulieu, de la Ville de Québec, s'étaient entendus pour créer une escouade commune.

— Je le sais, annonça Granger.

Duval invita finalement Granger à venir à la centrale où il lui fournirait tout ce qu'il avait en main et l'engagea à faire de même. Granger hocha affirmativement la tête, comme si le bon sens lui revenait aussi.

La chambre ressemblait à celle de Van Gogh. Layla l'avait décorée de couleurs pastel, toutes enjouées. Une reproduction d'un tableau naïf avait été accrochée : un petit camion vert lime livrant des fruits dans un marché de Bangkok. Une vieille chaise avait été peinte en jaune. Sur la table de chevet, le roman à l'eau de rose reposait près d'une photo dans un cadre blanc en plastique : Layla et sa mère, sans doute, pensa Duval.

La pièce était si exiguë que les hommes de l'Identité et les forces policières se marchaient sur les pieds. Heureusement, toutes les précautions avaient été prises pour éviter une contamination de la scène du crime. Une employée avec sa brosse récoltait des fibres et des poils sur le drap de Layla. Avec le nombre d'hommes qui y passaient, l'identification allait être ardue.

L'employée avisa Duval que la poignée avait été touchée par une des amies de Layla.

À quatre pattes sur le plancher, un autre spécialiste ramassa dans la corbeille une enveloppe et un condom qu'il ensacha.

Un policier de Québec avec une grosse tête d'aubergine casquée monta à la course. Une fois sur le palier, il s'adossa hors d'haleine contre la balustrade.

— Déziel vient de se rendre.

La nouvelle éclata comme un coup de grisou.

— Il y a dix minutes, ajouta le constable.

— Où est-il ? s'enquit Granger.

— À la centrale du boulevard Saint-Cyrille, répondit le policier au grand plaisir de Duval.

— J'y vais tout de suite, lança le lieutenant.

Il invita aussi Granger à le rejoindre et ce dernier s'empressa d'accepter. Il viendrait aussitôt qu'il aurait rempli les documents relatifs à cette enquête.

Sur le trottoir, Louis réconfortait les prostituées. Elles le remercièrent, les yeux pleins d'eau.

— Ça fait du bien de vous parler. Vous êtes un homme bon !

— C'est dommage que tous les beux soient pas comme vous, dit l'autre.

Louis sourit en regardant son confrère.

— C'est ce que je me dis depuis vingt ans. Vous allez voir, ce malade va ronger les murs de sa cellule pour le restant de ses jours.

Elles semblaient déjà familières avec Louis, qu'elles appelaient par son prénom.

Le Gros ouvrit son carnet et inscrivit le numéro de Jésus-Ouvrier.

— Demain, il y a une messe spéciale que j'ai organisée.

Il détacha la feuille avec les coordonnées et la remit à Marie.

— On répare les âmes en détresse.

Elle le gratifia d'un regard biblique à la Marie-Madeleine.

58

Le branle-bas de combat était général au poste. Entre les deux colonnes de marbre de l'entrée, Dallaire apostropha Duval. Le capitaine eut un rictus à la vue de la prune bleuie sur le front du lieutenant.

— Il ne t'a pas manqué !

— La portière était bleue !

— On a une mauvaise nouvelle.

Le visage de Duval se rembrunit.

Dallaire et le lieutenant grimpèrent l'escalier en troisième vitesse jusqu'au bureau du chef.

— Des parents ont appelé pour signaler que leur fille n'est pas rentrée ce matin. Elle était sortie au Fuzz. Elle s'appelle Dahlia Héroux. Vérifie si son nom figure sur les listes d'élèves. Les parents vont venir nous porter une photo. C'est peut-être la fille qui accompagnait le suspect.

Le visage de Duval devint livide.

— Hier, en allant au Fuzz, je pressentais quelque chose, mais je ne m'attendais pas à y trouver toute la galerie. À ma grande surprise, Sébastien Poirier et Déziel étaient là. Je ne m'attendais pas à les voir tous.

— Ça, je le sais. Laurence nous en a parlé.

— J'ai aussi croisé le type aux cheveux peinturlurés, très bizarre, que nous n'avons pu filer au cimetière. Malgré la couleur différente de ses cheveux, je l'ai reconnu. D'après les renseignements du portier du bar, c'est lui que j'ai dû suivre dans le stationnement, mais je n'ai jamais pu l'apercevoir. Laurence s'est fait draguer par lui. Le type a essayé de l'entraîner mais pas en utilisant la force. Et il semble qu'il se soit éclipsé avec une autre fille. Peut-être Dahlia Héroux?

— Une grande noire?

— Hier, elle avait les cheveux roses. Appelle Laurence, elle l'a vue.

— Je vais t'envoyer à l'Identité pour un portrait-robot du gars.

— Pas nécessaire, on l'a pris en photo aux funérailles de Rosalie.

— Oublie ça. À l'église, Boivert a essayé de le photographier, mais le suspect est sorti trop vite et cachait son visage pour dissimuler ses pleurs.

Complètement dégoûté, Duval fixa le plancher.

— Badeau t'attend. On se retrouve à la salle de conférences dans trente minutes.

Duval, qui avait hâte de voir Déziel, se pressa en direction de l'I.-J.

◆

Dans l'antichambre de la salle d'interrogatoire, une vitre teintée permettait d'observer Déziel, en garde à vue, sans qu'il le sache. Il ressemblait à un insurgé en attente d'être jugé par le tribunal d'une junte militaire. Assis sur son banc, menotté, le sinistre professeur se mirait dans la glace opaque. Il portait un jean noir et une chemise rouge en soie et des *shoe-claques* comme en portent les gamins. Il ne lui manquait qu'une fronde dans la poche arrière.

Duval, tout en jetant de fréquents coups d'œil en direction du philosophe, raconta à ses collègues « ses mémoires » de la veille. À sa gauche, Francis avait le cou tapissé de sucettes. Il avait été rapide en affaires. Adèle Marino lui avait téléphoné pour lui dire que le message inscrit dans le mausolée d'Angélique était tiré du *Hamlet* de Shakespeare.

— Ils ont passé la soirée à spéCULer, dit Louis en insistant sur la deuxième syllabe.

Duval regarda l'horloge.

Succion d'air : la porte capitonnée s'ouvrait. Dallaire apparut dans l'embrasure.

Derrière le capitaine, Granger était secondé par deux mastiffs. En constatant que Francis était aussi mal en point que Duval, le vieux limier fronça les sourcils. Qui les avait tabassés comme ça ? Un détective aux cheveux roux, Pascal Landry, fixait aux deux minutes sa montre de plongée sous-marine. Il louchait d'un œil et son regard fuyait quand il vous fixait. Son comparse, le lieutenant Jean Béland, était un hommage à l'univers sphérique : tête parfaitement ronde, yeux exorbités de gnome, lèvres lippues, cheveux bouclés collés aux oreilles et une panse hémisphérique. Il rongeait sans arrêt ses ongles et ses mains étaient couvertes d'eczéma. Dallaire annonça que le chef de police de la Ville de Sillery était parti à un tournoi de bridge à Windsor.

— Trop dommage, on vient de perdre une semaine ! ironisa Duval.

Il déballa ensuite tout ce qu'il avait appris depuis le début. De son côté, Granger révéla une information qui fit dresser les cheveux de Duval. Deux mois plus tôt, un étudiant de l'Université Laval avait menacé un professeur, une femme, qui donnait un cours de littérature. Il tenait l'information de la police de Sainte-Foy.

— On n'a jamais pu découvrir qui était l'expéditeur du colis. Le professeur donnait un cours devant cent cinquante élèves dans un amphithéâtre.

— Quelle sorte de menace ? s'enquit Duval.

— Elle a reçu à la maison, tenez-vous bien, un fœtus de porc dans une boîte à chaussures portant une inscription obscène.

— Le fœtus provenait sans doute d'un laboratoire de biologie du cégep ou de l'université, dit Duval.

— Ils ont vérifié. On a contre-vérifié, mais sans succès. On n'a jamais pu prouver d'où il venait, annonça Granger.

— Avez-vous vérifié, poursuivit Duval, si des étudiants en biologie suivaient un cours facultatif en littérature ? Angélique Fraser étudiait en biologie.

— Oui, on a fait tout ça. Mais on n'a rien trouvé.

— Il faudrait comparer la liste des étudiants de Déziel et celle du cours de lettres. Pouvez-vous me donner le nom et l'adresse du professeur de lettres ?

— Oui, j'ai ça ici : madame Louise Riendau.

Duval se mit à échafauder une multitude d'hypothèses. Mais avant, il lui fallait interroger Déziel qui marinait dans la salle d'interrogatoire.

Duval rappela à Francis et à Prince de se rendre aux funérailles de Mathieu à l'église Saint-Charles-Garnier. Prince râla à l'idée de se taper un deuxième service funéraire et Francis y alla la mort dans l'âme.

◆

Avant de passer à l'interrogatoire, Louis lut à Déziel ses droits. Assis derrière la table, le philosophe l'écouta avec ennui. Granger se leva. Il s'approcha de Déziel et lança une première salve de questions.

— Monsieur Déziel, pourquoi n'êtes-vous pas parti à New York ?

— J'ai changé d'idée. J'avais surestimé mes finances. Je devais me reloger. Je couche à l'hôtel depuis quelques semaines et je suis cassé. Et je me suis dit que je devais assister aux funérailles de Michaël. Lui, c'était mon élève.

— Où êtes-vous allé après l'hôtel ?

— J'ai loué plus tôt que prévu une maison de campagne à Saint-Ferréol-les-Neiges. J'ai le bail ici.

Déziel sortit le document signé la veille et le remit à Duval. Le lieutenant l'examina et constata que le professeur disait vrai.

— Qui est le gars qui est venu vous parler, l'autre jour, à votre bureau alors que j'arrivais avec mon collègue ? Si je me rappelle bien, vous lui faisiez des recommandations.

Déziel parut mal à l'aise.

— Tout le monde me connaît. Tout le monde me parle. Je ne sais pas de qui il est question.

— Vous ne vous rappelez pas ?

— Non.

— Hier, au Fuzz, il avait les cheveux verts et il est passé devant vous et vous vous êtes longuement regardés.

— Écoutez, il y avait trois cents personnes. Je connais tout le monde dans la boîte. Je ne sais pas de qui vous voulez parler.

— Monsieur Déziel, Sébastien Poirier est entré dans votre bureau pour prendre un document dans un classeur.

— Je vous l'ai dit, c'est mon correcteur.

— Qu'avez-vous à dire sur Sébastien ?

— Un charmant garçon, excellent correcteur.

— Revenons au gars aux cheveux verts qui se trouvait au Fuzz. C'était un de vos élèves. Quel est son nom ?

— Je n'ai pas de mémoire pour les noms des élèves. Il faudrait que je consulte ma liste.

— Ce garçon a aussi été aperçu aux funérailles de Rosalie Nantel. Vous le connaissez ?

Impatient, Déziel se raidit et haussa le ton.

— Écoutez, je n'y suis pas allé, aux funérailles de Rosalie. Je ne sais pas de qui vous parlez. Je n'ai pas la mémoire des noms. J'ai une centaine d'élèves par session, sans compter tous les anciens qui viennent me voir pour trouver un réconfort spirituel.

— Quelle forme prend ce réconfort spirituel ?

— Des encouragements, des conseils… Plusieurs étudiants font un transfert paternel sur ma personne.

— Alors, qui était ce garçon qui pleurait dans votre bureau ?

— À ce que je sache, je n'ai pas à révéler cette information.

— Ce garçon m'a agressé.

— Prouvez-le-moi.

Duval serra les dents, les poings, puis reprit contenance.

— Monsieur Déziel, nous allons vous faire subir un test sanguin et nous allons prélever un échantillon de vos cheveux.

— Allez-y, si ma déposition ne suffit pas. Et pourquoi pas le polygraphe…

— Chaque chose en son temps, râla Granger.

Duval aborda une question d'ordre littéraire qui le chicotait.

— Aimez-vous Baudelaire ?

— Bien sûr. Quel lettré n'aime pas Baudelaire ? « Le poète est semblable au prince des nuées qui hante la tempête et se rit de l'archer », déclama Déziel avec grandiloquence, pour le plus grand ennui des détectives. C'est comme de demander à un alpiniste s'il adore la montagne ! Ou à un policier s'il aime les armes à feu...

Duval n'apprécia pas la comparaison de Déziel, mais ne s'en formalisa pas.

— Et Shakespeare ?

— Lieutenant, pourquoi tournez-vous autour du pot ?

— Et Camus ? Nous avons examiné vos livres : certaines citations trouvées près des corps des victimes y ont été soulignées.

Déziel éclata de rire, leva de dépit ses bras.

— Voyons, lieutenant ! Si vous feuilletez tous mes livres, vous verrez que je suis un incorrigible marqueur de textes. Je les défigure, je les triture. Vous constaterez la même chose chez mes collègues du département.

Le mot « défigurer », dans la bouche de Déziel, donnait des frissons dans le dos.

Duval reprit son questionnaire sur la littérature.

— Des citations de textes célèbres trouvées sur les scènes de crime correspondent à des œuvres que vous mettez au programme et qui sont inscrites dans votre plan de cours. Étrange coïncidence...

— Je n'ai rien à voir dans tout ça. Lisez les plans de cours de mes collègues et vous constaterez qu'ils se ressemblent tous.

Duval sentit alors que Déziel cachait quelque chose.

— Avez-vous remis à Angélique Fraser une version ancienne des *Fleurs du mal* ?

— Non !

— Vous ne vous rappelez pas ?

— Non.

Duval sortit le livre.

— Pourtant, ce recueil découvert chez Angélique vous a appartenu.

Déziel afficha un sourire forcé.

— Vous me l'apprenez, alors. Vous savez, prêter un livre équivaut trop souvent à le donner : ils ne reviennent jamais. Et de toute façon, est-ce qu'Angélique a été tuée ? C'est un complot ou quoi ? hurla Déziel, qui devenait paranoïaque.

— Monsieur Déziel, j'ai remarqué dans votre bibliothèque un ouvrage traitant de dissection, de médecine anatomique.

Déziel roula des yeux exaspérés.

— Et les livres que vous possédez sur les armes à feu font-ils de vous un tueur ?

— Déziel, c'est moi qui pose les questions !

— Écoutez, lieutenant Duval, je suis passionné par cette période qu'on appelle la Renaissance. À cette époque, les leçons d'anatomie étaient fort courues. Les plus grands artistes, Vinci, Titien, Goya et Rembrandt, ont immortalisé par leurs illustrations les travaux de brillants médecins comme Vésale. L'ouvrage que je possède se trouve, dans sa version originale, à la bibliothèque de l'école depuis deux cents ans. C'est un des joyaux de notre collection. À ce que je sache, ça ne fait pas de moi un meurtrier. Si vous continuez d'ausculter ma bibliothèque, à l'école, vous vous apercevrez que j'ai des centaines de livres sur la Renaissance italienne. Cette période m'intéresse autant par l'esprit d'invention qui y prévalait que par l'humanisme qui s'en dégageait, ce que je ne ressens pas présentement dans cette pièce. Interrogez plusieurs de mes étudiants qui sont devenus médecins et ils vous diront tous que ces cours ont influencé leur orientation professionnelle.

Granger, une cigarette au coin des lèvres, s'assit au bord de la table, juste assez près pour s'immiscer dans la bulle de Déziel.

— Déziel, vous avez tué ces deux personnes. C'est écrit dans votre face, décréta le vieux.

Ses deux compères hochaient positivement la tête.

— Allez dire ça à un juge et il va vous corriger comme un mauvais élève.

— Vous êtes un tueur sadique !

— Je vous dis que je n'ai tué personne. Pourquoi j'aurais fait ça ?

— Pour le plaisir ?

— Voyons, c'est faux.

Déziel avait chaud. La sueur ruisselait sur son front.

— D'où vous vient cette obsession de la mort ? martela Granger.

— Monsieur, je suis professeur de philosophie et ce sujet est sans doute celui qui a le plus captivé les grands philosophes : d'où viens-je ? Où vais-je ? Qui suis-je ? L'âme est-elle immortelle ? Voilà ce que l'État me commande d'enseigner. Je suis payé pour discuter de la vie et de la mort. Descartes compte au nombre des philosophes dont je fais lire les textes. À ses amis qui s'informaient de ses dernières lectures, il montrait un veau écorché et répondait : « Voilà ma bibliothèque. » Et on n'est pas venu l'arrêter pour autant. Descartes, comme Léonard de Vinci, a pratiqué de nombreuses dissections qui ont fait progresser la médecine et les connaissances scientifiques.

Duval repensa à cette histoire de fœtus de porc mais laissa Déziel poursuivre son monologue.

— *La Fabrique du corps humain,* qui figure dans ma bibliothèque, n'est qu'un livre parmi tant d'autres. Je m'intéresse à tous les grands anatomistes. J'ai même remporté, pendant mon cours classique, le premier prix d'anatomie. Apprenez que la philo est une discipline enseignée dans les collèges avec la caution du Ministère.

Granger frotta son nez camus et plissé et se pencha vers Déziel, plantant ses yeux d'oiseau noir dans ceux bleu clair du philosophe.

— Êtes-vous nécrophile ?

— Et vous ? répliqua Déziel, exaspéré.

Granger lui balança une claque au visage qui fit plier Déziel. Duval s'interposa, dévisagea le détective en colère.

— Vous n'avez pas le droit, se plaignit Déziel. Vous n'avez rien compris à ce que je viens de dire. Votre question est aussi absurde que de demander à un policier s'il est assoiffé de meurtre parce qu'il porte une arme.

Le professeur suait de plus en plus. Duval, qui n'appréciait pas la méthode de Granger, relança la charge de questions.

— Monsieur Déziel, où étiez-vous cette nuit entre 2 h et 5 h ?

— J'étais chez un ami.

— Où ?

— Dans sa maison de Saint-Apollinaire. Je ne peux emménager avant la semaine prochaine à Saint-Ferréol. Je dois me remeubler.

Duval tourna le dos à Déziel, fit trois pas vers la glace teintée et se retourna. Il posa un index sur ses lèvres comme s'il cherchait ses mots et pointa son doigt en direction du suspect.

— Monsieur Déziel, plusieurs de vos élèves sont mêlés directement à ces histoires de meurtres et de nécrophilie. Comment expliquez-vous ce fait ?

Déziel se rembrunit.

— Je l'ignore. C'est votre travail de le découvrir. Je vous ai dit ce que je savais. Vous oubliez que d'autres professeurs enseignent aussi à ces élèves.

— Mais il semble que vous les ayez marqués funestement. La direction m'a affirmé que vous exerciez sur eux une forte influence.

— Écoutez, si vous voulez revenir sur la mort d'Angélique, je n'ai rien d'autre à ajouter. Un de mes collègues, il y a deux ans, a remis une copie avec un commentaire acerbe à un étudiant, et celui-ci s'est suicidé le soir même. Est-il responsable de son décès ?

Une fois de plus, Duval s'était fait clouer le bec.

— Alors comment expliquez-vous cette fascination que vous transmettez à vos étudiants ?

Le ton monta. Déziel n'appréciait pas le terme « fascination ».

— Je les fascine ? Eh bien, tant mieux ! C'est le signe d'une expérience d'enseignement réussie. Les jeunes sont naturellement captivés par ce sujet. Ne me prenez pas pour un monstre qui farcit d'idées noires la tête de ses élèves. Sinon, allez faire la morale au professeur qui leur enseigne la physique nucléaire. Sachez que, au fil des ans, j'ai enseigné à des classes fort différentes. Chacune d'elles possède un profil psychologique particulier. Au début de ma carrière, un cercle socratique s'était formé et les étudiants se fréquentent toujours. D'autres ont fait une obsession de Nietzsche au point de s'identifier à lui et d'autres encore se sont mis à écrire comme Camus. Des pro-Sartre et des pro-Camus s'affrontaient dans des débats passionnants et houleux au point de s'empoigner. Puis, les jeunes du cercle Thanatos se sont à leur tour nourris du mouvement romantique présenté dans leur cours de littérature.

— Vous dites « leur cours de littérature » : vous n'enseignez pas Baudelaire ?

— Non, il m'arrivait souvent de le citer, mais c'est tout.

— Mais ce livre apparaît dans votre plan de cours.

— Oui, mais pas comme ouvrage obligatoire.

— Et le professeur de littérature ?

— Vous le lui demanderez.

Granger voulut poser une question, mais Duval tint à poursuivre là-dessus.

— Auriez-vous eu des conflits avec certains élèves ?

— Non. Il y a toujours des cas d'indiscipline mais rien de majeur.

— Auriez-vous connu, à l'époque du cercle Thanatos, un élève qui aurait été le souffre-douleur des autres ?

— Je ne saurais dire. Il y a toujours eu des *nerds* ou des *weirdos*. Mais le cercle Thanatos comptait plusieurs spécimens dignes d'être mentionnés dans une anthologie d'excentriques.

Un agent entra et remit à Duval le portrait-robot du type qu'il avait aperçu la veille. Duval esquissa un sourire. Badeau avait un sixième sens pour reconstituer ce qu'avaient vu les autres. Duval mit le portrait devant le visage du professeur.

— Vous le connaissez ?

— Non.

— Ce n'est pas l'homme que j'ai vu sortir de votre bureau ?

— Non.

— Ce n'est pas le gars qui vous a toisé du regard, hier ?

— Je ne me rappelle pas.

Duval expira, passa une main sur son visage. L'endroit était chaud et l'air sec, irrespirable.

— Madame Généreux, de l'hôtel, m'a dit que des jeunes venaient vous voir. Mathieu vous a-t-il rendu visite dans les jours qui ont précédé sa mort ?

— Oui.

— Combien de temps avant sa mort ?

— Cinq jours.

— Et Rosalie ?

— Non.

— L'avez-vous rencontrée ailleurs ?

— Non.

— Que voulait Mathieu ?

— Jaser.

— Mathieu, dans son manuscrit, parle d'un dénommé Spleen qui teint ses cheveux en vert. Vous le connaissez ?

— Je n'ai jamais entendu ce nom.

— Dans son livre, Mathieu écrivait qu'un accident avait mis fin au cercle Thanatos.

— Je ne sais pas ce qui s'est passé.

— Vous êtes sûr ? Qui est Styx ?

— Il s'appelait Gabriel Cantin, un gars brillant. Il a chuté comme le héros de Nietzsche. Il incarnait à la fois Dionysos et Apollon. Sa culture latine et grecque était phénoménale, mais il était aussi bizarre, très autodestructeur.

— Pourquoi dites-vous ça ?

— Il était dur pour son corps. Il faisait beaucoup de sport, de culturisme, mais il consommait aussi beaucoup de drogues. Il savait s'imposer comme chef. Il se préparait pour son cours de philo comme pour un match de boxe. Il faisait en classe un redoutable maître de rhétorique. Aujourd'hui, il a de la difficulté à marcher et à parler. Il a tout perdu en quelques instants : beauté, éloquence, grâce et avenir.

— Et ses amis, comment se comportaient-ils avec lui ?

— Ils l'idolâtraient.

— Vous avez son adresse ?

— Il habite chez ses parents à Sillery. Vous le trouverez facilement dans l'annuaire. Les Cantin ne sont pas nombreux.

Duval tenta de le court-circuiter.

— Le type aux cheveux verts avait une petite cicatrice au front. Est-ce qu'on parle du même gars ?

— Je n'ai pas vu Gabriel hier. Mais vous allez le constater, Gabriel est un peu légume aujourd'hui. Ça m'attriste, car il avait un brillant avenir. Toutes les portes des universités lui étaient ouvertes. Il devait entrer en médecine.

Duval se rappela avoir lu que certains psychopathes avaient subi des blessures majeures au cerveau, ce qui tendait à expliquer leur désordre psychologique et les meurtres sadiques qu'ils pouvaient commettre.

— Madame Généreux m'a dit que votre fils venait vous voir à l'hôtel.

— La vieille délire. Je n'ai pas d'enfant.

On frappa à la porte. Méthot, l'assistant du chef, rapportait des nouvelles fraîches sur le meurtre de la rue Notre-Dame-des-Anges.

— Du nouveau ! Une prostituée qui attendait son client en épiant par la fenêtre de son appartement affirme avoir vu un gars bizarre, quelques minutes avant que Layla soit tuée. Il avait les cheveux longs, dans la quarantaine, et il cherchait une adresse.

Granger et ses hommes devaient se pointer d'urgence à la centrale du parc Victoria. Duval l'avisa qu'il le tiendrait au courant de la suite de l'interrogatoire. Granger partit en le saluant d'un signe de tête plus amical que tous les précédents réunis.

Duval prit le dessin et le posa de nouveau devant Déziel.

— Regardez-le encore une fois.

— Non. Ce visage ne me dit rien.

— Si je me rappelle bien, vous disiez à ce garçon de patienter, d'avoir du courage. Pourquoi ?

— Je ne sais pas.

Duval hocha la tête. Il se souvenait bien du regard que s'étaient lancé, la veille, les deux hommes. Il lui montra de nouveau le portrait.

— Vous ne le reconnaissez pas ?

— Non.

— Quel est son nom ?

Duval sentit Déziel sur le point de craquer.

— Je veux voir mon avocat, pesta le philosophe.

— Pourquoi le protégez-vous ?

— Je veux voir mon avocat.

— Qu'on le remette dans sa cellule.

— Vous n'avez pas le droit ! protesta Déziel.

Duval reprendrait l'interrogatoire un peu plus tard.

59

Duval descendit les marches qui menaient au sous-sol de l'église Saint-Charles-Garnier. Des cartons colorés avec des messages pastoraux tapissaient les murs de l'escalier : « Jésus t'aime », « Jésus pardonne ». L'humidité du lieu mordait la chair et indiquait un mauvais drainage. Une lourde fumée se mouvait au plafond, tandis que s'élevait la clameur d'une centaine de voix qui parlaient en même temps. Trois douzaines de tables pliantes étaient alignées d'un bout à l'autre de la salle. Attablés devant leurs assiettes, parents et amis de Michaël évoquaient le garçon disparu.

Duval, qui n'avait pas déjeuné, s'arrêta devant la table du buffet et s'apprêta à garnir une assiette mais changea d'idée. Pas question de jouer les pique-assiettes. Surtout que les buffets funéraires avaient un goût macabre qui l'écœurait. Il se versa un café dans un gobelet de styromousse et balaya l'assemblée du regard.

Tous les jeunes de l'âge de Mathieu s'étaient regroupés autour des tables qui longeaient le mur. Le jeu de la mort, qu'ils avaient trouvé « glamour », pensa Duval, les rattrapait. Comme si Thanatos les avait adoptés : Tod, Angélique, Rosalie, Michaël. Une véritable cuvée de la mort.

Les garçons et les filles avaient tous revêtu leurs habits sombres. Duval les trouvait déjà vieux pour leur âge. Une jeune fille aux cheveux châtains, le visage recouvert d'une voilette noire à mailles fines fixée à un chapeau, tenait une photo de Michaël dans sa main, celle que les parents avaient remise aux intimes de leur fils : le genre de cliché qu'offre le service de photo des grands magasins et qui fait la fierté des parents mais pas des enfants. Sur la photo, Mathieu, en complet-cravate, ressemblait à un enfant modèle, très bcbg, et non pas au rebelle punk qu'il était devenu. Voilà l'image qu'on désirait laisser de lui. Elle était loin de la figure que Duval avait vue dans un logement malfamé de la côte d'Abraham, une corde autour du cou.

Le lieutenant s'approcha de la table. Devant la fille à la voilette, le lieutenant identifia de biais Cantin du fait qu'il était défiguré. L'œil droit s'était affaissé et la moitié du visage refusait d'obéir aux commandes du cerveau. Dire que ce garçon avait été adulé et imité par ses amis ! Le surhomme avait déboulé de la cime.

Le lieutenant s'arrêta pour l'entendre parler, mais Cantin articulait à grand-peine ses phrases. Duval nota, malgré la laideur, une certaine ressemblance entre le garçon aperçu la veille et le jeune Gabriel. Mais le phénix *bleaché* avait perdu toute la prestance qui lui donnait aura et influence.

La jeune fille au côté de Cantin se leva et Duval, l'index relevé, l'intercepta du regard. La brunette aux traits fins et à la bouche en forme de cœur avait recouvert sa tête d'un châle noir et d'une fine dentelle.

— Bonjour, mademoiselle ; lieutenant Duval. Je m'excuse de vous déranger dans ces circonstances, mais j'ai quelques questions à vous poser.

— Vos amis étaient au service.

— Je sais, mais j'ai un portrait-robot à vous montrer.

Toutes les conversations cessèrent. Leurs regards semblaient paralysés par ce qu'ils allaient découvrir. Duval lui remit le dessin.

— Connaissez-vous ce garçon ? Il a assisté aux funérailles de Rosalie Nantel, hier.

Elle scruta attentivement le dessin et le passa à un camarade qui portait un foulard rouge en soie et une bague argentée montrant une tête de cobra.

— On dirait Ian-Antoine, un ancien du Séminaire.

— C'est Ian-Antoine, confirma la fille à la voilette.

— Quel est son nom de famille ?

— Maranda, répondit un garçon en complet Pierre Cardin.

Les lettres I.A.M., au bas de la dédicace à Angélique, clignotèrent comme des néons dans le cerveau de Duval.

— Voulez-vous dire qu'il a quelque chose à voir dans tout ça ? demanda la brunette en jouant avec son col drapé.

Duval ne répondit pas et leur retourna une question.

— Comment se comportait-il à l'école ?

Chacun y alla en vrac d'un commentaire.

— Il a failli être renvoyé pour indiscipline ou quelque chose du genre, argua bouche-en-forme-de-cœur. C'était un timide qui a fini par sortir de son cocon. Mais il avait des troubles de comportement. Il était antisocial de nature et ce trait de caractère le rattrapait. Il n'acceptait pas d'être contredit.

— De toute façon, il n'était pas assez fort pour le programme, laissa tomber une blonde.

— Vous vous rappelez, il avait fait des avances à Angélique, laissa échapper la jeune brune bcbg.

Cobra, qui avait les cheveux noir corbeau lissés avec du gel, en rajouta.

— Il avait aussi un œil sur Rosalie. Ça faisait bien rire Michaël. Pauvre Spleen ! C'est le nom que lui donnait Michaël.

— Elles l'avaient reviré de bord, ponctua la blonde.

Énervée, la brunette renversa son verre de café noir. Elle venait de faire le lien.

— Ah ! mon dieu ! C'est pas vrai ! Vous pensez…

— Il était aux funérailles, hier. Il pleurait… dit la blonde.

— Comment se comportait Déziel avec lui ? reprit Duval.

Cobra balaya d'une main sa chevelure et prit le relais.

— Distant. Il ne s'en occupait pas. Il aurait préféré ne pas l'avoir dans sa classe. Il le trouvait emmerdant. L'autre vouait un véritable culte à Victor.

Le voisin de Cobra, les cheveux ras et la tête engoncée dans son veston Pierre Cardin, se délia la langue.

— Tu te rappelles, Ian-Antoine s'est présenté un jour dans notre cercle de discussion.

— Gabriel l'avait une fois humilié à propos d'une histoire de courant philosophique, reprit la blonde. Il le détestait.

Quand il entendit son nom, Gabriel Cantin, alias Styx, se remémora l'épisode et s'esclaffa comme un être des profondeurs dont le rire surgit de façon mécanique.

Bouche-en-cœur-et-cils-au-vent intervint.

— En philo, il avait réussi à se faire admettre dans la classe de Victor. C'était un programme d'élite. Durant les cours, Victor lui faisait la vie dure. Il lui posait des questions vicieuses et l'autre ne savait pas quoi répondre. C'était un véritable exercice d'humiliation.

— Est-ce que les étudiants s'en prenaient à lui ?

— Oui, dit Cobra. Tout au long de son secondaire au Petit Séminaire, Ian-Antoine a souvent été la cible de railleries. Quand il est arrivé au collégial, il passait toujours pour un bizarre qui faisait jaser. Mais après sa première année au collège, il a changé. Il avait pris du muscle, grandi. Il avait un air intimidant, supérieur, mais demeurait tout aussi sauvage, inadapté. Il ne parlait pas. On aurait dit un fasciste : chemise noire, cheveux courts. Sur la piste de danse du Fuzz, il intimidait tout le monde. Il adorait *slammer* et cognait sur tout ce qui bougeait. Il était pire que Gabriel, à qui il essayait de ressembler. C'est ce qu'on trouvait.

— Il avait un air de conquérant, ajouta Bouche-en-cœur.

— On aurait dit un Zarathoustra ! dit la fille à la voilette.

— Dans le cours de français, il s'est passé quelque chose avec madame Belzile, parce qu'il a été suspendu deux semaines, se rappela la brunette.

— Qu'est-ce qui est arrivé ?

— Ce qu'on sait, poursuivit-elle, c'est que madame Belzile, la prof, a été très affectée. Je l'ai vue pleurer le jour où Ian-Antoine est retourné en classe. Faut dire qu'il était fort en lettres et qu'il l'affrontait tout le temps. Ce matin-là, devant la porte de la classe, elle a eu une longue discussion avec le directeur des études avant que le cours commence.

— Mais qu'est-ce qu'il lui a fait, à ce professeur ? demanda Duval.

Bouche-en-cœur-et-cils-au-vent leva un index qui annonçait qu'elle se rappelait.

— Je crois qu'elle s'est sentie menacée par lui.

Duval comprit que Maranda n'aimait pas voir des femmes commenter ce qu'il considérait comme une chasse gardée masculine.

Gabriel, qui avait peine à articuler, catapulta quelques mots à grand-peine. Entre deux syllabes, il sifflait comme un serpent.

— Au... dé... but du s'... condaire, il s'... faisait ap... pe... ler Peau-d'... satin... Ses oues... es... semblaient à elles d'un... bé... bé. Tout... monde le ca... essait à la blague. Et appelez-vous... l'inisation...

Un rire sadique émergea des profondeurs de son cerveau malade. Ailleurs, un silence gêné se répandit. Personne ne voulait parler. Duval sentit que Styx était allé trop loin.

— Racontez maintenant.

— Il voulait faire partie de notre groupe de discussion, dit Cobra.

— Le cercle Thanatos ?

— Comment ça que vous êtes au courant ? demanda la tête rase.

— On me paie pour ça.

— On l'a initié : une sorte de bacchanale, reprit Cobra. On avait déguisé un de nos amis en femme. L'illusion était parfaite. Maranda s'est fait prendre les culottes à terre. Et on s'est rendu compte qu'il avait un minuscule zizi et la rigolade a pris. Et on ne l'a plus jamais revu.

— Qui était cet ami déguisé ?

Devant Duval se dressa un mur de silence et les regards devinrent fuyants.

— Qui était-ce ?

Brunette bcbg finit par lâcher le morceau.

— Michaël.

— L'illusion était parfaite. Michaël avait des traits androgynes, confessa à son tour la blonde, qui posait en caressant l'ourlet de son oreille gauche.

Duval eut envie de les féliciter pour cette mise en scène qui avait sans doute contribué à faire de Maranda, de frustration en frustration jusqu'à la psychose, ce qu'il était devenu. Ian-Antoine Maranda qui revenait hanter ses anciens amis. Un autre silence sale de remords s'installa.

— Et pourquoi il a été viré ?

— On ne l'a jamais su, conclut Cobra en lissant sa chevelure vers l'arrière.

Les visages des survivants du cercle Thanatos s'étaient figés comme ceux d'un vieux film muet qui vient de se rompre. « Et si vous étiez la prochaine victime ? » avait envie de lancer Duval.

— Comment était Déziel comme professeur ?

Il s'ensuivit une bouillabaisse de compliments :

— Victor est génial ! C'est le meilleur professeur de philo ! Il a une approche originale. Il connaît tout. Contrairement aux autres profs, il est resté jeune tout en ayant la connaissance d'un sage.

— Connaissez-vous Dahlia Héroux ?

Un chœur spontané de « non » convainquit Duval qu'ils ne la connaissaient pas, ce qui voulait dire que la vengeance de Maranda pouvait se poursuivre sur un autre front que celui des anciens tortionnaires du collège. Rosalie lui avait dit non, et elle était morte. Angélique s'était-elle vraiment suicidée ou avait-on simulé un suicide comme pour Mathieu ? Elle aussi semblait avoir dit non à Ian-Antoine. Écarté également du cercle Thanatos, Maranda en était sorti cassé dans son orgueil démesuré alors qu'il était un expert de la mort. C'était lui le vrai pape noir qui aurait dû officier dans le cercle Thanatos.

— Je vous demande de vous tenir prêts à venir faire une déposition sous serment.

— Si on vous comprend bien, Ian-Antoine serait le meurtrier...

— Il est notre suspect numéro un.

Duval prit leurs numéros de téléphone et les remercia. Décidément, cette assemblée avait un goût morbide.

60

Duval contacta Bernard par radio pour lui demander de vérifier immédiatement si le nom de Ian-Antoine Maranda figurait parmi les étudiants inscrits au programme de littérature, et surtout dans une classe de lettres à la session d'automne 1979 à l'université.

— Le cours s'intitule *Les Symbolistes*. Le professeur s'appelle Louise Riendau.

— C'est sérieux comme piste ?

— Oui. Très. Maranda suit un cours de littérature.

— Comment je fais ? C'est samedi. Tout est fermé à l'université.

— Tu réveilles le recteur s'il le faut. Tu fais un appel à la sécurité, mais je veux la réponse d'ici une heure.

— OK !

À la hauteur de la rue Moncton, Duval reçut un appel de Louis. La chanson *That's the Way I Like It*, de KC and the Sunshine Band, jouait en arrière-fond dans le bureau.

— J'ai joint le directeur général, qui a fait sortir Boutin du lit. Une fois que je l'ai eu en ligne, je lui ai dit qu'il recevrait tous ses rendez-vous de lundi dans une cellule s'il continuait de jouer les carpes. Il doit se présenter au poste à 13 h.

— Louis, je ne veux plus voir Boutin, mais je veux absolument parler à Laure Belzile. Elle était prof de littérature au collège. Appelle Boutin pour lui demander son numéro. Ne cherche pas à comprendre.

— Mais tu te plains sans cesse de ne pas pouvoir discuter avec Boutin !

— Fais ce que je te dis. Toujours pas de nouvelles de la fille qui est disparue ?

— Oui. Je viens de recevoir sa fiche de disparition. Elle étudiait en littérature à l'université.

— En littérature ? Dis-le à Bernard. Demande-lui de vérifier si son nom est sur la liste de Louise Riendau, le cours s'intitule *Les Symbolistes*. Il s'occupe de cette piste.

— Oui, boss.

— Sait-on autre chose sur la fille ?

— Aucun antécédent de fugue. Une bonne petite fille de Saint-Louis-de-France. Un peu rebelle mais pas en guerre avec ses parents.

— J'arrive.

Duval pensa alors que son samedi en compagnie de Laurence était fichu. Il ne leur restait plus qu'à espérer, malgré leurs horaires de fou, un petit dimanche tranquille.

◆

En prenant d'assaut son bureau, Duval avait l'air d'un chien affamé qui a flairé un bon morceau. Derrière un monticule de dossiers, Louis lui tendit le mémo avec le numéro de téléphone de Laure Belzile.

— Elle habite à Moncton.

Duval, téléphone à la main, faisait les cent pas. Pendant qu'il attendait la communication, il se tourna vers Louis.

— Il s'appelle Ian-Antoine Maranda : I.A.M.

Le Gros ne pigeait pas.

— Les initiales dans le vieux livre d'Angélique ! Il est aussi sur la liste 5514. La même classe que Mathieu.

Après cinq sonneries, une voix répondit.

— Madame Belzile… Ici le lieutenant Duval, de la Sûreté du Québec… Ne vous inquiétez pas, il n'est rien arrivé de grave à un de vos proches. Vous avez enseigné au Petit Séminaire de Québec… On m'a dit que vous aviez eu des problèmes avec un certain Ian-Antoine Maranda… Pouvez-vous me dire ce qui s'est passé ?

Longue pause. Respiration angoissée. Et le début d'une crise à l'autre bout.

— Écoutez, monsieur, si je suis à Moncton aujourd'hui, c'est justement parce que vous n'êtes pas intervenu à ce moment-là. Appelez la psychologue du collège, Simone Labbé, elle va vous raconter tout ce que j'ai enduré, parce que Boutin, lui, va tout nier. Mais moi, après l'humiliation que j'ai vécue, je ne tiens plus à parler de cette histoire. C'est à elle à parler.

— Vous avez son numéro ?

— Il est dans le bottin du Séminaire.

— Je veux son numéro personnel. Comme c'est samedi… Vous pouvez me le donner ? C'est important.

— Un instant.

Au bout d'une minute, elle donna à Duval le numéro de téléphone de la psychologue et raccrocha dans l'oreille de l'enquêteur.

Francis entra. Duval lui lança le bloc-notes.

— Tiens, tu nous organises un rendez-vous immédiatement avec elle.

— Où ?

— N'importe où. Dans son lit, s'il le faut… mais de préférence à son bureau…

— Il me semblait que l'État n'avait rien à faire dans la chambre à coucher des citoyens…

— Nous, on est payés pour ça.

Francis leva l'index.

— J'avais oublié…

◆

La pièce offrait une vue splendide sur les élévateurs à blé du port de Québec. Le bureau était tapissé d'affiches produites par les ministères de la Santé et de l'Éducation. Francis, dont les hématomes prenaient une teinte compote de pommes, présenta Duval qui affichait, lui, ses blessures fraîches. On eût dit deux boxeurs au lendemain d'un combat de seize rounds avec George Foreman. Simone Labbé, la psychologue, les dévisagea, la mine horrifiée. Elle les invita à prendre place autour de la table ronde. Au centre, de gros lys en plastique s'élevaient dans un vase bleu.

— Vous avez passé tous les deux un mauvais quart d'heure, on dirait.

— Une mauvaise semaine, vous voulez dire, lança Duval d'une voix neutre.

Simone Labbé, la mi-quarantaine, enchaînait cigarette sur cigarette, café sur café, enroulait et déroulait sur son index ses longs cheveux cassés, poivre et sel. Lorsqu'elle ne parlait pas, elle avait un sourire tombant comme ceux des clowns tristes. Elle était en poste dans cet établissement depuis quinze ans.

La seule mention du nom de Ian-Antoine Maranda par Francis au téléphone avait fait dire à Labbé : « J'ai toujours pensé que ce cas-là nous rebondirait un jour en pleine face. » Et dire que Francis n'avait même pas mentionné les mots « suspect pour meurtres ».

Elle avait pris la peine de sortir le dossier de Ian-Antoine Maranda, qui n'avait rien d'une feuille de chou. Elle n'avait même pas eu besoin de feuilleter la liasse de documents pour se rappeler le cas.

— Je viens de parler à madame Belzile, qui a eu des ennuis avec Maranda.

Elle déroula la couette de cheveux autour de son index.

— Écoutez, j'ai tout fait pour appuyer Laure dans cette affaire. La crise a commencé à cause d'un texte écrit par Ian-Antoine, une véritable levée des inhibitions : dans l'histoire, un professeur de littérature incompétent est écrasé sous une bibliothèque. Le personnage de sa fiction, une femme, ressemblait trop à Laure, qui est handicapée. Le titre m'avait marquée : *Le Poids des mots !* On sentait dans cette nouvelle beaucoup de hargne à l'égard des femmes : Ian-Antoine insistait sur leur incapacité à comprendre l'univers masculin. Laure est féministe et n'hésite pas à dénoncer au passage la misogynie de certains écrivains. Elle met au programme des textes d'auteures féministes. Elle dérange ! Vous comprendrez que le discours réactionnaire d'Ian-Antoine passait mal, d'autant plus qu'il appuyait avec arrogance son discours sur ceux de grands écrivains. Son texte comportait aussi des menaces implicites que le professeur a prises au sérieux. Elle est venue me consulter en état de choc.

Elle s'arrêta un instant et Francis la relança :

— Et que s'est-il passé ?

— Ian-Antoine Maranda se préoccupait à peine d'atténuer son look punk dans une institution où la tradition exige une bonne tenue. Son allure inquiétait le professeur. Sa plainte a été adressée au directeur général. Laure a exigé que l'étudiant soit filé par la police, mais la direction l'en a dissuadée. Le directeur prétendait qu'il ne pouvait rien faire d'autre que de semoncer Ian-Antoine. On était en pleine campagne de recrutement et il lui a expliqué que mêler la police à cette histoire ternirait la renommée de l'institution. Vous devez aussi connaître une autre donnée importante. On fonctionne par inscriptions et il en coûte cher aux parents pour envoyer leur enfant dans notre école. La concurrence est féroce. En plus, on n'est pas syndiqués, ici. Le personnel ne bénéficie pas de la sécurité d'emploi qu'offrent les cégeps publics. Pour maintenir sa clientèle et la qualité de l'enseignement, le Séminaire a besoin de généreux donateurs. Si vous fouillez dans l'annuaire de la fondation du collège, vous verrez que, d'année en année, le beau-père d'Ian-Antoine a été un important mécène : 5 000, 7 000, 10 000 $ par année. Il était fier que son fils appartienne à ce nouveau programme d'élite.

Elle prit un air implorant.

— Ne dites pas que je vous ai donné cette information. Monsieur Maranda a étudié dans notre école et ne jure que par le Séminaire. C'est un fils d'ouvrier qui a réussi grâce à une bourse. Vous comprenez que le poids de son argent vaut plus que le poids d'une plainte de professeur. J'ai appuyé Laure de mon mieux à l'époque, mais Boutin m'a dit de ne pas faire de zèle. Dans le cas d'Ian-Antoine Maranda, il fallait protéger ses droits à la liberté d'expression. Si j'avais su… En fait, Boutin craignait que l'affaire ne devienne publique et redoutait une poursuite. Il pensait que les arguments du collège ne tiendraient pas en face d'un bon criminaliste : Ian-Antoine avait écrit une œuvre littéraire au même titre que ses idoles. J'ai eu beau rédiger des rapports avec les mises en garde d'usage, ça n'a rien donné.

— Pour protéger la réputation de l'établissement, la direction a donc étouffé l'affaire, résuma Duval.

Il comprenait pourquoi Boutin l'avait niaisé depuis le début. La réputation de l'école pesait plus lourd dans sa balance que la sécurité du personnel.

— La direction a suspendu momentanément Ian-Antoine du cours de Laure et, comme il réussissait très bien en français, il n'a pas eu de problème à passer son examen. Il a même refusé de s'excuser.

— Tout ça au nom de la liberté d'expression ! railla Francis.

— Je sais, c'est totalement aberrant, affirma Simone Labbé.

Elle enroulait et déroulait ses cheveux à une vitesse folle. La psychologue alluma au bout de ses lèvres gercées une autre cigarette avec le mégot précédent taché de rouge à lèvres. Puis elle aspira à fond et expira un voile de fumée qui l'embruma.

Francis chassa discrètement le nuage de la main.

— Et comment a réagi le professeur ?

— Laure n'a jamais accepté qu'on le réintègre dans sa classe. Elle a pris un congé de maladie puis elle a démissionné à la fin de l'année. L'affaire s'est tassée en laissant un goût amer à tout le monde. Quelque temps après, j'en ai reparlé à Boutin. J'aurais voulu qu'on

avertisse les parents, mais comme le garçon avait dix-
huit ans à l'époque, la direction ne pouvait même pas,
pour des raisons légales, communiquer avec ses parents
pour savoir ce qui se passait dans sa vie. On a essayé
d'en parler à Victor Déziel, mais il nous a rembarrés
en disant que, contrairement à la rumeur qui courait
dans le département, ce n'était pas son fils.

— Oh ! oh ! Un instant. Vous allez trop vite. Vous
me dites que Ian-Antoine Maranda serait le fils de
Victor Déziel ?

— C'est ce que le garçon croyait. Victor a été marié
à la mère de Ian-Antoine il y a longtemps. Le garçon
s'était créé un mythe avec cette histoire. Il s'identifiait
beaucoup à Victor, qui lui refusait toute affection alors
qu'il l'accordait facilement aux autres élèves qui l'adu-
laient. Victor affirmait que son ex-femme, qu'il décrivait
comme une névrosée, en avait l'entière responsabilité.
Il ne reconnaissait pas la paternité de Ian-Antoine. Il
l'a élevé pendant les cinq premières années de sa vie.
Puis il est parti. Victor disait que ce fils était le fruit
de la manipulation d'une femme qui l'avait conçu à son
insu avec un autre homme et que, pareil à la mère, il
empoisonnait sa vie. Son ex-femme s'est remariée
alors qu'Ian-Antoine avait douze ans. À plusieurs reprises, selon Victor, elle avait refusé que son nouveau
mari passe un test de paternité. Le beau-père adoptif,
monsieur Maranda, était apparemment toujours absent.
Comme Ian-Antoine continuait d'idolâtrer Victor, un
professeur très populaire, j'espérais que Vic puisse
l'approcher. Après son refus d'intervenir, je me suis
refusé à abdiquer, car je pensais que ce garçon avait
besoin d'un suivi clinique, et qu'il pouvait peut-être
même représenter un danger. Je l'ai reçu trois fois en
entrevue. Il prenait déjà des neuroleptiques et je sais
qu'il était affecté par des encéphalites. Il était suivi

par un psychiatre, le docteur Moisan, qui pratique à Robert-Giffard. Ian-Antoine craignait qu'on l'enferme un jour, mais il ne se croyait pas fou. J'avais aussi remarqué qu'il ne supportait pas le refus. Il détestait qu'on lui dise non. Je savais qu'il faudrait un jour envisager d'autres traitements. Après ma série de rencontres, j'en avais rediscuté avec Boutin. Il m'a menacée. Il ne fallait surtout pas en parler au beau-père. Il ne restait que quelques semaines avant la fin de la session. Il fallait tenir ça mort. Gardez ça pour vous, lieutenant, mais Boutin est un ami et un ancien confrère de classe de monsieur Maranda.

Elle réfléchit, expira sa fumée, écrasa sa cigarette en la tordant plusieurs fois.

— J'ai su que la mère biologique d'Ian est décédée il y a près d'un an. C'est le genre de choc qui peut entraîner un déraillement psychologique.

Duval nota la dernière phrase dans son calepin. Il se retint de lui révéler qu'on recherchait Ian-Antoine pour meurtres.

— Je veux l'adresse de Maranda.

Elle en releva deux au dossier : celle du chemin Saint-Louis, chez ses parents, où Duval s'était déjà rendu, et la plus récente, au 126 de la rue Saint-Réal.

— Chaque année, on fait une fête pour les anciens et son père nous a donné cette adresse dans Saint-Jean-Baptiste.

La rue Saint-Réal, nichée au sommet du coteau et qui offrait une vue sur les immeubles de la côte d'Abraham, était située à proximité du squat de Mathieu.

Duval s'empara du téléphone. Qu'avait à dire Déziel pour sa défense ? Le répartiteur établit le contact téléphonique avec l'agent responsable de la garde à vue. La voix granuleuse de Déziel résonna dans le combiné. Duval n'y alla pas par quatre chemins :

— Ian-Antoine Maranda, ce nom vous dit quelque chose ?

Un long silence d'étonnement s'ensuivit, puis :

— Un garçon discret. Il ne fréquentait pas le cercle, si c'est ce que vous voulez savoir, quoiqu'il ait adopté un look très marginal au fur et à mesure de ses études. Je crois que son attitude bizarre et sa timidité étaient un repoussoir pour les autres. En classe, il ne parlait pas. Ce que j'ai remarqué par la suite, d'une session à l'autre, c'est qu'il s'est mis à s'entraîner comme un fou pour passer peu à peu d'une constitution frêle à une colonne de muscles. Il a gagné en assurance. Il se donnait des airs supérieurs.

— Et vous me dites qu'il n'avait rien à voir avec le cercle Thanatos ?

— Non.

— Et avec vous ?

— Qu'est-ce que vous voulez insinuer, lieutenant ?

— Pourquoi cachez-vous votre paternité ?

— Nuance ! C'est le fils de ma première femme, pas le mien. Un enfant qu'elle a eu dans mon dos. Elle a toujours prétendu que c'était le mien pour me mettre l'enfant dans les pattes et me soutirer de l'argent avant de marier un riche commerçant.

Déziel s'impatienta et coupa court au sujet de Ian-Antoine.

— Quand allez-vous me sortir d'ici ?

— Monsieur Déziel, avez-vous l'impression que Ian-Antoine aurait pu commettre ces meurtres ?

— Non. Et je veux voir un avocat ! vociféra le professeur.

Il raccrocha.

Simone Labbé écarquilla les yeux en entendant le mot meurtre. Elle alluma une autre cigarette, les deux yeux louchant vers le foyer qui rougeoya.

Duval se tourna vers elle.

— Je vais vous demander de faire une déposition. Votre évaluation psychologique de Ian-Antoine est très importante.

— Oui, mais je risque…

— Pour ce qui est de la fondation, je vais mener l'enquête moi-même, ce qui ne vous impliquera pas.

— D'accord.

— Après ça, Boutin a besoin d'avoir un bon fonds de pension, remarqua Francis.

Les deux hommes remercièrent Simone Labbé et se lancèrent sur la piste de Maranda.

Le lieutenant communiqua avec Dallaire pour l'obtention du mandat de perquisition.

— On tient notre gars !

Il refila les deux adresses de Maranda à Dallaire et l'informa des soupçons qui pesaient sur Maranda.

— Demande au service de l'Identité de vérifier si Ian-Antoine Maranda possède un dossier judiciaire.

— Compte deux heures pour le mandat.

— D'ici là, on fait de la surveillance. J'envoie Louis et Bernard au 126, rue Saint-Réal. Moi, je me rends avec Francis à la résidence familiale.

61

Duval roula lentement dans un secteur boisé et sinueux du chemin Saint-Louis. Francis le suivait. Duval ralentit et repéra l'adresse des Maranda sur un écriteau blanc. Pour se rendre à la maison, il fallait emprunter une pente boisée, mais il clignota à gauche dans une rue adjacente. Il préférait garer la voiture ailleurs pour ne pas attirer l'attention. Francis l'imita. Alors que le lieutenant s'apprêtait à descendre de l'automobile, la voix de Bernard retentit à la radio.

— Daniel, tu as du flair. Maranda est bel et bien inscrit dans la classe de littérature de madame Riendau. On vient de recouper les renseignements de Granger. Elle habite au 42, rue de la Suète, à Sainte-Foy.

— Excellent, Bernard !

La chaîne blanche qui interdisait habituellement l'accès au terrain reposait sur le sol. Un raidillon en terre battue, magnifique et longue allée tapissée de feuilles mortes, serpentait entre arbres et fougères jusqu'au portique. À travers les ramures, au loin, la silhouette d'une maison cossue se détachait. Francis s'amena aux côtés de Duval et le lieutenant remarqua de nouveau les sucettes dans son cou.

— Tu as soupé avec ta belle Française ?

— Finalement, elle est née ici, de parents français.

— Vous avez passé une belle soirée ?

— Mes plaies me font déjà moins mal…

La colossale résidence à deux étages, tout en pierre, s'imposa bientôt à eux, massive et grise. C'était le genre de maison, avec son toit mansardé, sa rotonde, ses lucarnes et ses fenêtres à carreaux, qui aurait plu à Laurence, pensa Duval. Le bâtiment patrimonial avait été construit au siècle dernier : un arboretum entourait la construction. Le terrain de cent mille pieds carrés s'étendait jusqu'au cap et surplombait le fleuve. Duval appuya sur la sonnette. Rien ne semblait avoir bougé depuis la dernière fois. Aucun signe de vie à l'intérieur. Il regarda par les fenêtres, mais les draperies brunes l'empêchaient de distinguer quoi que ce soit.

Il sonna une seconde fois. Dans le stationnement était garée une Mercedes 450 SL. Duval trouvait étrange que la voiture soit là et qu'il n'y ait personne dans la maison. Il se pencha. Des ornières montraient clairement qu'un autre véhicule stationnait habituellement à côté de la Mercedes. Tapie sous les arbres, une petite maison, probablement celle qui était réservée à l'origine aux domestiques, semblait à l'abandon. Dans le garage adjacent à la maison, un véhicule avait été recouvert d'une bâche noire. Il s'agissait d'une compacte. Était-ce la BMW dont il avait goûté la portière ?

— Qu'est-ce qu'on fait ? demanda Francis.

— On fait le tour.

Duval leva la tête vers les lucarnes. Un bref instant, il crut voir bouger les draperies. Francis examina la boîte aux lettres et n'y trouva rien. Pendant que celui-ci patrouillait le boisé, Duval arpentait les abords de la résidence. Cette propriété devait bien valoir dans les 300 000 $. La piscine, à moitié remplie d'une eau limoneuse, était jonchée de feuilles et de branches mortes. Un ballon rouge dérivait à la surface.

L'endroit était complètement isolé par les arbres. C'était la campagne en ville. À l'arrière, un solarium ménageait une vue imprenable sur le fleuve. Duval arpenta la véranda, mais les lourdes tentures ne lui permettaient pas, là non plus, d'entrevoir l'intérieur. Il retourna au stationnement et découvrit Francis en train de fouiller dans les ordures.

— En tout cas, on ne mange que du surgelé dans cette maison. Regarde, c'est juste des plats Swanson, des boîtes de conserve, des pizzas.

Francis remarqua une bouteille de Winstrol, un stéroïde pour chevaux, ce qui expliquait la masse de muscles de Maranda. Puis il referma le couvercle de la poubelle.

— Qu'est-ce qu'on fait maintenant ? demanda-t-il.
Duval se gratta la tête.

— Je suis très inquiet du sort de Dahlia.

Duval hésitait entre continuer de faire le guet chez Maranda et se rendre chez le professeur Riendau.

— Puisqu'elle n'habite pas très loin, je vais aller chez madame Riendau. Reste ici. Je reviens dans une trentaine de minutes.

Duval jeta un dernier coup d'œil aux fenêtres. Il ne lui restait plus qu'à remonter la pente jusqu'à sa voiture.

La voix de Dallaire se fraya un chemin dans le grésillement de la radio.

— Salut, Daniel, on n'a rien dans nos dossiers contre Maranda.

— Maranda n'est pas à la résidence du chemin Saint-Louis. Je vais rencontrer le professeur de lettres de l'université.

— Bernard vient d'arriver dans la rue Saint-Réal. Ils entendent de la musique à l'intérieur. Une BMW qui correspond à celle que tu as décrite se trouve pas très loin de l'immeuble. En passant, Granger aurait arrêté un suspect dans le meurtre de la prostituée : une affaire de cœur et de stupéfiants.

— Il peut maintenant prendre sa retraite… Il faut craindre une baisse significative dans la résolution de crimes, blagua Duval.

Le grognement du chef en disait long : il n'appréciait pas l'arrogance de ses hommes.

62

Madame Riendau habitait un bungalow dans la paroisse Sainte-Geneviève. Derrière la maison, où s'étendait un terrain d'Hydro-Québec, des pylônes géants piquaient le ciel gris, et les fils qui couraient de l'un à l'autre grésillaient. Râteau à la main, la dame ramassait les feuilles d'automne qui s'accumulaient sous les érables. Elle avait déjà rempli deux sacs verts. La chargée de cours avait revêtu un coupe-vent K-Way bleu et un pantalon tartan. Un labrador noir à la queue folle la suivait partout. Elle s'arrêta un instant lorsqu'elle aperçut Duval marchant dans sa direction.

Le chien, à grandes foulées pataudes, s'élança au-devant du visiteur, qui le caressa.

— Vous êtes madame Riendau ?

— Oui, dit-elle en s'appuyant sur le manche du râteau.

— Je suis le lieutenant Daniel Duval, de la SQ.

Inquiète, la jeune femme fronça les sourcils.

— Rassurez-vous, il n'est rien arrivé.

— Ouf ! Vous m'avez fait peur.

Elle avait le teint d'une femme en santé, mais souffrait d'un léger embonpoint.

— Venez, on va s'asseoir derrière, à la table de pique-nique, dit-elle.

Malgré le couvert de nuages menaçants, le temps frisquet et la brise qui se levait, Duval accueillit l'idée avec plaisir. L'air sentait bon les feuilles. Une porte claqua. Le mari, en chemise à carreaux, s'avança jusqu'à la balustrade du patio. D'un geste de la main, elle lui signala que tout allait bien.

Elle offrit à Duval quelque chose à boire, mais il refusa.

— Madame Riendau, je vais sans doute vous rappeler de mauvais souvenirs en évoquant le nom de Ian-Antoine Maranda ?

Elle prit un air sombre.

— Oh non ! Ne me parlez pas de lui ! Je veux le chasser de mes pensées à tout jamais. J'étais sûre que c'était lui. Vous venez pour le colis suspect ?

— Nous savons qu'il vous a causé des ennuis et il semble qu'il en crée à d'autres. Nous le recherchons. Nous savons aussi qu'il vous a fait des menaces voilées et qu'il vous a envoyé, quoiqu'il n'y ait pas de preuves directes, un fœtus de porc dans une boîte à chaussures.

Elle ferma les yeux au rappel de ce cauchemar.

— Comment était-il en classe ? reprit le lieutenant.

— Bizarre. J'ai tout de suite compris que quelque chose n'allait pas chez lui. J'ai beau me retrouver devant cent cinquante élèves, lui, on ne le manque pas. Ses yeux qui vous scrutent et cet air pincé, hautain… Il me toisait comme une incompétente. Vous ne pouvez pas savoir à quel point il me méprisait. Je donne un cours sur la poésie française du XIXe siècle : il n'aimait pas ma façon d'enseigner. Il me reprenait fréquemment sur des détails insignifiants, il trouvait que j'insistais trop sur Lamartine et pas assez sur Baudelaire. Il levait la main à tout bout de champ ou m'interrompait soudainement sans demander la parole. Imaginez, devant cent cinquante élèves, être constamment corrigée sur des détails. Il connaissait tout de la vie des écrivains maudits, en particulier de Baudelaire, Rimbaud et Lautréamont. À croire qu'il en faisait un culte.

— Vous dites Baudelaire ?

— Oui. Il en était rendu à m'insulter à propos de mes analyses de poèmes. Il me disait devant toute la classe que je n'y comprenais rien, que *Les Fleurs du mal* rejoignaient les hommes et non les femmes, qui n'y voyaient que du romantisme. Il exploitait toute la misogynie baudelairienne dans ses travaux. Je songeais à un congé de maladie pour ne pas avoir à affronter cette classe. Puis, j'ai corrigé sa deuxième dissertation et je n'en revenais pas de la violence de son contenu.

— Vous avez conservé la copie ?

— Oui. Pour illustrer son travail, il avait découpé dans un livre d'art une peinture de Félicien Rops, ami et illustrateur de Baudelaire, où l'on voyait une femme crucifiée. Vous voyez le genre.

Le visage de Duval se figea. Il pensa tout de suite à Rosalie Nantel, les bras en croix.

Elle réfléchit un instant.

— Le travail s'intitulait *Le Jardin de la mort* et il faisait référence aux *Fleurs du mal*. Le propos était réducteur et misogyne, tout simplement inacceptable, mais écrit brillamment. Puis j'ai reçu cet animal putréfié et j'ai demandé l'intervention de la police. Maranda a abandonné le cours, mais on n'a jamais pu prouver que le colis venait de lui. J'enseignais à cent cinquante élèves dans cette classe et à cent vingt dans l'autre.

Le chien s'assit devant Duval.

— Depuis, l'avez-vous revu par hasard ?

— Non.

— Comment se comportait-il avec les autres étudiants ?

— Plutôt distant.

Duval caressa le chien, qui frottait sa grosse tête contre ses genoux.

— Vous le cherchez pourquoi ?

— Vous allez le savoir assez vite par le biais des journaux.

Un gros nuage perça et Duval reçut quelques gouttes sur les mains.

— Madame Riendau, connaissez-vous une étudiante appelée Dahlia Héroux ?

Elle demeura paralysée comme si elle comprenait soudainement la raison de cette visite.

— Dahlia ? Il ne lui est rien arrivé, j'espère ?

— Elle a disparu.

— Elle s'asseyait à côté de lui. Ils sont tous les deux des punks. C'était la seule personne à qui il parlait.

Duval regarda le ciel qui s'apprêtait à vomir ses eaux. Il se leva et remercia la dame. Elle n'affichait plus cette sérénité qu'il avait remarquée en arrivant. La visite d'un policier gâche trop souvent la journée des autres. Métier de mal-aimés. Messager de mauvaises nouvelles.

Une corneille traversa le ciel, croassa trois fois en luttant contre le vent et se laissa déporter au-dessus des pylônes pour se perdre dans l'écran gris de nuages.

◆

Duval frappa dans la vitre embuée de la voiture de Francis. La pluie l'avait forcé à regagner son véhicule. Il écoutait une tribune téléphonique à la radio.

— Puis ? demanda Duval.

— Ils ont annoncé qu'un suspect vient d'être arrêté pour le meurtre de la rue Notre-Dame-des-Anges.

— Je sais.

— En bas, les lumières sont toujours éteintes. Quand il s'est mis à pleuvoir, je suis venu m'abriter dans la voiture. Personne n'est entré ou sorti. Toi ?

— C'est lui, j'en suis sûr à cent pour cent. Il a fait à Riendau la même chose qu'à Belzile. Il faut établir une surveillance vingt-quatre heures sur vingt-quatre. Dahlia Héroux est sa compagne de classe dans un cours de littérature.

La noirceur couvrait la ville. Francis, qui avait pris rendez-vous avec Adèle, ne se voyait pas faire des heures supplémentaires en soirée, mais si Duval l'exigeait, il serait de la partie. Il espérait que l'arrestation de Maranda ne soit plus qu'une formalité. Était-il parti en cavale avec Dahlia? Était-elle la fleur de confiance, celle qu'il protégerait? Maranda n'avait pas toute sa tête mais, comme bien des déments, il faisait preuve d'intelligence et respectait une certaine logique. Il avait cherché à faire passer ses meurtres sur le dos de Mathieu et de Victor Déziel, le faux père qui l'avait renié, humilié, privé d'amour.

— J'ai appelé le patron, reprit Duval. Pas de voiture banalisée avant 20 h, ce qui veut dire que l'un de nous doit faire le guet. Le mandat ne tardera sans doute plus. Tu peux partir.

Duval, qui n'avait pas vu souvent Laurence au cours des derniers jours, s'inquiéta de la réaction de sa douce. Il lui avait gâché sa soirée de la veille et voilà qu'il passait son samedi à faire du temps supplémentaire sous la pluie. Puis il se rappela qu'il n'avait pas encore de texte pour la messe de Louis.

Il demanda à Francis d'appeler Laurence pour lui signaler où en était le déroulement de l'enquête et, par conséquent, son absence.

— Dis-lui qu'on brûle, elle va comprendre.

Francis tapota amicalement l'épaule du lieutenant pour le saluer. Pendant qu'il faisait la sentinelle sur le chemin Saint-Louis, Duval voulut coucher rapidement sur papier quelques phrases pour la messe de Loulou. Puisque le pardon était le thème de la cérémonie, il broderait quelques idées là-dessus, mais le manque d'inspiration freina rapidement ses bonnes intentions. Duval fourra son calepin dans son imperméable. Une pluie fine ruisselait sur le pare-brise. Dans la voiture, l'humidité transperçait les os et il régla la chaufferette au maximum. Il scruta les environs, mais personne ne franchissait l'entrée.

Chuintement à la radio.

— Daniel, c'est Loulou.

— Tu es toujours là ?

— Imagine-toi qu'on a retrouvé dans la rue d'Auteuil une Gremlin vert grenouille qui appartient à Dahlia Héroux. Ses parents paniquent. On a reçu le mandat et on fouille présentement la planque de la rue Saint-Réal, mais il n'y a personne. Toi ?

— Personne en vue.

— Sois prudent. Ton mandat ne devrait pas tarder.

— À tantôt.

Les lampadaires de la rue Saint-Louis émirent une faible lumière qui augmenta peu à peu. Pas question d'attendre le mandat, Duval était prêt à pénétrer à l'intérieur.

63

Il gara le véhicule dans la pente, à mi-chemin de la maison. Quitter la quiétude et la chaleur du véhicule exigeait un effort que la capture de Maranda récompenserait. Dans le boisé, l'obscurité enveloppait les lieux. Il fouilla dans la boîte à gants et pesta contre sa négligence. Il avait oublié d'acheter des piles pour la torche électrique. Il se réprimanda à voix haute : «Tant pis pour toi ! »

Il descendit le chemin. Le vent sifflait en agitant les dernières feuilles, rabattait les branches qui s'éperon-

naient entre elles. Un ciel chargé d'eau déversait ses
trombes. Duval pensa à la messe de Loulou. Les prêtres
devraient bénir les eaux qui tombent du ciel. Noyer le
monde d'eau bénite. Eau de misère. Eau de sang. Mais
ce monde crasseux, où l'on drogue les enfants, vole
et tue son prochain, agresse les femmes sadiquement,
n'avait que faire des goupillons et des chemins de croix
de son enfance. Le monde de la criminalité, comme
l'univers, semblait obéir à la loi de l'expansion.

La résidence se découpa devant lui, sinistre à cette
heure. Une faible lumière perçait de l'une des lucarnes. La pénombre lui permettait de voir ce qui
restait invisible au grand jour.

La voie légale avait trop tardé. Plus question d'attendre. Duval marcha lentement jusqu'à la porte, sonna
et toucha la crosse de son .38. Contact rassurant. Il
appuya une autre fois sur la sonnette. *Niet*. Il vérifia
une à une si les fenêtres du rez-de-chaussée étaient
déverrouillées mais pas de chance. Elles étaient toutes
bien closes.

La pluie redoubla d'ardeur. Le fleuve devant lui
n'existait plus : une tache entre deux rives. Au sud, les
chapelets de lumières épousaient les formes irrégulières
de la raffinerie et la torche qui flambait au sommet de
la structure faisait penser à une montagne russe infer-
nale.

Deux gros lions en ciment gardaient l'entrée de la
façade arrière. Duval monta sur la véranda parée de
boiseries anciennes. Devant la porte noire, il sortit sa
carte de la SQ. La serrure, de qualité supérieure, ne
serait pas une proie facile. Le lieutenant glissa sa carte
dans la rainure de la porte, mais cette dernière comportait deux verrous, ce qui compliqua l'opération lorsqu'il
parvint à sortir le pêne hors de la gâche.

Il contourna la maison, se rappelant avoir vu à
l'étage, du côté est, une fenêtre à guillotine légèrement

ouverte. La tête relevée, il examina les lieux et sou-
pesa ses chances d'y arriver. Après s'être hissé sur le
garage au toit en pignon, adjacent à la résidence, il
pourrait avec une branche ou un râteau pousser sur le
châssis et l'ouvrir davantage. Il scruta le sol du boisé,
repéra une branche assez longue, testa sa résistance,
l'émonda et se dirigea vers le garage. S'agrippant au
larmier, il accéda difficilement à la toiture en bardeaux.
Le toit recouvert de feuilles mouillées était glissant.
Les gouttières étaient encombrées de végétaux : branches, feuilles, samares. Décidément, cette maison de
riches manquait d'entretien. Prudemment, Duval monta
la pente abrupte. Une fois au sommet, il enjamba le
pignon. Il étira le bras et de toute sa force poussa le
châssis avec la branche. La fenêtre offrit beaucoup de
résistance, mais elle remonta pouce par pouce. Au
loin, il entendit une sirène. Il scruta la fenêtre, le mur
en pierres de taille, et se demanda comment il allait
s'y prendre. Il ne lui manquait que trois pieds pour
toucher le rebord de la fenêtre. Ses mains patinaient
sur les grosses pierres détrempées qui n'offraient
aucune prise solide. L'épaisseur du mortier rendait la
tâche difficile. Il tâta les pierres dont les saillies lui
paraissaient les plus sûres et entreprit l'ascension de
la façade.

Le bout d'une chaussure bien calé, il chercha un
appui et s'éleva jusqu'au bord de la fenêtre. La tête la
première, il se glissa sans bruit à l'intérieur. Il détendit
ses phalanges endolories par l'effort. Ses vêtements
mouillés lui collaient au corps. Il crut apercevoir une
ombre, mais c'était le rideau que fouettait le vent. La
pièce baignait dans l'obscurité, mais, sous le seuil de
la porte au bout du corridor, Duval distinguait un faible
rai de lumière. Il sortit son pistolet. Il regarda autour
de lui, appuya sur l'interrupteur du plafonnier. La pièce

servait de chambre d'ami. Duval renifla, intrigué par l'odeur bizarre qui se dégageait de la maison. Il avait l'impression qu'on avait oublié un sac d'ordures contenant de la viande. Il ouvrit la porte lentement.

Le carillon d'une pendule marqua la demie de la septième heure, ce qui lui causa une montée d'adrénaline. Il se figea, seuls ses yeux bougeant. Le tic-tac de l'horloge résonna en contrepoint des battements de son cœur. La gorge serrée, Duval observa les lieux. Son nez frétillait. D'où provenaient ces miasmes ? Un long corridor menait à six autres pièces ; au centre, une échelle abrupte conduisait au grenier. Une table avait été renversée ainsi que le vase de fleurs séchées qui avait dû s'y trouver. Il marcha lentement jusqu'à la salle de bains, leva le bouton de l'interrupteur. Un néon s'alluma par à-coups. La pièce était recouverte de tuiles blanches non lavées depuis longtemps. Un chandelier en bronze reposait sur la tablette de la lucarne.

Dans la poubelle s'accumulaient des produits de beauté : fards, tubes de rouge à lèvres. Sur la tablette vitrée, sous la pharmacie, Duval vit une crème antibiotique prescrite par le docteur Moisan : *Appliquez sur lésions*. Il se rappela le gant de latex que le chien avait découvert dans le cimetière et il établit aussitôt un lien avec l'onguent antidémangeaisons. Il se souvint qu'un odontologiste du labo avait dû cesser de pratiquer la chirurgie dentaire parce qu'il était devenu allergique au latex, plus particulièrement à cette poudre qui permettait d'enfiler les gants plus facilement. Il se demanda alors si c'était le cas du suspect.

La porte de la pharmacie était ouverte. Duval remarqua une boîte de gants de latex Johnson et Johnson. On semblait ne pas s'en être servi souvent. Il prit un flacon de médicaments. Il s'agissait de neuroleptiques, un médicament contre la schizophrénie prescrit par le même docteur Moisan. Le flacon était plein et la prescription datait d'un mois déjà. Trois fioles de Winstrol étaient alignées sur une tablette. À côté, un dentier était plongé dans un verre d'eau. Duval referma l'armoire à pharmacie et chancela en voyant, en surimpression de son image, un message inscrit sur la glace avec du rouge à lèvres.

MY GOD

I AM INSANE

MAD DOG IS INSIDE

GOT MAD

DAMN GOD

L'éclairage au néon rendait son visage blafard. Sous la lucarne, un bain sur pattes, crasseux, n'avait pas été récuré depuis des lustres. Les cernes incrustés dans l'acier levaient le cœur. Poils et cheveux s'enchevêtraient dans la bonde. La pente du bain ne laissait pas s'écouler l'eau totalement. Aucun ménage n'avait été fait là depuis longtemps.

De nombreux insectes, vestiges estivaux, s'étaient abîmés dans l'abat-jour du luminaire. La plante verte, dans la jardinière, avait fané comme toutes les autres. Le temps s'était arrêté dans cette maison.

Duval décida aussitôt d'appeler à la centrale. Ça ne sentait pas bon du tout. Il connaissait trop bien cette odeur, celle qu'un jeune policier n'oublie jamais : l'odeur de la mort qui colle aux tissus et à la peau.

Sur un secrétaire, il repéra un téléphone noir à cadran. Il saisit le combiné, mais n'entendit rien. Il appuya frénétiquement sur le bouton de l'interrupteur. L'absence de tonalité persista. Sa tension et ses fréquences cardiaques grimpèrent d'un cran. Il se surprit à serrer son arme dans le creux de sa main. Les rayures de la crosse s'étaient imprégnées dans sa peau. Décidément, quelque chose clochait dans la baraque de riches.

Il marcha vers la porte sous laquelle filtrait le rai lumineux. Les rideaux l'avaient sans doute empêché de voir la lumière de l'extérieur. L'odeur pestilentielle venait de là. Pour la forme, il frappa doucement, une fois, deux fois. Aucune réponse. Le mort dormait dur. La poignée en verre était verrouillée. Les miasmes putrides qui s'en échappaient laissaient présager le pire. Une musique symphonique sourdait faiblement d'une radio. Seuls les passages *forte* étaient audibles. Duval se pencha pour regarder par le trou de la serrure, mais ne distingua rien. La faible lumière provenait d'une veilleuse en vitrail rouge. Il fouilla dans le fond de sa poche, sortit un trombone, l'enfonça dans la serrure. Quelques mouvements de poignet et la porte s'ouvrit en grinçant. Au pied du lit, il discerna les contours d'une paire de souliers qui reposaient à la verticale. Duval crut d'abord que Maranda s'était suicidé, mais la réalité le rattrapa. Il appuya sur l'interrupteur et ce qui était flou devint un cas de plus pour le coroner. L'état apparent du corps en état de décomposition suggérait un décès remontant à plusieurs jours. Le lieutenant pensa soudainement au *Château de Barbe-Bleue*, ce conte que lui lisait sa mère. À deux mètres de lui, sur le lit, un homme obèse en sous-vêtements pourrissait sur le dos. Des lacérations étaient encore visibles à la hauteur du cou. Il pressentit que cet homme était le tuteur ou le beau-père d'Ian-Antoine Maranda.

Il tourna les talons vers la seule pièce dont la porte était ouverte. Ses lucarnes donnaient sur le fleuve. S'y trouvait une bibliothèque antique, vitrée. Duval chercha à tâtons le commutateur et le releva. Il remarqua qu'on y avait déplacé des livres mais sans essuyer la poussière. D'ailleurs, la poussière flottait partout dans la maison. À l'extérieur, un coup de vent balaya les branches sur la façade avant. Les ramures des arbres ressemblaient à de sombres artères connectant le ciel et la terre.

Il nota sur un secrétaire en merisier des coupures de journaux et de revues, notamment des *comics* dans lesquels on avait prélevé des lettres, comme l'avait déterminé Miljours. Le regard de Duval se posa sur un vieux livre à la couverture rigide. Il le prit et lut avec difficulté les lettres d'or qui avaient résisté aux assauts du temps : *Les Fleurs du mal*. L'exemplaire devait dater du siècle dernier. Dans un compartiment du meuble, une trentaine d'enveloppes au nom de Gérard Maranda n'avaient pas été décachetées. La première lettre avait été postée une quinzaine de jours plus tôt. Plusieurs d'entre elles venaient du même expéditeur et attirèrent l'attention de Duval : Hôpital Robert-Giffard, Hôpital Robert-Giffard, Hôpital Robert-Giffard. Il parcourut rapidement cette correspondance. Il comprit que le beau-père s'était finalement résigné à placer son embarrassant beau-fils. L'hôpital Robert-Giffard confirmait le placement et la date prévue.

D'un regard circulaire, Duval embrassa la pièce. Çà et là, des assiettes encroûtées de sauce n'avaient pas été ramassées. Sur une vaste étagère vitrée se trouvait une collection d'animaux empaillés ou squelettiques : corbeau, geai, faucon, pic, renard, castor et, pièce de résistance, un coyote aux dents acérées. « Tel père, tel fils », pensa Duval. L'odeur âcre, sucrée et capiteuse, devenait insupportable.

À travers la grande fenêtre à carreaux, le fleuve n'était plus qu'une tache sombre pointillée de quelques lumières, celles des timoneries et des bouées.

Le craquement d'une poutre amplifia l'anxiété qui le tenaillait.

L'échelle permettant d'accéder au grenier était recouverte d'un vernis sombre. Le lieutenant y monta, appuya sur l'interrupteur et les combles s'éclairèrent. De vieilles poutres fissurées soulignaient le plafond. Sur le plancher en larges lattes de pin roulait la poussière. La pièce était un véritable musée de mannequins d'étalage ayant appartenu à un ancien chapelier. Des moulages aux visages délavés, à la mode des années quarante et cinquante, le regardaient, figés pour l'éternité sur leurs podiums d'étalage. On aurait dit que cette douzaine de mannequins racontait l'histoire de la mode au vingtième siècle. On les avait coiffés avec goût ou fantaisie : coiffe d'infirmière avec une croix rouge, tambourin, cloche des années folles, capeline, turban. Certains portaient des lunettes aux montures transparentes et anguleuses. Étrangement, le dernier buste était revêtu d'une voilette noire à mailles fines et avait des lunettes fumées semblables à celles de Jackie Kennedy lors des funérailles de son mari en 1963. C'était lugubre et dans le ton général de la maison.

Un grand lit noir à baldaquin, ouvragé par un ébéniste de talent et décoré d'un volant de soie à sa base, frappa l'imagination de Duval. Le rideau de tulle jauni par le soleil dérobait l'intérieur du lit au regard, ce qui ne rassura pas le lieutenant. Il sortit son portefeuille, lourd de toutes ses cartes inutiles, et le lança dans le tissu, qui voleta. Personne ne s'y cachait. Il jeta un coup d'œil sous le sommier. Personne. La poussière s'y accumulait. Duval tira le voile : la literie défaite et souillée lui leva le cœur.

Devant le pied du lit se dressait un miroir ovale sur pied. Dans un coin, près d'une vieille armoire antique, il aperçut le panier en osier pour le linge sale. Il le renversa et un vêtement taché de sang roula sur le plancher, suivi d'un deuxième et d'un troisième.

Puis, il reconnut les vêtements que portait Maranda la veille, sa redingote prétentieuse.

Sur le mur qui faisait face aux mannequins de cha-pelier, on avait suspendu des cadres baroques de photos en noir et blanc. Insolite galerie de portraits où figuraient le Joker de la série *Batman*, Oscar Wilde, porte-cigarettes à la main, et Charles Baudelaire. Le personnage suivant était familier à Duval, car il s'agis-sait de Charles Manson. Entre Baudelaire et Manson, un cliché de Maranda, rouge aux lèvres et fard sur le visage, comme une star du cinéma muet. Il avait pris soin d'accentuer la volute de cigarette, ce qui créait un bel effet. Une image de Gloria Swanson, probablement tirée de *Sunset Boulevard*, s'ajoutait à la série.

Un bénitier, surmonté d'un ange en marbre, était accroché aux côtés de chandeliers baroques et lour-dauds qui provenaient d'une église. Des *ex-voto* devant les lucarnes et des petits lampions complétaient le décor. Le sacré et le profane se chevauchaient là comme sur les scènes de crime. Duval pensa que cette chambre avait tout d'un lieu de cauchemar, une chapelle dé-mente ayant la mort comme divinité.

Le lieutenant se tourna brusquement, effrayé, les sens en alerte. Les branches des arbres grattaient la façade et les fenêtres. Au-dessus de la pièce où se décomposait le cadavre, l'odeur était plus prégnante.

Un candélabre reposait sur la table de chevet. La cire des chandelles s'était consumée au point de re-couvrir totalement le pied du chandelier.

Une vaste collection de disques s'entassait sur deux tablettes fixées au mur de pierre : des disques punk mais aussi de la musique classique. Une chaîne stéréo de grand luxe s'étalait sur le plancher.

Duval ouvrit prudemment la penderie en chêne et y trouva une garde-robe à faire rougir un mannequin.

Soudain la lumière s'éteignit. Le noir complet. Duval se figea, caché derrière le lit. S'agissait-il d'une panne localisée? Mais il ne ventait pas assez fort, pensa Duval. Et il n'avait entendu aucune explosion de transformateur. Quelqu'un avait coupé l'alimentation électrique. Duval chercha des allumettes dans ses poches mais en vain. Il se rappelait en avoir vu dans la salle de bains. À tâtons, frôlant le mur, il se dirigea vers l'échelle, la descendit avec précaution. Il n'y voyait rien. À l'odeur, il sut qu'il ne devait pas aller à droite. Il entra dans la salle de bains et passa sa main à l'aveuglette sur un coin de la tablette de la pharmacie. Un objet tomba et éclata en morceaux: le verre et son dentier. Duval sentit sous ses phalanges le paquet d'allumettes. Il s'en empara, arracha une allumette, la frotta et le soufre étincela sans s'allumer. Trop humide. Il recommença avec une autre, sans plus de succès. Duval se dit qu'il lui fallait sortir de ce guet-apens.

Un bruit sourd comme celui d'une fournaise à l'huile que l'on frappe retentit. Maranda se terrait quelque part dans cette grande maison. Dahlia Héroux était-elle avec lui? Si Maranda avait pu couper l'électricité, il avait sûrement trouvé refuge au sous-sol, pensa Duval. Il déchira la dernière allumette, la coinça entre le grand rabat et le frottoir et la tira d'un geste vif. La flamme chétive s'embrasa lentement et Duval put allumer une à une les chandelles du chandelier à trois branches. Il fallait rester pour aider la jeune fille.

Puis quelqu'un se mit à jouer avec l'interrupteur de la boîte électrique, allumant et éteignant les lumières de la maison. Duval descendit à l'étage en tenant son pistolet fermement d'une main et le candélabre de l'autre. Son ombre lui dessinait une silhouette de criminel avec ce .38 pointé vers l'avant.

Duval tourna à droite, sa main frôlant le mur lui servant de guide.

Il avait une raideur au cou, probablement son ascension de la façade qui le rattrapait.

Un téléphone mural se trouvait accroché près de la porte d'entrée. Duval saisit le récepteur mais n'entendit pas la tonalité. Il regarda tout autour, sans découvrir la porte de l'escalier menant à la cave. Il avait beau chercher, il n'y comprenait rien. Mais il se rappela la maison ancienne de son grand-père à Sainte-Agathe. Il inspecta le parquet en approchant la lumière des bougies. Il distingua une poignée de cuivre encastrée dans une trappe dans le plancher de la cuisine. Il déverrouilla la porte arrière avant de tenter quoi que ce soit. Dans le miroir au-dessus du comptoir, il se vit à travers la lueur des chandelles. Il se pencha au-dessus de la trappe. La vaste superficie de la maison ferait de la cave un piège à chaque pas. Une fois la trappe en lattes de chêne soulevée, il faudrait descendre en enfer. Quant à sortir pour appeler les collègues, c'était un risque pour celle qu'on séquestrait sûrement dans la cave, d'autant plus que la voiture était loin. Mais il ne fallait pas jouer cette partie seul. Encore une fois, l'indécision le torturait. L'horloge sonna huit coups. Pendant le gong, il agrippa la poignée de la trappe et la souleva avec délicatesse. Mais elle résista puisqu'elle avait été barricadée par-dessous. Il se releva. Le tic-tac du pendule recommença tout près de là.

Les bruits devenaient de plus en plus inquiétants. Mais ils avaient quelque chose de faux aux oreilles du détective. Duval déposa le candélabre, passa une main dans ses cheveux.

Il sortit vérifier les soupiraux, mais leur étroitesse interdisait toute tentative de se glisser à l'intérieur. Il retourna dans la cuisine et poussa de tout son corps un gros bloc de boucher, qui faisait au moins cent livres, au-dessus de la trappe. Pendant qu'il réfléchissait à une autre solution, le prince des ténèbres ne sortirait pas du château.

Alors il pensa au garage adjacent à la maison. Il sortit à la course, brisa un carreau d'un coup de crosse et à l'aveuglette déverrouilla la porte. Une lampe de poche, toute petite, était accrochée à un clou. Il la prit et, malgré le pâle faisceau, il aperçut une scie ronde, mais se rappela qu'il n'y avait pas d'électricité. Scrutant fébrilement les lieux avec un sentiment d'urgence, il repéra une vieille hache suspendue au mur. Il la décrocha, mais la lame tomba tandis que le manche lui restait dans les mains. Son regard dévia vers une brouette dont la caisse contenait une vieille scie à chaîne. Il reprit espoir. En dévissant le bouchon, il constata au son et à l'odeur que le réservoir contenait assez d'essence.

Avant de tenter quoi que ce soit, il s'élança dans un sprint fou vers sa voiture. Il laissa rouler le véhicule au neutre jusqu'en bas : il ne voulait pas faire paniquer Maranda, qui risquait de disjoncter et d'achever Dahlia Héroux si, par chance, elle était encore en vie. Avant de sortir du véhicule, il lança un appel à l'aide par radio. Il se hâta de récupérer la scie à chaîne devant la porte de la maison.

Avant d'entrer, il tira sur la poignée du démarreur et l'appareil rota, cracha une poussière bleue et nauséabonde, mais sans démarrer. « Le *choke*. Où est le *choke* ? » se dit-il. Il chercha l'étrangleur, appuya sur la manette. Il tira avec force la corde du démarreur. Même résultat. Il tira de nouveau et l'engin pétarada dans une épaisse fumée. Scie à chaîne à la main, il se dirigea d'un pas enragé vers la demeure.

Duval sentit des papillons dans son estomac. Étrangement, il aimait cette sensation, cet état second. Tous ses réflexes et ses sens étaient affûtés au maximum.

L'ombre de géant qu'il créait faisait peur avec cet engin meurtrier. Le lieutenant déposa prudemment la scie et dégagea brusquement le bloc de boucher. Il appuya sur le levier et la scie rugit davantage. Il se pencha et perça une longue raie dans la trappe, faisant jaillir une gerbe de bran de scie. La lame découpa un deuxième segment. Il entendit un cri strident, mais ne put déterminer à cause du boucan s'il s'agissait de Maranda ou de Dahlia. Ce doute lui redonna espoir de sauver la captive. Il s'attaqua aux troisième et quatrième côtés du carré. L'essence, la fumée bleue et la sciure le firent toussoter.

Alors que tout allait bien, la scie tressauta dans ses mains en crachant une pluie d'étincelles. La chaîne se rompit sur un clou, fusa au plafond et faillit le décapiter. Il laissa tomber la scie à chaîne sur le plancher. Puis, il sauta sur la trappe mais, quoiqu'elle bougeât légèrement, elle refusait de céder. Son regard balaya les lieux à la recherche d'un objet lourd. Dans le passage, un buste en marbre de Duplessis reposait sur une colonne. Duval s'approcha, l'éclaira. L'objet requit toute sa force, mais il réussit à le transporter à petits pas jusqu'à la cuisine. Devant la trappe, il souleva la sculpture le plus haut qu'il put et la laissa choir. La trappe s'affaissa lourdement et le marbre alla débouler l'escalier en fracassant le bois dans un vacarme épouvantable. Duval arracha à coups de pied les dernières planches.

Le calibre .38 bien ancré dans sa paume, il descendit deux échelons abrupts. Il botta les débris éparpillés au milieu des marches branlantes. Rapidement, il scruta les lieux. La lampe de poche ne permettait pas de voir très loin. Les longues poutres crevassées nervuraient le plafond d'un mur à l'autre. La cave était devenue un capharnaüm d'antiquités, bric-à-brac de bourgeois.

Du plancher au plafond s'empilaient des armoires antiques, un harmonium, un sofa recouvert d'un drap blanc, des coffres et des boîtes par dizaines. Duval sursauta en voyant derrière lui un amas de vieux mannequins, bras, jambes, troncs et têtes enchevêtrés, fouillis inextricable. La famille possédait, se rappela Duval, un magasin à rayons. Il y avait aussi de vieux comptoirs vitrés et des caisses enregistreuses, vestiges de la Belle Époque. Une odeur de mazout imprégnait l'air humide. À gauche se trouvait une fournaise à l'huile.

Duval se demanda par où, comment et quand Maranda allait surgir. L'endroit était une fourmilière de recoins, un nid d'embuscades. Quelqu'un haletait. Était-ce la fille ? Maranda ? La montagne d'objets empêchait de voir qui que ce soit, mais les sons provenaient du coin sud-ouest.

Duval descendit les huit marches qui le séparaient de la dalle. Son pied droit toucha le ciment et il se cacha derrière un réfrigérateur. La guerre des nerfs s'intensifia. La tache qu'il vit sur le plancher ne rassura pas. Du sang ou de la peinture ?

— Maranda ! Sors de là ! La maison est cernée.

La voix du lieutenant était assurée et sans appel. Le silence qui suivit mit en évidence le bruit de l'eau qui s'écoulait dans le puisard.

Duval n'aimait pas les odeurs qui se mélangeaient à l'humidité. « Il te faut des yeux tout le tour de la tête », s'avisa Duval. Son postérieur accrocha un objet derrière lui, une porte d'armoire s'ouvrit en grinçant. Il se tourna et son regard se figea sur le miroir de la penderie : ce visage, le sien, trahissait la peur. Il tiqua en voyant un gros crucifix et une étole. Il referma la porte. Tel un commando, il devait avancer jusqu'au bout de cette interminable tranchée. Il envisagea un

certain nombre de scénarios, se prépara mentalement
à réagir. Il éteignit la lampe de poche et s'enfonça de
plusieurs mètres en territoire ennemi.

Soudain, un bruit au rez-de-chaussée attira son attention. Une porte qu'on ouvrait et une masse brinquebalante qui tentait de franchir le seuil. Maranda avait-il
pu remonter ? Les soupiraux ? Impossible. Du renfort ?

Il tourna la tête et se sentit perdre l'équilibre. Des
objets s'affaissaient autour de lui dans un affreux tintamarre. Un objet dur le sonna légèrement. Il eut le
temps de se glisser sous des meubles recouverts de
draps blancs et il rampa. Mais il constata qu'il avait
échappé son arme. Son visage reposait contre la dalle
de ciment. Sa lèvre saignait.

Puis il entendit en haut un bruit bizarre : une masse
qui rampait. Un faisceau lumineux dardait le mur de
ciment. Quelqu'un descendait les escaliers mais péniblement.

— Daniel ? T'es là ?

— Louis. Je suis ici. Méfie-toi. Maranda est quelque
part dans ce foutoir. Probablement le coin sud-ouest.

— Il va falloir que tu m'expliques où est le sud !
railla le Gros.

— Où est le renfort ?

— Pour l'instant, le renfort, c'est moi... J'étrenne
un Mauser, tonna Louis. Je l'ai testé au champ de tir et
ma cible ressemblait à l'homme invisible après deux
minutes.

Duval appréciait l'arrivée de Louis, mais n'aimait
pas l'entendre fanfaronner.

— T'es blessé ? reprit Louis en baissant le ton.

— Légèrement. Va chercher de l'aide.

Aucune réponse. Du Loulou tout craché. Duval
rampa vers le bout d'une table, leva le drap et aperçut
Louis qui descendait les marches sur les fesses en se

tenant avec les mains. Maranda n'était sûrement pas armé, car il aurait sans doute déjà fait feu sur Louis. Le faisceau lumineux de la torche du Gros balaya la cave. Quelqu'un poussa un son strident suivi d'un cri sourd. Duval eut alors la certitude que Maranda jouait en même temps le bourreau et la victime. Le dément avait regagné une position tactique dans le maquis d'objets. Le lieutenant poursuivit sa reptation et le dégoût l'envahit lorsque sa main toucha des cheveux. Mais, à la froideur et à la douceur du visage, il sut qu'il ne s'agissait pas d'un mannequin.

— Maranda, lança Louis, si tu veux pas aller rejoindre tes amis au cimetière, sors de là, les mains en l'air, sinon tu vas jouer pour de vrai avec les poignées de ton cercueil.

— Moi, j'ai pour principe de ne pas toucher aux handicapés.

La voix était hystérique, celle d'un esprit dérangé.

— Moi, je suis payé pour arrêter les handicapés mentaux de ton espèce.

— Je te ferai remarquer, Perry Mason, que j'ai un Q.I. de 140.

— Ton beau petit Q.I., je vais le faire gicler tout partout… M'en vais te le régler, ton problème. Les ambulanciers vont le ramasser à la pelle, ton Q.I. Tu vas être cuit-cuit quand je serai sorti d'ici. J'ai beau prêcher «Tu ne tueras point», là, je sens que le Seigneur me presse de te ramener à Lui. Tu peux pas savoir, fifille, comme tu me répugnes après ce que j'ai vu à la morgue.

Duval n'aimait pas que Louis provoque la bête assassine qui se cachait en face. Traquée à mort, elle n'avait plus rien à perdre.

Des bruits de pas. Une armoire tomba, un miroir se fracassa. Des éclats de verre glissèrent sur le meuble qui protégeait le lieutenant.

— Tu brises les meubles de ta maman, fiston ?

— Amène-toi, gros cloporte.

Duval souhaita voir Louis demeurer au bas de l'escalier alors qu'il se dirigeait vers Maranda, qu'il avait repéré au son. À tâtons, centimètre par centimètre, il continua de ramper, butant contre les objets.

Duval ramassa ce qui lui sembla un éclat de miroir assez tranchant pour s'en faire un couteau. L'éclairage de la torche que Louis orientait vers le mur du fond lui permettrait de repérer, à travers les pattes des meubles, les pieds de Maranda.

— Humpty Dumpty se dégonfle, là-bas ? fanfaronna le désaxé.

— Ton heure a sonné, mon garçon. L'heure où l'on couche les p'tits gars. T'aimes ça, de la charogne ? Je vais te faire manger de la charcuterie avariée.

— Toi, tu dois plus baiser, emmanché comme ça.

— Je connais des gars à Bordeaux qui vont rêver de mettre leur deux par quatre dans ton petit cul de charognard. Tu vas marcher les fesses serrées, ma poulette. À trente ans, tu vas porter des couches extra-absorbantes.

Duval espérait que Louis ne pousse pas Maranda à bout alors qu'il était à moins de dix pieds du prédateur.

— Écoute-toi parler. Tu fais tout faire par tout le monde, gros crisse d'impuissant !

Duval souhaita que Maranda n'entraîne pas Louis dans une escalade où le Gros péterait les plombs. Mais il croyait bien que son collègue avait changé. Louis tentait de gagner du temps avant l'arrivée des renforts. Une sirène retentissait enfin au loin.

Duval déboucha dans l'étroit passage qui permettait de circuler à travers le capharnaüm. Il pensa à Rosalie et Angélique, à Mathieu et à celle qui se trouvait là en ce moment. Il se sentit porté par une force hors du commun. Il se rappela l'image que Louis lui avait re-

mise. Ces enfants massacrés, ou profanés, il les imaginait rampant avec lui et se soulevant contre le monstre.
Duval aurait aimé lui faire subir une terreur égale à
celle qu'il avait infligée à ses victimes.

Le lieutenant avança de quelques pieds pendant que
Louis et l'autre échangeaient des insultes. Il y était
presque. Il lui faudrait surgir sans se tromper. Prendre
une chance. Frapper d'abord les jambes et ensuite
l'achever si nécessaire.

Louis éteignit sa torche. Si Maranda était armé, la
noirceur relative devenait une alliée. Mais que faisaient ses collègues? s'inquiéta Duval. Pourquoi Louis
agissait-il seul? Une manière de lui rendre la pareille
pour l'affaire Hurtubise?

Duval, lui, aurait aimé y voir clair au lieu d'avancer
à tâtons.

— Tu te rends calmement, Maranda, et rien ne t'arrivera, lança Louis.

— Je n'ai rien à gagner à me rendre.

— Un procès.

— Et la peine de mort.

— La peine de mort a été abolie, tu devrais savoir
ça avec ton Q.I. de 140. Si t'es pas apte à subir un
procès, on t'enverra à Saint-Michel-Archange.

— Ça s'appelle Robert-Giffard, maintenant.

Les harmonies funestes des sirènes suggéraient que
les voitures de patrouille étaient à proximité.

Une torche de feu jaillit du coin où se cachait
Maranda et fusa d'un bout à l'autre, puis explosa contre
le mur juste au-dessus de Louis. Une lueur violente
embrasa les lieux. Un cocktail Molotov. Le feu lécha
le plafond jusqu'en haut de la trappe.

Louis dégringola dans l'escalier alors que Maranda
s'élançait à la course. D'un geste vif, le bras du lieutenant, armé de son éclat de verre, surgit de sous une
table pour entailler le mollet du désaxé. Maranda poussa

un cri furieux. Duval sentit le sang gicler dans sa main. Il tenta de s'accrocher à lui, mais l'autre renversa la penderie vitrée, qui s'abattit dans un fracas de verre. La silhouette du dément se découpait à travers les flammes. Il botta le revolver que Louis tenait à la main. Le Gros s'agrippa à lui désespérément alors que l'autre tentait de se hisser dans les marches.

— Je le tiens, Daniel. Viens vite ! Y me varge dessus à coups de pied. Je suis plus capable. Dépêche-toi. Y m'échappe !

— Tiens bon, j'arrive.

Duval se fraya un passage dans l'allée. La fumée devenait insupportable. Ils s'asphyxiaient dans cet espace clos.

Au bas de l'escalier où le feu faisait rage, Louis résistait, mais l'acharnement de l'autre, la démence des coups le fit lâcher prise.

— Vite, y se sauve ! tonna Louis.

Duval enjamba l'armoire, aperçut la crosse de son arme à la lueur du feu. En se penchant pour la ramasser, il entrevit un long bras nu, maculé, et une chevelure rose.

Il repéra Louis, hors d'haleine, près des flammes, le souleva comme un sac de patates : « Accroche-toi ! »

Les lueurs des gyrophares, à l'extérieur, se reflétaient dans les soupiraux.

Dehors, il entendit quelqu'un crier à Maranda : « Hé ! Il y a d'autres personnes là-dedans ? Où vous allez ? Revenez ! »

Le bruit de pas des policiers qui prenaient d'assaut la cuisine rassura Duval.

— Y a quelqu'un ?

— Oui, ici, cria Duval en émergeant de la trappe.

Vision d'apocalypse pour le policier qui grimaça en voyant Louis dont les sourcils avaient roussi. L'agent lui porta secours.

— Ça va aller ?

— Oui, dit le Gros.

Duval déposa Louis dans son fauteuil roulant. Il aurait aimé sortir Dahlia Héroux, mais il craignait que les tablettes remplies de produits chimiques, gallons de peinture, solvants et autres substances, ne s'enflamment rapidement.

— Passe-moi ta lampe de poche, dit-il à Louis.

Duval sortit pour se retrouver face à un policier.

— Où est passé le gars ? s'enquit-il.

— Il a piqué à travers le petit sentier.

— Il y a un corps à l'étage et un autre au sous-sol. Dépêchez-vous avant que tout flambe, dit le lieutenant en s'éloignant. En bas, c'est assez risqué, à cause des produits inflammables.

D'une voix grave, le policier ordonna à ses hommes d'aller récupérer les victimes et appela les pompiers.

Duval se mit à courir vers l'est. Il traversa le boisé qui bordait la maison. Aux glapissements des chiens, il savait que Maranda sautait les clôtures. À ce jeu-là, le lieutenant pouvait courir longtemps et Maranda serait vite hors d'haleine.

Une première clôture blanche lui permit de constater que le fuyard venait de passer par là. Un filet de sang et des empreintes de mains ensanglantées maculaient le treillis. D'autres jappements retentirent devant lui. Duval se hissa à son tour sur la clôture comme s'il courait dessus. Une fois l'obstacle enjambé, il sauta trois mètres plus bas et absorba lourdement le choc de ses quatre-vingt-dix kilos. Il sortit son pistolet, scruta les lieux de ses yeux d'épervier : une piscine qu'on n'avait pas encore vidée de son eau saumâtre, des saules et des bouleaux pleureurs tout autour. La maison, bizarre, avec de grands pans inclinés percés de hublots, ressemblait à un aquarium pour humains.

Derrière l'une des baies, les membres d'une famille ne perdaient rien de la scène. À l'intérieur, un chien aboyait. L'homme éclaira le patio. Du sang. Il ne fallait pas être médecin légiste pour constater que la blessure s'aggravait. L'épreuve du 400 mètres haies se poursuivit sur le terrain adjacent. Duval gravit l'autre clôture, une Frost en broche – il les détestait, celles-là. Combien de fois depuis son enfance s'était-il accroché dans ce modèle !

Un hurlement de femme retentit. Autres jappements. Pourvu qu'il n'y ait pas de prise d'otages, appréhenda-t-il. Des lumières s'allumaient un peu partout. Un effet de dominos lumineux. Il entendit un homme crier au voleur. Le bruit des sirènes qui se rapprochaient le rassura. Derrière la porte-fenêtre d'une maison ancestrale, une famille épiait la justice en action. Duval regarda sur le toit mansardé, très bas.

— Il est parti par là, lui lança une voix sans visage.

Ces immenses terrains offraient de nombreux recoins pour se cacher. Le lieutenant ne comprenait pas pourquoi les voisins ne pouvaient s'entendre sur un modèle de clôture. « Pas une crisse de clôture pareille », pesta-t-il. Celle-ci, en fer forgé, s'apparentait au portail de Graceland. Elle culminait à trois mètres de hauteur. Les longs barreaux éperonnés n'avaient rien de rassurant. Impossible de voir de l'autre côté à cause de la vigne qui les recouvrait. Le lieutenant grimpa et d'en haut il aperçut Maranda, à cinquante mètres, buter contre une haie de cèdres. Le fuyard bifurqua à gauche entre deux maisons. Maranda courait en boitillant. Prudemment, Duval glissa, cramponné à un barreau, puis il piqua à son tour entre les deux résidences. Une petite clôture d'un mètre le séparait de la chaîne de trottoir.

De l'autre côté de la rue, les feux arrière d'une Jaguar s'allumaient dans l'entrée d'une maison. Duval entrevit

Maranda qui fonçait vers la voiture. Le monstre ouvrit la portière et agrippa l'automobiliste pour l'expulser du véhicule. L'homme se retrouva sur le derrière et poussa un juron. Maranda recula le véhicule à une vitesse folle. Il braqua si vite qu'il écrasa les cèdres qui bordaient le stationnement.

La Jaguar accéléra vers l'est. Le lieutenant déboucha enfin dans la rue. La lunette arrière de la voiture était déjà trop distante pour tirer d'un angle convenable. Mais la Jaguar n'irait pas très loin. Deux voitures de police bouchaient les intersections. De puissants phares s'allumèrent au bout de la rue. Les policiers s'étaient postés derrière les portières. À soixante mètres du stop, le fuyard braqua à cent quatre-vingts degrés. Il déborda sur la pelouse d'une résidence, laboura la tourbe, catapultant de longues mottes de gazon sur l'asphalte. Plainte hurlante des pneus sur l'asphalte. Duval se retrouva de biais par rapport aux phares avant de la Jaguar. Il se pencha, tendit le bras, mais, au dernier instant, il refusa d'appuyer sur la détente. Des têtes partout et lui dans l'impossibilité de tirer sans risque ! Trop de ménages suivaient le spectacle de leur perron. Il bondit au milieu de la rue. Il mira de nouveau et visa la lunette arrière qui éclata, ce qui fit hurler des gamins. La voiture avança par à-coups. La Jaguar semblait avoir des ratés, à moins que ce ne fût Maranda qui s'effondrait au volant. La voiture s'immobilisa devant l'entrée d'une maison. Maranda ouvrit la portière. Trop loin de la cible, Duval ne pouvait tirer.

Le lieutenant cavala, donnant tout ce qu'il avait dans un sprint fou. Dans la petite rue tranquille de ban-lieue, les talons résonnaient fortement sur la chaussée. Sur le pavé s'étirait un long filet de sang. Maranda n'en avait plus pour très longtemps, ce qui le rendait encore plus dangereux. La distance d'une maison le séparait du fuyard, qui lui parut de plus en plus chancelant. Quelques secondes encore. C'est alors que Maranda obliqua vers une résidence, y pénétra et claqua la porte. Une clameur s'éleva parmi les témoins de la scène. Duval s'immobilisa, refusant de prendre d'assaut la maison.

Il retraita chez le voisin d'en face, posté dans l'embrasure de sa porte. Duval demanda aussitôt à un quidam sur son perron :

— Qui habite là ?

— C'est le vieux docteur Bélair. Sa dame n'a pas une forte santé.

L'homme dans sa robe de chambre en ratine bleue avait été tiré de la douche. L'eau dégoulinait sur son visage. Tout en l'écoutant, Duval ne quittait pas des yeux la maison d'en face.

Rien de rassurant. On éteignit une à une les lumières du rez-de-chaussée des Bélair. La maison fut plongée dans le noir. Duval se frotta nerveusement le cuir chevelu. Les policiers détestaient les prises d'otages.

Le cottage de l'homme à la robe de chambre allait devenir le Q.G. improvisé de l'opération.

Les deux voitures de patrouille de la police de Sillery arrivèrent en trombe devant la maison du bon-Samaritain-malgré-lui.

— Établissez un très long cordon de sécurité, intima Duval.

L'agent le toisa, pas content de se faire donner un ordre sur son territoire par un officier de la SQ.

— Allez, ordonna Duval. Il est gravement blessé et il n'en a pas pour longtemps, ce qui en fait une bête enragée. Il ne faut pas l'énerver davantage.

Le chef adjoint de la police de Sillery s'approcha : un homme tout en longueur au visage encore jeune mais à la tignasse déjà toute blanche.

— Qu'est-ce qu'on fait ?

— Rien pour l'instant, dit le lieutenant d'un ton cassant. Appelez une ambulance. Et dites à vos gars de rester loin de la maison. Je vais tenter d'entrer en contact avec Maranda.

Duval se tourna vers l'homme à la robe de chambre.

— Je peux téléphoner ?

— Oui, ici, monsieur l'agent.

Le résident invita Duval à entrer. Alors qu'il allait refermer la porte, Duval lui demanda de la laisser ouverte. L'homme remit l'appareil au détective. Le fil de téléphone était assez long pour que le détective puisse s'installer sous le porche d'entrée. Son hôte, bottin à la main, lui dicta le numéro de téléphone du vieux docteur Bélair que Duval composa aussitôt. Après quatre sonneries, la voix chevrotante du médecin lui répondit.

Devant Duval, la maison de style Tudor, avec ses volumes triangulaires, n'avait de rassurant que les deux grands ormes qui se dressaient en sentinelle.

— Oui ?

— Docteur, je suis le lieutenant Duval.

— Il tient un couteau près du cou de ma femme. Si vous vous approchez, il dit qu'il va la tuer. Il saigne abondamment. Il est blessé à deux endroits.

Le hurlement de Maranda interrompit le docteur.

— D'abord, restez calme, reprit le lieutenant, Maranda est gravement blessé. Dites-lui que vous êtes médecin et offrez-lui de l'aider.

— C'est déjà fait. Il refuse.

— Dites-lui que nous sommes prêts à le conduire immédiatement par ambulance à l'hôpital.

— Il veut parler à son père.

— Son père ?

Le chef adjoint de la police de Sillery entra dans la maison.

Duval entendait indistinctement Maranda qui délirait.

— Docteur, d'après vous, il en a pour combien de temps ?

— Il va finir par tomber dans le coma.

— Passez-le-moi.

Silence. Une boursouflure motorisée d'une autre époque, avec le signe de la Croix-Rouge, s'amena, sirène stridente.

Au bout du fil, Duval percevait la voix calme du docteur qui parlait à Maranda. Puis à la respiration haletante, il sut qu'il avait le ravisseur au bout du fil.

— Maranda, on est prêts à te conduire à l'hôpital. On ne te fera pas de mal. Tu laisses sortir monsieur et madame Bélair et je vais entrer, paisiblement. Tu as besoin de soins.

— Parler... à mon père...

Le lieutenant demeura saisi par la requête. Duval comprit que, dans la tête de Maranda, Victor avait toujours été cette figure paternelle. Il envoya un agent appeler Dallaire afin qu'on amène sans délai Victor Déziel sur les lieux.

Un cri jaillit du récepteur téléphonique, suivi d'un bruit sec. Duval perdit le contact. Le récepteur avait été échappé sur le plancher. Après plusieurs secondes, la voix angoissée du médecin fut de nouveau audible :

— Il est tombé et a entraîné ma femme avec lui. Il y a du sang partout. Elle souffre d'hyperventilation. Je ne sais plus quoi faire. Il délire complètement.

— Tenez bon. J'arrive !

Un agent s'approcha.

— Lieutenant, le capitaine Dallaire me dit que Déziel est en route.

Duval répondit par un signe de tête et reprit la communication :

— Docteur Bélair… dites-lui que Victor Déziel va venir.

Il perdit une fois de plus le contact, puis entendit la tonalité.

Duval remit le récepteur à l'agent en lui demandant de téléphoner afin de rétablir la communication avec les Bélair et le ravisseur.

L'Econoline de Louis s'immobilisa devant la maison. Lentement, le Gros s'extirpa de son véhicule en déployant une gymnastique impressionnante. Devant la résidence, le cordon jaune du périmètre de sécurité était secoué par le vent. Les curieux étaient gardés à distance. Duval avait commandé aux policiers d'éteindre tous les gyrophares afin de ne pas exciter davantage Maranda. Derrière les vitres des maisons, les voisins attendaient le dénouement du drame.

Duval traversa la rue en courant tandis que Louis lui recommandait de faire attention. La poignée de la porte avant était verrouillée. Le lieutenant se posta derrière dans le garage. Comme le luminaire à l'extérieur était demeuré allumé, il distinguait à travers les mailles du rideau de dentelle la silhouette voûtée du docteur. Il apercevait aussi les jambes de la vieille dame et celles de Maranda collées les unes sur les autres. Tous trois se trouvaient dans la salle à manger. Il entendit le vieil homme implorer le ravisseur de ménager sa femme. Maranda bavait un flot de paroles incohérent. Duval aurait aimé faire un signe au docteur Bélair, mais ce dernier ne le voyait pas.

Il courut vers l'arrière et tomba sur une autre porte verrouillée. Puis la femme du docteur poussa un cri.

— Non, ne faites pas ça ! hurla le médecin.

Duval fracassa la fenêtre avec la crosse de son arme. D'une main nerveuse et tâtonnante, il saisit la poignée puis la tourna. Le .38 au creux de la main, il balaya la pièce du regard. Accroupi dans le noir, le mari soutenait sa femme. Maranda s'était volatilisé.

— Où est-il ?

— Dans la salle de bains. J'entends le ventilateur. Au bout du corridor.

La sonnerie du téléphone retentissait sans que personne réponde.

Les yeux révulsés par la terreur, la vieille dame avait du mal à reprendre son souffle. Sa robe de chambre était maculée de sang. Elle était assise sur le tapis, le dos appuyé contre un mur. Son mari la réconfortait. À côté, la flaque de sang témoignait de l'état de santé de Maranda.

La sonnerie du téléphone cessa enfin.

Un halo de lumière éclairait le bout du corridor. Duval sentit sous ses pieds une longue traînée de sang. À voir la largeur de la trace sanguinolente sur le plancher de bois franc, Maranda avait rampé. Mais Duval avait appris à se méfier des bêtes blessées à mort.

Il longea le mur jusqu'à l'endroit où la coulée rouge tournait dans la pièce. Il tenait à remettre le jeune homme à la justice. Il jeta un coup d'œil rapide dans la salle de bains.

Maranda avait tenté de se hisser sur les toilettes. Ses deux bras et sa tête étaient appuyés au siège de la cuvette. On aurait dit qu'il avait voulu disparaître par ce trou. Le couteau était tombé à ses côtés. Duval constata qu'il avait atteint d'une balle l'omoplate du jeune homme. Avait-il touché le poumon ? La lacération au mollet gauche était très profonde.

Duval empoigna Maranda, l'étendit sur le carrelage. Il prit le pouls du garçon mais ne sentit rien. Son t-shirt au nom de circonstance, *The Damned*, était barbouillé de sang. Alors qu'il se relevait, un Christ rougeaud et sanguinolent accroché au mur lui donna des frissons. Il courut à l'extérieur demander de l'aide puis retourna au chevet de Maranda. Il tenta de repérer un grain de vie dans le jeune homme mais en vain. Duval observa que ses mains portaient des lésions cutanées, ce qui confirma l'hypothèse d'une allergie au latex. Pourrait-on le réanimer ? Les signes vitaux ne répondaient plus. Duval comprit qu'il avait tué.

Il sortit pour laisser entrer les policiers et ambulanciers. La moue sceptique et indifférente de l'un des secouristes annonça que le séjour terrestre de Maranda venait de prendre fin.

Duval arpenta le salon en faisant attention de ne pas marcher dans la flaque rouge. Déjà le service de l'Identité judiciaire s'amenait par la porte de devant.

L'un d'eux s'adressa à Duval.

— Beau travail, lieutenant !

Duval trouva le compliment absurde, comme toujours. Un homme dément était mort au bout de son sang et on le félicitait, lui, l'architecte de cette enquête.

Louis arriva à son tour, aidé par un agent de la police de Sillery – ce qui ferait jaser à la centrale du boulevard Saint-Cyrille.

Le Gros avait perdu ses sourcils mais pas son humour.

— Après la moelle épinière et un rein, les sourcils… Ça va *fitter* avec le reste maintenant… ironisa le Gros en passant une main sur son crâne chauve. Toi, ça va ?

Duval tapota l'épaule de son ami.

— Je te remercie d'être venu.

— J'ai eu un pressentiment. Quand j'ai vu que tu ne répondais pas à la radio, j'ai pensé que t'avais pas pu t'empêcher d'entrer chez Maranda. J'ai téléphoné et il n'y avait plus de service. J'étais déjà en route quand tu as demandé du renfort. Les gars ont eu de la difficulté à trouver l'adresse.

— Et toi, tu es tombé lourdement.

— Je croyais bien retrouver l'usage de mes jambes après ça !

Les ambulanciers passèrent devant eux avec la civière. Ils amenaient Maranda au CHUL, où l'on constaterait le décès.

Duval s'approcha du docteur et de sa femme. Autant le premier avait conservé sa minceur, autant sa femme avait accumulé des strates de bourrelets. Monsieur Bélair avait des cheveux blancs et soyeux, des yeux d'un bleu de mer, et son visage avait conservé un air de jeunesse. Assise dans la cuisine, sa femme commençait à se ressaisir. Elle avait subi un violent choc nerveux. Un policier de Sillery s'entretenait avec eux. La dame refusa l'offre du policier de partir en ambulance.

Duval avait apprécié le flegme du docteur. Il n'avait jamais paniqué, même quand Maranda s'était écroulé avec sa femme.

— Monsieur Bélair, je veux vous remercier pour votre calme exemplaire.

L'homme se leva et tendit la main à Duval.

— Merci, lieutenant Duval, je trouvais rassurant de vous parler. À votre voix, je savais qu'on s'en tirerait. Vous êtes intervenu presque immédiatement.

En sortant, Duval aperçut Déziel qui n'osait pas approcher de la civière. Il observait la scène, sans émotion.

— Décidément, ce n'est pas l'instinct paternel qui vous remue, lança Duval au passage.

Le professeur pinça les lèvres. En arrière-plan, l'homme à la robe de chambre bleue attendait dans l'embrasure de sa porte.

Duval et Louis regagnèrent la résidence de Maranda. En roulant le long du chemin pentu qui menait à la maison, ils croisèrent le fourgon de la morgue. La lueur du brasier éclairait le boisé. À travers troncs et branches, c'était pareil à un vitrail embrasé de rouge, d'orange et de bleu. Le feu consumait l'immeuble dans sa totalité, les fenêtres crachaient le feu qui léchait le toit. Un vent tourmenté alimentait le bûcher.

Louis stationna son Econoline derrière un véhicule d'incendie.

Le crépitement du bois qui se consumait se mélangeait aux grésillements des radios.

Le brasier dégageait une chaleur intense. C'était comme une soirée d'août en automne. Les tuyaux, comme de gros boas, couraient sur le sol. Un pompier au sommet de l'échelle, derrière un canon à eau, arrosait le toit. Aucun plancher n'avait encore cédé. Les grosses poutres de ces maisons étaient plus solides que les poutres d'acier, qui fondaient et ne résistaient jamais longtemps à l'assaut des flammes.

Duval marcha vers le chef des pompiers, dont le visage suintait à travers la suie. Francis apparut dans le champ de vision du lieutenant.

— Daniel, ça va?

— Oui. Pas trop de mal, ici?

— On a trouvé un corps à l'étage : le corps d'un obèse en état de putréfaction.

— Vous connaissez son identité?

— Oui. Gérard Maranda. Un voisin a dit à un reporter qu'il croyait Gérard Maranda parti en vacances à Acapulco depuis une dizaine de jours.

— Et le corps de Dahlia Héroux a été récupéré?

— Non. Les flammes étaient trop fortes. On ne pouvait pas descendre. Quand les pompiers sont arrivés, le feu était pratiquement hors de contrôle.

Duval tiqua. Il faudrait s'assurer qu'il s'agissait bien de la jeune fille. La tête relevée, son regard fixait le brasier. Les flammes se reflétaient dans ses yeux.

— Maranda? demanda Francis.

— Mort.

Le caporal Tremblay montra une totale indifférence à l'annonce de cette nouvelle.

Duval, qui n'avait pas écrit son rapport sur les événements de la veille et qui devait rédiger celui de la journée, décida qu'il lui fallait rentrer à la centrale. Qui sait? Peut-être aurait-il enfin un instant libre à passer en famille dans quelques heures? Il s'imaginait à la campagne ou dans un chalet au fond des bois, loin de la classe criminelle, loin de la crasse humaine.

Pour la première fois en vingt ans de carrière, il avait tué un homme. Une fois la pression relâchée, derrière son volant, une douleur à l'épaule le tenailla. Une autre contusion à panser.